The Position of Roman Slaves

Dependency and Slavery Studies

Edited by
Jeannine Bischoff and Stephan Conermann

Volume 6

The Position of Roman Slaves

Social Realities and Legal Differences

Edited by
Martin Schermaier

DE GRUYTER

Gefördert durch die Deutsche Forschungsgemeinschaft (DFG) im Rahmen der Exzellenzstrategie des Bundes und der Länder – Exzellenzcluster Bonn Center for Dependency and Slavery Studies (BCDSS) EXC 2036/1-2020, Projektnummer: 390683433

Funded by the Deutsche Forschungsgemeinschaft (DFG, German Research Foundation) under Germany's Excellence Strategy – Cluster of Excellence Bonn Center for Dependency and Slavery Studies (BCDSS) EXC 2036/1-2020, Project No.: 390683433

ISBN 978-3-11-099868-9
e-ISBN (PDF) 978-3-11-098719-5
e-ISBN (EPUB) 978-3-11-098722-5
ISSN 2701-1127
DOI https://doi.org/10.1515/9783110987195

Library of Congress Control Number: 2022949292

Bibliographic information published by the Deutsche Nationalbibliothek
The Deutsche Nationalbibliothek lists this publication in the Deutsche Nationalbibliografie; detailed bibliographic data are available on the internet at http://dnb.dnb.de.

Cover image: Frescoe at Pompeii showing a parrot pulling a chariot driven by a cricket, lithograph by Giacomo Lenghi, Library of Congress, https://www.loc.gov/resource/pga.11496/
Typesetting: Integra Software Services Pvt. Ltd.
Printing and binding: CPI books GmbH, Leck

www.degruyter.com

Introduction

Roman law has a lot to tell us. It forms the basis for most private law systems in use today. It is an important source for the history of concepts and ideas in western civilisation. And it is, finally, a key with which to unlock our understanding of ancient Roman culture. Anyone who wants to study Roman slavery cannot ignore Roman slave law.

But work on the Roman legal texts involves a number of difficulties. They are easily accessible, both in print and digitally online. The most important texts have been translated into the most common modern languages. But not every historian will find it easy to engage with the complex legal questions posed by many of these texts. What they have to tell us about social conditions in Rome often only becomes intelligible after one has worked one's way through the hard shell of technical jargon and dogmatic subtleties. Another problem is that most extant legal texts do not discuss the legal position of slaves. Instead, they discuss slaves who, as persons or as things, became part of a legal dispute. These texts tell us only indirectly about the rights or duties of slaves, or about a slave's position vis-à-vis a free person. Only where Roman laws were used to discuss a specific conflict in concrete terms can we draw conclusions about what is commonly referred to as 'slave law.' Paul du Plessis has already described this conundrum: 'While Roman legal sources do not provide much information about the socio-economic context of slavery, they do contain interesting glimpses of such concerns and the way in which this affected juristic reasoning.'[1]

So, if we want to find out something about the legal and social position of slaves, we need to study Roman legal texts in terms of their purposes, as it were: only the ruling and the reasoning divulge some information about the roles of slaves in that specific conflict, and perhaps more generally. The project about the Roman legal sources of slavery, 'Corpus der römischen Rechtsquellen zur antiken Sklaverei (CRRS)',[2] supported by the Mainz Academy of Sciences and Literature, facilitates access to the relevant legal texts and so helps us to understand them. It is, however, beyond the scope (and indeed not the stated aim) of that excellent project to facilitate access also to underlying social conditions in Rome. The present volume hopes to fill that gap in terms of selected aspects of Roman slave law. The authors, all of whom are legal historians, hope to bore through the hard technical shell of legal texts in order to get at their social core.

In doing so, they start from a shared working hypothesis, namely that Roman slavery was more diverse than we might assume from the standard wording about servile legal status. Slaves were the property of their *dominus*, objects rather than persons, and largely without rights: these are some components of our basic knowledge

1 Paul J. du Plessis, "The Slave in the Window," in *By the Sweat of Your Brow. Roman Slavery in Its Socio-Economic Setting*, ed. Ulrike Roth (London: Institute of Classical Studies, University of London, 2010): 49–60, 59.

2 https://www.adwmainz.de/index.php?id=712 [accessed 04.08.2022].

https://doi.org/10.1515/9783110987195-202

about Roman slavery. Yet numerous inscriptions as well as literary and also legal sources reveal clear differences in the social structure of Roman slavery. At the lower end of the scale, we find the socially degraded penal slaves (*servi poenae*), at the top end the often wealthy and sometimes socially influential state slaves (*servi caesaris*). In between, there were numerous groups and professions who shared the status of being unfree while inhabiting very different worlds.

The papers in this volume now pose the question of whether and how legal texts reflected such social differences within the Roman servile community. Did the legal system reinscribe social differences, and if so, in what shape? Were exceptions created only in individual cases, or did the legal system generate privileges for particular groups of slaves? Did it reinforce and even promote social differentiation? Of course, the essays collected here cannot paint a complete picture of Roman slave law. But they all probe neuralgic points that have long been known to challenge the homogeneous image of Roman slave law that still dominates modern scholarship. In this way we hope to show that Roman slave law was a good deal more colourful than historical research has so far assumed.

This volume is the result of a conference held at the 'Bonn Center for Dependency and Slavery Studies' (BCDSS) in August 2020. Despite the uncertainties created by the Covid-19 pandemic, a large number of the authors gathered in person in Bonn to discuss their contributions in two intensive sessions. As such, this conference was one of only a few academic bright spots during a two-year period of widespread isolation. We would like to thank the responsible bodies at the University of Bonn and the BCDSS for their support. Our special thanks go to the BCDSS, which funded both the conference and this volume. Imogen Herrad translated most of the papers in this volume into English; she also reviewed and, where necessary, improved the few that were submitted in English. We would like to express our sincere thanks for her commitment and patience in exploring particular interpretations and meanings. We would also like to thank the staff of the Institute of Roman Law and Comparative Legal History at the University of Bonn, especially Tessa Spitzley, as well as Dr Janico Albrecht at the BCDSS, who compiled the indexes and typeset and prepared the manuscript for going to press.

Bonn, June 2022

Martin J. Schermaier
on behalf of all authors

Contents

Introduction — V

Martin Schermaier
Without Rights? Social Theories Meet Roman Law Texts — 1

Thomas Finkenauer
***Filii naturales*: Social Fate or Legal Privilege? — 25**

Pierangelo Buongiorno
Social Status 'Without' Legal Difference. Historiography and Puzzling Legal Questions About Imperial Freedmen and Slaves — 67

Richard Gamauf
***Peculium*: Paradoxes of Slaves With Property — 87**

Richard Gamauf
***Dispensator*: The Social Profile of a Servile Profession in the *Satyrica* and in Roman Jurists' Texts — 125**

Wolfram Buchwitz
Giving and Taking: The Effects of Roman Inheritance Law on the Social Position of Slaves — 165

Aglaia McClintock
***Servi poenae*: What Did It Mean to Be 'Condemned to Slavery'? — 187**

Jakob Fortunat Stagl
***Favor libertatis*: Slaveholders as Freedom Fighters — 203**

Martin Schermaier
Neither Fish nor Fowl: Some Grey Areas of Roman Slave Law — 237

Bibliography — 269

Authors — 297

Index of Sources — 299

Martin Schermaier

Without Rights? Social Theories Meet Roman Law Texts

The title holds out great promise: but it immediately becomes clear from the format that this paper does not address Roman slave law as a whole. For that purpose, we can still confidently turn to Buckland's masterwork,[1] which, despite the many recent, more narrowly focused studies, has not lost its value as an exhaustive survey of the topic. This paper does not address the question of slave law as such, but instead asks whether Roman legal texts can provide information about the social reality of Roman slavery.

To start with, there are methodological questions: what terms and concepts can we use to describe a society that we do not know from empirical observation but only from its artefacts? The term 'slave law' (1) is just as multi-layered and imprecise as the term 'slavery' (2). Both are modern, and as such have the potential to get in our way as we examine historical conditions. Awareness of this hermeneutical problem enables us to clarify in outline (3) how Roman jurists classified slaves and categorised them as objects or actors of property law. In doing so, we confront sociological concepts and socio-historical findings with modern exegesis. Unsurprisingly, not all Roman texts that are used to support popular arguments are in fact suitable for this purpose. Ideas about so-called 'Roman slave law' feed on narratives that emerged during the period of transatlantic slavery. However, the fact that Roman jurists also had very definite ideas about the social inferiority of Roman slaves emerges clearly even from a close reading of Roman legal sources. But it is not only the rules but also the nuances that deserve attention.

1 Was There Ever a Roman Slave Law?

This question will surprise many: was there ever a Roman slave law? There were slaves and there was a legal system, so there will have been slave law in Rome. How could Roman law, worked out with such great precision and in minute detail, have bypassed the millions of slaves[2] on whose very existence Rome's specialised

1 William Warwick Buckland, *The Roman Law of Slavery. The Condition of the Slave in Private Law from Augustus to Justinian* (Cambridge: Cambridge University Press, 1908).
2 For the proportion of slaves among the general population see for example Walter Scheidel, "Quantifying the Sources of Slaves in the Early Roman Empire," *Journal of Roman Studies* 87 (1997): 156–69; diverging slightly is William V. Harris, "Demography, Geography and the Sources of Roman Slaves," *Journal of Roman Studies* 89 (1999): 62–75; more recently Walter Scheidel, "The Roman Slave

https://doi.org/10.1515/9783110987195-001

economy was based in the first place? Have not thousands[3] of ancient legal texts on slavery[4] come down to us? Was Roman slave law not repeatedly used as a model for later rules[5] or codifications, such as Louis XIV's 'Code Noir'?[6] The parallel to the Roman model was certainly repeatedly invoked in the era of the transatlantic slave trade.[7] So did what was so often observed and described never even exist?

Not necessarily. For what we think of as slave law today builds on concepts that the Roman jurists probably were not even aware of. Each generation creates its own conception of what slavery is, of what law is. Both define what might be identified as 'slave law'. A Roman jurist would probably have classified early nineteenth-century wage labourers as slaves and might think of civil servants and agency workers today

Supply," in *The Cambridge World History of Slavery*, vol. 1, *The Ancient Mediterranean Worlds*, ed. Keith Bradley and Paul Cartledge (Cambridge: Cambridge University Press, 2011): 287–310.

3 Elisabeth Herrmann-Otto, "Die Sklaverei in antiken Theorien und deren Bedeutung für die moderne Menschrechtsdiskussion," in *Grundlagen der antiken Sklaverei. Eine Institution zwischen Theorie und Praxis*, ed. Elisabeth Herrmann-Otto (Hildesheim: Georg Olms Verlag, 2015): 39, 50 lists 'mehr als 5,000 Paragraphen allein in den 50 Büchern der Digesten'.

4 A considerable part has now been made accessible through the publications in the series *Corpus der römischen Rechtsquellen zur antiken Sklaverei* (*Corpus of Roman Legal Sources on Ancient Slavery*), founded by the Mainz Academy and edited by Tiziana Chiusi, Johanna Filip-Fröschl and Johannes Michael Rainer (Stuttgart, since 1999); an overview of the volumes so far published can be found at: https://www.adwmainz.de/index.php?id=712&L=4 [accessed 04.08.2022].

5 So David Mevius, *Ein kurtzes Bedencken über die Fragen so von dem Zustand, Abfoderung und verwiederter Abfolge der Bawrsleute zu welchen iemand Zuspruch zu haben vermeynet, bey jetzigen Zeiten entstehen und vorkommen* (Stralsund: Zachariä, 1645); see Marion Wiese, *Leibeigene Bauern und Römisches Recht im 17. Jahrhundert. Ein Gutachten des David Mevius* (Berlin: Duncker & Humblot, 2005).

6 *Code noir, ou recueil d'edits déclarations et arrets concernant les esclaves négres de l'Amérique* (1685), which Louis XIV enacted for the French colonies in the Caribbean; see for example Vernon V. Palmer, "Essai sur les origines et les auteurs du Code Noir," *Revue internationale de droit comparé* 50, no. 1 (1998): 111–40; Dominique A. Mignot, "Le droit romain et la servitude aux Antilles," *Bulletin de la Société d'Histoire de la Guadeloupe* 127–128, no. 1–2 (2001): 25–46; Dominique A. Mignot, "Du 'ius vetus' au code noir: Le délit de l'esclave aux îles françaises d'Amérique (XVIIe – XVIIIe siècle)," *Latomus* 64, no. 3 (2005): 733–41; Frédéric Charlin, "Droit romain et Code Noir. Quelques réflexions a posteriori," *Clio@Themis. Revue électronique d'histoire du droit* 8 (2015), https://publications-prairial.fr/cliothemis/index.php?id=1491?id=1491#toc [accessed 04.08.2022]; Linda De Maddalena, "Spuren des römischen Rechts im Code Noir," in *Sklaverei und Recht: Zwischen römischer Antike und moderner Welt*, Berner Universitätsschriften 61, ed. Iole Fargnoli and Thomas Späth (Bern: Haupt Verlag, 2018): 85–99. For the *Code Noir* in general and its history see Jean-François Niort, *Le Code Noir. Idées reçues sur un texte symbolique* (Paris: Le Cavalier Bleu, 2015).

7 Alan Watson, *Slave Law in the Americas* (Athens: University of Georgia Press, 1989); Sally Hadden, "The Fragmented Laws of Slavery in the Colonial and Revolutionary Eras," in *The Cambridge History of Law in America*, vol. 1, *Early America (1580–1815)*, ed. Michael Grossberg and Christopher Tomlins (Cambridge: Cambridge University Press: 2008): 253–87 and 646–57; Peter van den Berg, "Slaves: Persons or Property? The Roman Law on Slavery and Its Reception in Western Europe and Its Overseas Territories," *Osaka Law Review* 63 (2016): 171–88. More sophisticated is Robin Blackburn, "The Old World Background to European Colonial Slavery," *The William and Mary Quarterly* 54, no. 1 (1997): 65–102.

as slaves, too. Conversely, a modern jurist might waver in his assessment of Roman 'slave society'[8] if he was told that many masters kept and cared for their slaves even in old age and sickness.[9] Even if, in the seventeenth or eighteenth century, people thought that their own regulations on slavery would follow Roman law, this was not a historical claim. At the time, as in the *usus modernus iuris romani*[10] in general, the ancient texts were used to solve current legal questions. But these often had little or nothing to do with what we know today as historical Roman law.

Many modern studies of slavery in Roman law continue to make very similar mistakes. Even Buckland already rebuked this 'defect of the gravest kind'.[11] Some studies idealise the curbs on slave masters' despotism as an expression of the idea of *humanitas* in jurisprudence.[12] Others put Roman slavery on a par with transatlantic slavery;[13] yet others resort to purely legal terminology and define Roman slaves as their masters' objects and property.[14] While none of these approaches produces exclusively false insights, none quite does justice to the historical circumstances either.

They all share the same mistaken approach: they try to describe and classify ancient slavery with the help of modern concepts. Those who speak of 'humanity' will find it hard to distance themselves from the meaning this term acquired during the

8 The term originates in Marxist theory, but is still being used today, for example by Christian Delacampagne, *Die Geschichte der Sklaverei* (Düsseldorf/Zürich: Artemis und Winkler Verlag, 2004): 73 (for Rome): 'Sklavenhaltergesellschaft' ('société esclavagiste'). Cf. as well Wilfried Nippel, "Sklavenhaltergesellschaft," in *Handwörterbuch der Antiken Sklaverei*, ed. Heinz Heinen et al. (Stuttgart: Franz Steiner Verlag, 2017): 2601–3. It should however be noted that the term survived in the concept of a 'slave society', for example in Moses I. Finley, *Ancient Slavery and Modern Ideology* (New York: The Viking Press, 1980): 9, who identifies five 'genuine slave societies'. Critically on that Noel Lenski, "Framing the Question: What Is a Slave Society?," in *What Is a Slave Society? The Practice of Slavery in Global Perspective*, ed. Noel Lenski and Catherine M. Cameron (Cambridge: Cambridge University Press, 2018): 15–58.

9 See Stefan Knoch, *Sklavenfürsorge im Römischen Reich. Formen und Motive zwischen humanitas und utilitas* (Hildesheim: Georg OlmsVerlag, 2005): 119–42; succinctly Herrmann-Otto, "Sklaverei in antiken Theorien" (n. 3): 32, with reference to Sen. clem. 1.18.2.

10 On this topic see Franz Wieacker, *A History of Private Law in Europe, with Particular Reference to Germany*, transl. Tony Weir (Oxford: Clarendon Press, 1995): 159–67.

11 Buckland, *Law of Slavery* (n. 1): 2.

12 So for example Joseph Vogt, *Sklaverei und Humanität: Studien zur antiken Sklaverei und ihrer Erforschung* (Wiesbaden: Franz Steiner Verlag, 1983); largely in agreement with him are Wolfgang Waldstein, *Operae libertorum. Untersuchungen zur Dienstpflicht freigelassener Sklaven* (Stuttgart: Franz Steiner Verlag, 1986): 388; Johannes M. Rainer, "Humanität und Arbeit im römischen Recht," *Zeitschrift der Savigny-Stiftung für Rechtsgeschichte, Romanistische Abteilung* 105 (1988): 745–70, referring to Fritz Schulz, *Prinzipien des römischen Rechts* (Berlin: Duncker & Humblot, 1934).

13 Especially by Finley, *Ancient Slavery* (n. 8): 93–122. Delacampagne, *Geschichte der Sklaverei* (n. 8): 73–96, pursues a similar argument.

14 Such as Herrmann-Otto, "Sklaverei in antiken Theorien" (n. 3): 51.

Enlightenment,[15] and so struggle to separate its philosophical[16] from its socio-ethical significance.[17] What makes it all the more difficult to distinguish between the two is the fact that Roman jurists actually used *humanus* or *humanior* in a legal-ethical sense, correcting strict law.[18] 'Strict law', however, does not refer to the norms that regulated the positions and duties of slaves but to the formalised *ius civile* that was rigid in content and had come down from the ancestors. The *humanitas* of the Roman jurists is therefore not the one that we expect of humane law today.

Much the same is true for analogies with transatlantic slavery. Being a slave in the late Republic or the Empire was a deplorable fate for most. The vast majority of Roman slaves worked on latifundia, in quarries and mines or on galleys; their lives were joyless, miserable and usually short, and probably differed little from those of the slaves in the European colonies. But archaeological and literary evidence for the enslaved labouring masses is rare. We are, however, very well informed about the much smaller number of more advantaged domestic slaves. This may distort our view of ancient slavery. Even so, comparison with transatlantic slavery is misleading. One essential difference is that Roman slavery, unlike its transatlantic counterpart, had no racist basis.[19] In addition, the position of Roman slaves cannot be clearly described either in social or legal terms: 'Roman slaves were of many types', as Watson rightly noted.[20] This is also the subject of this paper. If we want to perceive and classify the differences, it helps to leave behind the stereotypes of transatlantic slavery. In this as in any historical study, moral judgements do more harm than good.

---

15 See Marc Laureys and Rolf Lessenich, "Humanität," in *Bonner Enzyklopädie der Globalität*, ed. Ludger Kühnhardt and Tilman Mayer (Wiesbaden: Springer Verlag, 2017): 1379–88; Rudolf Rieks, "Humanitas," in *Historisches Wörterbuch der Philosophie*, vol. 3, ed. Joachim Ritter, Karlfried Gründer and Gottfried Gabriel (Basel: Schwabe, 1973): 1231–32.

16 Jörg Splett, "Humanität: I. Philosophisch," *Staatslexikon online*, 04.01.2021, https://www.staatslexikon-online.de/Lexikon/Humanit%C3%A4t [accessed 04.08.2022].

17 Arndt Küppers, "Humanität: II. Sozialethisch," *Staatslexikon online*, 04.01.2021, https://www.staatslexikon-online.de/Lexikon/Humanit%C3%A4t [accessed 04.08.2022].

18 Cf. for example Antonio Palma, *Humanior interpretatio. 'Humanitas' nell'interpretazione e nella normazione da Adriano ai Severi* (Turin: Giappichelli, 1992); see also my review in *Iura. Rivista internazionale di diritto romano e antico* 44 (1993/1996): 343–51.

19 This was already observed by Alan Watson, *Roman Slave Law* (Baltimore/London: Johns Hopkins University Press, 1987): XVIII: '[N]on racist slavery is very different but may be no less horrifying in many regards than racist slavery'.

20 Alan Watson, "Seventeenth-Century Jurists, Roman Law, and the Law of Slavery," *Chicago-Kent Law Review* 68, no. 3 (1992): 1343, 1347.

2 Roman Slaves and 'Social Death'

Orlando Patterson, following Claude Meillassoux,[21] described slavery as 'social death'. He defined a slave as a person who has no kin, no origin and no home, who is at the mercy of his master and has 'no social existence outside his master',[22] arguing that this concept fully applied also to Roman slaves.[23] As fruitful as the concept of 'social death' can be in describing slavery, it is inaccurate as a description of Roman conditions. Patterson himself identified two possible objections to his hypothesis: for one thing, there were many Greek slaves in Rome and the esteem in which Greek culture was held could have been reflected in Roman attitudes towards them.[24] For another, certain slaves performed important tasks in the imperial administration, so that their social status may have equalled that of free men.[25]

Patterson rightly rejected the first objection: respect for everything Greek did not improve the social status of Greek slaves. But there is another dimension to this objection that Patterson did not sufficiently consider: many elite Roman families employed Greek tutors, many of whom were slaves.[26] While the social position of these educators was not unassailable,[27] it was much more assured than that of other slaves. In addition, it should be kept in mind (which is not Patterson's point[28]) that as part of the reception of Greek culture, stoic ethics found great favour among Rome's educated classes. This was probably the driving force behind the acceptance of the concept of the equality of all human beings[29] endorsed in learned

21 Claude Meillassoux, *L'esclavage en Afrique précoloniale* (Paris: François Maspero, 1975).

22 Orlando Patterson, *Slavery and Social Death. A Comparative Study* (Cambridge, MA: Harvard University Press, 1982, quoted from the 2018 edition): 35–76, at 38.

23 Patterson, *Slavery and Social Death* (n. 22): 40.

24 Patterson, *Slavery and Social Death* (n. 22): 88–92.

25 Patterson, *Slavery and Social Death* (n. 22): 300–308.

26 This is reported in detail by Lucian in his work *De mercede conductis*. Lucian assumed that tutors concluded contracts of employment that ran for a year at a time; but we may assume that the relationship with his master was probably not significantly different for a tutor who had been bought as a slave. See Markus Hafner, *Lucians Schrift 'Das traurige Los der Gelehrten'. Einführung und Kommentar zu De Mercede Conductis Potentium Familiaribus, lib. 36*, Hermes Einzelschriften 110 (Stuttgart: Franz Steiner Verlag, 2017); see also the overview in Ludwig Friedländer, *Darstellungen aus der Sittengeschichte Roms in der Zeit von August bis zum Ausgang der Antoninen*, vol. 3 (Leipzig: Hirzel, 1920): 280–91; briefly also Patterson, *Slavery and Social Death* (n. 22): 91–92.

27 See for example Luc. merc. cond. 39.

28 For a divergent opinion see Christian Delacampagne, *Geschichte der Sklaverei* (n. 8): 87–96.

29 D. 1.1.4 (Ulp. 1 inst.): [. . .] *iure naturali omnes liberi nascerentur* ('according to natural law all men are born free'). See for example Tony Honoré, "Ulpian, Natural Law and Stoic Influence," *Tijdschrift voor Rechtsgeschiedenis* 78, no. 1–2 (2010): 199–208.

discourses.[30] Such positions[31] were not without influence on the pertinent social norms, i.e. what was considered to be the right or decent way to act beyond legal stipulations in dealing with slaves. Even if the legal texts remain largely quiet on this front, we should not underestimate the 'inhibiting influence of social norms on the behavior of individual masters toward their slaves'.[32] The concept of *favor libertatis*[33] may show how this influence found expression in concrete legal terms. The same applies to a series of imperial measures that improved the legal position of slaves.[34]

The second objection, i.e. the prominent position of the *familia Caesaris*,[35] for example, is also not easy to refute. Patterson rightly points out that the members of the *familia Caesaris* were exposed to the whims of the emperor;[36] the ever-looming risk of falling from grace was one reason why the emperor could count on their absolute loyalty. But such loyalty arising from dependency alone does not make slaves. Freedmen or liegemen were dependent in a comparable manner. Moreover, empirical evidence shows that the vast majority of the *familia Caesaris* were not only financially well-off but also enjoyed social recognition.[37] Patterson has to concede this, and so he sums up the relationship between the emperor and his slaves or freedmen as being 'not wholly asymmetric'.[38]

Such slaves, whose occupation, training or special talents ensured their higher rank, as a rule were able to have their own families,[39] to count on later manumission,

---

30 Sen. benef. 3.18–20; epist. 47. Ulrich Eigler, "Familiariter cum servis vivere: Einige Überlegungen zu Inhalt und Hintergrund von Senecas Epistel 47," in *Seneca: philosophus et magister*, ed. Thomas Baier, Gesine Manuwald and Bernhard Zimmermann (Freiburg im Breisgau: Rombach, 2005): 63–79, pointed out that Seneca was not concerned with the protection of slaves but rather with the moral integrity of the *dominus*.

31 Egon Flaig, *Weltgeschichte der Sklaverei*, 3rd ed. (Munich: C.H. Beck, 2018): 75–76, refers to prestoic sources.

32 John Bodel, "Death and Social Death in Ancient Rome," in *On Human Bondage. After Slavery and Social Death*, ed. John Bodel and Walter Scheidel (Oxford: Wiley-Blackwell, 2016): 81–108, 87.

33 Cf. J.F. Stagl, "'Favor libertatis': Slaveholders as Freedom Fighters" (in this volume).

34 Cf. Martin Avenarius, "Einleitung," in *Stellung des Sklaven im Privatrecht*, vol. 3, *Erbrecht. Aktive Stellung: Personeneigenschaft und Ansätze zur Anerkennung von Rechten*, Corpus der römischen Rechtsquellen zur Sklaverei 4, ed. Martin Avenarius (Stuttgart: Franz Steiner Verlag, 2017): 14–19.

35 Still essential reading are Gérard Boulvert, *Esclaves et affranchis impériaux sous Haut-Empire. Rôle politique et administratif* (Naples: Jovene, 1970); Gérard Boulvert, *Domestique et fonctionnaire sous le Haut-Empire romain: La condition de l'affranchi et de l'esclave du prince* (Paris: Les Belles Lettres, 1974); Paul Richard Carey Weaver, *Familia Caesaris: A Social Study of the Emperor's Freedmen and Slaves* (Cambridge: Cambridge University Press, 1972). The role played by public slaves is no less remarkable, see Alexander Weiß, *Sklave der Stadt. Untersuchungen zur öffentlichen Sklaverei in den Städten des Römischen Reiches*, Historia Einzelschriften 173 (Stuttgart: Franz Steiner Verlag, 2004).

36 Patterson, *Slavery and Social Death* (n. 22): 300–301.

37 For numerous examples see the paper by Pierangelo Buongiorno in this volume.

38 Patterson, *Slavery and Social Death* (n. 22): 308.

39 Cf. the examples in Reinhard Willvonseder, *Stellung des Sklaven im Privatrecht*, vol. 1, *Eheähnliche Verbindungen und verwandtschaftliche Beziehungen*, Corpus der römischen Rechtsquellen zur Sklaverei

and to accumulate wealth of their own. These privileges were not legally protected. But both our extant epigraphic and legal evidence about such slaves testify to their comfortable social position. They do not seem to have experienced a 'social death', or to have lived their lives as social 'nobodies'. So Roman slaves were complex figures. Even most of the social criteria that Patterson and others see as typifying slavery fail wholly or in part when faced with the wide range of slave conditions in Rome. And if we start to look for legal criteria to define these relations, things get even more difficult.

3 The Legal Status of Roman Slaves

3.1 *Nullum caput*

It is only at first glance that the legal classification of slaves seems simple: all slaves were unfree, and as such unable to enter into valid marriages, to acquire property or even to undertake political tasks. In addition, they were the property of their masters. But what did 'unfreedom' really mean at Rome? And what did it mean to be the property of another person? The answer to these questions is more difficult than some modern historians or sociologists imagine. And even the answer given by jurists and legal historians often leaves out the grey area between social reality and legal rules.

Regardless of their social position, the legal status of all slaves was the same: *servile caput nullum ius habet*, as the jurist Paulus wrote.[40] But this sentence is easily misunderstood unless we take its context into account. The fragment is about changes in the legal status of a person. The Roman jurists distinguished three such statuses:[41] *status libertatis*, according to which a person was free and not a slave; *status civitatis*, according to which a person was a Roman not a foreigner; and *status familiae*, according to which a person was either under the authority of a *pater familias* or not.

4 (Stuttgart: Franz Steiner Verlag, 2010); Henrik Mouritsen, "The Families of Roman Slaves and Freedmen," in *A Companion to Families in the Greek und Roman World*, ed. Beryl Rawson (Chichester/Malden, MA: Wiley-Blackwell, 2011): 129–44; Jonathan Edmondson, "Slavery and the Roman Family," in *The Cambridge World History of Slavery*, vol. 1, *The Ancient Mediterranean World*, ed. Keith R. Bradley and Paul Cartledge (Cambridge: Cambridge University Press, 2011): 347–49.

40 D. 4.5.3.1 (Paulus 11 ad ed.).

41 Cf. John A. Crook, *Law and Life of Rome, 90 B.C. – A.D. 212* (New York: Cornell University Press, 1967): 36–45; Max Kaser, *Das römische Privatrecht*, vol. 1, *Das altrömische, das vorklassische und klassische Recht*, 2nd ed. (Munich: C.H. Beck, 1971): 271–72; Andrew Lewis, "Slavery, Family and Status," in *The Cambridge Companion to Roman Law*, ed. David Johnston (Cambridge: Cambridge University Press, 2015): 151–74.

Since the time of Cicero, a loss of status was called *capitis deminutio.*[42] But because there could be not only loss but also gain, the jurist Gaius noted succinctly, *capitis minutio est status permutatio.*[43] *Caput* here did not mean 'head' or 'person', but the legal categorisation of a person.[44] In this context, Paul considers the question of whether the manumission of a slave is also a *capitis minutio*, but rejects this because a slave, who has no status, cannot change it. Nothing more, but also nothing less, is meant by the strange sentence that 'a slave's *caput* is possessed of no right'. Justinian added a clarification by Modestinus, *hodie enim incipit statum habere.*[45] Status could only be discussed where it existed. From a strictly conceptual point of view, the acquisition of *status libertatis* can therefore not be described as a change of status. But Paul did not mean that a slave had 'no right'.

3.2 A Person or a Thing?

But how else, apart from their status, could the legal position of slaves be established? In legal texts, they were often treated as *res*, objects of law. But in many respects the slaves' ability to establish rights and obligations through their own actions was also taken into account. Jurists would ask under which conditions slaves could independently entitle or obligate their masters. But the fact that slaves were human beings who thought and acted is never generally addressed in the legal sources. It seems to have been taken for granted. This was probably why Gaius, when he distinguished in his textbook between objects of law (*res*) and legal subjects (*personae*), counted slaves among the *personae* (Gaius inst. 1):[46]

Gai. Inst. 1.8–9: Omne autem ius, quo utimur, vel ad personas pertinet vel ad res vel ad actiones. Et prius videamus de personis. 9. Et quidem summa divisio de iure personarum haec est, quod omnes homines aut liberi sunt aut servi.	Gai. Inst. 1.8–9: All our law is about persons, things or actions. We turn to persons first. 9. The main classification in the law of persons is this: all men are either free or slaves.[47]

42 Cic. top. 18 and 29; see also Max Kaser, review of *The Law of Persons in the Later Roman Republic*, by Alan Watson, *Tijdschrift voor Rechtsgeschiedenis* 36, no. 3 (1968): 429–33.
43 D. 4.5.1 (Gai. 4 ad ed. prov.): 'Capitis minutio is the change of status'.
44 Hermann Gottlieb Heumann and Emil Seckel, *Handlexikon zu den Quellen des römischen Rechts*, 9th ed. (Jena: G. Fischer, 1914): 56 accordingly note the meaning of 'Leben, Freiheit und Zivität einer Person', with reference to D. 48.11.7 pr.-1 and D. 37.14.10.
45 D. 4.5.4 (Mod. 1 pandect.): 'For now he begins to have status.' (MacCormack in Alan Watson, *The Digest of Justinian*, vol. 1–4 [Pennsylvania: University of Pennsylvania Press, 1985]).
46 The text is even conserved in the Digests of Justinian: Gai. inst. 1.8 (= D. 1.5.1) and Gai. inst. 1.9 (= D. 1.5.3) and also forms the backbone of Justinian's Institutes: I. 1.2.12–1.3 pr.
47 Transl. Gordon and Robinson in Watson, *Digest of Justinian* (n. 45).

The fact that Gaius also describes 'man' (*homo*) as a thing (*res*)[48] in his textbook does not prevent him from categorically classifying slaves as *personae*.[49] This double assignment,[50] so to speak, is an apt expression of the fact that the legal position of Roman slaves cannot be clearly described in modern terms. In any case, unlike other movable objects,[51] slaves were not considered 'merchandise' (*merx*);[52] but in certain circumstances Romans had no qualms legally to equate slaves with objects.

This understanding of persons as objects of law or of claims stands in stark contrast to our own liberal creed. We do not interpret the *vindicatio liberorum*, which in modern German law is represented by § 1632 para 1 of the German Civil Code (BGB),[53] as the parents' claim in rem but rather as an expression of their right of custody.[54] We do not construe as debt slavery the fact that a creditor can benefit from the debtor's labour until the debt is paid off but rather as a right enforced by the courts to satisfy the creditor.[55] Even so, if the court seizes a part of their wages for the creditor, the debtor in effect works for the creditor without having contracted about it. And the child, like a thing, can be demanded from anyone who withholds it from its parents (i.e. from any 'possessor'). In those cases, human beings become the objects of claims, but the legal constructions used to dress up such relationships[56] make them appear innocuous and civilised.

---

48 Such as Gai. inst. 2.13: (*Corporales*) *hae, quae tangi possunt, velut fundus, homo vestis, aurum argentum et denique aliae res innumerabiles* (transl. Gordon and Robinson in Watson, *Digest of Justinian* (n. 45): 'Corporeal things can be touched – land, a slave, clothes, gold, silver and of course countless others').

49 See for example Hans-Dieter Spengler, "Zugleich Person und Sache – vielleicht Arbeitstier oder Unternehmer: Rechtliche Aspekte der römischen Sklaverei," in *Recht der Wirtschaft und der Arbeit in Europa. Gedächtnisschrift für Wolfgang Blomeyer*, ed. Rüdiger Krause, Winfried Veelken and Klaus Vieweg (Berlin: Duncker & Humblot, 2004): 271–83; Hans-Dieter Spengler, "Homo et res," in *Handwörterbuch der Antiken Sklaverei*, vol. 2, ed. Heinz Heinen et al. (Stuttgart: Franz Steiner Verlag, 2017): 1444–48; Antonio Saccoccio, "Römische Sklaverei zwischen ius gentium und ius naturale," in *Sklaverei und Recht: Zwischen römischer Antike und moderner Welt*, Berner Universitätsschriften 61, ed. Iole Fargnoli and Thomas Späth (Bern: Haupt Verlag, 2018): 41, 45–50.

50 Concise and still relevant is Kaser, *Das römische Privatrecht*, vol. 1 (n. 41): 285.

51 D. 50.16.66 (Ulp. 74 ad ed.): *Mercis appellatio ad res mobiles tantum pertinet.*

52 D. 50.16.207 (Afr. 3 quaest.): *Mercis appellatione homines non contineri Mela ait: et ob eam rem mangones non mercatores, sed venaliciarios appellari sit, et recte.*

53 § 1632 para 1 BGB: 'The care for the person of the child includes the right to require surrender of the child from every person who is unlawfully withholding it from the parents or from one parent.' English translation by the German Federal Ministry of Justice and Consumer Protection and the Federal Office of Justice: https://www.gesetze-im-internet.de/englisch_bgb [accessed 04.08.2022].

54 Patterson, *Slavery and Social Death* (n. 22): 21–22 chooses as an example for US American law the fact that spouses are one another's 'property'.

55 Relevant regulations are to be found in §§ 850 ZPO (*Zivilprozessordnung* = Law on Civil Procedure).

56 Patterson, *Slavery and Social Death* (n. 22): 22, regards this as merely a 'social convention', or 'an exercise in semantics' or simple 'politeness'. With regard to a discussion of European civil law, this is however not the whole story.

But what does this oscillation of the legal position between 'person' and 'object' mean for historical research? First of all, classification as *persona* clearly does not mean that slaves were always treated as subjects. By the same token, even in those instances where slaves were objects, such as when a jurist counted them as a factor in their master's estate, they were not completely dehumanised. Buckland's decision not to use a modern term for Roman slaves but rather to consider them from two angles, as thing and as persons, was therefore correct.[57]

Okko Behrends[58] and Martin Avenarius[59] even believe that from the imperial period onwards, slaves had a 'partial legal capacity'. But rather than linking this partial legal capacity to the notion of person, they base it on the ability of slaves to litigate certain matters themselves. The best-known example is that of a slave manumitted by will (in the form of a *fideicommissum*), who could independently enforce the claim for liberation against the heir.[60] Buckland had previously already criticised those who applied the concept of rightlessness to Roman slaves. He pointed out that although the servile population lacked many of the rights that were readily available to the 'free', this did not apply to all matters; he added that those who speak of 'rightlessness' did so from a modern understanding of the term.[61]

It is however difficult to define the 'rights' of slaves in specific terms or case groups. What frequently happened in social practice was that slaves were granted favours. Such concessions created grey areas in legal terms because, while slaves could expect their masters to grant them certain privileges, there was no legal means of enforcing those privileges. We will need to look more closely at this 'soft law' in slave law.[62]

This leaves us with the preliminary conclusion that modern concepts of persons and things, of legal subjects and objects of law, cannot clearly describe the legal

57 Buckland, *Law of Slavery* (n. 1): 10–72 ('Slave as Res') and 73–238 ('Slave as Man'); so also Watson, *Roman Slave Law* (n. 19): 46–66 and 67–89.

58 Okko Behrends, "Prinzipat und Sklavenrecht. Zu den geistigen Grundlagen der augusteischen Verfassungsschöpfung," in *Rechtswissenschaft und Rechtsentwicklung*, ed. Ulrich Immenga (Göttingen: Schwartz, 1980): 56–62 [= in *Institut und Prinzip*, vol. 1, ed. Martin Avenarius (Göttingen: Wallstein Verlag, 2004): 417–55]; see also Wolfgang Waldstein, "Zur 'Teilrechtsfähigkeit der Sklaven nach Kaiserrecht'," in *Ars Iuris. Festschrift für Okko Behrends zum 70. Geburtstag*, ed. Martin Avenarius, Rudolf Meyer-Pritzl and Cosima Möller (Göttingen: Wallstein Verlag, 2009): 589–602.

59 Avenarius, "Einleitung" (n. 34): 1–5.

60 See for example Francesca Lamberti, "Fideicommissa libertas ancillae data," in *Femmes-esclaves. Modèles d'interpretation anthropologique, économique, juridique*, ed. Francesca Reduzzi Merola and Alfredina Storchi Marino (Naples: Jovene, 1999): 2385–94; Rolf Knütel, "Rechtsfragen zu den Freilassungsfideikommissen," in *Sklaverei und Freilassung im römischen Recht. Symposion für Hans Josef Wieling zum 70. Geburtstag*, ed. Thomas Finkenauer (Berlin: Springer Verlag, 2006): 131–51; Francesco Maria Silla, *La 'cognitio' sulle 'libertates fideicommissae'*, L'Arte Del Diritto 11 (Padua: Cedam, 2008).

61 Buckland, *Law of Slavery* (n. 1): 2.

62 See below at p. 237–268 (Martin Schermaier, "Neither Fish nor Fowl").

position of Roman slaves. This is not only due to the intricacies of Roman slave law but rather to the fact that the concepts that we apply to Roman law do not do justice to historical circumstances. Christianity and the western Enlightenment elevated humanity to the exalted position of 'crown of creation',[63] which deepened the chasm between 'person' and 'thing' to the extent of rendering it unbridgeable.[64] Those modern terms do not allow for any nuances in between. The concept of 'half-freedom', despite its popularity, cannot help us with classical law because the Romans had one consistent definition of servile legal status: a slave was a person without status.

3.3 Slaves as Their Masters' 'Property'

To say that slaves were the property of their masters also inadequately describes the legal position of slaves. Certainly, it is true that in Roman thinking slaves were property: *in persona servi dominium*, Paul wrote about the power relationship between masters and slaves:

> D. 50.16.215 (Paul. 1 ad legem Fufiam et Caniniam): 'Potestatis' verbo plura significantur: in persona magistratuum imperium: in persona liberorum patria potestas: in persona servi dominium. Et cum agimus de noxae deditione cum eo qui servum non defendit, praesentis corporis copiam facultatemque significamus. In lege Atinia in potestatem domini rem furtivam venisse videri, et si eius vindicandae potestatem habuerit, Sabinus et Cassius aiunt.

> D. 50.16.215 (Paul, Lex Fufia Caninia, sole book): The word "potestas" has many meanings; in the person of magistrates it means imperium; in the person of children it means parental power; in the person of a slave it means ownership. But when we are dealing over noxal surrender with someone who does not defend his slave, we mean the capacity and ability to hand over an actual body. In the lex Atinia, according to Sabinus and Cassius, something stolen seems to have come into the potestas of its owner if he has acquired the potestas of claiming it by vindicatio.[65]

Even if other jurists employed similar terms,[66] it does not follow that it was the fact of being a property of their master's that made the slave a slave. Even abandoned

63 The literature is vast; see as a representative example Theo Kobusch, *Die Entdeckung der Person. Metaphysik der Freiheit und modernes Menschenbild* (Darmstadt: Herder Verlag, 1997); so also, albeit with a different take on the history of ideas, Larry Siedentop, *Inventing the Individual. The Origins of Western Liberalism* (London: The Belknap Press, 2014).

64 Critically, Roberto Esposito, *Le persone e le cose* (Turin: Giulio Einaudi Editore, 2014).

65 Transl. Crawford in Watson, *Digest of Justinian* (n. 45).

66 D. 12.6.64 (Tryph. 7 disp.): [. . .] *dominatio ex gentium iure introducta est* ('The domination of slaves was introduced by the common law of nations'); D. 1.5.4.1 (Flor. 9 inst.): *Servitus est constitutio iuris gentium, qua quis dominio alieno contra naturam subicitur* ('Slavery is constituted by the common law of nations, according to which somebody is – contrary to natural justice – subjected

slaves, whose masters had given up their possession in them, remained slaves.[67] But if we look at it from the other side, the connection between slave status and property is quite correct: being a slave usually entailed belonging to the *dominium* of another.

But what is *dominium*? Paul describes it as that form of *potestas* which pertained to slaves and objects. But the children of the family[68] were under comparable *potestas*, as was the wife – who is not mentioned in D. 50.16.215 – in a *manus* marriage.[69] *Dominium*, *patria potestas* and *manus* were forms of being under the domestic power of the *pater familias*; those in it included all objects or persons of which or whom the head of the household could say, *mea sunt*, they belong to me. This in no way implies that he was able to exercise unlimited power over the person in question. The concept is better understood as the owner's ability to demand the return of the object or the person from anyone less entitled to possess it. *Meum est, quod ex re mea superest, cuius vindicandi ius habeo*, Celsus wrote.[70]

So Roman property was conceptualised from the possibility to bring an action, i.e. from *ius vindicandi*: whoever was able to demand the return of the thing (or person) in question from another was considered its (or their) owner. That is why – as we saw above (§ 1632 para 1 BGB) – a Roman jurist would regard twenty-first-century German parents as the owner of their child because he can reclaim it.

But we today do not understand property from the potential to bring a lawsuit, instead we define it materially, i.e. as comprehensive power of disposition. An owner is someone who can 'deal with the thing at his discretion'.[71] This does not apply to custody. So, according to our modern view, children are not the 'property' of their parents. With the same conviction, Article 1 of the Slavery Convention of the League of Nations (1926), which is still in force today, states,

---

to the ownership of another'); D. 1.5.5.1 (Marc. 1 inst): *Servi autem in dominium nostrum rediguntur* ('People are brought under our power as slaves', transl. based on MacCormick and Birks in Watson, *Digest of Justinian* [n. 45]).

67 Cf. D. 9.4.38.1 (Ulp. 37 ad ed.); D. 41.7.2 (Paul. 54 ad ed.); cf. Friedrich Affolter, *Die Persönlichkeit des herrenlosen Sklaven. Ein Stück aus dem römischen Sklavenrecht* (Leipzig: Von Veit, 1913).

68 Gaius (inst. 1.52 and 55) referred to the power over both slaves and over children as *potestas*, domestic power.

69 Gai. inst. 1.49 and 108–115b.

70 D. 6.1.49.1 (Cels. 18 dig.): 'Whatever remains from my property which I have a right to vindicate is itself mine'. (transl. Stein in Watson, *Digest of Justinian* [n. 45]); similar to the definition of *bona* in D. 50.16. 49 (Ulp. 59 ed.): [. . .] *aeque bonis adnumerabitur etiam, si quid est in actionibus petitionibus persecutionibus.* ('Among our goods will equally be reckoned also anything which is subject to actions, petitions, or claims', transl. Crawford in Watson, *Digest of Justinian* [n. 45]).

71 E.g. § 903 BGB: 'Der Eigentümer einer Sache kann, soweit nicht das Gesetz oder Rechte Dritter entgegenstehen, mit der Sache nach Belieben verfahren [. . .]'; engl. translation (n. 53): 'The owner of a thing may, to the extent that a statute or third-party rights do not conflict with this, deal with the thing at his discretion [. . .]'.

> (1) Slavery is the status or condition of a person over whom any or all of the powers attaching to the right of ownership are exercised.

Slavery is said to exist even if only some of the powers that constitute ownership are exercised. But this does not change the fact that the Slavery Convention is based on a clearly defined concept of ownership. It defines ownership according to how it is exercised. This both acuminates and narrows Roman *dominium*. Certain forms of control over things or persons are not covered by such a definition. What this means in practice is made clear by the 2005 decision of the European Court of Human Rights in the case of *Siliadin v France*: the case was that of a young woman who had been employed as an unpaid domestic worker by a French family for many years. The woman was unable to escape because the family had confiscated her passport. While the court ruled that she had been subjected to forced labour, it denied that she had been a 'slave':[72]

> Although the applicant was, in the instant case, clearly deprived of her personal autonomy, the evidence does not suggest that she was held in slavery in the proper sense, in other words, that Mr and Mrs B exercised a genuine right of legal ownership over her, thus reducing her to the status of an "object".

From this reasoning we can see not only that modern law makes a strict distinction between subject and object, but also that the concept of 'property' is being measured against this distinction: entitlement to treat someone as an object is what constitutes property.

This ruling makes clear what had already been pointed out by Orlando Patterson, i.e. that slavery cannot be accurately described by the legal concept of 'property'.[73] Moses I. Finley, probably one of the most distinguished scholars of ancient slavery, had implied the same for the conditions in Greek and Roman antiquity.[74] Most recently David M. Lewis casts doubt on Patterson's position. He believes that it

---

72 ECtHR, 28. June 2005, no 73316/01 para 122; on this decision cf. Rebecca J. Scott, "Under Color of Law. Siliadin v France and the Dynamics of Enslavement in Historical Perspective," in *The Legal Understanding of Slavery. From the Historical to the Contemporary*, ed. Jean Allain (Oxford: Oxford University Press, 2012): 152–64, as well as several other contributions in that volume, e.g. Robin Hickey, "Seeking to Understand the Definition of Slavery" in *The Legal Understanding of Slavery: From the Historical to the Contemporary*, ed. Jean Allain (Oxford: Oxford University Press, 2012): 220–41; James E. Penner, "The Concept of Property and the Concept of Slavery" in *The Legal Understanding of Slavery: From the Historical to the Contemporary*, ed. Jean Allain (Oxford: Oxford University Press, 2012): 242–52; Jean Allain, "The Definition of Slavery in International Law," *Howard Law Journal* 52, no. 2 (2009): 239–75.

73 Patterson, *Slavery and Social Death* (n. 22): 20–27.

74 Moses I. Finley, "Between Slavery and Freedom," *Comparative Studies in Society and History* 6, no. 3 (1964): 248: '[N]either the property-definition nor any other single test is really meaningful'.

is possible clearly to distinguish the rights of masters to their slaves from the rights to other dependents in ancient societies, citing Tony Honoré, who, in a short comparative survey of law listed the typical entitlements of owners.[75] Lewis argued that such typical entitlements could also be identified for the relationship between masters and slaves. But this argument, built on the 'bundle of rights-theory',[76] is still tied too closely to the concept of one person belonging to another. More promising is the approach – most recently advocated by Tony Honoré himself[77] – of looking for typical forms of social discrimination.

Moreover, Lewis misses the point of Patterson's argument. Patterson rejected the idea of defining the position of slaves in terms of 'ownership' or 'property'. He was not concerned with the material substance of these terms. Even so, Patterson's conceptual position is weak because he assumes that the 'conception of absolute ownership' originates in Roman law: '[T]he Romans invented the legal fiction of dominium or absolute ownership, a fiction that highlights their practical genius'.[78] He argues that this precisely expressed their understanding of slavery because *dominium* had derived from the word *dominus* in its meaning of slave master. Thus, he sums up:[79]

> It is not the condition of slavery that must be defined in terms of absolute notions of property, as is so often attempted: rather it is the notion of absolute property that must be explained in terms of ancient Roman slavery.

This sounds plausible and convincing, but the approach is wrong. Because what Patterson refers to as 'the notion of absolute property' is a product not of Roman but of late medieval law. It was only then, in the fourteenth century, that property as *dominium* became an 'absolute' concept, in which the right was founded on the owner's discretion in dealing with the thing in question.[80] Only then was property no longer defined in order to fend off third parties but also according to substantive criteria such as the way an owner was entitled to deal with slaves. This was where the modern concept of property originated. This is the basis of Article 1 of the Slavery Convention, quoted above, and, unfortunately, also the basis of modern historians' ideas about Roman property and the position of Roman slaves. The fact that Patterson even identifies the concept of *dominium* as based on Roman slavery completes the hermeneutic

---

75 Tony Honoré, "Ownership," in *Oxford Essays in Jurisprudence*, ed. Anthony Gordon Guest (Oxford: Oxford University Press, 1961): 107–47.

76 On this theory and the concept of property see e.g. James E. Penner, "The 'Bundle of Rights' Picture of Property," *UCLA Law Review* 43 (1995–1996): 711–820.

77 Tony Honoré, "The Nature of Slavery," *in The Legal Understanding of Slavery. From the Historical to the Contemporary*, ed. Jean Allain (Oxford: Oxford University Press, 2014): 10–16.

78 Patterson, *Slavery and Social Death* (n. 22): 31.

79 Patterson, *Slavery and Social Death* (n. 22): 32.

80 Cf. Martin Schermaier, "Dominus actuum suorum: Die willenstheoretische Begründung des Eigentums und das römische Recht," in *Zeitschrift der Savigny-Stiftung für Rechtsgeschichte, Romanistische Abteilung* 134 (2017): 49–105.

circle; his fallacy is perfect. What should have caught his attention is the fact that the *dominus* gets his name from the *domus*, the house or household he heads.[81] Although the terms *dominus* and *dominium* appear comparatively late,[82] it is reasonable to assume that both were derived from 'domestic property', that property which in contrast to gentile property was held exclusively by the *pater familias*, the master of all persons and objects in the household.[83]

It is a different matter that the classification of Roman slaves into their master's *dominium* – such as in Paul – resulted in a social discrimination[84] which must have occurred at the time of Rome's expansion in the third and second centuries BCE. But even this classification says little about the legal position of slaves. And it would be overstated even if we were to think of *dominium* as absolute property in the modern sense.

3.4 Servi pro nullo habentur

But it is not only the *dominium* that induces modern scholars to retroject later conditions back onto Roman slavery. There are numerous other, mostly short, sentences that also imply the inferior legal position of slaves. The same applies to them as to the *dominium* over slaves: they frequently do not contain as much as modern readers wish to find in them. A well-known example is Ulpian's statement that slaves counted *pro nullis*, as nothing, under civil law. It sounds unambiguous: slaves do not legally exist.[85] But that is probably not what Ulpian wanted to express. If we read the fragment to the end, we learn that it is a completely different matter according to natural law:

> D. 50.17.32 (Ulp. 43 ad Sab.): Quod attinet ad ius civile, servi pro nullis habentur: non tamen et iure naturali, quia, quod ad ius naturale attinet, omnes homines aequales sunt.

> D. 50.17.32 (Ulpian, Sabinus, book 43): As far as concerns the civil law slaves are regarded as not existing, not, however, in the natural law, because as far as concerns the natural law all men are equal.[86]

81 Cf. Alois Walde and Johann Baptist Hofmann, *Lateinisches Etymologisches Wörterbuch*, vol. 1, Indogermanische Bibliothek, 2. Reihe: Wörterbücher (Heidelberg: Carl Winter, 1938): 367; Richard P. Saller, "Familia, Domus, and the Roman Conception of the Family," *Phoenix* 38, no. 4 (1984): 342–49.
82 Still seminal is Max Kaser's *Eigentum und Besitz im älteren römischen Recht* (Weimar: Hermann Böhlaus Nachfolger, 1943): 306–12.
83 E.g. Plaut. Most. 661 (*nomen domini*) and 686 (*dominus aedium*); Pseud. 1140 (*dominus aedium*); Cat. Agr. 1,4 (*dominus agri*); for further examples see Kaser, *Eigentum und Besitz* (n. 83): 308 n. 6.
84 Concisely Luigi Capogrossi Colognesi, "Das Eigentum in Rom vom Ende der patriarchalischen Ordnung bis zur Blütezeit der Sklavereiordnung," in *Eigentum. Beiträge zu seiner Entwicklung in politischen Gesellschaften. Werner Sellnow zum 70. Geburtstag*, ed. Jens Köhn and Burkhard Rode (Weimar: Böhlau, 1987): 117–39, esp. 121–23.
85 This is how Patterson reads it: *Slavery and Social Death* (n. 22): 40.
86 D. 50.17.32 (Ulp. 43 ad Sab.) (transl. Crawford in Watson, *Digest of Justinian* [n. 45]).

According to natural law, all men were equal, both slaves and free. So, we now have put at least Ulpian's statement that *ius civile* regards slaves as nothing into perspective. To interpret it correctly, however, we need to know that the Roman jurists regarded *ius civile* as only one part of positive law. There was also *ius gentium* (international law) and *ius honorarium*, made up by edicts of the magistrates. When he referred to *ius civile*, Ulpian meant only a certain section of positive law. In addition, although the Roman jurists thought of *ius naturale* as a philosophical category, it was not meaningless for the way they understood and applied positive law. The terse statement *servi pro nullis habentur* merely means that according to this particular aspect of law, under *ius civile*, slaves counted as nothing.

In addition to these general considerations, it is worth paying attention to the context from which the sentence is taken. The forty-third book *ad Sabinum* also contains the following fragment:

D. 15.1.41 (Ulp. 43 ad Sab.): Nec servus quicquam debere potest nec servo potest deberi, sed cum eo verbo abutimur, factum magis demonstramus quam ad ius civile referimus obligationem. itaque quod servo debetur, ab extraneis dominus recte petet, quod servus ipse debet, eo nomine in peculium et si quid inde in rem domini versum est in dominum actio datur.	D. 15.1.41 (Ulpian, Sabinus, book 43): A slave cannot really owe or be owed anything, but we use the word loosely to indicate the facts rather than with reference to obligations at civil law. Thus, a master may sue third parties for what they owe the slave, and he may be sued for what the slave owes them up to the amount of the peculium, and for any benefit thereby accruing to him.[87]

Under *ius civile*, a slave could be neither a creditor nor a debtor. This was because slaves were not entitled to take legal action, i.e. they could not assert claims in court nor be sued for debt: *cum servo nulla actio est*, Gaius noted succinctly.[88] This is noteworthy because in Greek law, slaves were entitled to take legal action.[89] But even under Roman law the servile lack of entitlement did not exclude slaves from being able to establish debts or claims, as the text continues: their master could claim what they were owed; while, if a slave owed a debt to another person, their master would be liable for it from the slave's *peculium*.

To readers unversed in Roman law, the text sounds perplexing: a slave unable to be a debtor was able to owe; a slave unable to be a creditor could be owed a debt. Behind this aporia hides a problem specific to classical law, which originated as case law and was therefore oriented towards litigation and the procedural enforcement of

87 Transl. Weir in Watson, *Digest of Justinian* (n. 45).
88 D. 50.17.107 (Gai. 1 ad ed. prov.): 'There is no action with a slave' (Crawford in Watson, *Digest of Justinian* [n. 45]). Cf. Kaser, *Das römische Privatrecht*, vol. 1 (n. 41): 286.
89 See for example Alfons Bürge, "Lo schiavo (in)dipendente e il suo patrimonio," in *Homo, caput, persona: La costruzione giuridica dell'identità nell'esperienza romana; dall'epoca di Plauto a Ulpiano*, ed. Alessandro Corbino, Michel Humbert and Giovanni Negri (Pavia: IUSS Press, 2010): esp. 370–72.

law. In its scholarly treatment, however, this law only started on the path towards becoming an institutional system of substantive rights and claims with Masurius Sabinus' *ius civile*,[90] on which Ulpian comments here. We probably already have a merging of the procedural and the institutional views in this account by Sabinus, and we certainly do in Ulpian.[91] The procedural view is that no claim could be brought for the debts of slaves. They could, however, be effectively settled; from the 'natural' perspective they were still owed: and it was for this reason that the Roman jurists called them *obligationes naturales*.[92]

D. 15.1.41 is an eloquent testimony to this. If the two fragments D. 50.17.32 and D. 15.1.41 were originally closely associated,[93] *servi pro nullis habentur* merely means that from the point of view of procedural law, slaves were treated as non-existent persons – just as, incidentally, women were.

Ulpian's sentence that slaves did not participate in *ius civile* has a similar meaning:

D. 28.1.20.7 (Ulp. 1 ad Sab.): Servus quoque merito ad sollemnia adhiberi non potest, cum iuris civilis communionem non habeat in totum, ne praetoris quidem edicti.	D. 28.1.20.7 (Ulpian, Sabinus, book 1): It is also right that a slave cannot be used in solemn acts as he is totally excluded from participation in the civil law, and even in the praetor's edict.[94]

It is unclear how much of this text is Ulpian's own statement: *iuris civilis communionem non habeat in totum* could either mean that slaves could not fully participate in *ius civile*,[95] or that they could not participate in it at all.[96] In my view, the former translation is the correct one. But even if we were to prefer the second one, the text does not

90 Cf. as well D. 15.1.49.2 (Pomp. 4 ad Quint. Muc.); the manual on *ius civile* of Quintus Mucius Scaevola, which was later commented by Pomponius, is presumably the first institutional depiction of the *ius civile* (D. 1.2.2.41; Pomp. sing. ench.) and could have been the model for Sabinus' work.

91 The two schools of thought in classical jurisprudence can still be traced in the structure of the *Digest*, compare D. 41.1 (material preconditions of property acquisition) to D. 6.1 (acquisition of property as consequence of loss of the right to claim of previous owner).

92 See, in detail, Kaser, *Das römische Privatrecht*, vol. 1 (n. 41): 480–81, esp. 481 (on debts of slaves); Götz Schulze, *Die Naturalobligation. Rechtsfigur und Instrument des Rechtsverkehrs einst und heute – zugleich Grundlegung einer Forderungslehre im Zivilrecht* (Tübingen: Mohr Siebeck, 2008).

93 Otto Lenel, *Palingenesia iuris civilis*, vol. 2 (Leipzig: Bernhard Tauchnitz, 1889; repr. Aalen: Scientia Verlag, 2000): 1173 (Ulpian no. 2899) assumes that they were.

94 Transl. Gordon in Watson, *Digest of Justinian* (n. 45).

95 This is the translation by Carl E. Otto, Bruno Schilling and Carl F.F. Sintenis, *Das Corpus Juris Civilis in's Deutsche übersetzt*, vol. 3 (Leipzig: G. Focke, 1831): 10; likewise that by Dominique Gaurier, *Les 50 livres du Digeste de l'Empereur Justinien. Edition traduite et annotée*, vol. 2 (Paris: Éditions La Mémoire du Droit, 2017): 1036.

96 This is the translation by Rolf Knütel, Berthold Kupisch, Thomas Rüfner and Hans Hermann Seiler, *Corpus Iuris civilis. Text und Übersetzung*, vol. 5, *(Digesten 28–34)* (Heidelberg: C.F. Müller, 2012): 6; likewise Watson's (n. 94).

completely exclude slaves from the law. The starting point of the argument was that slaves and others who were subject to authority were incapable of witnessing a will. This included women. Solemn acts of law based on ancient tradition, like the *testamentum per aes et libram*, were not available to slaves. This legal incapacity to make or to witness a will[97] echoes the lack of entitlement to take legal action; both were formal requirements, and both were part of public law.[98] So *ius civile* and *ius praetorium*, which latter Ulpian rules out for slaves, do not mean civil law as a whole but merely that part of the law which concerned formalised, and therefore also procedural, acts.

The sources provide further evidence for both. A slave to whom an inheritance had accrued could not himself formally declare its acceptance: this had to be done by his master. In D. 28.8.1 we read:

D. 28.8.1 (Ulp. 60 ad ed.): Si servus fuerit heres institutus, utique non ipsi praestituimus tempus ad deliberandum, sed ei cuius servus est, quia pro nullo isti habentur apud praetorem.	D. 28.8.1 (Ulpan, Edict, book 6): If a slave has been instituted heir, we have certainly not provided [the slave] himself with time for consideration, but the person who owns the slave, because, before the praetor, those people [slaves] are regarded as non existent.[99]

Slaves could inherit,[100] but they could not themselves declare their acceptance of the inheritance. For this reason, it was not they themselves but instead their masters who were granted a suitable period of reflection.[101] Slaves were unable to make a corresponding application to the *praetor* because they were incapable of raising actions. So, the sentence *pro nullo isti habentur* does not mean, as Patterson assumed,[102] that slaves were without rights. It merely means that slaves could not bring effective procedural action.

We have already mentioned that in a legal system like the Roman one, in which entitlements were conceived of in terms of procedural enforceability, procedural capability determined substantive law. In this respect, it could be argued that slaves possessed no rights merely on the grounds that they were denied access to the

97 Cf. D. 28.1.8 (Gai. 17 ad ed. prov.); D. 28.1.19 (Mod. 5 pand.); however, a slave could be appointed as scribe of a will, D. 28.1.28 (Mod. 9 reg.).

98 For the making of a will see D. 28.1.3 (Pap. 14 quaest.): *Testamti factio non privati, sed publici iuris est* ('*Testamenti factio* is matter not of private, but of public law', transl. Gordon in Watson, *Digest of Justinian* [n. 45]).

99 Transl. Gordon in Watson, *Digest of Justinian* (n. 45).

100 Cf. Wolfram Buchwitz, *Servus alienus heres. Die Erbeinsetzung fremder Sklaven im klassischen römischen Recht* (Vienna/Cologne/Weimar: Böhlau, 2012); for the text see 125–26; for general points see Buckland, *Law of Slavery* (n. 1): 137–39.

101 Cf. D. 50.17.107 (Gai. 1 ad ed. prov.): *cum servo nulla actio est.* 'There is no action with a slave', transl. Crawford in Watson, *Digest of Justinian* (n. 45).

102 Cf. again Patterson, *Slavery and Social Death* (n. 22): 40.

courts. But this conclusion is fallacious for two reasons: firstly, it fails to recognise the legal reality, which – as we shall see – could diverge from formal law.[103] And secondly, the principle that slaves could not appeal to the praetor and the courts was broken several times. There is a description of one case in the following text:

D. 48.10.7 (Marc. 2 inst.): Nullo modo servi cum dominis suis consistere possunt, cum ne quidem omnino iure civili neque iure praetorio neque extra ordinem computantur: praeterquam quod favorabiliter divi Marcus et Commodus rescripserunt, cum servus quereretur, quod tabulae testamenti, quibus ei data erat libertas, subprimerentur, admittendum ad suppressi testamenti accusationem.	D. 48.10.7 (Marcian, Institutes, book 2): Slaves can in no way bring actions against their masters, since they are reckoned as altogether unable to raise actions in the jus civile most surely, and also not in praetorian law nor in cognito proceedings; except for [the case] of which as a concession the deified Marcus and Commodus wrote in a rescript, when a slave was making a complaint that the tablets of a will, in which he had been granted his freedom, were suppressed, that he should be allowed to bring an accusation concerning the suppression of the will.[104]

Marcian explains that slaves were unable to sue their masters, under neither *ius civile* nor *ius praetorium*, nor according to the *extraordinaria cognitio*. They were accordingly excluded from all forms of litigation that existed side by side during the empire: the *legis actio*, preaetorian litigation and the post-classical procedures of extraordinary inquiry.[105] However, Marcian continues, the emperors Marcus Aurelius and Commodus allowed an exception: if a slave had grounds to assume that their deceased master had set them free in his will, and if the heir denied access to the document, the slave could accuse the heir of withholding the will. A comparable *favor libertatis*[106] underlies cases in which emperors allowed slaves to bring cases against an heir for freedom granted by will or bequest.[107]

There are even exceptions for the exclusion of slaves from *ius civile* or *ius honorarium*, which was limited to procedural law and formal legal acts. So *pro nullo habere* should not be taken literally: for one thing, because of the exceptions mentioned; for another, and most importantly, because it says nothing about the material entitlement of slaves.

---

103 See for more detail p. 249–251.

104 Transl. Robinson in Watson, *Digest of Justinian* (n. 45).

105 On these forms of litigation see Max Kaser and Karl Hackl, *Das römische Zivilprozessrecht*, 2nd ed. (Munich: C.H. Beck, 1996): 25–51, 151–62 and 435–514; more concisely Ernest Metzger, *Litigation in Roman Law* (Oxford: Oxford University Press, 2005).

106 For information on other relevant texts, apart from Stagl (in this volume), see Liselot Huchthausen, "Zum Problem der Freiheitsbegünstigung (favor libertatis) im römischen Recht," *Philologus* 120, no. 1 (1976): 47–72. Thomas Finkenauer, Die Rechtsetzung Mark Aurels zur Sklaverei (Stuttgart: Franz Steiner Verlag, 2010): 13–26 is sceptic about the influence of favor libertatis.

107 Such as D. 40.7.34.1 (Pap. 21 quaest.); D. 47.4.1.7 (Ulp. 38 ad ed.).

3.5 Enslavement as 'Death'

Those legal texts in which slavery is being compared with death deserve particular attention as they seem to express what Patterson means by the concept of 'social death'. While Patterson does not discuss these texts, Bodel comments:[108]

> The figuring of slavery as social death, so far from being opposed to a legal definition of the institution, was built by the Romans into the law of persons, to characterize a status that was absolute but potentially temporary.

The institution of *postliminium* testifies to the fact that Roman law potentially understood slavery as a transitory, temporally limited event. This, at any rate, applied to Romans who had been taken captive in war and so – from the Roman point of view – lost all family and property rights through enslavement. Of those who died as captives, the time of capture was considered their time of death.[109] A will set up prior to capture would then become effective.[110] In the absence of a will, intestate succession would take effect.[111] Dependents who had been under *manus* or *potestats* attained their freedom, while slaves would go to the heirs or legatees unless their manumission had been decreed in the will. If, however, the captive returned, was released from slavery or ransomed, his old rights were restored (*ius postliminii*).[112]

Because enslavement could happen not only as a result of captivity, but also of a criminal sentence,[113] D. 35.1.59.2 provides for the same consequences for the latter case. It is again useful to consider the context fully to understand this text:

D. 35.1.59 (Ulp. 13 ad leg. Iul. et Pap.): Intercidit legatum, si ea persona decesserit, cui legatum est sub condicione. (1) Quid ergo, si non decesserit, sed in civitate esse desierit?	D. 35.1.59 (Lex Julia et Papia, book 13): A legacy fails if the person to whom it was left under a condition dies. 1. What, then, if he does not die but ceases to be a citizen?

108 Bodel, "Death and Social Death" (n. 32): 94.

109 D. 49.15.18 (Ulp. 35 ad Sab.): *In omnibus partibus iuris is, qui reversus non est ab hostibus, quasi tunc decessisse videtur, cum captus est* ('In every branch of the law, a person who fails to return from enemy hands is regarded as having died at the moment when he was captured', transl. Robinson in Watson, *Digest of Justinian* [n. 45]). We know from I. 2.12.5 that this regulation was based on a law of P. Cornelius Sulla's (*lex Cornelia de confirmandis testamentis*).

110 Cf. most recently Sebastian Lohsse, "Die Beerbung des Kriegsgefangenen. Entwicklungsstufen der Auslegung der lex Cornelia de confirmandis testamentis," in *Facetten des römischen Erbrechts*, ed. Jan Dirk Harke (Berlin/Heidelberg: Springer Verlag, 2021): 79–111; Carlos M. Sánchez-Moreno Ellart, "Die fictio legis Corneliae in P.Berol. 11753 A and 21294 A," *Archiv für Papyrusforschung und verwandte Gebiete* 67, no. 1 (2021): 102–9.

111 This conforms to the currently prevailing view, cf. D. 49.15.22 pr. (Iul. 62 dig.); D. 38.16.1 pr. (Ulp. 12 ad Sab.).

112 Still relevant is August Bechmann, *Das Ius Postliminii und die Lex Cornelia: Ein Beitrag zur Dogmatik des römischen Rechts* (Erlangen: Verlag von Andreas Deichert, 1872).

113 See Aglaia McClintock (in this volume).

114 Transl. Thomas in Watson, *Digest of Justinian* (n. 45).

puta alicui legatum 'si consul fuerit' et is in insulam deportatus est: numquid non interim exstinguitur legatum, quia restitui in civitate potest? quod probabilius esse arbitror. (2) Non idem erit dicendum, si ea poena in eum statuta fuerit, quae irrogat servitutem, quia servitus morti adsimulatur.	Suppose a legacy to someone, "if he becomes consul", and he be deported to an island; is it to be said that the legacy is not destroyed in the interim, because he could be restored to citizenship? I think this is the more acceptable view. 2. The same would not be said if he were subjected to a penalty entailing slavery; for slavery is equated with death.[114]

The examples dealt with here in brief[115] address the effectiveness of a bequest decreed under a conditional precedent. Did the heir have to wait for the condition to be met before fulfilling the bequest, or could he consider the bequest to be discharged if something befell the legatee? The *principium* states briefly that the legatee's death would cause the legacy to lapse unless the condition had occurred by then. If it already had, the case was different: in this case, the claim passed to the heir of the legatee. Only his premature death caused the legacy to lapse entirely. If the condition did not occur before the legatee's death, it was of no use to his heir. This was the starting point for the following deliberations.

In § 1, the legatee had not died, but been exiled as the result of a criminal conviction. In this case, the legacy was not extinguished even if the condition had not yet been met before banishment. Upon being exiled, the legatee would lose his citizen rights, which was why the condition that he becomes consul could not occur. There were good grounds for assuming that the legacy was extinguished, but, Ulpian countered, the exiled might yet be pardoned, and so regain his citizenship and become consul after all. So, the heir was required to wait and see whether this would happen during the legatee's lifetime.

This case discussed in § 1 was not dissimilar from the one in § 2: what applied if, before the stipulated condition had occurred, the legatee was given a punishment that entailed losing his freeman status? Ulpian's answer is clear and concise: because *servitus poenae* was equated with death (*servitus morti adsimulatur*), the legacy was going to expire. But could it not again be argued that the condemned might still be pardoned? This was indeed not impossible. But for one thing a pardon did not automatically result in the reinstatement of proprietary status.[116] And even if the ex-convict had been exceptionally[117] reinstated into all citizen rights by means of *restitutio in integrum*, this restitution could not completely erase the reduction in status: with death occurring as a result of the conviction, there was now no possibility of the condition ('that he becomes consul') occurring and the bequest

---

115 On the fragment see most recently Tommaso Beggio, *Contributo allo studio della 'servitus poenae'* (Bari: Cacucci Editore, 2020): 219–21.

116 Cf. Wolfgang Waldstein, *Untersuchungen zum römischen Begnadigungsrecht. Abolitio – indulgentia – venia*, Commentationes Aenipontanae 18 (Innsbruck: Universitätsverlag Wagner, 1964): 132.

117 Cf. Waldstein, *Begnadigungsrecht* (n. 116): 135–37 (on Paul. sent. 4.8.22).

claim being effective. A different decision would have resulted in significantly increased uncertainty for the heir: his obligation would no longer have depended solely on the condition occurring but also on the pardon, and even on whether the condition had occurred only *after* the pardon. This would go too far beyond the testator's stipulations. So, if a legatee had been sentenced to penal slavery before the stated condition had occurred, the heir was thereby freed from his obligation.

This is what Ulpian intended to say by the short sentence *servitus morti adsimulatur*: a liability that had not yet fallen effective would expire permanently with the creditor's enslavement, just as if he had died.

Another sentence of Ulpian's, D. 50.17.209, sounds much more universal: *Servitutem mortalitati fere comparamus* – 'In general, becoming a slave is compared with death'. We can be certain that this sentence – like all the rules contained under the heading of D. 50.17 (*De diversis regulibus iuris antiqui*) – had been phrased for a specific reason and now, without this context, appeared to have general validity and greater weight. Here too, however, we can reconstruct this context. Like fragment D. 35.1.59, the sentence originates in Ulpian's commentary on the *lex Iulia et Papia*. Augustus had passed these two laws[118] in order to promote marriage and encourage procreation. Especially the *lex Papia Poppaea* with its sanctions against the unmarried and the childless had a considerable impact on Roman inheritance law: anyone who was still unmarried at the stipulated age and had not already given birth to or fathered three (legitimate) children, could not receive anything from a will and a legacy. Those who were married but childless could only receive half of what they were left. The portions of inheritance or legacies thus released (the so-called *caducum*) went to married heirs or legatees with at least one child.[119] If there were none, the inheritance or legacy went to the state.

What does all this have to do with Ulpian's rule? The connection is revealed by the cases discussed in D. 35.1.59: the question is which persons could obtain the *caducum* before it went to the state.[120] If any among them were married with children but had lost their freedom at the time of the possible acquirement, they did not count as acquirers; the inheritance or legacy went to the next potential inheritor

118 *Lex Iulia de maritandis ordinibus* in 18 BCE and *lex Papia Poppaea* in 9 CE; see for example James A. Field, "The Purpose of the Lex Iulia et Papia Poppaea," *The Classical Journal* 40, no. 7 (1945): 398–416; Angelika Mette-Dittmann, *Die Ehegesetze des Augustus: Eine Untersuchung im Rahmen der Gesellschaftspolitik des Princeps* (Stuttgart: Franz Steiner Verlag, 1991); Susan Treggiari, *Roman Marriage: 'Iusti Coniuges' from the Time of Cicero to the Time of Ulpian* (Oxford: Oxford University Press, 1991): 60–80; Riccardo Astolfi, *La 'lex Iulia et Papia'* (Padua: Cedam, 1996).

119 For more details, see Kaser, *Das römische Privatrecht*, vol. 1 (n. 41): 319–21; Astolfi, *lex Iulia et Papia* (n. 118): 126–32; most recently Filippo Bonin, "Tra ius antiquum, lex Iulia e Lex Papia: Il complesso destino di caduca in età Augustea," *Teoria e Storia del diritto Privato* 12 (2019), https://dialnet.unirioja.es/servlet/articulo?codigo=7236855 [accessed 05.08.2022].

120 Lenel, *Palingenesia*, vol. 2 (n. 93): 948, puts D. 35.1.59 under the heading '*Quae lege Papia caduca fiant*'.

or to the state. D. 50.17.209 is a similar case: the few extant fragments from Ulpian's fourth book of *ad legem Iuliam et Papiam libri XX* discuss the question which children could be considered to be the testamentary beneficiary's. Did they include children born by his wife while he was a prisoner of war (and thus in slavery)?[121] Did they include the children fathered by a man while he was a prisoner of war?[122] The sentence contained in D. 50.17.209 can probably be placed in a similar context.[123] Here again, *servitus* is discussed with reference to the child and not to the person whose entitlement to inherit is being discussed. Children in captivity or slavery did not count in favour of their parents (in terms of the *lex Papia Poppaea*): it was as if they had been stillborn or died. This, and nothing more, is meant in Ulpian's pronouncement that 'becoming a slave is compared with death'.

4 Some Results

Such terse, formulaic sentences, which are sometimes used to illustrate sociological arguments or to express social-historical findings, often turn out to be unsuitable for this purpose. This has been shown by the deliberations in this paper on *nullum caput* (a), *pro nulla habentur* (d) or *servitus morti adsimulatur* (e). That is not to say that these phrases are meaningless for the legal classification of slaves. Whether it was slaves not being admissible to trial or to bring a formal action, or the fact that in Augustus' legislation to encourage population expansion only free persons were counted while slaves were not: all of these show quite clearly the legal discrimination against slaves that did exist. Even so, the legal context matters. It tells us whether something is the brief outline of a legal issue, or an actual rule that can be universalised.

But just like the description of slaves as the 'property' of their masters, these sentences also have an important significance in the history of ideas. Most of those who later wanted to understand and use the Roman sources were not concerned with their historical meaning.[124] The sentences and pronouncements stand for themselves, they are not *explanandum*, but *explanans*. They are just as normative as they are (being part of Roman law) authoritative. The concept of *dominium*, for example, took on a life of its own in the high middle ages, becoming a key concept not only in jurisprudence but also in moral theology and in political and social philosophy. In slave law, as indicated, it turned into an Archimedean point from which

121 D. 1.7.46 (Ulp. 4 ad leg. Iul. et Pap.).
122 D. 49.15.9 (Ulp. 4 ad leg. Iul. et Pap.).
123 Cf. Lenel, *Palingenesia*, vol. 2 (n. 93): 943–44.
124 In this sense, Patterson's observation in *Slavery and Social Death* (n. 22): 189 is quite correct: 'Roman legal theory, which probably did not depart much from practice, certainly influenced most subsequent slaveholding societies in the Western world'.

it became possible to conceptualise slavery for the first time. Much the same is true for the rules cited as examples. While they may not have contributed to legitimising asymmetrical dependencies, we use them to analyse dependency structures. This is unproblematic as long as we do not want to use them to explain Roman slavery itself. In other words: the fact that being a slave was tantamount to 'social death' can be proven with many details from Roman slave law but not with the dictum that jurists considered slaves *pro nullo* (or *pro nullis*).

If we try to understand Roman slavery from the experience of transatlantic slavery, we cannot do justice either to the social or the legal conditions in antiquity. The study of Roman slavery must begin *ab ovo*: we must first understand the role of the *servi* in the small-scale structures of early Rome because it was during this period that the rules governing status began to be developed, which would, centuries later, continue to provide the frame of reference for the legal status of slaves. Only from this point is it possible to explain the consequences of the prosperous slave economy of the late Republic and the Empire which turned slaves into 'merchandise'[125] while at the same time causing a strong social differentiation within the slave class. This is the period in which most of our sources originated, at the peak of the Roman slave economy. For Roman jurists, all *servi* still shared the same status, and so were essentially all in the same legal situation. But it would be absurd to understand them as a homogeneous class because of this. The social differences among the unfree were immense and were respected by contemporary law. The following contributions will examine this tension in more detail.

125 In an economic, not a legal, sense: cf. Mela in D. 50.16.207 (Afr. 3 quaest.), see above n. 52.

Thomas Finkenauer

Filii naturales: Social Fate or Legal Privilege?

1 Introduction

Roman law with its agnatic kinship concept is strictly oriented towards the *paterfamilias*, whether dead or alive: agnatic relatives are defined as all those who are (or would be) subject to the *patria potestas* of the father or another shared patrilineal ancestor (if alive).[1] A child who has been emancipated from *patria potestas* is no longer related to its sire; an adopted child is agnatically related to its adoptive father *only*: consanguinity is irrelevant.

Only Roman citizens can be or have agnates: unfree persons have no 'father',[2] because *patria potestas* is bound up with Roman citizenship; hence they have no agnates, no family. It is denied them even after manumission, which is why, for instance, the freed son of a freedman is not agnatically related to him, and so has no legal right to his father's inheritance on intestacy.[3]

While *paterfamilias* is not only a social but also a legal term, the expression for the natural father, *pater naturalis*,[4] although mentioned in legal sources, never acquired legal significance. The same is true for biological, 'natural', children (*liberi naturales*), grandchildren, siblings or grandparents. Nowhere is there any mention of a *familia naturalis*; also not with reference to slave families.[5] The legal sources stress the biological parentage of a 'natural' child only where they want to distinguish it from an adopted[6] or an emancipated[7] one. Such a *filius naturalis* may be *legitimus*, i.e. the child of a lawful marriage (*iustum matrimonium*); or an illegitimate child

1 Max Kaser, *Das römische Privatrecht*, vol. 1, *Das altrömische, das vorklassische und klassische Recht*, 2nd ed. (Munich: C.H. Beck, 1971): 58.

2 See also Plautus, *Captivi*, 574: *quem patrem, qui servos est?*

3 Reinhard Willvonseder, *Stellung des Sklaven im Privatrecht*, vol. 1, *Eheähnliche Verbindungen und verwandtschaftliche Beziehungen*, Corpus der römischen Rechtsquellen zur antiken Sklaverei 4 (Stuttgart: Franz Steiner Verlag, 2010): 2.

4 Hermann Gottlieb Heumann and Emil Seckel, *Handlexikon zu den Quellen des römischen Rechts*, 9th ed. (Jena: G. Fischer, 1914): s.v. *naturalis*, b.

5 Ulpian D. 38.8.1.4 (46 ad ed.) is the only place that references *familia naturalis patris*, as opposed to *familia adoptiva*. Heumann and Seckel, *Handlexikon* (n. 4): s.v. *naturalis*, b α, are not entirely precise.

6 Ulpian D. 38.8.1.4 (46 ad ed.).

7 Gaius ep. 1.6.4.

https://doi.org/10.1515/9783110987195-002

resulting from the union of two slaves, of a free man with a slave or a concubine (who may be free or unfree) or the illegitimate offspring of two Roman citizens.[8]

The lack of liberty and citizenship meant that sexual unions between slaves or free and unfree, such as between a male or female Roman with a female or male slave, could only ever be a *contubernium*,[9] in which the male partner was unable to be *maritus*, the female partner unable to be *uxor*. Their children were not *liberi*, but only *liberi naturales*.[10] This essay will explore the extent to which the law protected such unions and their offspring, in spite of the above.

In civil law, a slave was a mere thing, *res*, the property of his master. Slaves were the object of contracts about sale, custody or hire, transfer of ownership, pledge or usufruct, of legacies or inheritances. Their close ties to blood relatives, to what we would call their 'family', were not recognised in law. Late classical jurists like Ulpian[11] and Paul[12] at least are very clear about the irrelevance of *servilis cognatio*.[13] However, in classical law there are some texts that acknowledge the existence and even, to some degree, the significance of these ties.[14] They will be the subject of this investigation.

---

8 For more detail about (il)legitimacy see Giovanni Luchetti, *La legittimazione dei figli naturali nelle fonti tardo imperiali e giustinianee* (Milan: Giuffrè, 1990): 8–12; Heumann and Seckel, *Handlexikon* (n. 4): s.v. *naturalis*, b.

9 UE 5.5; PS 2.19.6; on *contubernium* see Elemér Pólay, *Die Sklavenehe und das römische Recht*, Acta Juridica et Politica, Universitatis Szegediensis 14/7 (Szeged: József Attila Tudományegyetem Szeged, 1967): 1–84, 38–39; Marcel Simonis, *Cum servis nullum est conubium: Untersuchungen zu den eheähnlichen Verbindungen von Sklaven im westlichen Mittelmeerraum des Römischen Reiches* (Hildesheim/Zurich/New York: Georg Olms Verlag, 2017): 17–33. The term *concubinatus* is also not infrequently found, although it is not technically available to slaves; cf. Simonis, *Cum servis nullum est conubium*: 39.

10 This term occurs in the legal sources for the first time in Julian D. 42.8.17.1 (49 dig.).

11 D. 38.8.1.2 (46 ad ed.). *Pertinet autem haec lex ad cognationes non serviles: nec enim facile ulla servilis videtur esse cognatio* ('But this law does not apply to servile relationships. For it is not easy to define any servile tie as a cognate relationship', transl. Jameson in Alan Watson, *The Digest of Justinian*, vol. 3 [Pennsylvania: University of Pennsylvania Press, 1985]). The sentence refers to the granting of *bonorum possessio*.

12 D. 38.10.10.5 (l. s. de grad. et adfin.). *Non parcimus his nominibus, id est cognatorum, etiam in servis: itaque parentes et filios fratresque etiam servorum dicimus: sed ad leges serviles cognationes non pertinent* ('We do not refrain from using these names, that is, the names of cognates; and so we talk about the parents and sons and brothers of slaves too, but servile relationships do not belong to [the realm of] the laws.', transl. Jameson in Watson, *Digest of Justinian* [n. 11]).

13 For details see Kaser, *Das römische Privatrecht*, vol. 1 (n. 1): 316; Pólay, *Die Sklavenehe* (n. 9): 23.

14 For more detail see Kaser, *Das römische Privatrecht*, vol. 1 (n. 1): 350–51.

1.1 Impediment to Marriage (*incestum*)

Roman law prohibited marriages between persons related in the direct line, as well as between collateral relatives, generally as far as the third degree. The prohibition also extended to illegitimate blood relatives as well as kinship ties of servile origin: of course, this only applied to freedpersons who, once manumitted, acquired Roman citizenship and thus a necessary requirement for marriage:

D. 23.2.14.2 (Paulus 35 ad ed.): Serviles quoque cognationes in hoc iure observandae sunt. igitur suam matrem manumissus non ducet uxorem: tantundem iuris est et in sorore et sororis filia. idem e contrario dicendum est, ut pater filiam non possit ducere, si ex servitute manumissi sint, etsi dubitetur patrem eum esse. unde nec volgo quaesitam filiam pater naturalis potest uxorem ducere, quoniam in contrahendis matrimoniis naturale ius et pudor inspiciendus est: contra pudorem est autem filiam uxorem suam ducere.

D. 23.2.14.2 (Paulus, Edict, book 35): Blood relationship between slaves must be considered in connection with this rule. So on manumission a man cannot marry his own mother, and the rule is the same for a sister and a sister's daughter. On the other hand, it must be said that a father cannot marry his daughter, if they have been manumitted, even where it is doubtful whether he is her father. So a natural father cannot marry his daughter who was born out of wedlock, because natural law and decency must be taken into consideration in marriage, and it is indecent to make a daughter into your wife.[15]

Paul invokes *ius naturale* and *pudor*, decency, to state clearly that *servilis cognatio* is among the impediments that prevent a marriage. Pomponius however cites the *mores maiorum* as prohibiting such a union.[16]

1.2 Summons (*in ius vocatio*)

Children were unable to summon to court their natural parents or other ascendants without express permission of the praetor.[17] The moral reason for this prohibition is the respect that is the due of parents:

D. 2.4.6 (Paulus 1 sent.): Parentes naturales in ius vocare nemo potest: una est enim omnibus parentibus servanda reverentia.

D. 2.4.6 (Paulus, Views, book 1): No one can summon natural parents to court; for the same respect should be observed toward all parents.[18]

---

15 Transl. McLeod in Watson, *Digest of Justinian* (n. 11).

16 Pomponius D. 23.2.8 (5 ad Sab.). For concubinage see Ulpian D. 23.2.56 (3 disp.).

17 Ulpian D. 2.4.4.1.2 (5 ad ed.).

18 Transl. MacCormack in Watson, *Digest of Justinian* (n. 11). See also PS 1.1b.1.

This ban prohibits, for example, an adopted child from suing its biological father.[19] But it also expressly includes servile family ties – which only assume significance, however, after manumission, because a slave cannot appear in court.[20]

D. 2.4.4.3 (Ulpian 5 ad ed.): Parentes etiam eos accipi Labeo existimat, qui in servitute susceperunt: nec tamen, ut Severus dicebat, ad solos iustos liberos: sed et si volgo quaesitus sit filius, matrem in ius non vocabit,	D. 2.4.4.3 (Ulpian, Edict, book 5): Labeo thinks that those who have produced children in slavery are also to be considered parents and that the term is not applicable, as Severus[21] said, only in the case where the children are legitimate. But if a son has been born in promiscuity, he shall not summon his mother to court,[22]

1.3 Murder (*parricidium*)

Originally, the penalty for killing another person's slave had only been the obligation to pay damages to the slave's owner. Not until the legal interpretation of Sulla's law on murder was it also considered murder in criminal law. Claudius ruled that killing one's own slave was murder only in the absence of sufficient reason.[23] The reform of *parricidium* in the *lex Pompeia* (after 80 B.C.) included the murderer's ascendants as well descendants, unless he was a *paterfamilias*; it also abolished the *poena cullei*, the penalty of death in the sack, although the latter point is contested among scholars.[24] In the high classical period, Venuleius believed the *lex Pompeia* applied to slaves, albeit indirectly and by analogy only, and so included the killing of natural parents under its regulations: *cum natura communis*

---

19 Ulpian D. 2.4.8 pr. (5 ad ed.).

20 Max Kaser and Karl Hackl, *Das römische Zivilprozeßrecht*, 2nd ed. (Munich: C.H. Beck, 1996): 205.

21 He lived during the first half of the second century, cf. Wolfgang Kunkel, *Herkunft und soziale Stellung der römischen Juristen*, 2nd ed. (Graz/Vienna/Cologne: Hermann Böhlaus Nachfolger, 1967): 154. So there is no need to emend Servius, *contra* William Warwick Buckland, *The Roman Law of Slavery: The Condition of the Slave in Private Law from Augustus to Justinian* (Cambridge: Cambridge University Press, 1908): 78.

22 Transl. MacCormack in Watson, *Digest of Justinian* (n. 11).

23 Theodor Mommsen, *Römisches Strafrecht* (Leipzig: Duncker & Humblot, 1899): 616–17.

24 Mommsen, *Römisches Strafrecht* (n. 23): 644–45; Hermann Ferdinand Hitzig, "Culleus," in *Paulys Realencyclopädie der classischen Altertumswissenschaft*, vol. 4/2 (Stuttgart: J.B. Metzler 1901): col. 1744–48, 1747; Herwig Stiegler, "Konkubinenkind, 'privignus', 'parricidium'?," in *Sodalitas. Scritti in onore di Antonio Guarino*, vol. 7, ed. Vincenzo Giuffrè (Naples: Jovene, 1984): 3191–214, 3208; Bernardo Santalucia, *Diritto e processo penale nell'antica Roma*, 2nd ed. (Milan: Giuffrè, 1998): 161; see also the more nuanced discussion in J.D. Cloud, "Parricidium: From the lex Numae lo the lex Pómpela de parricidiis," in *Zeitschrift der Savigny-Stiftung für Rechtsgeschichte, Romanistische Abteilung* 88 (1971): 1–66, 52.

est, similiter animadvertetur.[25] However, we do not know the extent to which the law was actually applied in this way.[26]

2 Manumission

2.1 *Manumissio apud consilium adprobata*

Manumission under Roman civil law not only gave liberty to the freedman, it also made him a Roman citizen. The *lex Aelia Sentia*, established under Augustus in 4 A.D., restricted manumissions by imposing age limits: the slave's owner had to be at least twenty, the manumittee at least thirty years of age. Manumission of a slave below the age of thirty or by a minor below twenty was permissible only if there was a *iusta causa*, a valid reason,[27] which had to be shown (*causae probatio*)[28] before the magistrate's *consilium.*[29] Gaius, also active in the high classical period, includes ties to a slave's natural family, *servilis cognatio*, among the valid reasons for such a privileged manumission.[30] He also lists a foster-child (*alumnus*[31]), a tutor or educator

25 Venuleius D. 48.2.12.4 (2 de iudic. publ.). [. . .] *item nec lex Pompeia parricidii, quoniam caput primum eos adpraehendit, qui parentes cognatosve aut patronos occiderint: quae in servos, quantum ad verba pertinet, non cadunt: sed cum natura communis est, similiter et in eos animadvertetur* [. . .] ('[. . .] Again, the *lex Pompeia* on parricide is not [applicable] since its first chapter covers those who have killed their parents, blood relations, or patrons; so far as the words go these do not apply to slaves, but because the laws of nature are common to [all humans], a similar punishment will be imposed on them also [. . .]', transl. Robinson in Watson, *Digest of Justinian* [n. 11]). For the text see Pia Starace, "Venuleio, il parricidio, i servi, la natura," in *Testi e problemi del giusnaturalismo romano*, ed. Dario Mantovani and Aldo Schiavone (Pavia: IUSS Press, 2007): 497–518, 515; Lucia Fanizza, "Il parricidio nel sistema della 'lex Pompeia'," *Labeo* 25, no. 3 (1979): 267–89, 268.

26 Cloud, "Parridicum" (n. 24): 52.

27 For this meaning of *iustus* see Thomas Finkenauer, "Die römischen Juristen und die Gerechtigkeit," in *Recht und Gerechtigkeit*, ed. Otfried Höffe (Freiburg im Breisgau/Berlin: Rombach, 2014): 11–46, 27.

28 Gaius inst. 1.18; Kaser, *Das römische Privatrecht*, vol. 1 (n. 1): 297; Johanna Filip-Fröschl, "Gefühle und Recht. Gedanken zur rechtlichen Relevanz von Gefühlen, ausgehend von den Bestimmungen zur römischen Sklavenfamilie," in *Vis ac potestas legum. Liber amicorum Zoltán Végh*, ed. Michael Rainer (Frankfurt am Main: Peter Lang Verlag, 2010): 9–33, 22 sqq.

29 For how the *consilium* was constituted at Rome and in the provinces, see Gaius inst. 1.20.

30 See also Gaius inst. 1.38–39.

31 Heumann and Seckel, *Handlexikon* (n. 4): s.v. *alumnus*; see Michael Memmer, "Ad servitutem aut ad lupanar . . .," *Zeitschrift der Savigny-Stiftung für Rechtsgeschichte, Romanistische Abteilung* 108 (1991): 21–93, 42. *Alumnus* could refer either to an abandoned child (*expositus*) who had been raised for the slave market, or to a nursling who had been sent away to be raised; see Elisabeth Herrmann-Otto, *Ex ancilla natus: Untersuchungen zu den 'hausgeborenen' Sklaven und Sklavinnen im Westen des römischen Kaiserreiches* (Stuttgart: Franz Steiner Verlag, 1994): 18. For our purpose the child must be unfree.

(*paedagogus*), a male slave intended to be employed as an asset manager, or a female slave the manumitter plans to marry, but he begins his list with the natural child or sibling:

Gaius inst. 1.19: Iusta autem causa manumissionis est, veluti si quis filium filiamve aut fratrem sororemve naturalem aut alumnum aut paedagogum aut servum procuratoris habendi gratia aut ancillam matrimonii causa apud consilium manumittat.

Gaius inst. 1.19: Now, a good reason for the grant of freedom exists, for instance, if a person frees before the committee his son or daughter or his real brother or sister, his foster-child or his teacher, or a slave to be made an asset manager, or a female slave for the purpose of marriage.[32]

A woman could also manumit a male slave *matrimonii causa*[33] in this privileged manner, as could a mother her natural son below the age of thirty.[34] Ulpian expressly underlines the consideration given to blood ties.[35]

Gaius only lists examples, his list is not exhaustive. In the late classical period, Ulpian also mentions the manumission of the 'bag carrier' (*capsarius*), milk-brother (*collactaneus*), tutor (*educator*) or wet nurse (*nutrix*):[36]

D. 40.2.13 (Ulpian libro de off. procons.): si collactaneus, si educator, si paedagogus ipsius, si nutrix, vel filius filiave cuius eorum, vel alumnus, vel capsarius (id est qui portat libros), vel si in hoc manumittatur, ut procuratorsit, dummodo non minor annis decem et octo sit, praeterea et illud exigitur, ut non utique unum servum habeat, qui manumittit. item si matrimonii causa virgo vel mulier manumittatur, exacto prius iureiurando, ut intra sex menses uxorem eam duci oporteat: ita enim senatus censuit.

D. 40.2.13 (Upian, Duties of Proconsul, book 6): that the slave is his foster brother or foster father or schoolmaster or nurse or son or daughter to any of these or his foster child or capsarius, that is, one who carries books, or that he is manumitted for the purpose of being his procurator provided that such a person is not under eighteen. It is a further requirement that the manumitter should not have just one slave. A virgin or woman may also be manumitted for marriage, provided that the master must first swear an oath to take her as his wife within six months; this was resolved by the senate.[37]

---

32 Translation based upon W.M. Gordon and O.F. Robinson, *The Institutes of Gaius* (London: Cornell University Press, 1988): 27.

33 Marcian D. 40.2.14.1 (4 reg.). For this entire topic see Andreas Wacke, "Manumissio matrimonii causa. Die Freilassung zwecks Heirat nach den Ehegesetzen des Augustus," in *Fünfzig Jahre Forschungen zur antiken Sklaverei an der Mainzer Akademie: 1950–2000. Miscellanea zum Jubiläum*, ed. Heinz Bellen and Heinz Heinen (Stuttgart: Franz Steiner Verlag, 2001): 133–58.

34 This option is attested from at least the time of Marcellus onwards, cf. D. 40.2.20.3 (Ulp. 2 de off. cons.).

35 D. 40.2.12 (Ulp. 2 ad l. Aeliam Sentiam). *Vel si sanguine eum contingit (habetur enim ratio cognationis).* ('Or that there is a connection by blood [for account is taken of kinship]', transl. Brunt in Watson, *Digest of Justinian* [n. 11]).

36 See also Inst. 1.6.5.

37 Transl. Brunt in Watson, *Digest of Justinian* (n. 11).

The privileged manumission of a foster child (*alumnus*), a tutor, milk-brother or wet nurse are, of course, quite outside the territory of *cognatio servilis* as a valid reason for manumission, as is the manumission of a female slave in order to marry her. What appears to be of primary concern to Gaius and Ulpian in determining the exceptions to the *lex Aelia Sentia* – and as such the privileged access to manumission for freedman or slave owner – are not ties of blood, but rather the close relationship between manumitter and manumittee evidenced by the will to bestow liberty.[38] The situation is different, however, in the case of the slave intended to be employed as manager of his master's assets, which seems driven mainly by utilitarian considerations: the manumitter was apparently not sufficiently mature to manage his property himself.

A remarkable addition to the circle of slaves with potentially privileged access to manumission is listed by Ulpian in D. 40.2.13: they include the *issue* of a milk-brother, tutor or wet nurse. Ulpian is clearly thinking here of the simultaneous manumission of parents and child. Sufficient grounds for privileged manumission was evidently also the existence of kinship ties to a slave who was close to the manumitter; this close relationship (to a person other than the manumitter) was justification enough.

When privileged manumission came under judicial scrutiny, the pivotal aspect – excepting only the freedman asset manager – was the affection, *affectus*. In accordance with the stated legal purpose of the *lex Aelia Sentia*, the only motive that should be disregarded was extravagance or excess: *Illud in causis probandis meminisse iudices oportet, ut non ex luxuria, sed ex affectu descendentes causas probent* [. . .].[39] For this reason the law did not support manumission of a slave favourite, the *servus delicatus*:[40] Roman society did not consider amorous affection the equal of affection between family members, and so did not recognise it in law.

2.2 *Redemptio servi suis nummis*

A slave could buy his own freedom by arranging for a third party to purchase and subsequently manumit him. If the money used was from the slave's own purse, a *constitutio* by Marcus Aurelius legally obliged the purchaser who broke the agreement to

---

38 Correctly Adriaan Johan Boudewijn Sirks, "The lex Junia and the Effects of Informal Manumission and Iteration," *Revue Internationale des Droits de l'Antiquité* 30 (1983): 211–92, 241; unconvincing Herrmann-Otto, *Ex ancilla* (n. 31): 85 n. 178.

39 Ulpian D. 40.2.16 pr. (2 ad l. Aeliam Sentiam): 'It is to be borne in mind by judges when approving grounds for manumission that they are to approve grounds that arise not from luxury but from true feeling [. . .]', transl. Brunt in Watson, *Digest of Justinian* (n. 11).

40 Martin Kindler, *Affectionis aestimatio. Vom Ursprung des Affektionsinteresses im römischen Recht und seiner Rezeption* (Berlin: Duncker & Humblot, 2012): 43.

manumit the slave.[41] The slave could take them to the prefect's or the provincial governor's court.[42] There were several legal curiosities about this transaction, the so-called *redemptio suis nummis* ('purchase with his own money'), such as the fact that slaves could not legally own money,[43] and that a manumission mandate issued by a slave was not legally valid.[44] These were disregarded, by Marcus Aurelius as much as by classical and later classical jurists. In order for the transaction and the duty to manumit to be legally recognised, the purchaser must not use any of his own assets for the purchase, and could only benefit by gaining the title of *patronus*, but not any economically relevant patronage rights. He could therefore neither demand services (*operae*) nor a right to any of the ex-slave's inheritance after his death.[45]

The sources emphasise the seller's emotional interest, *ratio affectus*, in the transaction, and give as example a case in which the slave in question is a natural son or brother:

D. 17.1.54 pr. (Papinian 27 quaest.): Cum servus extero se mandat emendum, nullum mandatum est. sed si in hoc mandatum intercessit ut servus manumitteretur nec manumiserit, et pretium consequetur dominus ut venditor et affectus ratione mandati agetur: finge filium naturalem vel fratrem esse (placuit enim prudentioribus affectus rationem in bonae fidei iudiciis habendam) [. . .]

D. 17.1.54 pr. (Papinian, Questions, book 27): When a slave gives a mandate to a third party to buy him, the mandate is of no effect. But if the mandate was for the purpose that the slave should be manumitted and [the buyer] does not manumit, the master will recover the price, as seller, and there will be an action on mandate by reason of affection; suppose that it is his natural son or his brother (for the more insightful jurists have agreed that account is to be taken of affection in actions of good faith) [. . .][46]

So despite the contract between the slave and the third-party purchaser having no legal force, it does have an effect in favour of the seller! He (or she) can bring an

41 Ulpian D. 40.1.4 pr. (6 disp.).

42 Rolf Knütel, "Freikauf mit eigenem Geld," in *Handwörterbuch der antiken Sklaverei*, vol. 1, ed. Heinz Heinen et al. (Stuttgart: Franz Steiner Verlag, 2017): coll. 1095–97, 1096.

43 A slave's special property, the *peculium*, was legally not owned by the slave but by his master; but Ulpian tells us that for this transaction the jurists turned a blind eye to regulations: *coniventibus oculis*, Ulpian D. 40.1.4.1 (6 disp.).

44 See the immediate reaction by Papinian, D. 17.1.54 pr. (27 quaest.). For a detailed treatment see Thomas Finkenauer, "Anmerkungen zur redemptio servi suis nummis," in *Festschrift für Rolf Knütel zum 70. Geburtstag*, ed. Holger Altmeppen, Ingo Reichard and Martin Josef Schermaier (Heidelberg: C.F. Müller, 2009): 345–57; Susanne Heinemeyer, *Der Freikauf des Sklaven mit eigenem Geld – Redemptio suis nummis* (Berlin: Duncker & Humblot, 2013).

45 Finkenauer, "Anmerkungen zur redemptio" (n. 44): 349–50.

46 Transl. Gordon, Robinson and Fergus in Watson, *Digest of Justinian* (n. 11).

action *affectus ratione* and sue for the slave's manumission.[47] That this cannot be a later emendation of or addition to the original text can be seen from Papinian's parenthetical, generalising comment in which he admits that the issue is contentious and lauds himself as one of the *prudentiores*.[48]

There are other references to kinship as grounds for *redemptio*, such as in C. 7.16.12 of 293 (the sale of a slave who was the son of his *dominus* by one of his female slaves), or in D. 40.1.19, where Papinian draws an explicit connection between a natural brother or father purchasing a slave's freedom and *redemptio*.[49] According to D. 40.1.4.8,[50] *redemptio* without reservation was granted even in cases where purchaser or seller were below the age of twenty. So for manumission by means of *redemptio* there was no need to prove the existence of one of the grounds of justification provided for in the *lex Aelia Sentia*,[51] because *redemptio* was based from the outset on a constellation in which even a minor under 20 could legally manumit. Evidently, kinship is an essential factor for the entire legal institution.

But why did a father sell his child to a third party instead of manumitting it himself? The key advantage was that the third-party purchaser did not gain any patronage rights, as outlined above, while all economically relevant rights would have gone to the manumitting father, and, in case of his death, from him to the children in his *patria potestas*, i.e. to the freed slave's siblings. *Redemptio* made it possible to evade this unwelcome legal consequence that the manumitted child should fall under its siblings' patronage.[52]

---

47 For a detailed discussion of this text see Rolf Knütel, "Das Mandat zum Freikauf," in *Mandatum und Verwandtes: Beiträge zum römischen und modernen Recht*, ed. Dieter Nörr and Shigeo Nishimura (Berlin/Heidelberg: Springer Verlag, 1993): 353–74, 368–70 see also Andreas Wacke, "Das Affektionsinteresse: Heute und in römischen Rechtsquellen," in *Ars iuris. Festschrift für Okko Behrends*, ed. Martin Avenarius, Rudolf Meyer-Pritzl and Cosima Müller (Göttingen: Wallstein Verlag, 2009): 555–88, 583.

48 Correctly Wacke, "Das Affektionsinteresse" (n. 47): 584; Kindler, *Affectionis aestimatio* (n. 40): 197.

49 Papinian D. 40.1.19 (30 quaest.). *Si quis ab alio nummos acceperit, ut servum suum manumittat, etiam ab invito libertas extorqueri potest, licet plerumque pecunia eius numerata sit, maxime si frater vel pater naturalis pecuniam dedit: videbitur enim similis ei qui suis nummis redemptus est.* ('If anyone has received cash from another person so that he may manumit his slave, the slave's freedom can be wrung even from the unwilling master, although very commonly it is the slave's money that has been paid out, especially if the money has been given by his natural brother or father; in fact, he will resemble the slave who has been purchased with his own cash', transl. Brunt in Watson, *Digest of Justinian* [n. 11]).

50 Ulpian D. 40.1.4.8 (6 disp.). [. . .] *sed et si minor sit viginti annis qui vendidit, interveniet constitutio. nec comparantis quidem aetas spectatur: nam et si pupillus emat, aequum est eum fidem implere, cum sine damno eius hoc sit futurum* [. . .] ('[. . .] But even if the vendor is under twenty, the constitution will still take effect. Nor is any regard paid to the age of the purchaser; for even if a *pupillus* purchases, it is fair that he should fulfill the trust, inasmuch as this involves him in no loss [. . .]', transl. Brunt in Watson, *Digest of Justinian* [n. 11]).

51 See section 2.1 above.

52 Finkenauer, "Anmerkungen zur redemptio" (n. 44): 354; so also Knütel, "Freikauf" (n. 42): col. 1097.

2.3 Imposed Manumission

If a slave was sold with a provision that he be subsequently manumitted by the purchaser (*lex dicta ut manumittatur*), and if the purchaser complied with that provision, he acquired rights of patronage over the freed slave. However, if he did not free the slave at the specified time, Marcus Aurelius ordered that manumission should then occur automatically.[53]

C. 4.57.2 (Alexander Augustus Eutychiano): Si ea lege Chreste servum, sed naturalem filium venumdedit, ut emptor eum manumitteret, quamvis non est manumissus, ex constitutione divorum Marci et Commodi ad Aufidium Victorinum liber est. PP. VI id. Nov. Alexandro A. cons. (222).	C. 4.57.2 (Alexander Augustus Eutychiano): If Chrestes sold his slave, who was his natural son, with a provision that the purchaser should manumit him, then, although he has not been manumitted, he is nevertheless free according to the constitution of the divine Marcus and Commodus directed to Aufidius Victorinus.[54]

Thus the slave acquired the legal status he would have had if he had been properly manumitted, while the purchaser got only limited patronage rights.[55]

But this provision for manumission appears strange: why did the seller not himself manumit the slave and thus secure patronage rights, instead of leaving them to a stranger? One possible explanation is that the seller may have wanted to obtain Roman citizenship for his slave. A seller who was mute or deaf, for example, was unable to perform *manumissio vindicta* and could only help his slave achieve the lesser Latin citizenship by means of praetorian manumission.[56] A non-citizen (*peregrinus*) master could give neither Roman nor Latin citizenship to his freedman or freedwoman. An effective alternative in both cases was the sale of the slave to a Roman citizen, who would subsequently free him in accordance with *ius civile*, and so make him a Roman citizen.[57] Although the legal institution of imposed manumission was not established to privilege the seller's kinship ties, it could play a role, as this rescript of Severus Alexander shows.

53 Cf. also Callistratus D. 40.8.3 (3 de cogn.); Scaevola D. 18.7.10 (7 dig.). For the subject as a whole see Thomas Finkenauer, *Die Rechtsetzung Mark Aurels zur Sklaverei* (Stuttgart: Franz Steiner Verlag, 2010): 37.

54 Based on the transl. of Blume in Bruce W. Frier, *The Codex of Justinian, A New Annotated Translation* (Cambridge: Cambridge University Press, 2016).

55 Finkenauer, *Mark Aurel zur Sklaverei* (n. 53): 38.

56 Cf. PS 4.12.2; Kaser, *Das römische Privatrecht*, vol. 1 (n. 1): 296.

57 For the subject as a whole see Philipp Lotmar, "Marc Aurels Erlaß über die Freilassungsauflage," *Zeitschrift der Savigny-Stiftung für Rechtsgeschichte, Romanistische Abteilung* 33 (1912): 304–82, 341–46.

3 Liability With Blood Relatives

Slaves, like land and livestock, are counted among the valuable assets (*res mancipi*). The option of raising capital by selling the slaves of an insolvent debtor is therefore highly important for creditors. However, classical law has some significant restrictions to their rights of access to a debtor's assets, namely with regard to execution in bankruptcy (3.1), the pledging of all the debtor's assets (3.2), and the debtor's liability from legacies (3.3).

3.1 The Master's Bankruptcy

In classical Roman law, the assets of a debtor unable or unwilling to meet an obligation will be seized as a whole (general execution) at the request of one of his creditors. This entailed his social death. Individual execution was unknown. As a result of the creditors' request, the debtor's entire property was seized (*missio in bona*) and his assets sold by the *magister bonorum* (*venditio bonorum*), usually by public auction.[58] General execution was very harsh: it did not even stop at the debtor's personal belongings such as clothes or provisions.[59] The only exemptions were his unfree concubine, and any children he might have by a female slave, as Paul tells us:

D. 42.5.38 pr. (Paulus 1 sent.): Bonis venditis excipiuntur concubina et liberi naturales.

D. 42.5.38 pr. (Paulus, Views, book 1): A concubine and natural child [of the debtor] are excluded from the sale of assets.[60]

The debtor's concubine and natural children are counted among his assets, so they must have been unfree: if not, Paul would not have expressly exempted them from sale by auction. In principle, the creditors are entitled to them, since they are part of his property; but it appears that in practice, the law was unwilling to separate the 'family' of debtor, concubine and *liberi naturales* – even though it was not legally recognised as such.

Because of the late transmission in the *Pauli Sententiae* – most scholars date them to around 300 A.D.[61] – this way of acknowledging the existence of servile family ties might appear a post-classical phenomenon, but there are good reasons for

58 Kaser and Hackl, *Zivilprozeßrecht* (n. 20): 397.
59 Cf. Cic., *Pro Quinctio* 15,49.
60 Transl. Thomas in Watson, *Digest of Justinian* (n. 11).
61 Detlef Liebs, "Jurisprudenz," in *Handbuch der lateinischen Literatur der Antike*, vol. 8/5, *Restauration und Erneuerung: Die lateinische Literatur von 284 bis 374 A.D.*, ed. Reinhart Herzog and Peter Lebrecht Schmidt (Munich: C.H. Beck, 1989): 66, § 507.1: Der Sentenzenverfasser (Pseudo-Paul I).

believing that it does, in fact, date to the classical era:[62] firstly, the *Sententiae* contain classical material, albeit in simplified form; mostly by Paul, Papinian and Ulpian.[63] Secondly, the content of our passage is indirectly confirmed by a sentence in Ulpian, D. 20.1.8, which I will come to in a moment. And thirdly, the fact that the Elder Seneca (54 B.C.–c.38 A.D.) writes – in a literary work – about family members being separated through auction indicates that the idea[64] that such cases ought to be prevented had been in currency for some time. Seneca writes about siblings:[65]

> Seneca rhet., Contr. 9.3.3: [. . .] in auctione fratres quamvis hostilis hasta non dividit. plus quiddam est geminos esse quam fratres: perdit uterque gratiam suam, nisi cum altero est.

> Seneca rhet., Contr. 9.3.3: At an auction the spear, however unfriendly, does not divide brothers. It is rather more to be twins than brothers – both lose their charm if they are separated.[66]

In one of his rhetorical *controversiae*, Seneca posits the case of a father who exposed his sons and now demands their return from the foster father. He wants to know where they are and comes to an arrangement with the foster father whereby the latter shall retain one of the boys in exchange for disclosing their whereabouts.[67] After he has returned both boys to their natural father, the fosterer demands one back, as agreed. The above sentence about a slave auction is being said on behalf of the natural father. So even in early classical law the separation of siblings in separate auction sales is prevented – at least in a rhetorical exercise. We may therefore assume with some certainty that classical law precluded the sale by auction of a debtor's unfree spouse and children.

62 So, correctly, Buckland, *Law of Slavery* (n. 21): 39; Siro Solazzi, *Il concorso dei creditori nel diritto romano*, vol. 2 (Naples: Jovene, 1938): 137; Kaser and Hackl, *Zivilprozeßrecht* (n. 20): 398 n. 25; Gérard Boulvert and Marcel Morabito, "Le droit de l'esclavage sous le Haut-Empire," in *Aufstieg und Niedergang der römischen Welt*, pt. 2, *Principat*, vol. 14, *Recht*, ed. Hildegard Temporini and Wolfgang Haase (Berlin: De Gruyter, 1982): 98–182, 138; Willvonseder, *Stellung des Sklaven* (n. 3): 72; Richard Gamauf, "§ 26 (Sklaverei)" marginal no. 18, in *Handbuch des römischen Privatrechts*, ed. Ulrike Babusiaux et al. (Tübingen: Mohr Siebeck, 2023).

63 Liebs, "Jurisprudenz" (n. 61).

64 At least in the form of 'moral advice', cf. Francesco de Martino, *Wirtschaftsgeschichte des alten Rom* (Munich: C.H. Beck, 1985): 297.

65 There is no proof that they were twins, *contra* Rosanna Ortu, "Costantino e la tutela giuridica della 'servorum agnatio'," in *Philia. Scritti per Gennaro Franciosi*, vol. 3, ed. Frederico Maria D'Ippolito (Naples: Satura Editrice, 2007): 1887–926, 1914 n. 86; Zoltán Végh, "Ex pacto ius," *Zeitschrift der Savigny-Stiftung für Rechtsgeschichte, Romanistische Abteilung* 110 (1993): 184–295, 239.

66 Transl. Michael Winterbottom, *Seneca the Elder, Declamations*, vol. 2, *Controversiae Books 7–10: Suasoriae, Fragments*, Loeb Classical Library 464 (Cambridge, MA: Harvard University Press, 1974).

67 For the possible content of this agreement and the difficulties of what Zoltán Végh termed a '*juristisches Monstrum*' ('legal monstrosity'), see Végh, "Ex pacto ius" (n. 65): 242.

3.2 Pledging With Slaves

Roman law provides for things being pledged individually, but also for a non-possessory general pledge involving all of the debtor's present and future assets. The latter is either agreed upon or, in some cases, arises by law.[68] Ulpian/Paul D. 20.1.6 and 7 exclude from the general pledge those of the debtor's assets which he would have been unlikely to pledge on an individual basis, such as his household effects, clothes and specific slaves, namely those to whom he is close or whose services he requires on a daily basis. As examples[69] Ulpian D. 20.1.8 lists an unfree concubine, the debtor's children by a female slave, his unfree foster children and/or his domestic slaves (*ministeria*[70]). A creditor may not take possession of them, lay a claim to or sell them:

D. 20.1.8 (Upian 73 ad ed.): Denique concubinam filios naturales alumnos constitit generali obligatione non contineri et si qua alia sunt huiusmodi ministeria.

D. 20.1.8 (Ulpian, Edict, book 73): For example it is accepted that a concubine, natural child, or foster child, and anyone belonging to the household in the same position is excluded from the general pledge.[71]

With this opinion Ulpian prioritises the debtor's attachment to these slaves over the creditor's interest in having the maximum of recoverable assets. The debtor's interest is based on an attachment (the existence of which is taken for granted) not only to his own children, but also his mate, his foster children and/or his domestic slaves. This is why the creditor has no claim to them, unless expressly granted by the debtor.[72] The reason lies in the interpretation of his intent: without any indication to the contrary it is highly improbable and indeed unlikely that he wanted to make these slaves the objects of a pledge.[73] The purpose of the law is to provide protection – not for the slaves (e.g. on humanitarian grounds), but for their owner's

---

68 Kaser, *Das römische Privatrecht*, vol. 1 (n. 1): 458, 466.

69 In D. 20.1.8, *denique* means 'for example', cf. Heumann and Seckel, *Handlexikon* (n. 4): s.v. *denique* 4; Herbert Wagner, *Voraussetzungen, Vorstufen und Anfänge der römischen Generalverpfändung* (Marburg: N.G. Elwert, 1968): 126.

70 Heumann and Seckel, *Handlexikon* (n. 4): s.v. *ministerium* 2; cf. Ulpian D. 33.7.12.31 (20 ad Sab.); Felix B.J. Wubbe, *Res aliena pignori data* (Leiden: Universitaire pers Leiden, 1960): 230. This meaning is found not just in Justinian, cf. Wagner, *Generalverpfändung* (n. 69): 125 n. 799; for an earlier, different view see Gerhard Beseler, "Unklassische Wörter," *Zeitschrift der Savigny-Stiftung für Rechtsgeschichte, Romanistische Abteilung* 57 (1937): 1–51, 43. Wagner, *Generalverpfändung* (n. 69): 127 n. 804 counts among the *ministeria* a female slave who, without necessarily being a long-term concubine, is a favourite of the debtor's.

71 Transl. Honoré in Watson, *Digest of Justinian* (n. 11).

72 It is of course quite possible for the owner expressly to arrange for such a special pledge; so, correctly, Wagner, *Generalverpfändung* (n. 69): 125 n. 798.

73 Wagner, *Generalverpfändung* (n. 69): 125.

interest in them. In the absence of an explicit agreement Ulpian ultimately focuses on the debtor's presumed intent.[74] This is no different to a statute issued in 197 A.D. by the imperial court:

C. 8.16.1 (Severus/Antoninus Augusti Optato): Alumnos tuos et ceteras res, quas neminem credibile est pignori specialiter datum fuisse, generali pacti conventione, quae de bonis tuis facta est, in causam pignoris non fuisse rationis est. <a. 197 pp. XII k. April. Laterano et Rufino conss.>

C. 8.16.1 (Severus/Antoninus Augusti Optato): It accords with reason that your foster-children (alumni), along with other property that is not credible anyone would specifically pledge, are not included as pledges in a general agreement made about your estate (bona).[75]

3.3 Legacies

By means of a *legatum per damnationem* (obligatory legacy) a testator can oblige his heir to deliver a thing to the legatee; the obligation is enforced by means of an action based on the will. Should the heir deny his liability, he is sued for double the value of the object or service in question (*lis infitiando crescit in duplum*).[76] The testator can also bequeath a thing that belongs to a third party.[77] In this case, the heir is obliged to purchase the object in order to convey it to the legatee. If the third party does not wish to sell the object or demands an excessive price for it, the heir is only liable to the legatee for the simple material value (*aestimatio*):[78]

D. 30.71.3–4 (Ulpian 51 ad ed.): Qui confitetur se quidem debere, iustam autem causam adfert, cur utique praestare non possit, audiendus est: ut puta si aliena res legata sit negetque dominum eam vendere vel immensum pretium eius rei petere adfirmet, aut si servum hereditarium

D. 30.71.3–4 (Ulpian, Edict, book 51): Whenever someone admits that something is due from him but adduces a cause why he cannot deliver it, the plea is to be heard, for instance, if property belonging to someone else has been bequeathed and he says the owner will not sell

74 Amalia Sicari takes a somewhat different view, cf. Amalia Sicari, *Leges venditionis. Uno studio sul pensiero giuridico di Papiniano* (Bari: Cacucci Editore, 1996): 223, 225; regarding the debtor's individual integrity as ultimately protected, and the exceptions as 'umanamente comprensibile'. However, integrity is protected only to the extent that Roman law protects a proprietor's private autonomy: it would readily recognise his right to pledge his son.

75 Transl. Blume in Frier, *The Codex of Justinian* (n. 54).

76 Gaius inst. 2.282; 4.9; Kaser, *Das römische Privatrecht*, vol. 1 (n. 1): 743; see now Lisa Isola, "Überlegungen zur Litiskreszenz bei der actio ex testamento," *Zeitschrift der Savigny-Stiftung für Rechtsgeschichte, Romanistische Abteilung* 137 (2020): 106–35.

77 Gaius inst. 2.202.

78 Gaius inst. 2.202. 262; Gaius D. 32.14.2 (1 fideicomm.): *immodico pretio*; Labeo-Iavolenus D. 32.30.6 (2 post. a Iav. epit.); Iavolenus D. 35.2.61 (4 epist.); Kaser, *Das römische Privatrecht*, vol. 1 (n. 1): 749.

neget se debere praestare, forte patrem suum vel matrem vel fratres naturales: aequissimum est enim concedi ei ex hac causa aestimationem officio iudicis praestare. § 4. Cum alicui poculum legatum esset velletque heres aestimationem praestare, quia iniquum esse aiebat id separari a se, non impetravit id a praetore: alia enim condicio est hominum, alia ceterarum rerum: in hominibus enim benigna ratione receptum est, quod supra probavimus.

it, or declares that he is demanding an exorbitant price, or if he says that he is not obliged to deliver a slave belonging to the estate such as, say, his father, mother, or natural brothers. The most equitable course in this case is for the judge to allow him to pay the value instead. § 4. When a cup was bequeathed to someone and the heir wished to pay its value, saying that it was unfair that he should be parted from it, he could not win the praetor's consent. For the case of persons is one thing, and that of things, another. An indulgent attitude is accepted in the case of persons, as we have shown above.[79]

Ulpian first discusses two cases in which a bequeathed object belongs to another person, who is either unwilling to sell or willing to do so but only at an excessive price. The third case concerns an estate which includes slaves who are blood relations of the heir – father, mother or siblings. Ulpian considers it most just (*aequissimum*) to hear the debtor, i.e. the heir, because he has given a *iusta causa* for being unable to convey the slaves to the legatee and should therefore have the option of paying their (single, not double) value. Ulpian contrasts this with a case concerning the emotional value claimed by the heir for a cup left to him: the praetor will regard with sympathy the attachment to persons, but is unlikely to do the same when the target of affection is an object.

Let us take a closer look at the different cases. If the third party is not willing to sell, the heir cannot be censured for not conveying the slave. He in no way refutes his obligation under the will, as Ulpian stresses in § 3. There is therefore no reason to treat him as a debtor who disputes the debt, and lets the case go to court.[80] A debtor who denies his obligations must be punished, but not one who is willing to oblige but prevented from doing so by an insurmountable obstacle. The Roman jurists balance the interests of heir and legatee: the heir[81] is not unduly punished (as he would be if he had to pay double the amount in dispute[82]) while the legatee does not have to go away empty-handed.[83] The second case is similar: should the third party demand a price for

79 Transl. Braun in Watson, *Digest of Justinian* (n. 11).

80 Nevio Scapini, *La confessione nel diritto romano*, vol. 1, *Diritto classico* (Turin: Giappichelli, 1973): 42.

81 Kaser and Hackl, *Zivilprozeßrecht* (n. 20): 139–40, 284.

82 Cf. also Labeo-Iavolenus D. 32.30.6 (2 post. a Iav. epit.).

83 Hugo Krüger, "Die humanitas und die pietas nach den Quellen des römischen Rechtes," *Zeitschrift der Savigny-Stiftung für Rechtsgeschichte, Romanistische Abteilung* 19 (1898): 6–57, 48.

its slave that is excessively high, the heir cannot be expected to comply with the testator's disposition. Ultimately, an equal treatment of both cases suggests itself.[84]

We may imagine the third case – relatives being left in a bequest – as e.g. a *dominus* who appoints as heir one of his freedmen, or one of his slaves whom he manumits in his will, while at the same time leaving certain other slaves, who turn out to be related to the heir, to a third party. If the heir does not have to convey his relatives to the legatee, the family can stay together. Some scholars have assumed that this solution is Justinianic because the crucial consideration is one of equity, similar to the one openly expressed in § 4.[85] However, the view that only Justinian's compilers – and not classical jurists – would have considered equity is no longer current.[86] We can assume that the distinction between mere objects, such as the favourite cup, and slaves, whose humanity – at least according to natural law – the same Ulpian stresses,[87] was just as clear to a late classical jurist. The result is that the heir purchases the freedom of his relatives at market price.[88]

Some scholars have denied the authenticity of the text;[89] however, since the methodological shift of the 1960s, the use of textual criticism on the basis chiefly of linguistic evidence has been discounted. A different reading due to an assumed Justinianic modification must be based on material reasons.[90] In the 1955 edition of his manual, Max Kaser accepted that the passage under discussion contained interpolations,[91] but

---

84 See also Gaius D. 32.14.2 (1 fideicomm.); Giuseppe Grosso, *I legati nel diritto romano. Parte generale*, 2nd ed. (Turin: Giappichelli, 1962): 249, argues in a similar vein to myself; Riccardo Orestano, "La valutazione del prezzo nel fedecommesso e nel legato di res aliena e nella fideicommissaria libertas," *Annali della Facoltà di Giurisprudenza. Università degli Studi di Camerino* 10 (1936): 225–56, 229–43, 241, 243.

85 Grosso, *legati* (n. 84): 251; probably also Pasquale Voci, *Diritto ereditario romano*, vol. 2, 2nd ed. (Milan, Giuffrè, 1963): 252 n. 4.

86 For decisions on the grounds of benevolence (*benignitas*) see Tobias Kleiter, *Entscheidungskorrekturen mit unbestimmter Wertung durch die klassische römische Jurisprudenz* (Munich: C.H. Beck, 2010): 18–19; for *aequitas* in classical decisions and *aequissimum* ibid. 30–37.

87 See below n. 236.

88 Although, strictly speaking, since he is the heir they will remain his property until he manumits them.

89 Emilio Albertario, "Conceptus pro iam nato habetur," *Bullettino dell'Instituto di Diritto Romano* 33 (1924): 1–77, 68–69; Emilio Albertario, "D. 21,1,35. 'Ulpian L. 1 ad edictum aedilium curulium'. Esempio di decomposizione di un testo giustinianeo nei suoi elementi costitutivi," in *Studi in onore di Salvatore Riccobono*, vol. 1 (Palermo: Arti Grafiche *Cav.* Giuseppe Castiglia, 1936): 641–51, 648; Gerhard Beseler, "Aequissimus," *Zeitschrift der Savigny-Stiftung für Rechtsgeschichte, Romanistische Abteilung* 45 (1925): 455–56, 456; Grosso, *legati* (n. 84): 248.

90 Max Kaser, *Zur Methodologie der römischen Rechtsquellenforschung*, Österreichische Akademie der Wissenschaften, Philosophisch-historische Klasse, Sitzungsberichte 277/5 (Vienna/Cologne/Graz: Böhlau, 1972).

91 Max Kaser, *Das römische Privatrecht*, vol. 1, *Das altrömische, das vorklassische und klassische Recht* (Munich: C.H. Beck, 1955): 428 n. 3.

no longer did so in the second edition of 1971.[92] Hence, there remains little doubt – subject to one final consideration[93] – that the whole text is classical.[94]

4 Separating the Slave Family

From quite early on, the authors of manuals on agriculture were opposed to separating slave couples joined in a *contubernium*, or of slave parents and their children. In the first century B.C. Varro recommends that *praefecti* (*vilici*?) of an estate be allowed to have their own special property (*peculium*), and a female companion with whom they may have children. In this way he will be more attached to the place, and as such more valuable to his owner.[95] Varro explains that the added value is due largely to the greater productivity of a slave who is satisfied with his work.[96] Columella makes a very similar point about the benefits of allowing slaves to form families. He advises the *paterfamilias* to give the *vilicus* a female companion who will help and look after him; and to reward very fertile slave women with exemption from work or even manumission: such justice and consideration will increase their master's estate.[97] We may assume that for Columella even more than for Varro the shortage of slaves in the first century A.D. made natural reproduction of slaves a prime consideration.[98]

There are also a number of passages in the Digest that provide protection for slave families. Even though strictly speaking the law does not recognise the servile family unit, legal rulings took care that slave spouses, parents and children, and even slave siblings, would not be separated.

92 Kaser, *Das römische Privatrecht*, vol. 1 (n. 1): 514 n. 4, 749 n. 45.

93 See below 4.4.

94 Similarly Kaser: Maria Gabriella Zoz de Biasio, "Nota minima sulla tutela dei nuclei familiari servili," in *Studi in onore di Arnaldo Biscardi*, vol. 4, ed. Franco Pastori (Milan: Istituto Editoriale Cisalpino-La Goliardica, 1983): 537–44, 543–44; Antonio Mateo, "La consideración clásica de la 'cognatio servilis' en la venta de esclavos (a propósito de D. 21,1,35)," in *Bullettino dell'Istituto di Diritto romano* 101–102 (2005): 335–83, 372; Willvonseder, *Stellung des Sklaven* (n. 3): 14; Gregor Albers, *Perpetuatio obligationis – Leistungspflicht trotz Unmöglichkeit im klassischen Recht* (Cologne: Böhlau, 2019): 204, 206; Gamauf, "§ 26 (Sklaverei)" (n. 62): marginal no. 18.

95 Varro 1.17.5; 2.10.6–7; on this topic see Pólay, *Die Sklavenehe* (n. 9): 18.

96 Ortu, "Costantino" (n. 65): 1900–1901.

97 Columella, *De re rust.* 1.8.5,19.

98 Ortu, "Costantino" (n. 65): 1903.

4.1 Rescinding the Purchase of a Slave

If someone sold a slave who had one of the defects mentioned in the edict of the curule aediles[99] without having made mention of it – such as disease or a propensity to run away – or if a defect developed contrary to what the seller had promised,[100] the purchaser had six months in which to bring an action for redhibition (*actio redhibitoria*). He could return the slave and demand a refund.

If several slaves were sold as a unit and a defect emerged in only one of them, the question arose as to whether the action for redhibition concerned the entire group or only the defective slave. It is a question of interpretation which solution is in line with the parties' interest: what did the parties agree – or what would they have agreed had they considered the defectiveness in only one slave? According to Julian, a jurist of the high classical period, one indicator was the question whether the purchase price had been agreed for the group or per individual. If it had been for the whole group, a demand for a partial refund would cause considerable difficulties. Had each part of the group been priced and sold individually, there would be as many sales contracts as there were slaves.[101] However, even with group members priced individually there might still have been a collective contract, for instance if the sale would not have gone ahead without the defective part. Julian cites examples: a four-horse team, a pair of mules, a troupe of slave actors (*comoedi*).[102] Or perhaps a connecting link between the parts, or the lead animal, is defective: if the purchaser returned only this part of the group, the rest would lose their function.[103] This is the context into which the compilers of the Digests place, first, a fragment of Ulpian and then a late fragment from Paul:

> D. 21.1.35 (Ulpian 1 ad ed. aedil. curul.): Plerumque propter morbosa mancipia etiam non morbosa redhibentur, si separari non possint sine magno incommodo vel ad pietatis rationem offensam. quid enim, si filio retento parentes redhibere maluerint vel contra? quod et in fratribus et in personas contubernio sibi coniunctas observari oportet.

> D. 21.1.35 (Ulpian, Curule Aediles' Edict, book 1): Healthy slaves are often returned on account of those who are diseased when they cannot be separated without great inconvenience or affront to human consideration (*pietatis ratio*). Suppose that I wish to return the parents but keep their son or vice versa. The same is true in respect of brothers and those linked in a servile quasi-matrimonial relationship.[104]

---

99 The edict dates to the third or second century B.C.
100 See the edict in Ulpian D. 21.1.1.1 (1 ad ed. aedil. curul.).
101 Africanus D. 21.1.34 pr. (6 quaest.).
102 Africanus D. 21.1.34.1 (6 quaest.).
103 Ortu, "Costantino" (n. 65): 1918.
104 Based on the transl. of Thomas in Watson, *Digest of Justinian* (n. 11).

Ulpian cites an economic reason why several slaves – including the defective ones – should be returned collectively (*sine magno incommodo*), and a humanitarian one: the return of all slaves prevents their being split up among different masters (*ad pietatis rationem offensam*). A rhetorical question – that finds a parallel in the *constitution* of Constantine CTh. 2.25.1, about which more below[105] – reminds us that a partial redhibition would separate spouses, siblings, or parents from children.

Paul agrees that siblings should not be separated. His dictum (a very brief passage of just two words) has been inserted into an Ulpian context by the compilers:

D. 21.1.38.14 (Ulpian 2 ad ed. aedil. curul.): Cum autem iumenta paria veneunt, edicto expressum est, ut, cum alterum in ea causa sit, ut redhiberi debeat, utrumque redhibeatur: in qua re tam emptori quam venditori consulitur, dum iumenta non separantur. simili modo et si triga venierit, redhibenda erit tota, et si quadriga, redhibeatur. [. . .] haec et in hominibus dicemus pluribus uno pretio distractis, nisi si separari non possint, ut puta si tragoedi vel mimi,
D. 21.1.39 (Paulus 1 ad ed. aedil. curul.): vel fratres:
D. 21.1.40 (Ulpian 2 ad ed. aedil. curul.): hi enim non erunt separandi. [. . .]

D. 21.1.38.14 (Ulpian, Curule Aediles' Edict, book 2): Now when matched beasts are sold, the edict states that if one be such as to be returnable, both are to be returned; this protects the interests of both purchaser and vendor and the animals are not separated; in like manner, a three- or four-horse team would have to be returned as a whole [. . .] We say the same of a batch of slaves sold at a single price, unless they cannot be split up, for example, serious or mimic actors,
D. 21.1.39 (Paulus, Curule Aediles' Edict, book 1): or siblings.
D. 21.1.40 (Ulpian, Curule Aediles' Edict, book 2): For these are not to be separated. [. . .][106]

Ulpian points out first that if one of a pair of draft animals is found to be defective, both must be returned in order to protect the interests of both vendor and purchaser. The same applies to a four-horse team, but not when a buyer purchases a dozen horses. Ulpian then cites a troupe of tragic (*tragoedi*) or mime (*mimi*) actors who must not be separated. To this list, the compilers added Paul's text about siblings.[107]

In both Ulpian D. 21.1.35 and Paul D. 21.1.39, the decisive factor for the extent of redhibition is whether or not the purchased animals or humans formed a functional team. However, in both there is also the humanitarian motive of preventing the separation of slaves who share a close bond. It is easy to see late-classical jurists arguing in terms of functionality, which is a reasonable interpretation of the parties' intent. The humanitarian motive, however, is often seen as a post-classical[108] or

105 See below 4.3.
106 Transl. Thomas in Watson, *Digest of Justinian* (n. 11).
107 For this meaning of *fratres* cf. Okko Behrends, Rolf Knütel, Bertold Kupisch and Hans Hermann Seiler, *Corpus Iuris Civilis, Text und Übersetzung*, vol. 4 (Heidelberg: C.F. Müller, 2005): 36–37.
108 Albertario, "D. 21,1,35" (n. 89): 648–51; Aldo Dell'Oro, *Le cose collettive nel diritto romano* (Milan: Giuffrè, 1963): 65; David Daube, "The Compilers' Use of a Revised Paul and Ulpian,"

Justinianic addition[109] following in the wake of Constantine's law in CTh. 2.25.1. Let us consider the arguments in detail.

One argument in favour of a later reworking of the dictum by Ulpian is its linguistic deficiency. Dell'Oro describes one sentence as being 'di una sconcertante scorrettezza',[110] and it is admittedly very uneven. The syntax in the phrase *sine magno incommodo vel ad pietatis rationem offensam* is odd; one would expect another *sine* instead of *ad*.[111] Even if we follow Charondas and the new German translation, both of which emend *ob* for *ad*, the sentence does not run quite smoothly. In the last sentence, the expression *in fratribus* being followed by *in personas* is similarly infelicitous.[112] However, these linguistic deficiencies do not render the text illegible, and scholars now agree that they are not sufficient grounds for assuming a later reworking. Where there is no motive for interpolation, the much more likely explanation is that such faults are due to abridgement: let us not forget that 95% of all classical law texts fell victim to the compilers' redaction.

In terms of content, scholars have critiqued both *magnum incommodum*[113] and *pietas* as being non-classical.[114] But the 'great inconvenience' referred to merely

---

Zeitschrift der Savigny-Stiftung für Rechtsgeschichte, Romanistische Abteilung 90 (1973): 359–60, 359; Pólay, *Die Sklavenehe* (n. 9): 67–68, 72, 79.

109 Silvio Perozzi, *Istituzioni di diritto romano*, vol. 1, 2nd ed. (Rome: Athenaeum, 1928): 201; Joseph Georg Wolf, "Interpolationen in den Digesten," in *Studia e Documenta Historiae et Iuris* 79 (2013): 3–80, 63. For the absence of classical characteristics see also Max Kaser, "rec. of Scritti in onore di Contardo Ferrini pubblicati in occasione della sua beatificazione, Milano 1947," *IURA* 2 (1951): 160–79, 169; Max Kaser, *Das römische Privatrecht*, vol. 2, *Die nachklassischen Entwicklungen* (Munich: C.H. Beck, 1959): 85 n. 18.

110 Dell'Oro, *Le cose collettive* (n. 108): 61; in a similar vein Albertario, "D. 21,1,35" (n. 89): 651, who argues that the text is the result of combining several glosses. See also Rodolfo Ambrosino, "Vel fratres (In margine all'editto degli Edili curuli)," *Studia e Documenta Historiae et Iuris* 16 (1950): 290–94, 291; Daube, "The Compilers' Use" (n. 108): 360.

111 Mateo, "cognatio servilis" (n. 94): 380, suggested emending *offensam* into the ablative *offensa*, but that is not wholly convincing without, again, repeating *sine*. *Plerumque*, on the other hand, does not indicate an interpolation, *contra* Albertario, "D. 21,1,35" (n. 89): 644; it simply means 'sometimes', cf. Heumann and Seckel, *Handlexikon* (n. 4): s.v. *plerumque*; Mateo, "cognatio servilis" (n. 94): 348.

112 See also Buckland, *Law of Slavery* (n. 21): 67 n. 6.

113 Albertario, "D. 21,1,35" (n. 89): 645; Dell'Oro, *Le cose collettive* (n. 108): 64–65.

114 Krüger, "humanitas und pietas" (n. 83): 52–53; Albertario, "D. 21,1,35" (n. 89): 645–47; Paul Jörs, "Digesta," in *Paulys Realencyclopädie der classischen Altertumswissenschaft*, vol. 5/1 (Stuttgart: J.B. Metzler, 1905): col. 483–543, 527 describes it as 'geschraubt', i.e. 'stilted'; Biondo Biondi, *Il diritto romano cristiano*, vol. 2 (Milan: Giuffrè, 1952): 438; vol. 3 (Milan: Giuffrè, 1954): 90; Siro Solazzi, "Il rispetto per la famiglia dello schiavo," *Studia e Documenta Historiae et Iuris* 15 (1949): 187–92, 187, 192; Dell'Oro, *Le cose collettive* (n. 108): 64–65.

indicates that splitting up a team can be economically senseless, and as such is not suspicious.[115] The same is largely true for *pietas*:

In fact, there are 21 allusions to *pietas* in Ulpian, plus a few more instances of *ratio pietatis*.[116] The context also makes a reference to *pietas* quite plausible: it can refer either to the relationship between the slaves who are kin (1), or to the relationship between master and slave (2).

(1) Moral duty is perceived primarily in terms of ascendants and descendants, siblings, collateral kin and spouses.[117] The term is almost always applied to the Roman family. But as early as the classical period, it may also increasingly refer to the bond between slave parents and children, or between servile spouses. Scaevola D. 32.41.2 (22 dig.) invokes *pietas* for the relationship of slave children to their natural father.[118] Ulpian, in assessing whether or not a case of manumission is legitimate, takes the relationship between a slave child and his slave parents into account;[119] and in D. 37.15.1.1 (1 opin.), Ulpian speaks of the *pietas* between a freedwoman and her child. Paul in D. 2.4.6 (1 sent.) describes the *reverentia* that is owed to one's parents.[120] In terms of terminology, too, there is some slippage between the servile and the Roman family: at times even an unfree mate is referred to as *uxor*, a term that usually refers to a Roman citizen wife.[121] Paul in D. 16.3.27 (7 resp.) uses the word *matrimonium* for a slave marriage – a term strictly reserved for a Roman

115 *Magnum incommodum* is found in other late classical texts, cf. Paul D. 4.4.24.1 (1 sent.); D. 40.7.20.6 (16 ad Plaut.); Ulpian D. 22.1.37 (10 ad ed.). In a similar vein Biondi, *DRC*, vol. 2 (n. 114): 438; Mateo, "cognatio servilis" (n. 94): 378; Lorena Manna, *Actio redhibitoria e responsabilità per i vizi della cosa nell'editto de mancipiis vendundis* (Milan: Giuffrè, 1994): 89.

116 Ulpian D. 3.2.23 (8 ad ed.); 25.3.5.15 (2 de off. cons.); 37.15.1 pr.1. (1 opin.); D. 34.1.14.1 (2 fideicomm.) has *pietatis intuitu*.

117 Heumann and Seckel, *Handlexikon* (n. 4): s.v. *pietas* 1 a–d; C. Koch, "pietas," in *Paulys Realencyclopädie der classischen Altertumswissenschaft*, vol. 20/1 (Stuttgart: J.B. Metzler, 1941): col. 1221–32, 1221–22.

118 See below 4.2.5.

119 D. 40.2.13 (libro de off. procons.); see above 2.1.

120 See above 1.2.

121 Cf. only Scaevola D. 33.7.20.4 (3 resp.); Ulpian D. 33.7.12.7.33 (20 ad Sab.); PS 3.6.38. Cato in *de agr.* 143 already employs *uxor* in this sense, as does Plautus e.g. at *Cas.* 109; *Mil. glor.* 1008. Plautus uses *maritus* to refer to the servile husband, cf. *Cas.* 291 (s. Simonis, *Cum servis nullum est conubium* [n. 9]: 37–38 with further references). Epigraphically, too, *uxor* and *maritus* are not infrequently attested for slave spouses, cf. Simonis, *Cum servis nullum est conubium* (n. 9): 38; Rosmarie Günther, *Frauenarbeit – Frauenbindung* (Munich: Wilhelm Fink, 1987): 142. For the credibility of this tradition see Willvonseder, *Stellung des Sklaven* (n. 3): 4; Sicari, *Leges venditionis* (n. 74): 225; Renato Quadrato, "'Maris atque feminae coniunctio'," *Index* 38 (2010): 223–52, 239; Ortu, "Costantino" (n. 65): 1910. *Coniux* occurs more frequently, although not limited to Roman marriage, cf. Simonis, *Cum servis nullum est conubium* (n. 9): 35.

marriage.[122] And even the 'dowry' given by the wife in a slave marriage is tacitly acknowledged as an effective dowry after manumission.[123] Why then should the Roman jurists not also designate the reciprocal loyalty between spouses or between servile relatives as *pietas*? The *pietas* in Ulpian D. 21.1.35 can be read in the same way, designating the close bond between the sold slaves.[124]

(2) On a second semantic level, *pietas* can be located outside the family, where e.g. a superior may display it towards an inferior,[125] or a beneficiary towards the deceased; in an even more general manner it can describe the sense of moral duty to be observed in human interactions.[126] The term is attested epigraphically for the relationship between patron and freedman – both by and towards the patron – from the time of Cicero onwards.[127] But as far as we can see, the concept of *pietas* was not used for the relationship between master and slave;[128] at most, a master might be exhorted to act kindly, amiably and justly towards his slave.[129] So, in the light of our extant sources it makes more sense to assume that what Ulpian means in D. 21.1.35 is not the sense of moral duty felt towards the slave by either the current *dominus* (i.e. the buyer) or previous *dominus* (i.e. the seller), but rather *pietas* between slaves.[130] In any case, one of those two explanations should suffice to make

---

122 Ulpian in D. 1.1.1.3 (1 inst.) similarly describes the union of man and woman in general as *matrimonium* in the context of his discussion of natural law.

123 Ulpian D. 23.3.39 (33 ad ed.); for the authenticity of this text see Ignazio Buti, "'Si serva servo quasi dotem dederit'. Matrimoni servili e dote," in *Schiavi e dipendenti nell'ambito dell''oikos' e della 'familia': Atti del 22. Colloquio Girea: Pontignano (Siena), 19–20 novembre 1995*, ed. Mauro Maggi and Giuseppe Cordiano (Pisa: ETS, 1997): 289–306; Filip-Fröschl, "Gefühle und Recht" (n. 28): 14.

124 So Mateo, "cognatio servilis" (n. 94): 348; Stefan Knoch, *Sklavenfürsorge im Römischen Reich* (Hildesheim: Georg Olms Verlag, 2005): 32. See also Ulpian D. 37.15.1.1 (1 opin.): *pietatis ratio secundum naturam.*

125 Gottfried Schiemann, "Pietas und patria potestas – Bemerkungen zu Marcian D. 48,9,5," in *Interpretationes Iuris Antiqui. Dankesgabe für Shigeo Nishimura*, ed. Thomas Finkenauer and Adriian Johan Boudewijn Sirks (Wiesbaden: Harrassowitz, 2018): 311–22, 315 points out that the popular topos of *pietas* as an important element in the relationship between ruler and ruled had been so regarded since the time of Augustus; Marco Melluso, *La schiavitù nell'età giustinianea* (Paris: Presses Universitaires Franc-Comtoises, 2000): 150–51.

126 Papinian D. 28.7.15 (16 quaest.).

127 Cf. Michael Hillen, *TLL*, 10.1.2098.21 und CLE 12.3 (*aet. Cic.*); CLE 371.2 from 16 A.D.; CIL V 2176.4 and CIL VI 2225.8 (both from the first century A.D.); CIL III 3658.7 (after 80 A.D.) and CIL XII 5130.6. However Callistratus D. 29.5.2 (5 de cogn.) is no supporting evidence, as *pietas pro servis* there refers to the *pietas* incumbent on the heir towards the testator with regard to the punishment of the slaves; see Finkenauer, *Mark Aurel zur Sklaverei* (n. 53): 81.

128 And so rejected by Pólay, *Die Sklavenehe* (n. 9): 42.

129 Seneca, *ep.* 47.13; *de clem.* 1.18.1; *de ben.* 3.21.2. Like him, Cicero had already stressed the importance of the *paterfamilias* practicing justice towards his slaves, Cic., *de off.* 1.41. For the reverse relationship, i.e. between slave and master cf. Val. Max. 6.8.2; Stat. Theb. 5.626–28.

130 See above (1) and below 4.2.1; similarly Jörs, "Digesta" (n. 114): 527; Knoch, *Sklavenfürsorge* (n. 124): 32, 147.

a classical-era use of the term plausible, rendering it unnecessary to speculate about a possible late textual change under the influence of Christianity.

In terms of the legal consequence of both texts, we should stress that neither bans a separation of the family members. Both buyer and seller retain full autonomy in how the contract is to be rescinded: but in case the buyer wishes to return the entire family or group of siblings, the seller must accept this and refund the total price; equally, the seller may refuse to take back only the defective slave.[131] However, if both parties wish to do so, they are free to agree the return only of the defective slave. Effectively, this late classical solution resolves a dissent between the parties about their return or take-back obligations,[132] or seeks to ascertain the presumed will of the parties on a question they have not clarified,[133] without affecting in any way their private autonomy. It places the parties' moral interest in preserving *pietas* on an equal footing with the economic interest in a complete redhibition. No damage accrues to either buyer or seller.[134]

Some scholars have questioned the classicality of the solution and pointed out that in classical law there was nothing to stop a vendor selling siblings to different buyers from the outset and so bring about a separation.[135] This is quite correct, but does not apply in our case, because both Ulpian and Paul assume that the family members were sold as a – functional or human – collective or *uno pretio*. There is no reason to suspect this solution (essentially a mere interpretation of the contract) of being a later reworking. If this law had been subject to a late intervention under the influence of Christianity, it would simply have prohibited a separation of the slave family (i.e. made it impossible to return only the defective slave without his defect-free family members),[136] most likely also the separate sale of slaves who were kin. But our texts show no such far-reaching infringement of the parties' autonomy at all. We shall therefore regard the two texts as mutually affirmatory and genuine; again subject to the result of an examination of the Constantinian Constitution CTh. 2.25.1.[137]

---

131 Correctly noted by Zoz de Biasio, "Nota minima" (n. 94): 541; Willvonseder, *Stellung des Sklaven* (n. 3): 36; Mateo, "cognatio servilis" (n. 94): 341. We might also quote Ulpian's sentence in D. 21.1.38.14: *in qua re tam emptori quam venditori consulitur.*

132 Zoz de Biasio, "Nota minima" (n. 94): 542.

133 Giambattista Impallomeni, *L'editto degli edili curuli* (Padua: Cedam, 1955): 82 n. 20; Mateo, "cognatio servilis" (n. 94): 348–49.

134 Also referenced in Krüger, "humanitas und pietas" (n. 83): 49.

135 Daube, "The Compiler's Use" (n. 108): 359.

136 See also Zoz de Biasio, "Nota minima" (n. 94): 542.

137 So also Buckland, *Law of Slavery* (n. 21): 78 with n. 3; Pier Silverio Leicht, "Il matrimonio del servo," in *Scritti in onore di Contardo Ferrini*, vol. 1, ed. Università cattolica del Sacro Cuore (Milan: Vita e pensiero, 1947): 305–17, 309; Boulvert and Morabito, "Le droit de l'esclavage" (n. 62): 138; Alfons Bürge, "Cum in familia nubas. Zur wirtschaftlichen und sozialen Bedeutung der familia libertorum," *Zeitschrift der Savigny-Stiftung für Rechtsgeschichte, Romanistische Abteilung* 105 (1988): 312–33, 324 n. 52; Alan Watson, "Religious and Gender Discrimination. St. Ambrose and the

4.2 Legacies

4.2.1 Many testators made testamentary arrangements that prevented slave families from being separated. Those leaving a country estate could bequeath it complete with its servile workforce, and expressly include the slaves' wives and children. This enabled relatives to remain together, in the possession of the legatee:[138]

D. 33.7.20.1 (Scaevola 3 resp.): Liberto suo quidam praedia legavit his verbis: 'Seio liberto meo fundos illum et illum do lego ita ut instructi sunt cum dotibus et reliquis colonorum et saltuariis cum contubernalibus suis et filiis et filiabus' [. . .]	D. 33.7.20.1 (Scaevola, Replies, book 3): Someone legated landed estates to his freedman in these words: "I give and legate to my freedman Seius my farms 'X' and 'Y', as instructi, together with accessories and rents due from tenants and the foresters with their companions, sons and daughters." [. . .][139]

Such bequests are not uncommon. It is not the women's and children's function on the estate that is decisive for their being included, but the family ties that link them to the male agricultural workers.

Instead of being bequeathed to a third party, women and children could also be willed to the manumitted father, a practice to which not a few texts attest. After his own manumission, which made him a Roman citizen, the father now owned the woman and children; he could manumit them in turn and so obtain Roman citizenship for them. He did not have *patria potestas* over them, because he was not legally married to his mate in a *matrimonium iustum* and their children were not born in wedlock. But as a freedman he was now their patron, a legal position similar to *patria potestas*.[140]

Valentiniani," *Studia e Documenta Historiae et Iuris* 61 (1995): 313–26, 325; Mateo, "cognatio servilis" (n. 94): 346, 382; Knoch, *Sklavenfürsorge* (n. 124): 32 and n. 45; Willvonseder, *Stellung des Sklaven* (n. 3): 36; Lauretta Maganzani, "Appunti sui concetti di dignità umana alla luce della casistica giurisprudenziale romana," *Studia e Documenta Historiae et Iuris* 77 (2011): 521–43, 538; Gamauf, "§ 26 (Sklaverei)" (n. 62): marginal no. 18; see also already Max Kaser, *Das römische Privatrecht*, vol. 2, *Die nachklassischen Entwicklungen*, 2nd ed. (Munich: C.H. Beck, 1975): 126 n. 22: classical concepts (updated from the earlier edition, cf. n. 109). There has been a great deal of learned speculation about those two words of Paul's, with many scholars suspecting pre-Justinianic modifications due to Christian influences, which turned twins (*fratres gemelli/gemini*) into simple brothers; cf. Ambrosino, "Vel fratres" (n. 110): 292–93; Dell'Oro, *Le cose collettive* (n. 108): 70. For a more detailed discussion see Thomas Finkenauer, "Der Schutz der Sklavenfamilie im klassischen römischen Recht," *Revue Internationale des Droits de l'Antiquité* 67/68 (2020/2021): 82–88.

138 For what follows see Filip-Fröschl, "Gefühle und Recht" (n. 28): 16–17.

139 Transl. Seager in Watson, *Digest of Justinian* (n. 11).

140 See e.g. Scaevola D. 34.1.20 pr. (3 resp.): the wet nurse's grandson is manumitted and is bequeathed his wife and their common children; Ulpian D. 36.1.11.2 (4 fideicomm.): being testamentarily manumitted, the slave Albina is left her daughter by *fideicommissum* and asked to manumit her. For Scaevola D. 32.37.7 (18 dig.) see below 4.2.4.

4.2.2 Roman jurists generally protect the intention of the deceased. His testamentary dispositions are upheld even if this results in slave relatives being separated: if e.g. the legatee is bequeathed a slave's wife but not the slave himself, she will go to the legatee while her husband stays with the heir. In the case of a testator who bequeaths to his disinherited daughter a legacy of ten unnamed slaves who are to be chosen by her mother (who together with the son is the heir), any children born to the ten slaves are not included in the legacy and thus remain with the heir.[141] The decision, harsh as it looks, is the direct result of the testator's intention:[142] in no place throughout the will does he think of the slave children, but expressly limits the number of slaves to be given to ten; his heirs are on no account to have to convey more than that number to the legatee. The decisive factors in this case are the wording and the interpretative guidance of *favor heredis*, which calls for the burden on the heir to be kept to a minimum.[143]

This echoes another decision by Scaevola, in which an unfree agent (*actor*) was bequeathed, but his *uxor* and his *filia* were not.[144] As an inevitable consequence the

141 Scaevola D. 33.5.21 (22 dig.). *Filium et uxorem heredes scripsit, filiam exheredavit et ei legatum dedit, cum in familia nuberet, centum et, cum in familia nupserit, his verbis: 'insuper arbitratu Semproniae matris eius mancipia decem, quae confestim post aditam hereditatem meam a Sempronia uxore mea eligi volo: quae mancipia, cum in familiam nupserit, dari volo. et si antequam nupserit, aliquod ex mancipiis decesserit, tunc in locum eius arbitratu Semproniae matris eius dari volo, dum ad eam plenus numerus perveniat. quod si Sempronia mater eius non elegerit, tunc ipsa sibi quae volet eligat'. quaesitum est, cum mater elegerit, an ea, quae ex his mancipiis ante nuptias adgnata sunt, ad puellam supra numerum decem mancipiorum pertineant. respondit, cum mancipiorum legatum in tempus nuptiarum testator transtulit, id quod medio tempore ancillae enixae sunt ad filiam non pertinere* [. . .] ('A man appointed his son and wife as heirs, disinherited his daughter, and gave her a legacy of a hundred, and added the following when she married within the family: "also, at the choice of her mother Sempronia, ten slaves, which I want to be chosen by my wife Sempronia as soon as my inheritance has been accepted; these slaves I want to be given when she has married into the family. And if, before she marries, any of the slaves dies, then I want another to be chosen by her mother Sempronia to be given in his place, so that the full number may come to her. But if her mother Sempronia does not make the choice, then let her choose which ones she likes for herself." It was asked, when the mother has made the choice, whether the children born from those slaves before the marriage would belong to the girl over and above the total of ten slaves. He replied that since the testator had postponed the legacy of slaves to the time of the marriage, the offspring produced by the slavewomen in the meantime did not belong to the daughter [. . .]', transl. Seager in Watson, *Digest of Justinian* [n. 11]).
142 So also Buckland, *Law of Slavery* (n. 21): 76.
143 So also Mateo, "cognatio servilis" (n. 94): 355; on *favor heredis* see Hans Wieling, *Testamentsauslegung im römischen Recht* (Munich: C.H. Beck, 1972): 23–28.
144 Scaevola D. 33.7.20.4 (3 resp.). *Idem quaesiit in actore legato, an uxor et filia legato cedant, cum actor non in praediis, sed in civitate moratus sit. respondit nihil proponi, cur cedant.* ('The same man asked, concerning the legacy of the agent, whether his wife and daughter went with the legacy, since the agent had lived, not on the estate, but in the town. He replied that no reason had been given why they should go with it', transl. Seager in Watson, *Digest of Justinian* [n. 11]).

slave family was to be divided between heir and legatee. The workplace of the bequeathed *actor* was in the town, not the countryside, so it was not a question of keeping together the economic unit of a *villa* and its workforce. In contrast to the cases to be discussed below, the jurist found no indication in the will of why any additional slaves should be left at the expense of the heir.[145] The testator's intent had to be respected. So it would be inaccurate to accuse Scaevola of being indifferent to the slaves' fate.[146]

4.2.3 But frequently the testator's intentions cannot be clearly ascertained; in those cases, the jurists used their scope of interpretation in favour of the servile family, especially if the will yielded indications for such an interpretation. If, for example, father, mother and their *filii* are bequeathed, the bequest will also include the grandchildren, as long as it cannot be shown that the testator intended the opposite.[147]

4.2.4 There are other cases where jurists from the high classical period onwards display benevolence towards slave families: if a testator bequeaths to all his manumitted slaves their children by *fideicommissum* – obviously so that the fathers can in turn manumit them and so gain patrons' rights over them[148] – the question arises about the fate of the children of those slaves whom he had previously manumitted while still alive. Scaevola's decision is sympathetic to those children, focusing on family reunion:

> D. 32.37.7 (Scaevola 18 dig.): Ex his verbis testamenti: 'omnibus, quos quasve manumisi manumiserove sive his tabulis sive quibuscumque aliis, filios filiasve suos omnes concedi volo' quaesitum est, an his, quos vivus

> D. 32.37.7 (Scaevola, Digest, book 18): "To all men and women whom I manumitted or shall manumit, either in this testament or in any other, I wish that their sons and daughters may be granted." Because of these words in a

145 Mateo, "cognatio servilis" (n. 94): 350.
146 Correctly Mateo, "cognatio servilis" (n. 94): 350; *contra* Albertario, "D. 21,1,35" (n. 89): 645. We should not accuse Scaevola of being indifferent to the slaves' fate; in fact some of his decisions were *pro libertate*, even against the testator's will, cf. Marcianus-Scaevola D. 40.5.50 (7 inst.), see also Pomponius D. 40.4.5 (3 ad Sab.) with Wieling, *Testamentsauslegung* (n. 143): 112–13, 148.
147 Scaevola D. 32.41.5 (22 dig.). The bequest ran: *'Fundum in Appia cum vilico suo et contubernali eius et filiis dari volo'* ('I wish her to be given my farm in Appia with its manager and his partner and their children.', transl. Braun in Watson, *Digest of Justinian* [n. 11]); see Josef Menner, "D. 33,7,18,4 – Vilicus und vilica als Objekte des Erbschaftsstreits," in *Sklaverei und Freilassung im römischen Recht. Symposium für Hans Josef Wieling zum 70. Geburtstag*, ed. Thomas Finkenauer (Heidelberg: Springer Verlag, 2006): 153–87, 177. Similarly Papirius Fronto in the account by Callistratus D. 50.16.220.1 (2 quaest.): *nisi voluntas testatoris aliter habeat*; see Voci, *Diritto ereditario romano*, vol. 2 (n. 85): 948. Willvonseder, *Stellung des Sklaven* (n. 3): 82, wrongly translates *filii* as 'sons' only, disregarding the daughters who are also included in the bequest, cf. Heumann and Seckel, *Handlexikon* (n. 4): s.v. *filius in fine* with reference to Callistratus D. 50.16.220.3 (2 quaest.) et al.
148 Willvonseder, *Stellung des Sklaven* (n. 3): 48.

manumississet, debeantur filii. respondit his quoque, quos quasve ante testamentum factum manumississet, filios filiasve ex causa fideicommissi praestari oportere.

will, the question was whether the sons of those whom he manumitted in his lifetime were due to them. He [Scaevola] replied that by virtue of the fideicommissum those men and women whom he had manumitted before making his will should also receive delivery of their sons and daughters.[149]

The clause chosen by the testator was as comprehensive as possible, including this will as well as any later dispositions, and both unfree sons and daughters. But it did not contain any information about what he intended to happen to the issue of the slaves he had already manumitted during his lifetime. The jurist could have interpreted this as an eloquent silence that deliberately overlooked the children. But the broadness of the clause and the testator's clear intention to keep the slave families together as far as possible enables Scaevola to decide in favour of their protection, and against a narrow interpretation. A testator who really does not wish servile families to be reunited must explicitly say so in his will.[150]

4.2.5 In a confirmed codicil – i.e. an informal but valid part of his testamentary disposition[151] – a testator bequeathed to all of his present and future freedmen their wives (*contubernales*) and children. Only the slaves he left to his wife were to be exempt. He then by way of a *fideicommissum* placed on his heirs the obligation to convey to his wife certain estates including *all* of the slaves on them. Dama had already been manumitted by the testator. His two unfree sons lived on those estates. Were they to go to Dama or to the testator's wife?

D. 32.41.2 (Scaevola 22 dig.): Codicillis confirmatis ita cavit: 'omnibus autem libertis meis et quos vivus et quos his codicillis manumissi vel postea manumisero, contubernales suas, item filios filias lego, nisi si quos quasve ad uxorem meam testamento pertinere volui vel ei nominatim legavi legavero'. idem postea petiit ab heredibus suis, ut regionem Umbriae Tusciae Piceno coheredes uxori suae restituerent cum omnibus, quae ibi erunt, et mancipiis rusticis vel urbanis et actoribus exceptis manumissis. quaesitum est, cum Eros et Stichus servi in diem vitae testatoris in Umbria in Piceno actum administraverint, sint autem Damae, quem testator

D. 32.41.2 (Scaevola, Digest, book 22): Someone provided as follows in a confirmed codicil: "To all my freedmen whom I have manumitted both in my lifetime and in this codicil or shall manumit in future, I bequeath their partners and their sons and daughters, with the exception of such persons of either sex that I have desired in my will to belong to my wife, or have bequeathed or shall bequeath to her by name." The same testator afterward asked [in a letter] his heirs to restore to his wife the territory of Umbria, Tuscia and Picenum together with all that was in it, and the rural and urban slaves with the agents, except for those manumitted.

149 Transl. Braun in Watson, *Digest of Justinian* (n. 11).

150 A very similar case is Scaevola D. 33.7.27.1 (6 dig.), where the jurist likewise decides in favour of the servile family.

151 Kaser, *Das römische Privatrecht*, vol. 2 (n. 137): 694.

vivus manumiserat, filii naturales, utrum eidem Damae ex verbis codicilli ab heredibus praestandi sint, an vero ad Seiam uxorem ex verbis epistulae pertineant. respondit ex codicillis ad patrem eos naturalem pietatis intuitu pertinere.

The question was whether Eros and Stichus, who had managed the testator's affairs in Umbria and Picenum to the last day of his life, should be delivered by the heirs, by virtue of the wording of the codicil, to Dama, because they were his natural sons and Dama had been manumitted by the testator in his lifetime, or should they belong to the testator's wife Seia by virtue of the wording of the letter. He [Scaevola] replied that they should belong to their father, following the codicil, out of respect for natural loyalty (pietatis intuitu).[152]

Scaevola finds against the widow and in favour of the father. This opinion is surprising, because the testator had expressly excluded from the bequest to his freedmen, including Dama, the slaves that were to go to his wife – which certainly included Dama's sons. If we are to take Scaevola at his word we must conclude that, for him, consideration of *pietas* was decisive. As we have already seen, *pietas* can relate to the relationship between a *dominus*/testator and his slaves,[153] or – and more plausibly – to the kinship ties between the father and sons.[154]

Scaevola does not even claim that his interpretation corresponds to the wording of the codicil and *fideicommissum*, or to the testator's intention. There was, however, the difficulty that the testator's disposition included all the slaves on a given estate, not just the *familia rustica*. Dama's sons had worked as agents (*actores*), so they did not strictly speaking belong to the estates that were to go to the widow. Perhaps the testator had simply not thought of them when he made his later disposition for his wife. But the disposition made it quite possible to infer the testator's intention not to separate slave families. So in this conflict between a literal reading and the topos of the family being inseparable,[155] the jurist finds in favour of *pietas*. It is probable that this interpretation was inspired by *favor libertatis*;[156] especially the jurists of the high classical period are inclined to favour manumission wherever possible: Dama gets his sons and can manumit them. In this way he acquires a patron's rights over them and, as such, a power similar to *patria potestas*. If, however, the testator had manumitted the children in question directly, together with their fathers, they would have been *his* freedmen. Scaevola's reading allows for 'indirect' manumission. This accords well with how wills were

152 Transl. Braun in Watson, *Digest of Justinian* (n. 11).
153 So Mateo, "cognatio servilis" (n. 94): 352.
154 See above 4.1.
155 See e.g. Ulpian D. 33.7.12.7 (below 4.2.6) und Ulpian D. 21.1.35 (above 4.1).
156 Similarly Willvonseder, *Stellung des Sklaven* (n. 3): 49–50.

likely to be interpreted in the high classical period[157] and renders implausible[158] the suspicion that *pietatis intuitu* or the decision might be later interpolations.[159] It is irrelevant for the authenticity of our *responsum* that Scaevola also made some 'hard' decisions in which he paid no heed to the slaves' fate (see above 4.2.2).[160] In those cases, the testators had given no indication that keeping slave families together was a matter close to their hearts – unlike the will under discussion here.

4.2.6 An estate (*villa*) could be bequeathed complete with all accessories (*instrumentum*). If a will made explicit mention of the estate slaves (*familia rustica*) to be bequeathed, the testator's intention was clear. But if the *villa* was to be left with accessories (*fundus cum instrumento*), a great number of delineation difficulties arose: The bequest certainly included the estate's work slaves,[161] because there was no doubt that the economic unity of estate and workers was to be preserved.[162] But what if some work slaves had been borrowed from another of the testator's estates, or sent to the town, or to another estate to be trained? Were those slaves to go with the property, or should they go to the heir charged with the legacy?[163] Then there were those slaves on the estate who did not directly contribute to its core economic activity, but who supported the work slaves, i.e. the agricultural workers, as bakers, cooks etc.[164] – where were they to go? Ulpian and some others opined that they were the accessories' accessories (*instrumenti instrumentum*) and affirm that they belong with

157 Wieling, *Testamentsauslegung* (n. 143): 112–16: The topos of *favor libertatis* was to become the prevailing one in the high classical period, even against a testator's intention.

158 Not only Willvonseder but also Filip-Fröschl, "Gefühle und Recht" (n. 28): 19, favours classicality; Bürge, "Cum in familia nubas" (n. 137): 324 n. 52; Riccardo Astolfi, *Studi sull'oggetto dei legati in diritto romano*, vol. 2 (Padua: Cedam, 1969): 24, also favours material authenticity; Mateo, "cognatio servilis" (n. 94): 353. See also below, 4.4.

159 Jacobus Cujacius, *Opera omnia*, vol. 7 (Naples: Michael Aloysius Mutius, 1758): col. 1019 B: *nostri auctores non solent ea ratione uti, nisi cum pietatis ratione receditur a iure communi*; Emilio Albertario, "I Tribonianismi avvertiti dal Cuiacio," *Zeitschrift der Savigny-Stiftung für Rechtsgeschichte, Romanistische Abteilung* 31 (1910): 158–75, 164; Krüger, "humanitas und pietas" (n. 83): 48; Biondi, *DRC*, vol. 2 (n. 114): 439; Solazzi, "famiglia dello schiavo" (n. 114): 190.

160 For a different reading see Albertario, "D. 21,1,35" (n. 89): 646; Krüger, "humanitas und pietas" (n. 83): 48.

161 The opinion of Alfenus in Ulpian D. 33.7.12.2 (20 ad ed.), that slaves cannot be accessories because they are living beings did not gain acceptance, cf. only Sabinus in Ulpian D. 33.7.8 pr. (20 ad Sab.) and Paul D. 33.7.19 pr. (13 resp.). The *vilicus* was included in the *instrumentum* only if the estate was administered because of his *fides dominica*; see Menner, "D. 33,7,18,4" (n. 147): 157.

162 See Marijan Horvat, "'Servi' e 'legatum fundi' nella giurisprudenza classica," in *Antologia giuridica romanistica ed antiquaria*, vol. 1, ed. Lorenzo Gagliardi (Milan: Giuffrè, 1968): 211–22, 214, 217 [= in *Studi in onore di Edoardo Volterra*, vol. 5 (Milan: Giuffrè, 1971): 89–97].

163 For these questions see Horvat, "'Servi' e 'legatum fundi'" (n. 162): 218–19.

164 Cf. the examples in Ulpian D. 33.7.12.5 (20 ad ed.).

the bequest.[165] In the early classical period, Trebatius still demanded that the wife of an estate manager (*vilicus*) must render assistance to her husband in some way in order to be counted as part of the bequest.[166] She would usually keep house for him and this will have sufficed, so that even in the early classical period, a separation of *vilica* and *vilicus* was probably the exception rather than the rule.[167] By contrast, Ulpian finds that the testator's intention includes without exception all the wives and children on the estate, not only those of the work slaves but also of the supporting slaves:

D. 33.7.12.7 (Ulpian 20 ad Sab.): Uxores quoque et infantes eorum, qui supra enumerati sunt, credendum est in eadem villa agentes voluisse testatorem legato contineri: neque enim duram separationem iniunxisse credendus est.	D. 33.7.12.7 (Ulpian, Sabinus, book 20): It should also be held that the testator wanted the wives and children too of those enumerated above, if they live in the same villa, to be included in the legacy; for it is not credible that he would have imposed a harsh separation.[168]

While during Trebatius' lifetime the wife of the *vilicus* was only included in the legacy if she performed specific services for him, Ulpian, living 200 years later, is more generous. He introduces a rule of interpretation that views the separation of spouses or of parents and children as hard-hearted, a *dura separatio*: instead, the whole slave family was to go to the legatee.[169] Of course, this rule only applied as long as the testator had not expressed contrary intentions. Some scholars regard Ulpian's rule as still following the testator's (presumed) intent.[170] However, this misses the point: Ulpian does not say that his reading in favour of the slaves reflected the testator's intention, either as it was or as it would have been had the latter thought of the slave family. Instead, Ulpian imputes a humanitarian aspect to the testator's intention (*credendum est*), namely the desire not to separate the slave family.[171] Nothing stood in the way of the testator having made wholly different dispositions at any time, including an acceptance of family separation.[172] As this intention is not made explicit, the

165 Ulpian D. 33.7.12.6 (20 ad ed.).

166 Cf. Ulpian D. 33.7.12.5 (20 ad ed.): *si modo aliquo officio virum adiuvet.* ('provided she assists her husband in some duty').

167 Menner, "D. 33,7,18,4" (n. 147): 165–66.

168 Transl. Seager in Watson, *Digest of Justinian* (n. 11).

169 Mateo, "cognatio servilis" (n. 94): 359 also underlines legal developments between the lifetimes of Trebatius and Ulpian.

170 Krüger, "humanitas und pietas" (n. 83): 48; Buckland, *Law of Slavery* (n. 21): 76; Voci, *Diritto ereditario romano*, vol. 2 (n. 85): 281 n. 53; Willvonseder, *Stellung des Sklaven* (n. 3): 50.

171 Wieling, *Testamentsauslegung* (n. 143): 182–83.

172 Voci, *Diritto ereditario romano*, vol. 2 (n. 85): 281 n. 53. Cf. just the two Scaevola texts D. 33.5.21; 33.7.20.4, above in section 4.2.2.

Roman jurist's interpretation is based on humanitarian grounds, as it so often is – take, for example, the case of *favor libertatis*.[173] Those, however, who argue that Ulpian's reading primarily aims to safeguard servile reproduction and so a sufficient supply of labour for the estates at a time when slaves were in short supply[174] ascribe to him an unduly restricted focus merely on economic aspects, something not consistent with his reasoning.

Some scholars have denied the classicality of this text, pointing to Constantine's constitution CTh. 2.25.1;[175] wrongly though.[176] For one thing, we know of classical texts that refer to a slave wife as *uxor* even though the term was restricted to Roman citizens wives; unfree wives are sometimes called *uxor* instead of *contubernalis*, and this quite early on.[177] Most importantly, we should assume that it is merely a *petitio principii*, to posit a later reworking because of similarities with Constantine's constitution. It is just as possible that his law was based on a classical predecessor, which accords with the textual tradition. Ulpian arrives at the same result here as he does for the question of the legacy of a *fundus instructus*, i.e. an estate duly equipped: there, too, he finds for the wives and children of the slaves being included in the legacy.[178]

---

173 Wieling, *Testamentsauslegung* (n. 143): 250.

174 So Maria Antonietta Ligios, *Interpretazione giuridica e realtà economica dell'"instrumentum fundi' tra il I sec. a.C. e il III d.C.* (Naples: Jovene, 1996): 192, 271; Astolfi, *legati*, vol. 2 (n. 158): 23; Mateo, "cognatio servilis" (n. 94): 359 n. 49, agrees cautiously.

175 Albertario, "D. 21,1,35" (n. 89): 648; Pietro Bonfante, *Corso di diritto romano*, vol. 1 (Rome: Attilio Sampaolesi, 1925; repr. Milano: Giuffrè, 1963): 151 n. 3; Gerhard Beseler, *Beiträge zur Kritik der römischen Rechtsquellen*, vol. 4 (Tübingen: Mohr Siebeck, 1920): 150; Biondi, *DRC*, vol. 2 (n. 114): 439; Kaser, "Contardo Ferrini" (n. 109): 169; Solazzi, "famiglia dello schiavo" (n. 114): 191; Pólay, *Die Sklavenehe* (n. 9): 65.

176 Its authenticity is confirmed by Krüger, "humanitas und pietas" (n. 83): 48; Perozzi, *Istituzioni* (n. 109): 201 n. 1; Buckland, *Law of Slavery* (n. 21): 76; Leicht, "Il matrimonio" (n. 137): 309; Horvat, "'Servi' e 'legatum fundi'" (n. 162): 217; Pólay, *Die Sklavenehe* (n. 9): 29; Wieling, *Testamentsauslegung* (n. 143): 182–83; Susan Treggiari, "Questions on Women Domestics in the Roman West," in *Schiavitù, manomissione e classi dipendenti nel mondo antico*, Pubblicazioni dell'istituto di storia antica 13, ed. Maria Capozza (Rome: L'Erma di Bretschneider, 1979): 185–201, 196–99; Boulvert and Morabito, "Le droit de l'esclavage" (n. 62): 139; Pasquale Voci, *Nuovi studi sulla legislazione romana del tardo impero* (Padua: Cedam, 1989): 49; Sicari, *Leges venditionis* (n. 74): 236; Filip-Fröschl, "Gefühle und Recht" (n. 28): 17; Willvonseder, *Stellung des Sklaven* (n. 3): 50, 82; Ortu, "Costantino" (n. 65): 1908; Martin Avenarius, *Stellung des Sklaven im Privatrecht*, vol. 3, *Erbrecht. Aktive Stellung: Personeneigenschaft und Ansätze zur Anerkennung von Rechten*, Corpus der römischen Rechtsquellen zur antiken Sklaverei 4 (Stuttgart: Franz Steiner Verlag, 2017): 7; Gamauf, "§ 26 (Sklaverei)" (n. 62): marginal no. 18. Material authenticity but post-classical reworking is assumed by Perozzi, *Istituzioni* (n. 109): 201 n. 1; Astolfi, *legati*, vol. 2 (n. 158): 23; Ligios, *instrumentum* (n. 174): 190; Mateo, "cognatio servilis" (n. 94): 361; cautious: Kaser, *Das römische Privatrecht*, vol. 2 (n. 137): 126 n. 22, who had previously argued against classicality (n. 175).

177 Cf. above n. 121.

178 D. 33.7.12.33 (20 ad Sab.); see also Mateo, "cognatio servilis" (n. 94): 365.

4.3 Actions for Division

In 325 (or 334[179]) the emperor Constantine passed a law prohibiting the separation of slave families in a strictly defined exceptional case:

CTh. 2.25.1 (Constantinus Augustus Gerulo rationali trium provinciarum): In Sardinia fundis patrimonialibus vel emphyteuticariis per diversos nunc dominos distributis, oportuit sic possessionum fieri divisiones, ut integra apud possessorem unumquemque servorum agnatio permaneret. Quis enim ferat, liberos a parentibus, a fratribus sorores, a viris coniuges segregari? igitur qui dissociata in ius diversum mancipia traxerunt, in unum redigere eadem cogantur: ac si cui propter redintegrationem necessitudinum servi cesserunt, vicaria per eum, qui eosdem susceperit, mancipia reddantur. Et invigilandum, ne per provinciam aliqua posthac querela super divisis mancipiorum affectibus perseveret. Dat. III. kal. Mai. Proculo et Paulino conss.

CTh. 2.25.1 (Constantinus Augustus Gerulo rationali trium provinciarum): With regard to the imperial or emphyteutic estates of Sardinia that have now been distributed to various owners, it is necessary that the division of the properties be effected in a way that relationships among slaves are preserved intact among each owner. For who could bear that husbands be separated from wives, brothers from sisters, or parents from children? Therefore those who have carried off slaves separated among different owners are to be compelled to bring them back together. And anyone whose slaves relocate on account of these required restorations shall receive back substitute slaves from the one who took them. Be on the alert, lest afterwards any grievances remain over the emotional separations of slaves throughout the province.[180]

The constitution was addressed to Gerulus,[181] the *rationalis* of the three provinces of Sardinia, Sicily and Corsica,[182] about whom nothing else is known. The law applied only to Sardinia, and there only to leasehold land from the imperial domain (*patrimonium Caesaris*) or the crown estate (*res privata*). The former was let on long-term but time-limited hereditary leases (emphyteutic lease), while the latter

---

179 The dating is problematic, cf. Otto Seeck, *Regesten der Kaiser und Päpste für die Jahre 311 bis 476 A.D.* (Stuttgart: J.B. Metzler, 1919): 428, who assumes 29 April 325 and amends the consuls to Paulinus and Julian (88–89, 174); in 334 Constantine was in the Danube provinces, which does not fit; Wolfgang Waldstein agrees, underlining the proximity to the Council of Nicaea, see his "Schiavitù e Cristianesimo da Costantino a Teodosio II," in *Atti dell'Accademia Romanistica Costantiniana*, vol. 8 (Naples: Edizioni Scientifiche Italiane, 1990): 123–45, 130. Piero Meloni argues for 334, *L'ammistrazione della Sardegna da Augusto all'invasione vandalica* (Rome: L'Erma di Bretschneider, 1966): 144.

180 Transl. Kyle Harper, *Slavery in the Late Roman World, AD 275–425* (Cambridge: Cambridge University Press, 2011): 271.

181 For Gerulus see Arnold H.M. Jones, John Robert Martindale and John Morris, *The Prosopography of the Later Roman Empire*, vol. 1, *A.D. 260–395* (Cambridge: Cambridge University Press, 2001): 394.

182 The *Notitia dignitatum* notes, *Rationalis summarum trium provinciarum, id est Siciliae, Saradiniae et Corsicae.*

was subject to a perpetual lease.[183] Recent divisions of land caused the emperor to declare a ban on dividing the *servorum agnatio* (!)[184] belonging to the individual plots of land among the leaseholders, the *possessores*.[185] It was intolerable, the emperor wrote, for children to be parted from their parents and siblings or spouses from each other.[186] If the divisions caused families to become separated, the divisions must be reversed; anyone losing a slave as a result is to receive one to replace him. It is the *rationalis'* task to make sure there are no complaints in the province about the separation of slaves who share a family tie.

The law's narrow scope[187] was not expanded when it was included in the Theodosian Code in 438,[188] where it is the only law under the heading of *actio communi dividundo*, the general action for dividing common property.[189] However, the fact that this is a regulation only applying to one individual case is often overlooked.[190]

---

183 For *patrimonium Caesaris* and *res privata* as well as emphyteutic leases see Kaser, *Das römische Privatrecht*, vol. 2 (n. 137): 152–53, 308–9; see also Voci, *legislazione romana* (n. 176): 46–47; Hans Wieling, "Grundbesitz I (rechtsgeschichtlich)," in *Reallexikon für Antike und Christentum*, vol. 12, ed. Theodor Klauser (Stuttgart: Anton Hiersemann Verlag, 1983): col. 1172–96, col. 1187–88.

184 For this odd term, which exclusively refers to the Roman family and does occur more commonly in the post-classical period, see their references in Ortu, "Costantino" (n. 65): 1892 n. 13. Clémence Dupont, *Les constitutions de Constantin et le droit privé au début du IVe siècle* (Lille: Université de Lille, 1937): 35–36 regards this, probably incorrectly, as the first legislative recognition of the servile family, and as such as a considerable advance for slaves.

185 Constantine and other emperors call them, imprecisely, *domini*; cf. Kaser, *Das römische Privatrecht*, vol. 2 (n. 137): 310.

186 For the background to the divisions Mateo, "cognatio servilis" (n. 94): 374–75 suggested that on the estates there were not only imperial slaves tied to those lands, but also slaves owned by the leaseholders, who could easily be taken from the estates. However, the constitution references the division of the estates themselves.

187 Correctly Manlio Sargenti, *Il diritto privato nella legislazione di Costantino* (Milan: Giuffrè, 1938): 57; Hans Langenfeld, *Christianisierungspolitik und Sklavengesetzgebung der römischen Kaiser von Konstantin bis Theodosius II* (Bonn: Habelt-Verlag, 1977): 212; Mateo, "cognatio servilis" (n. 94): 375; Harper, *Slavery* (n. 180): 272.

188 For this question see Peter Riedlberger, *Prolegomena zu den spätantiken Konstitutionen* (Stuttgart-Bad Cannstatt: Frommann-Holzboog Verlag, 2020): 151; incorrect: Zoz de Biasio, "Nota minima" (n. 94): 538.

189 Kaser rightly deplores our almost complete ignorance of the pre-Justinianic law of common ownership, except only for this one text which does not allow any generalisable statements: Kaser, *Das römische Privatrecht*, vol. 2 (n. 137): 409 n. 2.

190 So for example by Treggiari, "Women Domestics" (n. 176): 196; Jean Gaudemet, "Des 'droits de l'homme' ont-ils été reconnus dans l'Empire romain?," *Labeo* 33 (1987): 5–23, 15; Adalbert Polaček, "Diritti dell'uomo nell'epoca costantiniana," in *Atti dell'Accademia Romanistica Costantiniana*, vol. 8, ed. G. Crifò and S. Giglio (Naples: Edizioni Scientifiche Italiane, 1990): 95–102, 96; Jane F. Gardner, *Frauen im antiken Rom* (Munich: C.H. Beck, 1995): 221; Francesca Mencacci, "Relazioni di parentela nella comunità servile. Gli schiavi gemelli," in *Schiavi e dipendenti nell'ambito dell'"oikos' e della 'familia': Atti del 22. Colloquio Girea: Pontignano (Siena), 19–20 novembre 1995*, ed.

There has been much speculation about the emperor's motives. Some scholars assumed a link with CTh. 5.17.1 (332) about the flight of *coloni*, and view both as reflecting a social crisis in which the traditional structures of production were dissolving amid a growing shortage of servile workers. CTh. 2.25.1 is seen as an attempt to counter this crisis by tying a self-reproducing workforce to the soil.[191] The weakness of this economic reading is that such an imperial legal policy would certainly not have targeted just a single province.[192] The most common view is that Christian morality was a, or the, motivating factor for the law.[193] It has even been suggested that a connection runs from Ulpian through Lactantius who, inspired by Ulpian's *institutiones*, transported Ulpianic thinking all the way to the imperial court through the close ties he had there.[194] There is, however, no evidence that the emperor intended to prevent the separation of slave families *in general*, including *patrimonium* and *res privata* in other provinces, or private estates.[195] Also, the early church did not advocate the protection of slave families.[196] So there does not appear to have been a Christian, humanitarian motivation, at least not at the forefront of Constantine's mind when he drew up this slave legislation.[197] It makes much more sense to suppose that local events in Sardinia occasioned the constitution; the text itself opens with mentions of recent divisions. What is more, the final sentence makes clear that there were

Mauro Maggi and Giuseppe Cordiano (Pisa: ETS, 1997): 213–32, 214 n. 4; Waldstein, "Schiavitù e Cristianesimo" (n. 179): 130–31.

191 Angelo Puglisi, "Servi, coloni, veterani e la terra in alcuni testi di Costantino," *Labeo* 23 (1977): 305–17, 311–13; Harper, *Slavery* (n. 180): 272. Similarly Elisabeth Herrmann-Otto, "Sklaven und Frauen unter Konstantin," in *Konstantin der Große*, ed. Alexander Demandt and Josef Engemann (Trier: Philipp von Zabern Verlag, 2006): 83–95, 92, whose interpretation is however marred by her assumption that the slaves are still owned by the emperor, which is unlikely in the case of leasehold land; likewise Marcel Simonis, "Ehe," in *Handwörterbuch der antiken Sklaverei*, vol. 1, ed. Heinz Heinen et al. (Stuttgart: Franz Steiner Verlag, 2017): col. 767–74, 772.

192 The same is true for the link proposed by Dupont with *iugatio capitatio*, which was decisive for tax law, i.e. the fiscal unity of a property and its tied servile workforce. There is not necessarily a connection to the protection of slave spouses or children; Dupont, *Constantin* (n. 184): 37–38.

193 See for example Bonfante, *Corso*, vol. 1 (n. 175): 151; Leicht, "Il matrimonio" (n. 137): 306–7; Biondi, *DRC*, vol. 3 (n. 114): 90; Dupont, *Constantin* (n. 184): 37–38; Dell'Oro, *Le cose collettive* (n. 108): 65; Daube "The Compiler's Use" (n. 108): 360; Ortu, "Costantino" (n. 65): 1894; more cautiously: Waldstein, "Schiavitù e Cristianesimo" (n. 179): 131–32, 142, who cannot quite decide whether to credit Christian ideas or pagan thinking influenced by ideas from Stoicism and natural law. The Bible also prohibits the separation of slave spouses (2. Gen. 21.3), but allows exceptions (21.4).

194 Francesco Amarelli, *Vetustas – innovatio. Un'antitesi apparente nella legislazione di Costantino* (Naples: Jovene, 1978): 122–23 makes a (not immediately evident) reference to *divin. inst.* 5.15.3; Ortu, "Costantino" (n. 65): 1923.

195 Also highlighted by Sargenti, *Costantino* (n. 187): 58; similarly Mateo, "cognatio servilis" (n. 94): 377.

196 Pointed out by Harper, *Slavery* (n. 180): 273.

197 So apparently also Wolfgang Seyfarth, *Soziale Fragen der spätrömischen Kaiserzeit im Spiegel des Theodosianus* (Berlin: Akademie-Verlag, 1963): 140–41.

not just fears about potential grievances over the separation of slave families, but that such grievances already existed (*perseveret*). It seems therefore plausible to assume a connection with slave revolts, or the fear of revolt.[198]

In the West, there is an extensive interpretation of the imperial law: the *interpretatio Visigothorum*[199] omits reference to Sardinia.[200] The process of ever more extensive application goes even further in the East:

> C. 3.38.11 (Constantinus Augustus Gerulo): Possessionum divisiones sic fieri oportet, ut integra apud successorem unumquemque servorum vel colonorum adscripticiae condicionis seu inquilinorum proxima agnatio vel adfinitas permaneret. quis enim ferat liberos a parentibus, a fratribus sorores, a viris coniuges segregari? igitur si qui dissociata in ius diversum mancipia vel colonos traxerint, in unum eadem redigere cogantur. D. III k. Mai. Proculo et Paulino conss.

> C. 3.38.11 (Constantinus Augustus Gerulo): Divisions of property should be so made that all the near relatives or connections among slaves, serfs affixed to the soil, or tenants (inquilini), remain under one ownership. For who would tolerate that children should be separated from parents, brothers from sisters, husbands from wives? If slaves or serfs have, accordingly, been separated and placed under different ownerships, they must be reunited under one.[201]

The *Codex Iustinianus* lists the constitution in the title for *actio familiae erciscundae* as well as for the more comprehensive *actio communi dividundo*, i.e. the action for dividing an inheritance and the action for dividing common property.[202] By registering all the public and private properties of the empire, by referring to *successores* as

198 Puglisi, "Servi, coloni, veterani" (n. 191): 309; Camillo Bellieni, *Enfiteusi, schiavitù e colonato in Sardegna all'epoca di Costantino* (Cagliari: Edizioni della Fondazione Il nuraghe, 1930): 66; Meloni, *Sardegna* (n. 179): 144–45; Heinz Bellen, *Studien zur Sklavenflucht im römischen Kaiserreich* (Wiesbaden: Franz Steiner Verlag, 1971): 73–74; Ortu, "Costantino" (n. 65): 1891.

199 Cf. Lucia di Cintio, *L'"interpretatio Visigothorum' al 'Codex Theodosianus'* (Milan: LED Edizioni Universitarie, 2013): 11–16.

200 CTh. 2.25.1. Interpr. *In divisione patrimoniorum seu fiscalium domorum sive privatorum observari specialiter debet, ut, quia iniustum est, filios a parentibus vel uxores a maritis, cum ad quemcumque possessio pervenerit, sequestrari, mancipia, quae permixta fuerint, id est uxor cum filiis et marito suo, datis vicariis, ad unum debeant pertinere, cui necesse fuerit commutare, quod sollicitudo ordinantium debet specialiter custodire, ut separatio fieri omnino non possit.* ('Since it is unjust for children to be separated from parents or wives from husbands whenever a landholding has come to any person, when there is a partition of estates of the imperial patrimony or of homes belonging to the fisc or the privy purse, it must be particularly observed that substitute slaves must be given, so that the slaves who live together, that is, a wife with her children and husband, must belong to one person, upon whom the necessity rests of making the exchange. It must be the responsibility of the officials to guard with particular care that separations cannot take place at all'; transl. by Clyde Pharr, *The Theodosian Code* [Princeton: Princeton University Press, 1952]: 57).

201 Based on the transl. of Blume in Frier, *The Codex of Justinian* (n. 54).

202 Kaser, *Das römische Privatrecht*, vol. 2 (n. 137): 537–38.

individual and universal successors[203] and by extending it to *coloni* – tenant farmers who were tied to the soil (*coloni adscripticii*)[204] – the ban on dividing properties gained a much wider scope than it had had in Constantine's original constitution.[205]

4.4 A Methodological Problem: On Reconstructing Classical Sources

Narrowly limited in its scope, CTh. 2.25.1 by the emperor Constantine, which prevented the separation of servile families, addressed, as we have seen, a specific question that only concerned the imperial properties in a single province. This regulation was universalised first at the turn of the fifth to the sixth centuries in the Visigothic *interpretatio* issued on the subject, and subsequently in the Justinianic constitution C. 3.38.11. This led scholars, especially during the first half of the twentieth century, to conclude that certain slave-friendly regulations which sought to prevent the separation of servile spouses, parents and children, or siblings, had not been brought in until Justinian or at least pre-Justinianic glosses influenced by Constantine's ruling, and consequently under Christian influence.[206] Seen in this light, all passages in the Digest that recognise *cognatio servilis* in some way appear to be interpolated or at least the result of post-classical revision.[207]

This argument is no longer tenable. It is closely linked to methodological premises that most scholars ceased to hold in the late 1960s.[208] It is therefore not sufficient simply to count the number of votes for and against reworking;[209] an approach which overestimates the assertions of the 'interpolation hunters', i.e. so to speak the 'usual suspects' such as Beseler, Albertario or Solazzi. Excessive textual criticism has gone

---

203 This is, incidentally, the only time the compilers make a *successor* of a *possessor* (e.g. at CTh. 2.25.1), cf. Puglisi, "Servi, coloni, veterani" (n. 191): 307.

204 Wieling, "Grundbesitz I" (n. 183): col. 1189.

205 See also Mateo, "cognatio servilis" (n. 94): 375–76. In 542 A.D. in Novel 157 Justinian also introduced a punishable ban on the separation of slave families against large landowners and ordered that separations which had already been carried out must be reversed.

206 For the question of what motivated Constantine's laws see Dietrich V. Simon, "Zum Einfluß des Christentums auf die Gesetzgebung Kaiser Konstantins des Großen," in *Rom, Recht, Religion. Symposium für Udo Ebert zum siebzigsten Geburtstag*, ed. Kristian Kühl and Gerhard Seher (Tübingen: Mohr Siebeck, 2011): 73–88.

207 See esp. Albertario, "D. 21,1,35" (n. 89): 648; Bonfante, *Corso*, vol. 1 (n. 175): 151; Biondi, *DRC*, vol. 2 (n. 114): 438. Melluso's work, *La schiavitù nell'età giustinianea* (n. 125): 150–51, still maintains this antiquated standpoint of interpolation criticism.

208 Let me here once more refer to Kaser's epochal essay on methodology (n. 90). His change of position about our question between the first and second edition of his manual is significant (cf. n. 91, 137).

209 But this is ultimately the approach adopted by, among others, Herrmann-Otto, *Ex ancilla* (n. 31): 263.

out of fashion. Linguistic indications that a text has been disrupted are no longer taken to prove changes to the content. In view of the fact that Justinian's compilers cut some 95% of the original texts we should not be surprised to see evidence of edits. As long as there is no discernible material reason for a passage to have been changed, we should therefore assume that our texts are authentic.

An argument against a post-classical reworking is the fact that Constantine's law had not been generalised in the east until the Justinianic period; the *interpretatio*, being Visigothic, cannot be used as evidence. We know of no ambition of Constantine's to apply more broadly the constitution he had established for a single case. Why then should only Constantine's constitution have sown the seed for later reworking;[210] why cannot already classical jurisprudence have played this role?[211]

Current scholarly thinking requires a material reason for assuming content of the Digest was interpolated by the compilers. It might be tempting to see exactly this reason in C. 3.38.11.[212] But this falls short of the mark. Justinian's legislation is confined to actions for dividing common property, while in other respects, as we have seen, texts favourable to slaves in his Digest are sparse, isolated and, above all, not definitive enough to have been specifically revised.[213] Why, for example, would the emperor put words into the mouth of Paul instead of directly correcting Ulpian's text on the matter? Why – assuming that there was a general ban on separations – did Justinian not simply prohibit the sale of individual members of a slave family, or at least the redhibition of separated slave relatives? Scholars have pointed to many passages in the Digest that evidence maximum indifference to servile families.[214] Why were those passages not adapted in accordance with the presumed general plan? Finally, interpolation of *pietas* in Ulpian D. 21.1.35 and Scaevola D. 32.41.2 in pursuit of a general plan is unlikely, if for no other reason simply because different sub-committees worked on those two texts during the creation of the Digest.[215]

But if we take the texts seriously in their chronological tradition, we can see in them the traces of delicate juridical work, scrupulous interpretations and the weighing of interests, characteristic of classical jurisprudence. We can reasonably assume that the arguments against separation belong to the classical era[216] precisely because already then slave families had often been kept together by testamentary dispositions.[217]

210 Albertario, "D. 21,1,35" (n. 89): 647; Biondi, *DRC*, vol. 3 (n. 114): 90; Sargenti, *Costantino* (n. 187): 57–58.

211 Cf. already Leicht, "Il matrimonio" (n. 137): 309; Mateo, "cognatio servilis" (n. 94): 377; not dissimilar also Gamauf, "§ 26 (Sklaverei)" (n. 62): marginal no. 18.

212 One representative example (there are many) is Solazzi, "famiglia dello schiavo" (n. 114): 187.

213 Cf. again D. 33.7.12.7 (above 4.2.5); correctly Pólay, *Die Sklavenehe* (n. 9): 29.

214 Albertario, "D. 21,1,35" (n. 89): 645 (albeit incorrectly, cf. n. 146).

215 Cf. Tony Honoré, "Justinian's Digest: The Distribution of Authors and Works to the Three Committees," *Roman Legal Tradition* 3 (2006): 1–47, 14.

216 Similarly Filip-Fröschl, "Gefühle und Recht" (n. 28): 17.

217 See above 4.2.1.

5 Affection

According to two texts by Paul, the affection felt by the natural father for his slave child plays no role in calculating the value of the child.[218] General criteria must be employed to establish a slave's value, not the personal feelings of an individual.

Paul D. 9.2.33 pr. (2 ad Plaut.)[219] cites the first chapter of the *lex Aquilia*: someone kills another person's slave, whose owner demands damages from the killer. The evaluation of the loss – the highest value of the slave in the last year before his death – is to be based on general criteria, not on the possibly much higher price the natural father would have paid to the owner.[220] Paul refers to a rule by Sextus Pedius in the late first century A.D., which stated that the value of a thing ought not to be assessed *ex affectione nec utilitate singulorum*, but in a general way. The reason for this decision probably lies in the original Roman compensation system, which only knew fixed penalties and required standardised criteria because of its punitive character;[221] possibly also in an aversion to a law of damages that would have been too expensive for the economy at the time.[222]

A second text by Paul also uses the dictum by Sextus Pedius to rule out a subjective valuation:[223] if an heir who has inherited his own son wants to invoke the

218 See also Ulpian D. 7.7.6.2 (55 ad ed.).

219 D. 9.2.33 pr. (2 ad Plaut.). *Si servum meum occidisti, non affectiones aestimandas esse puto, veluti si filium tuum naturalem quis occiderit quem tu magno emptum velles, sed quanti omnibus valeret. Sextus quoque Pedius ait pretia rerum non ex affectione nec utilitate singulorum, sed communiter fungi: itaque eum, qui filium naturalem possidet, non eo locupletiorem esse, quod eum plurimo, si alius possideret, redempturus fuit* [. . .] ('If you kill my slave, I think that personal feelings should not be taken into account [as where someone kills your natural son whom you would be prepared to buy for a great price] but only what he would be worth to the world at large. Sextius Pedius says that the prices of things are to be taken generally and not according to personal affections nor their special utility to particular individuals; and accordingly, he says that he who has a natural son is none the richer because he would redeem him for a great price if someone else possessed him [. . .]', transl. Kolbert in Watson, *Digest of Justinian* [n. 11]). Cf. Fritz Raber, "Zum 'pretium affectionis'," in *Festgabe für Arnold Herdlitczka*, ed. Franz Horak and Wolfgang Waldstein (Munich/Salzburg: Wilhelm Fink, 1972): 197–213, 203; this is misunderstood by Herrmann-Otto, *Ex ancilla* (n. 31): 84–85, who wrongly assumes that the master is identical with the killed man's natural father, and that a 'lucrative deal' has been thwarted.

220 Kaser, *Das römische Privatrecht*, vol. 1 (n. 1): 621 n. 18; Thomas Finkenauer, "Pönale Elemente der lex Aquilia," in *Ausgleich oder Buße als Grundproblem des Schadenersatzrechts von der lex Aquilia bis zur Gegenwart. Symposium zum 80. Geburtstag von Herbert Hausmaninger*, ed. Richard Gamauf (Vienna: Manz, 2017): 35–71, 51.

221 Kindler, *Affectionis aestimatio* (n. 40): 90–93, 197; with further explanatory approaches.

222 Cf. Pierluigi Zannini, "In tema di regolamento di confini della sfera di risarcibilitá del danno aquiliano: Una lezione dei prudentes," in *Valori e principii del diritto romano*, vol. 3, ed. Andrea Trisciuoglio (Naples: Edizioni scientifiche Italiane, 2009): 117–27, 121.

223 D. 35.2.63 pr. (2 ad leg. Iul. et Pap.). *Pretia rerum non ex affectu nec utilitate singulorum, sed communiter funguntur. nec enim qui filium naturalem possidet tanto locupletior est, quod eum, si alius possideret, plurimo redempturus fuisset. sed nec ille, qui filium alienum possidet, tantum habet, quanti eum patri*

lex Falcidia vis-à-vis the legatee and keep one quarter of the inheritance, the valuation may only be based on the inheritance's objective value; not on a higher one based on the fact that the inheritance includes the heir's natural son:[224] the heir is not obliged to base his calculations of the worth of the estate (and the quarter in question) on more than its market value;[225] he is no richer than another would be owning the son. There is, again, a sound reason for this ruling; the point of the Falcidian quarter is to make sure – not least in the interests of the legatees – that there is an incentive for the heir to accept the inheritance, or to prevent his rejecting it. This purpose of the law could be subverted if, in calculating the value of the estate, a wholly unrealistic price unobtainable on the free market were to be fixed for a *filius naturalis* to whom the heir is entitled.[226]

Quite a different situation obtains in D. 17.1.54 pr. by Papinian, which we discussed above.[227] There the jurist explicitly invokes *affectio* in order to justify the bringing of an action based on good faith. We know of no other case where the jurists proceeded in this way, despite the general nature of the stated rationale.[228] The text demonstrates that the general statement in Pedius' dictum can be well justified in certain contexts, but does not apply in others; the rejection of compensating for affection was not a general dogma.[229]

---

vendere potest, nec exspectandum est, dum vendat, sed in praesentia, non qua filius alicuius, sed qua homo aestimatur [. . .] ('Things acquire their value from their general usefulness not from the particular approach (*affectus*) or utility of individuals. A man who possesses as a slave his own natural son is not thereby the richer because, did another hold the slave, he himself would pay a large ransom for him. Equally, a person who possesses the son of someone else does not have the value for which he can sell that son to his father nor the amount for which he might hope to sell him but his present value as a slave not as somebody's son [. . .]', transl. Thomas in Watson, *Digest of Justinian* [n. 11]). On the text see Voci, *Diritto ereditario romano*, vol. 2 (n. 85): 758; Wacke, "Das Affektionsinteresse" (n. 47): 573; Kindler, *Affectionis aestimatio* (n. 40): 83–84; misunderstood by Herrmann-Otto, *Ex ancilla* (n. 31): 44 n. 36.

224 Raber, "pretium affectionis" (n. 219): 202 and Kindler, *Affectionis aestimatio* (n. 40): 84, unconvincingly focus on the affection of the (deceased!) testator.

225 Even if the natural father of the slave in the inheritance is a third party, the heir who is allowed to keep the slave is not obliged to accept, as basis for the calculation, an excessive purchase price which this third man might be prepared to pay for his son.

226 Even if one were to agree with Otto Lenel, *Palingenesia iuris civilis*, vol. 1 (Leipzig: Bernhard Tauchnitz, 1889): col. 1127 n. 2, that because of the inscription this text should be read as referring to *computatio decimarum*, i.e. the calculation of the one tenth spouses were entitled to leave to one another, it does not change the fact that there was no material basis for a subjective valuation (Kindler, *Affectionis aestimatio* [n. 40]: 84). On *computatio* see Kaser, *Das römische Privatrecht*, vol. 1 (n. 1): 724.

227 See above 2.2.

228 Kindler, *Affectionis aestimatio* (n. 40): 143.

229 Raber, "pretium affectionis" (n. 219): 206; Hans Wieling, review of *Festgabe für Arnold Herdlitczka zu seinem 75. Geburtstag, dargebracht von seinen Schülern und Freunden*, ed. Franz Horak und Wolfgang Waldstein, *Zeitschrift der Savigny-Stiftung für Rechtsgeschichte, Romanistische Abteilung* 89 (1972): 464–71, 467; Wacke, "Das Affektionsinteresse" (n. 47): 587, who points to the possibility of the evaluation under oath.

6 Conclusion

There was never any legal recognition of 'the' servile family in the classical period. Enslaved persons who were kin were and continued to be objects of legal relations who could be separated arbitrarily. That, at least, is the theory. But some texts in individual sectors of law do acknowledge the existence of natural family ties among slaves – if only as reflections of the weighing and interpreting of interests.[230] The texts discussed in this essay presented the *filii naturales* and other 'natural' relatives as a distinct group of slaves who were granted multiple privileges that set them apart from other slaves. Other slaves who might also be the objects of affectionate ties such as wet nurses, foster children or tutors, are not nearly as privileged; only in terms of privileged manumission are they treated equally to natural family members. Domestic slaves are advantaged only with regard to pledging, while slave favourites do not enjoy any legal privileges at all.

The notion that slaves who share a familial tie should not be separated because they will reproduce and perform their tasks better goes back to the Republican period;[231] it reflects the profit motive of this slave-owning society.[232] In due time, from the high classical period onwards, a humanitarian motive was added to this utilitarian idea. Numerous wills from the classical period testify to efforts not to tear servile families apart: to bequeath to the beneficiary his spouse and children. Given this zeitgeist we should credit the classical jurists with the odd humanitarian decision. We encounter this same humanitarian aspect later in Constantine's law.

What is doubtful, however, is that these decisions also reflect Stoic thinking about the equality of all humans.[233] In our texts, the jurists themselves only sporadically argue on the basis of natural law;[234] and only as an exception do they argue that the institution of slavery is contrary to it[235] and that all human beings are

---

230 This idea is, however, taken much too far by Vojtěch Poláček, "Randbemerkungen zur Forschung über Staat und Recht im Altertum," in *Studi in onore di Edoardo Volterra*, vol. 3 (Milan: Giuffrè, 1971): 201–36, 229 n. 53.

231 See above 4 pr.

232 Stressed by Herrmann-Otto, *Ex ancilla* (n. 31): 264.

233 See e.g. Seneca, *ep.* 47.1: slaves are servants, but humans. Waldstein, "Schiavitù e Cristianesimo" (n. 179): 124, emphasises the strong influence of Stoicism. Reflecting my own more sceptical position is Gamauf, "§ 26 (Sklaverei)" (n. 62): marginal no. 7 n. 50, with numerous references to the various scholarly positions in this debate; see also Finkenauer, *Mark Aurel zur Sklaverei* (n. 53): 91.

234 We do encounter *ius naturale* in the reason given for the impediment to marriage in D. 23.2.14.2 and in the nature common to all in D. 48.2.12.4; see above 1.1 and 1.3. There is no reason to assume that the terminology – *filius, pater* etc. *naturalis* – references natural law; it is purely descriptive to denote biological descent; so correctly Heumann and Seckel, *Handlexikon* (n. 4): s.v. *naturalis*, a; Kaser, *Das römische Privatrecht*, vol. 1 (n. 1): 204.

235 Florentinus D. 1.5.4.1 (9 inst.). *Servitus est constitutio iuris gentium, qua quis dominio alieno contra naturam subicitur.* ('Slavery is an institution of the *jus gentium*, whereby someone is against

equal by nature, never forgetting to point out that civil law does not recognise this equality.[236] Nor did natural law lend itself to arguing in favour of privileging only *some* slaves over others;[237] the argument of equality might have been used to justify comparing the marriage of slaves with those of Roman citizens, but if this happened at all, it was only implicitly. The reasons given by the jurists in our context, such as they are, tend to be more modest. They refer to *pudor*,[238] to the *mores maiorum*,[239] to *aequitas*[240] or *affectio*.[241] Where they talk about relations between slaves, their decisions are based on the required *reverentia*[242] or on a borrowing of the concept of *pietas*,[243] accepted for relations between Roman family members. Occasionally they merely cite *benignitas*[244] or the need to prevent *duritia*, hardness of heart, which imposition of a separation would occasion.[245]

The dichotomy free – unfree did not apply to *affectio* between parents and children or between siblings: it was possible to love one's 'natural' child just as much as the legitimate one. It was for this reason, that within the law of manumission restrictions were eventually lifted wherever possible. The family in the social sense

---

nature made subject to the ownership of another.', transl. MacCormick in Watson, *Digest of Justinian* [n. 11]). See also Kaser, *Das römische Privatrecht*, vol. 1 (n. 1): 205.

236 Ulpian D. 50.17.32 (43 ad Sab.). *Quod attinet ad ius civile, servi pro nullis habentur: non tamen et iure naturali, quia, quod ad ius naturale attinet, omnes homines aequales sunt.* ('As far as concerns the civil law slaves are regarded as not existing, not, however, in the natural law, because as far as concerns the natural law all men are equal.', transl. Crawford in Watson, *Digest of Justinian* [n. 11]).

237 The difficulties of arguing on the basis of natural law may be seen from the following example: in the case concerning the child of an enslaved woman, classical jurisprudence ruled that it should not remain with her usufructuary but belonged to her master. Although this ruling almost inevitably resulted in the separation of mother and child, Gaius justified it on the grounds of *natura rerum*: Gaius D. 22.1.28.1 (2 rer. cott.). *Partus vero ancillae in fructu non est itaque ad dominum proprietatis pertinet: absurdum enim videbatur hominem in fructu esse, cum omnes fructus rerum natura hominum gratia comparaverit.* ('But offspring of a female slave are not fruits; so they belong to the owner. It seemed absurd that a human being should count as fruits, since nature provided all fruits for man.', transl. Honoré in Watson, *Digest of Justinian* [n. 11]). See also Ulpian D. 7.1.68 pr. (17 ad Sab.). *Vetus fuit quaestio, an partus ad fructuarium pertineret: sed Bruti sententia optinuit fructuarium in eo locum non habere: neque enim in fructu hominis homo esse potest* [. . .] ('The question was raised in times gone by whether the offspring of a female slave belonged to the usufructuary. However, the opinion of Brutus, that the rules of usufruct are not applicable to this case, has prevailed; the fact is that one human being cannot be treated as being among the fruits of another [. . .]', transl. Fergus in Watson, *Digest of Justinian* [n. 11]). Likewise sceptical Gamauf, "§ 26 (Sklaverei)" (n. 62): marginal no. 18 n. 107.

238 See above 1.1.

239 See above 1.1.

240 See above 3.3.

241 See above 2.1, 2.2; 3.2, 3.3.

242 1.2.

243 4.1, 4.2.5.

244 See above 3.3.

245 See above 4.2.6.

went far beyond the limits of what was legally recognised. Referring to *pietas* as a typical Roman obligation between servile parents and their child, or between servile siblings, not only meant societal acceptance of kinship ties that lay outside the law, but in some cases even legal recognition for them.

What can we finally say about the social status of *filii naturales*? The legal sources are not best suited to being the basis for a judgement. If the *dominus* of a slave son occupied an elevated position in society, it is likely that his *filius naturalis* also commanded considerable social prestige; it is likely that his father arranged for him to be bought and manumitted. The son of a poor *dominus*, on the other hand, probably enjoyed little prestige even as a freedman. The sources tell us of poor *domini*, such as the debtor who had to secure his debt through a general pledge on all his property or suffer social death through bankruptcy. If the *pater naturalis* was a third party, his social standing only came into play if he was able to purchase freedom for his child. The degree to which the social and as such also the legal position of *filii naturales* depended on external factors is clearly shown in a dictum by Ulpian, D. 36.1.18.4,[246] where the testator's *dignitas* is one of the factors that will decide whether or not his estate should pass to his natural children – or to an external third party.

246 Cf. D. 36.1.18.4 (Ulp. 2 fideicomm.). *Si quis rogatus fuerit, ut, si sine liberis decesserit, restituat hereditatem, Papinianus libro octavo responsorum scribit etiam naturalem filium efficere, ut deficiat condicio: et in libertino eodem colliberto hoc scribit. mihi autem, quod ad naturales liberos attinet, voluntatis quaestio videbitur esse, de qualibus liberis testator senserit: sed hoc ex dignitate et ex voluntate et ex condicione eius qui fideicommisit accipiendum erit.* ('If one be asked to restore the inheritance should he die without children, Papinian, in the eighth book of his *Replies*, writes that even a natural son will defeat the condition, and in the case of a freedman, a son born in slavery and manumitted with his father. This is his opinion. To me, however, it would seem that where natural children are concerned, it is a question of intention what kind of children the testator had in mind; but this is to be judged according to the dignity and the intention and the situation of the creator of the *fideicommissum*', transl. Barton in Watson, *Digest of Justinian* [n. 11]). For more detail see Finkenauer, "Der Schutz der Sklavenfamilie" (n. 137): 103–4.

Pierangelo Buongiorno

Social Status 'Without' Legal Difference. Historiography and Puzzling Legal Questions About Imperial Freedmen and Slaves

1 Historiography

> In den drei Dezennien, die seit dem Erscheinen der ersten Auflage dieses Buches beinahe verflossen sind, ist die Forschung auf dem hier behandelten Gebiet nicht stehen geblieben.

With these words the German historian Otto Hirschfeld opened, in 1905, the introduction to the second edition of perhaps his most famous work, *Die kaiserlichen Verwaltungsbeamten bis auf Diocletian.*[1] Through the systematic and painstaking investigation of sources, especially epigraphic and papyrological ones, this study had reconstructed – since its first edition (Berlin 1877) – the development of the imperial administration: from the first nucleus that emerged in the Julio-Claudian period, through the well-structured administration under Claudius to the considerable reforms in the age of Diocletian.

By Hirschfeld's own admission, the subject necessarily ended up being influenced by the progress in the auxiliary sciences of epigraphy and papyrology.

In the pages of Hirschfeld, the *familia Caesaris*, i.e. the ensemble of slaves and freedmen of the emperors, was not investigated *ex professo* but could be perceived as a constant presence in some ways. In the same way that an extensive group of slaves and freedmen carried out the most diverse tasks in private households, the emperor's slaves and freedmen could be called upon to carry out palace tasks as well as, broadly speaking, tasks connected to the management of the emperor's property and, *lato sensu*, of entire spheres of the growing imperial administration. Hirschfeld mainly focused on the first important evidence concerning the *familia Caesaris*, namely its activities to ensure the water supply of Rome, in imitation of a model that tradition says was introduced by Agrippa. This led to the creation of a

1 Otto Hirschfeld, *Die kaiserlichen Verwaltungsbeamten bis auf Diocletian*, 2nd ed. (Berlin: Weidmann, 1905): VI. The book, whose first edition had appeared in 1877, was projected as part of a monumental history of the Roman administration, to be published under the title *Untersuchungen auf dem Gebiete der roemischen Verwaltungsgeschichte*.

Note: The following pages develop the paper delivered in Bonn in August 2020, with some modifications and the addition of a concise apparatus of footnotes and useful bibliography.

https://doi.org/10.1515/9783110987195-003

position of *procurator aquarum*, which was at first entrusted to imperial freedmen (e.g. such as *Ti. Claudius Aug. lib. Bucolas*, *CIL* XI 3612).[2]

Nevertheless, he emphasized the involvement of the emperor's slaves and freedmen in the newborn imperial administration,[3] which reached its peak during the first Antonine age. At a later time these administrative apparatuses saw a progressive 'professionalization', in the course of which the slaves and freedmen at the top of these hierarchies were replaced by members of the equestrian rank. This was due in part to a change in the social perception of the emperor's role (of which slaves and freedmen were the most obvious manifestation) in relation to the administration of the empire:

> Die Person des Kaisers tritt aus der Reichsverwaltung zurück, an Stelle der kaiserlichen Freigelassenen und Sklaven wird der so lange vom Staatsdienste gänzlich ausgeschlossene dritte Stand zu den niederen Stellen zugelassen, es bildet sich eine Subalternenkarriere im modernen Sinne und ein in sich geeinigter Reichsbeamtenstand.[4]

Hirschfeld's study was in its own way pioneering, a sign of a proudly 'Mommsenian' period: a time in which sources and evidence were the core of scholarly thought, in which historical and legal investigations were not seen as divided by insurmountable obstacles but perceived as parts of the same whole. In addition to historians, the work was also appreciated by that generation of jurists such as Leopold Wenger and Paul Koschaker who, influenced above all by scholars such as Ludwig Mitteis, would shortly open new paths of romanistic research.[5]

In any case, Hirschfeld's work set the standard, remaining – for method and results – a point of reference for many decades. Arnold Mackay Duff's study on *Freedmen in the Early Roman Empire*,[6] for example, was a strong tribute to Hirschfeld's work: the same was also the study on imperial freedmen, and even the overall structure of § V of the entry *Libertus* in the *Dizionario Epigrafico*, edited by Giovanni

2 Hirschfeld, *Die kaiserlichen Verwaltungsbeamten* (n. 1): 275–84.

3 Hirschfeld, *Die kaiserlichen Verwaltungsbeamten* (n. 1): 457–65.

4 Hirschfeld, *Die kaiserlichen Verwaltungsbeamten* (n. 1): 486.

5 It is interesting to note that in the Nachlass Paul Koschaker (stored in the Rechtshistorische Bibliothek of the WWU Münster), there is a copy (signature ROM VI E 8) of the newly published second edition of Hirschfeld's book, given to the younger Paul Koschaker by the elder Leopold Wenger on the occasion of their teaching in Graz in WS 1905/06 (Wenger as außerordentlicher Professor, Koschaker as Privatdozent, freshly habilitated by Gustav Hanausek). The title page bears the dedication: "Meinem lieben Freunde Koschaker bei Beginn der gemeinsamen Dozentur. Graz, Oktober 1905. L. Wenger." The book was evidently at the center of the debate among these scholars, certainly not ruled by the anxiety to distinguish by labels what is history and what is law, a concern that unfortunately governs much historical-legal research today. On the relations between Koschaker and Wenger see Tommaso Beggio, *Paul Koschaker (1879–1951). Rediscovering the Roman Foundations of European Legal Tradition*, 2nd ed. (Heidelberg: Winter, 2018): 33–34, with bibliography.

6 Arnold Mackay Duff, *Freedmen in the Early Roman Empire* (Oxford: Clarendon Press, 1928; repr. 1958).

Vitucci: it was organized, after a preamble, according to the tasks of the imperial freedmen, and broadly followed the *Gliederung* of Hirschfeld's work.[7]

But Vitucci, who concluded his work in October 1958, more than half a century after Hirschfeld, was able to consider the further progress of epigraphic research, made up of discoveries and new text readings, and this allowed him to specify how the number of imperial slaves and freedmen involved in the administration grew progressively and disproportionately, and how these servants and officials were actually not small in number even under the first emperors. From the examinations of the epigraphic evidence, diligently annotated by Vitucci, it became clear that from the start of the Julio-Claudian period, imperial freedmen were employed in almost all the branches of administration, both in Rome and in the provinces, in parallel with the progressive expansion of imperial interference in the spheres of competence of the ancient magistracies. Often this led to the creation of new administrative apparatuses, especially from the age of Claudius.[8]

Vitucci's work, soon to be counted among 'the best general treatments on freedmen',[9] provided a solid documentary basis for several works on slaves and imperial freedmen that were published soon after. These studies were now being written from a perspective of social history. All of them were conducted during the following decade, and, while coming to light in different cultural and academic contexts, brought about a season of profound rethinking of the categories of historical research, with a greater openness toward social history, evidently driven by that climate of democratization that pervaded the western world.

As is well known, the distinguished scholar Gérard Boulvert (1936–1984) dedicated almost his entire research activity to analyzing the role of imperial slaves and freedmen in the first centuries of the current era. His monumental two-volume doctoral dissertation was written under the direction of Jacques Macqueron and then discussed at the University of Aix-en-Provence in 1964. It was awarded with the *Premio Vincenzo Arangio-Ruiz*; after this exploit of such a young scholar the first volume was published in 1970 in Napoli (Jovene) under the title of *Esclaves et affranchis impériaux sous le Haut-Empire romain. Rôle politique et administrative*, while the second volume, concerning the work of *servi* and *liberti principis*, appeared as a stand-alone volume in Paris (Les Belles Lettres) in 1974 under the title *Domestique et fonctionnaire sous le haut-Empire romain.*

---

7 Giovanni Vitucci, s.v. "Libertus," in *Dizionario Epigrafico*, vol. 4/1 (Rome: L'Erma di Bretschneider, 1958): 905–46, mainly 933–46.

8 Vitucci, "Libertus" (n. 7): 934. On this point see also § 2, below.

9 Thus Paul Richard Carey Weaver, *Familia Caesaris. Social Study of the Emperor's Freedmen and Slaves* (Cambridge: Cambridge University Press, 1972): 4 n. 2.

The research of Boulvert on *servi* and *liberti principis* was not an isolated case.[10] In fact, the 1960s were the years in which this subject came to the fore, even in other cultural contexts. If the participation of slaves and imperial freedmen in the Roman imperial administration had been understudied for a long time, despite its obvious importance for early Imperial social and administrative history, the reconstruction of the multiple profiles of interest that arose from it was in the 1960s again the focus of other cultural contexts, such as the Anglo-Saxon and West German ones.

As Hans-Georg Pflaum pointed out, between the 1960s and 1970s 'les recherches sur l'esclavage' were 'à la mode', mainly because of many inscriptions that constituted the base for fruitful investigations.[11] But without doubt it was also the cultural effect of the processes of decolonisation investing society after the end of the Second World War: such processes implied and indeed somewhat required a better knowledge of the phenomena of imperialism also in an historical perspective. Thus, in the same years in which Boulvert worked on his topic, two other scholars published books on the same subject.

In Germany, under the supervision of Hans Ulrich Instinsky, a brilliant scholar as Heinrich Chantraine (1929–2002) in 1964 submitted his Habilitationsschrift entitled *Freigelassene und Sklaven im Dienst der römischen Kaiser. Studien zu ihrer Nomenklatur*. This research was part of the growing interest of the *Akademie der Wissenschaften und der Literatur Mainz* in slavery in the ancient world, and in fact it was published, after review, in 1967 as the inaugural volume of the series *Forschungen zur Antiken Sklaverei*; this series had been founded by Instinsky himself together with Joseph Vogt with the aim of publishing the results of the monumental project of the same name. This project was recently completed under the auspices of the *Kommission für Geschichte des Altertums* of the *Akademie* in Mainz, without, however, treating in a systematic fashion the themes of *liberti* and *servi* in the imperial administration.[12]

Boulvert had already stressed in his thesis the necessity of focusing attention on the one hand on the role of slaves and freedmen in the nascent imperial bureaucracy, and on the other on their legal status (especially, of course, the freedmen) in terms of Roman private law.[13] Chantraine meanwhile drew attention to some important matters: mainly the close ideological connection between slaves and freedmen; he also drew attention to the possibility of better defining their legal status based

10 See already Luigi Labruna, "Gérard Boulvert (1936–1984)," *Index* 15 (1987): XIII–XXII.

11 Hans-Georg Pflaum, "Préface," in *Domestique et fonctionnaire sous le haut-Empire romain*, vol. 3, ed. Gérard Boulvert (Paris: Les Belles Lettres, 1974): 3.

12 Except for the synthetic encyclopedic voice of Werner Eck, s.v. "Familia Caesaris," in *Handwörterbuch der Antiken Sklaverei*, vol. 1, ed. Heinz Heinen et al. (Stuttgart: Franz Steiner Verlag, 2017): 907–8.

13 Gérard Boulvert, "Les esclaves et les affranchis impériaux sous le Haut-Empire romain" (PhD diss., CRDP Aix-en-Provence, 1964): vol. 1, 2–7, 455.

on a systematic study of the 'Nomenklatur', largely in the light of the epigraphic documentation.[14] As Chantraine himself recalls, such an approach took advantage of the rich epigraphic heritage collected in the *Corpus Inscriptionum Latinarum*, using the prosopographical method employed by Hermann Dessau and, mainly regarding the *uterque ordo*, by Edmund Groag and Arthur Stein.[15]

This formidable season of studies was completed by the research of Paul Richard Carey Weaver (1927–2005), an Australian professor of classics, who in 1972 published a relevant volume, *Familia Caesaris. A Social Study of the Emperor's Freedmen and Slaves*.[16] The text combined social history with an account of the actual practice of a Roman law of slavery concerning imperial servants. Weaver's monograph was preceded by several short essays, all of which appeared in the 1960s and which emphasized some preliminary[17] methodological problems. Weaver mainly tried to verify whether and in what way the framework of epigraphic documentation could confirm the reality of some aspects of the Roman law of persons.

The rapid succession of wide-ranging studies by Boulvert, Chaintraine and Weaver produced, by the mid-1970s, the consolidation of a base, not only of data, but also (and perhaps above all) of reflective perspectives on which the investigations of the following decades were based. More detailed investigations, which allowed us to deepen our knowledge of individual aspects and problems of the role of slaves and freedmen within the dynamics of imperial power, sometimes even examined on a temporal basis. One is the synthesis by Fergus Millar in his *Emperor in the Roman World*. Another good example is Aloys Winterling's *Aula Caesaris*, a study on the institutionalization of the imperial court that investigated the role of freedmen, especially in the second half of the Julio-Claudian age.[18]

Over time, our dossier on the subject has been enriched by new epigraphic evidence which allowed us to increase our knowledge, updating the picture outlined by Vitucci's studies. Until the early years of the twenty-first century a constant survey of epigraphic evidence was carried out by Paul Weaver who, practically until the end of his life, worked on the preparation and constant updating of a repertoire of sources on imperial servants and freedmen, which included reassessing the interpretation of already known texts. After Paul Weaver's death (he passed away on 2 January 2005), Alleeta French, his widow, handed over his *Repertorium Familiae*

---

14 Heinrich Chantraine, *Freigelassene und Sklaven im Dienst der römischen Kaiser* (Wiesbaden: Franz Steiner Verlag, 1967): 14–41.
15 Chantraine, *Freigelassene und Sklaven* (n. 14): VII.
16 See above n. 9.
17 Cf. mainly Paul Richard Carey Weaver, "The Status Nomenclature of the Imperial Freedmen," *Classical Quarterly* 13, no. 2 (1963): 272–78; Paul Richard Carey Weaver, "Irregular Nomina of Imperial Freedmen," *Classical Quarterly* 15, no. 2 (1965): 323–26.
18 Fergus Millar, *The Emperor in the Roman World, 31 B.C.–A.D. 337* (London: Duckworth, 1977): 69–83; Aloys Winterling, *Aula Caesaris: Studien zur Institutionalisierung des römischen Kaiserhofes in der Zeit von Augustus bis Commodus (31 v. Chr.–192 n. Chr.)* (Munich: C.H. Beck, 1999).

Caesarum to Werner Eck. Only a few parts of the *Repertorium* were not yet ready and sometimes just sketched out, but Werner Eck's team made it ready for publication in only a few short months. It was published in September 2005.[19] As Eck writes in the introduction to the *Repertorium*, Weaver

> knew all the problems associated with this group of people, and he knew above all how important this group is for understanding the imperial period. For, without knowledge of it, the politics, administration and society of the Principate cannot be analysed and understood. Above all, however, he saw that many general statements concerning this group often were not supported by the sources, at least if one takes all the sources into consideration comprehensively. Of course, he also knew that it was very laborious to obtain a complete overview of the relevant sources; for a comprehensive collection of the sources did not exist. From an early time, therefore, he turned himself to the task of constructing a *repertorium* which would render it unnecessary for others to make such a laborious collection.[20]

2 Social Condition and Political Relevance of Imperial Slaves and Freedmen: Some Remarks

The results of the historiographical framework outlined above made it possible to consolidate and refine our knowledge. There is no doubt that imperial slaves and freedmen were very numerous. There were various routes by which slaves came into the imperial patrimony: purchase in the markets through intermediaries assigned to look after the emperor's interests in his various possessions, confiscation of the goods of convicted criminals, testamentary bequests, and especially the birth of *vernae* from slaves already belonging to the emperor's patrimony (often – but not always, as we will see – as a result of endogamic phenomena within the *familia Caesaris*).

All of these slaves, as well as the freedmen manumitted by the emperor, are generally referred to as the *familia Caesaris*, an expression that synthetizes the nexus *liberti servive*. But, above all during the initial phase of the principate, there was an elite of freedmen from the more restricted circle close to the first emperors, who stood out for their importance.

One can certainly agree with Mouritsen in the consideration that 'the Roman emperor had literally hundreds if not thousands of freedmen, and it was of course

19 Paul Richard Carey Weaver, "Repertorium Familiae Caesarum," *Universität zu Köln*, 09.07.2013, https://alte-geschichte.phil-fak.uni-koeln.de/personal/ehemalige-emeriti/eck-prof-dr-werner/weaver-repertorium [accessed 23.08.2022].

20 Werner Eck, *Information Regarding Paul Weaver's Repertorium of Imperial Freedmen and Slaves* (Cologne: Universität zu Köln, 2005): 1, https://alte-geschichte.phil-fak.uni-koeln.de/personal/ehemalige-emeriti/eck-prof-dr-werner/weaver-repertorium [accessed 23.08.2022].

only a handful of them who ever came near the centre of power and only for what seems to be a relatively short period during the first century CE',[21] but on the other hand it should be noted that, although the number of servants who emerged and reached important positions was proportionally very low, we can speak of these persons as 'servants and officials' at the same time.

The beginnings of an imperial power apparatus, the primitive nucleus of a bureaucracy, was run by the freedmen from the *familia Caesaris*. This privileged existence gradually faded away, from the early Antonine age onwards, coming to a definitive end during the principate of Hadrian, in which the bureaucracy was run by equestrians.

The principate of Claudius, as numerous sources and evidence confirm, undoubtedly marked the highest point of this process. In other words, Claudius accelerated the processes of bureaucratisation of imperial power, and he did so through the active involvement of freedmen. Despite the critical attitude of senatorial historiography, these freedmen were nearly always selected for their outstanding managerial and political skills, which promoted them to head departments as *a cognitionibus, a studiis, a rationibus, ab epistulis, a libellis*, where they supervised the various areas of management of imperial power, from the treasury to the chancellery.[22] In the same period we also find imperial freedmen placed in charge of the government of some provinces entrusted to the emperor (e.g. Marcus Antonius Felix, procurator of Judea from 52 to 60 CE), or of parts of them.[23]

These activities were accompanied by substantial monetary donations to imperial freedmen who had risen to top positions, as well as *ornamenta* (*quaestoria, praetoria, consularia*), i.e. honours comparable to those of senators (of quaestorian, praetorian or consular rank).

It lasted only for a brief period. Gradually the imperial freedmen slipped more and more into subordinate or middle-management positions, often connected to the peripheral management of the imperial wealth, and not infrequently having slaves belonging to the emperor[24] as their dependents, especially when it came to managing the landed estates and the related production chains.[25] This wealth was, moreover, expanding due to phenomena that, for the first imperial age, were reproduced on a large scale: the hereditary succession of the emperor to private individuals and

21 Henrik Mouritsen, *The Freedman in the Roman World* (Cambridge: Cambridge University Press, 2011): 93.

22 The key text remains Suet. *Claud.* 28. See already Vitucci, "Libertus" (n. 7): 935–36. But now see also Pierangelo Buongiorno, *Claudio. Il principe inatteso* (Palermo: 21 Editore, 2017): 107–14.

23 For Felix see *PIR*[2] A 828; but already in the age of Tiberius a freedman is reported as vice-prefect of Egypt (Cass. Dio. 58.19.6).

24 Vitucci, "Libertus" (n. 7): 936.

25 The study by Marco Maiuro, *Res Caesaris. Ricerche sulla proprietà imperiale nel principato* (Bari: Edipuglia, 2012), deserves to be mentioned.

above all the legislation relating to *bona caduca* and the numerous confiscation procedures connected to criminal repression.

Thus, while the imperial slaves, who legally were counted among the *res Caesaris*, were often relegated to the most menial tasks, the freedmen were increasingly promoted to be procurators of the emperor's wealth, thus participating in a concrete way in the construction of the imperial order, now in open dialectic with the republican one.[26]

A relevant element of this process was the establishment of the jurisdiction of the imperial procurators and the rapid alignment of their judgements with those of the emperor. The *procuratores*, or at least some of them, had from the outset had a circumscribed focus of jurisdictional authority, albeit limited *in servitia et pecuniae familiares*, that is, over the *familia Caesaris* itself and the personal property of the emperor.

Within a few decades, however, this authority increased, as a matter of practice, to exponentially affect conflicts with private individuals. We have evidence of this – perhaps for the principate of Caligula, and certainly early on during the principate of Claudius[27] – in relation to matters previously entrusted to praetorian jurisdiction. It is likely, therefore, that there were frequent conflicts of authority between the jurisdiction of the magistrates and the judicial functions of the *procuratores*, now established in practice.

At the end of this process, a senatorial decree passed already in 53 CE determined that the sentences issued by the imperial procurators were recognized as equivalent to those issued by the imperial court.[28] This had the effect of acknowledging the existence of two constitutional orders (the republican and the imperial one) and, by means of the link constituted by the *princeps* (almost a Cartesian pineal gland), connecting them through the delegation to the imperial order of functions traditionally being the responsibility of the republican order. As Tacitus tells us (*ann.* 12.60.1), after this senatorial decree of 53 CE the imperial order, which was expressed through the procurators, was recognized more fully and abundantly than before (*plenius quam antea et uberius*).

26 For the connection wealth-*procuratores*, see Peter Astbury Brunt, *Roman Imperial Themes* (Oxford: Oxford University Press, 1990): 353–432. But see now also the important work of Sabine Schmall, *Patrimonium und Fiscus. Studien zur kaiserlichen Domänen- und Finanzverwaltung von Augustus bis Mitte des 3. Jahrhunderts n. Chr.* (PhD diss., Universität Bonn, 2011).

27 Suet. *Cal.* 47.1; *CIL* V 5050 = *ILS* 206.

28 Pierangelo Buongiorno, *Senatus consulta Claudianis temporibus facta. Una palingenesi delle deliberazioni senatorie dell'età di Claudio (41–54 d.C.)* (Naples: Edizioni scientifiche Italiane, 2010): 77, 349–52, with bibliography.

3 Roman Jurisprudence and the *liberti servive principis*

In the light of what I have outlined so far, it can be seen how the *familia Caesaris*, i.e. the slaves belonging to the *fiscus Caesaris* and the freedmen deriving from this patrimonial asset, all of who promoted the emperor's economic interests, assumed an almost autonomous connotation even in the eyes of the jurists.

This is confirmed by an examination of the mentions of *servi* and *liberti Caesaris* in Roman jurisprudence. This is an aspect that has been somewhat neglected by previous studies, but which requires further reflection.

First of all, it should be noted that the expression *familia Caesaris* or *familia principis* is never attested in jurisprudential sources. In fact, the Roman jurists mainly refer to individual imperial slaves, and to indicate them they prefer formulations such as *servus principis*, *servus Caesaris* and even *servus fisci*, whereby *fiscus* is seen as an element of continuity in the principate.[29] This is explained above all by the fact that the attention of jurists often focused on the conduct of the *servus* as an individual, and not of the emperor's *familia* as a whole.

But even this interest is always functional to the investigation of an individual emperor's prerogatives in the field of private law. This is confirmed, for example, by the evidence (*e.g.* Ulp. 16 *ad ed.*, D. 1.19.1.2; Pomp. 12 *ex var. lect.*, D. 28.5.42) concerning the emperor's power to purchase an inheritance through his slaves.

In other words, the sources of classical jurisprudence overall show how, at least on a formal level, slaves (and freedmen) of the emperor, especially when considered *uti singuli*, did not enjoy a privileged position compared to slaves and freedmen of private individuals. By way of further proof, it is sufficient to recall how even pseudo-Ulpian, in the *Liber singularis regularum*, recalled (1.12) how the provisions on the annulment of manumissions ordered by minors under thirty years of age under the *lex Aelia Sentia* included imperial slaves (*ideo sine consilio manumissum Caesaris servum manere putat*).

However, the circumstances (admittedly not many) in which the emperor's slaves and freedmen were considered in their entirety lead us back to a perhaps somewhat different scenario. A significant clue comes from Callistratus, 2 *quaest.*, D. 47.9.7 [*Pal.* 107 Lenel]. Callistratus wrote the *quaestiones* in the early years of the principate of Septimius Severus, roughly between 193 and 200 CE.

---

29 Ulp. 8 *ad Sab.* D. 29.2.25.2. From this list should be excluded the *servi poenae* who, as mentioned in a rescript of Antoninus Pius, were separated from the *servi fisci* (see D. 34.8.3; D. 29.2.25.3; D. 49.14.12: *magis poenae servos quam fisci*). On this matter see, efficaciously, already Annarosa Gallo, s.v. "Strafsklaverei," in *Handwörterbuch der Antiken Sklaverei*, vol. 3, ed. Heinz Heinen et al. (Stuttgart: Franz Steiner Verlag, 2017): 2963, and now, widely, also Tommaso Beggio, *Contributo allo studio della 'servitus poenae'* (Bari: Cacucci Editore, 2020), 15–17, 59–60, 115–120, 288–292.

This casuistic work intended to resolve several practical cases, arranged according to relevant themes.

In the second book the jurist also focused at length on naval trade and shipwrecks. In the palingenetic reconstruction of Otto Lenel, in fact, D. 47.9.7 is immediately followed by D. 14.2.4 (*Pal.* 108 Lenel), i.e. a text about the risks involved in the loss of cargo by a cargo ship. Such topics often attracted the interest of Callistratus, as we can see for example (with specific reference to shipwreck) in texts such as 1 *de ed. monit.* D. 47.9.6, and 1 *de cogn.*, D. 50.6.6.3–6. On the other hand, Callistratus was a jurist who was attentive to certain aspects of provincial administration and the risks and responsibilities connected with overseas traffic were evidently part of his horizon of interests.[30]

Justinian's commissioners cut off the fragment without modifying it (there is no reasonable trace of interpolation) and put it under the heading D. 47.9.7, *De incendio ruina naufragio nave rata expugnata* ('Concerning fire, destruction, and shipwreck, where a boat or a ship is taken by force'):

D. 47.9.7 (Call. 2 quaest.): Ne quid ex naufragiis diripiatur vel quis extraneus interveniat colligendis eis, multifariam prospectum est. nam et divus Hadrianus edicto praecepit, ut hi, qui iuxta litora maris possident, scirent, si quando navis vel inficta vel fracta intra fines agri cuiusque fuerit, ne na naufragia diripiant, in ipsos iudicia praesides his, qui res suas direptas queruntur, reddituros, ut quidquid probaverint ademptum sibi naufragio, id a possessoribus recipiant. de his autem, quos diripuisse probatum sit, praesidem ut de latronibus gravem sententiam dicere. ut facilior sit probatio huiusmodi admissi, permisit his et quidquid passos se huiusmodi queruntur, adire praefectos et ad eum testari reosque petere, ut pro modo culpae vel vincti vel sub fideiussoribus ad praesidem remittantur. a domino quoque possessionis, in qua id admissum dicatur, satis accipi, ne cognitioni desit, praecipitur. sed nec intervenire naufragiis colligendis aut militem aut privatum aut libertum servumve principis placere sibi ait senatus.

D. 47.9.7 (Callistratus, Questions, book 2): Many precautions have been taken to hinder property from being stolen during a shipwreck, or to prevent strangers from coming in and taking possession of it. For the Divine Hadrian provided by an edict that those who owned land on the shore of the sea should, when a ship either badly damaged or broken up within the boundaries of any of them, see that nothing was stolen from the wreck; and that the governors of provinces should grant actions against them in favor of those who were searching for the property of which they had been deprived, to enable them to recover anything which they could prove had been taken from them during the shipwreck, by those who had possession of the same. With reference to such as are proved to have taken the property, the governor should impose a severe sentence upon them, as upon robbers. And to render proof of the commission of crimes of this kind easier, he permitted those who complained of having suffered any loss to go before the prefect and give their evidence, and search for the guilty parties, in order that they might be sent before the governor either in chains, or under bond, in proportion to the gravity of their offences. He also directed

30 Salvatore Puliatti, *Callistratus. Opera* (Rome: L'Erma di Bretschneider, 2019): 107, 219–20.

> that security be taken from the owner of the property alleged to have been stolen not to desist from the prosecution. The Senate also decreed that neither a soldier, nor any private individual, nor a freedman or a slave of the emperor, should interfere in the collection of articles dispersed by shipwreck.

Callistratus' text recalls two regulatory measures: firstly, an edict of Hadrian, datable to between 117 and 138 CE, which is said to have introduced as a main regulatory provision the establishment of a *cognitio* in charge of provincial governors in matters of shipwrecks, which also prohibited the owners of coastal land from taking possession of goods resulting from a shipwreck (*ne* [. . .] *quis extraneus interveniat colligendis eis* [*naufragiis*, scil.]). This measure was in continuity with an older senatorial decree, approved at the time of the emperor Claudius (*Claudianis temporibus*),[31] which forbade the removal of any kind of shipwrecked goods and provided for liability for the entire value of the cargo and the boat (the synecdoche *si quis ex naufragio clavos vel unum ex his abstulerit, omnium rerum nomine teneatur* is vivid).[32] But evidently the measure introduced by the Senate under Claudius must have been disregarded, so that the edict of Hadrian made it easier to sanction such stealthy conduct by defining a particular procedural regime, which lightened plaintiff's burden of proof and increased the penalty while providing a safeguard for the plaintiff to prevent him from withdrawing the accusation.

However, Callistratus adds at the end of his fragment[33] that the Senate further decreed that neither a soldier nor a private citizen, nor (of particular interest to us) even 'a freedman or a slave of the emperor' could interfere in the collection of goods lost in a shipwreck. The dating of this senatorial decree, not recorded by Volterra and referred to only in passing by Talbert,[34] fluctuates at first glance between the principate of Hadrian and the advent of Septimius Severus. The aim of the decree, in any case, was the same as that of the above-mentioned edict, i.e. to sanction interference in the recovery of goods lost due to a shipwreck. This has led some scholars to believe that this decree aimed to clarify Hadrian's edict,[35] even to specify how the regulation

---

31 Cf. Buongiorno, *Senatus consulta Claudianis temporibus facta* (n. 28): 370–71, 421–22.

32 The text is not mentioned in the portion of Callistratus' text that has come down to us but is known to us from Ulp. 56 *ad ed.*, D. 47.9.3.8.

33 Strangely enough, however, the interesting book by Sara Galeotti, *Mare monstrum. Mare nostrum. Note in tema di pericula maris e trasporto marittimo nella riflessione della giurisprudenza romana (I secolo a.C. – III secolo d.C.)* (Naples: Jovene, 2020) does not address this senatorial measure.

34 Edoardo Volterra, *Senatus consulta*, eds. Pierangelo Buongiorno, Annarosa Gallo and Salvatore Marino (Stuttgart: Franz Steiner Verlag, 2017); Richard J.A. Talbert, *The Senate of Imperial Rome* (Princeton, NJ: Princeton University Press, 1984): 452 no. 159.

35 Antonino Pinzone, "Naufragi, fisco e trasporti marittimi nell'età di Caracalla (su CJ 11,6,1)," *Quaderni Catanesi* 4, no. 7 (1982): 64–109.

introduced by this emperor sanctioned not only the conduct of private individuals, but also that of soldiers and *liberti servive principis*. In other words, in the event of a shipwreck near a *castrum* or imperial property, those who claimed rights to the shipwrecked property could be deprived of it with impunity.

What is certain is that while the distinction *privati/milites* is well attested after Marcus Aurelius, the explicit reference to a third *genus* of persons, the *liberti servive principis*, clearly alludes to the privileged role of *fiscus* and leads me to prefer a dating of this senatorial decree in the age of Pertinax (193 CE). Given the fact that the wording *ait senatus* could lead us to place the measure in a period not far from the one in which Callistratus wrote, it should also be noted that during the brief principate of Pertinax the Senate experienced a period of relevance and centrality, while certain arbitrary acts of imperial power were more limited.[36] The fact that the Senate intervened to interpret an imperial edict at the end of the second century CE also has a not inconsiderable relevance, which leads us, once again, to the principate of Pertinax.

Finally, the expression *liberti servive principis* deserves a few more comments. The disjunctive enclitic *-ve* closely links the *servants* and *freedmen* of the emperor, almost like two parts of the same whole. Here, then, the notion of *familia Caesaris*, never attested in the sources of jurisprudence, appears in another form, indicating the two cores (slaves of the emperor and freedmen bound to him by *officia*) around which this *familia is* articulated: we are standing at the threshold of what in the *Pauli sententiae* will be qualified as *familia fiscalis*.[37]

The group of imperial delegates is thus understood as a living body, composed of both slaves and ex-slaves, all of them ideologically linked to the emperor and his wealth: the slaves are a part of it, the ex-slaves help to administer it. The *familia* of the emperor has then its own recognised social status which is quite distinct from that of private individuals (and, obviously, from the *milites*). On a strictly legal level, a *libertus* of the emperor was not significantly distinct from a *libertus* manumitted by a *privatus*; and all slaves were indiscriminately slaves. In short: being part of the *liberti servive principis* was a social status but without legal difference.

---

36 On this point Mario Mazza see, "Il breve regno (in)felice di Publio Elvio Pertinace: Considerazioni sull'impero romano alla svolta dell'età severiana," in *Fides Humanitas Ius, 9 maggio 2007*, ed. Cosimo Cascione and Carla Masi Doria (Naples: Editoriale Scientifica, 2008): 161–86.

37 *Paul. Sent.* 5.1.3: *Descriptio ingenuorum ex officio fisci inter fiscalem familiam facta ingenuitati non praeiudicat.*

4 Status Nomenclature, Imperial Freedmen and Roman Private Law

As part of the *fiscus*, the slaves were transferred from an emperor to his successor. The *operae libertorum* were also due to the emperor (no matter who he was): this scheme is already clear under the emperor Claudius, who received *operae* from imperial freedmen who had been manumitted by previous emperors and even by other members of the dynasty, such as C. Iulius Callistus, a freedman of Caligula; or M. Antonius Pallas and M. Antonius Felix (freedmen of Antonia minor).

The epigraphic evidence confirms that imperial freedmen were proud to state that they received the status of free person from an emperor, an *Augustus* (this 'status' is usually indicated in the inscriptions with the nomenclature *Augusti libertus*). The most relevant trace remains in the use of the *tria nomina*, as the freedmen retained part of the emperor's nomenclature in their private names (*praenomen+nomen;* while the servile name is preserved in the *cognomen*). The system is the same for private individuals; so a name such as *Ti. Claudius Aug. lib. Classicus* means that *Classicus* was the freedman of a *Ti. Claudius* (this could have been either Claudius or Nero); *Ti. Iulius* leads us back to Tiberius, *C. Iulius* to Augustus or Caligula, *M. Antonius* to Antonia minor, *T. Flavius* to a member of the Flavian dynasty, *M. Ulpius* to Trajan, *P. Aelius* to Hadrian, *Ti. Aelius* to Antoninus Pius and so on. This structure is probably the product of unwritten rules but it is nevertheless interesting to note that in the epigraphic evidence we have some irregularities[38] that can be listed in two groups:

1. non-imperial *nomina*; inscriptions pertaining to some imperial freedmen who have a name at least apparently not connected with the emperors and their relatives.
2. irregular imperial *nomina*: inscriptions pertaining to some imperial freedmen who have names that do not chronologically correspond to the period in which they lived.

Many solutions were proposed for each of these inscriptions, but these solutions need to be examined under the light of the juridical system. Even though some scholars, such as Heikki Solin, think that such an activity is only 'an exercise in hermeneutic nihilism',[39] we shall try to reconsider the most relevant part of this evidence, paying attention to other aspects such as law and even political history.

38 Partially recorded and discussed first by Weaver, "Irregular Nomina" (n. 17) and then updated in *Familia Caesaris* (n. 9): 35–37; but see also Chantraine, *Freigelassene und Sklaven* (n. 14): 67–89; for other possible updates of this dossier see also Weaver, *Repertorium* (n. 19).

39 Heikki Solin, "Abuso dell'onomastica nella ricerca epigrafica," in *Usi e abusi epigrafici. Atti del Colloquio Internazionale di epigrafia latina (Genova 20–22 settembre 2001)*, ed. Maria Grazia Angeli Bertinelli and Angela Donati (Rome: Quasar, 2003): 279–86. This statement, as well as speaking for itself because of its staggering relativism, expresses the *Isolierung* – just to use a polite expression –

In the dossier of non-imperial *nomina* we have first of all *CIL* VI 12533 = 34057 = *CIL* X 2112 = EDR177121:[40]

> D(is) M(anibus) / C(aio) Asinio Aug(usti) lib(erto) / Paramythio / Festiano / Falconia Hedone / marito bene m(erenti)

The inscription was dedicated to the *manes* of C. Asinius Paramythius Festianus, freedman of an emperor, by his widow Falconia Hedone. It comes from Rome and its chronology is uncertain, but it could maybe be dated to the end of the first century CE on the basis of paleography. Hirschfeld pointed out that this evidence seems to be connected to the possibility that the emperor could have been instituted as heir of a C. Asinius, with the consequence that, at the time of his manumission, the slave Paramythius had attained the name of his original master. Mommsen criticized this thesis with this argument: 'Si in principe per exceptionem eiusmodi patronatus admissus esset, exempla similia abundarent'.[41]

An example of a slave manumitted *ex legato* by the emperor who was appointed as heir seems instead to be, for example, *CIL* X 6318 = *ILS* 2815 = EDR127089:

> Ti(berio) Iulio Aug(usti) l(iberto) / Optato / Pontiano / procuratori et / praefect(o) classis / Ti(berius) Iulius / Ti(beri) f(ilius) Fab(ia) / Optatus IIvir.

Optatus senior could have been originally a slave of a Pontius, who appointed the emperor Tiberius as his heir.

Coming back to C. Asinius Paramythius Festianus, it is then possible also to think of a *servus alienus* instituted as heir. Such an *heredis institutio* was conditional upon *manumissio*: see Cels. 16 *dig.* D. 28.7.21 (*Servus alienus ita heres institui potest 'cum liber erit'* et rell.) and the main purpose was to preserve the *sacra privata* of the *de cuius*, in application of the principle *sacra cum pecunia* (already known by Cic. *leg.* 2.52: *Nam sacra cum pecunia pontificum auctoritate, nulla lege coniuncta sunt*).[42] The *de cuius* could then have been a C. Asinius Festus (see the *agnomen Festianus*), and Paramythius (who already was an imperial slave) the *servus alienus*.

---

in which some of the so-called "epigraphists" have been confined for some time now, being convinced of the absolute self-sufficiency and epistemological primacy of their field of study.

40 See also Chantraine, *Freigelassene und Sklaven* (n. 14): 67–68; Weaver, *Familia Caesaris* (n. 9): 36–37.

41 Hirschfeld, *Die kaiserlichen Verwaltungsbeamten* (n. 1): 276; *contra* Theodor Mommsen, "Observationes epigraphicae," in *Ephemeris epigraphica: Corporis inscriptionum Latinarum supplementum*, vol. 5, ed. Instiuti Archaeologici Romani (Romae-Berolini: Georgium Reimerum, 1884): 109 n. 7. On this matter see also Paul Richard Carey Weaver, "Augustorum libertus," in *Historia* 13, no. 2 (1964): 189.

42 On this topic see Wolfram Buchwitz, *Servus alienus heres. Die Erbeinsetzung fremder Sklaven im klassischen römischen Recht* (Vienna/Cologne/Weimar: Böhlau, 2012).

Another similar case is the *CIL* VIII 12922:[43]

D(is) M(anibus) s(acrum) / M(arcus) Macrius Trophimus / Aug(usti) lib(ertus) medicus pius / vixit annis XXXXV / fecer(unt) lib(erti) eius patrono / bene de se merenti

In this case the inscription – which was found at Carthage and can be dated to the first or second century CE only because of its reference to the *Dis Manibus* – is dedicated to the *manes* of M. Macrius Trophimus, freedman of an emperor and pious doctor. He died 45 years old and the inscription was put up by his freedmen.

But I would add to this category also the controversial case of *C. Pompilius Caesaris libertus*, from Rubi (today Ruvo di Puglia), who is attested in *CIL* IX 313 = EDR104467 (presumably first half of the first century CE).[44]

So we can assume that in all of these cases the imperial slaves could have been instituted *heredes* as *servi alieni* under the condition of gaining their freedom.

The case of *CIL* VI 24316 = AE 2006, 173 seems to be more puzzling:

D(is) M(anibus) / C(aius) Plotius Aug(ustae?) lib(ertus) Gemellus / et Flavia Arescusa se vivi / comparaver(unt) sibi et fil(iis) suis / libert(is) libertab(us)q(ue) posterisq(ue) / eorum

The inscription comes from Rome and can be dated to the beginning of the second century CE. It was vowed to the *manes* of C. Plotius Gemellus, an imperial freedman, and of Flavia Arescusa (his wife). They acquired the tomb for themselves and for their children and their freedmen and freedwomen and even for their descendants.

It is not certain if C. Plotius Gemellus was a *servus principis* who was instituted as *heres*[45] or simply a freedman of the wife of Trajan, Pompeia Plotina (who was the daughter of a Plotia). Perhaps, as François Chausson suggested,[46] Gemellus received the *patrimonium* of Plotina through her mother, and in this case the nomenclature of C. Plotius would be no exceptional case.

Let us now look at the cases of inscriptions apparently including one or more irregular imperial *nomina*, beginning with the puzzling evidence of *CIL* VI 15317 = EDR151983.[47]

---

43 See also Chantraine, *Freigelassene und Sklaven* (n. 14): 79–80; Weaver, *Familia Caesaris* (n. 9): 35–36; but already Herman Gummerus, *Der Ärztestand im römischen Reiche nach den Inschriften* (Helsingfors: Societas Scientiarum Fennica, 1932): no. 308.

44 On which see also Marcella Chelotti, "Rubi," in *Supplementa Italica*, vol. 5, ed. Unione Accademica Nazionale (Rome: Quasar, 1989): 17, with bibliography.

45 As Chantraine, *Freigelassene und Sklaven* (n. 14): 79–80 hypothesized.

46 François Chausson, "De Domitia Longina aux Antonins: Le règne de Nerva," *Bulletin de la Société nationale des Antiquaires de France* 2002 (2008): 203.

47 See also Chantraine, *Freigelassene und Sklaven* (n. 14): 86–87; Weaver, *Familia Caesaris* (n. 9): 35–36 and Weaver, *Repertorium* (n. 19): 69, no. 373, 259–61, no. 1604. Useless is Solin, "Abuso dell'onomastica nella ricerca epigrafica" (n. 39).

> D(is) M(anibus) / Ti(berio) Claudio Vitalioni filio / karissimo qui vix(it) ann(os) XI / m(enses) VII d(ies) XIII fecit / P(ublius) Aelius Aug(usti) lib(ertus) Ianuarius pater / et Claudiae Successae coniugi / bene merenti et incomparabili feminae / cum qua vix(it) ann(os) XXXI cuius nulla(m) cupiditate(m) / est expert(us) et Ti(berio) Claudio Aug(usti) l(iberto) Censorino filio / karissimo et sibi et suis lib(ertis) libertabusq(ue) poster(is)q(ue) / eorum

We are again at Rome, and the inscription is dedicated to the *manes* of a child, Ti. Claudius Vitalio, who lived for 11 years, 7 months and 13 days. His father was P. Aelius Ianuarius, imperial freedman, who put up the inscription for himself, his wife Claudia Successa, 'a meritorious wife and wonderful woman, with whom he lived for 31 years without having experienced her bad side', and for Ti. Claudius Censorinus, freedman of the emperor, and also for all their freedmen and freedwomen and for their descendents.

In this inscription we have two imperial freedmen, a *Ti. Claudius* and a *P. Aelius*. But the date of the inscription clearly leads us back to the second century, after 117 CE (i.e. the earliest possible date for a manumission of an imperial freedman named P. Aelius) and it is also important to stress that the latest date for a manumission of an imperial freedman 'regularly' named *Ti. Claudius* had been in the first half of 68 CE.

The most reasonable hypothesis is then that this inscription is an example of a late application of the *senatus consultum Claudianum* of 52 CE. As is well known, through this decree the Senate had established that if a woman who had carnal relations with a slave did not cease this relationship after three warnings of the slave's master, she herself became a slave of the same master.[48] But as Gai. *inst.* 1.84 shows, in accordance with the norms of the same *senatus consultum* a woman who was a Roman citizen and had sexual intercourse with the slave of another with the consent of her slave partner's master could remain free herself, but any children she had would be slaves. However, Hadrian was displeased by the injustice and impropriety of this norm and so decided to restore the rule of the *ius gentium* so that as the woman herself remained free, her child was also born free.[49]

We can then assume that Claudia Successa was a free woman who had sexual intercourse with Ianuarius, who was a slave of the emperor Hadrian. Because of the consent of the master (maybe not the emperor personally but some procurator whose *servus vicarius* Ianuarius had been?[50]), Claudia Successa remained free, but her first son Censorinus became a slave, being born before Hadrian's reform.

---

48 Buongiorno, *Senatus consulta Claudianis temporibus facta* (n. 28): 311–25.

49 Gai. inst. 1.84: *Ecce enim ex senatus consulto Claudiano poterat civis Romana, quae alieno servo volente domino eius coiit, ipsa ex pactione libera permanere, sed servum procreare; nam quod inter eam et dominum istius servi convenerit ex senatus consulto ratum esse iubetur. Sed postea divus Hadrianus iniquitate rei et inelegantia iuris motus restituit iuris gentium regulam, ut cum ipsa mulier libera permaneat, liberum pariat.*

50 On this matter see, in general, Heinrich Erman, *Servus vicarius. L'esclave de l'esclave romain* (Naples: Jovene, 1986).

Censorinus attained his freedom as *Augusti libertus*, but because of the free condition of his mother he could use her name.

But Successa and Ianuarius also had a second son, Ti. Claudius Vitalio, who was not an *Augusti libertus* but seems to have been a freeborn. So we can speculate that he was born after the reform of the *senatus consultum Claudianum* passed under Hadrian and almost certainly before the manumission of his father Ianuarius, who is clearly an imperial freedman of Hadrian.

Another interesting case is the one of an inscription from Rome, *NSc* 1917, p. 291 no. 7 = EDR000144,[51] which can be securely dated after 138 CE because of palaeography, names, and archaeological context.

> Ti(berio) Cl(audio) Aug(usti) / l(iberto) Eutrapelo / patri piissi/mo et dulcis/simo T(itus) Aelius / Aug(usti) l(ibertus) Paris / filius b(ene) m(erenti) f(ecit)

This inscription was dedicated to the memory of Ti. Claudius Eutrapelus, a freedman of the emperor, by his son Ti. Aelius Paris, who was also freedman of the emperor.

In this case again the latest possible date for the manumission of an imperial freedman 'regularly' named *Ti. Claudius* is 68 CE, while the earliest possible date for the manumission of an imperial freedman named *Ti. Aelius* is 138 CE.

It is extremely unlikely that a father could have been manumitted 70 years before his son. It seems therefore better to consider again the application of the *senatus consultum Claudianum* before the reform passed under Hadrian for Eutrapelus (who had been son of a Claudia who had remained free). Eutrapelus had then (at least) one son, Paris, with a *serva Caesaris* whose name remains unknown. Paris was then manumitted by Antoninus Pius.

Let us turn now to two more puzzling cases. *CIL* VI 376 = *ILS* 3670 = EDR179457:[52]

> Iovi Custodi / et Genio / thesaurorum / aram / C(aius) Iulius Aug(usti) lib(ertus) / Satyrus / d(onum) d(edit) // dedic(avit) XIII K(alendas) Febr(uarias) / M(arco) Civica Barbaro / M(arco) Metilio Regulo / co(n)s(ulibus).

The inscription comes from Rome and was placed at an alter vowed as a gift to *Iuppiter Custos* and to the *Genius thesaurorum*. The vower was C. Iulius Satyrus, freedman of the Emperor.

He dedicated it on 20 January under the consulship of Marcus Civica Barbarus and Marcus Metilius Regulus (i.e. in 157 CE). The latest possible date for a manumission of an imperial freedman 'regularly' named *C. Iulius* is January 41 CE. In this case

---

51 See also Chantraine, *Freigelassene und Sklaven* (n. 14): 77; Weaver, *Familia Caesaris* (n. 9): 25, 35–36.

52 See also Chantraine, *Freigelassene und Sklaven* (n. 14): 77–78; Weaver, *Familia Caesaris* (n. 9): 25, 35. Different view in Gérard Boulvert, *Esclaves et affranchis impériaux sous le Haut-Empire romain. Rôle politique et administrative* (Naples: Jovene, 1970): 95–96 no. 29.

again the simplest solution would be then the application of the *senatus consultum Claudianum* before the reform of Hadrian: Satyrus could have been son of a Iulia. Nothing is said about the age of Satyrus and it is not unlikely to think that he was not very young in 157 CE.

But we do not possess much information, and an alternative could be that Satyrus could have been instituted as a *servus alienus heres* according to the will of an otherwise unknown C. Iulius. But this is merely speculative.

We can conclude our overview with the analysis of the most puzzling inscription, *CIL* VI 8634 = *ILS* 1697 = EDR171345:[53]

> Ti(beri) Claudi Aug(usti) / lib(erti) Aviti imbi/tatoris et T(iti) Ae/li Aug(usti) lib(erti) Theo/doti adiuto/ris a cognit(ionibus) / et Scetasiae / Octaviae fili(i)s / carissimis / Antonia Rhodine / mater fecit.

The inscription[54] was found at Rome, in the archaeological context of the so-called *Sepolcreto Salario*, and is a funerary text in memory of Ti. Claudius Avitus, imperial freedman, who worked as *invitator*; of T. Aelius Thedotus, *adiutor a cognitionibus*, imperial freedman; and of Scetasia Octavia. They all were children of an Antonia Rhodine, who made the tomb. The dating is unclear but must be in either the first or the second century CE. In any case, the reference to a *T. Aelius* suggests (but does not prove) a dating after 138 (as we have seen, the earliest possible date for the manumission of an imperial freedman named *T. Aelius*).

If we accept a dating after 138 CE, we could describe this scenario: Antonia Rhodine was freeborn or a freedwoman of an Antonius. She had three children with different partners. Two of them were conceived with one or two imperial slaves (and so we would have an application of the *senatus consultum Claudianum* before Hadrian's reform). The third, Octavia, clearly a freeborn, would have been then coinceved in Rhodine's marriage to a Scetasius. This hypotesis, however, does not explain why the two sons have different *nomina*. As we saw, the latest possible date for a manumission of an imperial freedman 'regularly' named Ti. Claudius had been the first half of year 68 CE; and because of the *nomen* of Rhodine (Antonia!) there is no plausible argument for the use of *Ti. Claudius* instead of Antonius with reference to Avitus.

Although the palaeographic aspects of the inscription could seem to be closer to the second century CE,[55] I would like then to put forward another (not certain, but plausible) hypothesis that brings us back to the imperial slaves and freedmen of the Julio-Claudian dynasty.

---

53 See also Chantraine, *Freigelassene und Sklaven* (n. 14): 78–79; Weaver, *Familia Caesaris* (n. 9): 35.

54 On the *monumentum*, see Dietrich Boschung, *Antike Grabaltäre aus den Nekropolen Roms* (Bern: Stämpfli, 1987): 65, 82.

55 But obviously the paleographical argument is not definitive; and in any case, the inscription in question does not explicitly mention the invocation to the *Dii Manes* but only the genitive form for the names of the departed.

Antonia Rhodine, who seems not to be an imperial freedwoman, could have been directly related to a freedman of Antonia Minor, the mother of the future emperor Claudius. After the approval of the *senatus consultum Claudianum* in 52 CE, she had sexual intercourse with one imperial slave but with the consent of his master. So she remained free and the two children, Avitus and Theodotus, were born slaves. One of them, Ti. Claudius Avitus, could have been then manumitted already by either Claudius or more likely by Nero. Theodotus may instead have become part of the patrimony of Claudia Antonia, the daughter of Claudius and of his second wife Aelia Paetina. The strange *nomen* of Theodotus (Aelius) could be attributed to such a context and he could have been qualified as *Augusti libertus* because of the manumission by Claudia Antonia, who was daughter of Aelia Paetina and half-sister of the emperor Nero.[56] This hypothesis is however entirely speculative and there is unfortunately no evidence of the identity (and so of the *praenomen*) of the father of Aelia Paetina.

In any case, we should note that the names of all the protagonists are close to the context of the imperial family in the age of Claudius (even the *cognomen* of the freeborn daughter of Antonia Rhodine: Octavia!); this would be moreover supported by the fact that the *gens* Scetasia, originally from Iguvium, with whom Rhodine became related, seems to be attested only for the first century CE.[57]

5 Conclusions: The Rank of Imperial Slaves and Freedmen

In summary, we can conclude that being an imperial slave (and moreover an imperial freedman) could imply a relevant social status. Originally, this relevance was limited only to a few leading freedmen, later for the *familia Caesaris* as a whole, as it was perceived as expression of *fiscus* itself.

Imperial freedmen, and moreover slaves, were proud to state their connection with the imperial house. In some inscriptions the slaves used expressions such as *Caesar noster, Augustus noster*, to refer to 'their' emperor.

Such a proud statement of social status did not produce any appreciable forms of legal difference in comparison with the slaves and freedmen of private citizens;[58] in other words, there were no privileged norms for slaves and freedmen who belonged

56 Could the decision to use the *nomen* Aelius, instead of *Claudius*, indicate a form of political opposition of Claudia Antonia against Nero? It seems likely that the woman was involved in the Pisonian conspiracy in 65 CE.

57 *CIL* XI 5898 = EDR138067; *CIL* VI 26007; *CIL* VI 26008 = EDR158684.

58 Except for the fact that we have no information about imperial slaves who were killed in the application of *senatus consultum Silanianum* after the violent death of an emperor (such as Caligula or Domitian), perhaps because of an interest to protect the *fiscus*.

or had belonged to the emperor and the imperial family. The affair concerning the *restitutio natalium* of powerful imperial freedmen such as the brothers M. Antonius Pallas and Felix, connected to Claudius, confirms that: all the freedmen, even if they were tied to the emperor and had received the *ornamenta consularia*, were legally subjected (albeit only formally) to freeborn persons: unless there had been a *restitutio natalium*, a freedman remained a freedman.[59]

It is for this reason (as I pointed out above) that after the middle of the first century CE the political role of a small group of leading freedmen was no longer tolerated. The construction of a new imperial bureaucracy, in which the leading roles were now reserved for equestrian officers led to freedmen soon being excluded from political games and leading political roles. They nevertheless retained economic relevance as *procuratores* of the emperor, and in some cases also played a role in the administration of justice through *cognitiones* at their first stage:[60] and this seems to be an aspect that still requires systematic analysis.

59 With reference to M. Antonius Pallas see also the scepticism of Plinius in *ep.* 8.16.
60 Cf. Tac. *ann.* 12.60.1; Suet. *Cl.* 12.1.

Richard Gamauf

Peculium: Paradoxes of Slaves With Property

1 Focus of this Paper

Legal historians tend to identify *peculium* primarily with what they find in the Roman jurists' discussions of the *actio de peculio vel de in rem verso* or the *legatum peculii*.[1] The available sources, together with the legal intricacies of the *actio de peculio*,[2] frequently reduce the study of *peculium* exclusively to discussions of complex questions of law. This is understandably the province of legal historians,[3] who

1 Its name appears in two Digest titles, D. 15.1 *De peculio* / 'The *peculium*' and D. 33.8 *De peculio legato* / 'The legacy of a *peculium*'. This paper is a synthesis of findings regarding *peculium* from a number of earlier studies on various aspects of slave-*peculium*.

2 In the edict, there was a single combined action, the *actio de peculio vel de in rem verso* (cf. Gai. 4.74a). Over time, the jurists treated its elements as independent actions. This state of late classical law was preserved in the multi-volume commentaries on the edict, and determined the distribution of the material between two Digest titles, D. 15.1 *De peculio* / 'The *peculium*' and D. 15.3 *De in rem verso* / 'Benefit taken' (Transl. Weir in Alan Watson, *The Digest of Justinian*, vol. 1–2 (Philadelphia: University of Pennsylvania Press, 1998]).

3 References are primarily to recent studies in English; an extensive bibliography is in Richard Gamauf, "§ 102. Klage aufgrund Sonderguts oder Bereicherung des Gewalthabers (actio de peculio vel de in rem verso)," in *Handbuch des Römischen Privatrechts*, ed. Ulrike Babusiaux et al. (Tübingen: Mohr Siebeck, 2023); still unsurpassed on all legal aspects of slavery is William Warwick Buckland, *The Roman Law of Slavery: The Condition of the Slave in Private Law from Augustus to Justinian* (Cambridge: Cambridge University Press, 1908). Recent studies on *peculium* in English include: Ireneusz Żeber, *A Study of the Peculium of a Slave in Pre-Classical Roman Law* (Wrocław: Wydawnictwo Uniwersytetu Wrocławskiego, 1981); Aaron Kirschenbaum, *Sons, Slaves and Freedmen in Roman Commerce* (Jerusalem: Hebrew University Magnes Press, 1987): 31–88; Alan Watson, *Roman Slave Law* (Baltimore/London: Johns Hopkins University Press, 1987): 90–101; Luuk de Ligt, "Legal History and Economic History: The Case of the actiones adiecticiae qualitatis," *Tijdschrift voor Rechtsgeschiedenis* 67, no. 3–4 (1999): 205–26; David Johnston, "Peculiar Questions," in *Thinking Like a Lawyer: Essays on Legal History & General History for John Crook on His Eightieth Birthday*, ed. Paul McKechnie (Leiden: Brill, 2002): 173–84; Willem J. Zwalve, "Callistus's Case: Some Legal Aspects of Roman Business Activities," in *The Transformation of Economic Life under the Roman Empire: Proceedings of the Second Workshop of the International Network Impact of Empire (Roman Empire, c. 200 B.C.–A.D. 476), Nottingham, July 4–7, 2001*, ed. Lukas de Blois and John Rich (Amsterdam: J.C. Gieben, 2002): 116–27; David Johnston, "Suing the Paterfamilias: Theory and Practice," in *Beyond Dogmatics: Law and Society in the Roman World*, ed. John W. Cairns and Paul J. du Plessis (Edinburgh: Edinburgh University Press, 2007): 173–84; Jean-Jacques Aubert, "Dumtaxat de

Note: I would like to thank Mag.a Karina Jasmin Karik, BA (Vienna) for her help in preparing this article, and to acknowledge the unending friendliness of Dr Benjamin Spagnolo (Cambridge) who rendered my English slightly more idiomatic.

https://doi.org/10.1515/9783110987195-004

treat non-legal aspects or social ramifications of *peculia*, if they notice them at all, as of secondary importance compared to their legal consequences.[4] One common exception is where legal historians note the *peculium's* role in financing manumissions by way of *suis nummis emere* / buying (freedom) with one's own money. In this instance, too, however, the discussion is dominated by the legal problems of such arrangements.[5]

To some extent, the ancient sources do foster – and may even justify – a predominantly legal approach: surviving legal texts mention *peculia* over a thousand times, whereas non-legal writings hardly ever refer to the institution.[6] The bulk of material comes from discussions about who is liable for slaves' 'debts'. Accordingly,

peculio: What's in a Peculium, or Establishing the Extent of the Principal's Liability," in *New Frontiers: Law and Society in the Roman World*, ed. Paul J. du Plessis (Edinburgh: Edinburgh University Press, 2013): 192–206; Andreas M. Fleckner, "The Peculium: A Legal Device for Donations to personae alieno iuri subiectae?," in *Gift Giving and the 'Embedded' Economy in the Ancient World*, ed. Filippo Carlà and Maja Gori (Heidelberg: Winter, 2014): 213–39.

4 Some legal historians, however, are aware of social aspects: Alfons Bürge, "Lo schiavo (in)dipendente e il suo patrimonio," in *Homo, caput, persona: La construzione giuridica dell'identità nell'esperienza romana; dall'epoca di Plauto a Ulpiano*, ed. Alessandro Corbino, Michel Humbert and Giovanni Negri (Pavia: IUSS Press, 2010): 369–91; Wolfram Buchwitz, "Fremde Sklaven als Erben: Sozialer Aufstieg durch Dritte," in *Homo, caput, persona: La construzione giuridica dell'identità nell'esperienza romana; dall'epoca di Plauto a Ulpiano*, ed. Alesandro Corbino, Michel Humbert and Giovanni Negri (Pavia: IUSS Press, 2010): 393–425; Wolfram Buchwitz, *Servus alienus heres: Die Erbeinsetzung fremder Sklaven im klassischen römischen Recht* (Vienna/Cologne/Weimar: Böhlau, 2012); Wolfram Buchwitz, "Servus servo heres: Testierfreiheit für Sklaven," in *Fontes Iuris: Atti del VI Jahrestreffen Junger Romanistinnen und Romanisten Lecce, 30–31 marzo 2012*, ed. Pierangelo Buongiorno and Sebastian Lohsse (Naples: Edizioni Scientifiche Italiane, 2013): 141–49. Fleckner, "Peculium" (n. 3): 213–39. See also the paper by Buchwitz in this volume.

5 Henrik Mouritsen, *The Freedman in the Roman World* (Cambridge: Cambridge University Press, 2011): 159–80; Thomas Finkenauer, "Anmerkungen zur redemptio servi suis nummis," in *Festschrift für Rolf Knütel zum 70. Geburtstag*, ed. Holger Altmeppen, Ingo Reichard and Martin Schermaier (Heidelberg: C.F. Müller, 2009): 345–57; Susanne Heinemeyer, *Der Freikauf des Sklaven mit eigenem Geld – Redemptio suis nummis* (Berlin: Duncker & Humblot, 2013); Rolf Knütel, "Freikauf mit eigenem Geld," in *Handwörterbuch der Antiken Sklaverei*, vol. 1, ed. Heinz Heinen et al. (Stuttgart: Franz Steiner Verlag, 2017): 1095–97; more literature in Richard Gamauf, "§ 36. Sklaven (servi)," in *Handbuch des Römischen Privatrechts*, ed. Ulrike Babusiaux et al. (Tübingen: Mohr Siebeck, 2023): n. 63. For a social history point of view, cf. Ulrike Roth, "Peculium, Freedom, Citizenship: Golden Triangle or Vicious Circle? An Act in Two Parts," in *By the Sweat of Your Brow: Roman Slavery in Its Socio-Economic Setting*, ed. Ulrike Roth (London: Institute of Classical Studies, University of London, 2010): 91–120.

6 This is the count according to Fleckner, "Peculium" (n. 3): 218; Kyle Harper, *Slavery in the Late Roman World, A.D. 275–425* (Cambridge: Cambridge University Press, 2011): 223 assumes only few privileged slaves had *peculia*, whereas Andreas Wacke, "Die libera administratio peculii: Zur Verfügungsmacht von Hauskindern und Sklaven über ihr Sondergut," in *Symposium für Hans Josef Wieling zum 70. Geburtstag*, ed. Thomas Finkenauer (Berlin: Springer Verlag, 2006): 268 takes the complex legal regime developed in this context as indicating a certain ubiquity of substantive *peculia*.

numerous studies based on texts that explicitly mention the term confine *peculium* for the majority of legal historians to questions of whether the *actio de peculio* could be employed against the legal superior.

Historically as well as socially, however, this action was the result of the existence of *peculium* – meaning the institution, as well as the funds held by a slave in an individual case – as a fact of everyday life. By focusing predominantly (and sometimes even exclusively) on the *actio de peculio*, legal history misses something crucial: contemporaries outside the legal profession did not take note of the (probably) widespread phenomenon of property entrusted to slaves because of a possible *actio de peculio*; rather, they looked at *peculium* because of what it was socially and economically, namely property available to persons *alieni iuris* to use according to their own wishes.[7]

In this regard, Ulrike Roth's paper on *peculia* of slaves in Roman agriculture is a notable exception.[8] She does not follow the usual strictly legalistic approach; but nor does she ignore the jurists' concepts.[9] The central difference in her treatment is the selection of sources. She draws heavily upon texts that do not mention the term directly, and puts greater emphasis on less-studied social consequences of *peculia* that are, nonetheless, acknowledged by some legal definitions (especially in the context of *legatum peculii*[10]). In Roth's work, *peculium* stands for any (agricultural) property used by slaves for their own personal purposes.

Objections to such an approach from a legal historian's standpoint are easy: a slave exploiting property for himself or his 'family' did not necessitate a formal division of a household's assets between the *peculium* and the master's property / *res dominicae*.[11] But to Roman jurists, this was the essential step in the creation of a *peculium*. In economic terms, only property available for use in business outside the household qualified as *peculium*; this was presumably rare in agricultural contexts.[12] Without property used externally, the problems to which the *actio de peculio* was addressed could not arise; it was only external commercial activities of slaves that necessitated the legal regime of *peculium*.

---

7 *Peculia* of children-in-power are not discussed. Sons in military service owned their acquisitions; on the development of the so-called *peculium castrense* / 'camp *peculium*', cf. Dominik Rodak, *Entwicklungslinien des militärischen Sonderguts (peculium castrense) von Augustus bis Hadrian* (Göttingen: V&R unipress, 2022).

8 Ulrike Roth, "Food, Status, and the Peculium of Agricultural Slaves," *Journal of Roman Archaeology* 18 (2005): 278–92.

9 Roth, "Food" (n. 8): 278–79.

10 See below after n. 97.

11 Examples of separate accounting: D. 11.3.1.5 (Ulp. 23 ad ed.); D. 15.1.49.2 (Pomp. 4 Quin. Muc.); D. 15.3.3.5 (Ulp. 29 ad ed.); D. 33.8.6.4 (Ulp. 25 Sab.); D. 33.8.23.1 (Scaev. 15 dig.); D. 35.1.40.3 (Iav. 2 post. Lab.); D. 40.1.6 (Alf. 4 dig.); D. 40.7.3.2 (Ulp. 27 Sab.); D. 41.1.37.1 (Iul. 44 dig.); Inst. 2.20.20.

12 See below at n. 127.

It is precisely the different method adopted that makes Roth's contribution noteworthy, as well as essential to better understand both *peculium* as a legal institution and the jurists' bickering about 'correct' terminology. As her paper makes clear, *peculium* as 'slaves' patrimony' existed long before the *actio de peculio*. It is scarcely surprising, then, that some jurists hint at the original (and for slaves always the primary) social role of *peculium* in their definitions, though they rarely mention that role in analysing cases.

The socio-economic transformation of *peculium* from the personal property of slaves into business capital led to the creation of the action. Even after this shift, slaves' personal interests in *peculia* remained vital for the institution, and their personal interests also defined the meaning of *peculium*. The discourse about *peculium* in our sources is, however, overwhelmingly legal, and this distorts our perspective. Social aspects deserve close attention in legal studies of *peculium*, because such aspects can also gain legal significance.

This paper studies *peculium* mostly from legal texts. Some texts address the differences between the jurists' technical understanding of the term and a broader colloquial meaning that included property besides that administered by slaves. Jurists denounced such language as imprecise, misleading, or simply wrong. Here, legal historians have followed suit and unhesitatingly accepted the jurists' technical understanding, without paying sufficient attention to the fact that, despite the jurists' efforts, this never became the primary meaning of *peculium* more generally. Existing scholarship treats evidence of a broader understanding outside the legal profession as relatively unimportant, or as documenting only a secondary meaning.[13] The present article reconsiders and challenges that hitherto uncontested traditional interpretation.

2 Introduction: What is a Peculium?

The oldest known legal definition of *peculium*[14] goes back to the late Republican jurist Q. Aelius Tubero, who emphasised its legal characteristics. The significance of a *peculium* for a slave was of no concern to him. Owing to its sophistication, his definition served as a model for later jurists' concepts of *peculium*:

D. 15.1.5.4 (Ulpian 29 ad ed.): Peculium autem Tubero quidem sic definit, ut Celsus libro sexto digestorum refert, quod servus domini

D. 15.1.5.4 (Ulpian, Edict, book 29): According to Celsus in the sixth book of his Digest, Tubero defines a peculium as the property which

13 Literature in Gamauf, "Klage aufgrund Sonderguts" (n. 3): n. 10.

14 On definitions of *peculium* cf. Luigi Amirante, "Lavoro di giuristi sul peculio: Le definizioni da Q. Mucio a Ulpiano," in *Studi in onore Cesare di Sanfilippo*, vol. 3 (Milan: Giuffrè, 1983): 3–15; see also Żeber, *Study* (n. 3): 24–25; for more literature cf. Gamauf, "Klage aufgrund Sonderguts" (n. 3): n. 11.

permissu separatum a rationibus dominicis habet, deducto inde si quid domino debetur.	the slave, with the master's permission, keeps in a separate account of his own, less anything owed to the master.[15]

Ulpian quoted Tubero in his commentary on the *actio de peculio*. In this action, the *peculium* was the value of assets that a slave held with the master's consent in a separate account. From the value of such assets, the judge then deducted what a slave 'owed' to his master (or other persons in the *familia*). Ulpian reduced *peculium* to the outcome of complex accounting operations – operations that had regard to horizontal as well as vertical economic relationships within a Roman household.[16] In this sense, *peculium* was nothing more than the maximum amount available to meet a master's liability to his slave's creditors.

Roth, however, studies situations where slaves use property primarily *within* their master's household, or on his estate. In such situations, the juristic concept of *peculium* was meaningless, though the same types of property (livestock, land etc.) might be involved in both scenarios.[17]

While property of a 'merely domestic' *peculium* benefitted slaves' personal lives, it had no repercussions outside the *familia*. The need to transform a 'domestic' into a legal *peculium* arose when the slave no longer operated exclusively inside the *familia* but transacted with eternal third parties. Only then did the internal economic structures of a household or the financial status of a *peculium* gain relevance for outsiders: for third parties doing business with slaves, the *peculium* was, like the estate of a free person, the pool of assets available to satisfy their potential claims.[18]

Roman legal literature on *peculium* (discussing either the *actio de peculio* or a *legatum peculii*[19]) does not explicitly mention how the availability of assets in *peculia* changed slaves' lives. The jurists were not blind to this consequence but focussed on what was legally relevant, and ignored what was not – e.g., benefits to slaves, an improved economic situation for masters, or the role of *peculia* in facilitating control over slaves.

In a successful *actio de peculio* or a trial involving a *legatum peculii*, the judge had to determine the amount to pay to the claimant; with this purpose in mind, jurists advised how to calculate a *peculium*'s value. The interest of a Roman judge in a *peculium* (and that of most other actors in Roman law) did not go beyond its

15 Transl. Weir in Watson, *Digest of Justinian* (n. 2).

16 Richard Gamauf, "Slaves Doing Business: The Role of Roman Law in the Economy of a Roman Household," *European Review of History/Revue européenne d'histoire* 16, no. 3 (2009): 331–46.

17 Plots of land in *peculia*: D. 6.1.41.1 (Ulp. 17 ad ed.); D. 15.1.7.4 (Ulp. 29 ad ed.); D. 33.8.6 pr. (Ulp. 25 Sab.); Petron. 53.2; livestock: C. 4.26.10 pr. (Diocl., a. 294).

18 D. 15.1.19.1 (Ulp. 29 ad ed.); D. 15.1.32 pr. (Ulp. 2 disp.); D. 15.1.47.6 (Paul. 4 Plaut.); literature in Gamauf, "Klage aufgrund Sonderguts" (n. 3): n. 25, n. 148.

19 For the difference see below after n. 97.

value. He needed to transform a *peculium* into a number, detached from the economic and social complexities involved in its daily operations and heedless of the slave's personal reasons for wanting it. Tubero's *definitio* accomplished precisely this, and did so in a model manner, as its presence in jurists' discourse centuries later indicates. The *actio de peculio* essentially reduced *peculium* to the outcome of an account: the (imaginary) credit column contained the slave's items and his claims against other household members; the debit side consisted of what he 'owed' to the master and others in the *domus*. This is what the books would reveal to the judge. At the last stage before a *condemnatio*, the value of assets removed from the *peculium* (with the master's acquiescence) to the prejudice of a claimant would be reinstated.

This operation was not designed to unveil *peculium* as an aggregate of goods and claims offering various – legitimate as well as illegitimate – possibilities to a slave. Digest 15.1.5.4 (Ulp. 29 ed.) removed all social, emotional, and economic meanings (and entanglements) from *peculium*, and stripped it down to the result of – at times intricate – calculations.

Tubero's *definitio* shaped the perspective of Roman jurists on *peculium*. Accordingly, its impacts on the holders' personal lives, how slaves utilised *peculia* for their own purposes – in other words, many of the aspects that Roth's approach unpacks – caught the jurists' attention only under exceptional circumstances. Jurists noted slaves' uses (and abuses) of 'their' property outside business only where it implicated a third party (i.e., a party other than the master and the slave[20]). Such a third party might be: the recipient of property embezzled by a slave from his *peculium*;[21] someone trying to recover a 'dowry' given in a slave's 'marriage';[22] or perhaps a slave-dealer, as when a buyer considered the spending habits of his recently acquired slave as actionable character flaws.[23]

20 This answers the question implied in the following statement by Mouritsen, *Freedman* (n. 5): 175: 'Although the *peculium* probably often exceeded the slave's value, the legal sources barely hint at the possibility that it might be used for self-purchase. Thus, book fifteen of the *Digest*, entirely dedicated to the *peculium*, mentions its use as payment for freedom on only three occasions, all linked to situations where a slave had borrowed money which was then offered to the master in return for manumission' (references omitted). As legal relationships exclusively existed between *personae sui iuris*, deals of masters and slaves were of legal interest only if they had an impact on another free person besides the master.

21 D. 11.3.16 (Alf. 2 dig.). For more on this case, see the study on *dispensatores* in this volume after n. 114.

22 E.g., D. 23.3.39 pr. (Ulp. 33 ad ed.); D. 16.3.27 (Paul. 7 resp.); Gamauf, "Sklaven (servi)" (n.5): n. 12, n. 73.

23 Examples in Richard Gamauf, "Erro: Suche nach einem verschwundenen Sklaven: Eine Skizze zur Interpretationsgeschichte des ädilizischen Edikts," in *Inter cives necnon peregrinos: Essays in Honour of Boudewijn Sirks*, ed. Jan Hallebeek et al. (Göttingen: V&R unipress, 2014): 282–84.

For a judge establishing the extent of liability in an *actio de peculio*, the slave's share in his *peculium* could sometimes matter, too (although direct documentation in this regard is lacking). A master was liable for dishonestly tolerating the devaluation of a *peculium* by his slave to the detriment of a claimant.[24] Unfortunately, Ulpian gives few indications of what amounts to *dolus* in this context; the possibilities were probably many and manifold. However, a judge might regard a sudden increase in a slave's spending on family or hobbies as suspicious. Such an increase was illegitimate when motivated by anticipated defeat in a lawsuit *de peculio*. If he stood to lose the *peculium* anyway, a master had no further personal interest in keeping it intact. Why not let the slave enjoy it, at the expense of the creditors? In such circumstances, the slave also had good reasons for trying to do so, because defeat in an *actio de peculio* diminished or even extinguished his *peculium*[25] and, with it, many or all of the present and future benefits they hoped to derive from it.

Slaves' 'private' interests in having *peculia* were not unappreciated by Roman jurists but – unless amounting to abuses connived at by a fraudulent *dominus* / master – they remained irrelevant to an *actio de peculio*. The situation in the case of a *legatum peculii* differed in this regard.[26] Nevertheless, it was a given that slaves usually had their masters' consent for some private expenditure, and were not expected to reserve the *peculium* exclusively for business activities. This influenced jurists' conception of *peculium* too. Jurists did not view *peculium* from a slave's perspective, but they did live in the same world. By the time jurists began to work out their characteristic concept, *peculium* was already a long-standing social institution with various purposes and readily understood impacts on the lives of both slaves and masters: it was a common means of social control and an economic factor of the highest importance. The jurists could hardly ignore this, and it shaped their reasoning.

In legal discussions, however, the interests of masters trumped the welfare of slaves. The treatment of slaves' food and clothes in an *actio de peculio* is instructive. As Roth demonstrates, for slaves, *peculium* basically meant better access to food, clothing and other necessities.[27] Having a *peculium* – or not – might mean the difference between life and death (sometimes not only their own). Of course, masters and jurists understood what slaves considered primarily as 'theirs'. The *actio de*

---

24 D. 15.1.21 pr. (Ulp. 29 ad ed.); see Aubert, "Dumtaxat de peculio" (n. 3): 192–206; for more literature, cf. Gamauf, "Klage aufgrund Sonderguts" (n. 3): n. 38.

25 What a master paid in an *actio de peculio* reduced a *peculium* (D. 33.8.16 Afr. 5 quaest.), because creditors were paid in the chronological order of the judgments delivered in their favour; see Gamauf, "Slaves Doing Business" (n. 16): 337–38; Gamauf, "Klage aufgrund Sonderguts" (n. 3): nos. 33, 36.

26 See below after n. 97.

27 Put in a nutshell by Roth, "Food" (n. 8): 288 as follows: 'To have (*peculium*) was to be (a slave family).'

peculio, however, looked at it exclusively from a master's perspective:[28] the question was[29] whether the master increased his liability (to the slave's creditors) by that which he provided to his slaves for maintenance.[30] What a slave needed to exist was not business capital, and so not *peculium* in terms of the *actio*.[31] However, this was indirectly helpful for slaves, because it meant that the law did not indirectly encourage a master to parsimony.[32]

3 Roman Jurists and Peculium

3.1 Roman *familia* and *peculia*

As a technical legal term, *peculium* referred to property that a slave or a son-in-power administered on his own, based on a grant by his *dominus* / master (or *pater familias* / father.) *Peculium* was rooted in the economic organisation of the Roman family unit. In an agnatic *familia*,[33] the head of the household alone held (all) rights of monetary value. Persons (free and unfree) subject to the power of another / *alieni iuris* (Gai. 1.51)[34] – in this case, the *pater familias* or *dominus* – were legally incapable of possessing or owning property, or holding legal claims.[35] Therefore, the concession of a *peculium* and a transfer of things to (the account of) a slave[36] gave the latter only factual control. From a legal point of view, nothing changed: the master

28 Food for *familia* or the slave himself was a typical example of a *versio in rem*; e.g., D. 15.3.3.1, 3, 7, 10 (Ulp. 29 ad ed.).

29 D. 15.1.40.1 (Marcian. 5 reg.); D. 15.1.25 (Pomp. 23 Sab.).

30 This discussion reveals that, in the context of the *actio*, the underlying concept of *peculium* was primarily as a fund intended for business purposes.

31 See Gamauf, "Slaves Doing Business" (n. 16): 333–34.

32 See below n. 158.

33 On the various meanings of *familia* cf. D. 50.16.195.2 (Ulp. 46 ad ed.). Etymology links *familia* to *famulus* / 'servant'; a *familia* – wife, children, slaves, chattels – was everything at the service of the head of the household / *pater familias* (or *dominus* in case of slaves). See Michiel de Vaan, *Etymological Dictionary of Latin and the Other Italic Languages* (Leiden: Brill, 2008): s.v. famulus.

34 Roman law treated slaves as persons and as chattels. Slaves were owned, sold, leased etc. like any other movable (e.g., slave / *homo* was a stock example for a *res corporalis* / 'corporeal thing'; cf. Gai. 2.13). The near absolute power of the master (for ideological reasons named *vitae necisque postestas* / 'right over life and death') was not a consequence of ownership but was understood as a separate legal power over the slave as a *persona* (Gai. 1.52). Legally, little difference existed between *patria potestas* / 'father's power' and *dominica potestas* / 'master's power' (this term is attested in D. 21.1.17.10 Ulp. 1 ed. aed. cur.); literature in Gamauf, "Sklaven (servi)" (n. 5): n. 9.

35 D. 41.1.54.4 (Pomp. 31 Q. Muc.); D. 50.17.118 (Ulp. 11 ad ed.); D. 50.16.182 (Ulp. 27 ad ed.); Gai. 2.87, 96.

36 D. 15.1.4.1 (Pomp. 7 Sab); D. 15.1.8 (Paul. 4 Sab.); in the household accounts, such items 'belonged' to the slave: D. 15.1.16 (Iul. 12 dig.); D. 40.7.39.2 (Iav. 4 post.).

still owned or possessed the goods in the *peculium* and acquired claims in connection with agreements entered into by the slave.[37] By law, slaves were mere *de facto* holders, albeit sometimes[38] with full powers to dispose of assets.[39]

3.2 Acquisitions for the Master and Liability *de peculio*

Designating some of his estate as the *peculium* of his slave brought a master many benefits. A *peculium* allowed its holder to acquire for the master (possession and, in consequence[40]) ownership, without express prior order or subsequent ratification.[41] *Personae alieni iuris* were incapable of holding rights, so every gain immediately accrued to the master. The regime of *peculium* gave a master these benefits while simultaneously sparing him full responsibility for resulting burdens. A master who was not familiar with his slaves' dealings – e.g., because he let them operate far away[42] – never risked incalculable losses.

The master's liability was limited in the praetorian *actio de peculio*, the action against him for undischarged debts of a slave with a *peculium*. The *actio de peculio vel de in rem verso* was one of the so-called *actiones adiecticiae qualitatis*.[43] These 'additional' actions were created between the third and first centuries BCE, presumably in response to a steep increase in business activities undertaken by slaves. They addressed several interrelated problems inherent in doing business with slaves: (1) The *ius civile* did not recognise agreements with slaves as valid contracts, and so other parties had no enforceable claims; (2) Slaves lacked legal personality and could not be sued; (3) Slaves were technically property-less, and so had nothing to satisfy creditors. Taken together, these factors restricted access to credit and to business opportunities; both masters and slaves lost out, because economically gifted slaves could

37 These nevertheless formed part of the *peculium*: D. 15.1.7.4 (Ulp. 29 ad ed.).

38 Jurists speak of (*naturaliter*) *tenere* / '(factually) hold': D. 41.2.1.5 (Paul. 54 ad ed.); D. 41.2.24 (Iav. 14 epist.); D. 41.2.49.1 (Pap. 2 def.); D. 45.1.38.7 (Ulp. 49 Sab.) or *habere* / 'have': D. 15.1.5.4 (Ulp. 29 ad ed.); D. 15.1.37.3 (Iul. 12 dig.). Some authors assume a legal claim of a slave in respect of his *peculium*: for Roberto Pesaresi, *Ricerche sul peculium imprenditoriale* (Bari: Cacucci Editore, 2008): 80–120, the slave was possessor; Ignazio Buti, *Studi sulla capacità patrimoniale dei 'servi'* (Naples: Jovene, 1976): 5–6 sees partial legal capacity; and Johannes Jacobus Brinkhof, *Een studie over het peculium in het klassieke Romeinse recht* (Meppel: Krips Repro B.V., 1978): 53, 83, 229 argues for a legally acknowledged wider independence.

39 The underlying idea in Roman slave law was that a slave should only be able to improve the master's position; see also Johnston, "Suing the Paterfamilias" (n. 4): 183. Therefore, donations were outside their powers; see Gamauf, "Klage aufgrund Sonderguts" (n. 3): n. 22 and the paper on *dispensatores* in this volume at n. 201.

40 Watson, *Roman Slave Law* (n. 3): 102–14; Kirschenbaum, *Sons* (n. 3): 7–26.

41 D. 41.2.44.1 (Pap. 23 quaest.).

42 See below after n. 167.

43 The term was coined in the Middle Ages on the basis of D. 14.1.5.1 (Paul. 29 ad ed.).

not develop their potential, and because business had to be transacted by the *dominus* personally.

To resolve these problems, creditors needed the ability to sue the master. Economic expedience and legal principle[44] excluded out of hand attribution to the master of full responsibility for all of a slave's obligations. The interests of masters and creditors were opposed: masters wished to limit liability but not supervise daily operations, while creditors sought security when dealing with slaves. The Roman jurists developed a perfectly balanced solution: the finely-tuned system of *actiones adiecticiae qualitatis*, based on the 'idea [. . .] of apportioning risks according to benefits: the master takes the benefits to be derived from his slave's activities, and he should therefore take the burdens'.[45] Unlimited liability required the master's explicit or implicit authorisation of specific transactions, or else his appointing slaves to certain functions of general management.[46] In the case of an absentee master and a slave not appointed to a position of general management, the *actio de peculio vel de in rem verso* limited liability to the value of the *peculium* at the time of judgment, or to the subsisting gain derived from a transaction.[47]

An *actio adiecticiae qualitatis* was therefore not a free-standing substantive claim but, rather, a procedural device to enforce a claim arising out of a slave's transaction (which was not binding according to the strict *ius civile*) against the master (who, under the Roman concept of 'privity of contract', the principle of *vinculum iuris*,[48] was not a party to the transaction). Sale and purchase to a slave with a *peculium*, for example, enabled the seller to sue for the price using an *actio venditi* with a *formula*

44 In Roman law, there was no direct representation, not even in the case of slaves; see immediately at n. 48.

45 Barry Nicholas, *An Introduction to Roman Law* (Oxford: Clarendon Press, 1962): 202.

46 If a master himself permitted someone to contract with his slave, he was fully liable under the *actio quod iussu* / 'action based on authorisation'; this was also the consequence of appointing a business manager (*actio institoria* / 'action for a manager') or a sea captain (*actio exercitoria* / 'action against a ship owner'); cf. Kirschenbaum, *Sons* (n. 3): 90–121; Jean-Jacques Aubert, *Business Managers in Ancient Rome: A Social and Economic Study of Institores, 200 B.C.–A.D. 250* (Leiden: Brill, 1994); de Ligt, "Legal History" (n. 3): 205–26; Zwalve, "Callistus's Case" (n. 3): 116–27; Alfons Bürge, "§ 101 Klage aufgrund Weisung des Gewalthabers (actio quod iussu)," in *Handbuch des Römischen Privatrechts*, ed. Ulrike Babusiaux et al. (Tübingen: Mohr Siebeck, 2023); Alfons Bürge, "§ 104 Klagen aufgrund Bestellung eines Geschäftsleiters oder Kapitäns (actio institoria, actio exercitoria)," in *Handbuch des Römischen Privatrechts*, ed. Ulrike Babusiaux et al. (Tübingen: Mohr Siebeck, 2023). A different regime applied regarding the part of a *peculium* that a slave employed for commerce with his master's knowledge (*merx peculiaris*) under the *actio tributoria*; see Richard Gamauf, "§ 103. Klage wegen Verteilung (actio tributoria)," in *Handbuch des Römischen Privatrechts*, ed. Ulrike Babusiaux et al. (Tübingen: Mohr Siebeck, 2023).

47 See below after n. 164.

48 Reinhard Zimmermann, *The Law of Obligations: Roman Foundations of the Civilian Tradition* (Oxford: Oxford University Press, 1996): 45–54.

adapted to refer to the *peculium*.[49] The claimant then had to prove: (1) a transaction with a slave in the defendant's power that (2) would have grounded a valid claim had the transaction been concluded with a free person instead of the slave; and (3) a sufficient balance in the *peculium* to meet the claim at the time of judgment. He did not need to demonstrate the master's prior or subsequent knowledge or consent for the transaction. On the other side, the master could not escape responsibility *de peculio* by prohibiting third parties from contracting with slaves to whom he had granted *peculia*.[50]

Consequently, the debts (and potential losses) of a slave that his master might be liable to meet never grew to unexpected amounts. Irrespective of the total 'debt', and of the number of creditors of a slave, a master would never ultimately be liable for more than the money value of the *peculium* / *dumtaxat de peculio*[51] (after settling intra-household debts as a priority creditor), unless the master had immediately made, and retained, a gain from the underlying transaction. Thus, the inexperience, negligence, or even malice of slaves never cost the master more than the value of goods in the *peculium* he had conceded; the slave and the *peculium* constituted a limited liability trading vehicle.

4 Of Persons and Things, and a Moral Reckoning

One purpose of the law is to bring into order into the world by reducing its many facets to a few manageable categories.[52] Something of that kind was probably the Roman jurist Gaius's aim when, around 161 CE, he taught the basics of the law of persons:

> D. 1.5.3 (= Gaius Inst. 1.9): Summa itaque de iure personarum divisio haec est, quod omnes homines aut liberi sunt aut servi.

> D. 1.5.3 (Gaius, Institutes, book 1): Certainly, the great divide in the law of persons is this: all men are either free men or slaves.[53]

This *divisio* / classification was intended to be all-encompassing. It excluded a person partly free and partly slave; it left no room for the statuses between free and unfree that other legal orders accepted, even though slavery was based on *ius gentium*[54] and

49 The *intentio* of the *formula* named the slave as buyer and ordered the judge to treat him 'as if he were free' / *si liber esset*. According to the *condemnatio*, the master had to pay not more than the *peculium*'s value; details in Gamauf, "Klage aufgrund Sonderguts" (n. 3): nos. 1–2.

50 D. 14.3.17.1, 4 (Paul. 30 ad ed.); D. 15.1.29.1 (Gai. 9 ed. prov.); D. 15.1.47 pr. (Paul. 4 Plaut.).

51 See above after n. 14.

52 Hans Kelsen, *Reine Rechtslehre*, 2nd ed. (Vienna: Franz Deuticke, 1960): 3–4.

53 Transl. MacCormack in Watson, *Digest of Justinian* (n. 2).

54 D. 1.1.4 (Ulp. 1 inst.); D. 1.5.4.1 (Flor. 9 inst.).

not a uniquely Roman institution.[55] In Gaius's opinion, this clear-cut Roman concept embraced *omnes homines*.

All the same, the Roman jurists coped quite well with a more complicated and irregular world. Papinian noted (surprisingly casually, as if not worth mentioning at all) that free persons were sold and bought as slaves almost daily. His pupil Paul explained that this happened because it was hard to tell the difference between free persons and slaves.[56] The confusion of the real world sometimes blurred the clear-cut dichotomy of the *summa divisio de iure personarum*; in an extreme case (however exceptional), a slave might even serve as *praetor*.[57]

Some legal and non-legal sources likewise create the impression that the *summa divisio* into freemen and slaves had a counterpart in property law. There, however, the difference was not categorical but merely terminological. Two generations after Gaius, Ulpian advised how to label property correctly in relation to the holder's status:[58]

D. 50.16.182 (Ulpian 27 ad ed.): Pater familias liber 'peculium' non potest habere, quemadmodum nec servus 'bona'.	D. 50.16.182 (Ulpian, Edict, book 27): The head of the household who is free cannot have a peculium, just as a slave cannot have "property".[59]

Bona (or *patrimonium*) was the proper term for goods held by a free *pater familias*; *peculium* was only appropriate for slaves. Accordingly, a *pater familias* should never speak of 'my *peculium*'. The reason to stress this terminological point in a commentary on the *edictum de pecunia constituta* (a promise to pay an existing debt) remains unknown. A common use of *peculium* that often ignored this difference probably prompted problems of interpretation similar to those connected with wills.[60] For the purposes of D. 50.16 (*De verborum significatione* / The meaning of expressions; transl. Michael Crawford), the compilers truncated the snippet of Ulpian's commentary to make it look like a definition – omitting the underlying

55 D. 40.12.9.2 (Gai. ed. praet. urb.); D. 40.5.31.1 (Paul. 3 fideic.); D. 40.12.30 (Iul. 5 Min.); literature in Gamauf, "Sklaven (servi)" (n. 5): n. 2.

56 D. 41.3.44 pr. (Papinian 23 quaest.) [. . .] *propter adsiduam et cottidianam comparationem servorum* [. . .] *nam frequenter ignorantia liberos emimus* [. . .] / Papinian, Questions, book 23: '[. . .] by reason of the regular, daily traffic in slaves [. . .] we frequently in ignorance buy freemen [. . .]' (transl. Thomas in Watson, *Digest of Justinian* [n. 2]); D. 18.1.5 (Paulus 5 Sab.) *Quia difficile dinosci potest liber homo a servo* / Paul, Sabinus, book 5: 'Because it can be difficult to distinguish a freeman from a slave' (transl. Thomas in Watson, *Digest of Justinian* [n. 2]).

57 D. 1.14.3 (Ulp. 38 Sab.); Rolf Knütel, "Barbatius Philippus," in *Handwörterbuch der Antiken Sklaverei*, vol. 1, ed. Heinz Heinen et al. (Stuttgart: Franz Steiner Verlag, 2017): 342–44.

58 Cf. Generoso Melillo, *Categorie economiche nei giuristi romani* (Naples: Jovene, 2000): 77–93; for more literature, see Gamauf, "Klage aufgrund Sonderguts" (n. 3): n. 15 nos. 84–85.

59 Transl. Crawford in Watson, *Digest of Justinian* (n. 2).

60 See below after n. 73.

reason, i.e. that only free persons could technically own an estate, whereas slaves could only be said to hold a *peculium*. Jurists regarded the term *peculium* as applicable solely to goods administered by slaves. The same Digest title preserves a supplementary 'definition' of *bona*:[61]

D. 50.16.49 (Ulpian 59 ad ed.): 'Bonorum' appellatio aut naturalis aut civilis est. naturaliter bona ex eo dicuntur, quod beant, hoc est beatos faciunt: beare est prodesse. in bonis autem nostris computari sciendum est non solum, quae dominii nostri sunt, sed et si bona fide a nobis possideantur vel superficiaria sint. aeque bonis adnumerabitur etiam, si quid est in actionibus petitionibus persecutionibus: nam haec omnia in bonis esse videntur.

D. 50.16.49 (Ulpian, Edict, book 59): The designation "goods" can be either natural or prescribed by the civil law. The natural designation of goods derives from the fact that they beatify, that is, they make people happy; to beatify is to benefit. The designation of goods under the civil law consists of those things which form part of our patrimony. One must realize that among our goods must be reckoned not only those things in the case of which we have ownership but also any goods which are held by us in trust or which are superficiary. Among our goods will equally be reckoned also anything which is subject to actions, petitions, or claims; for all these things seem to form part of our goods.[62]

Ulpian contrasts the wider meaning of the term *bona* with *dominium* / ownership. In addition to items owned, *bona* also encompassed things possessed in good faith (by a person erroneously believing he owned them),[63] plus various kinds of actionable claims.

61 Cf. Ulrike Babusiaux, "Funktionen der Etymologie in der juristischen Literatur," *Fundamina: A Journal of Legal History* 20, no. 1 (2014): 56.

62 Transl. Crawford in Watson, *Digest of Justinian* (n. 2).

63 Michael Crawford's translation of *et si bona fide a nobis possideantur* with 'held by us in trust' does not make that clear. For the details, see Eric Pool, "Lateinische Syntax und juristische Begriffsbildung: In bonis 'alicuius' esse und bonitarisches Eigentum im klassischen römischen Recht," *Zeitschrift der Savigny-Stiftung für Rechtsgeschichte, Romanistische Abteilung* 102 (1985): 481; Hans Ankum, Marjolijn van Gessel-de Roo and Eric Pool, "Die verschiedenen Bedeutungen des Ausdrucks in bonis alicuius esse/in bonis habere im klassischen römischen Recht (I)," *Zeitschrift der Savigny-Stiftung für Rechtsgeschichte, Romanistische Abteilung* 107 (1990): 293–96, 331–32, 347–48; Hans Ankum, Marjolijn van Gessel-de Roo and Eric Pool, "Die verschiedenen Bedeutungen des Ausdrucks in bonis alicuius esse/in bonis habere im klassischen römischen Recht (III)," *Zeitschrift der Savigny-Stiftung für Rechtsgeschichte, Romanistische Abteilung* 107 (1990): 203–96, 212–13; the interpretation advocated by Alfred Söllner, "Bona Fides – Guter Glaube," *Zeitschrift der Savigny-Stiftung für Rechtsgeschichte, Romanistische Abteilung* 122 (2005): 34–35 seems too narrowly technical.

Ulpian explains the term extensively: he resorts to the word's 'natural' meaning, i.e., to serve the 'pursuit of happiness'.[64] Linking *bona* to *beare* / make happy seems etymologically far-fetched,[65] but Ulpian does not seek to make a point about language. The *summa divisio* of humans into free persons and slaves necessitated adapting property terminology to status: as a result, *bona* was the property of a holder *sui iuris* and *peculium* that of a slave.

Digest 50.16.49 (Ulp. 59 ed.) adds an economic and moral varnish to the term *bona*: a thing causes 'happiness' primarily by virtue of its qualities; the holder's legal status is prima facie irrelevant. By looking to the 'natural meaning' of *bona*, Ulpian connects that term for property to Roman ideas about natural law (*ius naturale*) and a hypothetical state of nature. The Romans assumed that, during the so-called Golden Age, neither laws[66] nor ownership nor slavery existed.[67] Originally – before the *summa divisio* had come into being – a thing had inherent potential to make all people equally happy. Therefore, because of its 'natural meaning', *bona* in theory seemed a fitting term for property in relation to *omnes homines*. Ulpian's world, however, was one where *liberi* and *servi* (co-)existed. The exclusive enjoyment of a thing and gaining 'happiness' from it required the protection of law. Legal protection, however, depended on the holder's legal status. Accordingly, slaves were excluded from a relationship with *bona*; instead of having legally protected interests in property, they were reduced to having *peculia* that masters could revoke at will,.[68]

In his early seventh-century encyclopaedia, Isidore of Seville added a further moral element to the discourse correlating socio-legal status and correct property terminology:

Isid. etym. 5.25.4–5: (4) Bona sunt honestorum seu nobilium, quae proinde bona dicuntur, ut non habeant turpem usum, sed ea homines ad res bonas utantur. (5) Peculium proprie minorum est personarum sive servorum. nam peculium est quod pater vel dominus filium suum vel servum pro suo tractare patitur [. . .]

Isid. etym. 5.25.4–5 (4) Goods are the possessions of honourable or noble people, and they are called "goods" (bona) for that reason, because they have no base use, but people make use of them for good (bonus) purposes. (5) A peculium, properly speaking, relates to younger persons or slaves, for a peculium is something that a father allows his son, or a master his slave, to handle as his own [. . .][69]

64 For the relationship between ownership and 'the pursuit of happiness' in the US Declaration of Independence, see, e.g., Carli N. Conklin, *The Pursuit of Happiness in the Founding Era. An Intellectual History* (Missouri: University of Missouri, 2019).

65 Cf. de Vaan, *Etymological Dictionary* (n. 33): s.v. beō -āre, bonus.

66 Ovid Met. 1.89–94 and 127–31.

67 D. 1.1.4 (Ulp. 1 inst.); D. 1.5.4 (Flor. 9 inst. = Inst. 1.3.1–3); D. 40.11.2 (Marcian. 1 inst.); D. 50.17.32 (Ulp. 43 Sab.); D. 12.6.64 (Tryph. 7 disp.); Gamauf, "Sklaven (servi)" (n. 5): n. 7.

68 See below at n. 151.

69 Transl. Stephen A. Barney, W.J. Lewis, J.A. Beach and Oliver Berghof, eds., *The Etymologies of Isidore of Seville* (Cambridge: Cambridge University Press, 2006): 121.

Isidore derived the term *bona* from a moral evaluation of the possible uses of things. In the case of persons of superior rank, good and non-reprehensible usage could be expected, and that made the term *bona* appropriate. He contrasted *bona* with *peculium*, which for him signified property in the hands of lesser people or slaves. The logic he applied to *bona* would require explaining *peculium* based on the humbler usages of property held by lower-ranking persons or slaves. Such an etymology, however, did not exist. Instead, Isidore invoked the legal meaning of *peculium* and clarified that *minores* meant persons of lesser age, not lower social standing.[70]

Ulpian repeatedly called for precision, to avoid misunderstandings arising from the non-technical everyday usage of *peculium*. In part, the problem originated with jurists themselves: they sought to confine *peculium* to property held by *personae alieni iuris*, and to keep it distinct from *bona* / *patrimonium*, because indiscriminate usage would render statements including the term *peculium* ambiguous, unless the holder's status was also known.

Ironically enough, the 'abuse' of language is nowhere better documented than in Justinian's Digest, because jurists found it offensive, and Ulpian repeatedly repudiated it. Ulpian himself offers the clearest surviving example in his commentary on the *actio de peculio*, in a text preceding Tubero's highly technical definition of *peculium* (D. 15.1.5.4 Ulp. 29 ad ed.):[71]

D. 15.1.5.3 (Ulpian 29 ad ed.) Peculium dictum est quasi pusilla pecunia sive patrimonium pusillum.	D. 15.1.5.3 (Ulpian, Edict, book 29) A peculium is called so because of the picayune nature of the money or property in it.[72]

In context, this was originally perhaps no more than a reminder that legal *peculia* might often contain much more[73] than the minor assets (*pusilla pecunia*[74]) which everyday usage associated with *peculium*. In a different context, Ulpian criticised

70 *Minores* was misleading, because it was not age but *patria potestas* that reduced children-in-power during their father's lifetime to holding *peculia*; on the age at which slaves started having *peculia*, cf. Gamauf, "Klage aufgrund Sonderguts" (n. 3): n. 17, n. 104.

71 See above after n. 12.

72 Transl. Weir in Watson, *Digest of Justinian* (n. 2).

73 D. 15.1.7.4 (Ulp. 29 ad ed.).

74 On *pusillus*, see Richard Gamauf, "Ideal Freedmen-Lives? On the Construction of Biographies in the Cena Trimalchionis," in *Le realtà della schiavitù: Identità e biografie da Eumeo a Frederick Douglass. Les réalités de l'esclavage: Identités et biographies d'Eumée à Frederick Douglass. Atti del XL Convegno internazionale del GIREA (Napoli, 18–20 dicembre 2017)*, ed. Francesca Reduzzi Merola, Maria Vittoria Bramante and Adelaide Caravaglios (Naples: Satura Editrice, 2020): 289–90.

how many people (*plerique*) referred to their estates (in testaments) incorrectly as *peculia* instead of *patrimonia*:

D. 36.1.17 pr. (Ulpian 4 fideic.): [. . .] et si 'peculium meum' testator dixerit, quia plerique ὑποκοριστικῶς patrimonium suum peculium dicunt [. . .]

D. 36.1.17 pr. (Ulpian, Fideicommissa, book 4): [. . .] and should the testator have said "my peculium", since most people use the word peculium as a diminutive for their patrimony [. . .][75]

Such false modesty on the part of a testator created problems, given the narrow interpretation of *peculium* by the legal profession. According to Ulpian's strict criteria, an expression like *peculium meum* in a testament was devoid of content. The narrow notion of *peculium* in legalese provided only a pretext to challenge the validity of a *fideicommissum* containing words like 'my *peculium*'.[76] Applying the jurists' terminological yardstick, the testator, as a free person, could rightfully call nothing in his estate by that term. But in order to respect the clear intentions in such a case, jurists, despite their linguistic misgivings, accepted the testator's carelessly chosen words as effective.[77]

A real-life example of one of those *plerique* was the imperial freedman Publius Aelius Onesimus, who died during Hadrian's reign and bequeathed the substantial sum of 200,000 *sesterces*[78] to his hometown.[79] Self-confidently, he recorded his benevolence and parts of his testament in an inscription. Its wording exemplifies the objectionable style criticised by Ulpian. Publius blamed 'the mediocrity of his tiny *peculium*' (*pro mediocritate tamen peculioli mei*) for not leaving as much as he owed (*quamvis plurimum debeam*) to his most beloved hometown (*amatissima patria*). This statement of a freedman might still echo a façon-de-parler of his slave days,

75 Transl. Barton in Watson, *Digest of Justinian* (n. 2).

76 *Peculium meum* is unique; regarding slave-*peculium*, legal texts represent masters' perspectives and commonly call it *peculium suum*. Contexts include: payments for freedom D. 24.1.9.1 (Ulp. 32 Sab.); D. 35.1.57 (Pomp. 9 Q. Muc.); C. 7.11.2 (Alex., undated); legacy or *fideicommissum*: D. 15.1.18 (Paul. 4 quaest.); D. 33.8.8.2 (Ulp. 25 Sab.); D. 33.8.14 (Alf. 5 dig.); D. 33.8.23 pr. (Scaev. 15 dig.); D. 40.1.6 (Alf. 4 dig.); D. 40.7.17 (Ner. 3 membr.); D. 40.7.40.3 (Scaev. 24 dig.); D. 33.8.6.3 (Ulp. 25 Sab.); and validity of other payments: D. 46.3.35 (Alf. 2 dig.); D. 46.3.84 (Proc. 7 epist.).

77 See Hans Wieling, *Testamentsauslegung im römischen Recht* (Munich: C.H. Beck, 1972): 140.

78 For comparison: from the reign of Commodus, legionnaries received an annual pay of 1,500 *sesterces*; cf. Kai Ruffing and Hans-Joachim Drexhage, "Antike Sklavenpreise," in *Antike Lebenswelten: Konstanz – Wandel – Wirkungsmacht: Festschrift für Ingomar Weiler zum 70. Geburtstag*, ed. Peter Mauritsch, Werner Petermandl, Robert Rollinger and Christoph Ulf (Wiesbaden: Harrassowitz, 2008): 341.

79 CIL III 6998 = CIL III 13652. Compare CIL VI 19175 *de mea pauperte* with the reference to an estate by *paupertas* in D. 36.1.80.12 (Scaev. 21 dig.). Thomas McGinn, "Celsus and the Pauper: Roman Private Law and the Socio-Economic Status of Its Consumers," in *Scritti per Alessandro Corbino*, vol. 4, ed. Isabella Piro (Tricase: Libellula, 2016): 631–33 thinks the testator was not poor but of modest means.

when *peculium* had been correct for 'his money'. Probably his wish to sound modest (which Ulpian identified as a reason for such locutions) followed a tendency of freedmen to downplay their actual wealth in inscriptions.[80]

Moreover, even people without discernible servile background used the term *peculium* for their property. Proculus, for instance, reported overhearing old peasants claiming in conversations that 'money without *peculium* was worthless'. This admonition always to keep some property safely hidden shows that country folk called such a nest egg *peculium*.[81]

An obvious choice in the search for the word in a non-legal context are Petronius's *Satyrica*. The *cena Trimalchionis* documents both freedmen life[82] and first-century CE vernacular Latin / *sermo vulgaris*.[83] The *Satyrica* mention *peculia* four times but never with reference to a slave's *peculium*, which some slaves in the *cena Trimalchionis* surely had.[84] Once, the Senate is ridiculed as miserly for an inappropriately small dedication to Jupiter, the size of a *peculium*. Twice, freedmen in the *cena* call their now substantial fortunes *peculia*.[85]

---

80 Gamauf, "Ideal Freedmen-Lives" (n. 74): 290.

81 D. 32.79.1 (Celsus 9 dig.): [. . .] *Proculus ait* [. . .] *et audisse se rusticos senes ita dicentes pecuniam sine peculio fragilem esse, peculium appellantes, quod praesidii causa seponeretur.* / Celsus, Digest, book 9: '[. . .] Proculus says [. . .] he had heard aged country folk saying that "no reliance could be placed on money without peculium", meaning by *peculium* what was put aside for safety' (transl. Braun in Watson, *Digest of Justinian* (n. 2). A comparable inscription of a *rusticus* and his *peculium* is: AE 1903,140; for further examples, cf. Johannes Platschek, "Das Nebengut der Ehefrau in D. 23.3.9.3 (Ulp. 31 Sab.): Quae Gaiae peculium appellantur," *Quaderni Lupiensi* 5 (2015): 131. When Trimalchio's business failed, his wife Fortunata sold her jewels and clothes, i.e., what would have been a slave's savings. With that kind of money, he finally became successful (Petron. 76.7); see Richard Gamauf, "De nihilo crevit – Freigelassenenmentalität und Pekuliarrecht," in *Der Bürge einst und jetzt: Festschrift für Alfons Bürge*, ed. Ulrike Babusiaux, Peter Nobel and Johannes Platschek (Zürich: Schulthess, 2017): 280–81.

82 See my paper on *dispensatores* in this volume, nn. 2 and 3.

83 On colloquialisms in the *cena*, cf. Martin S. Smith, ed., *Petronius: Cena Trimalchionis* (Oxford: Oxford University Press, 1975): 220–24, XX–XXI; Victoria Rimell, "Letting the Page Run On: Poetics, Rhetoric, and Noise in the Satyrica," in *Petronius: A Handbook*, ed. Jonathan R.W. Prag and Ian D. Repath (New York: Wiley-Blackwell, 2009): 65–67; Gareth L. Schmeling, *A Commentary on the Satyrica of Petronius* (Oxford: Oxford University Press, 2011): XXVI–XXIX.

84 Petron. 30.7–10, 53, 75.4.

85 Petron. 75.3, 76.8; cf. Gamauf, "De nihilo" (n. 81): 235. This can be understood as reminiscent of the slave language of their past, as, e.g., Edward Courtney, *A Companion to Petronius* (Oxford: Oxford University Press, 2001): 78, assumes. Using *peculium* for 'their money', however, was not the style of slaves but typically of masters (see at n. 181). Petronius probably showed how quickly former slaves switched code and referred to as *peculium* what before had been only *suum*. Now, besides *peculium*, former slaves could speak of *bona* or *patrimonium*, as well; there are no instances of slaves' using such terms for their property. On Petron. 43.5, see Gamauf, "Ideal Freedmen-Lives" (n. 74): 293 n. 109.

Most interestingly, however, is the first use of *peculium* in Petronius's text.[86] Ascyltos, one of the novel's protagonists, was lost on the way to his lodgings. A respectable *pater familiae* offered to help but then abducted the boy to a brothel and attempted to rape him. Petronius describes the assault by *prolatoque peculio coepit rogare stuprum* / and showing (holding out) a *peculium*, he asked for sex.

Here, *peculium* creates different double-entendres: *peculium* can stand for 'a little money' but also 'a penis'.[87] This double meaning unmasks the *pater familiae* as a social impostor, as well as a sexual predator. If a holder's morals and his purposes determined the correct term for his property (as Isidore or his sources reasoned), then *bona* was inappropriate here, for more than one reason. Such shameful ends excluded *bona* and left *peculium* as the alternative designation for money. The impression of a cultivated *pater familiae*[88] is displaced, leaving a slave (or a son-in-power) – or, in any case, a red-light-district regular – who fits into the *Satyrica*'s demimonde. The author skilfully reveals the rift between words and intentions in just one concept: *peculium*. *Peculio prolato* serves to deconstruct the figure of the *pater familiae humanissimus*. This was a joke for an audience fully aware of the semantic trapdoors of *peculium*, familiar with lawyers' jargon,[89] and expecting surprises and ambiguities.

86 Petron. 8.2–4: *At ille deficiens: Cum errarem, inquit, per totam civitatem nec invenirem quo loco stabulum reliquissem, accessit ad me pater familiae et ducem se itineris humanissime promisit. per anfractus deinde obscurissimos egressus in hunc locum me perduxit, prolatoque peculio coepit rogare stuprum* [. . .] / 'He faltered affectingly and said, "I was wandering all over the city and couldn't figure out where I'd left our silly lodging. But then a fatherly type came up to me and offered himself – with a torrent of kind words – as a guide. He led me through the darkest twists and turns and finally to this place, where he took out some cash and proposed an assault on my virtue. [. . .]"' (transl. Sarah Ruden, *Petronius: Satyricon* (Indianapolis: Hackett Publishing, 2000): 6).
87 Schmeling, *A Commentary* (n. 83): 27; Natalie Breitenstein, *Petronius: 'Satyrica 1–15': Text, Übersetzung, Kommentar* (Berlin: De Gruyter, 2009): 111–12. Translations usually miss this point; an exception is the recent German translation by Niklas Holzberg, *Petronius Arbiter: Satyrische Geschichten* (Berlin: Akademie-Verlag, 2013): 19: 'zog sein teures Ding raus'.
88 Breitenstein, *Petronius* (n. 87): 111.
89 In this, Petronius's approach is similar to that of his contemporary C. Cassius, who used the word *patrimonium* for a slave's money in a pun with very cruel consequences; see below after n. 182.

5 Speaking About Law to Non-Lawyers, or, Was *peculium* the *patrimonium* of a Slave?

In contrast to his approach to *bona*, Isidore's definition of *peculium* avoided moral undertones. Etymology led him back, as in the case of *pecunia* / money, to *pecu(s)* / flock, herd:[90]

Isid. etym. 5.25.5: Peculium proprie minorum est personarum sive servorum. nam peculium est quod pater vel dominus filium suum vel servum pro suo tractare patitur. peculium autem a pecudibus dictum, in quibus veterum constabat universa substantia.	Isid. etym. 5.25.5: A peculium, properly speaking, relates to younger persons or slaves, for a peculium is something that a father allows his son, or a master his slave, to handle as his own. And it is called peculium from "livestock" (pecus), of which all the wealth of the ancients consisted.[91]

According to Isidore, properly / *proprie*, the word referred to property of slaves and sons-in-power[92] alone. The characteristic of such property was that persons *alieni iuris* could treat it as their own / *pro suo tractare* (one manuscript even has *suo iure tractare* / according to one's own right, in this passage[93]). He did not unveil the reasons (the incapacity of *personae alieni iuris* to own) and likewise ignored most of what D. 15.1.5.4 (Ulp. 29 ad ed.) listed as the essential prerequisites of a *peculium* for the purposes of an *actio de peculio* (book-keeping, domestic claims etc.). Isidore writes here not as a lawyer but as someone more familiar with the perspective of the holder of a *peculium*.

Nevertheless, to fully appreciate what Isidore was discussing, his audience required prior knowledge of matters he left unmentioned: the existence of a broader (but legally improper) everyday use of the word; and the restriction of *peculia* to *personae alieni iuris*, whom the Roman jurists regularly characterised as unable 'to have something of their own' (*nihil suum habere posse*).[94] Isidore's seventh-century Visigothic contemporaries were hardly familiar with this background. The omissions likely reflect the intellectual horizon of the original addressees of his sources, legally trained readers of the works of the classical jurists.[95] The lexicographer surely drew on writings that, like Ulpian's, advocated adhering to the technically

90 de Vaan, *Etymological Dictionary* (n. 33): s.v. pecu.

91 Transl. Barney, Lewsi, Beach and Berghof, *Etymologies* (n. 69): 120.

92 On the capacity of children-in-power to have property in post-classical law, cf. Max Kaser, *Das römische Privatrecht*, vol. 2, *Die nachklassischen Entwicklungen* (Munich: C.H. Beck, 1975): 214–19.

93 Buti, *Studi* (n. 38): 14 n. 3.

94 See below n. 182.

95 For Isidore and his sources, cf. Franz Wieacker, *Römische Rechtsgeschichte: Quellenkunde, Rechtsbildung, Jurisprudenz und Rechtsliteratur*, vol. 1, *Einleitung, Quellenkunde, Frühzeit und Republik* (Munich: C.H. Beck, 1988): 103 n. 117; Leopold Wenger, *Die Quellen des römischen Rechts* (Vienna: Holzhausen, 1953): 213.

precise meaning of *peculium*, instead of using the term synonymously with *patrimonium pusillum* / tiny patrimony,[96] or patrimony in general.[97] Closest to Isidore's approach among legal writers was the late classical jurist Florentinus:

D. 15.1.39 (Florentinus 11 inst.): Peculium et ex eo consistit, quod parsimonia sua quis paravit vel officio meruerit a quolibet sibi donari idque velut proprium patrimonium servum suum habere quis voluerit.	D. 15.1.39 (Florentinus, Institutes, book 11): A peculium is made up of anything a slave has been able to save by his own economies or has been allowed by a third party in return for meritorious services or has been allowed by his master to keep as his own.[98]

Florentinus's analysis differed fundamentally from Tubero's and Ulpian's concept in D. 15.3.3.4 (Ulp. 29 ad ed.). In D. 15.1 *De peculio*, his text appears amidst a discussion of the *actio de peculio*. The topic of the eleventh book of Florentinus's Institutes, however, was the law of bequests / *de legatis*.[99] In an *actio de peculio*, a judge had to establish the *peculium*'s abstract value, a limit of a master's liability for his slave's debts. In a bequest (or *fideicommissum*[100]) of *peculium*, the heir was not asked to pay a sum of money but to hand over to the *libertus* 'his *peculium*'[101] in its entirety – for example, a workshop complete with implements, slave personnel, stock etc. Florentinus therefore guided a judge to identify which of the goods administered by the slave at the time of his master's demise had been in 'his *peculium*'.[102]

This precision was necessary because not everything that a master allowed his slave to use formed part of the *peculium*. For example, items could also be 'loaned' or 'leased' to the slave who would be able to use them without thereby increasing the master's maximum liability *de peculio*.[103] Just as free borrowers or tenants did not own property transferred to them under those contracts, slaves in comparable situations could not treat such property 'as their own'; consequently, it was not included in the *peculium*.

Florentinus's sociological approach facilitated the identification of items prima facie belonging to a *peculium*. He started with what, from a servile point view, was

96 D. 15.1.5.3 (Ulp. 29 ad ed.).
97 D. 36.1.17 pr. (Ulp. 4 fideic.).
98 Transl. Weir in Watson, *Digest of Justinian* (n. 2).
99 Otto Lenel, *Palingenesia iuris civilis*, vol. 1 (Leipzig: Bernhard Tauchnitz, 1889): 178.
100 On which cf. Nicholas, *Introduction* (n. 45): 267–68.
101 E.g., D. 15.1.18 (Paul. 4 quaest.); D. 33.8.8.2 (Ulp. 25 Sab.); D. 33.8.14 (Alf. 5 dig.); D. 33.8.23 pr. (Scaev. 15 dig.); D. 40.1.6 (Alf. 4 dig.); D. 40.7.40.3 (Scaev. 24 dig.).
102 This was essential in such a case, even though the physical transfer of goods was not enforceable and the verdict specified a sum of money only.
103 D. 15.1.16 (Iul. 12 dig.); D. 15.3.16 (Alf. 2 dig.); D. 40.7.14 pr. (Alf. 4 dig.); Colum. 11.1.24; cf. Buti, *Studi* (n. 38): 29–30; Andreas Wacke, "Faktische Arbeitsverhältnisse im Römischen Recht? Zur sogenannten 'notwendigen Entgeltlichkeit', besonders bei Arbeitsleistungen vermeintlicher Sklaven," *Zeitschrift der Savigny-Stiftung für Rechtsgeschichte, Romanistische Abteilung* 108 (1991): 134–35.

typically and undeniably *peculium*: property not given by the master but acquired by the slave himself through saving rations, and from tips or rewards for extra services etc.[104] If a master (or a supervising slave[105]) intentionally left 'acquisitions' from such sources with slaves, a *peculium*, a pool of assets functioning as their 'own property' / *proprium patrimonium*, came into being.[106] It is hardly surprising that, niceties of the law aside, both sides – slaves as well as masters – unhesitatingly accepted that certain assets somehow 'belonged' to slaves.

Such a view filters through in Ulpian's struggle with the terminological inconsistencies of *servus sui nummis emptus* / a slave bought with his own cash. In such a transaction, a slave gave money from his *peculium* to a so-called *redemptor*, by whom he would be purchased and then manumitted.

D. 40.1.4.1 (Ulpian 6 disp.): Et primo quidem nummis suis non proprie videtur emptus dici, cum suos nummos servus habere non possit: verum coniventibus oculis credendum est suis nummis eum redemptum, cum non nummis eius, qui eum redemit, comparatur. proinde sive ex peculio, quod ad venditorem pertinet, sive ex adventicio lucro, sive etiam amici beneficio vel liberalitate vel prorogante eo vel repromittente vel se delegante vel in se recipiente debitum redemptus sit, credendum est suis nummis eum redemptum: satis est enim, quod is, qui emptioni suum nomen accommodaverit, nihil de suo inpendit.

D. 40.1.4.1 (Ulpian, Disputations, book 6): Now at first sight the expression "purchased with his own cash" seems improper, since a slave cannot have cash of his own; but we are to close our eyes and suppose him to have been bought with his own cash, when it is not the cash of the purchaser which is used to pay the price. So then whether he has been purchased with his peculium, which belongs by right to the vendor, or from profit obtained by chance, or by the kindness or generosity of a friend, or by the slave's carrying a charge to his own account, or giving an undertaking, or accepting a liability or the obligation to pay a debt, we are to suppose that he was purchased with his own cash; it is enough that the nominal purchaser laid out no money of his own.[107]

Given the legal implications of such cases, Ulpian's terminological objection – that one could not properly / *non proprie*[108] say that a slave had his own cash / *suos nummos servus habere non possit* – seems of minor importance. Ulpian, however, claimed to suffer almost physically from such abuse of language.[109] Nevertheless,

---

104 Peter P. Spranger, *Historische Untersuchungen zu den Sklavenfiguren des Plautus und Terenz*, 2nd. ed. (Stuttgart: Franz Steiner Verlag, 1984): 67–69; Gamauf, "De nihilo" (n. 81): 239–43.
105 D. 15.1.4.6 (Pomp. 7 Sab.); D. 15.1.6 (Cels. 6 dig.); Francesca Reduzzi Merola, *'Servo parere': Studi sulla condizione giuridica degli schiavi vicari e dei sottoposti a schiavi nelle esperienze greca e romana* (Naples: Jovene, 1990): 68–75.
106 D. 15.1.3.4 (Ulp. 29 ad ed.); D. 15.1.7.1 (Ulp. 29 ad ed.); D. 15.1.49 pr. (Pomp. 4 Q. Muc.).
107 Transl. Brunt in Watson, *Digest of Justinian* (n. 2).
108 Cf. similar wording in Isid. etym. 5.25.4.
109 Ulpian termed it abuse in D. 15.1.41 pr. (Ulp. 43 Sab.); comparably worded is D. 46.1.16.4 (Iul. 43 dig.); for which cf. Gamauf, "Slaves Doing Business" (n. 16): 333.

his discussion of the term *sui nummi* – legally meaningless in relation to a slave – is highly revealing. He showed that masters did perceive items in a *peculium* in different ways. Ulpian discerned two types of property: one he called *peculium* belonging to the seller / *quod ad venditorem pertinet*; the other consisted of money gained by the slave in business with persons other than the master (*adventicio lucro*)[110] or from gifts by extraneous persons. This distinction was not drawn for the benefit of the terminologically hypersensitive: legally, the source made no difference and, technically, all of the assets belonged to the seller / *ad venditorem pertinet*. All the same, not even Ulpian, with his declared preference for terminological clarity, could ignore the different social perception attaching to goods acquired for the slave's *peculium* in different ways.

On the one hand, there was property acquired by the slave – *patrimonium servi*; on the other, there was capital from the master's 'own' coffers, invested to enlarge the slave's 'own' *pusilla pecunia* / *peculium*, according to the needs of his enterprise. (An investment made, as with any investor, with a view to profit.) The master intended to retain the capital component in the event of alienation (hence the characterisation *ad venditorem pertinet* in D. 40.1.4.1 Ulp. 6 disp.) or manumission *inter vivos*,[111] while the rest of the *peculium* followed the slave.[112]

---

110 Technically, *adventicius* was property in a *peculium* not coming from the master; cf. Hermann Gottlieb Heumann and E. Seckel, *Handlexikon zu den Quellen des römischen Rechts*, 11th ed. (Graz: Akademische Druck- und Verlagsanstalt, 1971): 20; Adolf Berger, *Encyclopedic Dictionary of Roman Law* (Philadelphia: American Philosophical Society, 1953): 352. The *ius commune* distinguished, as with dowries, between *peculium adventicium* and *peculium profecticium*; see Hans-Georg Knothe, "Das gemeine Kindesvermögensrecht: Zur Anwendung römischer Rechtsquellen unter gewandelten Familienstrukturen und Berufsbildern," *Zeitschrift der Savigny-Stiftung für Rechtsgeschichte, Romanistische Abteilung* 98 (1981): 255–302.

111 Because of the limited liability it entailed, some treat *peculium* as a forerunner of modern capital companies (see the literature in Gamauf, "Klage aufgrund Sonderguts" (n. 3): n. 13). As a type of enterprise, *peculium* most likely resembled modern sole-trader businesses. The person of the holder was essential for success; cf. Gamauf, "De nihilo" (n. 81): 227–30. Therefore, keeping a *peculium* after sale or a manumission of the slave made little sense; without the holder as its 'soul', *peculium* could be worthless; it was not a structure – an organisation independent of the holder – like a modern firm, in which the leadership might be changed. The jurists' standard example for a slave whose value depended on his personal skills was a painter: e.g., D. 9.2.23.3 (Ulp. 18 ed.). It was quite natural that he kept his tools, which were worthless without his talent, when he was manumitted (D. 33.7.17 Marcian. 7 inst.; PS 3.6.63). The same may have held true for other artisans (see also above at n. 150) or whenever a business depended on the personality of the person running it. This could explain why a *peculium* was regarded the accessory of a slave even when he was worth less than it was; see D. 21.1.44 pr. (Paul. 2 ed. aedil. curul.) [. . .] *nam et plerumque plus in peculio est quam in servo, et nonnumquam vicarius qui accedit pluris est quam is servus qui venit.* / Paul, Curule Aediles' Edict, book 2: '[. . .] For it may often be that his *peculium* is worth more than the slave himself and sometimes the *vicarius*, who goes with him, is worth more than the slave actually being sold' (transl. Thomas in Watson, *Digest of Justinian* (n. 2).

112 On such cases, see in Gamauf, "Klage aufgrund Sonderguts" (n. 3): n. 15.

In his approach to property that was incorrectly but commonly referred to as *sui nummi*, Ulpian did not substantially differ from Florentinus's treatment of the case of *legatum peculii*. In both situations, the objective was to identify which property counted as '*patrimonium servi*'; in the case of *suis nummis emere*, this denoted assets that the slave might use to purchase his freedom.

The terminology at the conclusion of the passage is noteworthy: Ulpian demanded that the *redemptor* use none of his own money: *nihil de suo impendit*. When slaves paid for something with 'their own money', they expressed this in inscriptions by *de suo* or *sua pecunia*.[113] However, Ulpian was confronting a situation for which jurists lacked a better, more technically apposite terminology. *Patrimonium*, *bona* and even *peculium* were useless, because, legally, the 'slave's money' belonged to the *redemptor*. At the same time, however, it was not *suum* in the way that property in a *peculium* was *suum* for a slave. This was a manner of speaking about property distinct from that of the jurists; property was not classified in accordance with personal status but rather by its origin or the purpose for which it was intended.

6 Minima on the Development of *peculium*

Here follows not an attempt at a history of slave *peculium* but, rather, a few observations. The Romans saw in *peculium* an ancient institution. According to Livy 2.41.10, *peculia* of sons-in-power were at least as old as the Republic. The *peculium* of slaves, too, long predated the *actio de peculio*. Its earliest trace (though dubious in some details) is the claim that the XII Tables protected *statuliberi* (slaves freed subject to a condition) in the case of alienation:

Ulpian epit. 2.4: Sub hac condicione liber esse iussus: 'si decem milia heredi dederit' etsi ab herede abalienatus sit, emptori dando pecuniam ad libertatem perveniet; idque lex duodecim tabularum iubet.	Ulpian epit. 2.4: If someone was ordered to be free under the condition "if he will give ten thousand to the heir", and the heir sells him, he will attain freedom by giving the money to the buyer. So orders the law of the XII Tables.

A *statuliber* was a slave freed in a will upon condition of, for example, paying a certain sum to the heir.[114] As in the case of *suis nummis emere*, the slave became free upon payment – in this instance, even against the will of his master, because of the testator's order. The provision protected a slave sold by an heir so that the

113 See below n. 136.
114 Alan Watson, *The Law of Persons in the Later Roman Republic* (Oxford: Oxford University Press, 1967): 201–17; Gamauf, "Klage aufgrund Sonderguts" (n. 3): n. 10; Gamauf, "Sklaven (servi)" (n. 5): n. 71.

latter could retain his full value (it is likely that the sum specified in the will was usually lower). Following such a sale, the slave would nevertheless be free if he paid the original sum to his buyer. It is hardly credible that this was the position in Rome in the fifth century BCE.[115] What is certain, however, is that, for the unknown author of the *epitome Ulpiani*, the situation was commonplace, and he could not imagine that the early beginnings of the *ius civile* were any different.

No inquiry into the development of *peculium* can bypass the last part of Isidore's definition, which explicitly addresses the origins of the institution:

Isid. etym. 5.25.5: [. . .] Peculium autem a pecudibus dictum, in quibus veterum constabat universa substantia.	Isid. etym. 5.25.5: [. . .] And it is called peculium from "livestock" (pecus), of which all the wealth of the ancients consisted.[116]

It is only a small etymological step from *peculium* back to *pecus.*[117] In his claim that the earliest *peculia* consisted of livestock, Isidore followed the example of agricultural writers;[118] as an idea, this seems as natural today as it did in the seventh century.[119] The agricultural writer Varro saw *peculium* as the permission accorded to slaves to graze cattle on their master's land:[120]

Varro rust. 1.2.17: [. . .] peculium, quibus domini dant ut pascant [. . .]	Varro rust. 1.2.17: [. . .] and the slaves' peculium, the grazing which their master allows them [. . .]
1.17.7: Studiosiores ad opus fieri liberalius tractando aut cibariis aut vestitu largiore aut remissione operis concessioneve, ut peculiare aliquid in fundo pascere.	1.17.7: They are made to take more interest in their work by being treated more liberally, in respect either of food, or of more clothing, or of exemption from work, or of permission to graze some cattle of their own on the farm, or other things of this kind.
1.19.3: In hoc genere semivocalium adiciendum de pecore ea sola quae agri colendi causa erunt et quae solent esse peculiaria	1.19.3: Under this head of inarticulate equipment, it is to be added that of other animals only those are to be kept which are of service

115 No doubt regarding the authenticity oft he rule is expressed in Martin Avenarius, *Der pseudo-ulpianische liber singularis regularum: Entstehung, Eigenart und Überlieferung einer hochklassischen Juristenschrift: Analyse, Neuedition und deutsche Übersetzung: Quellen und Forschungen zum Recht und seiner Geschichte* (Göttingen: Wallstein Verlag, 2005): 208.
116 Transl. Barney, Lewis, Beach and Berghof, *Etymologies* (n. 69): 120.
117 See above at n. 90.
118 E.g., Fest. s.v. *peculium* (p. 290 Z. 34f. Lindsay) [. . .] *servorum peculium ex pecore item dictum est* [. . .] / 'slaves' *peculium* is also named after cattle [. . .]'.
119 See, e.g., Roth, "Food" (n. 8): 280; Żeber, *Study* (n. 3): 9–10; Gamauf, "Klage aufgrund Sonderguts" (n. 3): n. 10, n. 58.
120 Roth, "Food" (n. 8): 279–83.

pauca habenda quo facilius mancipia se tueri et assidua esse possint.

in agriculture, and the few which are usually allowed as the private property of the slaves for their more comfortable support and to make them more diligent in their work.[121]

For Varro, *peculium* (and similar terms) denoted animals raised by slaves and used by them for their own benefit.[122] By this concession, a landowner who primarily produced wine or oil for the market saved money when he let his slaves produce their own food on the side (ideally in their 'spare time'). Roman agricultural writers preached self-sufficiency, which meant producing as much as possible on the estate and purchasing as little as possible from outside.[123] Against this background, *peculia* facilitated more intensive exploitation of slaves without provoking resentment. The slaves' work for their own food (which saved the master expense) would be undertaken more willingly when the (extra) burden was accorded under the guise of a sort of privilege.[124] With intensive cultivation by a highly motivated workforce, comparatively small parcels of land could produce high yields (not least because slaves might divert effort from regular work into caring for their *peculia*).[125]

Peculium likely began to evolve when masters first allowed slaves to use land and keep the produce for themselves. This posed little risk of embezzlement or damage through neglect. Once this approach proved efficient, the grant came to include livestock as well. This was the first acknowledged 'property' of slaves (the question never arose in relation to the land), hence the term *peculium*. Both crops and animals were originally intended primarily to provide for the slaves' upkeep; later, surpluses allowed for barter or sale within and outside of the estate. If a master provided a slave with, for example, seed, on the understanding that it would be replaced after the harvest, this was like a '*mutuum*' / loan for consumption,[126] and a

121 Transl. William Davis Hooper and Harrison Boyd Ash, *Marcus Porcius Cato: On agriculture. Marcus Terrentius Varro: On agriculture* (Cambridge: Harvard University Press, 1935): 177, 227, 233.

122 For references to Roman sources and comparative material from American slavery, see Gamauf, "De nihilo" (n. 81): 240; additional parallels in Leslie Howard Owens, *This Species of Property: Slave Life and Culture in the Old South* (New York: Oxford University Press, 1976): 53–54, 65–66, 68 and Kenneth M. Stampp, *The Peculiar Institution: Slavery in the Ante-Bellum South* (New York: Vintage Books, 1956): 79, 103, 164–65.

123 Cato. agr. 2.7.

124 See also Roth, "Food" (n. 8): 282.

125 In Stalin's USSR after 1934, 10–12% of arable land was privately cultivated, producing almost two thirds of the marketed (!) produce; cf. David R. Shearer, "Stalinism, 1928–1940," in *The Cambridge History of Russia*, vol. 3, *The Twentieth Century*, ed. Ronald Grigor Suny (Cambridge: Cambridge University Press, 2006): 205–6. Owens, *This Species of Property* (n. 122): 68 summarises in relation to the US, 'It should be understood that the slave's private labours were not merely of supplementary benefit to the diet. They were often a vital part of his upkeep.'

126 Legal relationships between a master and his slaves were impossible. This was, however, the language used to describe such relationships in a Roman household; see also above n. 109.

'claim' against the *peculium* was entered into the books. Surpluses from the *peculium* were probably marketed at first by the master or a *vilicus* / steward, because agricultural writers strongly advised against allowing slaves to leave an estate, especially to attend markets.[127] Depending on the arrangement, the master or *vilicus* then 'owed' the slave from a 'sale' or 'mandate', and registered this, too, as a 'claim' in the accounts.[128] In the *actio de peculio*, such accounting claims increased the value of a *peculium* (in the case of claims against the master or another slave) or decreased it (in the case of claims against the slave). To understand the possible problems and solutions in such economic arrangements, it is helpful to compare experiences in the southern United States of America. Antebellum masters 'debited the slaves for items purchased for them during the year and made cash settlement at the end of the year'; in addition, they 'acted as bankers for their slaves and kept careful accounts in their plantation records'.[129] As texts on the *actio de peculio* show,[130] the internal structures of Roman households with slave *peculia* functioned in a very similar manner; so, too, would the accounts.

The idea of *peculium* did not remain confined to the countryside. The term and the institution appear in Plautus's comedies (c. 254–184 BCE). There, urban slaves also have *peculia*, if they are well-behaved (and sometimes if they are not).[131] Plautus could already rely for word-play on his audience's familiarity with the more restricted notion of *peculium* as what a slave had earned himself, or been given by his master to keep for himself. In this way, wisecracks could turn lashes into *peculium*: in the comedy *Asinaria*, two slaves discuss how thrashings increased the *peculium*, the treasure each slave carried on his back;[132] in *Persa*, a slave receives a warning that his misdeeds might earn him a *peculium* – i.e., lashes.[133]

127 Varro rust. 1.13.2; 1.16.5; s. also Petron. 28.7 and n. 154 in the paper on *dispensatores* in this volume.

128 On 'contracts' between household members, see Gamauf, "Slaves Doing Business" (n. 16): 332–33.

129 Kenneth M. Stampp, *The Peculiar Institution: Slavery in the Ante-Bellum South* (New York: Vintage Books, 1956): 165.

130 Gamauf, "Klage aufgrund Sonderguts" (n. 3): n. 23.

131 Emilio Costa, *Il diritto privato romano nelle commedie di Plauto* (Turin: Bocca, 1890): 104–8.

132 Plaut. Asin. 276: *Etiam de tergo ducentas plagas praegnatis dabo. Largitur peculium, omnem in tergo thensaurum gerit.* / 'I'll even give you two hundred fat whip-strikes off my back. He is giving away his *peculium*, he carries his whole fortune on his back' (transl. Amy Richlin, *Slave Theater in the Roman Republic: Plautus and Popular Comedy* [Cambridge: Cambridge University Press, 2017]: 165).

133 Plaut. Persa. 192: *Scelus tu pueri es, atque ob istanc rem ego aliqui te peculiabo.* / 'You're a rascal of a boy and that's why I'll give you some present today' (transl. Wolfgang de Melo, *Plautus: The Merchan. The Braggart Soldier. The Ghost. The Persian* [Cambridge: Harvard University Press, 2011]: 475). On a sexual connotation of *peculium* in this passage, see Breitenstein, *Petronius* (n. 87): 112 and Richlin, *Slave Theater* (n. 132): 183.

This was something masters laughed about, not slaves. Masters might also enjoy hearing slaves mimic 'master language' by speaking of *peculium. Peculium* was not the term preferred in the language of slaves, who tended to speak of *meum (esse)* and the like for 'their property'.

Albeit taken from a different context, comparison between two testamentary provisions regarding *peculia* in *manumissiones testamento* in the Digest title on *statuliberi* provides later confirmation of this observation:

D. 40.7.40.1 (Scaevola 24 dig.): 'Pamphilus liber esto peculio suo heredibus vere dato.'	D. 40.7.40.1 (Scaevola, Digest, book 24): "Let Pamphilus be free on faithfully giving his peculium to the heirs."[134]
D. 40.7.21 pr. (Pomponius 7 ex Plaut.): '[. . .] Calenus [. . .] liber esto suaque omnia et centum habeto [. . .]'	D. 40.7.21 pr. (Pomponius, from Plautius, book 7) "[. . .] Let Calenus be free and have all that belongs to him plus one hundred [. . .]"[135]

Pamphilus had to deliver what his late master's books showed as his *peculium*; Calenus was allowed to keep what had been 'his' during slavery. With Ulpian's differentiation in D. 40.1.4.1 (Ulp. 6 disp.) in mind, the semantic variation between *peculium suum* and *sua omnia* might be telling. These clauses regard *peculia* from different angles and, consequently, could mean different sets of items. In Pamphilus's case, the order could have required return of the 'master's share' – i.e., the business capital part of a *peculium* (referred to in D. 40.1.4.1 (Ulp. 6 disp.) by *ad venditorem pertinet*) – but not his 'personal belongings'. Calenus, however, was to keep precisely (and only) that part of his *peculium*, because he was accorded all what was 'his'. As *dispensator*, Calenus had surely controlled much more of his master's estate than what he had held as *peculium* in the strict sense – *pro suo tractare*. These two clauses do not show standardised language but they perhaps reveal a pattern: *peculium* was the legal term, and the one masters used for property administered by their slaves. A slave regarded *suum* or (above all) *sua pecunia* as what (in such a *peculium*) he could use as he pleased. In addition, in inscriptions, slaves quite clearly preferred *sua pecunia* or *de suo* to *de suo peculio*.[136]

134 Transl. Brunt in Watson, *Digest of Justinian* (n. 2).

135 Transl. Brunt in Watson, *Digest of Justinian* (n. 2).

136 A search in the Clauss–Slaby epigraphical database (http://www.manfredclauss.de/ [accessed 24.08.2022]) shows ten inscriptions with *de suo peculio*, of which three can unequivocally be ascribed to slaves (CIL 11.6314, CIL 2–07.981; AE 2009, 1256). In comparison, 1,785 inscriptions contain *de suo*, and *sua pecunia* appears in 1,817 (a detailed social analysis of the material is not possible here). For a précis of the phenomenon, see Christer Bruun, "Slaves and Freed Slaves," in *The Oxford Handbook of Roman Epigraphy*, ed. Christer Bruun and Jonathan Edmondson (New York: Oxford University Press, 2015): 615; more literature on *peculia* in inscriptions in Gamauf, "Klage aufgrund Sonderguts" (n. 3): n.15, n. 92.

7 Conclusions

7.1 Functions of *peculium*

Mere force was no way to secure loyalty, discipline, or the economic efficiency required when slaves worked independently far away and without supervision. As Keith Bradley pointed out decades ago,[137] the Romans believed in a mix of measures for the social control of their slaves: they wielded heavy sticks, like the *SC Silanianum*,[138] but they did not deny their slaves a few carrots, such as the chance of enjoying a *peculium*. The *peculium* gained special importance where slaves' tasks hinged on their disposition to cooperate.[139]

Peculium did not exist simply for the benefit of individual masters and slaves; there was also a strong public interest in its institutional workability. As a legal regime, it allowed a slave unlimited acquisitions without unpredictable losses or the necessity of daily supervision. The enlarged economic spheres and enhanced motivation of slaves under such a regime benefitted the Roman economy as a whole.

To slaves, a *peculium* offered new horizons: a higher standard of living for them and their 'families',[140] release from the constraints present in the master's house;[141] and, if everything went well, ultimately, the prospect of manumission.[142] By these means, a *peculium* rewarded collaboration and might convince potential troublemakers that loyalty was the better option, because only the master could grant freedom.

In addition to rewarding loyalty, *peculia* helped masters to keep their slaves under control. *Servi ordinarii* were responsible to the *dominus* for 'their slaves'[143] – i.e. *servi vicarii* held in their *peculia*; losses caused by a *vicarius* reduced the *peculium* of his *servus ordinarius* 'master'.[144] Intelligent slaves who were also naturally good at

137 Keith R. Bradley, *Slaves and Masters in the Roman Empire: A Study in Social Control* (Brussels: Latomus, 1984).

138 In addition, see below at n. 184.

139 See also Stefan Knoch, *Sklavenfürsorge im Römischen Reich: Formen und Motive zwischen humanitas und utilitas*, 2nd ed. (Hildesheim: Georg Olms Verlag, 2017): 187–96. From the comparison of 44 slave societies, Orlando Patterson, *Slavery and Social Death: A Comparative Study* (Cambridge, MA: Harvard University Press, 1982): 186, concluded that systems with *peculium* were generally more 'humane' than societies without.

140 Roth, "Food" (n. 8): 281–92.

141 This could be an existential advantage if the master was assassinated, because under the *SC Silanianum* all slaves 'under the same roof' were to be tortured and (most probably) executed; see below at n. 184.

142 See also below n. 149.

143 For the social relevance of slaveholding by slaves see Patterson, *Slavery and Social Death* (n. 139): 184.

144 Gamauf, "Slaves Doing Business" (n. 16): 338.

deploying others for their own ends were thus apt to be granted *peculia*. Self-interest turned slaves with *peculia* into 'talent scouts', who searched and trained candidates[145] for 'better positions': slaves had under-slaves / *vicarii* in their *peculia*; those, in turn, had other slaves in theirs, and so forth. In theory, a vertical structure in a *familia* could develop on the initiative of the slaves alone, without any prior planning by the master: slaves with slaves in their *peculia* led to a hierarchy: *ordinarius* / 'master'-slave; *vicarius* / under-slave; *vicarii vicarius* / under-slave's under-slave; *vicarius vicarii vicarii* / under-slave of an under-slave's under-slave, etc.[146] Every 'slave' master took some of his under-slaves' profits, which included those of further under-slaves. With *manumissio* as a possible reward if they performed as expected, slaves at all levels in the hierarchy tried to enlist capable support for their endeavours.[147]

At the economic apex of a *familia* stood the *dominus*. It was to him that profits from all of the slaves and under-slaves were ultimately funnelled. He needed to know neither how many slaves he actually owned, nor how the members of his *familia servorum* operated at any given moment. He had no need to ensure, personally, the productivity of slaves (to him probably anonymous) in lower positions or on far-away estates. The *servi ordinarii* at each level took care of this. Theoretically he might interact only with the top-ranking *servus ordinarius* of his household, who ultimately reported for all others.[148] On the other hand, *vicarii* at all levels hoped for promotion when a better position within the *familia servorum* became vacant by the advancement or manumission of their 'slave master'; this, too, offered motivation to collaborate.[149] Providing a replacement could be included in the agreement

145 For slaves training slaves see Plut. Cat. 21.7.

146 Gamauf, "Klage aufgrund Sonderguts" (n. 3): n. 14; Gamauf, "Sklaven (servi)" (n. 5): n. 19.

147 The *servus ordinarius* could grant a *peculium* to his *servus vicarius* (D. 15.1.4.6 Pomp. 7 Sab.; D. 15.1.6 Cels. 6 dig.).

148 Cf. Trimalchio's claim that only ten percent of his slaves had ever seen him in person (Petron. 37.6); see the paper on *dispensatores* in this volume, n. 139 and subsequent nn.

149 However, the majority of slaves were probably too old, serving on estates that a master never visited, or in lower positions, and their efforts went unnoticed. They could not expect to be rewarded with manumission. In order that they might, nevertheless, 'play by the rules' and do whatever they could to increase and keep safe their *peculia*, some masters allowed their slaves to 'give' 'their property' to others when they died by means of 'testaments'; see Plin. epist. 8.14 and Gamauf, "De nihilo" (n. 81): 243; for Pliny's practice also Buchwitz, "Servus servo heres" (n. 4): 146–48 and Buchwitz's paper in this volume, n. 42 and subsequent nn. Cato's advice to sell old and sick slaves (Cato 2.7. [. . .] *servum senem, servum morbosum* [. . .] *vendat*. / 'Sell [. . .] an old slave, a sickly slave [. . .]', transl. Hooper and Ash, *Cato* (n. 121): 9; cf. also Plut. Cato 4.4) probably often fell flat, because buyers were hardly interested; however, in such situation, a slave might be willing to give up his until now well-hidden savings (and perhaps motivate his friends to come forward in support) in order to die in freedom and so soften the loss.

suis nummis emere – e.g. a slave with an essential function could be manumitted on condition that he had trained up a *vicarius* to replace him.[150]

The master could revoke a *peculium* any time he wished.[151] Such an *ademptio peculii* often put an end to a slave's aspirations. Sometimes, however, the loss of (only) all that was 'his' could be advantageous. If slaves broke something precious or caused other damage, masters regularly resorted to – sometimes barbaric[152] – physical punishments. In his *peculium*, a slave had something 'of his own' from which to compensate the master for 'his' loss, and so evade physical punishment.

7.2 The Social Practice of *peculium*

The legal methods of creating *peculia* were flexible enough to accommodate variations in, for example, their economic objectives, the capabilities and character of slaves, and the interests and needs of masters.[153] Masters (or higher-ranking slaves in larger households) were always on the lookout to identify who in a *familia servorum* might qualify for more responsibilities and, therefore, for a *peculium*.[154]

In the following scenario, though not taken from one single source, all of the central elements are authentically Roman. Experiences of slavery in the United States of America, where structurally comparable problems existed,[155] are used to fill gaps.

A slave might first catch his master's eye,[156] perhaps because he looked better fed or clothed[157] than his comrades (even though the master follows Cato's advice and keeps rations short[158]). Enquiries exclude theft from the master (or others) as

150 Sometimes, the deal regarding a manumission obliged the slave to give another slave in his stead; see Mouritsen, *Freedman* (n. 5): 170–71; Gamauf, "Sklaven (servi)" (n. 5): n. 64.
151 Gamauf, "Klage aufgrund Sonderguts" (n. 3): nos. 28–29.
152 A famous example is that of Vedius Pollio, who wanted to feed a slave to his lampreys for breaking an expensive cup; for sources and literature on this – even by Roman standards – outrageous and therefore memorable event, see Gamauf, "Sklaven (servi)" (n. 5): n. 34, n. 198.
153 See Gamauf, "Klage aufgrund Sonderguts" (n. 3): nos. 19–20.
154 For a comparative sociological perspective on *peculium*, see the ground-breaking work of Patterson, *Slavery and Social Death* (n. 139): 182–86
155 Gamauf, "De nihilo" (n. 81): 225–45 and above after n. 125.
156 Petron. 75.4.
157 'Rich' slaves did not go unnoticed, see Gamauf, "De nihilo" (n. 81): 241 n. 118.
158 Cato. agr. 5.56–59; Spranger, *Historische Untersuchungen* (n. 104): 68; Alfons Bürge, "Cibaria: Indiz für die soziale Stellung des römischen Arbeitnehmers?," in *Ars boni et aequi: Festschrift für Wolfgang Waldstein zum 65. Geburtstag*, ed. Martin Josef Schermaier and Zoltán Végh (Stuttgart: Franz Steiner Verlag, 1993): 63–78; Richard Gamauf, *Ad statuam licet confugere: Untersuchungen zum Asylrecht im römischen Prinzipat* (Frankfurt am Main: Peter Lang Verlag, 1999): 92.

the explanation for the slave's condition.[159] Those enquiries might further reveal that the slave earns funds in his spare time, by running errands for neighbours or making repairs, cultivating minor land etc.[160] In sum, the master identifies someone who seeks out every extra *nummus*. The *pusilla pecunia* accumulated so far is, as experience has taught the master, beyond his reach, even though it is legally his.[161] Exploiting the slave's economic talent for himself requires a detour. The master might reduce the slave's chores and observe what ensues. If this results in satisfactory growth of the slave's 'business', master and slave discuss future strategies in 'common'[162] and their respective 'shares' in the profits.

It was by no means impossible (and might be theoretically expedient for the master, in view of an *actio de peculio*), to allow a slave to operate a *peculium* consisting solely of self-accumulated funds. However, a master who manifested trust by 'investing' his 'own' money in the *peculium* did not just accelerate the growth of the business but also made it palatable for the slave to give up some of the profits. As soon as the household accounts document the new situation, the 'slave's money' becomes a fully-fledged *peculium*. Whatever the slave acquires is acquired for the master. The alienation of property still requires the master's prior consent; presumably, however, this is unnecessary for less valuable or self-acquired goods.[163] Most importantly, already at this early stage, creditors have the protection of the *actio de peculio (vel de in rem verso)*.

From now on, whenever items pass from slave to master (i.e., by transfer recorded in the accounts[164]), the slave is compensated (and, if he is lucky, makes a little profit); the rules are the same in horizontal or vertical business transactions between two slaves. If the master drains a *peculium* by taking from it without reimbursement, he hurts his own interests. He does not decrease his potential liability, because the reduced liability *de peculio* is counteracted by a reciprocal increase in liability under the second clause of the *actio de peculio vel de in rem verso*: for the value of property taken from the slave without compensation, creditors might sue *de in rem verso*.[165] In addition, the slave's business suffers from the drain of capital. Finally, seeing his efforts go unrewarded also puts a damper on a slave's enthusiasm.

159 Plaut. Trin. 413; Truc. 461–62; Dion. Hal. 4.24.4; D. 15.1.4.2 (Pomp. 7 Sab.); D. 19.1.30 pr. (Afr. 8 quaest.); D. 47.2.68.4 (Cels. 12 dig.). Goods taken from the master did not count as *peculium* (for purposes of the *actio*); other booty, however, did.

160 For the sources of a *peculium* and the income of slaves, see Gamauf, "De nihilo" (n. 81): 239–43.

161 Plaut. Rud. 929; cf. Spranger, *Historische Untersuchungen* (n. 104): 86–87.

162 In D. 33.8.22.1 (Lab. 2 post. a Iavoleno epit.), master and slave 'co-own' a *servus (vicarius)*.

163 For Rome, this is no more than an assumption but it is probable in a comparative perspective; see Wacke, "Die libera administratio" (n. 6): 310–11; Patterson, *Slavery and Social Death* (n. 139): 182.

164 Petron. 53.6–8.

165 Gamauf, "Klage aufgrund Sonderguts" (n. 3): n. 40.

After a further period of economic success, the final promotion to full autonomy is the grant of *libera administratio*. Now, almost all the slave's dispositions regarding property in 'his' *peculium* are legally binding, as if he himself owned it.[166] The capacities now attained with respect to the *peculium* fully justify Isidore's term *pro suo tractare*. The arrangements might specify how much the slave might use for personal purposes and perhaps some sort of 'career plan', ultimately spelling out the conditions (and the price) for obtaining his freedom *suis nummis*.[167]

The Digest illustrates trust[168] put in slaves with *peculia* and with their high levels of independence. Slaves travelled to Africa or Gaul to collect debts, buy things, or run businesses; slaves from the provinces established branch operations for their masters at Rome.[169] One instance records a slave who probably did no more for his master directly than pay him a sum of money once a year.[170] All these situations involve *peculia* – but surely not merely as the basis for business activities. In any case, even a slave who functioned as his master's *institor* / business manager, or

---

166 Use of the *peculium* for gifts was not covered; see above n. 39.

167 This could lead to a double bind: the more competent a slave appeared, the higher was his price! Slaves therefore tried to keep the master in the dark to some extent; see Plaut. Rud. 929 and Spranger, *Historische Untersuchungen* (n. 104): 86–87.

168 D. 40.9.10 (Gaius 1 rer. cott. sive aur.) *In fraudem creditorum manumittere videtur, qui vel iam eo tempore, quo manumittit, solvendo non est vel datis libertatibus desiturus est solvendo esse. saepe enim de facultatibus suis amplius, quam in his est, sperant homines. quod frequenter accidit his, qui transmarinas negotiationes et aliis regionibus, quam in quibus ipsi morantur, per servos atque libertos exercent: quod saepe, adtritis istis negotiationibus longo tempore, id ignorant et manumittendo sine fraudis consilio indulgent servis suis libertatem.* / Gaius, Common Matters, book 1: 'It is deemed that a man manumits to the detriment of creditors if he is insolvent at the time of manumission or would become insolvent after the grants of freedom; for men often hope that their assets are greater than they actually are. This frequently happens to persons who carry on business through slaves and freedmen beyond the sea or in regions where they are not living themselves; they are often ignorant of losses incurred over a long period and bestow the favor of freedom on their slaves, manumitting without fraudulent intent.' (transl. Brunt in Watson, *Digest of Justinian* [n. 2]) – Topic of the discussion was the *lex Aelia Sentia* of 4 CE. It voided manumissions when the *dominus* intended to deprive creditors of satisfaction by reducing his estate through the *manumissio* of slaves (Gai. 1.37, 47); see Gamauf, "Sklaven (servi)" (n. 5): n. 54; literature there in n. 312. Gaius wanted to illustrate how this might happen frequently without involving fraud, e.g., if losses were caused by slaves running businesses in far-away regions. The text is remarkable in revealing the trust put in slaves and the interrelated fates of slaves in a *familia*. The master not only trusted slaves enough to let them conduct *transmarinas negotiationes*, which necessitated losing contact for long periods, but, in the case under discussion, the *transmarinas negotiationes* involved so much of his estate that, after their failure, he depended on the value of the slave, whom he actually wanted to become free, to pay for his other debts. Under such circumstances, the outcome would not be different, if the slave had paid the master for his manumission.

169 D. 45.1.141.4 (Gai. 2 verb. oblig.; cf. the paper on *dispensatores* in this volume, n. 50 and subsequent nn.); D. 28.5.35.3 (Ulp. 4 disp.); D. 14.3.13 (Ulp. 28 ad ed.); D. 41.2.1.14 (Paul. 54 ad ed.); D. 40.9.10 (Gai. 1 rer. cott. sive aur.); D. 5.1.19.3 (Ulp. 60 ad ed.).

170 D. 33.7.19.1 (Paul. 13 resp.).

who went abroad as a *magister navis* / sea captain, needed a *peculium* for his daily needs, or to relax with a cup of wine after work. Unsupervised slaves, when away on business trips for months,[171] needed incentives, not only to ignore the short-term temptation of running away with the money entrusted to them, but also in order not to waste too much time and money on the good life of the metropolis, or the lures of the circus, art galleries, taverns, prostitutes, or the like. Legal sources attest to such risks[172] but say little about the measures taken against them.

It helped to send more than one slave abroad: the putative miscreant feared betrayal by the others.[173] The strongest incentive was probably the reliable prospect of manumission. Slaves lived according to the logic of slavery, and dreamed of dying free. Additional reasons for returning might include an informal family left behind (whose members' freedom was possibly included in the deal *suis nummis emere*[174]) or the fact that most slaves had no 'home' other than the master's *domus*, where their friends and social relations were to be found.[175] All this made returning more appealing (and therefore more probable) than a life on the run among strangers. The availability of legal enforcement of *suis nummis emere* – an agreement between master and slave that was, by definition, devoid of legal consequence[176] – proves public awareness of, and interest in maintaining, the prospect of freedom as viable and appealing for slaves.

Even in macro-economic terms, *peculia* were of the utmost importance. The legal framework permitted use of more than merely the muscle power of slaves, and so enhanced their economic potential and value.[177] At the same time, strictly limited liability and personal incentives involved for slaves reduced the costs of supervision. Because of *institores*, *magistri navis* and slaves acting with *peculia*, the lack of a legal regime for free people to act as direct representative agents[178] never caused economic problems.[179] Unless the basic assumption that any managerial

---

171 According to D. 15.1.48 pr. (Paul. 17 Plaut.), a *libera administratio* ended if a slave escaped or his fate was unknown; cf. Aubert, "Dumtaxat de peculio" (n. 3): 196–97.

172 D. 11.3.1.5 (Ulp. 23 ad ed.); D. 21.1.65 (Ven. 5 act.); D. 21.1.4.2 (Ulp. 1 ed. aed. cur.); to similar effect, against employing slaves given to such pleasures, was Colum. 1.8.1. On how slaves viewed such distractions, see Hor. Ep. 1.14.15.

173 D. 21.1.17.7 (Ulp. 1 ed. aed. cur.) discusses the case of a *servus vicarius* who unwittingly joined his superior in the latter's escape.

174 Mouritsen, *Freedman* (n. 5): 170.

175 As the focal point of social relations, Pliny (Plin. epist. 8.16) called the master's household the slaves' state (*civitas*); cf. Gamauf, "Slaves Doing Business" (n. 16): 331 and above n. 149.

176 That is how the jurist C. Cassius Longinus judged such arrangements in 61 CE; see below at n. 188.

177 See above at n. 169.

178 Sociological reasons for the lack of free agents are given by Patterson, *Slavery and Social Death* (n. 139): 183.

179 See, e.g., Dennis P. Kehoe, "Agency and Growth in the Roman Economy," in *New Frontiers: Law and Society in the Roman World*, ed. Paul J. du Plessis (Edinburgh: Edinburgh University Press,

position in the Roman economy could theoretically be filled by a slave is wrong, *peculium* must have been crucial. Masters, after granting *peculia* to appropriate slaves, had time for politics, philosophy, and pleasure, while their businesses were being taken care of.

7.3 The Strangeness of the Language of *peculium*

Peculium was a point of convergence of the state, of individual slave-owners and, in case of *peculia* that served purposes beyond more mere maintenance, for a small group of elite slaves.[180] In everyday language, *peculium* meant 'slave property'; slaves referred to the assets included in it simply as 'their own'. This terminology was the outcome of a process in which a once broader meaning of *peculium* (= property in general) was gradually restricted, first to property of lesser value (*pusilla pecunia*) and, ultimately, since it (originally) readily qualified as property of little value, to the property of slaves (*patrimonium servi*). Without doubt, the avid supporters, if not the authors, of this linguistic evolution were the Roman jurists. They dealt with *peculium* most commonly in the context of the *actio de peculio*. They therefore sought to restrict the general notion of *peculium* to its signification in this specific legal context. When they failed to propagate their terminological preference in society at large, they continued to complain when the 'wrong' kind of property was referred to as *peculium*. Though perhaps a (slight) exaggeration, it appears that the group least likely to call 'their property' *peculium* was, paradoxically, slaves.[181] Slaves and freemen wanted the same thing: they longed for something to call 'their own' – *suum*. However, a slave, in saying words like '*meum esse*', ignored the '*summa divisio*' of free people and slaves. (Part of the problem may be that the Romans lacked a succinct definition of an owner's legal powers; the formula of the *legis actio sacramento in rem* used the words *meum esse* for claiming ownership.) Jurists were more sensitive in this regard that the average Roman. They endorsed precision, and insisted on a language in which *peculium* and *patrimonium* had opposing meanings.

For jurists, the everyday life *peculium* was not a straightforward topic to discuss. A set of terse textbook phrases, probably all ultimately attributable to Gaius,

2013): 177–91; Dennis P. Kehoe, "Agency, Roman Law, and Roman Social Values," in *Ancient Law, Ancient Society*, ed. Dennis P. Kehoe and Thomas McGinn (Ann Arbor: University of Michigan Press, 2017): 105–32; Barbara Abatino and Giuseppe Dari-Mattiacci, "Agency Problems and Organizational Costs in Slave-Run Business," *Amsterdam Law School Legal Studies Research Paper* 2011–40/*Amsterdam Center for Law & Economics Working Paper Paper* 2011–2013, 13.10.2011, https://papers.ssrn.com/sol3/papers.cfm?abstract_id=1942802 [accessed 25.08.2022].

180 See the diverging opinions on the distribution of *peculia* in n. 6.

181 See also above n. 85.

declared that 'slaves could not have anything of their own'.[182] Everyday definitions of *peculium* for circumscribing the capacities of slaves used exactly the same words. The situation did not improve when jurists demanded that the term *peculium* be reserved for property under the control of slaves; and they muddled such situations even further by using its antonym *patrimonium* to outline the slave's position vis-à-vis such property.

The language of property features conspicuously but unexpectedly (and is therefore easily overlooked) in one of the gloomiest moments of Roman slavery. In 61 CE, Roman senators discussed the execution of 400 innocent slaves. The reason was the assassination of one of the senators' own class, the *praefectus urbi* Pedanius Secundus, by one of his slaves. Tacitus ponders two possible triggers for the crime: a broken promise to manumit a slave who had already paid for freedom; or an erotic rivalry between the master and a slave for the favours of another slave boy.[183] Following a master's violent death in such cases, the *SC Silanianum* ordered the execution of all slaves under the same roof at the time of the crime. In a top upper-class household such as that of Pedanius Secundus', this could mean death for more than 400 people. The free *plebs* staged street protests against that imminent massacre, which in turn led to a debate in the senate where some opposition was voiced against applying the *SC Silanianum*[184] against so many innocents. Decisive in this discussion was the contribution of the eminent jurist C. Cassius Longinus. Tacitus composed it as a dazzling display of oratory,[185] in which the contemporary of Petronius and Seneca delivered one of his rhetorical drumbeats by means of an *argumentum ad absurdum*. Polemically but effectively, he distorted compassion for innocents into an endorsement of the killer's motives. He dared senators who contemplated clemency to pronounce as well that the master had been deserving of death. For Longinus, even entertaining discussion of the killer's motives was as good as condoning them (which, by the way, no

---

182 Gai. 2.87 (*nihil suum habere potest*), 96 (*nihil suum esse possit/posse*); D. 41.1.10.1 Gai. 2 inst. (*nihil suum habere potest*); Inst. 2.9.3 (*nihil suum habere potest*); Epit. Ulp. 20.10 (*nihil suum habet*).

183 Tac. Ann. 14.42.1.

184 On the *SC Silanianum*, see Olivia F. Robinson, "Slaves and the Criminal Law," *Zeitschrift der Savigny-Stiftung für Rechtsgeschichte, Romanistische Abteilung* 98 (1981): 233–35; Watson, *Roman Slave Law* (n. 3): 134–38; Jill Harries, "The Senatusconsultum Silanianum: Court Decisions and Judicial Severity in the Early Roman Empire," in *New Frontiers: Law and Society in the Roman World*, ed. Paul J. du Plessis (Edinburgh: Edinburgh University Press, 2013): 51–70; Joseph Georg Wolf, "Senatus Consultum Silanianum," in *Handwörterbuch der Antiken Sklaverei*, vol. 3, ed. Heinz Heinen et al. (Stuttgart: Franz Steiner Verlag, 2017): 2543–45; for more literature see Gamauf, "Sklaven (servi)" (n. 5): n. 38.

185 Dieter Nörr, "C. Cassius Longinus: Der Jurist als Rhetor (Bemerkungen zu Tacitus, Ann. 14.42–45)," in Dieter Nörr, *Historiae iuris antiqui: Gesammelte Schriften*, vol. 3, ed. Tiziana J. Chiusi, Wolfgang Kaiser and Hans-Dieter Spengler (Goldbach: Keip, 2003): 1585–620; Joseph Georg Wolf, *Das Senatusconsultum Silanianum und die Senatsrede des C. Cassius Longinus aus dem Jahre 61 n. Chr.* (Heidelberg: Winter, 1988).

one had suggested). To him, the whole discussion was utterly absurd; accordingly, he reframed the issue in property terms to ridicule attempts even to consider the slave's motives:

Tac. ann. 14.42.1: [. . .] seu *negata libertate, cui pretium pepigerat, sive amore exoleti incensus* et dominum aemulum non tolerans [. . .]	Tac. ann. 14.42.1: Either Secundus had refused him his freedom, after negotiating the price for it, or the man, fired with passion for a catamite, could not bear having his master as a rival. [. . .]
Tac. ann. 14.43.4: An, ut quidam fingere non erubescunt, iniurias suas ultus est interfector, quia *de paterna pecunia transegerat aut avitum mancipium detrahebatur*? pronuntiemus ultro dominum iure caesum videri.	Tac. ann. 14.43.4: Or (since some do not blush to fabricate stories) was the murderer avenging wrongs he had himself suffered? Had he been dealing with money left him by his father, or was a family slave being filched from him? Let us go all the way and declare that the master's murder appears justified![186]

Nothing highlights the institutional abnormality of slavery, the devastating impact it had on individuals, and the law's deep entanglement[187] with it, better than Tacitus's – purportedly verbatim – report of a discussion of mass-murder under the guise of justice. Taking centre-stage is the leading legal mind of the period. He not only defended the slaughter of 400 unquestionably innocent slaves as a legal necessity; in Cassius's opinion, sparing 400 innocent human beings was not clemency (or justice) but would have amounted to making the victim the real culprit. A vote to absolve the slaves, according to Cassius, acknowledged Pedanius's killing as lawful. However, for Cassius, no cause imaginable could justify such a reaction by a slave.[188] Then, in a mounting rhetorical crescendo, he dismissed the rumoured causes as insubstantial. His argument climaxed in two rhetorical questions that he wanted to sound like jokes. What was a broken promise of manumission, even after payment of the money? – Nothing, because a slave's money was no *paterna pecunia*, owned by his father and inherited from him. How about the rumours of a quarrel concerning the slave boy? –

186 Transl. John Yardley and Anthony Barret, *Cornelius Tacitus: The Annals: Reigns of Tiberius, Claudius, and Nero* (Oxford: Oxford University Press, 2008): 324, 325.

187 On the logical inconsistencies of Roman thinking in such matters, see Richard Gamauf, "'Cum aliter nulla domus tuta esse possit . . .': Fear of Slaves and Roman Law," in *Fear of Slaves – Fear of Enslavement in the Ancient Mediterranean: Peur de l'ésclave – Peur de l'ésclavage en mediterranée ancienne (Discours, representations, pratiques)*, ed. Anastasia Serghidou (Besançon: Presses Universitaires de Franche-Comté, 2007): 145–64.

188 The Emperor Augustus came closest to doing so when he suspended vindictive measures following the killing of a sexually deviant master whom he considered unworthy of revenge (Sen. Nat. 1.16.1). The emperor stopped short of declaring him *iure caesum videri* / 'killed according to the law'; these very words were also used by Cassius. See Gamauf, *Ad statuam licet confugere* (n. 158): 19.

Irrelevant, because this boy was no *avitum mancipium* that had belonged to the slave's father's father[189]!

It is noteworthy that the extreme circumstances – the murder of the officer in charge of public safety at Rome and of the control of its slaves;[190] and the prospect on this occasion of killing 400 slaves – made a jurist code-switch to the language of property in order to deliver a decisive argument and mock the very idea of a pardon. He wanted to show a distinction between master and slave so essential that it justified the slaughter of 400 innocent slaves after the killing of one (likewise guiltless) master. Doubtless, the language was chosen with care – by Tacitus but just as probably by Cassius himself, given the line of reasoning. Coming from a highly respected jurist, the words must have sounded utterly absurd; and this intensified his message: mercy, Cassius reasoned, after such an outrage was as perverse as the notion of a slave's protecting family heirlooms against his *dominus*. The enormity of the case under discussion, the importance of the audience he needed to convince, and the fact that Cassius weighed in with his full authority[191] add significance to his argumentation and choice of words (the legalistic nature of which suggests authenticity). To accentuate the gap between a Roman nobleman and one of his slaves, he pointed to the lack of *familia* and *patrimonium* of the latter, what Orlando Patterson called the slave's 'social death'. The *summa divisio* categorically distinguished freemen and slaves. The strongest legal means for upholding this distinction was the *SC Silanianum*; and at no other known moment in history was this enactment or its underlying ideology more 'celebrated' than on the day of C. Cassius Longinus's speech.

Cassius and Petronius surely knew one another; and Roman senators understood the language of property and status well enough to understand Cassius's joke and Petronius's suggestive hints concerning the *peculium prolatum*. For reasons of ideology, however, it was intolerable to blur distinctions of status through language, even in a grey zone, and to use the term *peculium* indiscriminately. Much more was at stake here than in the interpretation of testaments. Those might, as Cassius showed in his speech with shocking fervour, erode the dividing line between master and slave. Some, like Cassius, saw the imminent danger of a slippery slope: the confusion caused by not differentiating who held *peculium* and who *patrimonium* was a potential first step towards breaking down the assigned social roles of slaves and masters. A misguided pardon might first instigate disobedience among slaves and, ultimately, even incite murder of their masters.

---

189 This was, besides being legally impossible, also practically absurd in this case. In Catull. 25, the poet chastises the thief of his cloak for the extra impudence of showing it in public *tamquam avita* / 'as if it were his own heirloom'.

190 Gamauf, "Sklaven (servi)" (n. 5): n. 37.

191 Tac. ann. 14.43.1–2.

Like the other senators present when Cassius resumed his seat, all (or at least all slave-owning) Romans were in agreement that this outcome must never be allowed to happen.[192] Assuming they are authentic, his words reinforce the profound importance of upholding the underlying distinction: that 'we can live one amongst many, in safety amongst their fears' ([. . .] *possumus singuli inter plures, tuti inter anxios* [. . .] *agere*; Tac. ann. 14.44.2).[193]

192 Tac. ann. 14.45.1.

193 Transl. Yardley and Barret, *Cornelius Tacitus* (n. 186): 326.

Richard Gamauf

Dispensator: The Social Profile of a Servile Profession in the *Satyrica* and in Roman Jurists' Texts

1 Introduction

Petronius' *Satyrica*[1] occupy a special position, both as a work of literature and as a source for the (social) history of the early Imperial Age.[2] The work's central episode, the *cena Trimalchionis*/Trimalchio's Dinner, is set in the everyday world of freedmen and slaves; and we never feel as close to them as when the host and his guests – all of whom are fictional *liberti*/freedpeople – boast about their careers and freely give their opinions. This makes the *Satyrica* an ideal text to be interrogated about the lives of slaves and freedmen.[3] The work has been mined by numerous studies on

---

1 Most scholars accept Tacitus' (ann. 16.17–19) attribution of the work to the consular Petronius (*praenomen* Titus, Gaius or Publius?) and its origin during the reign of Nero; see Gareth L. Schmeling, *A Commentary on the Satyrica of Petronius* (Oxford: Oxford University Press, 2011): xiii–xvi; Edward Courtney, *A Companion to Petronius* (Oxford: Oxford University Press, 2001): 5–11; Jonathan R.W. Prag and Ian D. Repath, "Introduction," in *Petronius: A Handbook*, ed. Jonathan R.W. Prag and Ian D. Repath (New York: Wiley-Blackwell, 2009): 5–10; Thomas Völker and Dirk Rohmann, "Praenomen Petronii: The Date and Author of the Satyricon Reconsidered," *Classical Quarterly* 61, no. 2 (2011): 660–76; Heinz Hofmann, "Petronius, Satyrica," in *A Companion to the Ancient Novel*, ed. Edmund P. Cueva and Shannon N. Byrne (Chichester: Wiley-Blackwell, 2014): 98–100. For a later dating, see Pierre Flobert, "Considérations intempestives sur l'auteur et la date du Satyricon sous Hadrien," in *Petroniana: Gedenkschrift für Hubert Petersmann*, ed. József Herman and Hannah Rosén (Heidelberg: Winter, 2003): 109–22; Hofmann, "Petronius" (as above): 99; Ulrike Roth, "Liberating the cena," *Classical Quarterly* 66, no. 2 (2016): 614–34. Arguments in favour of a later date from a legal historical point of view are summarized in Leopold Wenger, *Die Quellen des römischen Rechts* (Vienna: Holzhausen, 1953): 231–32.

2 For the current state of research and the recent scholarship (which is vast) see Schmeling, *A Commentary* (n. 1); Courtney, *Companion* (n. 1); Jonathan R.W. Prag and Ian D. Repath, eds., *Petronius: A Handbook* (New York: Wiley-Blackwell, 2009); for references up to 2018 see the Petronian Society Newsletter (https://ancientnarrative.com/article/view/32035 [accessed 25.08.2022]).

3 An overview of the topic is given by Antonio Bravo García, "El 'Satiricón' como reflejo de la esclavitud de su tiempo," *Cuadernos de filología clásica* 6 (1974): 195–208; Gaetano Puglisi, "Il microcosmo di C. Pompeius Trimalchio Maecenatianus: Schiavi e liberti nella casa di un mercante romano (Petr. 27–78)," *Index* 15 (1987): 207–26; Jean Andreau, "Freedmen in the Satyrica," in *Petronius: A Handbook*, ed. Jonathan R.W. Prag and Ian D. Repath (New York: Wiley-Blackwell, 2009):

Note: A German version of this paper appeared in *Index* 49 (2021): 112–42 ("Dispensator: Sozialprofil eines Sklavenberufes in den Satyrica und römischen Juristentexten").

https://doi.org/10.1515/9783110987195-005

first-century economic[4] and social history, and on the history of mentalities.[5] Legal historians similarly hope that the *Satyrica* preserve some information on the legal practice of the time.[6]

Literary scholars or classical philologists regularly voice scepticism[7] about such a 'realistic' reading of this picaresque novel, despite the fact that details in

114–24; Ulrich Eigler and Rebecca Lämmle, "Trimalchio," in *Handwörterbuch der Antiken Sklaverei*, vol. 3, ed. Heinz Heinen et al. (Stuttgart: Franz Steiner Verlag, 2017): 3103–10.

4 Such as Elio Lo Cascio, "La vita economica e sociale delle città romane nella testimonianza del Satyricon," in *Studien zu Petron und seiner Rezeption. Studi su Petronio e sulla sua fortuna*, ed. Luigi Castagna and Eckard Levèvre (Berlin: De Gruyter, 2007): 3–14; Koenraad Verboven, "A Funny Thing Happened on My Way to the Market: Reading Petronius to Write Economic History," in *Petronius: A Handbook*, ed. Jonathan R.W. Prag and Ian D. Repath (New York: Wiley-Blackwell, 2009): 125–39. For Trimalchio and economic history see John H. D'Arms, *Commerce and Social Standing in Ancient Rome* (Cambridge: Harvard University Press, 1981): 97–120; Lo Cascio, "La vita economica" (as above): 8–9, and Kathrin Jaschke, *Die Wirtschafts- und Sozialgeschichte des antiken Puteoli* (Rahden: Leidorf, 2010): 247–50.

5 D'Arms, *Commerce* (n. 4): 97–120; Paul Veyne, "Vie de Trimalcion," *Annales: Economies, sociétés, civilisations* 16 (1961): 213–47.

6 Wenger, *Quellen* (n. 1): 231–32; Franz Wieacker, *Römische Rechtsgeschichte: Quellenkunde, Rechtsbildung, Jurisprudenz und Rechtsliteratur*, vol. 1, *Einleitung, Quellenkunde, Frühzeit und Republik* (Munich: C.H. Beck, 1988): 86 n. 9; Peter Gröschler, "Die pompejanischen und herkulanensischen Urkunden als Erkenntnisquelle für das römische Recht," in *Hermeneutik der Quellentexte des Römischen Rechts*, ed. Martin Avenarius (Baden-Baden: Nomos, 2008): 44 hopes to gain 'einen Eindruck vom wirklichen Leben'. On law in the *Satyrica* see Louis Debray, "Pétrone et le droit privé romain," *Nouvelle revue historique de droit français et étranger* 43 (1919): 5–70 and 127–86; Richard Gamauf, "Petronius 97: Quaestio lance et licio oder Rechtspraxis des ersten Jahrhunderts?," in *Fides humanitas ius: Studii in onore di Luigi Labruna*, vol. 3, ed. Cosimo Cascione and Carla Masi Doria (Naples: Editoriale Scientifica, 2007): 2037–45; Richard Gamauf, "Aliquid de iure gustare: Portrayal and Criticism of Lawyers in Petronius," in *Ius Romanum Schola Sapientiae: Pocta Petrovi Blahovi k 70. narodeninám*, ed. Peter Mach, Matúš Nemec and Matej Pekarik (Trnava: Právnická fakulta Trnavskej university, 2009): 151–65; Alessando Barchiesi, "Extra legem: Consumo di letteratura in Petronio, Arbitro," in *La letteratura di consumo nel mondo greco-latino: Atti del convegno internazionale Cassino, 14–17 Settembre 1994*, ed. Michael Paschalis and Stelios Panayotakis (Eelde: Groningen University Library, 2013): 191–208.

7 Cf. Schmeling, *A Commentary* (n. 1): 82: 'Social historians often use him [i.e. Trimalchio] as a model for the freedman-businessman, as though the character from the *Cena* were real and not fictional; [. . .] T. as an approximation of a real ancient businessman must be dealt with cautiously.' and Flobert, "Considérations" (n. 1): 116: 'Rien n'est plus faux, ni l'assignation à cette date [i.e. a Neronian date], ni la qualification de réaliste.' Those who agree that the work is basically realist include Lo Cascio, "La vita economica" (n. 4): 3–14 and Eckart Olshausen, "Soziokulturelle Betrachtungen zur Cena Trimalchionis," in *Studien zu Petron und seiner Rezeption. Studi su Petronio e sulla sua fortuna*, ed. Luigi Castagna and Eckard Lefèvre (Berlin: De Gruyter, 2007): 15–31.

the text match[8] the cultural background and the material culture from the Neronian age.[9]

2 Purpose and Method of This Study

Such fundamental differences of opinion appear irreconcilable. But historical research into this text does not require *a priori* proof that every scene and every detail can claim to be credible.[10] There is indisputably grotesque exaggeration in the *cena Trimalchionis.*[11] The world is distorted into a caricature of itself.[12] But these are mere

---

8 Trimalchio's projected grave monument (Petron. 71.5–12) is very similar to actual first-century freedman tombs; see D'Arms, *Commerce* (n. 4): 108–16; Courtney, *Companion* (n. 1): 114; Lauren Hackworth Petersen, *The Freedman in Roman Art and History* (Cambridge: Cambridge University Press, 2006): 68–69, 84–120; John R. Clarke, *Art in the Lives of Ordinary Romans: Visual Representation and Non-Elite Viewers in Italy, 100 B.C.–A.D. 315* (Berkeley: University of California Press, 2003): 184–87. There, is, however, exaggeration in the passage: 'Petronius [. . .] conjured up an image of Trimalchio's excess in commemoration that matched the excess of his famous banquet' (quoting Clarke, *Art*: 187). Schmeling, *A Commentary* (n. 1): 290–303 is undecided whether the description of monument and inscription is 'social history or literature' (quote at 300). Still of fundamental importance is Theodor Mommsen, *Gesammelte Schriften*, vol. 7, *Philologische Schriften*, 3rd ed. (Zürich: Weidmann, 1994): 191–205 (= "Trimalchios Heimath und Grabinschrift," *Hermes* 13 (1878): 106–21).

9 Cf. Gilbert Bagnani, *Arbiter of Elegance: A Study of the Life and Works of C. Petronius* (Toronto: University of Toronto Press, 1954): 6–26; J.P. Sullivan, "Petronius' 'Satyricon' and Its Neronian Context," in *Aufstieg und Niedergang der römischen Welt*, pt. 2, *Principat*, vol. 32.3, *Sprache und Literatur (Literatur der julisch-claudischen und der flavischen Zeit)*, ed. Hildegard Temporini and Wolfgang Haase (Berlin: De Gruyter, 1985): 1666–86; Victoria Rimell, "Petronius' Lessons in Learning – The Hard Way," in *Ordering Knowledge in the Roman Empire*, ed. Jason König and Tim Whitmarsh (Cambridge: Cambridge University Press, 2007): 108, 112; Barchiesi, "Extra legem" (n. 6): 203–4.

10 Cf. Prag and Repath, "Introduction" (n. 1): 2: 'However, one of the main problems when approaching the *Satyrica* is the frequently sharp divide between literary and historical studies [. . .] It can be read as a literary text, as a social document, or as evidence for historical reality, but none of these readings can properly exist without the others.' Urging caution in general is Sandra R. Joshel, "Slavery and Roman Literary Culture," in *The Cambridge World History of Slavery*, vol. 1, *The Ancient Mediterranean World*, ed. Keith R. Bradley and Paul Cartledge (Cambridge: Cambridge University Press, 2011): 238: 'As a mirror of social reality [. . .] Roman literature reflect[s] a reality shaped primarily by the interests, hopes and anxieties of its elite authors and audience.'

11 The births at Petron. 53.2 would require 1.5 million slaves living on Trimalchio's estate, while the amount of wheat harvested in a day would have been enough to feed ten thousand people for a year; see Martin S. Smith, ed., *Petronius: Cena Trimalchionis* (Oxford: Oxford University Press, 1975): 142; for the exorbitant fortunes of freedmen see Schmeling, *A Commentary* (n. 1): 184–85; further examples in Rimell, "Petronius' Lessons" (n. 9): 110.

12 E.g. D'Arms, *Commerce* (n. 4): 99: '[T]he text of the *Satyricon* [. . .] sometimes faithfully reflects, sometimes comically distorts, contemporary Roman institutions and social realities.' and Henrik Mouritsen, *The Freedman in the Roman World* (Cambridge: Cambridge University Press, 2011): 291: 'While the comic exaggeration is apparent, the basic "realism" of Petronius' portrayal of the freedmen has

superimpositions: we can still search for historicity underneath.[13] We cannot differentiate between truth and fiction in the context of the *Satyrica* alone. Nor is coherence in terms of content enough in itself to warrant the assumption that an episode is anchored in reality. A passage in a literary text may sound probable, but nevertheless be wholly fictitious. If we want to investigate the degree of historicity of a given text, what we need is an external, but thematically comparable frame of reference; a source or a body of sources that is unlikely to cloud the issue with irony or literary ambiguities.

For the *dispensatores*[14] in the *cena* a suitable frame of reference can be Roman jurists' writings.[15] There are repeated mentions of *dispensatores* in jurists' texts written roughly contemporaneously with the *Satyrica* (however we may decide to date the latter). In these, the perspective is unlikely to be fundamentally different since jurists and their readers shared the social background of Petronius and his audience.

Particularly valuable for us is the casual mention of mundane matters in legal texts, because jurists did not frame descriptions of their cases as nuanced portraits of social situations. They usually provided the minimum[16] of information necessary to understand the case at issue (indeed, frequently not even that). Unexpected background information, such as mention of the fact that a slave involved was a *dispensator* and not some other, unspecified type,[17] stands out. It deserves our attention even if at first glance it appears to be irrelevant to the legal problem. In contrast to Anglo-American case law, in the casuistic Roman legal discourse the authority of a *responsum* did not depend on an actual case. It is therefore advisable not to reject

been widely accepted.' and 292: 'Petronius seized on the – indisputable – existence of wealthy "independent" freedmen in Roman society and created a fictional "underworld" entirely inhabited by members of this particular sub-category. The effect was both "realistic" and highly unreal.' For further discussion of realism in the *Satyrica* see Courtney's summary of the *cena* in *Companion* (n. 1): 123–26.

13 D'Arms, *Commerce* (n. 4): 97: '[I]t remains open to anyone to argue that a given passage is not material from which we can legitimately extract historical information'; Courtney, *Companion* (n. 1): 115: '[W]hile in many respects Trimalchio is surreal, in others he is simply social reality writ large, and beneath the exaggeration Petronius intends us to see him as representative of a certain stratum in society [. . .].' See also John Bodel, "The cena Trimalchionis," in *Latin Fiction: The Latin Novel in Context*, ed. Heinz Hofmann (London: Routledge, 1999): 41–43.

14 For the sake of consistencey the Latin term remains untranslated (even if in the translation quoted it has been rendered into English). For the *dispensator*'s role see after n. 23 below.

15 For Barbara Stelzenberger, *Kapitalmanagement und Kapitaltransfer im Westen des Römischen Reiches* (Rahden: Leidorf, 2008): 30, 'erlauben vor allem die Digesten einen – zum Teil äußerst detaillierten – Blick in die Lebenswelten dieser Menschen'.

16 For Petronius' criticism of terse legal language see John A. Crook, "'Si parret' and a Joke in Petronius," in *Sodalitas: Scritti in onore di Antonio Guarino*, vol. 3, ed. Antonio Guarino and Vincenzo Giuffrè (Naples: Jovene, 1984): 1353–56; Gamauf, "Aliquid" (n. 6): 57–58.

17 Cf. the categorizations of slaves in D. 47.10.15.44 (Ulp. 77 ed.) [. . .] *multum interest, qualis servus sit,* [. . .] *dispensator* [. . .] *an qualisqualis*; see n. 208 below, see also Marcel Simonis, *Cum servis nullum est connubium: Untersuchungen zu den eheähnlichen Verbindungen von Sklaven im westlichen Mittelmeerraum des Römischen Reiches* (Hildesheim: Georg Olms Verlag, 2017): 103.

out of hand 'superfluous' information as mere local colour in otherwise laconic juristic discourse, but to consider instead what additional information its intended ancient readers could have derived from it.

3 The Question

For this reason the present essay will combine information from the *cena Trimalchionis* with legal texts. Anecdotes in Petronius mention elements that also occur in the descriptions of facts in the jurists or that could presumably be in the background of the cases they discuss. Occasionally, the similarity extends to terminology and word usage.[18]

The novel and the legal texts have opposing but complementary perspectives: the *cena*'s internal narrative eludes straightforward 'fact checks', while the jurists' expositions do not require them. The realism of their writings is beyond question. Some cases are taken from the life,[19] and even discussions of hypothetical cases[20] rely on the audience's familiarity with the practical work of *dispensatores*. Wholly fictitious cases would have been useless for jurists' purposes.

Looking at both fiction and legal sources together produces not only insights into the degree of realism in passages from the *cena*, but also different readings of legal texts. These can occasionally go beyond the literal wording,[21] but may take us closer to the original problem's *Sitz im Leben*.[22]

---

18 See below n. 91. Identical terms were employed to describe positive slaves qualities; cf. Richard Gamauf, "De nihilo crevit – Freigelassenenmentalität und Pekuliarrecht," in *Der Bürge einst und jetzt: Festschrift für Alfons Bürge*, ed. Ulrike Babusiaux, Peter Nobel and Johannes Platschek (Zürich: Schulthess, 2017): 231–33.

19 This is shown by the backgrounds of cases or from incidental details (D. 11.3.16 Alf. 2 dig.; n. 115), direct quotations from wills, and the use of individual slave names instead of the usual placeholder names (D. 40.5.41.15 Scaev. 4 resp.; see below n. 169; D. 40.7.21 pr. Pomp. 7 ex Plaut.; see below n. 182).

20 D. 45.1.141.4 (Gai. 2 de verb. oblig.) see below n. 50.

21 See the synopsis of the 'anecdotal' material below in the Conclusion.

22 See also Richard Gamauf, "Kindersklaven in klassischen römischen Rechtsquellen," in *Kindersklaven – Sklavenkinder: Schicksale zwischen Zuneigung und Ausbeutung in der Antike und im interkulturellen Vergleich: Beiträge zur Tagung des Akademievorhabens Forschungen zur antiken Sklaverei (Mainz, 14. Oktober 2008)*, ed. Heinz Heinen (Stuttgart: Franz Steiner Verlag, 2012): 231–32.

4 Dispensator as a Slave Profession

The main duties[23] of (usually male)[24] slave *dispensatores* were financial[25] (cash management, collecting outstanding debts, etc.).[26] The decisive factor was usually

23 Basic information gives Wilhelm Liebenam, "Dispensator," in *Paulys Realencyclopädie der classischen Altertumswissenschaft*, vol. 5 (1905): 1189–98; more recently Joaquín Muñiz Coello, "Officium dispensatoris," *Gerión. Revista de Historia Antigua* 7 (1989): 107–19; Elisabeth Herrmann-Otto, *Ex ancilla natus: Untersuchungen zu den 'hausgeborenen' Sklaven und Sklavinnen im Westen des römischen Kaiserreiches* (Stuttgart: Franz Steiner Verlag, 1994): 369–98; Jean-Jacques Aubert, *Business Managers in Ancient Rome: A Social and Economic Study of Institores, 200 B.C.–A.D. 250* (Leiden: Brill, 1994): 196–99; Jesper Carlsen, *Vilici and Roman Estate Managers until A.D. 284* (Rome: L'Erma di Bretschneider, 1995): 147–58; Jean Andreau, *Banking and Business in the Roman World* (Cambridge: Cambridge University Press, 1999): 26–27, 64–65; Alexander Weiß, *Sklave der Stadt: Untersuchungen zur öffentlichen Sklaverei in den Städten des Römischen Reiches*, Historia Einzelschriften 173 (Stuttgart: Franz Steiner Verlag, 2004): 39–42; Gérard Minaud, *La comptabilité à Rome: Essai d'histoire économique sur la pensée comptable commerciale et privée dans le monde antique romain* (Lausanne: Presses polytechniques et universitaires romandes, 2005): 174–77; Stelzenberger, *Kapitalmanagement* (n. 15): 29–72; Leonhard Schumacher, "On the Status of Private Actores, Dispensatores and Vilici," in *By the Sweat of Your Brow: Roman Slavery in Its Socio-Economic Setting*, ed. Ulrike Roth (London: Institute of Classical Studies, University of London 2010): 31–47; Koenraad Verboven, "Dispensator," in *The Encyclopedia of Ancient History*, vol. 4, ed. Roger S. Bagnall et al. (Malden: Wiley, 2013): 2166–67; Jesper Carlsen, *Land and Labour: Studies in Roman Social and Economic History* (Rome: L'Erma di Bretschneider, 2013): 193–202; Christoph Schäfer, "Dispensator I. Allgemeines," in *Handwörterbuch der Antiken Sklaverei*, vol. 1, ed. Heinz Heinen et al. (Stuttgart: Franz Steiner Verlag, 2017): 736–38; Gottfried Schiemann, "Dispensator II. Einzelne juristische Aspekte," in *Handwörterbuch der Antiken Sklaverei*, vol. 1, ed. Heinz Heinen et al. (Stuttgart: Franz Steiner Verlag, 2017): 738–39. Additional scholarship lists Schmeling, *A Commentary* (n. 1): 99.

24 For the scholarship see Simonis, *Cum servis nullum est conubium* (n. 17): 98, 104. Occasional *dispensatrices* are mentioned in inscriptions; cf. Carlsen, *Vilici* (n. 23): 148 n. 492; Herrmann-Otto, *Ex ancilla* (n. 23): 369–96; *contra* Simonis, *Cum servis nullum est conubium* (n. 17): 95. Weiß, *Sklave* (n. 23): 41–42 and Schiemann, "Dispensator II" (n. 23): 738–39 do not exclude the possibility of free *dispensatores*. Muñiz Coello sums up arguments why the function was performed only by slaves: "Officium" (n. 23): 113–14; see also below n. 34 and following.

25 For an overview of the roles of slaves involved in finance see Maria Antoinetta Ligios, "'Ademptio peculii' e revoca implicita del legato: Riflessioni su D. 34.4.31.3 (Scaev. 14 dig.)," *Index* 34 (2006): 514–15.

26 For overlapping fields of activity in case of *dispensatores* and *actores* see John A. Crook, *Law and Life of Rome, 90 B.C.–A.D. 212* (New York: Cornell University Press, 1967): 187; Herrmann-Otto, *Ex ancilla* (n. 23): 377; Christoph Schäfer, "Die Rolle der actores in Geldgeschäften," in *Fünfzig Jahre Forschungen zur antiken Sklaverei an der Mainzer Akademie 1950–2000: Miscellanea zum Jubiläum*, ed. Heinz Bellen and Heinz Heinen (Stuttgart: Franz Steiner Verlag, 2001): 215; for *actores* in exclusively agricultural contexts see Carlsen, *Vilici* (n. 23): 147–58; Aubert, *Business Managers* (n. 23): 192; Puglisi, "Il microcosmo" (n. 3): 219 (n. 33) believes they also performed other tasks. The tasks of the *servus pecuniis exigendis praepositus*, so called after his job, also included debt collection. He would have been an *actor* (D. 44.4.5.3 Paul. 71 ed.) or *institor* (D. 13.7.11.5 Ulp. 28 ed.; D. 14.1.1.12 f. Ulp. 28 ed.; D. 26.7.37.1 Pap. 11 quaest.; D. 14.1.1.13 Ulp. 28 ed.; D. 47.2.67.3 Paul. 7 ad Plaut.). He is, however, viewed as a *dispensator* by Giuseppe Giliberti, *Legatum kalendarii. Mutuo feneratizio e*

the configuration of the *domus*: in some rare and untypical cases, large households[27] – the most prominent example, and at the same time an exceptional case, was the *familia Caesaris* – could have several *dispensatores*, each with their own area of operations,[28] who were under the authority of one *procurator*.[29] 'Secondary employment'[30] in elite households and the *familia Caesaris* could be highly profitable.[31] Their *peculia* regularly included slaves of their own (*vicarii*).[32] A *dispensator* needed to have his master's trust and was difficult to replace. This is why most scholars believe that *dispensatores* were rarely if ever freed, and only later in life.[33]

---

struttura contabile del patrimonio nell'età del principato (Naples: Jovene, 1984): 80–81; Andreas Wacke, "Die adjektizischen Klagen im Überblick. Erster Teil: Von der Reeder- und der Betriebsleiterklage zur direkten Stellvertretung," *Zeitschrift der Savigny-Stiftung für Rechtsgeschichte, Romanistische Abteilung* 111 (1994): 322 and Giovanna Coppola Bisazza, *Lo iussum domini e la sostituzione negoziale nell'esperienza romana* (Milan: Giuffrè, 2003): 108 n. 56. For the liability arising from a *dispensator*'s *stipulatio* see Ralf Michael Thilo, *Der Codex accepti et expensi im Römischen Recht: Ein Beitrag zur Lehre von der Litteralobligation* (Göttingen: Muster-Schmidt, 1980): 315–16. There were various legal forms for the collection of debt by free agents (esp. mandate); cf. D. 17.1.12.16 (Ulp. 31 ed.); D. 17.1.34 pr. (Afr. 8 quaest.); D. 19.5.5.4 (Paul. 5 quaest.); D. 26.7.37.1 (Pap. 11 quaest.); see on this topic Schäfer, op. cit., 216. On *tributum* cf. D. 50.1.17.7 (Pap. 1 resp.).

27 In smaller households *dispensatores* were assigned a greater range of tasks; see Andrew Garland, "Cicero's Familia Urbana," *Greece & Rome* 39, no. 2 (1992): 166.

28 Trimalchio owned either two or three, depending on whether Petron. 30.2–3 and 30.7–10 talk about the same *dispensator* (namely Cinnamus). Herrmann-Otto, *Ex ancilla* (n. 23): 370–71 believes it is only one man; see also Schmeling, *A Commentary* (n. 1): 104.

29 Debray, "Pétrone" (n. 6): 47–48; Giliberti, *Legatum* (n. 26): 26–27; 30; Schmeling, *A Commentary* (n. 1): 104; for these hierarchies see also Aubert, *Business Managers* (n. 23): 322–23.

30 D. 14.3.12 (Iul. 11 dig.); CIL 6.3687 mentions a slave who is both *dispensator* and *negotiator*/manager.

31 For the earnings of imperial stewards see Ludwig Friedländer, *Darstellungen aus der Sittengeschichte Roms in der Zeit von August bis zum Ausgang der Antonine*, vol. 1, 9th ed., ed. Georg Wissowa (Leipzig: Hirzel, 1919): 69; Andreau, *Banking and Business in the Roman World* (n. 23): 65; Stelzenberger, *Kapitalmanagement* (n. 15): 63–64; she also stresses the different circumstances prevailing in imperial and private households (as above: 31, 63).

32 See Herrmann-Otto, *Ex ancilla* (n. 23): 381 n. 76; Stelzenberger, *Kapitalmanagement* (n. 15): 49–52; Jonathan Edmondson, "Slavery and the Roman Family," in *The Cambridge World History of Slavery*, vol. 1, *The Ancient Mediterranean World*, ed. Keith R. Bradley and Paul Cartledge (Cambridge: Cambridge University Press, 2011): 341.

33 Muñiz Coello, "Officium" (n. 23): 114; Carlsen, *Vilici* (n. 23): 151; Herrmann-Otto, *Ex ancilla* (n. 23): 386–87, 390–91; Schumacher, "Status" (n. 23): 36; Carlsen, *Land* (n. 23): 195; Mouritsen, *Freedman* (n. 12): 199–200. Trimalchio's own manumission was testamentary, as were those of most *dispensatores* in the Digest. Stelzenberger, *Kapitalmanagement* (n. 15): 58–63 suggests that as a rule *dispensatores* were comparatively young when they were manumitted ('in aller Regel noch in jungen Jahren freigelassen', 66); as does Schiemann, "Dispensator II" (n. 15): 738. There are few manumitted *dispensatores* in inscriptions, see Carlsen, *Vilici* (n. 23): 149–50; Liebenam draws different conclusions: "Dispensator" (n. 23): 1191–92.

In this way, *dispensatores* continued to make acquisitions as slaves[34] and could be subjected to torture;[35] slaves themselves may often have been keen to retain this lucrative position.[36]

Of a *dispensator*'s core tasks, the jurists only discuss his role in making and accepting payments for the *dominus*. For this, he would be appointed in several stages. Once a slave suitable for *dispensatio*[37] had been found, he was first given an internal *permissus* to fulfil the role.[38] He became legally entitled to receive payments as soon as debtors had been informed about his appointment;[39] from then on payment made to him was as good as directly to the *dominus*.[40] His removal was construed as an *actus contrarius* and followed the exact pattern in reverse: permission was first revoked internally, which became effective once the debtors had been notified. From that point on, payments to the former *dispensator* led no longer to a discharge of debt. Unsurprisingly, jurists were not consulted about such clear-cut cases. They came into play when payment had been made to a *dispensator* whose revocation had not yet been communicated to the debtors:

D. 46.3.51 (Paulus 9 ad ed.): Dispensatori, qui ignorante debitore remotus est ab actu, recte solvitur: ex voluntate enim domini ei solvitur, quam si nescit mutatam qui solvit liberatur.	D. 46.3.51 (Paul, Edict, book 9): Payment is validly made to a *dispensator* who, unknown to the debtor, has been removed from office; for he is paid with the consent of the master, and if the payer does not know that the master has changed his mind, he will be released.[41]

34 Aubert, *Business Managers* (n. 23): 197.

35 Leonhard Schumacher, *Sklaverei in der Antike: Alltag und Schicksal der Unfreien* (Munich: C.H. Beck, 2001): 292–93; Wolfram Buchwitz, "Servus servo heres: Testierfreiheit für Sklaven," in *Fontes Iuris: Atti del VI Jahrestreffen Junger Romanistinnen und Romanisten Lecce, 30–31 marzo 2012*, ed. Pierangelo Buongiorno and Sebastian Lohsse (Naples: Edizioni Scientifiche Italiane, 2013): 158; Mouritsen, *Freedman* (n. 12): 219–20.

36 Schumacher, "Status" (n. 23): 38, 43–47.

37 The terms is used for example in Cic. ad Att. 15.15.3; cf. Crook, *Law* (n. 26): 187; Stelzenberger, *Kapitalmanagement* (n. 15): 43–45.

38 See below n. 58 and subsequent nn.

39 This, however, is attested only in D. 45.1.141.4 (Gai. 2 verb. oblig.) where creditor and debtor immediately contracted with each other; see below n. 52 and subsequent nn.

40 Cf. Debray, "Pétrone" (n. 6): 47; for a brief discussion see also Gérard Boulvert and Marcel Morabito, "Le droit de l'esclavage sous le Haut-Empire," in *Aufstieg und Niedergang der römischen Welt*, pt. 2, *Principat*, vol. 14, *Recht*, ed. Hildegard Temporini and Wolfgang Haase (Berlin: De Gruyter, 1982): 147. Such payments were recorded in the *rationes dominicae*, which contained property that slaves administered under the master's direct control (and not autonomously as *peculia*); on this point and on accounting see Debray, "Pétrone" (n. 6): 48; Thilo, *Codex* (n. 26): 137–38, 122–23.

41 Transl. Beinart in Alan Watson, *The Digest of Justinian*, vol. 1–2 (Philadelphia: University of Pennsylvania Press, 1998).

Paul held the debtor to be liberated in this case too. This decision in the debtor's favour was based on the fact that even after having been recalled as *dispensator* a slave could still make his *dominus* possessor and owner of any monies he collected. Once it had been made public that a slave was authorized to receive payment, the thus manifested *animus possidendi* of the *dominus* was not cancelled by a merely internal revocation.[42] The protection of debtors' interests required that the revocation be made public. Payments made in good faith prior to this point by debtors of the slave's *dominus* were still made *ex voluntate domini*. After a manumission, however, property law rules strictly applied (*stricta iuris ratione*) and excluded such a construction:

> Gaius inst. 3.160: [. . .] et huic simile est, quod plerisque placuit, si debitor meus manumisso dispensatori meo per ignorantiam solverit, liberari eum, cum alioquin stricta iuris ratione non posset liberari eo, quod alii solvisset quam cui solvere deberet.

> Gaius inst. 3.160: As most people accept, this is a similar case to that in which my debtor makes payment to my *dispensator* without knowing that the *dispensator* has been freed. He is discharged by his payment despite the fact that in the strict sense of the law he could not be released, in that he paid to the wrong person.[43]

In the High Classical period it remained a matter of dispute among jurists whether payment to a former *dispensator* terminated the debtor's obligation. Manumission impeded the former master immediately becoming owner of the money paid. However, in this situation, the majority of jurists prefered to protect a creditor's good faith over a consistent application of property law rules: even though ownership of the money had not passed to the creditor, the debtor had paid in accordance with his obligation to a person designated to receive it. By this he had discharged his obligation and it was up to the creditor to get his due from his *libertus*. The contrary opinion, regarded by Gaius as too strict, placed a higher priority on the impossibility of a *libertus* to acquire ownership for his *patronus* than on good faith/*bona fides*. In consequence the debtor's obligation remained, but he could reclaim from the freedman the sum he had handed over without legal grounds.[44]

---

42 See the brief discussion in Ignazio Buti, *Studi sulla capacità patrimoniale dei 'servi'* (Naples: Jovene, 1976): 161–62. The intent to possess, which had been manifested by granting a *peculium*, was not cancelled when a master became insane or died (D. 41.2.1.5 Paul. 54 ed.); contrariwise a change of mind without external manifestation also remained irrelevant in terms of possession (D. 41.2.3.18 Paul. 54 ed.).

43 Transl. William M. Gordon and O.F. Robinson, *The Institutes of Gaius Translated with an Introduction; With the Latin Text of Seckel and Kuebler* (London: Duckworth, 1988): 359.

44 Because the case is treated as one comparable with a mandate, an obvious assumption would be that the creditor, in lieu of actual payment, was assigned the action against the *libertus* as in D. 17.1.29.3 (Ulp. 7 disp.).

The controversy continued until Justinian ruled in Inst. 3.26.10 in favour of a cancellation of the debt. Paul therefore still discussed both positions[45] in a comparable case: in D. 46.3.62 (Paul. 8 ad Plaut.)[46] a *dispensator* had been freed by testament and been bequeathed his *peculium.*[47] Subsequent to this, he had accepted payments from debtors who had owed money to the deceased without any relation to the *dispensator*'s *peculium.* On the question of whether the heir was entitled to deduct such sums from the *peculium* that had been left to the *libertus*, Paul answered that it depended on when the payments had been made. The heir could not deduct from the *peculium* monies received after his acceptance of the estate, because such were owed to him by the freedman himself. Any payments received prior to acceptance were owed from the *peculium* in accordance with the rules of unauthorized management and mandate, and the heir might simply retain the sum in question. If, however, the heir had approved payments made to the former *dispensator* after the

45 At the time when Paul had to deliver his opinion it was yet unknown which of the opposing views the future judge would follow in deciding the preliminary question as to the effects of the payment; so he discussed both.

46 D. 46.3.62 (Paulus 8 ad Plaut.): *Dispensatorem meum testamento liberum esse iussi et peculium ei legavi: is post mortem meam a debitoribus pecunias exegit: an heres meus retinere ex peculio eius quod exegit possit, quaeritur. et si quidem post aditam hereditatem exegerit pecuniam, dubitari non debet, quin de peculio eo nomine retineri nihil debeat, quia liber factus incipit debere, si liberantur solutione debitores. cum vero ante aditam hereditatem pecuniam accepit dispensator, si quidem liberantur debitores ipsa solutione, non est dubium, quin de peculio id retinendum sit, quia incipit debere hic heredi quasi negotiorum gestorum vel mandati actione. si vero non liberantur, illa quaestio est: cum negotium meum gerens a debitoribus meis acceperis, deinde ego ratum non habuero et mox agere velim negotiorum gestorum actione, an utiliter agam, si caveam te indemnem futurum. quod quidem ego non puto: nam sublata est negotiorum gestorum actio eo, quod ratum non habui: et per hoc debitor mihi constituitur.* / 'Paul, Plautius, book 8: In my will, I gave my *dispensator* his freedom and bequeathed his *peculium* to him; he exacted money from [my] debtors after my death; the question is: Can my heir retain out of the *peculium* what [the *dispensator*] exacts? Now, if, indeed, it be after the inheritance has been accepted that he exacts the money, there should be no doubt that no retention should be made from the *peculium* on that score because, having become free, he himself becomes a debtor [to the heir], if debtors are released by payment to him. But should the *dispensator*, before the inheritance is accepted, accept money, then, if their payment discharges the debtors, there is no doubt that retention thereof from the *peculium* is to be made because [the *dispensator*] then incurs liability to the heir by the action for unsolicited administration or that on mandate. If, however, the debtors are not thereby released, this question does arise. When, in conducting my affairs, you accept payment from my debtors, I do not ratify and presently wish to bring the action for unsolicited administration; can I successfully so proceed, if I undertake your indemnity? I for one think not; for the action for unsolicited administration is excluded by my nonratification, and thereby a debtor to me is created' (transl. Beinart in Watson, *Digest of Justinian* [n. 41]). The question is discussed extensively by David Daube in *Collected Studies in Roman Law*, ed. David Cohen and Dieter Simon (Frankfurt am Main: Klostermann, 1991): 963–72.

47 Cf. Gamauf, "Peculium" (in this volume): paradoxes of slaves with property.

latter's manumission (and so released his debtors),[48] the freedman as manager/*negotiorum gestor* owed the monies he had received directly to the heir.

To a debtor, a *dispensator* represented his master. Payment given to him was as a payment made directly to the creditor, as the debtor paid at the risk and with the consent of the *dominus*. Changes in the relationship between *dominus* and *dispensator* (e.g., an internal removal from office), or any abuse of powers regarding money collected by the latter in breach of his duties, did not affect the debtor. Such risks burdended him only when dealing with slaves who acted independently; a *dispensator*, however, stood *in loco domini.*[49]

A hypothetical textbook example such as D. 45.1.141.4[50] would make no sense unless *dominus* and *dispensator*[51] usually worked in close collaboration: creditor and debtor, both being in Rome, arrange by stipulation that payment is to be made that same day in Carthage.[52] Some (unnamed) jurists did not regard as wholly impossible (*non semper*) the completion (and validity) of such agreements.[53] In order

48 For *ratihabitio* see Hans Hermann Seiler, *Der Tatbestand der negotiorum gestio im römischen Recht* (Cologne: Böhlau, 1968): 61–62.

49 So also Daube, *Collected Studies* (n. 46): 967. Where slaves acted autonomously, a business partner who gave credit to a slave risked that no benefit (*versio*) had accrued to the master from the transaction (D. 15.3.3.9 Ulp. 29 ed.) or that the slave's *peculium* might not have been sufficient to cover his loan; see Richard Gamauf, "§ 102. Klage aufgrund Sonderguts oder unmittelbare Zuwendung in das Vermögen des Gewalthabers (actio de peculio vel de in rem verso)," in *Handbuch des Römischen Privatrechts*, ed. Ulrike Babusiaux et al. (Tübingen: Mohr Siebeck, 2023): nos. 42 and 33.

50 D. 45.1.141.4 (Gaius 2 de verb. oblig.): *Si inter eos, qui Romae sunt, talis fiat stipulatio: 'Hodie Carthagine dare spondes?', quidam putant non semper videri impossibilem causam stipulationi contineri, quia possit contingere, ut tam stipulator quam promissor ante aliquod tempus suo quisque dispensatori notum fecerit in eum diem futuram stipulationem ac demandasset promissor quidem suo dispensatori, ut daret, stipulator autem suo, ut acciperet: quod si ita factum fuerit, poterit valere stipulatio.* 'Gaius, Verbal Obligations, book 2: If a stipulation is made by parties at Rome thus, 'do you promise to pay today at Carthage', in the view of some the stipulation does not necessarily depend on an impossibility. It may be that both stipulator and promisor have, some time before, told their *dispensatores* that there would be a stipulation on that day, and the promisor has asked his *dispensator* to pay, the stipulator is to accept, the sum in question. If so, the stipulatio can be valid' (transl. Hart, Lewis and Beinart in Watson, *Digest of Justinian* (n. 41). *Contra* Stelzenberger, *Kapitalmanagement* (n. 15): 36–37, 48–49 and Aubert, *Business Managers* (n. 23): 197 a *iussum* was not involved in this situation. This text is regarded as evidence for Gaius' activities at Rome; see Detlev Liebs, "Römische Provinzialjurisprudenz," *FreiDok plus: Universitätbibliothek Freiburg*, https://freidok.uni-freiburg.de/fedora/objects/freidok:10556/datastreams/FILE1/content [accessed 25.08.2022].

51 However Minaud, *La comptabilité* (n. 23): 175, also believes that *dispensatores* enjoyed certain freedoms.

52 This is a popular geographical constellation for textbook cases, cf. D. 13.4.2.6 (Ulp 27 ed); D. 19.5.5.4 (Paul. 5 quaest.); D. 45.1.73 pr. (Paul. 24 ed.).

53 Differently decided Julian; see D. 13.4.2.6 (Ulpian 27 ad ed.): [. . .] *quare verum puto, quod Iulianus ait eum, qui Romae stipulatur hodie Carthagine dari, inutiliter stipulari.* [. . .] / 'Ulpian, Edict, book 27: 6. [. . .] Thus, I agree with Julian's view that one who stipulates at Rome for something "to be given at Carthage today" makes a stipulation which is void' (transl. Birks in Watson, *Digest of*

to comply with their obligations, both parties need merely have instructed their *dispensatores* in advance to hold themselves ready for payment and receipt, respectively, at Carthage on that day. The scenario is obviously contrived, but it would have defeated its purpose had it struck readers as altogether impossible.[54] In any case, this clearly shows how *dispensatores* were assumed to follow detailed instructions even overseas.

Another piece of information we can glean from D. 45.1.141.4 is how third parties were informed of a *dispensator*'s authorisation to make payments for his master.[55] Such became immediately ineffective as soon as it was internally revoked; then the slave was no longer authorised to make payment on his master's behalf or dispose of his property.[56] In the absence of evidence in the sources we cannot assume that such situations were treated analogous to the internal revocation of authorisation to accept payment.[57]

5 How to Become a *dispensator*

For Gaius, too, the term *dispensator* was associated first and foremost with the management of money. In his excursus about the so-called *negotia per aes et libram*/ transactions by bronze and balance (Gai. 1.119–122), the jurist mentions the word as an etymological relic[58] of this archaic payment method: slaves allowed to handle money were still called *dispensatores* (*unde servi* [. . .] *appellati sunt*), because once upon a time payment had been made by weighing out metal.

Gaius inst. 1.122: [. . .] qui dabat olim pecuniam non numerabat eam sed appendebat; unde servi, quibus permittitur administratio	Gaius inst. 1.122: [. . .] In those times a person paying money would not count it but weigh it. This is why slaves who are permitted the

Justinian [n. 41]). Cf. Gregor Albers, *Perpetuatio obligationis: Leistungspflicht trotz Unmöglichkeit* (Cologne: Böhlau, 2019): 332–33.

54 It would only have needed one messenger who would deliver instructions to both to bring off the scheme.

55 For payments made by *dispensatores* see Ps. Quint. decl. min. 345.10; Debray, "Pétrone" (n. 6): 46–47; Aubert, *Business Managers* (n. 23): 197.

56 Cf. Andreas Wacke, "Die libera administratio peculii: Zur Verfügungsmacht von Hauskindern und Sklaven über ihr Sondergut," in *Sklaverei und Freilassung im römischen Recht: Symposium für Hans Josef Wieling zum 70. Geburtstag*, ed. Thomas Finkenauer (Berlin: Springer Verlag, 2006): 256–66.

57 The recipient's acquisition of ownership was barred by the *dispensator*'s lack of power to dispose of the money, and the resulting *furtum*.

58 For the etymology see also Alfred Gudeman, "Dispensator," in *Thesaurus Linguae Latinae*, vol. 1 (1909–1934): 1399–400, and Liebenam, "Dispensator" (n. 23): 1189.

pecuniae, dispensatores appellati sunt et adhuc vocantur.	administration of money are called in Latin *dispensatores*, that is, weighers-out.[59]

Reference to the familiar job title made these ancient legal acts appear less antiquated. Unfortunately the learned anecdote makes no mention of what precisely was included under the heading of *administratio pecuniae*,[60] or what a *dispensator*'s powers consisted of.[61] A glance at jurists' discussions of the *actio de peculio* fleshes out the phrase *administratio permittitur*: there, *permissus* (*domini*) referred to concession of a *peculium*,[62] while *administratio*[63] (*libera*) described the free disposal of it. In inscriptions, *permissus* could also denote consent to a slave's (generous) spending on his own affairs.[64] In all such cases the slave enjoyed the privilege of disposing of his master's property, to a greater or lesser extent; at least sometimes this included spending for his own benefit.

Beyond these rather vague comments, the jurists provide no further information about the internal procedure of appointing a *dispensator*. The use of *permittere*[65] allows us to infer that slaves actively sought *dispensatio* and thought of it as a privilege.[66] This is consistent with the anecdotal evidence in the *cena*, which gives a prominent place to the career of a *dispensator*, because this was how Trimalchio had risen.[67]

---

59 Transl. Gordon and Robinson, *The Institutes of Gaius* (n. 43): 83. Similarly Isid. Etym. 10.67: *Dispensator vocatur, cui creditur administratio pecuniarum. Et ideo dispensator quia prius qui dabant pecuniam non numerabant eam, sed adpendebant* / '*Dispensator* is the name for a person entrusted with the administration of money, and such a one is a *dispensator* because in former times the person who dispensed money would not count it but "weigh it out" (*appendere*)' (transl. Stephen A. Barney, W.J. Lewis, J.A. Beach and Oliver Berghof, eds., *The Etymologies of Isidore of Seville* [Cambridge: Cambridge University Press, 2006]: 217).

60 More on *administratio pecuniae* in Stelzenberger, *Kapitalmanagement* (n. 15): 43–49; *administratio* occurs also in Gai. 1.53 (*interdictio* of *prodigi*), which may however be a later addition, cf. Richard Gamauf, *Ad statuam licet confugere: Untersuchungen zum Asylrecht im römischen Prinzipat* (Frankfurt am Main: Peter Lang Verlag, 1999): 96–102.

61 Aubert, *Business Managers* (n. 23): 196 assumes the content of a *permissus* was standardised, similar to a *praepositio*. Since a *permissus* became effective through individual notifications to debtors, the protection of third party interests did not necessitate legal standardisation.

62 D. 15.1.5.4 (Ulp. 29 ed.); D. 20.3.1.1 (Marcian. form. hyp. sing.); D. 41.2.1.5 (Paul. 54 ed.).

63 E.g. D. 15.1.7.1 (Ulp. 29 ed.); D. 15.1.16 (Iul. 12 dig.); D. 15.1.24 (Ulp. 26 Sab.); D. 15.1.46 (Paul. 60 ed.); D. 15.1.48 pr.-1 (Paul. 17 Plaut.); cf. Gamauf, "Klage aufgrund Sonderguts" (n. 49): nos. 18–21.

64 Constructing a tomb with consent/*ex permissu*, e.g. CIL 3.3172; CIL 10.26; AE 2009, 1256.

65 The same expression is used to report a slave's promotion to the post of *vilicus* (the highest-ranking slave on a rural estate) in Apul. met. 8.22: *Servus quidam, cui cunctam familiae tutelam dominus permiserat.* / 'There had been a slave whose owner entrusted him with the supervision of the entire household' (transl. Sarah Ruden, *The Golden Ass. Apuleius* (New Haven: Yale University Press, 2011): 175).

66 Gaius also uses *permittere* on several occasions in connection with privileges: Gai. 1.7 (*ius respondendi*); 1.102 (*adoptio impuberis*); 1.150, 173, 176 (*tutoris optio*) etc.

67 Marcel Simonis believes this is to some extent realistic. Simonis, *Cum servis nullum est conubium* (n. 17): 103.

Information about his biography is scattered across a number of different passages: his beginnings[68] are depicted in mythologizing[69] frescoes in the entrance area of his house[70] (arrival at Rome,[71] sale in the slave market). The next scenes are more realistic:[72] he

---

68 Petron. 75.10–11: *Tam magnus ex Asia veni, quam hic candelabrus est.* [. . .] *tamen ad delicias ipsimi annos quattuordecim fui. nec turpe est, quod dominus iubet. ego tamen et ipsimae satis faciebam. scitis quid dicam: taceo, quia non sum de gloriosis.* (76.1) *Ceterum, quemadmodum di volunt, dominus in domo factus sum, et ecce cepi ipsimi cerebellum. quid multa? coheredem me Caesari fecit, et accepi patrimonium laticlavium.* / 'When I first came out of Asia, I was as tall as that lamp stand. [. . .] I was the master's favorite for fourteen years. It's not wrong if the master makes you do it. Anyway, I managed to do my own mistress as well. You know what I'm talking about. But I won't talk about it, because I don't like to brag. At any rate, the gods must be okay with it, 'cause I got in charge of the whole place, and the master was crazy about me. To make a long story short, he made me his heir (along with the emperor, of course), and I got a senator's fortune' (transl. Sarah Ruden, *Petronius: Satyricon* [Indianapolis: Hackett Publishing, 2000]: 164–65).

69 For the symbolism see Courtney, *Companion* (n. 1): 76; Schmeling, *A Commentary* (n. 1): 98–100, and Petersen, *Freedman* (n. 8): 4.

70 Gilbert Bagnani, "The House of Trimalchio," *American Journal of Philology* 75, no. 1 (1954): 16–39; Burkhardt Wesenberg, "Zur Wanddekoration im Hause des Trimalchio," in *Studien zu Petron und seiner Rezeption. Studi su Petronio e sulla sua fortuna*, ed. Luigi Castagna and Eckard Lefèvre (Berlin: De Gruyter, 2007): 267–83; Rose MacLean, *Freed Slaves and Roman Imperial Culture* (Cambridge: Cambridge University Press, 2018): 14–15, 25. This was probably based on tomb decorations; s. Bodel, "The cena Trimalchionis" (n. 13): 46; Gianpiero Rosati, "Trimalchio on Stage," in *Oxford Readings in the Roman Novel*, ed. Stephen J. Harrison (Oxford: Oxford University Press, 1999): 103–4; Hofmann, "Petronius" (n. 1): 106. For the placing inside the house see Wesenberg as above: 267–68. Trimalchio was a nouveau-riche, 'self-made' man, and as such had no *imagines*, portraits of illustrious ancestors, to show off there (see Wilhelm Kierdorf, "Imagines maiorum," in *Der neue Pauly: Enzyklopädie der Antike*, vol. 5, ed. Hubert Cancik and Helmuth Schneider (Stuttgart: J.B. Metzler, 1998): 946–47); instead his paintings told his own life story.

71 Puglisi, "Il microcosmo" (n. 3): 207–8, changes the chronology: he relocates the *dispensator* training to Chios and regards Trimalchio's sale to Rome as punishment for his affair with the *domina* (see n. 81). However, this is improbable because not a single sale or purchase of a *dispensator* is attested; it seems that masters entrusted this work exclusively to slaves already in the household, see n. 73.

72 Petron. 29.3–4. *Erat autem venalicium <cum> titulis pictis, et ipse Trimalchio capillatus caduceum tenebat Minervaque ducente Romam intrabat. hinc quemadmodum ratiocinari didicisset, deinque dispensator factus esset, omnia diligenter curiosus pictor cum inscriptione reddiderat.* / 'There was a slave market, with the slaves all carrying signs describing themselves, and Trimalchio as a long-haired boy was entering the city. Minerva led him, and he held a herald's wand like the one of Mercury carries. Then you saw him learning how to keep accounts, then becoming *dispensator* – the conscientious painter had shown it all and put captions everywhere' (transl. Ruden, *Petronius* (n. 68): 20). Gesine Manuwald believes the *tituli* offer insights about literacy, Gesine Manuwald, "Der Dichter in der Gemäldegalerie: Zur Diskussion über Kunst und Literatur in Petrons Satyrica," in *Studien zu Petron und seiner Rezeption. Studi su Petronio e sulla sua fortuna*, ed. Luigi Castagna and Eckard Lefèvre (Berlin: De Gruyter, 2007): 262; see also Nicholas Horsfall, "'The Uses of Literacy' and the Cena Trimalchionis II," *Greece & Rome* 36, no. 2 (1989): 202–3, while Smith, *Petronius* (n. 11): 60, interprets them as ridiculing the painter's incompetence who failed to create an intelligible painting and had to add explanations. For visually conspicuous *dispensatores* see below n. 212 and subsequent nn.

learns arithmetic[73] – like other (child) slaves in the *cena* – and achieves the pinnacle[74] of a slave career[75] by being made *dispensator.*

In recounting Trimalchio's biography, Petronius again employs the stylistic device of deliberately contrasting 'fact and fiction':[76] the host himself describes a version of his rise that differs from his 'official CV' as depicted in the frescoes. He brags how he finally (because he had been made *dispensator*?) came to run both the household (*dominus in domo factus sum*) and his master (*cepi ipsimi cerebellum*), attributing this not to arithmetic skills, but solely to the fact that he enjoyed his *dominus*' favour, which he had won by other means.

6 Sex and the *dispensator*

A result of the fourteen years[77] in which Trimalchio had been the 'darling'/*delicatus*[78] of his master, whose every wish he had fulfilled (*nec turpe est, quod dominus iubet*[79]), were *dispensatio*, testamentary manumission and a vast inheritance (*patrimonium*

---

73 For arithmetic and accounting see Thilo, *Codex* (n. 20): 53–59; Minaud, *La comptabilité* (n. 23): 176; Schmeling, *A Commentary* (n. 1): 193. In the *cena*, only the prospect of higher earnings can lend attraction to education and careers; see n. 72, 194–209; Rimell, "Petronius' Lessons" (n. 9): 119–20 – Slave children in the *cena*, all of whom are also their masters' *delicati*, are praised for their arithmetic skills (Petron. 46.3; 75.4), while the ability to calculate percentages appears to be more desirable than being educated (Petron. 58.7). Similar abilities are mentioned in an epitaph for a deceased eight-and-a-half-year-old boy in CIL 5.7274. For the internal recruitment of *dispensatores* see Muñiz Coello, "Officium" (n. 23): 109; Herrmann-Otto, *Ex ancilla* (n. 23): 370.

74 Stelzenberger, *Kapitalmanagement* (n. 15): 41.

75 Career paths that progress from *vilicus* or *actor* to *dispensator* may be seen in CIL 6.278; CIL 9.4186; cf. Aubert, *Business Managers* (n. 23): 192–93.

76 Courtney, *Companion* (n. 1): 124; Rimell, "Petronius' Lessons" (n. 9): 116.

77 For this and for his age see John Bodel, "Trimalchio and the Candelabrum," *Classical Philology* 84, no. 3 (1989): 224–31; Kort Bydraes, "The Young Trimalchio," *Acta Classica* 36 (1993): 143–46; MacLean, *Freed Slaves* (n. 70): 15.

78 For *delicati* see Christian Laes, "Desperately Different? Delicia Children in the Roman Household," in *Early Christian Families in Context: An Interdisciplinary Dialogue*, ed. David K. Balch and Carolyn Osiek (Grand Rapids: Eerdmans, 2003): 298–324; Martin Kindler, *Affectionis aestimatio. Vom Ursprung des Affektionsinteresses im römischen Recht und seiner Rezeption* (Berlin: Duncker und Humblot, 2012): 40–45.

79 See also Sen. contr. 4 praef. 10: *Impudicitia in ingenuo crimen est, in servo necessitas, in liberto officium* / Losing one's virtue is a crime in the free-born, a necessity in a slave, a duty for the freedman (transl. Michael Winterbottom, *Seneca the Elder: Declamations*, vol. 1, *Controversiae Books 1–6: Suasoriae, Fragments*, Loeb Classical Library 464 (Cambridge, MA: Harvard University Press, 1974): 431). See, e.g., Anita Vittoria Nettis, "Padroni, sesso e schiavi," *Index* 28 (2000): 156 f.; Gamauf, *Ad statuam licet confugere* (n. 60): 87; Mark Masterson, "Studies of Ancient Masculinity," in *A Companion to Greek and Roman Sexualities*, ed. Thomas K. Hubbard (Hoboken: Wiley-Blackwell, 2014): 27–28; Craig A. Williams, *Roman Homosexuality* (Cary: Oxford University Press, 2010): 31–32.

laticlavium). In a company of former slaves this admission broke no taboos.[80] Trimalchio could make it quite openly, because his tale ended with a triumph: he had cuckolded the master with his *domina*![81] When Trimalchio made that revelation, the guests had already learned about the former's reaction:

Petron. 69.3: [. . .] Sic me salvum habeatis, ut ego sic solebam ipsumam meam debattuere, ut etiam dominus suspicaretur; et ideo me in vilicationem relegavit. sed tace, lingua . . .	Petron. 69.3: [. . .] So help me, I used to bang my own mistress. The master actually suspected, so he sent me off to run one of his farms. But here goes my mouth again.[82]

A Pompeian graffito testifies to the basic realism of Petronius' account even in this context: *Hic ego cum domina resoluto clune peregi; tales sed versus scribere turpe fuit.*[83] A slave reports with pride and assumed coyness about having sex with his *domina*.[84]

80 For sexual services as a means of career advancement elsewhere in the *cena* see Richard Gamauf, "Ideal Freedmen-Lives? On the Construction of Biographies in the Cena Trimalchionis," in *Le realtà della schiavitù: Identità e biografie da Eumeo a Frederick Douglass. Les réalités de l'esclavage: Identités et biographies d'Eumée à Frederick Douglass. Atti del XL Convegno internazionale del GIREA (Napoli, 18–20 dicembre 2017)*, ed. Francesca Reduzzi Merola, Maria Vittoria Bramante and Adelaide Caravaglios (Naples: Satura Editrice, 2020): 282–86.
81 Sexual relations between slaves and free women are discussed in Holt Neumon Parker, "Free Women and Male Slaves, or Mandingo Meets the Roman Empire," in *Fear of Slaves – Fear of Enslavement in the Ancient Mediterranean: Peur de l'ésclave – Peur de l'ésclavage en mediterranée ancienne (Discours, representations, pratiques)*, ed. Anastasia Serghidou (Besançon: Presses Universitaires de Franche-Comté, 2007): 281–98 (see 292–93 for Trimalchio).
82 Transl. Ruden, *Petronius* (n. 68): 52.
83 CIL 4.9246b; on which see Edward Courtney, *Musa Lapidaria. A Selection of Latin Verse Inscriptions* (Atlanta: Scholars Press, 1995): 310. 'Here, with my mistress, her butt opened, I did it. But it was naughty to write such verses' translates Holt Parker, "Sex, Popular Beliefs, and Culture," in *Cultural History of Sexuality in the Classical World*, ed. Mark Golden and Peter Toohey (London: Bloomsbury, 2014): 139; the German translation by Wilhelm Weeber, *Decius war hier . . . Das beste aus der römischen Graffiti-Szene*, 3rd ed. (Düsseldorf/Zürich: Artemis und Winkler, 2003): 55, is similar: 'Hier habe ich die Zeit mit meiner Herrin verbracht, indem ich ihr Hinterteil auseinanderzog, aber solche Verse zu schreiben, wäre schändlich.' Less aggressive wordings are those by Courtney (who reconstructs in the second line *cetera sed versu*): 'Here with my mistress, my haunches heaving, I performed – but to write out (the rest?) in verse would have been shameful' (op. cit. 101 f.) and Eva Cantarella, *Gli amori degli altri. Tra cielo e terra, da Zeus a Cesare* (Milan: La nave di Teseo, 2018): 162 who also finds 'ingenua tenerezza' in the text: 'Io qui, con le natiche al vento, ho fatto l'amore con la mia donna: ma scrivere queste cose è stato turpe.'
84 *Domina* can also refer to a mistress or lover, see Maria Wyke, "Mistress and Metaphor in Augustan Elegy," in *Sexuality and Gender in the Classical World: Readings and Sources*, ed. Laura K. McClure (Oxford: Blackwell, 2002): 193–219.

This parallels the relevant terms used by Trimalchio in terms of both content and style.[85]

In Trimalchio's telling, the affair becomes his ultimate success: he claims that he took the initative[86] and presents it as an act of revenge for his sexual humiliations.[87] By using the term *debattuere*[88] he assumes the active, masculine role[89] and transforms the swift encounter into a deliberate status transgression, almost as if he had coerced the *ipsima*.[90]

In Trimalchio's world, the master reacted quite mildely, by merely 'banishing him to the country'. Signigficantly, in speaking about such matters, both Petronius and Ulpian employ a legal term, *relegare*.[91] Under the Empire, temporary *relegatio* was the penalty for adultery for *honestiores* (something that satisfied Trimalchio's self-image!). In reality, such a relocation from the *familia urbana*[92] significantly worsened a slave's sitation and living conditions.[93] The hard work, to which they were unaccustomed, constituted grave risks to urban slaves. Consequently, an usufructuary would exceed his rights (*abuti videbitur*) to a use of the property without impairing its substance/

85 Petron. 69.3, 75.11 (n. 68).

86 From Petron. 75.11 (*satis faciebam*, n. 68) it appears to be the *domina* who makes the inital demand.

87 Occasionally Petronius attempts to portray a slave's emotional reaction to degrading treatment: he has Hermeros tell the guests that he redeemed his *contubernalis*/'slave wife' so that no one might wipe his hands on her hair (Petron. 57.6). Trimalchio does exactly that, quite unabashedly (Petron. 27.6); cf. Smith, *Petronius* (n. 11): 56; Schmeling, *A Commentary* (n. 1): 90. To use a slave as an animate 'towel' degraded them to the status of mere inanimate objects, cf. Courtney, *Companion* (n. 1): 74.

88 From *battuere* 'to beat, to pound'. According to the *Thesaurus Linguae Latinae*, the only classical attestation is the one in Petronius; the *lex Salica* (between 507 and 511) uses it synonymously with *verberare*. For the sexual connotation see Smith, *Petronius* (n. 11): 191 and Schmeling, *A Commentary* (n. 1): 284.

89 Parker, "Free Women" (n. 81): 292. Generally Michel Foucault, *Histoire de la sexualité*, vol. 3, *Le souci de soi* (Paris: Gallimard, 1984); Eckhard Meyer-Zwiffelhofer, *Im Zeichen des Phallus: Die Ordnung des Geschlechtslebens im antiken Rom* (Frankfurt am Main: Campus Verlag, 1995): 64–88; Evelyn Höbenreich and Giunio Rizzelli, *Scylla: Fragmente einer juristischen Geschichte der Frauen im antiken Rom* (Vienna: Böhlau, 2003): 197–98; Marilyn B. Skinner, *Sexuality in Greek and Roman Culture* (Malden: Blackwell, 2005): 195–97; Paul Veyne, *Sexe et pouvoir à Rome* (Paris: Tallandier, 2005); Parker, "Sex" (n. 83): 134–42; Masterson, "Studies" (n. 79): 16–17; Williams, *Roman Homosexuality* (n. 79): 17–19, 179–245.

90 For this term see Smith, *Petronius* (n. 11): 175; Schmeling, *A Commentary* (n. 1): 284.

91 D. 28.5.35.3 (Ulpian 4 disp.): [. . .] *si servus fuerit missus in villam interim illic futurus, quia dominum offenderat, quasi ad tempus relegatus* [. . .] / 'Ulpian, Disputations, book 4: [. . .] if a slave has been sent to a country house to stay there for the time being because he had offended his master, being as it were exiled for a period [. . .]' (transl. Gordon in Watson, *Digest of Justinian* [n. 41]).

92 The *dipensator* was universally counted among its members; see D. 34.2.1 pr. (Pomp. 6 Sab.); D. 50.16.166 (Pom. 6 Sab.).

93 Sen. ira 3.29.1; for other sources see Schmeling, *A Commentary* (n. 1): 284; for the comparatively privileged situation of the *familia urbana* cf. Edmondson, "Slavery" (n. 32): 340–41.

salva rerum substantia by ordering such changes.[94] Trimalchio's work during his 'exile' in the country is not specified in the novel.[95] Theoretically, it might have remained the usual because Pomponius mentions the employment of *dispensatores* on rural estates.[96]

Trimalchio was fortunate enough to retain his master's affections, be freed and become his former master's heir. The gossiping freedmen tell of another *dispensator*[97] in a similar situation (he, too, had had relations with his *domina*), who faced a very different fate:

> Petron. 45.4: [. . .] Et ecce habituri sumus munus excellente in triduo die festa; familia non lanisticia, sed plurimi liberti. [. . .] iam [. . .] habet (= lanista) [. . .] dispensatorem Glyconis, qui deprehensus est cum dominam suam delectaretur. [. . .] (8) Glyco autem, sestertiarius homo, dispensatorem ad bestias dedit. hoc est se ipsum traducere. quid servus peccavit, qui coactus est facere? magis illa matella digna fuit quam taurus iactaret. sed qui asinum non potest, stratum caedit.

> Petron. 45.4: [. . .] Anyway, we're gonna have a great show in three days, on the holiday. It's not some pack of slaves from the gladiatorial school, but mostly freedmen. [. . .] He's got Glyco's *dispensator*, who got caught entertaining the mistress. But Glyco's a two-bit character for giving his *dispensator* to the wild animals. He's just making a fool of himself. The poor slave only did as she ordered him. That piss pot of a woman is the one the bulls should be tossing. But if you can't beat the donkey, you beat the saddle.[98]

They were looking forward to the upcoming games, when the *dispensator* of Glyco, a freedman, would be put into the arena. He had cuckolded his master with the latter's wife and been sold *ad bestias*. The freedmen do not blame the slave (*quid servus peccavit, qui coactus est facere?*), and they have no sympathies for the wife[99] or for Glyco, who had made a big song and dance about the affair.

---

94 D. 7.1.15.1 (Ulp. 18 Sab.), see also Gamauf, *Ad statuam licet confugere* (n. 60): 113–14. The principle of observing due moderation is named in D. 7.1.15.3 (Ulp. 18 Sab.).

95 The following assume that he works as a *vilicus:* Aubert, *Business Managers* (n. 23): 151–52; Stelzenberger, *Kapitalmanagement* (n. 15): 42 n. 200; Schmeling, *A Commentary* (n. 1): 99 (but Schmeling wrongly understands it as a 'promotion' at 187); Mouritsen, *Freedman* (n. 12): 199. So also the translation by Ruden, see above n. 82.

96 D. 50.16.166 (Pom. 6 Sab.). For rural *dispensatores* see Carlsen, *Vilici* (n. 23): 153–58; Muñiz Coello, "Officium" (n. 23): 108. It is likely that the 'accused' in Petron. 53.10 was one such (see below n. 139). Mart. 6.73.1 f. juxtaposes *colonus* – *dispensator* to embody the contrast between town and country; cf. Stelzenberger, *Kapitalmanagement* (n. 15): 39.

97 The banishment to Baiae (Petron. 53.10) is wholly ironic; cf. Smith, *Petronius* (n. 11): 145. Schmeling, *A Commentary* (n. 1): 219 suggests that 'the *atriensis* was bonking Fortunata and T. quietly removed him' (however, such restraint seems hardly in character for Trimalchio).

98 Transl. Ruden, *Petronius* (n. 68): 32.

99 Calling her a *matella* (chamberpot – cf. Petron. 27.5) is a misogynistic and sexually derogatory slur; see Smith, *Petronius* (n. 11): 118; Schmeling, *A Commentary* (n. 1): 188.

The sorry fate of Glyco's *dispensator* made Trimalchio's triumph shine all the brighter. The unnamed *dispensator* had been seduced and punished; his passivity conformed to the slave stereotype. Just as cliched are the wanton wife,[100] and the greedy *libertus*[101] who tries to squeeze profit out of the slave to the last, by selling him *ad bestias*.[102] As a result, he suffered ridicule as a husband and a *dominus*[103] who was unable to enforce propriety[104] or discipline in his own house, and so became the butt of gossip all over town.

Petronius' noble audience would more readily sympathise with the restraint – not due to a lack of evidence (*suspicaretur*[105]) – shown towards an adulterous *dispensator* by Trimalchio's senatorial master, than with the severity of the freedman Glyco. *Relegatio* (instead of execution) meant the master kept a valuable slave and, even more important, the affair was not made public.[106] A senator had to avoid gossip, even if in the privacy of his home he might tolerate his wife taking the same sexual liberties with slaves as himself. In the event of adultery, the *lex Iulia de adulteriis* required the husband to divorce his wife and bring criminal charges against her; if he failed to do so, third parties could accuse him of *lenocinium*/pimping, which carried a risk to his reputation, his status and his assets.[107] If the main witness to the crime was no longer at hand, there was little to fear for the husband.

100 For the fear of being cuckolded by slaves see Kyle Harper, *Slavery in the Late Roman World, A. D. 275–425* (Cambridge: Cambridge University Press, 2011): 336–37; for adultery with slaves in satire cf. Meyer-Zwiffelhofer, *Im Zeichen* (n. 89): 96–97.

101 Christopher Star, *The Empire of the Self: Self-Command and Political Speech in Seneca and Petronius* (Baltimore: Johns Hopkins University Press, 2012): 194–96.

102 This was banned by a *lex Petronia*; cf., with references, Richard Gamauf, "§ 36. Sklaven (servi)," in *Handbuch des Römischen Privatrechts*, ed. Ulrike Babusiaux et al. (Tübingen: Mohr Siebeck, 2023): no. 34.

103 The law allowed the husband to simply kill any adulterous slave, either as the latter's master or, in case of an outsider, on the basis of a special *ius occidendi*; cf. Thomas McGinn, *Prostitution, Sexuality and the Law in Ancient Rome* (New York: Oxford University Press, 1998): 202–7; Olivia F. Robinson, *The Criminal Law of Ancient Rome* (London: Duckworth, 1995): 60–61.

104 The *domus* as 'focus of honor' is discussed by Richard P. Saller, *Patriarchy, Property and Death in the Roman Family* (Cambridge: Cambridge University Press, 1994): 88–95.

105 For investigations into suspected infidelity between a wife and a slave see Harper, *Slavery* (n. 100): 336–37. The prohibition of torturing slaves in a trial against their masters did not apply in a case of *adulterium*; see Leonhard Schumacher, *Servus index: Sklavenverhör und Sklavenanzeige im republikanischen und kaiserzeitlichen Rom* (Wiesbaden: Franz Steiner Verlag, 1982): 166; Anna Bellodi Ansaloni, *Ad eruendam veritatem: Profili metodologici e processuali della quaestio per tormenta* (Bologna: Bononia University Press, 2011): 225–47.

106 Parker, "Free Women" (n. 81): 293, assumes that most such cases went undetected.

107 McGinn, *Prostitution* (n. 103): 171–94; Robinson, *The Criminal Law* (n. 103): 67–68.

It is no accident that on both occasions in the novel the slave who gains his *domina*'s favour is a *dispensator.*[108] Their role meant that *dispensatores* had close contact with both master and mistress, as well as access to the household's money (a fact that did not harm their sex appeal).[109] The *cena* presents them – in their own perception as well as that of others – as having higher self-esteem than regular slaves.[110] In other words, they were probably the least slave-like among a household's slaves. And in fact free women did not shy away from relationships with them, as funerary inscriptions show:[111] the partners of *dispensatores* were more often free than unfree.[112] If there is poetic license (or exaggeration) in the portrayal of such relationships in the *Cena*, it is in Petronius' choice of free women from the own households as sexual partners for his fictional *dispensatores*.[113]

In private law, only a relationship with a partner from outside the household could become relevant.[114] In D. 11.3.16 (Alf. 2 dig.),[115] a *dominus* freed a *dispensator* without a prior rendering of accounts[116] and so learned too late about the latter's

108 Mart. 6.39 lists the slaves with whom a wife has already betrayed her husband; there is no *dispensator* among them. Was this omission deliberate irony?

109 Herrmann-Otto, *Ex ancilla* (n. 23): 387; Simonis, *Cum servis nullum est conubium* (n. 17): 103. Nor did the intimate details of their master's and mistress' lives remain a secret to slaves; cf. Michele George, "The Lives of Slaves," in *The World of Pompeii*, ed. John J. Dobbins and Pedar W. Foss (London: Routledge, 2007): 540; Harper, *Slavery* (n. 100): 335.

110 See Herrmann-Otto, *Ex ancilla* (n. 23): 370–71 for Cinnamus; Petron. 76.1: *dominus in domo* (text in nt. 68); 30.10: *superbus* (text in n. 131); see also n. 220.

111 Family relations of *dispensatores* are discussed by Herrmann-Otto, *Ex ancilla* (n. 23): 383–84; Stelzenberger, *Kapitalmanagement* (n. 15): 64–72.

112 Simonis, *Cum servis nullum est conubium* (n. 17): 101–2; Stelzenberger, *Kapitalmanagement* (n. 15): 66–69.

113 In Apul. met. 8.22 a fateful drama of jealousy ensues when a *vilicus* (the steward of an estate) begins an affair with a free woman outside the estate; see Simonis, *Cum servis nullum est conubium* (n. 17): 137.

114 How reflections of domestic relations can be detected in legal sources is shown by Alfons Bürge, "Cibaria: Indiz für die soziale Stellung des römischen Arbeitnehmers?," in *Ars boni et aequi: Festschrift für Wolfgang Waldstein zum 65. Geburtstag*, ed. Martin Josef Schermaier and Zoltán Végh (Stuttgart: Franz Steiner Steiner, 1993): 67; Gamauf, *Ad statuam licet confugere* (n. 60): 105–15; Wacke, "Die libera administratio" (n. 56): 271.

115 D. 11.3.16 (Alfenus 2 dig.): *Dominus servum dispensatorem manumisit, postea rationes ab eo accepit et cum eis non constaret, conperit apud quandam mulierculam pecuniam eum consumpsisse: quaerebatur, possetne agere servi corrupti cum ea muliere, cum is servus iam liber esset. respondi posse, sed etiam furti de pecuniis quas servus ad eam detulisset.* / 'Alfenus Varus, Digest, book 2: An owner manumitted a *dispensator*, and subsequently received the accounts from him; since they did not balance, he discovered that the slave had spent the money on a woman who was not very reputable. The question was asked whether the owner could sue the woman for making a slave worse, when the slave in question was now a free man. I replied that he could, but he could also sue for theft in respect of the money which the slave had handed over to her' (transl. Hine in Watson, *Digest of Justinian* [n. 41]).

116 See Thilo, *Codex* (n. 20): 124–30; Herrmann-Otto, *Ex ancilla* (n. 23): 375.

misappropriations. He had squandered (*consumpsisse*)[117] the money entrusted to him on 'a little woman' (*muliercula*), to whom he had handed over some of it (*ad eam detulisset*). Alfenus opined that the former master could bring an *actio servi corrupti*/action for 'making a slave (morally) worse' as well as an *actio furti*/action for theft over the sums handed over to the woman. Contrary to the fears expressed by the *dispensator*'s former master, the jurist found that manumission was no hindrance to bringing the *actio servi corrupti*.[118] It demanded double the amount involved (*quanti ea res erit*). This included both embezzled and spent money.[119] In addition, the woman could also be held accountable for the sums she had received as an accessory to a *furtum*.[120]

From Alfenus referring to her as *muliercula* Venturini assumed that the woman was a prostitute and the dispute was over her pay.[121] This is not very likely. The outraged master may have disparaged her as *muliercula*; but the use of diminutives was also Alfenus' personal style.[122] The *dispensator* cannot have been a 'john' or client of the woman because payment to a sex worker could not be legally reclaimed in Alfenus' time.[123] This *dispensator* had hardly embezzled funds for sex, but to finance his long-term relationship and a future together after manumisison.

The act of cohabiting with a slave from another household could be subsumed under both forms of corruption in the *formula* of the action: *recepisse persuasisseve*/

---

117 Similar terms (*muliercula, consumere*) also apperar in other sources reviewed by Georges Fabre, *Libertus. Recherches sur les rapports patron-affranchi à la fin de la république romaine* (Rome: École française de Rome, 1981): 183 at n. 128.

118 Otto Lenel, *Das Edictum Perpetuum: Ein Versuch zu seiner Wiederherstellung*, 3rd ed. (Leipzig: Bernhard Tauchnitz, 1927): 175. D. 11.3.5.4 (Ulpian 23 ad ed.): *Haec actio refertur ad tempus servi corrupti vel recepti, non ad praesens, et ideo et si decesserit vel alienatus sit vel manumissus, nihilo minus locum habebit actio, nec extinguitur manumissione semel nata actio.* / 'Ulpian, Edict, book 23: This action relates to the date when the slave was made worse or was harbored, not to the present; so even if the slave has died or has been disposed of or manumitted, the action still lies, and once there are grounds for the action, it is not extinguished by manumission' (transl. Hine in Watson, *Digest of Justinian* [n. 41]). S. Barbara Bonfiglio, *Corruptio servi* (Milan: Giuffrè, 1998): 117–21; Carlo Venturini, "Der dominus, der servus und die muliercula – Anmerkungen zu D. 11,3,16," in *Sklaverei und Freilassung im römischen Recht: Symposium für Hans Josef Wieling zum 70. Geburtstag*, ed. Thomas Finkenauer (Berlin: Springer Verlag, 2006): 244–45; Jan Dirk Harke, *Corpus der römischen Rechtsquellen zur antiken Sklaverei*, vol. 2, *Rechtspositionen am Sklaven*, pt. 2, *Ansprüche aus Delikten am Sklaven* (Stuttgart: Franz Steiner Verlag, 2013): 104.

119 Bonfiglio, *Corruptio* (n. 118): 121–32; Venturini, "Dominus" (n. 118): 245–50.

120 See also Paolo Ferretti, *Complicità e furto nel diritto romano* (Milan: Giuffrè, 2005): 234–38.

121 Venturini, "Dominus" (n. 118): 243–44.

122 Vgl. D. 9.2.52.4 (Alf. 2 dig.); D. 40.1.7 (Alf. 7 dig.) and Hans-Jörg Roth, *Alfeni Digesta: Eine spätrepublikanische Juristenschrift* (Berlin: Duncker und Humblot, 1999): 62, 74.

123 The earliest jurist dealing with the problem is Labeo in D. 12.5.4.3 (Ulp. 26 ed.), a generation later than Alfenus. He, however, based the decision not to allow a claim on a new reason. The principle as such was therefore older and certainly known to Alfenus. The woman could not benefit from not bringing this argument (in order to avoid disclosing her status as *infamis* because of her profession), as condemnation for *furtum* that she faced would then bring her *infamia*.

having harboured or persuaded.[124] In the case under discussion, *recipere*/harbouring was not applicable, as the slave had not fled.[125] However, the woman could still be held accountable for *corruptio servi*, as the definition of *persuadere* included any moral support of an act of embezzlement.[126]

Free women sought relationships with slaves in more favourable economic or social positions, a fact that greatly displeased the latters' masters – as is demonstrated by our case. That was why the *SC Claudianum*[127] of 52 CE punished with unusual severity (namely with the loss of her liberty) any woman who persisted in such a relationship against the master's will.[128] This would have prevented the problem of the case discussed by Alfenus: ownership of the money handed over to the woman would have reverted *ipso iure* to the *dominus* upon her enslavement.[129]

The economic consequences of a straying *dispensator* could not always be legally remedied. This is what Martial alludes to when he lists among inevitable disasters not only shipwreck, failed harvests or defaulting debtors, but also a *dispensator* 'fleeced by [his] crooked girlfriend'/*dispensatorem fallax spoliabit amica* (Mart. 5.42).

The Roman take on such delinquency[130] was clouded by a 'slaveholder mentality' not only in the cases of Petronius or Martial, who failed to grant even a *dispensator* sufficient agency to carry out embezzlement, theft, or adultery on his own initiative. (The proverbial exception was, once more, Trimalchio.) For the masters, this perspective/approach had the advantage of allowing them to pass any losses inflicted by their own slaves on to third parties, for example by means of the *actio servi corrupti*.

7 The *dispensator* as 'Master'

If they were uncovered in time, a *dispensator*'s dishonest dealings would be punished privately, as in the case of Trimalchio's adultery or the 'prosecution' of a *dispensator* for unknown offences (Petron. 53.10). In large households with a division of labour

124 Lenel, *Edictum* (n. 118): 175.

125 Cf. Georg Klingenberg, *Corpus der römischen Rechtsquellen zur antiken Sklaverei*, vol. 10, *Juristisch speziell definierte Sklavengruppen 6: Servus fugitivus* (Stuttgart: Franz Steiner Verlag, 2005): 13–19.

126 D. 11.3.1.4 (Ulp. 23 ed.); cf. Bonfiglio, *Corruptio* (n. 118): 58–65; Venturini, "Dominus" (n. 118): 244; Klingenberg, *Corpus* (n. 125): 52; Harke, *Corpus* (n. 118): 100.

127 For its content and literature see Gamauf, "Sklaven (servi)" (n. 102): no. 26.

128 Adriaan Johan Boudewijn Sirks, "Der Zweck des Senatus Consultum Claudianum von 52 n. Chr," *Zeitschrift der Savigny-Stiftung für Rechtsgeschichte, Romanistische Abteilung* 122 (2005): 138–49 regards enhanced control over male slaves as its primary purpose.

129 For *dispensatores* and the *SC Claudianum* cf. Simonis, *Cum servis nullum est conubium* (n. 17): 104.

130 An overview is provided by Stelzenberger, *Kapitalmanagement* (n. 15): 55–59.

among the servile population, even punitive powers could be delegated to slaves. That is why the protagonists in the *cena* are able to intercede with a *dispensator* in favour of his *vicarius* who faced a whipping over having lost the *dispensator*'s clothes.[131] None of the elements in this case is unrealistic: both inscriptions[132] and a text by Julian[133] attest to *dispensatores* having *vicarii*.[134] Theft of clothes was a frequent occurrence in the baths[135] (although jurists – unlike the *dispensator* in the *cena* – did not take a theft by itself as a proof of the keeper's negligence). The autonomous exercise of disciplinary powers – a central constituent of the master's power/*dominica potestas* – over a *servus vicarius* supports Ulpianus' treatment of the *servus ordinarius*/principal slave as the *vicarius*' actual master.[136] There is another example for this in the *cena*. A statement of accounts[137] read out at the meal lists not only the

131 Petron. 30.7–10: [. . .] *servus nobis despoliatus procubuit ad pedes ac rogare coepit, ut se poenae eriperemus: nec magnum esse peccatum suum, propter quod periclitaretur; subducta enim sibi vestimenta dispensatoris in balneo, quae vix fuissent decem sestertiorum.* [. . .] *dispensatoremque in atrio aureos numerantem deprecati sumus ut servo remitteret poenam. superbus ille sustulit vultum et: 'Non tam iactura me movet, inquit, quam neglegentia nequissimi servi. vestimenta mea cubitoria perdidit, quae mihi natali meo cliens quidam donaverat, Tyria sine dubio, sed iam semel lota. quid ergo est? dono vobis eum.'* / '[. . .] a stripped slave collapsed before us and launched into a plea before us to deliver him from a whipping. He hadn't sinned greatly, he claimed, or not in proportion to the punishment threatened. He had been left to watch the *dispensator*'s clothes in the public bath – scarcely a ten sesterces' worth of clothes [. . .] Locating him [i.e. the *dispensator*] in a little office counting gold coins, we delivered our entreaties on the slave's behalf. Haughtily, he lifted his face to us and said, "It isn't the material loss that troubles me, as much as the carelessness of that worthless chattel. He lost my evening clothes, which a client of mine gave me for my birthday – Tyrian-dyed fabric and all, you know – but they'd already been washed once. Oh well. I'll let him off as a favor to you"' (transl. Ruden, *Petronius* (n. 68): 21).

132 E.g. AE 1993, 911; especially imperial *dispensatores* frequently had their 'own' slaves.

133 D. 14.3.12 (Iul. 11 dig.); masters' liability for *dispensatores* is discussed by Stelzenberger, *Kapitalmanagement* (n. 15): 35–39.

134 For references see Francesca Reduzzi Merola, "I vari livelli della dipendenza: il vicarius vicarii," in *I diritti degli altri in Grecia e a Roma*, ed. Alberto Maffi and Lorenzo Gagliardi (Sankt Augustin: Academia Verlag, 2001): 249–54.

135 See D. 16.3.1.8 (Ulp. 30 ed.); D. 3.2.4.2 (Ulp. 6 ed.) as well as D. 47.17 *De furibus balnearis*/'Thieves Who Lurk about Baths'; see also Smith, *Petronius* (n. 11): 64. Clothes are the most frequently named stolen items on curse tablets that ask for divine help or revenge after a theft; see Markus Scholz, "Verdammter Dieb – Kleinkriminalität im Spiegel von Fluchtäfelchen," in *Gefährliches Pflaster: Kriminalität im Römischen Reich*, ed. Marcus Reuter and Romina Schiavone (Mainz: Philipp von Zabern Verlag, 2011): 89–105; most recently discussed by Paul J. du Plessis, "Trouble at the Baths," *RIDROM* 26 (2021): 308–33, https://ruidera.uclm.es/xmlui/bitstream/handle/10578/28461/touble.pdf?sequence=1&isAllowed=y [accessed 26.08.2022]. Stolen clothes are also addressed in Catull. 25.6 and, ostensibly at least, Petron. 12–15; s. Gamauf, "Aliquid" (n. 6): 153–57.

136 D. 15.1.17 (Ulpian 29 ad ed.): [. . .] *dominus eorum, id est ordinarius* [. . .] / 'Ulpian, Edict, book 29: [. . .] their master, the principal slave' (transl. Weir in Watson, *Digest of Justinian* [n. 41]).

137 The otherwise similar account P. Zen. 3.59398 does not contain such details; cf. Thilo, *Codex* (n. 20): 122–23.

settlements of disputes among the slaves, but also punitive measures that apparently had not required prior consultation with the master:[138] an 'indictment' against a *dispensator* and the crucifixion of a slave who had insulted his master's *genius*.[139]

In the case of absentee masters, supervision lay in the hands of the servile steward/*vilicus*, another 'manager' or a *servus ordinarius*.[140] An illustration of an 'absentee landowner'[141] is Trimalchio's boastful claim that nine-tenths of his slaves had never set eyes on him.[142] But the landowner himself was supposed to keep overall control personally even in those cases: the agricultural writer Columella, a contemporary of Petronius, advised landowners to inspect on a regualar basis the measures adopted by their *vilici*, and to to have an open ear for subordinate slaves' complaints.[143] A *senatus consultum* against harbouring *fugitivi* also assumed that regular reviews were carried out by the masters themselves. A landowner saved himself a considerable

138 Too much personal involvement in the punishment of his slaves cast a master's character in a bad light; cf. Hist. Aug. Elag. 49.3.

139 Petron. 53.1: *Et plane interpellavit saltationis libidinem actuarius, qui tanquam Vrbis acta recitavit:* '[. . .] (3) *Mithridates servus in crucem actus est, quia Gai nostri genio male dixerat.* [. . .] *iam etiam edicta aedilium recitabantur* [. . .] (10) *iam reus factus dispensator, et iudicium inter cubicularios actum.* / 'In any case, he was distracted from his lust for dancing by an accountant, who had read what sounded like the daily news at Rome. [. . .] The slave Mithridates was crucified for cursing the guardian spirit of our Gaius. [. . .] Now the aediles read their reports. [. . .] a *dispensator* had been indicted, and a dispute between two valets had gone to court' (transl. Ruden, *Petronius* [n. 68]: 38–39). The purpose of worshipping his master's *genius* was to increase a slave's attachment to him; see George, "Lives" (n. 110): 540; a *dispensator*'s dedication to his master's genius is preserved in AE 1990, 51.

140 See Colum. 11.1.25; cf. M.E. Sergeenko, "Villicus," in *Schiavitù e produzione nella Roma repubblicana*, ed. Iza Biezunska-Malowist (Rome: L'Erma di Bretschneider, 1986): 193–94; Silke Diederich, "Sklaverei bei den römischen Agrarschriftstellern," in *Unfreie Arbeit: Ökonomische und kulturgeschichtliche Perspektiven*, ed. Mustafa Erdem Kabadayi and Tobias Reichardt (Hildesheim: Georg Olms Verlag, 2007): 155–61; Tiziana J. Chiusi, "Vilicus," in *Handwörterbuch der Antiken Sklaverei*, vol. 3, ed. Heinz Heinen et al. (Stuttgart: Franz Steiner Verlag, 2017): 3213. The inscriptions in the *columbarium* of the Statilii, which was in use during the first half of the first century CE, testify to as many as 61% of slaves who were subordinate to a slave or a freedman, see Henrik Mouritsen, "Slavery and Manumission in the Roman Elite: A Study of the Columbaria of the Volusii and the Statilii," in *Roman Slavery and Roman Material Culture*, ed. Michele George (Toronto: University of Toronto Press, 2013): 56. The fact that Trimalchio's slaves were sorted into *decuriae* (Petron. 47.12 f.) might have served to assign them supervisors.

141 See D'Arms, *Commerce* (n. 4): 117.

142 Petron. 37.6. Puglisi, "Il microcosmo" (n. 3): 208 infers from this passage that 10% were house slaves; he estimates that Trimalchio owned 400 slaves altogether, which was not excessive. For hierarchies within the *familia urbana* see also Sandra R. Joshel, *Slavery in the Roman World* (Cambridge: Cambridge University Press, 2010): 192–93.

143 Colum. 1.8.15–17; cf. Carlsen, *Vilici* (n. 23): 76–78; Gamauf, *Ad statuam licet confugere* (n. 60): 92–93; Diederich, "Sklaverei" (n. 140): 155–61; Joshel, *Slavery* (n. 142): 174–79.

fine if he handed over (to their masters or to the authorities) fugitive slaves harboured by his *vilicus* or *procurator* as soon as he discovered such on his estate.[144]

Deducting the damages caused by an under slave directly from the *peculium*[145] of the slave manager also served to prevent solidarity between slaves at different hierarchy levels, or servile supervisors to become too lenient or lax in conducting their supervisory functions.[146] Such a deduction instantly reduced the 'standard of living' of the senior slave, as well as his chances of future manumission. But *vicarii* also showed themselves willing and grateful if their unfree superiors treated them with moderation.[147]

Nouveau-riche Trimalchio did not observe all of Columella's rules for the noble landowner. He was content (in the *cena*, at least) to rely on reports about his estates.[148] Of course this does not completely rule out the possibility that he may have also conducted personal inspections from time to time[149] as advised by agricultural writers. Perhaps also not all *domini* gave up their punitive powers to the extent that the *cena* portrayed Trimalchio as doing. According to Plutarch,[150] the elder Cato added slaves to his *consilium*/advisory body when deciding about the death penalty for slaves.[151]

It would be easier to reconstruct the handling of conflict with or disobedience of slaves if we could be certain that the echos of criminal procedure in the terminology[152] used in the *cena* were not mere figures of speech. We might then consider

144 D. 11.4.1.1 f. (Ulp. 1 ed.); Klingenberg, *Corpus* (n. 125): 55–56; Christopher J. Fuhrmann, *Policing the Roman Empire: Soldiers, Administration, and Public Order* (Oxford: Oxford University Press, 2012): 30–34.

145 Cf. D. 33.8.16 pr. (Afr. 5 quaest.) and Richard Gamauf, "Slaves Doing Business: The Role of Roman Law in the Economy of a Roman Household," *European Review of History/Revue européenne d'histoire* 16, no. 3 (2009): 337–38.

146 Diederich, "Sklaverei" (n. 140): 159, uses the term 'kapo system.'

147 CIL 9.3028 = ILS 7367: *Hippocrati Plauti vilico familia rustica quibus imperavit modeste* / 'To Hippocrates, steward of Plautus; from the rural slaves, whom he ruled with moderation.' This is not mere formulaic praise (for an example of the latter see CIL 6.1747; CIL 9.825), but clear and concrete emphasis on Hippocrates' exercise of his capacity as *vilicus* (see also Gamauf, *Ad statuam licet confugere* (n. 60): 94 n. 88). Columella stressed that a *vilicus* should master the *scientia imperandi* (Colum. 11.1.6). The term *imperare* bundles the different aspects of the exercise of power over slaves; s. Plaut. Cas. 103; Varro rust. 1.17.5; Colum. 1.8.10; Sen. contr. 5.5.1; Sen. clem. 1.18.1; D. 14.3.5.10 (Ulp. 28 ed.); D. 33.7.12.3 (Ulp. 20 Sab.); see also Carlsen, *Vilici* (n. 23): 77–78.

148 Trimalchio had already felt like the real head of the household as *dispensator* (see above n. 76 and subsequent nn.); as a master he seems to be under his slaves' thumb.

149 Varro rust. 1.16.5; Colum. 1.8.

150 Plut. Cat. Ma. 21.2. For literature on the subject see Gamauf, "Sklaven (servi)" (n. 102): no. 33.

151 The standard reading is that Cato consulted the slaves before making his decision. But in the case of an owner of several estates, it could also mean that the harshest punishments should only ever be pronounced in his presence and not by slaves alone.

152 Petron. 53.10 (*iudicium*); 70.5 (*ius dicere, sententia*); Cato agr. 5.1: *Litibus familia(e) supersedeat; siquis quid deliquerit, pro noxa bono modo vindicet.* / 'He must settle disputes among the slaves; and if anyone commits an offence he must punish him properly in proportion to the fault'

whether large households approached such cases in the form of 'quasi-legal' procedures in which slaves held 'offices', so to speak.[153] The consistent implementation of pre-determined rules[154] – a *ius domesticum* for the *iudicium domesticum* – would certainly have had advantages for decentralised households where slaves exercised disciplinary powers on a largely independent basis.[155]

Trimalchio's *dispensator* was obviously one of those who knew how to play the *dominus*: he pardoned the *servus vicarius* as requested by the dinner guests. Trimalchio himself theatrically reenacts this several times over during the meal: he pardons a cook,[156] a careless waiter, and a clumsy acrobat.[157] (In addition, the cook is presented with a gift and the acrobat manumitted![158]) This was not fiction, but merely the actions of a parvenu who aped the customs of the nobility:[159] Cato as well as Petronius (the latter even in his last hours) chastised their slaves in front of guests,[160] respectively during and after dinner.[161] Pardons as a result of the intervention of guests followed an *exemplum* of the Emperor Augustus, who famously saved a slave from being fed to lampreys.[162] Jurists dealt with interventions under less sensational circumstances; they

(transl. William Davis Hooper and Harrison Boyd Ash, eds., *Marcus Porcius Cato: On Agriculture. Marcus Terentius Varro: On Agriculture* (Cambridge: Harvard University Press, 1935): 13); on *relegare* see n. 91.

153 Veyne, "Vie" (n. 5): 237 in n. 2 suggests parallels with the internal structures of *collegia*.

154 Similar to the rule in Petron. 28.7: *Quisquis servus sine dominico iussu foras exierit accipiet plagas centum* / 'Any slave who goes out without the master's permission will receive a hundred lashes' (transl. Ruden, *Petronius* (n. 68): 19). For the language see Smith, *Petronius* (n. 11): 58; the number is exaggerated: Schmeling, *A Commentary* (n. 1): 93–94 and Joshel, *Slavery* (n. 142): 192; Hofmann advocates in favour of a symbolic reading, "Petronius" (n. 1): 106. Ancient agricultural writers stressed the importace of preventing unauthorised slave absences but did not suggest concrete penalties (Varro rust. 1.16.5).

155 There was no fundamental divergence of view on what constituted appropriate treatment between masters and slaves; see Gamauf, *Ad statuam licet confugere* (n. 60): 94 n. 88.

156 See also Mart. 8.23; Plut. Cat. Ma. 21.3. For the standards expected by guests of their host's servile staff see Cic. Piso. 67 and Joshel, *Slavery* (n. 142): 184–85.

157 The topical character of these scenes is stressed by Joshel, "Slavery" (n. 10): 224–26.

158 Petron. 49.6–50.1; 52.4–6; 54.3–4; Courtney, *Companion* (n. 1): 98–99; see the individual notes in Schmeling's, *A Commentary* (n. 1); Joshel, "Slavery" (n. 10): 224–27. For manumission *per mensam*/'at the table' see Gamauf, "Sklaven (servi)" (n. 102): no. 75.

159 Cf. Clarke, *Art* (n. 8): 161: '[A]nalysis of what's funny about Trimalchio reveals what the elites derided and detested about up-from-under people. [. . .] Petronius' *Satyricon* becomes a compendium of elite values.'

160 The latter acted like a spontaneous domestic court. For the functions of so-called domestic courts see Paola Ombretta Cuneo, "Hausgericht (iudicium domesticum)," in *Handwörterbuch der Antiken Sklaverei*, vol. 2, ed. Heinz Heinen et al. (Stuttgart: Franz Steiner Verlag, 2017): 1339–41.

161 Plut. Cat. Ma. 21.3; Tac. ann. 16.19.

162 For references see Gamauf, *Ad statuam licet confugere* (n. 60): 20–21.

ruled that such interventions should carry no negative legal consequences for slaves asking for mercy or the free persons who acted on their behalf.[163]

8 Master and *dispensator*

Inheritance and manumission law show both appreciation of *dispensatores* and dependency on their services. Rich masters like Trimalchio perhaps really did not know many of their slaves face to face. But the opposite could be assumed in the case of a *dispensator*. A case in point is an opinion by Gaius, who considered a testamentary manumission that ran, 'Let my *dispensator* be free' as in accordance with the *lex Fufia Caninia*,[164] even though this law demanded that slaves being freed should be mentioned *nominatim*/by name. Gaius' reasoning was that the *dispensator*'s (unique) function unmistakably identified which slave was meant.[165]

Socially, the experiences of masters and their *dispensatores* consisted of a combination of appreciation, trust, and dependencies. Testamentary manumissions highlight the complexity of such situations. Gaius Cassius Longinus[166] wanted to release heirs or legatees from the fideicommissary duty to manumit their own

---

163 D. 21.1.17.4 f. (Ulp. 1 ed. aed. cur.); D. 11.3.5 pr. (Ulp. 23 ed.); see Richard Gamauf, "Onesimus: fugitivus errove. Einsichten für die Bibelexegese aus der Digestenexegese? (Rechtshistorische Anmerkungen zum Umgang mit römischen Rechtstexten in der neueren Philemon-Auslegung)," in *Constans et perpetua voluntas: Pocta Petrovi Blahovi k 75. narodeninám*, ed. Peter Mach, Matej Pekarik and Vojtech Vladár (Trnava: Právnická fakulta Trnavskej university, 2014): 163–68.

164 Gai. 2.239; Ulp. reg. 1.25; for literature see Gamauf, "Sklaven (servi)" (n. 102): no. 53.

165 D. 40.4.24 (Gaius 1 rer. cott. sive aur.): *Nominatim videntur liberi esse iussi, qui vel ex artificio vel officio vel quolibet alio modo evidenter denotati essent, veluti 'dispensator meus' 'cellarius meus' 'cocus meus' 'Pamphili servi mei filius'.* / 'Gaius, Common Matters or Golden Words, book 1: Slaves ordered to be free are thought to be expressly designated, if they have been unambiguously identified by their craft, office, or in some other way, for example, "my *dispensator*", "my butler", "my cook", "the son of my slave Pamphilus" (transl. Brunt in Watson, *Digest of Justinian* [n. 41]).

166 D. 40.5.35 (Maecianus 15 fideic.): *Gaii Cassii non est recepta sententia existimantis et heredi et legatario remittendam interdum proprii servi manumittendi necessitatem, si vel usus tam necessarius esset, ut eo carere non expediret, veluti dispensatoris paedagogive liberorum, vel tantum delictum est, ut ultio remittenda non esset* [. . .] / 'Maecianus, Fideicommissa, book 15: Gaius Cassius thought that on occasion both heir and legatee should be excused the obligation to free their own slave, if either his service were so necessary that its loss would be inexpedient, as in the case of a *dispensator* or teacher for the children, or if he had committed an offense so serious that retribution should not be spared [. . .]' (transl. Brunt in Watson, *Digest of Justinian* [n. 41]). This opinion did not prevail; see also William Warwick Buckland, *The Roman Law of Slavery: The Condition of the Slave in Private Law from Augustus to Justinian* (Cambridge: Cambridge University Press, 1908): 520; on the role of a *paedagogus* see Mima Maxey, *Occupations of the Lower Classes in Roman Society as Seen in Justinian's Digest* (Chicago: University of Chicago Press, 1938): 56.

slaves[167] if their services were indispensable. On top of his list of such indispensable slaves, Cassius put *dispensatores.*[168]

Management by slaves only functioned with their willing cooperation. A *responsum* by Scaevola[169] is concerned with how best to conserve this willingness: in his will, a testator appointed as sole heir his nine-year-old son, Severus, and at the same time manumitted his *dispensator* December and the *vilicus/vilica* couple Severus and Victorina. However, the manumissions were not to take effect at his death, but after a waiting period of eight years. The question at issue was how to calculate those eight years. The content and style of the will show the father's concern for his child's economic well-being,[170] which after his death would depend primarily on the loyalty of the three slaves.[171] He also made arrangements that sought to resolve the dilemma arising from

---

167 Otherwise he would have had to renounce his inheritance or legacy.

168 The also-mentioned *ultio* conforms to the character of the jurist who in Tac. ann. 14.43 f. vehemently demanded that 400 innocent slaves be executed under the *SC Silanianum*; see Dieter Nörr, "C. Cassius Longinus: Der Jurist als Rhetor (Bemerkungen zu Tacitus, Ann. 14.42–45)," in *Historiae iuris antiqui: Gesammelte Schriften*, vol. 3, ed. Dieter Nörr, Tiziana J. Chiusi, Wolfgang Kaiser and Hans-Dieter Spengler (Goldbach: Keip, 2003): 1585–620.

169 D. 40.5.41.15 (Scaevola 4 resp.): *Herede filio suo ex asse instituto libertatem dedit in haec verba: 'December dispensator meus, Severus vilicus et Victorina vilica Severi contubernalis in annos octo liberi sunto: quos in ministerio filii mei esse volo: te autem, Severe fili carissime, peto, uti Decembrem et Severum commendatos habeas, quibus praesentem libertatem non dedi, ut idonea ministeria haberes, quos spero te et libertos idoneos habiturum'. quaero, cum eo tempore, quo Titius testamentum faciebat, filius natus annorum fuerat novem et Titius post biennium et sex menses decesserit, anni octo, in quos libertas erat dilata, ex testamenti facti tempore an vero ex mortis numerari debeant. respondit posse videri testatorem eos annos octo dilatae libertatis comprehendisse, qui computandi sunt a die testamenti facti, nisi aliud voluisse testatorem probaretur.* / 'Scaevola, Replies, book 15: A man instituted his son as sole heir and made a grant of freedom in these terms: "My *dispensator*, Decembrius, my bailiff, Severus, and Victorina, my housekeeper and Severus's *contubernalis*, are to be free after eight years; I wish them to be in the service of my son, but I request you, my dearest son, Severus, to take Decembrius and Severus into your favor, as I have not given them freedom with immediate effect in order that you might have satisfactory services, and I hope that you may also find them satisfactory freedmen." Given that at the time when Titius was making his will, his son had been aged nine and that Titius died two and a half years later, should the term of eight years for which freedom was deferred run from the time that the will was made or from the time of death? He replied that it might appear that the testator had fixed a total period of eight years for the deferment of freedom, which were to be counted from the date of the will, unless it were proved that he had wished something different' (transl. Brunt in Watson, *Digest of Justinian* [n. 41]). For further examples see Thomas E.J. Wiedemann, "The Regularity of Manumission at Rome," *Classical Quarterly* 35, no. 1 (1985): 172–75. For the legal background cf. Buckland, *Law of Slavery* (n. 166): 479–80; 518.

170 A minor was in the care of his guardian/*tutor*, who had only limited possibilities to assign independent tasks to slaves, cf. D. 15.1.3.3 (Ulp. 29 ed.); likely reasons are discussed by Gamauf, "Slaves Doing Business" (n. 145): 355 in n. 90.

171 The *dispensator* headed the hierarchy of the *familia urbana*, while *vilicus* and *vilica* managed the rural estate: these three slaves were pivotal for the son's economic future. In Mart. 7.71 and Mart. 11.39.6, *dispensator* and *vilicus* respectively together represent all the slaves, or the entire

the long delay of the efficacy of manumissions and the doubtlessly resulting demotivation[172] of the slaves: the son would have the slaves' services while they, provided they conducted themselves well, already had an irrevocable prospect of freedom. During that time, they also were to be given preferential treatment (*commendatos habeas*).[173] The seemingly pointless passage *quos in ministerio filii mei esse volo* could be interpreted in two ways: by the slaves as prohibiting their sale,[174] and by the son as a condition that made liberty contingent on their cooperation. The point of these measures was to enable continued administration of the estate, since only as slaves[175] December, Severus and Victorina were able to make acquisitions directly for the heir.[176]

Manumission by the father did not make his son the patron of the freed. December, Severus, and Victorina therefore became independent *liberti orcini*/freedpersons of the deceased (literally, of the Orcus, the abode of the dead).[177] A continued 'transfer of loyalty' (*te et libertos idoneos habiturum*) would then require their willingness.[178] Perhaps to achieve that the father had chosen this complex form of testamentary manumission 'in advance', hoping that his son would derive more benefit from the slaves if their support remained formally voluntary, rather than having the character of legally enforcable *operae*.

The wish to maintain Victorina's, December's and Severus' continued motivation explains the time span specified: in Scaevola's reading they gained their freedom

---

household. Dependency on slaves whose *domini* were unable to control them was accepted in cases such as when slaves of *infantes* (children) or *furiosi* (the mentally ill) independently administered their *peculia* (D. 41.2.1.5 Paul. 54 ed.). The jurists appear not to have worried about *servi callidi*/cunning slaves taking advantage of their masters. For this cliché in literature see Joshel, "Slavery" (n. 10): 220.

172 For the violent reactions of slaves who were deprived of their promised freedom see Gerhard Horsmann, "Die divi fratres und die redemptio servi suis nummis," *Historia* 35, no. 3 (1986): 318–21.

173 See also Edward Champlin, *Final Judgements: Duty and Emotion in Roman Wills, 200 B.C.–A.D. 250* (Berkeley: University of California Press, 1991): 139. For the legal meaning of *commendare* see D. 17.1.12.12 (Ulp. 31 ed.) and Francesco Maria Silla, *La 'cognitio' sulle 'libertates' fideicommissae* (Padua: Cedam, 2008): 111–14. The term is found in wills discussed by Scaevola (D. 33.1.18.1 Scaev. 14 dig.; D. 33.1.21.2 Scaev. 22 dig.) as well as in Trimalchio's will (Petron. 71.3).

174 For the social risks of a sale see Gamauf, *Ad statuam licet confugere* (n. 60): 127; Joshel, *Slavery* (n. 142): 152; testamentary bans on sales are in D. 40.5.12 pr. (Mod. l. sing. de manumiss.); D. 40.5.21 (Pap. 19 quaest.); D. 40.5.41.1 (Scaev. 4 resp.).

175 See above n. 33.

176 Wishing to give them custody of the minor would not have stood in the way of manumission: a freedman could be appointed as *tutor* (PS 4.13.3; Inst. 1.14.1); cf. Rolf Knütel, "Rechtsfragen zu den Freilassungsfideikommissen," in *Sklaverei und Freilassung im römischen Recht: Symposium für Hans Josef Wieling zum 70. Geburtstag*, ed. Thomas Finkenauer (Berlin: Springer Verlag, 2006): 143–45.

177 Gamauf, "Sklaven (servi)" (n. 102): no. 69.

178 In D. 35.1.71.1 (Pap. 18 quaest.), freedmen were given additional financial incentives to stay with the heir.

eight years after the making of the will. At this time the son, who had been nine years old when the will was written, would be seventeen and so hardly helpless, but still another eight years short of his 'majority' at twenty-five.[179] The fact that they were to attain their liberty exactly at this half-way point is probably the result of a compromise negotiated between the testator and the slaves.

We do not know whether the jurist was consulted by one of them or perhaps by a third party, nor for what purpose: but it was in everybody's interests to clarify the exact time. The most likely point for a dispute to arise was eight years after the making of the will. According to the more favourable interpretation (shared by Scaevola), this was the moment when the slaves would be free. If the son wanted to hold on to them, they would then need the help of an *adsertor libertatis* to bring a lawsuit for their freedom.[180] The certainty that in this eventuality somebody would act on their behalf would have reassured the slaves, and made it more likely that the testator's plan would succeed. So, to be on the safe side, *dominus* and slaves could, in advance of the drafting of the will, have asked a person who was trusted by both sides to intervene as *adsertor* should the necessity arise.

The trust invested in *dispensatores* was based on their reliability and correctness. The nature of legal sources allowed for discussing such aspects only indirectly and retrospectively. A *manumissio* might be an occasion to discuss internal matters of a master-slave relationship also under a legal perspective. On the topic of accounting,[181] jurists merely repeated the obvious: Scaevola included in the rendering of accounts the duty to reimburse any shortfalls discovered (D. 40.5.41.11 Scaev. 4 resp). Accuracy was to be measured in accordance with the master's interests, as Labeo remarked in a comment on the manumission of the *dispensator* Calenus, who was to be free if he had 'handled [the] accounts with care'.[182] If he fulfilled this requirement,

179 In C. 7.4.9 (Alex., a. 231) the time of services was limited until the testator's son reached the age of twenty-five; for the age limit in general see Max Kaser, Rolf Knütel and Sebastian Lohsse, *Römisches Privatrecht: Ein Studienbuch*, 22nd ed. (Munich: C.H. Beck, 2021): 142.

180 Gamauf, "Sklaven (servi)" (n. 102): no. 56–61; for the difficulty of finding *adsertores* see there, no. 57 n. 330.

181 For the *dispensator*'s accounting cf. Thilo, *Codex* (n. 20): 315–17.

182 D. 40.7.21 pr. (Pomponius 7 ex Plaut.): *Labeo libro posteriorum ita refert: 'Calenus dispensator meus, si rationes diligenter tractasse videbitur, liber esto suaque omnia et centum habeto'. diligentiam desiderare eam debemus, quae domino, non quae servo fuerit utilis.* [. . .] / 'Pomponius, From Plautius, book 7: In a book of his Posthumous Works Labeo cites the case: "Let my *dispensator* Calenus be free and have all that belongs to him plus one hundred, if it shall appear that he handled my accounts with care." The care we should require is that which will have been in the master's interest, not the slave's' (transl. Brunt in Watson, *Digest of Justinian* [n. 41]). Cf. Ireneusz Żeber, *A Study of the Peculium of a Slave in Pre-Classical Roman Law* (Wrocław: Wydawnictwo Uniwersytetu Wrocławskiego, 1981): 64. See also the humorous account in Quint. inst. 6.3.93: [. . .] *et dispensatori, qui, cum reliqua non reponeret, dicebat subinde 'non comedi; pane et aqua vivo', 'passer, redde quod debes'* / 'And when his *dispensator* failed to pay back the balance on his account and kept saying "I didn't eat it; I live on bread and water," Afer said "Sparrow, pay what you owe."' (transl. Donald

Calenus was also to receive his *peculium*[183] plus an additional one hundred. This was not the sort of fortune inherited by the fictional *dispensator* Trimalchio, but probably more start-up capital than many of his peers would have got.[184]

9 The *dispensator* and the City

Dispensatores were no 'ordinary'[185] slaves, neither in social nor in economic terms. This enabled them to invest more than just zeal into the relationship with their masters. Special occasions demanded that slaves show their respect for their masters with presents. Unlike his less fortunate peers, a *dispensator* could provide a gift without needing to scrimp and save:[186] he simply dipped into his *peculium*.[187] However, even these most privileged of slaves could only 'gift' to their master something that formally already belonged to him.[188] But because this might affect pecuniary interests of persons outside the *familia*, the cultivation of relations *intra domum* came under jurists' scrutiny. A gift changed the internal division of property within a household, between *res dominicae*/the master's immediate property and *peculia*, and therefore gained relevance in case of an *actio de peculio vel de in rem verso* against the master, because of the decrease in the *peculium*'s value.[189] By a 'gift' to the master the internal allocation of property was altered without compensating the *peculium* (in real or in accounting terms).[190] In an *actio de peculio vel de in rem verso*, this might have increased the master's liability for a so-called *versio*/benefit to the master. If, e.g., the seller had sold the

---

A. Russel, *Quintilian: The Orator's Education*, vol. 3, *Books 6–8* [Cambridge, MA: Harvard University Press, 2001]: 113).

183 Just as the *dispensator* in D. 46.3.62 (Paul. 8 ad Plaut.) had done; see above n. 46.

184 Żeber, *Study* (n. 182): 64, argues that in this case the sum was meant to be substantial.

185 See above n. 17, and below n. 206 and subsequent nn.

186 S. Gamauf, "De nihilo" (n. 18): 241 at n. 218.

187 By the same token, slaves also expected tips, gifts and so forth; see Gamauf, "De nihilo" (n. 18): 241–42.

188 For slaves' capacity to buy and sell see Gamauf, "Sklaven (servi)" (n. 102): no. 14; for gifts made to slaves see Andreas M. Fleckner, "The Peculium: A Legal Device for Donations to personae alieno iuri subiectae?," in *Gift Giving and the 'Embedded' Economy in the Ancient World*, ed. Filippo Carlà and Maja Gori (Heidelberg: Winter, 2014): 213–39; Stefan Knoch, *Sklavenfürsorge im Römischen Reich: Formen und Motive zwischen humanitas und utilitas*, 2nd ed. (Hildesheim: Georg Olms Verlag, 2017): 205.

189 For a comprehensive treatment including a review of the scholarship see Gamauf, "Klage aufgrund Sonderguts" (n. 49).

190 Cf. Gamauf, "Klage aufgrund Sonderguts" (n. 49): no. 23–24.

item intended as a 'gift' to the slave on credit, he would then have been able to bring an *actio venditi* against the slave's master for the payment of the price (up to the amount covered by the *versio*).[191] This, however, the jurists did not allow and thereby treated the 'gift' as if the slave had actually 'owed' it to the master.[192] In doing so, they assigned the same importance to a social duty as to a so-called natural obligation from a 'business transaction'[193] between master and slave.

This detail in D. 15.3.7 pr. (Ulp. 29 ed.), which might strike a casual observer as highly technical, is in fact testimony to the prevalence of this 'relationship economy' and its broader social acceptance. The cultivation of internal relations would never have become a legal issue if such occurrences had remained isolated and economically insignificant.[194] Equating 'munificence' within a *familia* with the settling of natural obligations in the *actio de in rem verso* demonstrates how widely established these practices were.

On these occasions the slaves in Trimalchio's household rather overdid it, either on their own initiative or because they knew of their master's predilections:[195] the doorway to his dining room was decorated, unusually, with *fasces* and ship's rams, both of which had been gifts from his *dispensator* Cinnamus.[196] Probably less flamboyant, in comparison at least, were the 'gifts' mentioned in the inscriptions.[197]

Such 'oiling of social wheels' continued outside the *domus*. Slaves received gifts from family friends and asked them for help when they feared punishments.[198] In

191 A transfer of property from a *peculium* to the *res dominica* could not increase the master's *de in rem verso*-liability towards the slave's creditors if the slave 'owed' him.

192 Gamauf, "Klage aufgrund Sonderguts" (n. 49): no. 40 and n. 243.

193 Cf. Gamauf, "Slaves Doing Business" (n. 145): 333.

194 The *peculia* of the slaves of wealthy families were substantial; this is especially well documented for the *familia Caesaris*; see above n. 27 and subsequent nn.

195 Petron. 30.1; cf. F.S. Naiden, "Embola Petroniana," *Classical Quarterly* 53, no. 2 (2003): 637–39; Petersen, *Freedman* (n. 9): 18–19; Minaud, *La comptabilité* (n. 23): 176; Jonathan R.W. Prag, "Cave Navem," *Classical Quarterly* 56, no. 2 (2006): 538–47; Smith, *Petronius* (n. 11): 62; Schmeling, *A Commentary* (n. 1): 103–4; Ulrike Roth, "An(other) Epitaph for Trimalchio: Sat.30.2," *Classical Quarterly* 64, no. 1 (2014): 422–25.

196 Actual historical *dispensatores* named Cinnamus are attested in four inscriptions; see Muñiz Coello, "Officium" (n. 23): 115 n. 17; Joseph Georg Wolf, *Neue Rechtsurkunden aus Pompeji. Tabulae Pompeianae Novae. Lateinisch und deutsch* (Darmstadt: Wissenschaftliche Buchgesellschaft, 2010): 27.

197 Beneficences by *dispensatores* paid for *de suo* are documented in inscriptions such as CIL 3.4797; CIL 6.239; CIL 6.3739 CIL 6.9320; CIL 6.39568; CIL 9,5177; CIL 11.7092; CIL 13.5194; CIL 14.2856; CIL 14.3033; AE 1973, 471; AE 1975, 232; AE 1980, 247; AE 1990, 51; AE 2005, 1107.

198 See above n. 131 and subsequent nn.

return, they thanked their benefactors according to their means.[199] In this manner, social networks[200] with persons outside the master's household were being maintained by gifts[201] and favours. Trimalchio's *dispensator* described the lost clothes as an expensive birthday present from one of his (!) clients. However, there are reasons to doubt the *dispensator*'s side of the story. The author lets the *vicarius* voice doubts about their ascribed high value. The purported occasion appears just as questionable. Might it not rather have been a bribe to the *dispensator* for being admitted to the master?[202] For his part, Trimalchio's *dispensator* also tried not to appear stingy. If we take literally how he ends the conversation after pardoning the *vicarius*, he even 'gave away' this 'good-for-nothing' slave to the dinner guests. The jurists, at any rate, regularly did not attribute such extensive powers over their *peculia* to slaves.[203]

The *dispensator*'s[204] elite standing within the household was recognised even in law. While the jurists postulated the same legal status of all slaves,[205] they nevertheless differentiated according to a slave's position within their *familia servorum*.[206] Social prestige was most clearly reflected in the handling of the offence of *iniuria*/insult (Inst. 4.4.7): certain behaviours were qualified as *iniuria*/insult or *iniuria atrox*/grave insult either by their nature, their public visibility or by the difference in rank of those involved. A defamatory attack against a slave primarily insulted the slave's master and so was considered an *iniuria* against the latter.[207] But in exceptional cases and after a preliminary examination/*causae cognitio*, the praetor would grant an action also in the

199 The *dispensator*'s *vicarius* returned the *beneficium* by serving his benefactors with 'the master's wine' (instead of the regular-quality wine that guests usually received; Petron. 31.2); also cf. Star, *Empire* (n. 101): 204–6.

200 For friendship of a slave with a person outside the master's *domus* see D. 3.5.5.8 (Ulp. 10 ed.).

201 The ban on slaves making gifts from their *peculia* (see next n. 202) allowed their master to control social relationships nurtured by such gifts; see Alfons Bürge, *Römisches Privatrecht: Rechtsdenken und gesellschaftliche Verankerung. Eine Einführung* (Darmstadt: Wissenschaftliche Buchgesellschaft, 1999): 186; Wolfram Buchwitz, "Fremde Sklaven als Erben: Sozialer Aufstieg durch Dritte," in *Homo, caput, persona: La costruzione giuridica dell'identità nell'esperienza romana; dall'epoca di Plauto a Ulpiano*, ed. Alessandro Corbino, Michel Humbert and Giovanni Negri (Pavia: IUSS Press, 2010): 234.

202 Gamauf, "De nihilo" (n. 18): 241–42; Cinnamus' claim to being a *patronus* is accepted in Star, *Empire* (n. 101): 205–6.

203 Gamauf, "Klage aufgrund Sonderguts" (n. 49): no. 22.

204 See Liebenam, "Dispensator" (n. 23): 1192; Muñiz Coello, "Officium" (n. 23): 116–17.

205 D. 1.5.5 pr. (Marc. 1 inst.); cf. Gamauf, "Sklaven (servi)" (n. 102): nos. 16–18.

206 Servile *dignitas* is aknowledged by Ulpian in D. 7.1.15.2 (Ulp. 18 Sab.); cf. Knoch, *Sklavenfürsorge* (n. 188): 28–31. For privileged slaves in general see Marcel Morabito, "Les esclaves privilégiés à travers le Digeste témoins et acteurs d'une société en crise," *Index* 13 (1985): 477–90.

207 Gai. 3.222; Matthias Hagemann, *Iniuria: Von den XII-Tafeln bis zur Justinianischen Kodifikation* (Cologne: Böhlau, 1998): 84–87.

name of the slave/*servi nomine*. An actionable insult against a slave/*iniuria servo facta* required the presence of a more severe form of attack and of particular personal characteristics in the victim.[208] Slaves worthy of such protection[209] were those of 'the best quality'/*bonae frugi,*[210] such as a *servus ordinarius*[211] or a *dispensator*.

An action *servi nomine* for an attack could be brought only if the *dispensator* had been recognisable as such.[212] This might be on the grounds of his clothing, appearance, typical professional attributes (e.g. account books,[213] money-bag, cash box etc.)[214] or the presence of *vicarii*.[215] The law of *iniuria* frequently took clothes as status markers.[216] Clothes similarly served as status symbols for slaves in the *cena* that they used to draw attention to themselves.[217] But these social markers also made such slaves vulnerable. An action *servi nomine* responded to this vulnerability in public which was caused by the ambiguous position of slaves who in some ways were members of the elites.

208 D. 47.10.15.44 (Ulpian 77 ad ed.): [. . .] *puto causae cognitionem praetoris porrigendam et ad servi qualitatem: etenim multum interest, qualis servus sit, bonae frugi, ordinarius, dispensator, an vero vulgaris vel mediastinus an qualisqualis.* [. . .] / 'Ulpian, Edict, book 77: [. . .] I think that the praetor's investigation into the matter should take into account the standing of the slave; for it is highly relevant what sort of slave he is, whether he be honest, regular, and responsible, a steward or only a common slave, a drudge or whatever' (transl. Thomas in Watson, *Digest of Justinian* [n. 41]). Literature in Gamauf, "Sklaven (servi)" (n. 102): no. 43–44.

209 The sanction was a penal action for money by the master.

210 Cf. Éva Jakab, *Praedicere und cavere beim Marktkauf: Sachmängel im griechischen und römischen Recht* (Munich: C.H. Beck, 1997): 190–95 (quotation at 191) and Gamauf, "De nihilo" (n. 18): 231.

211 For the term cf. Francesca Reduzzi Merola, *'Servo parere'. Studi sulla condizione giuridica degli schiavi vicari e dei sottoposti a schiavi nelle esperienze greca e romana* (Naples: Jovene, 1990): 59–60.

212 The necessary intent to insult someone/*animus iniuriandi* depended on the visibility of the protected status of the victim.

213 Cf. Thilo, *Codex* (n. 20): 42–52.

214 In Petron. 30.9, the *dispensator* can easily be identified because he counts money.

215 The best-known example are the sixteen *vicarii* accompanying the imperial *dispensator* Musicus Scurranus (CIL 6.5197 = ILS 1514).

216 D. 47.10.15.15 (Ulp. 77 ed.); Hagemann, *Iniuria* (n. 207): 72–74; Harper, *Slavery* (n. 100): 334.

217 Conspicuous clothing of a *dispensator* and a doorman catches visitors' eyes in Petron. 30.11 and Petron. 28.8; cf. Smith, *Petronius* (n. 11): 64 and 58.

With his self-dramatisation,[218] his display of wealth[219] and his elite habitus[220] a *dispensator* visually laid claim to what his 'social death',[221] his slave status, denied him.[222] This was sometimes a provocation to free men who might regard such flaunting of social and economic superiority as inappropriate and offensive. Envy, resentment or just a desire to put a slave in his place[223] could escalate into attack. For members of the *plebs*, a *dispensator* was not a slave and comrade who deserved support in times of distress,[224] but a member of the elite whose slave status deprived him of protection against their anger. Therefore, especially slaves in elevated positions needed additional protection against attacks targeting them directly, and not their masters. For such situations the *actio iniuriarum servi nomine* was the designated remedy.

10 Conclusion

Dispensatores were some of the most colourful among those Roman slaves who are known by name to us:[225] Trimalchio, larger than life, the private *dispensator* in an opulent senatorial household, was a fictitious character (albeit with much to teach the historian[226]). But even he would very nearly have been eclipsed in an encounter with his real-life almost-contemporary, the imperial *dispensator* Musicus Scurranus.[227] This slave of Tiberius travelled in grand style with an entourage of sixteen *vicarii* (including one *vicaria*). In the *Satyrica*, not only Trimalchio but also his own

218 '[P]ersons on the rise were dressing above their station', Skinner, *Sexuality* (n. 89): 250; see also Jeremy Hartnett, *The Roman Street: Urban Life and Society in Pompeii, Herculaneum, and Rome* (Cambridge: Cambridge University Press, 2017): 88–89. The freedman Hermeros even claimed no one had been able to tell he was a slave (Petron. 57.9).

219 For the perception of 'wealthy' slaves in public see Harper, *Slavery* (n. 100): 336; for similarily negative reactions in the American South see Kenneth M. Stampp, *The Peculiar Institution: Slavery in the Ante-Bellum South* (New York: Vintage Books, 1956): 209; Kathleen M. Hilliard, *Masters, Slaves, and Exchange: Power's Purchase in the Old South* (New York: Cambridge University Press, 2014): 64.

220 Star, *Empire* (n. 101): 205 on the *dispensator* Cinnamus: '[H]e looks down upon those freeborn guests'.

221 Orlando Patterson, *Slavery and Social Death: A Comparative Study* (Cambridge, MA: Harvard University Press, 1982); see also Gamauf, "Sklaven (servi)" (n. 102): no. 12 n. 71.

222 The dissonance between social position and legal status is visualized by a diagram in Geza Alföldy, *Römische Sozialgeschichte*, 4th ed. (Stuttgart: Franz Steiner Verlag, 2011): 196.

223 Hartnett, *Roman Street* (n. 218): 89.

224 Gamauf, *Ad statuam licet confugere* (n. 60): 17–20; MacLean, *Freed Slaves* (n. 70): 2–3.

225 There are thirteen texts featuring *dispensatores* in the Digest; two of them seem to give their real names.

226 Veyne, "Vie" (n. 5): 213.

227 See above n. 215.

dispensator Cinnamus is given the chance to make one or perhaps two flamboyant appearances.[228] That he represented a type can be seen from no fewer than four namesakes in inscriptions who shared his profession. December, who is mentioned in the Digest,[229] enjoyed a higher standard of living than was average for a slave. This is not mentioned explicitly, but we may assume that the heir would have followed his father's instruction to treat him well, if only out of self-interest. The freedman Calenus[230] became wealthy when a will grated him 'all that belongs to him'. The enamoured *dispensator* who had pampered his 'little woman' at his master's expense[231] would not have been out of place among Trimalchio's dinner guests. But only the imaginary, topsy-turvy world of the *cena* offered a safe enough space for wealthy freedmen to taunt even a Roman knight.[232] When they appeared in public, posers like Musicus Scurranus or Trimalchio's Cinnamus sometimes needed their 'bodyguard' of *servi vicarii* to keep the haters at bay. *Dispensatores* who lacked such protection had to hope that respect for their *dominus* and the risk of a *poena* for *iniuria*[233] would shield them from physical expressions of resentment.

From this synopsis it is not immediately obvious which anecdote originates in the microcosm of the Dinner of Trimalchio and which in the legal texts. The setting for *dispensatores* appears to be the same in both. The *dispensator*'s affair with the *muliercula* would probably have been grist to Petronius' mill, as would the foreseeable friction between Severus, the heir, and the slaves December, Severus and Victorina, who very probably resented serving him after their (testamentary) release by his father. Petronius might have found Calenus' accounting tricks less suitable material for entertainment.[234] Splinters from these lives are preserved in our sources. None of them are quite enough to reconstruct the biography of a three-dimensional *dispensator* (be he real or fictional), but if we combine them all they allow us to identify common features typical for this profession that set apart even an average *dispensator* from other slaves.

There continue to be gaps in our knowledge, because neither novelist nor jurists were interested in all aspects of a *dispensator*'s life. A particularly striking difference is the appointment to the post. The jurists are not concerned with the reasons for it; and without additional information from other sources we would not be able to draw any conclusions from *permittitur* in Gai. 1.122.[235] But in the *cena*, Trimalchio's

228 See above n. 28.
229 See above n. 169 and subsequent nn.
230 See above n. 182.
231 See above n. 194.
232 Petron. 57.4; Smith, *Petronius* (n. 11): 155–56; Schmeling, *A Commentary* (n. 1): 233.
233 See above n. 206 and subsequent nn.
234 See immediately below n. 247.
235 See above n. 59.

rise to *dispensator* is part of a central plot line.[236] Even so, the historical interpretation of Trimalchio's career is no simple matter: some see it as obvious that he[237] (perhaps like real-life *dispensatores*)[238] had deliberately furthered his career with his sexual availability. But even if there is some distortion to this very conspicuous element, it still allows us to see how some masters must have prepared their favourites, some from a very young age, for this important and prestigious position.[239] What the *cena* demonstrates without a doubt is that candidates for positions of trust had first to prove themselves.[240] We know from the *familia Caesaris* that slaves helped their advance with bribes.[241]

The sources under examination almost completely ignore mundane, everday business processes. Jurists were interested in what happened after a *dispensator*'s revocation from his position or manumission.[242] They assumed that in his dealings he always followed detailed instructions.[243] In the *Satyrica*, Trimalchio's profession is addressed explicitly only in the frescoes;[244] on one other occasion we see a *dispensator* counting money.[245] There is no more information about his everyday tasks. The sources are also largely silent about the nuts and bolts of *dispensatores* breaching their duty.[246] Only Martial draws attention to the potentially serious consequences of such acts.[247] Reassuringly for his audience, he does not attribute such grave dereliction of duty to the *dispensator* alone, but points the finger of blame at the woman who led him astray. Both for Martial and the *dominus* in D. 11.3.16 (Alf. 2 dig.), the fault lay not

---

236 See above n. 67 and subsequent nn.

237 So Parker, "Free Women" (n. 81): 293 ('[H]e sleeps his way to the top.'); similarly Skinner, *Sexuality* (n. 89): 249. By analogy this is also explained by the reflections on sex as a vehicle for the upward social mobilty of female slaves in Matthew J. Perry, *Gender, Manumission, and the Roman Freedwoman* (New York: Cambridge University Press, 2014): 51.

238 Simonis, *Cum servis nullum est conubium* (n. 17): 103; see also Edmondson, "Slavery" (n. 32): 341 and John Bodel, "Slave Labour and Roman Society," in *The Cambridge World History of Slavery*, vol. 1, *The Ancient Mediterranean World*, ed. Keith R. Bradley and Paul Cartledge (Cambridge: Cambridge University Press, 2011): 334: 'What mattered more than training or talent [. . .] was winning the master's favour.'

239 See above n. 73 and Gamauf, "De nihilo" (n. 18): 231–32. Trimalchio gives his favourite slave an education (Petron. 75.3 f.). Echion, a *libertus*, does the same for his favourite, modestly hoping that he might have a career in law (Petron. 46.3–8; Schmeling, *A Commentary* [n. 1]: 193; Gamauf, "Aliquid" [n. 6]: 160–61).

240 For the granting of a *peculium* see Gamauf, "De nihilo" (n. 18): 228–33 and Gamauf, "Ideal Freedmen-Lives" (n. 80): 286–87.

241 A slave of Galba's paid one million sesterces to procure a post as *dispensator* (Suet. Otho 5.2).

242 See above n. 41 and subsequent nn.

243 See above n. 51 and subsequent nn.

244 See above n. 68 and subsequent nn.

245 See above n. 131.

246 No flight by a *dispensator* is attested.

247 See above n. 129 and subsequent nn.

with the *dispensator*, but with her. When it came to misconduct, 'cherchez la femme' was also the unspoken motto in the *Satyrica*, where slaves did cheat their masters, but only in matters sexual. We may doubt that Trimalchio's master would have treated his 'toy boy' just as leniently, setting him free and making him his heir, if he had taken not his wife but his money. The latter scenario did have literary potential. Labeo warned the *dispensator* Calenus not to risk his freedom over 'creative accounting'.[248] Martial feared that disaster would ensue once a *dispensator* gave way to temptation; it is likely that this did not happen in Alfenus' case.[249] What stands out here is the identity of the culprit. For Petronius, there was probably good reason why even that arch trickster Trimalchio at least kept his hands off his master's money.

There is scarce mention in the sources of fraud and suchlike by Roman *dispensatores*: an indicator for their honesty (and, indirectly, the successful deterrent of torture?) – or their craftiness? Or is there a completely different explanation? It is quite possible that a master who was satisfied with his *dispensator*'s work just did not watch him too closely. Skilfully concealed transgressions would have been difficult to discover in any case. A combination of both phenomena might explain the enormous fortunes of imperial *dispensatores*.

The former *dispensator* in Alfenus' case was already free, and thus safe from the rack. Torture was used only against slaves; and many scholars believe its availability was a maior reason for the pervasive employment of slaves in finance.[250] However, there is no unambigous evidence for torture of *dispensatores* specifically other than the title of a declamation attributed to Quintilian, '*Dispensatores torti*/Tortured *dispensatores*' (Ps. Quint. decl. 353). This alone, however, is hardly reliable: The scenario of the *declamatio* is not realistic as it violates the applicable rules of Roman law,[251] which did not allow for a slave's torture and testimony against his own master in civil proceedings about money. For a Roman audience, this 'false' detail enhanced the unrealistic character of the declamation, a desired effect in such exercises in forensic oratory. There is no evidence either for the non-judicial torture of *dispensatores*, which is why many scholars combine reports about transgressions by *dispensatores* with those on the torture or punishment of slaves for financial misconduct to shore up their argument.[252] There can be no doubt that *dispensatores* under suspicion could be

248 See above n. 182.

249 The humorous tale in Quint. inst. 6.3.93 suggests the consequences were harmless (see above n. 182).

250 See above n. 33.

251 Vera Isabella Langer, *Declamatio Romanorum: Dokument juristischer Argumentationstechnik. Fenster in die Gesellschaft ihrer Zeit und Quelle des Rechts?* (Frankfurt am Main: Peter Lang Verlag, 2007): 174.

252 See the ancient texts given in Carlsen, *Vilici* (n. 23): 152 n. 514 and Aubert, *Business Managers* (n. 23): 190. The following passage is striking, but again does not reference the slave's professional capacity; Sen. epist. 122.15: *Audio, inquit, flagellorum sonum. quaero quid faciat: dicitur rationes accipere.* / 'I hear the sound of lashes. I ask what he is doing and I am told he is reviewing his

tortured[253] and severely punished. But there is as yet no proof that they were at greater risk in this respect than other slaves. In the *cena*, Glyco is criticised for the imminent execution of his *dispensator*.[254] The fact that such a thing can happen in the *cena* does not automatically mean that reality is being subverted. In the novel, *dispensatores* who hand out punishments stand out more than those on the receiving end. And the one detail that must not be overlooked in this context is that the tortured *dispensatores* in the *declamatio* are not suffering because of disloyalty against their *domini*.

There are good reasons why this risk and its possible remedies received so little attention in the sources. For legal discussions, the most interesting situations were those in which the responsibility for a *dispensator*'s misdeeds could be shifted to third parties. Brutality against one's own slaves, such as torture, concerned jurists in exceptional cases only; but no master should be blamed for an abuse of *dominica potestas*[255] when investigating or punishing a delinquent slave. The author of the *Satyrica* probably had different motives for treating with eloquent silence the misdeeds *dispensatores* were in fact most likely to commit. He wanted to entertain his noble peers and not make them wonder what their *dispensatores* might be getting up to behind their backs. Masters had no choice but to trust such slaves; therefore topical *exempla* with *dispensatores* who demonstrated outstanding loyalty in extreme situations, and long after manumission, were used for reassurance.[256] In Trimalchio, Petronius had created a *dispensator* who, while an arch trickster, was without fault in financial matters, and who had earned his freedom through professional reliability. This was welcome fare for masters, while any *dispensatores* secretly reading Petronius' tale found in it the message that a *patrimonium* (not necessarily *laticlavium*) at the end of a professional career would only be forthcoming as the result of loyal service.

accounts' (transl. Elaine Fantham, ed., *Seneca: Selected Letters* [Oxford: Oxford University Press, 2010]: 266).

253 This may be what happens at Petron. 53.10 (*iam reus factus dispensator* / 'a dispensator had been indicted'; transl. Ruden, *Petronius* [n. 68]: 39). This is not yet the punishment, but the launching of an investigation which could include the use of torture to identify e.g. accomplices (D. 9.2.23.4, Ulp. 18 ed.).

254 See above n. 97 and subsequent nn.

255 Cf. Gamauf, *Ad statuam licet confugere* (n. 60): 81–86.

256 The *dispensator* Argivus ensured that Galba's head and body were buried together (Suet. Galba 20.2; Tac. hist. 1.49.1). In Ps. Quint. decl. 388, a *dispensator* who had been manumitted years earlier assumes the role of *adsertor libertatis* (cf. above at n.180) to win freedom for the son of his former master, whom he still regards as his master (*adulescentem, quem dominum diceret*). For unknown reasons Tonia Wycisk, *Quidquid in foro fieri potest: Studien zum römischen Recht bei Quintilian* (Berlin: Duncker & Humblot, 2008): 52–53 believes this case furnishes evidence for a *manumissio vindicta*.

Wolfram Buchwitz

Giving and Taking: The Effects of Roman Inheritance Law on the Social Position of Slaves

1 Introduction

In the Roman world, the factors that had an influence on the social position of slaves are manifold. We can assume that their situation was to a large extent determined by the functions they exercised and by the social position of their masters. A slave who was living in a large senatorial household had his share in the prestige of his master. Slaves in the *familia Caesaris* held important public offices, could become very wealthy and lived in quasi-matrimonial relationships with free women.[1] On the other hand, the slave of a poor peasant who had merely a few acres of land could never climb to higher positions, and slaves working in the mines did not even have a chance of a better life. These differentiations in the social reality of slavery however had no counterpart in the legal system. The rules governing slavery as a legal institution do not distinguish between different groups of slaves – with the notable exception of *servi publici*[2] – but instead treat slavery as a homogeneous legal status.

In light of these circumstances, it could seem expedient to assess the social position of slaves mainly on the basis of their masters' social status, their position in the household and their general living conditions, such as wealth, occupation, urban or rural situation, provincial or Italian origin etc. However, the mere fact that the Roman legal system has not developed specific rules for slaves in different social situations does not mean that the law is irrelevant altogether. Rather, it can be observed that the general legal rules which apply indistinctively to all persons have specific impacts on different groups of persons and slaves. The actual social situation and living condition of a Roman slave is not only dependent on factual circumstances, but is influenced by legal factors as well, although these are more difficult to determine, as they are hidden behind the abstract rules of Roman law which equally apply to everyone.

For the purposes of the present research project on the rank of slaves in ancient Roman society, it is therefore necessary to go into the details of the Roman legal

1 See Pierangelo Buongiorno, in this volume, and Paul Richard Carey Weaver, *Familia Caesaris: A Social Study of the Emperor's Freedmen and Slaves* (Cambridge: Cambridge University Press, 1972); Paul Richard Carey Weaver, "Social Mobility in the Early Roman Empire – The Evidence of the Imperial Freedmen and Slaves," *Past & Present* 37 (1967): 3–20.

2 See below 4.2 and 6.

https://doi.org/10.1515/9783110987195-006

sources and identify the legal rules that actually have an impact on the social position of slaves. As it is not feasible to cover the whole area of private law in one contribution, I have chosen the field of inheritance law as a first object of study. Inheritance law plays an extremely important role in Roman society. In antiquity, as in all pre-modern societies, inheritance laws had a vast influence on the social position of all people concerned, as inheriting a fortune was the most important way of gaining an advanced social position. This is also reflected in the sources: About one third of all texts comprised in Justinian's digest are from the law of inheritance. Therefore, it is expedient to analyse if and how slaves had a share in inheritance law and thereby a way of raising their social status.

Methodologically, the present contribution will show that the traditional approach of 'law and society' studies, focusing on the influence of societal norms on the law, has to be complemented by a different research perspective that lays an emphasis on the influence of the legal rules on society. Only if taken together, these two approaches will give a complete picture of the complex interrelations between society and law in ancient Rome.

2 General Position of Slaves in Roman Inheritance Law

The starting point of all observations on the status of slaves in inheritance law must be the two guiding principles that have been developed by the Roman lawyers: First, slaves cannot make a valid will. Second, slaves can be instituted as heirs or legatees by free persons in their wills. There is a famous testimony for these two basic rules in the following source:

D. 28.1.16 pr. (Pomp. *l.s. reg.*): Filius familias et servus alienus et postumus et surdus testamenti factionem habere dicuntur: licet enim testamentum facere non possunt, attamen ex testamento vel sibi vel aliis adquirere possunt.	D. 28.1.16 pr. (Pomponius, Rules, sole book): A son-in-power, the slave of another person, a *postumus*, and a deaf person are said to have *testamenti factio*; for although they cannot make a will, they can still acquire by will for themselves or for others.[3]

This is an excerpt from the book *regulae* (legal rules) by Pomponius (second century Roman lawyer). It shows that there existed a general rule in Roman law according to which a slave had the so-called *testamenti factio* (testamentary ability). Pomponius explains the meaning of this rule: Slaves cannot make a will, but they are capable of

3 Transl. Hart in Alan Watson, *The Digest of Justinian*, vol. 1–4 (Philadelphia: University of Pennsylvania Press, 2009).

being instituted in another person's testament. In general legal language, the expression *testamenti factio* has two implications: it refers to the legal ability of drafting a valid will, which is sometimes called *testamenti factio activa*, as well as to the legal ability of receiving something from another person's will, which is called *testamenti factio passiva*.[4] Slaves do not enjoy *testamenti factio activa*, but only *testamenti factio passiva*.[5] The legal expression of *testamenti factio* may therefore be used in connection with slaves, but only in its second meaning.

The legal rule thus expressed by Pomponius is a specification of the more general legal principle according to which a slave is *res et persona*, a thing and a person at the same time. This general description of the status of a slave in Roman law is a legal principle rather than a legal rule,[6] but it explains the specific nature of the slave status well: A slave is characterised as a thing, because he or she can be sold like any other good on the market and the owner has the same power (*dominium/proprietas*) over a slave like over any other personal property. However, a slave is also characterised as a person, because he or she can enter into agreements with other slaves or free persons and these agreements are recognised by the law insofar as they may give rise to a claim against the slave's owner if the owner has consented to the agreement or has provided the slave with a personal de facto property (*peculium*).[7]

In the ambit of inheritance law, the nature of slaves as things is reflected in their inability to have any property of their own and consequently in their inability to draw up a will. If someone is unable to own property and unable to have family relationships, there is no point in making a will. On the other hand, the nature of slaves as persons is shown by their ability to be instituted as heirs in other persons' wills. The legal act of making a will was originally considered a two-sided legal relationship by Roman inheritance law,[8] although in classical times it was technically made unilaterally by the testator without any involvement of the heirs. Nevertheless, a slave was a person and therefore considered capable of being a party to this legal relationship with the testator. It is only due to the slave's inability to hold property that the factual acquisition of the goods bequeathed to him takes place in the person of his

---

4 For the (more complex) history of this expression see Hugo Krüger, "Testamenti factio," *Zeitschrift der Savigny-Stiftung für Rechtsgeschichte, Romanistische Abteilung* 53 (1933): 505–8.

5 Cf. also Gai. 17 ed. prov. D. 28.5.31 pr.: *testamenti factio cum servis ex persona dominorum introducta est.* ('Gaius, Provincial Edict, book 17: *testamenti factio* with slaves has been introduced through the person of their masters', transl. Gordon in Watson, *Digest of Justinian* [n. 3]).

6 Cf. in more detail Pietro Bonfante, *Corso di diritto romano*, vol. 1 (Rome: Attilio Sampaolesi, 1925; repr. Milan: Giuffrè, 1963): 143; Max Kaser, *Das römische Privatrecht*, vol. 1, *Das altrömische, das vorklassische und klassische Recht*, 2nd ed. (Munich: C.H. Beck, 1971): 285; Olis Robleda, *Il diritto degli schiavi nell'antica Roma* (Rome: Pontificia Università Gregoriana, 1976): 68–102.

7 Cf. book 15 of the digest.

8 Cf. Wolfram Buchwitz, *Servus alienus heres: Die Erbeinsetzung fremder Sklaven im klassischen römischen Recht* (Vienna/Cologne/Weimar: Böhlau, 2009): 28–29.

or her master or mistress.[9] This is expressed by Pomponius' last words, according to which some of the persons he mentions can only acquire for others (*aliis*).

It is important to note in this context that Pomponius treats slaves, sons-in-power, *postumi* (children born after the testator's death) and deaf persons equally. Although the legal and social situations of these groups of persons differ vastly, they all have one thing in common, for they can acquire from a testament but are unable to make a testament themselves. Therefore, the principle of *testamenti factio passiva* applies equally to all of them. Pomponius' reasoning shows the high level of abstraction which Roman jurisprudence has reached in the classical age: Persons belonging to totally different social groups are treated equally because they share an abstract legal ability.

3 Bequests by a Master to His Own Slave

A special category of slaves who benefitted from hereditary transmission of property are slaves who were instituted as heirs by their own masters. This situation is frequent in the sources and presents questions as to the 'how' and the 'why'. I will first address the 'how': How can a testator institute his or her own slave as an heir if the general rule says that only slaves belonging to other persons have *testamenti factio*, as expressed by Pomponius in D. 28.1.16 pr.? The answer lies in the concept of *res* and *persona*: As long as a person is in the slave status, he is also a *res* and cannot have any property of his own. It is only for this reason that an institution as heir is impossible. However, the owner of the slave has the possibility to free him and thereby make him a person capable of owning property. In this case, there is no impediment for an institution as heir. It is therefore generally accepted by the Roman lawyers that a slave belonging to the testator can be instituted if he is freed at the same time in the same testament:

Gai. inst. 2.185: Sicut autem liberi homines, ita et servi tam nostri quam alieni heredes scribi possunt. (186) Sed noster servus simul et liber et heres esse iuberi debet, id est hoc modo: Stichus servus meus liber heresque esto, vel: heres liberque esto.

Gai. inst. 2.185: Not only freemen but slaves, whether belonging to the testator or to another person, may be instituted heirs. (186) A slave belonging to the testator must be simultaneously instituted and enfranchised in the following manner: 'Stichus, my slave, be free and be my heir'; or: 'Be my heir and be free.'[10]

In his institutes (about 160 CE), Gaius describes how a testator may institute his own slave by writing in his testament not only the institution as heir, but also the

9 Gai. inst. 2.87.

10 Transl. Poste in Edward Arthur Whittuck, ed., *Gai institutiones or Institutes of Roman Law by Gaius*, 4th ed. (Oxford: Clarendon Press, 1904): 222.

enfranchisement. This is the special form of enfranchisement *ex testamento*, requiring the words *liber esto* in the will.[11]

The answer to the second question – why should a testator at all wish to free a slave and leave him his property as an heir – is more complex. At first glance, it seems strange that a Roman citizen should choose a person whose social status is much lower than his own as his successor. However, Gaius informs us that these types of hereditary transmissions served a specific legal purpose:

> Gai. inst. 2.153: Necessarius heres est servus cum libertate heres institutus, ideo sic appellatus, quia sive velit sive nolit, omni modo post mortem testatoris protinus liber et heres est. (154) Unde qui facultates suas suspectas habet, solet servum suum primo aut secundo vel etiam ulteriore gradu liberum et heredem instituere, ut si creditoribus satis non fiat, potius huius heredis quam ipsius testatoris bona veneant, id est ut ignominia, quae accidit ex venditione bonorum, hunc potius heredem quam ipsum testatorem contingat; quamquam apud Fufidium Sabino placeat eximendum eum esse ignominia, quia non suo vitio sed necessitate iuris bonorum venditionem pateretur; sed alio iure utimur. (155) Pro hoc tamen incommodo illud ei commodum praestatur, ut ea quae post mortem patroni sibi adquisierit, sive ante bonorum venditionem sive postea, ipsi reserventur. et quamvis pro portione bona venierint, iterum ex hereditaria causa bona eius non venient, nisi si quid ei ex hereditaria causa fuerit adquisitum, velut si Latinus [. . .] adquisierit, locupletior factus sit; cum ceterorum hominum, quorum bona venierint pro portione, si quid postea adquirant, etiam saepius eorum bona veniri solent.

> Gai. inst. 2.153: A necessary successor is a slave instituted heir with freedom annexed, so called because, willing or unwilling, without any alternative, on the death of the testator he immediately has his freedom and the succession. (154) For when a man's affairs are embarrassed, it is common for his slave, either in the first place (*institutio*) or as a substitute in the second or any inferior place (*substitutio*), to be enfranchised and appointed heir, so that, if the creditors are not paid in full, the property may be sold rather as belonging to this heir than to the testator, the ignominy of insolvency thus attaching to the heir instead of the testator; so as Fufidius relates, Sabinus held that he ought to be exempted from ignominy, as it is not his own fault, but legal compulsion, that makes him insolvent; this, however, is not in our view the law. (155) To compensate this disadvantage he has the advantage that his acquisitions after the death of his patron, and whether before or after the sale, are kept apart for his own benefit, and although a portion only of the debts is satisfied by the sale, he is not liable to a second sale of his acquired property for the debts of the testator, unless he gain anything in his capacity as heir, as if he inherit the property of a *Latinus Junianus* [another freedman of the testator]; whereas other persons, who only pay a dividend; on subsequently acquiring any property, are liable to subsequent sales again and again.[12]

---

11 Cf. William Warwick Buckland, *The Roman Law of Slavery: The Condition of the Slave in Private Law from Augustus to Justinian* (Cambridge: Cambridge University Press, 1908): 137, 460–61; and recently Berthold Kupisch, "Der Sklave als Zwangs-Erbe. Ulpian/Julian 4 ad Sab. (D. 28,5,6,4)," *Tijdschrift voor Rechtsgeschiedenis* 84, no. 3–4 (2016): 379–400, 396–99.

12 Transl. Poste in Whittuck, *Gai institutiones* (n. 10): 209–10.

From this detailed explanation, it can be derived that the institution of a slave belonging to the testator as an heir was mainly used in cases where the testator's estate was overindebted. Any other heir would not have accepted an inheritance which consisted mainly in debts, but the slave had to, because he was an *heres necessarius*, a mandatory heir. The ignominy of insolvency thus fell on the freed slave, not on the testator himself. The freedman however had the possibility of separating his own property from the property he received by the hereditary transmission so that the testator's creditors could only sell the part of his fortune that he inherited and not any later acquisitions that he made after the succession had taken place.

In sum, if a master makes a bequest to his own slave, this is in most cases not an expression of mere liberality or gratitude, but rather a convenient way of disposing of an overindebted inheritance by giving it to a person who could not decline to accept it. However, as a side effect, this also gave the slave freedom and a considerable degree of independence, as he was able to keep all future acquisitions for himself and did not lose them to the deceased master's creditors. The economical and social position of the freed slave was thereby improved, even though this was not the primary motive of the testator.

The special case of a slave being instituted as heir by his own master already shows the main characteristic of Roman slave law: The legal rules were for the most part not made to benefit the slaves, but rather for the convenience of their masters. However, as a side effect, they very often also had a great influence on the position of the slave himself. This type of secondary effect is very typical for the other situations as well, which will be treated in the following paragraphs.

4 Bequests by a Free Person to Another Person's Slave

Even more interesting for assessing the social reality of slavery is another type of hereditary succession: the *institutio servi alieni* (institution of another person's slave).[13] As we have seen in the quotations from Pomponius (D. 28.1.16 pr., *supra*) and Gaius (Gai. inst. 2.185, *supra*), it is technically possible to name another person's slave as an heir. The slave then acquires the deceased's estate for his master. A slave belonging to another person can therefore be instituted even without an enfranchisement. If the testator however does not want the slave's owner to acquire the estate, he may institute the slave conditional upon manumission:

13 Cf. Buckland, *Law of Slavery* (n. 11): 137; Buchwitz, *Servus alienus heres* (n. 8).

4.1 Conditional Upon Manumission

There are frequent occurrences in the sources where the de cuius institutes another person's slave under the condition that the slave is freed by his owner.[14] Celsus (second century Roman lawyer) explicitly asserts the possibility of such a testamentary disposition:

D. 28.7.21 (Cels. 16 *dig.*): Servus alienus ita heres institui potest 'cum liber erit': proprius autem ita institui non potest.

D. 28.7.21 (Celsus, Digest, book 16): A slave belonging to someone else can be instituted heir like this, "when he is free"; but one's own cannot be so instituted.[15]

The testator may add the words *cum liber erit* to the institution as heir and thereby make the slave his heir only in case of enfranchisement. It is obvious that such a type of institution greatly improves the position of the slave as it gives his owner a powerful motive for enfranchisement: Only if he frees the slave will the property pass over from the deceased's estate. It can reasonably be assumed that in such a situation slave-owners negotiated a certain 'price' to be paid by the slave for his freedom and thereby gained a certain share of the property the slave was going to inherit. This reduced the slave's benefit from the institution as heir, but nevertheless was a favourable situation for him, as he gained his freedom.

The conditional institution of another one's slave is a legal strategy first and foremost, but it allows for very important insights into the social history of slavery in Rome as well. We can assume that a testator who institutes the *servus alienus* only upon manumission has the intention to benefit the slave himself and not his master. In which situation did a testator have such an interest in benefitting another person's slave? There are some answers to this question in the sources passed down to us in the digest where we can see that testators actually employed this strategy in practice in order to benefit their family relations:

D. 31.83 (Paul. 11 *quaest.*): Latinus Largus: Proxime ex facto incidit species talis. libertinus patronum ex semisse heredem instituit et filiam suam ex alio semisse: fidei commisit filiae, ut quibusdam ancillis patroni restitueret, cum hae manumissae essent, et, si eadem filia heres non esset, substituit ei easdem ancillas. quoniam filia non voluit heres exsistere, ancillae iussu domini, id est patroni, adierunt defuncti hereditatem. post aliquantum temporis ab eo manumissae quaerebant, an fideicommissum petere ab eodem patrono possint. rogo ergo, quid de

D. 31.83 (Paul, Questions, book 11): Latinus Largus: Recently, the following case occurred. A freedman appointed his patron heir to half his estate and his own daughter as heiress to the other half. He charged his daughter with the *fideicommissum* of making restoration to certain female slaves of his patron on their manumission, and in case his daughter should not become heiress he substituted these female servants for her. Because the daughter did not wish to accept the inheritance, the female servants at the direction of their master, that

14 For more evidence from epigraphic sources see Pierangelo Buongiorno, in this volume.
15 Transl. Gordon in Watson, *Digest of Justinian* (n. 3).

hoc existimes rescribas. respondi nec repetitum videri in hunc casum fideicommissum, sed alterutrum datum vel fideicommissum vel ipsam hereditatem. melius autem dici in eundem casum substitutas videri, in quem casum fideicommissum meruerunt, et ideo ad substitutionem eas vocari. cum enim servo alieno fideicommissum ab uno ex heredibus sub condicione libertatis fuerit datum idemque servus ei heredi substituatur, licet pure substitutio facta sit, tamen sub eadem condicione substitui videtur, sub qua fideicommissum meruit.

is, the patron, accepted the inheritance of the deceased. After some time, they were manumitted by him and inquired if they could claim the *fideicommissum* from their patron. Therefore I ask you to write to me what you think of this. I replied that the *fideicommissum* did not seem to have been repeated in this case, but one or the other had been given, either the *fideicommissum* or the inheritance itself. But I would be better to say that they were made substitutes for the same eventuality under which they would have been entitled to the *fideicommissum*, and were therefore called to the substitution. For when a *fideicommissum* is charged on one of the heirs in favour of the slave of another, on condition of his freedom, and this same slave is substituted for that heir, even if the substitution is unconditional, he is held to have been substituted on the same condition under which he was entitled to the *fideicommissum*.[16]

As we can see from the first words (*ex facto*), this is a real case showing the actual testamentary practice: A freedman has instituted his patron and his daughter, each in a half share of the estate. This shows that the freedman probably was a rich person with a property of more than 100,000 sesterces, because a freedman who had less fortune was not obliged by the *lex Papia* to institute his patron if he had children of his own.[17] The freedman's daughter in this case was not to benefit from the institution, though, because she was asked by way of *fideicommissum* to hand over the inheritance to three slave girls who were owned by the deceased's patron. It can be assumed that the daughter had been otherwise compensated earlier for not receiving anything upon the death of her father. Maybe her father had given her a dowry when she had married. In any case, the daughter was to hand over the inheritance to the slave girls only in case of their manumission (*cum hae manumissae*

16 Transl. Braun in Watson, *Digest of Justinian* (n. 3).

17 Gai. inst. 3.42: *Postea lege Papia aucta sunt iura patronorum, quod ad locupletiores libertos pertinet. Cautum est enim ea lege, ut ex bonis eius, qui sestertiorum centum milium plurisve amplius patrimonium reliquerit, et pauciores quam tres liberos habebit, sive is testamento facto sive intestato mortuus erit, virilis pars patrono debeatur. Itaque cum unum filium unamve filiam heredem reliquerit libertus, proinde pars dimidia patrono debetur, ac si sine ullo filio filiave moreretur* ('At a still later period the lex Papia Poppaea augmented the rights of the patron against the estate of more opulent freedmen. For by the provisions of this statute whenever a freedman leaves property of the value of a hundred thousand sesterces and upwards, and not so many as three children, whether he dies testate or intestate, a portion equal to that of a single child is due to the patron.', transl. Poste in Whittuck, *Gai institutiones* [n. 10]: 284).

essent). This factor links the case to the rules laid down by Celsus in D. 28.7.21. We can therefore draw the conclusion that the testator, in making the *fideicommissum*, did not want to profit his patron, who would have acquired all bequests to his slaves while they were still in the slave status, but rather the slaves themselves in the moment they were released from slavery.

Much guesswork may be made as to the social background of such a testamentary disposition, but to my mind it is not overspeculative to assume that the three slave girls are the testator's own children and were born earlier during a time when he and their mother were slaves. Due to this situation, they are not the testator's children in a legal sense. The other daughter, whom he instituted as heir, was born later at a time when he and the mother were already freed and had married so that he could have legitimate children of his own. Against this background, the dispositions in the will are entirely reasonable: The freedman intended to benefit his natural children, but only in case they became free and could thus have the financial gain for themselves and not for their master, his patron, whom he had instituted already in an equal share of his estate.

However, the testator's daughter derailed his plan by not accepting the inheritance. In this case, the testator had foreseen in his will that the three slaves become his heiresses instead. Such a substitute institution was frequent in Roman testamentary practice because Roman testators tried to avoid intestate succession wherever possible.[18] The refusal of the daughter thus made the three slaves heiresses, but due to their slave status, they acquired everything for their master, the patron. Their master, on his part, freed them some time later (*post aliquantum temporis*). The freed slave women were probably not entirely happy in this situation, as they had not received anything from their natural father, and their patron was now in possession of the whole of the estate. Roman jurist Paul (second/third century) comes to a very audacious decision: He interprets the testator's will as though the condition under which the *fideicommissum* was made also applied to the substitution. In this way, the slaves' institution as heiresses is conditional upon their manumission. The fact that they previously accepted the inheritance for their master is legally irrelevant and void. The freed slaves therefore have the possibility to claim their share in the inheritance once they are freed from the person who possesses the goods, i.e. their patron. This is an extremely ample interpretation of the will, but it realises the testator's intentions, as he wanted to benefit the three slave girls who were probably his natural children.

The case shows that hereditary bequests to slaves were probably made because of family relations to the testator. It also shows that a testator who intended to benefit the slaves themselves was best advised to make the institution conditional upon their manumission. However, even if he omitted a clear statement in this

18 Cf. Kaser, *Das römische Privatrecht*, vol. 1 (n. 6): 688–89.

regard in his will, the Roman jurists made their best efforts to put into effect the supposed intention to benefit the slaves personally.

4.2 Without Manumission

Most bequests to slaves who belonged to other persons were not made conditional upon their manumission. In these cases, there is no actual possibility of benefitting the slave himself, because while he is a slave, he is unable to have any property of his own and the bequests become his master's property. However, the master is under a certain obligation to credit the assets to the slave's *peculium* (a de facto personal property of the slave[19]). This obligation was not a legal one, nor a strict social obligation, but it was recognised in some instances by the law and thus had its effects on the actual position of the slave in Roman society:

D. 15.1.7.5 (Ulp. 29 *ad ed.*): Sed et si quid furti actione servo deberetur vel alia actione, in peculium computabitur: hereditas quoque et legatum, ut Labeo ait.	D. 15.1.7.5 (Ulpian, Edict, book 29): If proceeds of an action of theft or other suit are owed to the slave, they should be included in the *peculium*; so also, according to Labeo, should any inheritance or bequest.[20]

According to first century Roman jurist Labeo, an inheritance or a legacy given to a slave were to be credited into his *peculium*, thereby separating these assets from his master's *patrimonium*. The master was the owner of all the goods in a technical legal sense, but the slave had the factual disposition over them.

It cannot be assumed that the legal rule laid down by Labeo and confirmed by Ulpian was a mere liberality towards slaves. The Roman ruling classes knew well how to exploit slave labour and slave status for their own benefit. Rather, the rule is a protection for third parties who contract with the slave. If someone concludes a contract with a slave – e.g. for the sale of goods or for the provision of services – he or she cannot sue the slave in case of non-performance because the slave lacks the ability to stand in court (*cum servo nulla actio est*).[21] However, the contractual partner of the slave can sue the slave's master if the master has given the slave a *peculium*. The maximum liability of the master under this *actio de peculio* is limited to the amount of the *peculium*.[22] Crediting certain assets to the *peculium* is therefore a

19 For details on *peculium*, see Richard Gamauf, in this volume.

20 Transl. Weir in Watson, *Digest of Justinian* (n. 3).

21 Gai. 1 ad ed prov. D. 50.17.107; cf. also Max Kaser and Karl Hackl, *Das römische Zivilprozessrecht*, 2nd ed. (Munich: C.H. Beck, 1996): 205.

22 Gai. inst. 4.72a: *Est etiam de peculio et de in rem verso actio a praetore constituta. Licet enim negotium ita gestum sit cum filio servove, ut neque voluntas neque consensus patris dominive intervenerit, si quid tamen ex ea re, quae cum illis gesta est, in rem patris dominive versum sit, quatenus in*

legal operation for the benefit of a third party, not for the slave himself. It is only to a certain, extenuated degree that slaves may personally profit from this legal operation of the *actio de peculio*. As the master is legally obliged towards a third party, this may have a side effect on the position of the slave. However, we cannot say in which cases this also lead to an actual increase in the goods the slave had under his disposition or whether the master still exercised control over them.

A certain inference may be drawn from a very similar legal situation regarding sons who are under paternal authority (*in potestate*):

Suet. Tib. 15.2: Nec quicquam postea pro patre familias egit aut ius, quod amiserat, ex ulla parte retinuit. Nam neque donavit neque manumisit, ne hereditatem quidem aut legata percepit ulla aliter quam ut peculio referret accepta.	Suet. Tib. 15.2: And from that time on he ceased to act as the head of a family, or to retain in any particular the privileges which he had given up. For he neither made gifts nor freed slaves, and he did not even accept an inheritance or any legacies, except to enter them as an addition to his personal property.[23]

Suetonius describes how Tiberius behaved after his adoption by Augustus: He did no longer receive inheritances and legacies as his personal property, but credited them to his *peculium* instead.[24] The legal situation regarding sons and slaves is identical in this respect: Both are unable to have any personal property and can therefore only have a *peculium*. It is interesting to note that Tiberius thus really behaves as a son *in potestate* after his adoption, as opposed to the time before his adoption when he was *sui iuris* and could credit all bequests made to him to his personal property.

The social situation of a son *in postestate*, however, is not equal to the situation of a slave. It is to be assumed that slave owners exerted much more influence over the *peculium* of their slaves than fathers over the *peculium* of their sons. The legal rules were the same, though.

In order to better assess the actual social practice of instituting slaves, we have to take into consideration the evidence from non-legal sources. There is relatively sparse evidence in the epigraphic sources, probably because slaves belonged to a

---

rem eius versum fuerit, eatenus datur actio. [. . .] At si nihil sit versum, praetor dat actionem dumtaxat de peculio ('There has also been instituted the action in respect of Peculium (*de peculio*) and of what has been converted to the profit of the father or master (*de in rem verso*), since notwithstanding the fact that a contract has been made without the consent of the father or master, yet if any portion has been converted to his profit, he ought to be altogether liable to that amount; [. . .] or if no portion has been converted to his profit, he ought to be liable to the extent of the *peculium*.', transl. Poste in Whittuck, *Gai institutiones* [n. 10]: 381).

23 Transl. John Carew Rolfe, *Suetonius. Lives of the Caesars*, vol. 2, *Julius. Augustus. Tiberius. Gaius. Caligula* (Cambridge, MA: Harvard University Press, 1914): 337.

24 Cf. Alfred Pernice, *Labeo – Das römische Privatrecht im ersten Jahrhunderte der Kaiserzeit*, vol. 1 (Halle: Verlag der Buchhandlung des Waisenhauses, 1873): 140.

disadvantaged social group and for the most part did not have sufficient means to erect tombstones with inscriptions. It is therefore not surprising that the only inscriptions mentioning the institution as heir come from the privileged groups of public slaves (*servi publici*) and imperial slaves (*servi Caesaris*):

CIL VI 2307 = D 4980 (Roma): Firviae C(ai) f(iliae) Primae / Antiocho publico p(opuli) R(omani) / Aemiliano pontificali / Primus publicus Tusculanorum / arcarius vir heres Primaes f(aciendum) c(uravit)	CIL VI 2307 = D 4980 (Roma): For Firvia Prima, Gaius' daughter, and for Antiochus, public slave of the people of Rome, and for Aemilianus, priest's slave, erected by Primus, public slave of the people of Tusculum, cashier, Prima's spouse and heir.
CIL VI 11390 (Roma): Alexander Caesar(is) / ser(vus) Atticianus / Sextiliae / Priscae contubernali / cuius heres est / merenti et / libertis libertabus eius / fecit	CIL VI 11390 (Roma): Built by Alexander Atticianus, emperor's slave, for Sextilia Prisca, his wife, whose heir he is, meritorious, and for her freedmen and freedwomen.

The first source shows that a free woman, Firvia Prima, had instituted as her heir the public slave Primus, who was married to her in a de facto marriage-like union. After her death, Primus had erected this tombstone for her and for two other slaves.[25] The second source shows a similar situation where a free woman, Sextilia Prisca, has instituted her slave husband Alexander Atticianus, an imperial slave. It is noteworthy that the terminology in both inscriptions is technically correct: The marriages between the free women and their slave husbands are legally invalid, because slaves cannot enter into a marriage. However, male and female slaves lived together with each other or with free persons in de facto marriage-like relationships, which were usually called *contubernia*.[26] Consequently, Alexander Atticianus calls himself a *contubernalis* and Primus calls himself simply *vir*. The word *maritus* is not used. On the other hand, both slaves explicitly declare that they are *heres*, which is the technical term for an heir, and correctly used, because slaves have *testamenti factio* and are thus able to receive inheritances and legacies (see above D. 28,1,16 pr.).

These examples from the inscriptions and from the digest show that slaves were instituted as heirs because of their family relationship to the testator. This is an imitation of the ordinary testamentary habits in the free population of Rome, where the partner in marriage also usually was the first person to be instituted as heir.[27]

---

25 I no longer uphold my earlier opinion on this inscription that there was only one other slave who moreover shared Primus' profession, see Buchwitz, *Servus alienus heres* (n. 8): 235–36.

26 Cf. PS 2.19.6: *Inter servos et liberos matrimonium contrahi non potest, contubernium potest.* ('Slaves and free persons cannot enter into a marriage, but into a contubernium.').

27 Cf. Richard P. Saller, *Patriarchy, Property and Death in the Roman Family* (Cambridge: Cambridge University Press, 1994): 178–80.

There are more reasons, however, for instituting slaves than a personal relationship between the slave and the testator:

Suet. Iul. 27.1: Omnibus vero circa eum [i.e. Pompeium] atque etiam parte magna senatus gratuito aut levi faenore obstrictis, ex reliquo quoque ordinum genere vel invitatos vel sponte ad se commeantis uberrimo congiario prosequebatur, libertos insuper servulosque cuiusque, prout domino patronove gratus qui esset.

Suet. Iul. 27.1: When he had put all Pompey's friends under obligation, as well as the great part of the senate, through loans made without interest or at a low rate, he lavished gifts on men of all other classes, both those whom he invited to accept his bounty and those who applied to him unasked, including even freedmen and slaves who were special favourites of their masters or patrons.[28]

Suetonius describes how Julius Caesar tried to gain influence by making gifts to other persons' favourite slaves (*servuli*). It is interesting to keep in mind that from a legal perspective these gifts were made to the slave owners. A slave who receives a gift acquires it for his owner in the same way as he acquires an inheritance for his owner. However, there is no doubt that Caesar actually preferred to make gifts to the slaves themselves rather than to their owners so that the slaves could exercise their influence on their masters and help Caesar's causes. We can thus draw the conclusion that these gifts benefitted the slaves themselves and fell into their de facto property, the *peculium*. The situation must have been similar in regard to inheritances and legacies. Whoever instituted a slave usually had the intention in mind that the slave's gratefulness would afterwards help his descendants in their relationship to the slave's master. In such a situation, the institution as heir is not made for the purpose of promoting the social status of the slave himself, but it nevertheless has such an effect: The slave gains de facto assets and social influence.

There are many more reasons for instituting slaves as heirs which shall not be addressed here in detail.[29] For our purposes, it is only important to know whether the institution had an influence on the social position of the slaves. This can be assumed only in those instances where the inheritance was credited to the slave's *peculium*. In all other cases where it was credited to the master's *patrimonium*, the slave did not have any advantage of his own but was instead used as an instrument of acquisition only. The following example is very illustrative in this regard:

D. 37.11.2.9 (Ulp. 41 *ad ed.*): Si servus heres scriptus sit, ei domino defertur bonorum possessio, ad quem hereditas pertinebit: ambulat enim cum dominio bonorum possessio. quare si mortis tempore Stichus heres institutus fuit servus Sempronii nec Sempronius eum iussit adire,

D. 37.11.2.9 (Ulpian, Edict, book 41): If a slave has been appointed heir, *bonorum possessio* is offered to the master to whom the inheritance will belong; for *bonorum possessio* moves with ownership. Wherefore, if at the time of [the testator's] death Stichus, the instituted heir, was the

28 Transl. Rolfe, *Suetonius*, vol. 2 (n. 23): 69.

29 For details see Buchwitz, *Servus alienus heres* (n. 8): 245–302.

sed vel decessit vel etiam eum alienavit et coepit esse Septicii: evenit, ut, si Septicius eum iusserit, Septicio deferatur bonorum possessio: ad hunc enim hereditas pertinet. unde si per multos dominos transierit servus tres vel plures, novissimo dabimus bonorum possessionem.

slave of Sempronius and Sempronius did not instruct him to accept the inheritance but died or even transferred his property in the slave and he came into the ownership of Septicius, it turns out that if Septicius has given him the instruction, *bonorum possessio* is offered to Septicius; for the inheritance belongs to him. Whence, if the slave has passed through the hands of many masters, three or more, we shall grant *bonorum possessio* to the most recent.[30]

This source deals with *bonorum possessio*, a second form of hereditary succession under Roman law.[31] The text shows the interesting legal effects of instituting a slave: If the slave is sold and transferred to a new owner, the slave may accept the inheritance on the instruction (*iussum*) of the new owner and thereby acquires the inheritance for him. A slave-owner (in this text: Sempronius) whose slave has been instituted as heir thus has the possibility of transferring the inheritance to another person (in this text: Septicius) simply by selling and handing over the slave to that person. The new owner then can order the slave to accept the inheritance. In the alternative, he may again sell the slave to another person and thereby give the newest owner (*novissimus*) the possibility to acquire the inheritance. This legal phenomenon is expressed in the source with the figurative expression that an inheritance (or a *bonorum possessio*) ambulates with the property in the slave (*ambulat cum dominio*).[32]

The situation of a slave who has been instituted heir by another person who is not his master is therefore clear-cut from a legal point of view: The institution is valid, the slave may be transferred to a new owner, and the slave acquires for the person who is his owner at the time of the acceptance of the inheritance. However, the actual social situation is more difficult to ascertain: It depends on whether the master allows his slave to have a *peculium* and on whether he credits the inheritance into the *peculium* or rather takes it for himself into his *patrimonium*. The slave's master had an almost unlimited freedom in deciding upon these two questions. The only parameter that may have had an actual legal influence on the autonomy of the slave-owner was the will of the testator: My thesis is – I have laid this down in detail and cannot repeat it here – that a slave-owner was obliged to credit the inheritance to the slave's *peculium* if the testator in his will had expressed a

30 Transl. Jameson in Watson, *Digest of Justinian* (n. 3).

31 Cf. Pasquale Voci, *Diritto ereditario romano*, vol. 1 (Milan: Giuffrè, 1960): 177–78; Burkard Wilhelm Leist, *Ausführliche Erläuterung der Pandecten nach Hellfeld. Ein Commentar begründet von D. Christian Friedrich von Glück*, vol. 4, Serie der Bücher 37/38 (Erlangen: Palm & Enke, 1879): 140–300.

32 Cf. also Buckland, *Law of Slavery* (n. 11): 138.

clear intention to benefit the slave personally.[33] There is admittedly only vague evidence in this regard in the legal sources, but plausibility accounts for such a solution.

5 Extra-Patrimonial Effects of the Institution as Heir

The institution as heir entails more complex effects than a mere transfer of property. In Roman society, an heir had the special obligation of representing the deceased and continuing to some degree his position in society. Although the extent of this phenomenon should not be overestimated and it is highly questionable if the *heredis institutio* indeed had the purpose of continuing someone's personality,[34] the appointment as heir is at least a certain sign of distinction for the heir and honours him as a person. This is known by the term *honor institutionis*, which even appears in legal sources. The honour given to the heir does not correspond with the assets, so it is an extra-patrimonial effect of the institution as heir.

The institution as heir, or giving a legacy, are signs of respect towards the recipient. Roman testators made many bequests to family, friends, and political allies, and thereby expressed their reverence towards these persons.[35] In the case of the institution of a slave, it is noteworthy that the person receiving this honour is in many cases the slave himself and not his master. This can be derived from the following source:

> D. 37.5.3.2 (Ulp. 40 *ad ed.*): Hoc autem solum debetur, quod ipsis parentibus relictum est et liberis: ceterum si servo eorum fuerit adscriptum vel subiectae iuri eorum personae, non debetur: nec enim quaerimus, cui adquiratur, sed cui honor habitus sit.

> D. 37.5.3.2 (Ulpian, Edict, book 40): But that alone is due which has been left to the parents themselves and the children; but if it has been given to one of their slaves or to a person legally subject to them, it is not due; for we do not inquire for whose benefit it is acquired but whom it was intended to favor.[36]

33 Wolfram Buchwitz, "Fremde Sklaven als Erben: Sozialer Aufstieg durch Dritte," in *Homo, caput, persona: La costruzione giuridica dell'identità nell'esperienza romana; dall'epoca di Plauto a Ulpiano*, ed. Alessandro Corbino, Michel Humbert and Giovanni Negri (Pavia: IUSS Press, 2010): 393–425, 412–24.

34 Cf. Andreas Wacke, "Erbrechtliche Sukzession als Persönlichkeitsfortsetzung?," *Zeitschrift der Savigny-Stiftung für Rechtsgeschichte, Romanistische Abteilung* 123 (2006): 197–247, 208–30.

35 Cf. Alfons Bürge, "Vertrag und personale Abhängigkeiten im Rom der späten Republik und der frühen Kaiserzeit," *Zeitschrift der Savigny-Stiftung für Rechtsgeschichte, Romanistische Abteilung* 97 (1980): 105–56, 142–43; Christoph Paulus, *Die Idee der postmortalen Persönlichkeit im römischen Testamentsrecht. Zur gesellschaftlichen und rechtlichen Bedeutung einzelner Testamentsklauseln* (Berlin: Duncker & Humblot, 1992): 58–59, 68–69, 83–84.

36 Transl. Jameson in Watson, *Digest of Justinian* (n. 3).

This text is from the ambit of the *bonorum possessio contra tabulas*, a special legal regime that was foreseen in the praetor's edict and granted the 'possession of the goods' to persons who were not instituted in the testament ('against the testament'). Such a right was granted to the testator's children.[37] However, in case the disinherited children claimed the inheritance as a *bonorum possessio contra tabulas*, they had to fulfil certain types of legacies that the testator had given to other children or to his parents. In his commentary on this edict, Ulpian decides that only legacies which were given to children or parents personally had to be fulfilled, not those legacies which were given to these persons' slaves. Ulpian also provides us with a reason for this decision: It is not of relevance who acquires the legacy, but who receives the honour of the bequest.

From this decision, it can clearly be derived that the honour entailed by receiving a legacy was with the slave himself, not with his master. The master in effect does not even receive the legacy under the praetor's edict if it is not given to him personally but only to his slave. For the sake of clarity, it must be added that the slave does not receive the legacy either, as he is not a person falling under the edict.

There are, however, exceptions to this rule. The *honor institutionis* does not always befall the slave or other subordinate person:

D. 26.2.28 pr. (Pap. 4 *resp.*): Qui tutelam testamento mandatam excusationis iure suscipere noluit, ab his quoque legatis summovendus erit, quae filiis eius relicta sunt, modo si legata filii non affectione propria, sed in honorem patris meruerunt.

D. 26.2.28 pr. (Papinian, Replies, book 4): When a man refuses, by claiming an exemption, to undertake a tutelage assigned to him by will, the legacies which have been left to his sons must also be withheld, as long as the sons have acquired the legacies not through affection toward themselves, but as a compliment to their father.[38]

In Roman inheritance law, the testator had the possibility to assign the guardianship over his children to a person by testament (*tutela testamentaria*). The guardian had to exercise this duty unless he could avail himself of a valid excuse (e.g. his age, absence, overburdening with other guardianships etc.). If the guardian relied on such an excuse (*excusatio*), he was denied the claim to the legacies made in the same testament, probably because it was assumed that the testator had given him these legacies as a compensation for the efforts he had with the guardianship.[39] In the case at hand, the legacies however were not given to the guardian himself but to his sons. Papinian nevertheless decides that there is no claim to the legacies, as the sons would acquire the legacies for their father. He puts this decision under

37 For details see Kaser, *Das römische Privatrecht*, vol. 1 (n. 6): 707–8.

38 Transl. Hart in Watson, *Digest of Justinian* (n. 3).

39 For details see Pasquale Voci, *Diritto ereditario romano*, vol. 2, 2nd ed. (Milan: Giuffrè, 1963): 906–7.

a condition, though: The claim for the legacies is denied only if they were given to honour the father. In the alternative, if the legacies were given to the sons because of an affection for them, there is a valid claim.

This decision shows that the legacy to a subordinate person – sons and slaves are treated equally in this respect – could be meant by the testator either to give honour to the subordinate person (son or slave) himself or to his father or master. The father or master only loses his claim to the legacy if it was intended to esteem himself and not his son or slave.

Although the source D. 26.2.28 pr. limits the rule of D. 37.5.3.2, making clear that a bequest to a slave is not always an honour to the slave himself,[40] the basic fact remains that a slave's institution as heir or his reception of a legacy may in many cases qualify as a distinction to the slave himself, which is quite a striking result in the ambit of a legal system which qualifies slaves as things and makes their masters the only persons capable of owning property. The honour which slaves acquire by their institution as heir or by the legacies given to them is certainly a factor that has to be taken into consideration when assessing the social position of a slave. Even though the slave could not legally own the assets from the bequest, he could praise himself vis-à-vis everybody as a person who obtained a special distinction from the testator. From the epigraphic sources, which frequently mention the position as an heir (*heres*), it can be seen that this was indeed a social advantage. An institution as heir was thus a clear improvement of the social position of a slave also in a non-monetary respect.

6 Bequests by Slaves to Other Slaves or to Free Persons

Lastly, a very revealing aspect of the relationship between slavery and law shall be discussed: bequests made by slaves. From a legal point of view, this is an impossibility: As slaves do not have the (active) right to make a will, but only the (passive) right to receive from a will,[41] they cannot make any bequests of their own. However, it was a common practice in Roman social life that slaves nevertheless disposed over their de facto property by quasi-testamentary documents. This is described by Pliny the Younger:

Plin. ep. 8.16: Solacia duo [. . .] alterum quod permitto servis quoque quasi testamenta facere eaque ut legitima custodio. Mandant	Plin. ep. 8.16: Two facts console me [. . .] and I allow even those who remain slaves to make a sort of will which I treat as legally binding.

40 See also D. 29.4.26 pr. (honour to the daughter).

41 See above 2.

rogantque, quod visum; pareo ut iussus. Dividunt, donant, relinquunt, dumtaxat intra domum; nam servis res publica quaedam et quasi civitas domus est.	They set out their instructions and requests as they think fit, and I carry them out as if acting under orders. They can distribute their possessions and make any gifts and bequests they like, within the limits of the household: for the house provides a slave with a country and a sort of citizenship.[42]

Pliny writes to a relative of his, Plinius Paternus,[43] informing him about the death of some young slaves. He expresses his sorrows about their dying young, but at the same time his solace about the fact that he had allowed them to make testaments. This is very instructive, as it shows how important the right to make a testament was in Roman society. Romans had the idea that they somehow lived on in these last wishes. This explains the quite frequent occurences where testaments were made public and inscribed into the funerary monuments.[44] The factual possibility of making a testament, granted to his slaves by Pliny, was therefore an important aspect to increase the slaves' social position and personal satisfaction.

The slaves' testaments were of course not recognised by the law. Pliny thus calls them *quasi testamenta*. However, Pliny upholds them as a matter of respect towards the deceased and fulfils the wishes of his slaves, as long as they only make bequests within his household and not to exterior persons (*dumtaxat intra domum*). This restriction greatly reduces the alleged generosity to which Pliny seeks to lay claim: As the slaves can only make dispositions in favour of other members of Pliny's household, he will usually remain the owner of the assets. The transfer will in most cases take place from one slave's *peculium* into another slaves's *peculium*,[45] but the legal ownership will remain with Pliny. Only in certain cases, such as bequests to freedmen or freedwomen, the slaves' quasi testaments will lead to an actual transfer of ownership. However, the text at least shows that the factual possibility of making a testament was an important addition to the social situation of a slave within his (limited) group of peers.

---

42 Transl. Betty Radice, *Pliny the Younger. Letters*, vol. 2, Loeb Classical Library 59 (Cambridge, MA: Harvard University Press, 1969): 47, 49.

43 See Adrian Nicholas Sherwin-White, *The Letters of Pliny: A Historical and Social Commentary* (Oxford: Clarendon Press, 1966): 135; Detlef Liebs, "Töchter klassischer Juristen," in *Festschrift für Ernst von Caemmerer zum 70. Geburtstag*, ed. Hans Claudius Ficker et al. (Tübingen: Mohr Siebeck, 1978): 34 n. 73: The addressee is probably mentioned in the inscription AE 1916, 116 from Como.

44 See e.g. the so-called testament of Dasumius, in: Salvatore Riccobono, Vincenzo Arangio-Ruiz and Giovanni Baviera, eds., *Fontes iuris Romani antejustiniani*, vol. 3 (Florence: S.A.G. Barbera, 1968): no. 48; cf. Werner Eck, "Grabmonumente in Rom und im Rheinland: Reflex von sozialem Status und Prestige?," in *Social Status and Prestige in the Graeco-Roman World*, ed. Annika B. Kuhn (Stuttgart: Franz Steiner Verlag, 2015): 165.

45 According to Martin Schermaier, "Neither Fish Nor Fowl" (in this volume, 257), however, Pliny's slaves were only allowed to dispose of small personal belongings outside of the *peculium*.

The phenomenon of slaves making bequests is furthermore attested in some inscriptions regarding slaves in the imperial administration (*familia Caesaris*):

CIL VIII 7076 (Constantine/Numidia): D(is) M(anibus) / Aprilis Aug(usti) n(ostri) / verna ad/iutor ta/bulari(i) / v(ixit) a(nnos) XX diebus / XXXII / [Th]esmus h(eres) // posuit	For the ghost-gods. For Aprilis, our emperor's home-born slave, assistant accountant. He lived twenty years and thirtytwo days. Erected by Thesmus, his heir.
AE 1985,143 (Roma): D(is) M(anibus) / Primo Caes(aris) n(ostri) ser(vo) / M(arcus) Ulpius Threptus / et Heracla Caes(aris) n(ostri) ser(vus) / amico b(ene) m(erenti) her(edes) fec(erunt)	For the ghost-gods. For Primus, our emperor's slave. Erected by Marcus Ulpius Threptus and Heracla, our emperor's slave, for their friend, very meritorious, whose heirs they are.

These two tombstone inscriptions were erected for two imperial slaves, Aprilis and Primus respectively. They had both instituted another slave as their heir, Thesmus and Heracla respectively. Primus also joined a free person in his testament, Marcus Ulpius Threptus, as a co-heir. The fact that this free person may call himself an 'heir' is clear evidence for a legally valid institution. This distinguishes the case from Pliny's description of non-enforceable slave testaments. When a third person, a free man, is instituted as an heir, he may claim the inheritance by a *hereditatis petitio* in court.

However, this raises the question of how a slave could make such a legally valid testament. In my opinion, it is to be assumed that imperial slaves (*servi Caesaris*) were given a special privilege in this respect.[46] A similar privilege is attested in the sources in respect to public slaves (*servi publici*):

Tit. Ulp. 20,16: Servus publicus populi Romani partis dimidiae testamenti faciendi habet ius.	Tit. Ulp. 20, 16: A public slave of the Roman people has the right to make a will concerning half [his property].

The unknown author of this classical text from Roman legal literature explains that public slaves have a special right to make a testament with regards to half of their estate. They may give one half to other persons while the other half necessarily remains with their master upon their death. Legal practice shows that this right was in fact exercised by some Roman public slaves:

CIL VI 2354 (Roma): Bithi publici / Paulliani fecit / Aemilia Prima / concubina eius et heres	For Bithus Paullianus, public slave, erected by Aemilia Prima, his concubine and heiress.

46 Cf. in detail Wolfram Buchwitz, "Servus servo heres – Testierfreiheit für Sklaven," in *Fontes iuris – Atti del VI Jahrestreffen Junger Romanistinnen und Romanisten, Lecce, 30–31 marzo 2012*, ed. Pierangelo Buongiorno and Sebastian Lohsse (Naples: Edizioni Scientifiche Italiane, 2013): 141–59, 153–55.

CIL X 4687 (Cales): Primogeni pub[lico] / minori Primogene(s) maio[r et] / Urbanus posuerunt he [redes]	For Primogenes minor, public slave, erected by his heirs Primogenes maior and Urbanus.

These two inscriptions show testamentary dispositions by public slaves (*servi publici*). Bithus Paullianus has instituted Aemilia Prima as his heiress (*heres*). She is correctly named a *concubina* on this inscription because her marriage with Bithus Paullianus is legally invalid due to his slave status. However, the institution as heiress is valid because of the special rights granted to public slaves, so she has correctly employed the term *heres* here.

In the second inscription, we have a similar type of institution as heir by a public slave. The beneficiaries in this case are two other (probably public) slaves.

The two inscriptions show that public slaves in fact made use of their right to make valid wills. The comparison with CIL VIII 7076 and AE 1985,143 also shows that the practice employed by imperial slaves was comparable. This leads to the assumption that the privilege was extended to this group of slaves, although there is no explicit testimony in this regard in the legal sources.

According to a recent contribution, we also have to consider the *testamentum porcelli* as a metaphor of a slave's testament.[47] This seems to me an overinterpretation of a comical text, but the source at least shows the importance of testamentary succession in Rome: If a late antique author can describe the possibility of making a testament as a relief for a pig that was to be slaughtered, it is very clear that there was a similar relief for slaves who had the practical or (in case of public and imperial slaves) even the legal possibility to draft a testament and thus remain in contact with their friends and relatives after their deaths.

7 Conclusions

In a comprehensive perspective, the legal framework and the information from the epigraphic sources provide us with a colourful picture of the participation of Roman slaves in the exchange of inheritances and legacies. We have seen that privileged groups of slaves, such as public and imperial slaves, can validly make bequests, and that all groups of slaves can at least receive from testaments of free people or even from testaments of these privileged slaves. In making wills and receiving from wills, Roman slaves thus more or less imitate the economic and social role of inheritance law in Roman society: It is well known that testaments in Roman society did not only have the purpose of

47 Daisuke Shinomori, "Testamentum porcelli: Ein von Sklaven errichtetes Testament?" in *Aus der Werkstatt römischer Juristen: Vorträge der Europäisch-Ostasiatischen Tagung 2013 in Fukuoka*, ed. Ulrich Manthe, Shigeo Nishimura and Mariko Igimi (Berlin: Duncker & Humblot, 2016): 353–73, 362–73.

transmitting property to one's relatives, as is their function in today's societies. Rather, Roman testators usually made many different bequests to various people, to their friends, family, and business partners. The exchange of inheritances and legacies was a way of forming alliances and strengthening relationships between families. Slaves had a small share in these social habits, as they were at least to a certain degree able to participate in the exchange of testamentary dispositions. The – albeit limited – recognition of inheritance rights for slaves thus provided them with a very important instrument to express their personality in relationship to other members of the servile groups, but also in relationship to free people. In some instances, this gave Roman testators the possibility to benefit slaves who were their family members.

On the other hand, it has to be kept in mind that Roman inheritance law recognises the legal capacity of slaves only in some narrow and specific situations. In the end, the slaves' masters almost always had the last word to say in regards to the quasi-fortune of their slaves and it was not possible for a slave to dispose over his de facto property or to receive from another person without the consent of his master. The institution of a slave was even used in many cases to benefit the master and circumvent rules of inheritance law rather than to benefit the slave himself. Moreover, there were probably only very few slaves from the privileged group of slaves living in the domestic sphere who took part in the exchange of inheritances and bequests. The vast majority of the Roman slave population who lived as workers on the fields or, even worse, in the mines never had anything to do with this special phenomenon of Roman slave society. For the privileged groups of slaves, however, inheritances and legacies were an important means of gaining wealth and social status.

For the purposes of slavery studies, it is important to note that legal factors have a significant influence on the actual social position of slaves. The conditions of slave life were not only dependent on the economic and social reality, but also on certain aspects of the respective legal system which either recognised slaves' ability to participate or denied slaves' legal personality partially or in total. Roman law took a mixed approach here, which is vested in the principle of *res et persona*. The social historian must keep in mind that the social circumstances not only lead to certain legal rules, but that the legal system also has a reality of its own and legal rules thus have a decisive influence on society.

Aglaia McClintock

Servi poenae: What Did It Mean to Be 'Condemned to Slavery'?

Roman legal science continues to exert its influence on Western legal thinking also on a symbolic level. These influences, generally unrecognized, continue to work covertly in the 'underground of our time'.[1] The never-abolished penal slavery is one element of these holdovers. Forced labor is still a feature of several prison systems around the world, whether it is considered punishment or direct reparation for the costs of imprisonment. Suffice it to recall that in the United States involuntary servitude as punishment for a crime, i.e. penal servitude, survived the abolition of slavery and involuntary servitude sanctioned by the Thirteenth Amendment in 1865.

It is noteworthy that today in many countries modern prisons have developed, on a model consistent with the Roman method of exploitation of convicts, a system for generating capital: prison workshops, manufacturing, and the packaging of goods. And those who have not developed such a system of exploitation of convict work from now and then initiate public debates on the opportunity of putting criminals to work. The same expression we use today 'penal servitude/slavery' comes with surprising continuities from the Roman world. It descends in my opinion from the rare expression *servitus poenalis*,[2] that in its turn shares a strong connection with the Latin *servus poenae*, a legal label devised during imperial Rome.

---

1 See Roberto Esposito, "Il dispositivo della persona," in *Homo, caput, persona. La costruzione giuridica dell'identità nell'esperienza romana*, ed. Alessandro Corbino, Michel Humbert and Giovanni Negri (Pavia: IUSS Press, 2010): 50–63, 51: 'Ma vorrei aggiungere che in questo sempre più frequente incontro tra la filosofia contemporanea e il diritto romano c'è forse qualcosa di più di un'esigenza specifica. C'è qualcosa che attiene alla costituzione stessa di quella che fu chiamata civiltà cristiano-borghese in una forma che sembra ancora sfuggire sia all'analisi storica sia a quella antropologica – come un resto nascosto che si sottrae alla prospettiva dominante, ma che, proprio per questo, continua a 'lavorare' in maniera sotterranea nel sottosuolo del nostro tempo.'

2 Tert. *Apol.* 27.7. *Itaque cum vice rebellantium ergastulorum sive carcerum vel metallorum vel hoc genus poenalis servitutis erumpunt adversus nos, in quorum potestate sunt, certi et inpares se esse et hoc magis perditos, ingratis resistimus ut aequales et repugnamus perseverantes in eo quod oppugnant et illos nunquam magis detriumphamus quam cum pro fideli obstinatione damnamur.* Aug. *De civitate Dei* 19.5. *Prima ergo servitutis causa peccatum est, ut homo homini condicionis vinculo subderetur; quod non fit nisi Deo iudicante, apud quem non est iniquitas et novit diversas poenas meritis distribuere delinquentium. Nullus autem natura, in qua prius Deus hominem condidit, servus est hominis aut peccati. Verum et poenalis servitus ea lege ordinatur, quae naturalem ordinem conservari iubet, perturbari vetat; quia si contra eam legem non esset factum, nihil esset poenali servitute cohercendum.* On the reception of the concept of *servus poenae* in the modern age see Aglaia McClintock, "The Concept of servus poenae in Roman Law and Its Reception in the Early Modern Period," in *Le realtà della schiavitù: Identità e biografie da Eumeo a Frederick Douglass. Atti del XL Convegno Internazionale GIREA Napoli, 18–20 dicembre 2017*,

https://doi.org/10.1515/9783110987195-007

Jurists, starting from the mid-second century CE, call *servi poenae* those who are sentenced to the penalties of decapitation, exposure to wild animals or gladiatorial combat in the arena, burning alive, hard labour for life in the mines, and crucifixion. They introduce a new type of slavery in which the slave's owner is not clearly determined and, as we will see, the consequences are not exactly the same as in regular slavery.

I will try to address five points: 1) origin of the terminology and concept of *servus poenae*; 2) the role played by the institution in the history of the potential conflict between the punitive power of the *dominus* on his slaves and the punitive power of the emperor on all the inhabitants of the empire, both free and slaves; 3) the importance of the new label in order to distinguish the legal condition of the people who were, respectively, working, being exploited, or being executed in the arena; 4) the religious beliefs as well as the ideology of the amphitheatre as background for the executions; 5) the ambiguity of the expression *servus poenae* that allows to exploit without owning.

1 Origin of the Terminology and Concept of *servus poenae*

Scholarship generally traces the origins of the terminology to a rescript by the emperor Antoninus Pius.[3] The emperor answering to a legal case advanced by private individuals stated the (in)capacity of a condemned person to receive bequests as heir or legatee in consideration of his or her new condition of *servus poenae*. Thus, by distinguishing these convicts from the *servi Caesaris* (who enjoyed special rights and participated in the administration of the *res publica*)[4] he created a new and specific legal category of persons.

D. 49.14.12 (Call. 6 de cogn.): In metallum damnatis libertas adimitur, cum etiam verberibus servilibus coercentur. sane per huiusmodi personam fisco nihil adquiri divus Pius re-	D. 49.14.12 (Callistratus, Judicial Examinations, book 6): Freedom is stripped away from those condemned to the mines, since they may also be flogged like slaves. The deified Pius re-

ed. Francesca Reduzzi Merola, Maria Vittoria Bramante and Adelaide Caravaglios (Naples: Satura Editrice, 2020): 519–31.

3 For scholarship on Roman law and a discussion of *servus poenae* see Aglaia McClintock, *Servi della pena. Condannati a morte nella Roma imperiale* (Naples: Edizioni Scientifiche Italiane, 2010): 20–23. Cf. now also Tommaso Beggio, *Contributo allo studio della 'servitus poenae'* (Bari: Cacucci Editore, 2020).

4 See the contribution in this volume by Pierangelo Buongiorno, *Social Status 'Without' Legal Difference. Historiography and Puzzling Legal Questions About Imperial Freedmen and Slaves*, 67–86.

scripsit: et ideo quod legatum erat ei, qui postea in metallum damnatus erat, ad fiscum non pertinere rescripsit magisque ait poenae eos quam fisci servos esse.	sponded that the Fiscus certainly did not acquire anything through such a kind a person; and, therefore, he answered that anything bequeathed to someone who had been subsequently condemned to the mines did not belong to the Fiscus, since, he says they are more slaves of the *Punishment/Penalty* than slaves of the Fiscus.[5]
D. 29.2.25.3 (Ulp. 8 ad Sab.): Si quis plane servus poenae fuerit effectus ad gladium vel ad bestias vel in metallum damnatus, si fuerit heres institutus, pro non scripto hoc habebitur: idque divus Pius rescripsit [. . .].	D. 29.2.25.3 (Ulpian, Sabinus, book 8): If someone who has become a slave of the *Punishment/Penalty*, because he was condemned to be executed or to fight with beasts or to work in the mines, has been instituted heir, it will be considered as if it had not been written; and this the deified Pius stated by rescript.
D. 48.19.7 pr. (Marcian. 1 inst.): Sunt quidam servi poenae, ut sunt in metallum dati et in opus metalli: et si quid eis testamento datum fuerit, pro non scriptis est, quasi non Caesaris servo datum sed poenae.	D. 48.19.17 pr. (Marcian, Institutes, book 1): Some [convicts] are *servi poenae* such as those sentenced the mines or to the *opus metalli*; and if anything is left to them in a will, it is treated as though it had not been written, as if it had been left not to a slave of Caesar but to a slave of the *Punishment/Penalty*.
D. 34.8.3 pr. (Marcian. 11 inst.): Si in metallum damnato quid extra causam alimentorum relictum fuerit, pro non scripto est nec ad fiscum pertinet: nam poenae servus est, non Caesaris: et ita divus Pius rescripsit. 1. Sed et si post testamentum factum heres institutus vel legatarius in metallum datus sit, ad fiscum non pertinent.	D. 34.8.3 pr. (Marcian, Institutes, book 11): Anything, apart from provision of maintenance, left to someone condemned to the mines is considered not to have been written but does not belong to the Fiscus, since he is a slave of the Penalty not of the emperor. The deified Pius states this in a rescript.

Roman capital punishments differed greatly one from another. As one can imagine, for reasons grounded in the particulars of each punishment, but also in the bureaucratic sclerosis of everyday life, death by no means followed straightaway: a fairly long time could elapse between the sentencing and the actual execution. Individuals condemned to fight in the arena could survive match after match, as could those who were thrown to the beasts, and the convicts who were waiting to die in the quarries might work there for some time. Both free persons and slaves became *servi poenae* as a consequence of a capital sentence. The legal authorities needed to know exactly which rights – if any – the convicts would have during that time.

5 Translations of the Latin and Greek texts are always mine if not otherwise stated. For Justinian's *Digesta*, I have used the well-known translation by Alan Watson (Philadelphia: University of Pennsylvania Press, 1985), amending it where necessary.

And this certainly was a preoccupation for the jurists, as we can see from an excerpt by Gaius included in the *Digest*:

D. 48.19.29 (Gai. 1 ad l. Iul. et Pap.): Qui ultimo supplicio damnantur, statim et civitatem et libertatem perdunt. itaque praeoccupat hic casus mortem et nonnumquam longum tempus occupat: quod accidit in personis eorum, qui ad bestias damnantur. saepe etiam ideo servari solent post damnationem, ut ex his in alios quaestio habeatur.

D. 48.19.29 (Gaius, Lex Julia et Papia, book 1): The condemned to the worst kind of torments lose their citizenship and freedom and this happens immediately; therefore this new "condition" (*hic casus*) precedes their death, sometimes for a long time, as happens in the case of the persons condemned to the beasts. Often they are kept alive after the condemnation, so that they can be tortured to provide information against others.

The increasing number of convicts must have been a pressing issue. I maintain that this peculiar kind of dependency – the new condition described by Gaius – although sharing the name '*servus*' and some common traits with slavery, set itself apart from regular 'classical' slavery because of its extreme harshness and irreversibility. In the age of the Antonines, jurists created a form of subjugation that did not even ideally aim to progress toward the status of the free. They excluded once and for all from the legal system those who had been found guilty in a formal trial. Free persons were branded on their faces, were deprived of freedom and citizenship, lost their property (which was seized by the imperial treasury), and their marriages were dissolved. They could not manumit their slaves, nor could they make a will or be written into one, or receive anything through intestate succession. Slaves lost the hope of being freed by a master, since the condemnation made them masterless. At least formally, all *servi poenae* were masterless because as convicts they could not hope to regain freedom (except if their sentence were overturned and they were restored to their previous condition). This is the great difference with regular slavery. Slavery inflicted during the republic meant becoming slave of a private individual, slavery inflicted from the reign of Antoninus Pius onwards meant becoming a criminal convict, a death row inmate waiting to die.

As we can see in other contributions in this volume, slavery in the ancient world was a complex phenomenon and the condition of slaves varied: some were exploited till death in the worst ways, but many were employed in businesses, some were teachers, some philosophers, some worked in the empire's bureaucracy as imperial slaves who enjoyed special privileges.

I have argued that the etymology of *servus poenae* must be searched in Roman religion.[6] I took up an insight by Gottlieb Francke elaborated in *De servis poenae apud Romanos usitatis (viro Ioanni Gottlieb Alberti apprecatur deque felicissimo natali gratulatur)* (Lipsiae 1727), and I believe that *servus poenae* meant 'sacred to the

6 McClintock, *Servi della pena* (n. 3): 75–77.

Poena', that is, to the Fury (infernal goddess) embodiment of vengeance and torture. There are many literary and iconographical sources[7] attesting the existence of a tradition regarding the goddess *Poena*, dating at least from the fifth century BCE (the earliest extant evidence, Italiote kraters), to the beginning of the second century CE (the poet Valerius Flaccus). The Furies are present in a fragment of a lost tragedy by Ennius.[8] The existence of this ancient tradition supports the thesis that the correct etymology of *servus poenae* was 'slave of the infernal goddess *Poena*.'

If found guilty of a capital offence, both citizens and slaves were called slaves of *Poena* – a divinity of the Underworld. The jurists decided to employ an artificial expression to recall the belief that by transgressing, wrongdoers had crossed the threshold of the living. This linguistic solution devised by the jurists tapped into the religious tradition of the fate awaiting the guilty, while maintaining an implicit ambiguity. The emperor declined to call such convicts *servi Caesaris*, slaves of the emperor, consigning them instead to the aforementioned infernal goddess. Whatever their previous condition, whether citizen or non-citizen, free or slave, they were now masterless. As we will see, formerly or still privately owned slaves in the rare cases of liberation from their sentence were not returned to their previous owners, nor were the latter compensated. The jurists created a formulation that simultaneously deprived citizens of their rights and slaves of the hope of being released. But the jurists were clear: these criminals, although called *servi*, did not belong to the emperor or to the state. Nevertheless, the emperor did use them as a workforce or as a means for entertainment.

In the past, modern scholarship has linked the origins of the institution to the condemnation to a life of hard labour in the mines, which at that time were owned and operated by the emperor. I have questioned this reconstruction. I believe that the origins of *servus poenae* must be sought elsewhere, and more precisely in the amphitheatre.

The amphitheatre in the second century CE was the location where all the death penalties producing convicts who were *servi poenae* occurred with the exception of life hard labour in the mines (*ad metalla* and *in opus metalli*). Let us also not forget that the sources compare and closely link both the mines and the amphitheatre to the Underworld.[9]

---

7 Cf. the *Unterweltsvasen*, a group of Apulian vases with scenes of the Underworld, VI–IV cent. BCE, Christian Aellen, *A la recherche de l'ordre cosmique. Forme et fonction des personnifications dans la céramique Italiote*, vol. 1–2 (Kilchberg/Zürich: Akanthus, 1994).

8 Enn. *Alexander*, 69–71 = *Ennianae poesis reliquiae*, ed. Johannes Vahlen, 2nd ed. (Leipzig: Teubner, 1928) = The Tragedies of Ennius, ed. Henry David Jocelyn (Cambridge: Cambridge University Press, 1967): 47–49.

9 The comparison between the mines and the Underworld is a classical literary trope. By way of example cf. Plaut. *Capt.* 5.4. *Vidi ego multa saepe picta, quae Acherunti fierent / cruciamenta, verum enim vero nulla adaeque est Acheruns / atque ubi ego fui, in lapicidinis. illic ibi demumst locus, / ubi labore lassitudo est exigunda ex corpore*. Cf. also Diodorus Siculus (5.38.1) who describes the mines

We are brought to believe that the imperial criminal repression was harsher and crueller than the republican one and also that the emperors displayed a certain creativity in devising new forms of punishments. A closer analysis shows how there is continuity in the violent ways of execution between the republic and the empire. All the imperial capital punishments of the first two centuries CE already existed in the republican era. Many of them (*crux, ad bestias, in ludum venatorium, ad metalla*) came from the military sphere[10] and were usually inflicted on slaves, enemies vanquished in war and deserters. Clearly during the republic, the jurists had found no interest in determining the legal condition of such kind of individuals. But since the beginning of the principate the situation became more complicated. Slaves could be condemned both by the judicial authorities and by the *dominus* on the basis of his powers, producing a coexistence of 'jurisdictions'. Furthermore, when a *dominus* punished his slave (for example by sending him to fight against wild animals) he retained the right to release him if it pleased him. Thus, during the first principate, the close connection between *dominus* and slave was not severed from the ability to inflict a punishment.

Emperors started to impose systematically the ancient military and servile punishments also on citizens and political opponents. During the republic, the death penalty did not necessarily entail the loss of *civitas*: convicts kept the capacity to draw up a valid will and could in certain cases avoid execution by choosing exile.

Since the reign of Augustus, both citizens and slaves found themselves subject to a same punitive power. The imperial courts (*cognitio*) worked alongside the older *iudicia publica* whose punishments were predetermined and fixed by the law. They were more flexible and their sentences could be lightened or exacerbated depending on the circumstances of the particular case. Not to mention that the emperor could also modify or cancel the penalties set by pre-existing laws.

in Sardinia as a hell on earth. See Francesco Salerno, *Ad metalla. Aspetti giuridici del lavoro in miniera* (Naples: Jovene, 2003).

10 According to Katherine E. Welch, *The Roman Amphitheatre. From Its Origins to the Colosseum* (Cambridge/New York: Cambridge University Press, 2007): 19, gladiatorial combats, the *venationes* and the condemnation *ad bestias*, as other forms of capital penalty came from a military context. Welch reprises, extending it, the well-known reconstruction by Keith Hopkins, *Death and Renewal*, Sociological Studies in Roman History 2 (Cambridge: Cambridge University Press, 1983): chapter "Murderous Games," 1–30, according to whom during peace amphitheatres were conceived as a safety valve for the violence of a war-oriented population. As evidence for the close relation between the Roman arena and the military sphere, Welch, *The Roman Amphitheatre*: 27–29, cites the presence of many military amphitheatres built in the legionary camps, and the oath taken voluntarily by gladiators. 'The Roman Empire was realized by means of controlled violence and obsessive military discipline. One way in which commanders chose to discipline their armies was through decimation [. . .].' Welch recognizes an 'amphitheatric' character in military disciplinary actions.

2 The Potential Conflict Between the *dominus* and the Emperor

The conflict underlying private punitive powers and the growing and expanding imperial power to punish becomes all the more evident in the amphitheatre, where the emperor visually represents his power and where, with the execution of the condemned, he presides over the conclusive phase of justice.[11] Augustus, by an express provision, decreed that the imperial games must surpass in splendour those organized by individuals. The emperor was the *patronus* for excellence.[12] As Donald Kyle[13] writes 'to suggest the scale of the phenomenon, some studies calculate the number of days of festivals (and of games within these) per year, e.g. sixty-five (under Augustus) and ninety-three (under Claudius) state-funded games days of 159 days of festivals in the early empire; 135 of 230 under M. Aurelius.' If we look at the numbers, we can see how the emperor was the largest sponsor of the games, as well as owner of the *ludi*,[14] special schools where gladiators were recruited and trained.

Audiences as large as 20,000 or 50,000 people, according to the venue, attended a spectacle of death, witnessing the fulfilment of justice. The emperors who executed innocent people or whose crimes didn't deserve the death penalty were perceived as cruel and unjust.[15]

The *princeps* must also be able to show mercy to those who had been able to win the favour of the crowd. Marcus Cornelius Fronto warns in a letter the 23-year-old Marcus Aurelius of the inevitability of meeting people's moods by releasing

---

11 Kathleen M. Coleman, "Fatal Charades: Roman Executions Staged as Mythological Enactments," *Journal of Roman Studies* 80 (1990): 44–73, 72.

12 Coleman, "Fatal Charades" (n. 11): 51 and nt. 63, observes how with rare exceptions, the *munerarii*, i.e. the public officials or private individuals appointed to organize *munus* had a way of strove to outdo one another. Augustus limited private expenditure to 120 gladiators (Cass. Dio. 54.2.4.). In the *Res Gestae* (22), he says that he employed 10,000 gladiators in eight spectacles and 3500 animals in twenty-six hunting games. This means his games surpassed more than ten times the maximum private expenditure. Cf. Erik Gunderson, "The Ideology of the Arena," *Classical Antiquity* 15, no. 1 (1996): 132 nt. 67; Donald G. Kyle, *Spectacles of Death in Ancient Rome* (London/New York: Routledge, 1998): 71 nt. 121. For sources showing the concern and the interest of the emperors to control the spectacles see Aglaia McClintock, "Nemesis, dea del νόμος. Modalità e simboli della repressione criminale nei primi secoli dell'impero," *Revue Internationale des Droits de l'Antiquité* 62 (2014): 289–306.

13 Kyle, *Spectacles of Death* (n. 12): 77, 103 n. 6.

14 The *ludus Iulianus* in Capua was founded by Caesar (with 5000 gladiators) and was passed on from emperor to emperor. Nero changed its name to *Ludus Neronianus*, see Luciana Jacobelli, *Gladiatori a Pompei* (Rome: L'Erma di Bretschneider, 2003): 19. According to Thomas Wiedemann, *Emperors and Gladiators* (London/New York: Routledge, 1992): 170–71, one must imagine a network of *familiae gladiatoriae* in the provinces of the empire.

15 Cf. Wiedemann, *Emperors and Gladiators* (n. 14): 78. A famous example is Caligula, who allegedly threw a number of spectators to the beasts: Cass. Dio 59.10.1.

criminals and by manumitting those who had killed fighting wild beasts in the amphitheatre.[16] These were obviously exceptional cases that increased the suspense. *Clementia* was thus an important means of self-representation and persuasion.[17] This representation was perceived as effective and just, if the power of choice between life and death – as a *ius vitae ac necis* of the father over his children and on his subordinates indefinitely amplified in the arena – remained firmly in the hands of the emperor.

As abovementioned, during the first principate, the punitive power of the *princeps* and the *dominus* coexisted on slaves. In this respect the *leges libitinariae* from Campania in force in Pozzuoli and Cuma are remarkable evidence of this situation. They are datable to Augustan age or slightly later, and are so called from the name of the goddess *Libitina* who in the ancient Roman world oversaw everything that had to do with death. These local statutes regulating in detail the contracts for burial services and for the carrying out of death sentences (public and private), show clearly that, if the owners did not want to punish or kill their slaves at home, they could require a public service at a fee, even if the execution was included in *spectacula.*[18]

The opposition between coexisting punitive powers manifested itself during the *ludi*, when the *princeps*, on his own initiative or to meet the favour of the audience, wished to free a slave[19] who was in the arena because he had been sent there on a whim or as a punishment by a private *dominus*. The owner's power, including the

16 Fronto, *Ad M. Caes.* 2.1.2. *Quorsum hoc retuli? Uti te, Domine, ita conpares, ubi quid in coetu hominum recitabis, ut scias auribus serviendum; plane non ubique nec omni modo, attamen nonnumquam et aliquando. Quod ubi facies, simile facere te reputato atque illud facitis, ubi eos, qui bestias stenue interfecerint, populo postulante ornatis aut manumittitis, nocentes etiam homines aut scelere damnatos, sed populo postulante conceditis* (Marcus Cornelius Fronto, *The Correspondence of Marcus Cornelius Fronto*, vol. 1, Loeb Classical Library, ed. and transl. C.R. Haines [Cambridge, MA: Harvard University Press, 1919]: 118–21).

17 Sen. *de clem.* 1.21.2. *Uti itaque animose debet tanto munere deorum dandi auferendique vitam potens. In iis praesertim, quos scit aliquando sibi par fastigium obtinuisse, hoc arbitrium adeptus ultionem implevit perfecitque, quantum verae poenae satis erat; perdidit enim vitam, qui debet, et, quisquis ex alto ad inimici pedes abiectus alienam de capite regnoque sententiam exspectavit, in servatoris sui gloriam vivit plusque eius nomini confert incolumis, quam si ex oculis ablatus esset. Adsiduum enim spectaculum alienae virtutis est; in triumpho cito transisset.*

18 The *lex Cumana*, incomplete and difficult to read (face A, col. II, ll. 3–5), speaks of the *editio* of *spectacula* in which the *carnifex* participates in the execution of convicts. It seems that the price to pay differed depending on whether the execution was booked by a private person or a by a public official, cf. Sergio Castagnetti, *Le 'leges libitinariae' flegree: Edizione e commento* (Naples: Satura Editrice, 2012): 20, 31, 214–15.

19 The case of slaves sent to work in the arena (by their owners) is conceptually different from the slaves who were in the arena as a punishment (inflicted by the *dominus* or by the emperor). For a full discussion of the topic and on the cases of conflict between emperor and private owner cf. McClintock, "Nemesis, dea del νόμος" (n. 12): 294–97.

possibility to free his slaves even after he had condemned them to die, could potentially undermine the stature of the *princeps.*

The emperors appear reluctant to override the powers of slave owners under the audience pressure. To the requests of the people to free a slave who was working as an actor during the games, Tiberius agreed only after obtaining the permission of the man's master and the assurance that the price of the slave had been paid (Cass. Dio. 57.11.6). To the public who demanded loudly to free a slave engaged in the chariot race, Hadrian replied, by circulating a sign in the arena, that it was not possible to interfere with a slave of others or force the master to liberate him.

Augustus issued regulation to control manumissions occurred in similar conditions with the *lex Aelia Sentia*[20] (4 CE): slaves who had been put in chains by their masters as a punishment, who had been branded with a hot iron, who had been found guilty as a result of torture, or who had been destined to fight in the arena with a sword or against wild beasts, did not become Roman citizens if set free by their master or someone else, but acquired only a condition compared to that of the *peregrini dediticii.*

From the start of the principate, emperors issued frequent rules aimed at limiting the arbitrariness of the owners' punitive powers, both also aimed at gaining control over the *damnati.* The *lex Petronia*[21]– whose date is encompassed between 19 and 61 CE and can therefore be placed in the Julio-Claudian age[22] – forbade owners to send their slaves *ad bestias* on a whim, sanctioning not only the sellers but also buyers who did not comply, but granting the application of the penalty if the owner's request to the magistrate was substantiated. However, the specific mention of *senatusconsulta* integrating the law and the number of imperial rescripts that followed, lead to believe that a series of cases were not included in its provisions, making it still possible for the *dominus* to send slaves directly *ad bestias* without the need of 'state' control. As for example if they were caught in the act of committing a crime one would say today on the spot.

---

20 Gai 1.13. *Lege itaque Aelia Sentia cavetur, ut, qui servi a dominis poenae nomine vincti sunt, quibusve stigmata inscripta sunt, deve quibus ob noxam quaestio tormentis habita sit et in ea noxa fuisse convicti sunt, quive ut ferro aut cum bestiis depugnarent traditi sint, inve ludum custodiamve coniecti fuerint, et postea vel ab eodem domnino vel ab alio manumissi, eiusdem condicionis liberi fiant, cuius condicionis sunt peregrini dediticii.*

21 Giovanni Rotondi, *Leges publicae populi Romani* (Hildesheim: Georg Olms Verlag, 1990): 468, with some hesitancy places it in 61 CE. See the discussion in McClintock, "Nemesis, dea del νόμος" (n. 12): 297–98 n. 34; cf. Pierangelo Buongiorno, "Lex (Iunia?) Petronia de servis," in *Handwörterbuch der antiken Sklaverei*, vol. 2, ed. Heinz Heinen et al. (Stuttgart: Franz Steiner Verlag, 2017): 1763–64, who opts for 19 CE under the reign of Tiberius.

22 Cf. Bernardo Santalucia, *Studi di diritto penale romano* (Rome: L'Erma di Bretschneider, 1994): 81 n. 126; Valerio Marotta, *Multa de iure sanxit. Aspetti della politica del diritto di Antonino Pio* (Milan: Giuffrè, 1988): 305.

The *lex Petronia* (and subsequent amendments) attest to the attempts to control the punishment *ad bestias* limiting private initiative:

D. 48.8.11.1 (Mod. 6 reg.): Servo sine iudice ad bestias dato non solum qui vendidit poena, verum et qui comparavit tenebitur. 2. Post legem Petroniam et senatus consulta ad eam legem pertinentia dominis potestas ablata est ad bestias depugnandas suo arbitrio servos tradere: oblato tamen iudici servo, si iusta sit domini querella, sic poenae tradetur.

D. 48.8.11.1 (Modestinus, Rules, book 6): If a slave be thrown to the beasts without [having been before] a judge, not only he who sold him but also he who bought him shall be liable to punishment. 2. Following the *lex Petronia* and the *senatusconsulta* relating to it, masters have lost the power of handing over at their own discretion their slaves to fight with the beasts; but after the slave has been produced before a judge, if his master's complaint is just, he shall in this case be handed over to punishment.

The *lex Petronia* is in line with the other imperial measures aimed at controlling every aspect of the games. Only in the third century CE provincial governors will be forbidden from indulging the people by releasing condemned *ad bestias*.

D. 48.19.31 pr. (Mod. 3 de poen.): Ad bestias damnatos favore populi praeses dimittere non debet: sed si eius roboris vel artificii sint, ut digne populo Romano exhiberi possint, principem consulere debet. 1. Ex provincia autem in provinciam transduci damnatos sine permissu principis non licere divus Severus et Antoninus rescripserunt populo.

D. 48.19.31 pr. (Modestinus, Punishments, book 3): The governor should not discharge those who have been sentenced to the beasts to please the audience: but if they are of such strength or ability that they can worthily be exhibited to the people of Rome, he should consult the emperor. 1. The deified Severus and Antoninus wrote in a rescript that convicts should not be transferred from one province to another without the *princeps*' permission.[23]

If some convicts possessed physical qualities that could make their exhibition worthwhile in Rome, the governors must seek the opinion of the *princeps* on the opportunity to transfer them.

Antoninus Pius' reign represents a turning point in the history of the relations between the power of private owners and that of the emperor. The imperial interventions become more cohesive and intense. Antoninus Pius' rule that 'he who killed a slave without just cause will be punished severely as he who killed a slave of others' combined and with the rescript that groups together a series of different condemnations (*ad gladium*, *ad metalla* and *ad bestias*) helps shed light on the emperor's motivation. On one hand he wanted to limit the owner's power of life and death over slaves, on the other he wanted to gain full control of the

23 Cf. Hopkins, *Death and Renewal* (n. 10): 10; Kyle, *Spectacles of Death* (n. 12): 119 n. 125.

power to punish *and* to set free individuals living in the empire, whether they be citizens, foreigners or slaves. Only the Emperor could have the last word on the *servi poenae*. And even if imperial rhetoric despised criminals it is noteworthy that the emperor had an economic interest for convicts which he exploited in mines and in the arena.

3 Distinguishing the *status* of Those Who Worked, Were Exploited or Executed in the Arena

The arena was a microcosm populated by people of every class and condition: professionals, citizens, freedmen, slaves, imperial slaves and obviously convicts who before the criminal verdict could have been either slaves or citizens. Even for ancient authors it was not always easy to determine the legal status of individuals who fought as *gladiators*, *harenarii* and *bestiarii*.

Just think of the confusion arising from the fact that the same word *bestiarius* could mean a trainer of animals who was working in the arena by his own choice, or a professional fighter, as well as a criminal who had been condemned to fight if he had the physique du rôle or the necessary abilities, or just an ordinary criminal who had been sentenced to die eaten by the beasts. Many individuals worked or performed in the arena voluntarily retaining their citizenship, others were slaves of the emperor, of the impresario, or of private individuals involved in the games. Others still had been sold to the *ludus* (understood here as a centre for recruiting and training) or to a *lanista* from a *dominus* as a punishment or just on a whim. Sources speak of owners who threw their slaves in the arena so they could brag of their servants' abilities or attractiveness. Finally, many (both citizens and slaves) were in the amphitheatre as convicted criminals, sent there by the public authority. The emperors had to face the confusion that could arise and make clear that although the arena was considered a polluted place where blood was shed, the voluntary workers retained their freedom and citizenship:

Severus Alexander (a. 224) CI. 3.28.11. In harenam non damnato sed sua sponte harenario constituto legitimae successiones integrae sunt, sicuti civitas et libertas manet.	CI. 3.28.11: The legitimate successions of someone working in the arena by his own choice and not because he has been condemned remain intact, just as he maintains citizenship and freedom.

4 The Religious Apparatus of the Executions

We must not forget that public executions took place during religious festivals. The legal evidence by itself is not able to provide the answers we seek. A judicious comparative use of other types of evidence may help fill in some of these gaps. The shrines of the goddess Nemesis that predominated in amphitheatres support in my opinion this reconstruction. This goddess of retribution, a *Poena* in a technical sense, was closely tied to the imperial ideology of dramatic displays of the punishments of those who opposed the imperial order.

It is important to consider the symbolic repertoire of the amphitheatre where capital punishments were enacted in a form of ritual transition to the Underworld. Romans considered the amphitheatre the threshold to the Underworld, as a place polluted by blood and dominated by infernal divinities. As we have seen the presence in the arena was both voluntary (as for some types of gladiators) and compulsory as for convicts.

Plutarch in *De sera numinis vindicta* describes the divinities punishing criminals. Adrastea (here identified a Nemesis)[24] has the supreme function of avenging every type of fault, and no small or large criminal can escape her by fraud or force. 'The swift *Penalty* (*Poiné*) deals with those who are immediately punished in the body or concerning the body [. . .]. Those who require more intensive care to recover from their evil are entrusted to Dike.[25] The goddess Penalty inflicts punishments to 'bodies and possessions'.[26]

The worship of the goddess Nemesis, genealogically linked to *Poena*, in second- and third-century CE prevails in amphitheatres, providing additional useful

---

24 As Michael B. Hornum, *Nemesis, the Roman State and the Games* (Leiden/New York/Cologne: Brill, 1993): 7, remarks, Nemesis is associated with Adrasteia already in the fifth century BCE by Antimachus (52–53) and Adrasteia is associated with Artemis (Demetrius Scepsius in the Suida, *Adrasteia*), and deer appear on the crown of the Nemesis cult statue at Rhamnous (Pausanias, *Graece descriptio* 1.33.3).

25 *De sera numinis vindicta* 25 (564 e–f) [. . .] ὡς Ἀδράστεια μέν, Ἀνάγκης καὶ Διὸς θυγάτηρ, ἐπὶ πᾶσι τιμωρὸς ἀνωτάτω τέτακται τοῖς ἀδικήμασι: καὶ τῶν πονηρῶν οὔτε μέγας οὐδεὶς οὕτως οὔτε μικρὸς γέγονεν, ὥστ' ἢ λαθὼν διαφυγεῖν ἢ βιασάμενος ἄλλη δ' ἄλλη τιμωρία τριῶν οὐσῶν φύλακι καὶ χειρουργῷ προσήκει: τοὺς μὲν γὰρ εὐθὺς ἐν σώματι καὶ διὰ σωμάτων κολαζομένους μεταχειρίζεται Ποινὴ ταχεῖα, πράῳ τινὶ τρόπῳ καὶ παραλείποντι πολλὰ τῶν καθαρμοῦ δεομένων: ὧν δὲ μεῖζόν ἐστιν ἔργον ἡ περὶ τὴν κακίαν ἰατρεία, τούτους Δίκη μετὰ τὴν τελευτὴν ὁ δαίμων παραδίδωσι: τοὺς δὲ πάμπαν; ἀνιάτους ἀπωσαμένης τῆς Δίκης, ἡ τρίτη καὶ ἀγριωτάτη τῶν Ἀδραστείας ὑπουργῶν Ἐρινύς μεταθέουσα πλανωμένους καὶ περιφεύγοντας ἄλλον ἄλλως, οἰκτρῶς τε καὶ χαλεπῶς ἅπαντας ἠφάνισε.

26 *De sera numinis vindicta* 25 (565 a): 'τῶν δ' ἄλλων' ἔφη 'δικαιώσεων ἡ μὲν μετὰ τὴν ἐν τῷ βίῳ ποινὴν ταῖς βαρβαρικαῖς ἔοικεν. ὡς γὰρ ἐν Πέρσαις τῶν κολαζομένων τὰ ἱμάτια καὶ τὰς τιάρας ἀποτίλλουσι καὶ μαστιγοῦσιν, οἱ δὲ παύσασθαι δακρύοντες ἀντιβολοῦσιν: οὕτως αἱ διὰ χρημάτων καὶ διὰ σωμάτων κολάσεις ἁφὴν οὐκ ἔχουσι δριμεῖαν οὐδ' αὐτῆς ἐπιλαμβάνονται τῆς κακίας, ἀλλὰ πρὸς δόξαν αἱ πολλαὶ καὶ πρὸς αἴσθησιν αὐτῶν εἰσιν.

information on the symbolic system adopted by the emperors in the building considered unanimously by scholars as the highest expression of Rome in every province of the empire.

Her cult is present in Rome from the very beginning of the imperial age. Nemesis was worshipped throughout the empire, from Hispania to Noricum, from Africa to Britannia, but there is a clear concentration of shrines in the Spanish and in the Danubian provinces. The most important Greek temple of Rhamnous was dedicated to Livia, the very first first-lady of the empire.[27]

During the second century CE, Nemesis acquires new features and only sometimes resembles the ancient woodland goddess. Nemesis accentuates in her features the repressive nature. In the Roman provinces she is often pictured as a winged goddess trampling over prostrate people.

A significant piece of evidence for my reconstruction is a small marble statue of a winged Nemesis, part of the Getty Villa Collection, dating from ca. 150 CE She is portrayed, unusually, to say the least, with the facial features and hairstyle of Faustina the Elder, beloved wife of the very emperor Antoninus Pius to whom the new condition and terminology of *servus poenae* was linked. The goddess of retribution stands with her right foot on the head of a fallen victim; her left hand holds the wheel of fortune on top of a globe and small altar. Yet another empress chose to be depicted in the guise of this particular mythological figure.

Archaeologists interpret the figure under Nemesis' foot as a personification of hybris, false pride, every excess of human action contrary to divine law. Interpretations are not unanimous. In other representations Nemesis is trampling over figures of women. The features of the prostrate persons vary greatly while generally 'personifications' are more typical and less variable. In my opinion it is more probable that the prone figure represented the criminals punished in the arena: the *servi* and *servae poenae*.

This is another strong clue linking the birth of the terminology *servi poenae* to the reign of Antoninus Pius and to the symbolic repertoire of amphitheatres. Nemesis/Faustina appears as the personification of imperial justice, a protectress of the legal system that the emperor is enforcing in every province. Her avenging nature is visually clear. Women and men under the foot of Nemesis/Faustina represent as in a mirror a dynamic of power: the absence of every right and prerogative versus the combination of every power.

This trait of protector of the law will be visually emphasized especially from the third century onwards, when among her attributes she will include also Dike's scales and sword. This powerful combination – scales and sword – still defines state justice today.

---

27 Cf. Aglaia McClintock, "Giustizia senza dèi," in *Giuristi nati. Antropologia e diritto romano*, ed. Aglaia McClintock (Bologna: Il Mulino, 2016): 73–95, 85 n. 45.

5 Exploiting Without Owning

Having delved into the background that led to the elaboration of the concept of *servus poenae*, I would like to conclude my contribution by drawing your attention to Justinian's classification of *capitis deminutio maxima*, i.e. of loss of freedom and citizenship included in his *Institutes*, published and promulgated in 533:

I. 1.16. Maxima est capitis deminutio, cum aliquis simul et civitatem et libertatem amittit. quod accidit in his qui servi poenae efficiuntur atrocitate sententiae, vel liberti ut ingrati circa patronos condemnati, vel qui ad pretium participandum se venumdari passi sunt.	I. 1.16. The greater *capitis deminutio* is when a man loses both his citizenship and freedom. This happens to those who become *servi poenae* as a consequence of of the atrocity of the sentence; and to the freedmen condemned to slavery because they were ungrateful to their patrons; and to all who allow themselves to be sold in order to share the price of the sale.[28]

Justinian presents three cases: a condition of *servus poenae* as a consequence of a particularly serious sentence; and two cases of regular slavery inflicted as punishment to the freedman (*libertus ingratus*) who was ungrateful to his patron and to the free man who allowed fraudulent sale of himself to obtain part of the price. This classification overtly groups together traditional slavery inflicted as punishment in which the felon becomes the slave of another individual (the person offended, i.e. the patron in the case of the ungrateful freedman; the buyer in the case of the fraudulent sale) with *servus poenae*, a condition of servitude, as we have seen, at least formally without an owner. At the time of Justinian, slaves and penal slaves can be included in the same group without the necessity of subtle distinctions, so it seems that a clear-cut separation into categories was no longer needed.

The new grouping reflects a changed world and propels the concept of *servus poenae* towards modernity as a form of slavery if yet peculiar. Justinian's classification will be reprised in the juristic discussion of the modern era.[29] Grotius[30] will devote important reflections on penal servitude, which he calls *servitus imperfecta*, since during his age it could be limited for a period of time and also in hardship (considering the kind of labours and subjugation it entailed).

The Dutch jurist Noodt in his turn will consider *servus poenae* a brilliant way of Romans of avoiding the problem of executing citizens.[31] Criminals were made

28 Transl. Thomas Collett Sanders, *The Institutes of Justinian*, 5th ed. (London: Longmans, 1874): 59.

29 See McClintock, "The Concept of servus poenae in Roman Law" (n. 2).

30 Hugo Grotius, *De jure belli et pacis*, vol. 2 (Utrecht: Ex officina Ioannis a Schoonhoven & Soc., 1625): chapter V § XXXII.

31 Gerardus Noodt, *Probabilium Juris Civilis*, vol. 4, 3rd ed. (Lugduni Batavorum: Ex officiana Fredericum Haaring, 1705).

slaves so that their lives unprotected by citizenship became disposable. Although maybe not philologically accurate, Noodt's merit is to accentuate how sovereignty, citizenship as a guarantee, capital punishment, the right to punish and to kill intertwine in the philosophical debate. Heineccius will spread Noodt's clever theory all over continental Europe.[32]

The Roman law concept of *servus poenae* found its legitimation and purpose in imposing civil death upon a person sentenced as guilty. Servitude as retribution for an offence is deeply embedded in our culture and the ambiguity devised by the Roman jurists of never openly declaring an owner whilst exploiting felons would be in course of time attractive to both liberal and conservative thinkers. A government would not openly declare a felon its property, but it could and would impose servitude.

Once the concept of penal servitude was included in the arsenal of jurists and politicians it never left it and with different intentions and political inclinations it would resurface in Cesare Beccaria, Gaetano Filangieri, Jeremy Bentham, Benjamin Franklin, Thomas Jefferson, William Blackstone – to quote just the most prominent thinkers.

32 Johann Gottlieb Heineccius, *Antiquitatum Romanarum iurisprudentiam illustrantium syntagma*, 1st ed. (Halle: 1719).

Jakob Fortunat Stagl

Favor libertatis: Slaveholders as Freedom Fighters

Favor libertatis is a principle of jurisprudence according to which, in cases of doubt, the decision has to be made in favour of the freedom of the slave. This principle is a contradiction and a menace to slavery itself, an institution that stood at the very basis of Roman society. *Favor libertatis* is so strong that it has precedence over all kinds of rules, its only limit being third party interests. A principle with such momentum cannot be simply the product of jurisprudence. Indeed, it must have had a stronger legal basis. But which legal basis could it be? This question has never been posed, and scholarship has simply taken the *favor libertatis* for granted. As a form of redress for this situation, therefore, the main purpose of the present study is to establish a group of legislative acts, especially the *lex Iunia Petronia* and the *lex Iunia Norbana*, as the sources from which the momentum of the *favor libertatis* was derived. The methodological stance taken here can be described as a re-legification of Roman law; that is, to give more importance to the phenomenon of *leges publicae* previously neglected due to a policy to minimise their presence in the Digest.

1 A Peculiar Institution

Favor libertatis is the name of a guiding principle in Roman jurisprudence concerning slaves, according to which in cases of doubt, decisions are to be made 'in favour of liberty'.[1] This principle called into question slavery itself – the most important means

1 Some scholars have taken the *favor libertatis* to be a Justinianic interpolation, for example Fritz Pringsheim, "Ius aequum und ius strictum," *Zeitschrift der Savigny-Stiftung für Rechtsgeschichte, Romanistische Abteilung* 42 (1921): 643–55, n. 5. but in Gaius' *Institutions* there is a text (Gai. 4.14) that argues against this, the authenticity of which can hardly be doubted: [. . .] *eadem lege [XII tabularum] cautum est favore scilicet libertatis, ne onerarentur adsertores* ('this [Law of Twelve Tables] showed a disposition to favour freedom, so that those who claimed him to be free should not be burdened', transl. W.M. Gordon and O.F. Robinson, *The Institutes of Gaius* [London: Duckworth, 1988]: 409). On the authenticity of this text see now Dario Mantovani, *Les juristes écrivains de la Rome antique: Les œuvres des juristes comme literature* (Paris: Les Belles Lettres, 2018): 185. It ought to be mentioned that Fritz Schulz, a stalwart 'interpolationist', probably on the basis of this

Note: The present article is part of the project 'The Temple of Justice. A Foundation of a Systematic Interpretation of the Digest', 2020/38/A/HS5/00378, funded by the Narodowe Centrum Nauki, Poland.

https://doi.org/10.1515/9783110987195-008

of production in the Roman economy[2] and one of the fundamental institutions underpinning its legal system.[3] What was behind this initiative? Who authorised the jurists to act in this fashion? Did they themselves devise the principle, or were they implementing a legal mandate? This raises the question of the legal basis of *favor libertatis*.

An even greater riddle is the question of what motivated the creators of *favor libertatis*, whether this was the emperor, the jurists or even the Roman people. Why did it exist at all? Romans accepted slavery (*servitus*), but at the same time they developed a principle according to which the law had to be aligned with liberty. It is intriguing to imagine the coexistence of *servitus* and *favor libertatis*.

To understand *favor libertatis* properly, it is important to be aware of two features of Roman *servitus*: The legal relationship of the master and his slave (women could, of course, own slaves as well) is that of ownership.[4] The master can, in theory, do whatever he pleases with the slave who is considered a chattel (*res mancipi*).[5] Ownership also entails the ability to enfranchise a slave (*manumissio*), an act that makes the slave a *libertus* or *liberta*, a free person with limited political and civic rights.[6] During the Republic, three forms of manumission existed: *vindicta, censu, testamento*.[7] All three were formal and cumbersome. The first took place before the praetor; the second consisted in inscribing the former slave into the list of citizens; the third was a clause in a will such as, 'Stichus, my slave, shall be free' (*Stichus servus meus liber esto*).[8] The formalities of wills were intricate,[9] and all the hazards that befell a will could befall these clauses (see the case in D. 28.4.3 under 5.5). A safer and common alternative was developed at the beginning of the empire, the *fideicommissum*, in which a master 'entrusted' a friend to enfranchise a slave after his death (which could be done in one of the previously mentioned procedures).[10] At the same time, the *praetor* granted freedom if he had come to the conclusion that

---

and other passages, considered this guiding principle to be authentic; Fritz Schulz, *Principios de derecho romano*, transl. Manuel Abellan Velasco (Madrid: Universidad Complutense, 1990): 240.

2 Francesco de Martino, *Storia della costituzione romana*, vol. 4, 2nd ed. (Naples: Jovene, 1974): 337.

3 The unsurpassed study on Roman slavery as a legal institution is still William Warwick Buckland, *The Roman Law of Slavery: The Condition of the Slave in Private Law from Augustus to Justinian* (Cambridge: Cambridge University Press, 1908). From the perspective of social history, the classical work is Geza Alföldy, *Römische Sozialgeschichte*, 4th ed. (Stuttgart: Franz Steiner Verlag, 2011). A new overview has been provided by Richard Gamauf, "§ 36: Sklaven (servi)," in *Handbuch des Römischen Privatrechts*, ed. Ulrike Babusiaux et al. (Tübingen: Mohr Siebeck, 2023): 914–84.

4 Gaius 1 *inst* D. 1.5.1.

5 Gai. 2.13; Max Kaser, *Das Römische Privatrecht*, vol. 1, *Das altrömische, das vorklassische und das klassische Recht* (Munich: C.H. Beck, 1971): 284.

6 On this and the following Kaser, *Das Römische Privatrecht*, vol. 1 (n. 5): 293–97.

7 On the republican era see Kaser, *Das Römische Privatrecht*, vol. 1 (n. 5): 115–19.

8 Gai. 2.267.

9 An overview can be found in Jakob Fortunat Stagl, "Das 'testamentum militare' in seiner Eigenschaft als 'ius singular'," *Revista de Estudios Histórico-Jurídicos* 36 (2014): 129–57.

10 Gai. 2.263–66.

the master had had the volition (*voluntas*) to enfranchise the slave, *inter amicos*, for example, or *per epistulam*.[11] Initially, these factual *liberti* enjoyed no protection at all if their master claimed them back, but already in the republican era the praetor began to acknowledge these informal liberations as legally valid.[12] This situation was fully recognised by a *lex Iunia Norbana* from 19 CE,[13] which we will discuss further on.

There has been no full-length scholarly investigation of *favor libertatis* since the work by Ivo Pfaff from the late nineteenth century,[14] although scholars have published important shorter works on the subject,[15] especially Hans Ankum[16] and Andreas Wacke.[17] But they all approach *favor libertatis* as a given, as though it came out of nowhere and was essentially based on nothing. An exception to this lack of investigative *élan* and a particularly meticulous and astute work is the essay by Liselot Huchthausen,[18] a classical philologist whose East German background gave her a much more political perspective on this subject which is, of course, of prime importance for Marxist theory.[19]

---

11 On the former see Gai. 1.41;44; on the latter Fr. Dos. 15; Iul. D. 41.2.38pr.

12 A. Steinwenter, "Latini Iuniani," in *Paulys Realencyclopädie der classischen Altertumswissenschaft*, vol. 12 (1925) (Stuttgart: J.B. Metzler, 1925): 911.

13 The main source is I. 1.5.3.

14 Ivo Pfaff, *Ein Beitrag zur Lehre vom favor libertatis* (Vienna: Manz, 1894).

15 See the studies by Gérard Boulvert and Marcel Morabito, "Le droit de l'esclavage sous le Haut-Empire," in *Aufstieg und Niedergang der römischen Welt*, pt. 2, *Principat*, vol. 14, *Recht*, ed. Hildegard Temporini and Wolfgang Haase (Berlin: De Gruyter, 1982): 98, 119–23; Jacob Giltaij, *Mensenrechten in het Romeinse recht?* (Nijmegen: Wolf Legal, 2011): 49; Jean Imbert, "Favor libertatis," *Revue historique de droit français et étranger* 26 (1949): 274; Pfaff, *favor libertatis* (n. 14); Olís Robleda, *Il diritto degli schiavi nell'antica Roma* (Rome: Pontificia Universita Gregoriana, 1976): 96; Pia Starace, *Lo statuliber e l'adempimento fittizio della condizione. Uno studio sul favor libertatis fra tarda Repubblica ed età antonina* (Bari: Cacucci Editore, 2006): 23; Andreas Wacke, "Der favor libertatis: Skizze eines Forschungsvorhabens," in *Vorträge gehalten auf dem 28. Deutschen Rechtshistorikertag Nimwegen 23–27 September 1990*, ed. Paul Nève and Chris Coppens (Nimwegen: Gerard Nood Instituut, 1992): 21–23; Andreas Wacke, "Favor libertatis," in *Handwörterbuch der antiken Sklaverei*, vol. 1, ed. Heinz Heinen et al. (Stuttgart: Franz Steiner Verlag, 2017): 923.

16 Hans Ankum, "Der Ausdruck favor libertatis in den Konstitutionen der römischen Kaiser," in *Sklaverei und Freilassung im römischen Recht: Symposium für Hans Josef Wieling zum 70. Geburtstag*, ed. Thomas Finkenauer (Berlin/Heidelberg: Springer Verlag, 2006): 1–17.

17 Wacke, "Der favor libertatis" (n. 15): 21–23; Wacke, "Favor libertatis" (n. 15): 923.

18 Liselot Huchthausen, "Zum Problem der Freiheitsbegünstigung (favor libertatis) im römischen Recht," *Philologus* 120, no. 1 (1976): 47–72.

19 Robert A. Padgug, "Problems in the Theory of Slavery and Slave Society," *Science & Society* 40, no. 1 (1976): 3–27; Friedrich Vittinghoff, "Die Theorie des historischen Materialismus über den antiken 'Sklavenhalterstaat'," *Saeculum* 11 (1960): 89–131. Georg Prachner, "Zur Bedeutung der antiken Sklaven- und Kolonenwirtschaft für den Niedergang des römischen Reiches (Bemerkungen zur marxistischen Forschung)," *Historia: Zeitschrift für Alte Geschichte* 22 (1973): 732–56.

Having touched on the sensitive issue of ideology, it might be appropriate to remind readers of how ancient slavery has been assessed in modern times.[20] From the already mentioned Marxist point of view, slavery is a mode of production and could only be overcome by changing production itself. The law regulating slavery is just the superstructure, while something like *favor libertatis* is a narcotic that pales into insignificance in the inherent, un-redressable cruelty and blight of bondage. Slavery becomes a metaphor for the condition of the workers and Spartacus a 'proletarian hero'. The opposite view is based on the doctrine of natural law and has its base in another kind of materialism, that of the sources. Florentinus states at the beginning of the Digest (D. 1.5.4pr.-1), 'Freedom is one's natural power of doing what one pleases, save insofar as it is ruled out either by coercion or by law. Slavery is an institution of the *ius gentium* [the law of nations or peoples], whereby someone is against nature made subject to the ownership of another.'[21] From this point of view, slavery was not rooted in the production process but rather in the law: it could be redressed, and there loomed the possibility of abolishing it altogether since it was 'against nature'.[22] From the latter point of view, *favor libertatis* was not so illogical even though everybody involved was, as a member of the *élite*, necessarily a slaveholder:[23] 'Natural law', the set of rules derived from nature which we will discuss later, is the basic legal and ideological tool for some kind of reform policy consisting in a piecemeal alleviation of the slaves' condition. From the opposite point of view, however, it is simply absurd to own slaves and to fight for their welfare, an endeavour which must ultimately result in the abolition of slavery. Those who do so must

20 In the scholarly debate about the absolute versus the relative evil of slavery, the former position was argued by Moses I. Finley, *Ancient Slavery and Modern Ideology*, 2nd ed. (New York: Markus Wiener, 1980), the latter by Joseph Vogt, *Sklaverei und Humanität: Studien zur antiken Sklaverei und ihrer Erforschung* (Wiesbaden: Franz Franz Steiner Verlag, 1983). For this debate see Johannes Deissler, "Cold Case? Die Finley-Vogt-Kontroverse aus deutscher Sicht," in *Antike Sklaverei: Rückblick und Ausblick. Neue Beiträge zur Forschungsgeschichte und zur Erschließung der archäologischen Zeugnisse*, ed. Heinz Heinen (Stuttgart: Franz Steiner Verlag, 2010): 77.

21 *Libertas est naturalis facultas eius quod cuique facere libet, nisi si quid vi aut iure prohibetur. Servitus est constitutio iuris gentium, qua quis dominio alieno contra naturam subicitur* (transl. MacCormick in Alan Watson, *The Digest of Justinian*, vol. 1–4 (Philadelphia: University of Pennsylvania Press, 1998).

22 Still fundamental is Wolfgang Waldstein, "Entscheidungsgrundlagen der römischen Juristen," in *Aufstieg und Niedergang der Antiken Welt*, pt. 2, *Principat*, vol. 15, *Recht*, ed. Hildegard Temporini and Wolfgang Haase (Berlin: De Gruyter, 1982): 3, 78. Ample references can be found now in Gamauf, "Sklaven (servi)" (n. 3): 7; see also Jakob Fortunat Stagl, *Camino desde la servidumbre* (Madrid: Editorial Dykinson, 2021): 42–46.

23 On the interaction of masters and servants see Paul Veyne, "Vie de Trimalcion," in *Annales: Economies, sociétés, civilisations* 16 (1961): 213–47 and Keith R. Bradley, "Roman Slavery and Roman Law," in *Historical Reflections/Réflexions Historiques* 15, no. 3 (1988): 477–95, on the lifestyle of the *ordo senatorius* and *equester* from a sociological point of view see Alföldy, *Sozialgeschichte* (n. 3): 150–69.

be diagnosed with a 'false consciousness'; they are strange and have no real place in history. The only redress for slavery is abolition, not only of slavery but of the production process which engenders it. Any intent to make slavery more humane is ridiculous insofar as this is impossible and pernicious, for the reason that it hampers the drive to root out the evil completely.[24] What is at stake with *favor libertatis* is nothing less than the question of whether we have an inbuilt moral compass that is independent of whichever conditions we happen to live under, or whether these conditions determine everything. Just consider the latest truly comprehensive description of Roman slavery by Richard Gamauf: He mentions the *favor libertatis* only occasionally and considers *ius naturale* to be a revery about a fictitious past that has no repercussions whatsoever for the law of slavery.[25] This stance appears to be peculiar given the sheer amount and force of the sources which we will encounter in the course of this investigation.

The two central questions of this study are, accordingly, firstly, 'What is the legal basis for the tendency to privilege liberty?' and secondly, 'What is the rationale of this privilege?'

2 The Morphology of the *favor libertatis*

In Justinian's institutions, there is a reference in I. 2.7.4 to 'liberty, in favour of which the ancient legislators enacted in many instances manifestly against the common rules' (*libertas cuius favore et antiquos legislatores multa etiam contra communes regulas statuisse manifestum est*). This definition tells us that *favor libertatis* concerned exceptions to the general rule and that these exceptions were based on formal legal provisions like *leges publicae, senatus consulta* etc.[26] Flowing from a legal directive, this guiding principle for the administration of justice is clearly expressed in Pomp. D. 50.17.20: 'Wherever there is a doubt in interpreting liberty, an interpretation shall be given that enhances liberty' (*Quoties dubia interpretatio libertatis est, secundum libertatem respondendum erit*). A comparison between these two texts illustrates the central point of the present investigation: whereas the emperor, who since the reign of Augustus had the constitutional authority to create law,[27] states that his predecessors had legislated in favour of liberty (*legislatores* [. . .]

24 On these two attitudes concerning slavery as a historical problem see Stagl, *Camino* (n. 22): 124–26.

25 Gamauf, "Sklaven (servi)" (n. 3): 24 and 27.

26 As indicated by Herman Gottlieb Heumann and Emil Seckel, *Handlexikon zu den Quellen des römischen Rechts*, 9th ed. (Jena: G. Fischer, 1914): s.v. legislator 2, indicate, this word can also mean 'jurist', but together with *statuere* it should mean the creation of a formal source of law.

27 Ulp. 1 *inst.* D. 1.4.1pr.: *Quod principi placuit, legis habet vigorem: utpote cum lege regia, quae de imperio eius lata est, populus ei et in eum omne suum imperium et potestatem conferat.*

regulas statuisse), Pomponius states that a jurist should 'respond' in favour of liberty; giving one's opinion, *respondere*, is the quintessential activity of a jurist.[28] Both pursue the same goal, and both remain within their respective spheres; the only difference is the scope of their authority: one acts as a *legifer*, a creator of the law; the other gives *responsa*, that is to say acts as an interpreter of the law.

There are forty-three instances in the sources where the *favor libertatis* (or linguistic variants thereof) is explicitly cited as the basis for a decision;[29] a further four passages speak of a *humanior* or *benigna interpretatio* with regard to slaves, which amounts to the same thing.[30] Another question are the texts where decisions are based on *favor libertatis* without explicit reference to it.[31] There are many possible reasons for the absence of a referential explanation. The first is literary: the original author may have been very succinct or wanted to avoid repetition. Then there is the question of textual transmission, both in the pre-Justinianic period and in the compilation itself. Based on my experience with the not unrelated phenomenon of *favor dotis*,[32] I would assume that we should multiply the extant cases by a factor of ten to arrive at the total *corpus* of texts that feature *favor libertatis*, that is to say about 500. Under these premises, it is no exaggeration to say that we are dealing with a phenomenon of the utmost importance since 5% of the total of 9,139 texts in the Digest refer to it. Given the fact that about a quarter of all the fragments in the Digest, that is to say about 2,250 texts, address aspects of slavery,[33] this estimate seems probable.

28 Adolf Berger, *Encylopaedic Dictionary of Roman Law* (Philadelphia: American Philosophical Society, 1953): s.v. Responsa.

29 Gai. *inst.* 4.14; I. 3.11.1; Gai. *ad ed. prov.* D. 4.7.3.1; Paul. 13 *ad ed.* D. 4.8.32.7; Paul. 5 *quaest.* D. 18.7.9; Ulp. 61 *ad ed.* D. 29.2.71; Marcell. 12 *dig.* D. 29.5.16; Paul. 4 *ad Vitell.* D. 31.14; Maec. 9 *fideicomm.* D. 35.2.32.5; Iul. 39 *dig.* D. 36.1.26.2; Iul. 42 *dig.* D. 40.2.4; Ulp. 4 *ad Sab.* D. 40.4.1; Ulp. 4 *ad Sab.* D. 40.4.10.1; Iul. 36 *dig.* D. 40.4.16; Iul. 42 *dig.* D. 40.4.17.2; Marcian. 1 *reg.* D. 40.4.26; Scaev. 23 *dig.* D. 40.4.29; Ulp. 60 *ad ed.* D. 40.5.4.16; Ulp. 5 *fideicomm.* D. 40.5.24.10; Ulp. 5 *fideicomm.* D. 40.5.26; Paul. 5 *ad Sab.* D. 40.7.4.6; Ulp. 28 *ad Sab.* D. 40.7.9.3; Ulp. 14 *ad ed.* D. 40.7.19; Ulp. 14 *ad ed.* D. 40.7.20.3; Iav. 6 *ex Cass.* D. 40.7.28; Paul. 5 *quaest.* D. 40.8.9; Iul. 5 *ex Minic.* D. 40.12.30; Paul. 15 *resp.* D. 40.12.38.1; Ulp. 71 *ad ed.* D. 43.29.3.9; Marcian. 2 *inst.* D. 48.10.7; Tryph. 4 *disp.* D. 49.15.12.9; Tryph. 18 *disp.* D. 49.17.19.5; Paul. l. *s. ad reg. Caton.* D. 49.17.20; Pomp. 7 *ad Sab.* D. 50.17.20; Gai. 5 *ad ed. prov.* D. 50.17.122; Paul. 16 *ad Plaut.* D. 50.17.179; Diocl. y Maxim. C. 4.6.9; Gord. C. 7.2.6; Valer. and Gallien. C. 7.4.10; Diocl. y Maxim C. 7.22.2; PS. 2.23.2; PS. 2.24.2.

30 Ulp. 6 *disp.* D. 34.5.10.1; Ulp. 12 *ad Sab.* D. 38.17.1.6; Ulp. 6 *fideicomm.* D. 40.5.37; Scaev. 4 *resp.* D. 40.5.41.10; Marcell 29 *dig.* D. 28.4.3; Ant. C. 6.27.2.

31 E.g. Lab. *post. a Iav. epit.* D. 32.29.4; Pomp. 3 *ad Sab.* D. 40.4.5; Ulp. 27 *ad Sab.* D. 40.7.3.16; further examples in Huchthausen, "Freiheitsbegünstigung" (n. 18): 49.

32 Jakob Fortunat Stagl, *Favor dotis: Die Privilegierung der Mitgift im System des römischen Rechts* (Vienna/Cologne/Weimar: Böhlau, 2009): 91–234; this explains the silence regarding Frg. Vat. 106. to which Rolf Knütel drew attention in his "Uxores constrictae," *Fundamina* 20, no. 1 (2014): 467–74.

33 Boulvert and Morabito, "Le droit de l'esclavage" (n. 15): 98, 154.

Bearing in mind these numbers should impede any attempt at marginalizing the *favor libertatis*: it is, in fact, a central feature of a central institution of Roman law.

One example for such an implicit application of *favor libertatis* is Pomp. D. 40.4.11.2: *Quum testamento servus liber esse iussus est, vel uno ex pluribus heredibus institutis, adeunte hereditatem statim liber est.* The inheritance 'rests', as the jurists say, until the formal *aditio*.[34] This requires an answer to the question of how to proceed when several persons have been appointed as heirs, but not all have acceded to the inheritance at the same time. Does the slave have to wait until all the heirs have taken possession of their inheritance, or would it suffice for one to have done so? Under ordinary conditions, all co-heirs would have needed to accede in order to activate the inheritance;[35] but in our case, one *aditio* suffices. This decision is made *in favorem libertatis*, even though Pomponius does not explicitly say so. Here now is an explicit example for *favor libertatis*, Iul. 36 *dig*. D. 40.4.16:

D. 40.4.16 (Iulian 36 dig.): Si ita scriptum fuerit: 'quum Titius annorum triginta erit, Stichus liber esto, eique heres meus fundum dato', et Titius, antequam ad annum trigesimum perveniret, decesserit, Sticho libertas competet, sed legatum non debebitur; nam favore libertatis receptum est, ut mortuo Titio tempus superesse videretur, quo impleto libertas contingeret; circa legatum defecisse conditio visa est.	D. 40.4.16 (Julian, Digest, book 36): If it has been written in the will, "when Titius reaches the age of thirty, let Stichus be free and let my heir give him a farm", and if Titius has died before reaching his thirtieth year, freedom belongs to Stichus, but the legacy will not be due. For by the principle favoring freedom, it has been accepted that after Titius's death a period of time evidently remained on whose expiry freedom accrued; regarding the legacy, the condition is thought to have failed.[36]

The testator wrote in his will: 'When Titius reaches the age of thirty, let Stichus be free and let my heir give him a farm.' Titius dies before he turns thirty, but in favour of freedom for Stichus – *in favorem libertatis* – it is assumed that he lived, although this fiction does not extend to the estate; in this respect, Titius did not reach the age of thirty. The heir, accordingly, lost ownership of the slave but kept the estate undiminished; the slave obtained his freedom but not a means of subsistence.

We might characterise *favor libertatis* as a guiding principle according to which, when in doubt, the decision is to be made in favour of the slave, regardless of

34 Kaser, *Das Römische Privatrecht*, vol. 1 (n. 5): 715, 720.
35 Kaser, *Das Römische Privatrecht*, vol. 1 (n. 5): 716.
36 Transl. Brunt in Watson, *Digest of Justinian* (n. 21).

whether the question is one of interpreting a will or applying a regulation extensively or even analogously. From a methodological point of view, *favor* is a fertile and dynamic principle naturally prone to extension;[37] so by referring to *favor*, the jurist appeals to the reader's obedience to the emperor and his legislative acts, an obedience that includes broad interpretations or analogies.[38] The topos of *favor* oscillates between the jurist's rhetorically construed self-justification for his bold interpretation and the implied argument that it is methodically correct to pay attention to the spirit as opposed to the letter of the law.[39] When the jurists speak of *favor liberatis*, which requires this or that decision overturning the established rules, they justify themselves as being in accord with the emperor and his forbears who did likewise.

Impressive as it was, the scope and power of *favor libertatis* were not boundless. It seems that there was a general principle according to which one was allowed to diminish one's own or rather one's heirs' estate, but not a third person's. This conclusion can be drawn from a text by Paul, D. 40.1.3: *Servus pignori datus, etiamsi debitor locuples est, manumitti non potest.*[40] A debtor had pledged a slave, but later wanted to set him free, which would have resulted in the pledgee losing his pledge, since a free man cannot be a pledge. The manumission would have the *de facto* effect of the loss of a surety which the parties had agreed upon previously, and thereby would have endangered the creditor's position who wanted to secure the payment due to him. His interests in this regard are stronger than those of the slave, even in the case that the debtor is creditworthy, which implies that the pledge is more of a formal than a substantial value.

---

37 Antonio Palma, *Humanior interpretatio: 'Humanitas' nell'interpretazione e nella normazione da Adriano ai Severi* (Turin: Giappichelli, 1992): 46 with regard to *humanitas*.

38 See the observations by Pfaff, *favor libertatis* (n. 14): 3; and esp. Huchthausen, "Freiheitsbegünstigung" (n. 18): 60.

39 In general D. 1.3.17 (Cels. 26 dig.): *Scire leges non hoc est verba earum tenere, sed vim ac potestatem.* ('Knowing laws is not a matter of sticking to their words, but a matter of grasping their force', transl. MacCromick in Watson, *Digest of Justinian* [n. 21]). Due to its palingenetical context the text originally maybe referred only to stipulations.

40 'A slave in pledge cannot be manumitted, even if the debtor can provide security for repayment.', transl. Brunt in Watson, *Digest of Justinian* (n. 21). See also D. 40.9.4 (Ulpianus libro tertio disputationum): *Servum pignori datum manumittere non possumus* ('We cannot manumit a slave given in pledge.', transl. Brunt in Watson, *Digest of Justinian* [n. 21]).

3 The Legal Basis of *favor libertatis*

3.1 Constitutional Requirements for Laws Changing Slavery

Favor libertatis disrupts Roman slave law and transgresses one of its fundamental principles:[41] above all the qualification of the relationship between master and slave as one of ownership.[42] It is difficult to imagine how the jurists could have changed this institution on their own, given the fact that they could not have created it, 'for a civilian ratio may degrade civilian rights, but with natural rights, this, indeed, cannot be done' (*quia civilis ratio civilia quidem iura corrumpere potest, naturalia vero non potest*), as Gaius proclaims.[43] The same holds true for the departure from slavery, *manumissio*, as we are told by Ulpian (1 *inst*. D. 1.1.4):

D. 1.1.4 (Ulpian 1 inst.): Manumissiones quoque iuris gentium sunt. est autem manumissio de manu missio, id est datio libertatis: nam quamdiu quis in servitute est, manui et potestati suppositus est, manumissus liberatur potestate. quae res a iure gentium originem sumpsit, utpote cum iure naturali omnes liberi nascerentur nec esset nota manumissio, cum servitus esset incognita: sed posteaquam iure gentium servitus invasit, secutum est beneficium manumissionis.	D. 1.1.4 (Ulpian, Institutes, book 4): Manumissions also belong to the *ius gentium*. Manumission means sending out of one's hand, *de manu missio*, that is, granting of freedom. For whereas one who is in slavery is subjected to the hand (*manus*) and power of another, on being sent out of hand he is freed of that power. All of which originated from the *ius gentium*, since, of course, everyone would be born free by the natural law, and manumission would not be known when slavery was unknown. But after slavery came in by the *ius gentium*, there followed the boon (*beneficium*) of manumission.[44]

Ius gentium was a law common to all peoples that allowed the Romans to cut out the deadwood in their own legal system, expand Roman law *imperio rationis*[45] and justify awkward institutions like slavery.[46] What Ulpian and other lawyers had in mind here was a sort of legal 'rock paper scissors': natural law is stronger than civil law; slavery

41 Pfaff, *favor libertatis* (n. 14): 15.
42 Flor. D. 1.5.3.1.
43 Gai. 1.58.
44 Transl. MacCromick in Watson, *Digest of Justinian* (n. 21).
45 Fritz Sturm, "Ius gentium. Imperialistische Schönfärberei römischer Juristen," in *Römische Jurisprudenz – Dogmatik, Überlieferung, Rezeption. Festschrift für Detlef Liebs zum 75. Geburtstag*, ed. Karlheinz Muscheler (Berlin: Duncker & Humboldt, 2011): 663–69.
46 Max Kaser, *Ius gentium* (Cologne/Vienna: Böhlau, 1993); Jacob Fortunat Stagl, "Eine Flucht nach Rom: Der geistige Weg Ernst Rabels," *Tijdschrift voor Rechtsgeschiedenis* 79, no. 3–4 (2011): 533, 545–48.

is against natural law and cannot, therefore, be regulated by civil law; but the law of nations is so strong that it can overcome civil law. From this, we can conclude that the stakes concerning slavery are high: anybody who wanted to tamper with this institution, and be it by means of *manumissio*, had to have a solid mandate.

As these deliberations prove, an antithetical guiding principle like *favor libertatis* cannot be simple jurisprudence: there must be a normative source[47] and a societal belief from which it draws its validity and momentum.[48] Enfranchising a slave is significant for the public interest in so far as it creates a new Roman citizen.[49] Nevertheless, manumission was treated during the republic as merely an act of private law.[50] Olís Robleda, one of the great authorities on the law of slavery, observes that legislation to curb manumission restricts this freedom in the interests of *status rei Romanae*,[51] and in consequence, transforms what was originally a category of *ius privatum* into *ius publicum*.[52] As a result, slavery as a whole is transformed into an institution of public law,[53] a phenomenon typical for the Augustan age, which also saw a transformation of the – originally wholly private – family into an institution of public law.[54] Given the public-law nature of slavery, it is clear that this institution cannot be changed merely by means of simple *responsa prudentium*, since this is the weakest form of legal source, while the *lex publica* is the strongest, as we can see from this list in Gaius:[55] *Constant autem iura populi Romani ex legibus, plebiscitis, senatus consultis, constitutionibus principum, edictis eorum, qui ius edicendi habent, responsis prudentium.*[56] Only a *lex publica*

---

47 Boulvert and Morabito, "Le droit de l'esclavage" (n. 15): 121: 'Where the lawyers do not dare to go, the emperors will go'.

48 See Carlo Castello, "'Humanitas' e 'favor libertatis'. Schiavi e liberti nel I secolo," in *Sodalitas. Scritti in onore di Antonio Guarino*, vol. 5, ed. Antonio Guarino and Vincenzo Giuffrè (Naples: Jovene, 1984): 2175–89, 2183, with regard to the *lex Iunia Petronia*; see in general, Stagl, *Camino* (n. 22): 317–36.

49 Kaser, *Das Römische Privatrecht*, vol. 1 (n. 5): 294.

50 Kaser, *Das Römische Privatrecht*, vol. 1 (n. 5): 293.

51 Ulp. 1 *inst.* D. 1.1.1.2.

52 Robleda, *Il diritto* (n. 15): 149–153.

53 Antonio Fernández de Buján, "Conceptos y dicotomías del ius," *Revista Jurídica Universidad Autónoma de Madrid* 3 (2000): 9, 42; in general see Juan Manuel Blanch Nougués and Carmen Palomo Pinel, "Ius publicum y ius priuatum en la experiencia histórica del derecho. Un ejemplo insólito en las distinciones de Bártolo expuestas a través de esquemas," *Revista General de Derecho Romano* 18 (2012): 1–68.

54 See also Paul. 60 *ad ed.* D. 23.3.2; Pomp. 15 *ad Sab.* D. 24.3.1; Stagl, *Camino* (n. 22): 295 ss.

55 Gai. 1.2.

56 Álvaro D'Ors, *Los romanistas ante la actual crisis de la ley* (Madrid: Ateneo, 1952): 9; Dario Mantovani, "Mores, leges, potentia. La storia della legislazione romana secondo Tacito (Annales III 25–28)," in *Letteratura e civitas. Transizioni dalla Repubblica all'Impero. In ricordo di Emanuele Narducci*, ed. Mario Citroni (Pisa: ETS, 2012): 353–404.

can derogate or modify[57] a *ius publicum* because only a *lex publica* can claim to be, in the words of Papinian, *communis rei publicae sponsio.*[58]

The politicization of private law under Augustus occurs in the legal form of a *lex publica*, the adequate form for implementing a 'public interest.' Justinian obscures this tendency through the de-legislating process recently identified by Dario Mantovani:[59] we have lost this precise component of Roman law because Justinian either left it out altogether or manipulated the passages which he did include. The main argument for a greater presence of *leges publicae* in the original writings of the jurists is the comparison between Gaius and the Digest. Whereas Gaius' Institutes, which were not tampered with by Justinian, mentions 39 *leges publicae*, the Justinian Digest only knows 23, and this is the case even though the Digest is sixteen times the size of the Institutes. How little do we really know from our legal sources about a law like the *lex Iulia et Papia*, which was after all so important that Julian devoted at least eighteen complete *libri* of his *digesta* to it? Justinian's 'de-legislating' obscures the 'juridification' under Augustus; the methodologically correct answer must be a 're-legislation' of the study of Roman law. And this is precisely what we are attempting here.

3.2 *Lex duodecim tabularum*: Republican *favor libertatis*

The first normative basis of this Roman custom seems to go back to a provision that is found in the Twelve Tables. We are told this in a passage in Gaius (Inst. 4.14) which states,

> But if the subject in dispute was a man's freedom then, even if he was a highly valuable slave, the same law provided that the action in oath was for a fine of fifty. This showed a disposition to favour freedom, so that those who claimed him to be free should not be burdened [text missing].[60]

There are special features to the manumission proceeding as part of a *legis actio*: the *vindicia* are given *secundum libertatem*, i.e. the presumptive slave is not transferred

---

57 D. 1.3.28 (Paulus libro quinto ad legem Uliam et Papiam): *Sed et posteriores leges ad priores pertinent, nisi contrariae sint, idque multis argumentis probatur.* ('But later laws also refer to earlier ones, unless they contradict them; there are many proofs of this.', transl. MacCromick in Watson, *Digest of Justinian* [n. 21]).

58 Pap. *def.* 1 D. 1.3.1.

59 Dario Mantovani, *Legum multitudo: La presencia de las leyes públicas en el derecho privado romano* (Valencia: Tirant Lo Blanch, 2022): 39–75.

60 *At si de libertate hominis controversia erat, etiamsi pretiosissimus homo esset, tamen ut l assibus sacramento contenderetur, eadem lege [XII tabularum] cautum est favore scilicet libertatis, ne onerarentur adsertores*, transl. Gordon and Robinson, *The Institutes of Gaius* (n. 1): 409.

to either party for the duration of the trial,[61] and the Twelve Tables provided that the *sacramentum* should be merely fifty asses, which according to Gaius is due to *favor libertatis*, so that the *adsertor libertatis* should not be unduly burdened.[62]

It is likely that behind this pre-Augustan *favor libertatis* stood the fact that in fifth-century Rome, the status of slavery could befall anybody who suffered financial collapse. A rule that favoured freedom might well one day benefit its creators – a sort of wager for one's liberty. It seems probable, however, that the term *favor liberatis*, i.e. the general principle of favouring liberty which is being constituted and generalised in this term, dates to the post-Augustan period.[63] The phenomenon of jurists who are no longer aware of the *ratio legis* of an old *lex* – and so in the position to invent one – is widespread.[64] Nevertheless, the idea of *favor libertatis* found the first expression in this provision of the Twelve Tables.

As slavery changed over the course of Roman history, the presumed rationale of republican *favor libertatis* increasingly lost its capacity to explain and sustain rules that favoured slaves: it had been devised for a certain kind of society and had to evolve as society itself evolved.[65] Enslaving the debtor in the course of personal execution fell out of use, and the right of a father to sell his children as slaves required a sale outside the city of Rome (*trans Tiberim vendere*).[66] There were few chances even in the high republican era of Romans being enslaved at Rome. On the other hand, the Roman conquest of the Mediterranean produced an influx of slaves from totally different nations[67] for whom the rustic chivalry of the Twelve Tables was out of place.[68] Varro Reatinus (116–27 BCE) refers in his treatise on agriculture to a common classification of slaves as 'talking equipment' for farm work,[69] and the jurist Labeo, who lived

61 Max Kaser and Karl Hackl, *Das römische Zivilprozeßrecht* (Munich: C.H. Beck, 1996): 74, 83, 101. For the archaeology of *favor libertatis* and this text cf. Huchthausen, "Freiheitsbegünstigung" (n. 18): 51.

62 Kaser and Hackl, *Römisches Zivilprozeßrecht* (n. 61): 103; now Gamauf, "Sklaven (servi)" (n. 3): 57.

63 See Buckland, *Law of Slavery* (n. 3): 438.

64 Iul. 55 *dig.* D. 1.3.20: *Non omnium, quae a maioribus constituta sunt, ratio reddi potest.* ('It is not possible to find an underlying reason for everything which was settled by our forebear.', transl. MacCromick in Watson, *Digest of Justinian* [n. 21]).

65 Alföldy, *Sozialgeschichte* (n. 3): 85–95.

66 Kaser and Hackl, *Römisches Zivilprozeßrecht* (n. 61): 145; Kaser, *Das Römische Privatrecht*, vol. 1 (n. 5): 291.

67 Concrete data, Siegfried Lauffer, review of *Struktur der antiken Sklavenkriege*, by Joseph Vogt, *Vierteljahrschrift für Sozial- und Wirtschaftsgeschichte* 46, no. 3 (1959): 395.

68 On the actual living conditions of rural slaves, their inclination to flee and the corresponding repression by the authorities, Heinz Bellen, *Studien zur Sklavenflucht im römischen Kaiserreich* (Stuttgart: Franz Steiner Verlag, 1971): 5.

69 Varro. rust. 1.17.

in the times of Augustus, considered slaves to be 'self-moving things'.[70] No other fact illustrates better the massification of slavery, and the estrangement between master and servant it entailed, than the slave revolts of 120–71 BCE.[71] Whereas in the good old days, *favor libertatis* was a wager on one's own freedom, it became a wager on the survival of Rome: it had become clear that slaves had to be treated differently if Rome wanted to evade the dangerous humiliation and even critical military situation such revolts or 'wars' brought about.[72]

3.3 *Lex Iunia Petronia*: Imperial *favor libertatis* I

As stated above, only a *lex publica* or another law in the broader sense can be considered to be the source of force of *favor libertatis*. In an analogy to the *favor dotis*, which can be traced back to the *lex Iulia et Papia Poppaea*,[73] I believe that the second normative basis of the *favor libertatis* is, among others, the *lex Iulia Petronia de servis*,[74] which probably dates to 19 CE.[75] The most important factor characterising scholarly work on this law is how very little we know about it. The reason for this aridity of our sources is the already mentioned 'de-legislating' (*delegificazione*) that happened under Justinian.

The first of our two sources about this law is Hermogenianus D. 40.1.24pr.-1: *Lege Iunia Petronia, si dissonantes pares iudicum existant sententiae, pro libertate pronuntiari iussum* (The *lex Iunia Petronia* ordains that in the case of two contradicting votes on an equal footing, the decision must be made in favour of liberty). In the case of a tied vote in a *causa liberalis*, the *lex Iunia Petronia* recommends that the result be freedom for the slave.[76] This should be interpreted as a decision *in favorem libertatis*. The term used here, *iussum*, is frequently found in descriptions of the content of *leges*

---

70 Ulp. 1 ad ed. aedil. curul. D. 21, 1, 1pr.: *Labeo scribit edictum aedilium curulium de venditionibus rerum esse tam earum quae soli sint quam earum quae mobiles aut se moventes* (transl. Thomas in Watson, *Digest of Justinian* [n. 21]).

71 Joseph Vogt, *Struktur der antiken Sklavenkriege* (Stuttgart: Franz Steiner Verlag, 1957); John Pentland Mahaffy, "The Slave Wars against Romen," *Hermathena* 7, no. 16 (1890): 167–82.

72 Good on this point, Barry Baldwin, "Two Aspects of the Spartacus Slave Revolt," *The Classical Journal* 62, no. 7 (1967): 289, 293–94.; see also Jean Christian Dumont, *Servus: Rome et l'esclavage sous la rèpublique* (Rome: École française de Rome, 1987): 102–205.

73 Stagl, *Camino* (n. 22): 27.

74 This opinion is shared by Castello, "'Humanitas'" (n. 48): 2183.

75 Pierangelo Buongiorno, "Lex (Iunia?) Petronia de servis," in *Handwörterbuch der antiken Sklaverei*, vol. 2, ed. Heinz Heinen et al. (Berlin: De Gruyter, 2017): 1763–64. Gilbert Bagnani's theories in *Arbiter of Elegance: A Study of the Life and Works of C. Petronius* (Toronto: University of Toronto Press, 1954) are unconvincing; cf. Robert Browning, review of *Arbiter of Elegance: A Study of the Life and Works of C. Petronius*, by Gilbert Bagnani, *The Classical Review* 6, no. 1 (1956): 45–47.

76 Buckland, *Law of Slavery* (n. 3): 36; Kaser and Hackl, *Römisches Zivilprozeßrecht* (n. 61): 121, 199.

publicae,[77] which can be explained by the manner in which they were passed. The presiding magistrate asked the popular assembly, *velitis iubeatis?*,[78] i.e. a given law.[79] This *iussum* by the *populus Romanus* can explain why *favor libertatis*, assuming it to derive from a *lex*, is strong enough to override all other rules or principles of *ius commune*. So Tomasz Giaro's observation that decisions in *favorem libertatis* are enthymemic,[80] i.e. that they presuppose a premise that is not explicitly stated, is correct: this premise of *favor libertatis* is the sovereignty of the Roman people. The second text is Mod. 6 *reg*. D. 48.8.11.1–2: 'If a slave be thrown to the beasts without [having been before] a judge, not only he who sold him but also he who bought him shall be liable to punishment. 2. Following the *lex Petronia* and the *senatus consulta* relating to it, masters have lost the power of handing over at their own discretion their slaves to fight with the beasts; but after the slave has been produced before a judge, if his master's complaint is just, he shall in this case be handed over to punishment'.[81] By the same *lex Petronia*, the slave's owner can no longer sell the slave *ad bestias* without the consent of a judge.[82] This means that the 'state' assumes control over the slave, and this, in turn, means that it is no longer correct to say that the master is the proprietor of the slave in the fullest sense of the word.

The *lex Petronia*, which I believe is identical to the *lex Iunia Petronia*,[83] likewise decrees in favour of the slaves, albeit not *in favorem libertatis*. Improving a slave's living conditions is not necessarily the same as *favor libertatis*, although they are related. It is, however, conceivable that this law was a sort of general provision for servile legal relationships and that the jurists arrived at *favor libertatis* by way of inductive reasoning from the law's general tendency. I assume that these *leges publicae*, the most important source of law for the Romans,[84] were the basis on which

77 Heumann and Seckel, *Handlexikon* (n. 26): s.v. '*iubere*' a).

78 Gell. 5.19.9.

79 Antonio Guarino, *Storia del diritto romano* (Naples: Jovene, 1998): §§ 133.

80 Tomasz Giaro, *Römische Rechtswahrheiten Ein Gedankenexperiment* (Frankfurt am Main: Klostermann, 2007): 320, cites as an exception to the rule Marcian. 7 *inst*. D. 40.5.50, which however also presupposes *favor libertatis*.

81 *Servo sine iudice ad bestias dato non solum qui vendidit poena, verum et qui comparavit tenebitur. Post legem Petroniam et senatus consulta ad eam legem pertinentia dominis potestas ablata est ad bestias depugnandas suo arbitrio servos tradere: oblato tamen iudici servo, si iusta sit domini querella, sic poenae tradetur.* (transl. Robinson in Watson, *Digest of Justinian* [n. 21]). See also Pomp. 22 *ad Sab*. D. 12.4.15 and Marcian. 1 *inst*. D. 18.1.42.

82 Buckland, *Law of Slavery* (n. 3): 36; Robleda, *Il diritto* (n. 15): 84.

83 Some scholars have contested the identity of the laws mentioned in these sources; but on balance the reasons in favour of identity are better, although they are too intricate to be discussed here. This view has been supported by Otto Karlowa, *Römische Rechtsgeschichte*, vol. 1 (Berlin: Von Veit, 1885): 624; Jean-Louis Ferrary, "La législation augustéenne et les dernières lois comitiales," in *Leges publicae. La legge nell'esperienza giuridica romana*, ed. Jean-Louis Ferrary (Pavia: IUSS Press, 2012): 569, 583–85.

84 Arg. Gai. 1.2 and Pap. 2 def. D. 1.1.7.

emperors enacted further rules in favour of slaves in the form of *constitutiones*. An allusion to this can be found in one of the two texts on the *lex Petronia* cited above: 'After the *lex Petronia* and other decrees of the Senate belonging to the same *lex*, the power was taken away from the master [. . .]' (*Post legem Petroniam et senatus consulta*[85] *ad eam legem pertinentia dominis potestas ablata est* [. . .]).[86] In this context, we must also consider a rescript by Antoninus Pius (138–161), which prohibits the killing of a slave without just cause, and masters are obliged to sell a slave in the case of maltreatment.[87] Another trace of the wider repercussions of this law can be found in a text from Marcian's *Institutes* (D. 18.1.42): 'Owners can, neither directly nor through procurators, sell their recalcitrant slaves to fight wild animals. The deified brothers [161–169 CE] so provided by rescript'.[88] This looks like a radicalization of *lex Petronia*.[89]

3.4 *Lex Iunia Norbana*: Imperial *favor libertatis* II

The other legal basis of *favor libertatis* seems to be the *Lex Iunia Norbana*.[90] The sources on this statute are scarce, and dating it is a most intricate problem.[91] As I have mentioned above, it grants freedom but not citizenship to those who were informally freed by their masters. The main sources concerning its content are I. 1.5.3 and Gai. 3.56: 'Subsequently, however, as a result of the Junian Act, all those whose liberty the praetor protected came to be free and were called Junian Latins: [. . .]'.[92]

85 The most recent work on this law, Buongiorno, "Lex" (n. 75): 1764; identified the *senatus consulta* mentioned in SHA Hadr. 18.7: *servos a dominis occidi vetuit eosque iussit damnari per iudices, si digni essent*, as well as the passage already cited in D. 48.11.1.1 and the *Edictum divi Claudii* about medical care for seriously ill slaves; Suet. *Claud.* 25.2. For this edict see Pierangelo Buongiorno, "Edictum divi Claudii," in *Handwörterbuch der antiken Sklaverei*, vol. 1, ed. Heinz Heinen et al. (Berlin: De Gruyter, 2017): 764.

86 Kaser, *Das Römische Privatrecht*, vol. 1 (n. 5): 285.

87 Gai. 1.53. On this text see Gamauf, "Sklaven (servi)" (n. 3): 34 with n. 209; and Richard Gamauf, *Ad statuam licet confugere: Untersuchungen zum Asylrecht im römischen Prinzipat* (Frankfurt am Main: Peter Lang Verlag, 1999): 81–84.

88 *Domini neque per se neque per procuratores suos possunt saltem criminosos servos vendere, ut cum bestiis pugnarent. et ita Divi Fratres rescripserunt* (transl. Thomas in Watson, *Digest of Justinian* [n. 21]).

89 Gamauf, "Sklaven (servi)" (n. 3): 34, seems to consider it to be rather a restatement, which is also possible.

90 This opinion is shared by Castello, "'Humanitas'" (n. 48): 2185, 2187.

91 A comprehensive study is now available by Luigi Pellecchi, "Loi Iunia Norbana sur l'affranchissement," *Leges Populi Romani*, 15.04.2020, http://telma.irht.cnrs.fr//outils/lepor/notice490/ [accessed 01.09.2022].

92 [. . .] *postea vero per legem Iuniam eos omnes, quos praetor in libertate tuebatur, liberos esse coepisse et appellatos esse Latinos Iunianos* [. . .] (transl. Gordon and Robinson, *The Institutes of Gaius* [n. 1]: 293); See also Fr. Dos. 5.

The dominant interpretation of this source is that only those slaves who were formally manumitted – a cumbersome procedure and in the case of a testamentary manumission littered with pitfalls – gained freedom and full citizenship (with, however, limited political participation), whereas those slaves who were informally manumitted did not obtain citizenship but only freedom; they belonged to a group which was called *Latini Iuniani.*[93] Concerning the dating, we do not have the slightest reason to mistrust Justinian's denomination of it as *lex Iunia Norbana*. This being the case, the *lex* must have been past in the year 19 CE for the simple reason that only in this precise year was there a pair of magistrates (consuls in this case) with the *nomen gentilicium* Iunius and Norbanus respectively.[94] From this we can conclude that both *leges Iuniani*, the Petronian and the Norbanian, share a common origin. And the *lex Iunia Norbana*, just like its sister law, gave rise to more legislation to mend loopholes, contradictions and *lacunae*: López Barja de Quiroga, the scholar who most exhaustively studied the *latinitas* of slaves in recent years, counts three *leges publicae* concerned with manumission (we will discuss the other two below), twelve *senatus consulta* (the type of formal legislation which replaced the *lex publica* during the empire) and fourteen *rescripta* (informal imperial legislation), with one case being dubious.[95]

3.5 *Cognitio principis*: Imperial *favor libertatis* III

This legislation does not address the *favor libertatis* as such; its aim is rather to alleviate the life and lot of slaves, yet there is a *tertium comparationis*, namely the principle of humanity. Both of these *leges publicae* are based on a recognition of slaves as fellow human beings. The most successful expression of this idea is to be found in Petronius' *Satyricon*,[96] that is to say, during the early Principate: 'slaves are also humans, and they drank the same mother's milk even though a hex will torment them'.[97] The idea that slaves and their masters had the same foster mother in common can also be read as an allusion to Romulus and Remus, to the very founding myth of Rome and the *nutrix lupa*[98] which fed them. The suckling future slave and

93 Steinwenter, "Latini Iuniani" (n. 12): col. 911; Kaser, *Das Römische Privatrecht*, vol. 1 (n. 5): 296. Now Gamauf, "Sklaven (servi)" (n. 3): 76; Pedro Manuel López Barja de Quiroga, "Latinus iunianus una aproximación," *Studia Historica. Studia Antigua* 4–5 (1986–1987): 125–26; Pellecchi, "Loi Iunia" (n. 91): passim.
94 Steinwenter, "Latini Iuniani" (n. 12): col. 910.
95 López Barja de Quiroga, "Latinus iunianus" (n. 93): 126–28.
96 Michael von Albrecht, *Geschichte der römischen Literatur: Von Andronicus bis Boethius und ihr Fortwirken*, 3rd ed. (Berlin: De Gruyter, 2012): 1028–50.
97 Sat. 71.1: *et servi homines sunt et aeque unum lactum biberunt etiam si illos malus fatus oppresserit*, transl. Michael Heseltine.
98 For example in Aug. civ. Dei. 22.6.28.

master repeat the founding myth of Rome and imply a *fraternitas*[99] among all its inhabitants.

Just as the emperors developed further the idea of brotherhood by enacting norms in favour of slaves,[100] so the jurists developed this notion further by *interpretatio*.[101] The emperors set a shining example, as in the following case (Marcell. 29 dig. D. 28.4.3[102]): a testator had invalidated a will by blotting out the names of the heirs, whose appointment was fundamental for the validity of wills in general. But the will also contained legacies in favour of the heirs and third persons, as well as the order to enfranchise slaves to both categories of legatees. In a dramatic session at the imperial council, the counsellors exchanged arguments for and against the validity of the will. If the will was considered valid, it would entail a severe breach of the fundamental rule of the Roman law of succession: 'and accordingly the institution of an heir is deemed the beginning and foundation of a will' (*caput et fundamentum intellegitur totius testamenti heredis institutio*).[103] If the testament is void, the treasury will benefit from it but, of course, the legatees will receive nothing, which would be a breach of the principle of justice: 'Justice is the constant and enduring will to give everybody what is due to him' (*Iustitia est constans et perpetua voluntas ius suum cuique tribuendi*).[104] Put before this dilemma, the emperor secludes himself from the quarrelling councillors in order to ponder the alternatives: (*Antoninus Caesar remotis omnibus cum deliberasset et admitti rursus eodem iussisset*). After having called back his council, he pronounces his decision: This case requires a 'very humane decision' (*causa praesens admittere videtur humaniorem interpretationem*) which respects the will of the deceased; therefore, the legacies have to remain intact. Concerning the original disposition by which the testator had manumitted a certain slave whose name he later blotted out, the emperor decrees that the slave should be free: *quod videlicet favore constituit libertatis* ('what is obviously to be derived from the *favor libertatis*').

---

99 Ps. Quint. decl. 16.4.

100 See Gamauf, "Sklaven (servi)" (n. 3) and Kaser, *Das Römische Privatrecht*, vol. 1 (n. 5): 285, with references and literature.

101 Mantovani, *Legum multitudo* (n. 59): 76–86.

102 On this text see recently Martin Avenarius, "Marc Aurel und die Dogmatik des römischen Privatrechts. Kaiserliche Rechtspflege im System der Rechtsquellen und die Ausfüllung von Gestaltungsspielräumen in einer Übergangszeit der Rechtsentwicklung," in *Selbstbetrachtungen und Selbstdarstellungen*, ed. Michael van Ackeren and Jan Opsomer (Wiesbaden: Reichert, 2012): 216; Thomas Finkenauer, *Die Rechtsetzung Mark Aurels zur Sklaverei* (Stuttgart: Franz Steiner Verlag, 2010): 17; Tony Honoré, *Emperors and Lawyers* (Oxford: Clarendon Press, 1994): 17; Jakob Fortunat Stagl, "Glanz der Rhetorik und Finsternis der Logik in einer Entscheidung Marc Aurels (Marcell. D. 28, 4, 3 pr.–1)," in *Meditationes de iure et historia: Essays in Honour of Laurens Winkel*, = *Fundamina: A Journal of Legal History* 20, ed. Rena van den Bergh et al. (Pretoria: Unisa Press, 2014): 871–80.

103 Gai. 2.229 '[. . .] the force of the will flows from the heir's appointment, which is its foundation or corner-stone', transl. Gordon and Robinson, *The Institutes of Gaius* (n. 1): 239.

104 Ulp. 1 reg. D. 1.1.10.

In a first step, Marcus Aurelius overrides an intricacy of Roman law of wills and testaments which declared the testator's volition the supreme consideration. The application of this principle, though, would lead to the slave not acquiring freedom since the testator had blotted out his name. So, in a second step, which blatantly contradicts the first, the emperor declares the *favor libertatis* to be a principle which is even stronger than the testator's volition. In Marcus Aurelius' heart, the *favor libertatis* had borne fruit.

3.6 *Legum fertilitas*

The defining feature of a slave's legal status is that they were their master's property, meaning, as was already pointed out, that he could do with them whatever he wanted. This consequence of legal logic is unacceptable in a society where anybody could become a slave due to debt. Even at the time of Twelve Tables, therefore, there had been a necessity to favour liberty. This is how the republican *favor libertatis* came into being. The later republic saw a substantial influx of slaves from all over the Mediterranean to Italy, a massification that changed slavery – a phenomenon we shall discuss further on. The next legislative initiative about which we know are the *leges Iunia Petronia* and *Iunia Norbana*, the first of which openly restricted a master's legal competencies over a slave, while the second radically changed the *régime* of manumission from a cumbersome formal into an effective informal procedure, thereby significantly promoting servile chances of gaining freedom. In retrospect both of these *leges publicae* were the starting point for an ever-growing avalanche of legislation in the more modern forms of *senatus consulta* and *rescripta* by the emperors *in favorem libertatis*. I would be inclined to call this phenomenon *fertilitas legum* since the impression is of one initial legal idea engendering a whole family of legislative acts[105] such as, for example, the Augustan legislation on marriage: This legislation dates from around the same time as the legislation on slaves, and also deals with demographic policy: essentially aiming to increase both the numbers and the morals of the old Roman stock.[106] The starting point was the *lex Iulia de maritandis ordinibus* 18 BCE,

---

105 Boulvert and Morabito, "Le droit de l'esclavage" (n. 15): 104: 'jurisprudence, sénatus consultes, lois, constitutions impériales [. . .] un véritable code de l'esclavage'.

106 The classical studies are Dieter Nörr, *Recht und Gesellschaft. Festschrift für H. Schelsky zum 70. Geburtstag* (Berlin: Duncker & Humbolt, 1978): 309 [= *Historia iuris antiqui: Gesammelte Schriften*, 3 vols., ed. Tiziana J. Chiusi, Wolfgang Kaiser and Hans-Dieter Spengler (Goldbach: Keip, 2003): vol. 2, 1093], and Leo Ferrero Raditsa, "Augustus' Legislation Concerning Marriage, Procreation, Love Affairs and Adultery," in *Aufstieg und Niedergang der römischen Welt*, pt. 2, *Principat*, vol. 13, *Recht*, ed. Hildegard Temporini and Wolfgang Haase (Berlin: De Gruyter, 1980): 278; Spagnuolo Vigorita, *Casta Domus. Un seminario legislazione matriminiale augustea* (Indiana: Indiana University Press, 2002). A recent bibliography can be found in Anna Dolganov, "Imperialism and Social Engineering: Augustan Social Legislation in the Gnomon of the Idios Logos," in *Studien zum 'Gnomon des Idios Logos':*

followed by the *lex Iulia et Papia Poppea* 9 CE; both were seen already in antiquity as a unit and may be referred to as the *lex Iulia et Papia.*[107] These two were accompanied by the *lex Iulia caducaria* as well as the *lex Iulia de fundo dotali* (both probably initially a chapter of the *lex Iulia et Papia*) and *lex Iulia de adulteriis* (18 CE).

Why does it have to be a *lex publica* or a *senatus consultum*, though, which brought about the *favor libertatis*? It is obvious that any fundamental change to property and formal procedures like *manumissio* could only have been brought about by a legal act strong enough to change *ius civile*, the ancient common law of the City of Rome, of which property is the basic legal framework.[108] The early empire is known for strict observance of the republican constitution even though it was considered only a form.[109] From this perspective, the only alternative to a *lex publica* or a *senatus consultum* is that the *favor libertatis* was a legal creation by the praetor.[110] The praetor, however, had no authority over measures of such magnitude,[111] especially not an issue of political importance;[112] and after the slave revolts any changes to the regulations of slavery doubtlessly were considered to be of such political import. Exaggerating only slightly, we might say that *favor libertatis* transforms the ownership of a slave, which is by definition perpetual,[113] into a temporary institution by creating something like a default rule according to which it is presumed that the master wanted to enfranchise his slaves after his death.[114] He may do otherwise, but in this case, the burden of expressing himself clearly rests on him. This kind of temporary ownership is a violation of the principles of *ius civile* just like a testament without an

Beiträge zum Dritten Wiener Koloquium zur Antiken Rechtsgeschichte, ed. Thomas Kruse (Vienna: Holzhausen, 2022): 1–39.

107 On both as a *lex* see Philippe Moreau, "Loi Iulia de maritandis ordinibus," *Leges Populi Romani*, 12.03.2020, http://www.cn-telma.fr/lepor/notice449/ [accessed 01.09.2022].

108 On the old *ius civile* see Kaser, *Das Römische Privatrecht*, vol. 1 (n. 5): 198–202.

109 Franz Wieacker, *Römische Rechtsgeschichte*, vol. 2, *Die Jurisprudenz vom frühen Prinzipat bis zum Ausgang der Antike* (Munich: C.H. Beck, 2006): 3–13.

110 This is the opinion of Boulvert and Morabito, "Le droit de l'esclavage" (n. 15): 119.

111 Wolfgang Kunkel, *Die Magistratur*, vol. 2, *Staatsordnung und Staatspraxis der römischen Republik* (Munich: C.H. Beck, 1995): 235.

112 Franz Wieacker, *Römische Rechtsgeschichte*, vol. 1, *Einleitung, Quellenkunde Frühzeit und Republik* (Munich: C.H. Beck, 1989): 413.

113 Pap. D. 8.1.4; Iust. C. 6.37.26 with regard to legacies. Diocl. u. Max. Frg. vat. 283; Pasquale Voci, *Diritto ereditario romano*, vol. 2 (Milan: Giuffre, 1967): 204.

114 This conclusion has indeed been drawn. Other scholars interpret the relationship between master and slave more as an issue of the 'law of persons' (*ius personarum*), from this point of view the rules mentioned above would imply a limitation to an originally unlimited status-related power of the slave. The text is ambiguous in this respect: Flor. 9. *inst.* D. 1.5.4.1 speaks of *dominium* but under the heading of 'De statu hominum' just as Marc. 1 inst. D. 1.5.5.1. Ownership is certainly a primordial juridical category and the 'law of persons' seems to be a rather later construction by jurists in order to find a common category for all kinds of dependency of a *pater familias*. On the evolution of and significance of the 'law of persons' see now Stagl, *Camino* (n. 22): 21–46; on the aforementioned discussion see Gamauf, "Sklaven (servi)" (n. 3): 97–102.

heir in the case of Marcus Aurelius discussed above. The emperor may turn the law upside down, but certainly not the praetor,[115] especially not under the empire. By the logic of Roman constitutional law, we may conclude that *favor libertatis* cannot be simply the invention of *iuris consulti* advising the praetor, who then turned their advice into jurisprudence (*Juristenrecht*). Since we have two *leges publicae* from the same year decreeing fundamental rules in favour of slaves and their offspring in the guise of *senatus consulta* or *rescripta* we are not only allowed but even compelled to consider them as the fountainhead of *favor libertatis*.

4 *Ius singulare*: A Theoretical Clarification

The mode of action of *favor libertatis*, in so far that it limits the scope of general rules and contradicts them, is something which must have been developed after the general rules had been established – otherwise, they would have been drafted in a way which incorporated the exceptions from the beginning. This makes it difficult to believe that this principle was just the product of the praetor who, even if he had the authority to 'correct' law for the sake of public interest on such a scale.[116] This kind of irruption from the outside as produced by the *favor*, a form of *utilitas publica*, which will tend to express itself in the form of a *lex publica*,[117] is what the Romans call *ius singulare*. The term describes a guiding principle which was decreed a) against the grain of common law, i.e. against that which would have been the rational solution from its perspective (*contra tenorem rationis*); b) for the sake of the public interest and related policies (*propter aliquam utilitatem*); and c) on the solid basis of formal authority (*auctoritate constituentium introductum*).[118] This last category, which was only descriptive, nevertheless served one important purpose: it tried to insulate the normal 'common' law (*ius commune*) from the destructive power of the 'special' law, the *ius singulare*. The exception had to be prevented from becoming the rule, as Julian (27 dig.) says in D. 1.3.15: 'From those [provisions] which have been constituted against the reason of

115 Boulvert and Morabito, "Le droit de l'esclavage" (n. 15): 121.

116 Pap. 2 def. D. 1.1.7.1: *Ius praetorium est, quod praetores introduxerunt adiuvandi vel supplendi vel corrigendi iuris civilis gratia propter utilitatem publicam* [. . .] ('Praetorian law [*jus praetorium*] is that which in the public interest the praetors have introduced in aid or supplementation or correction of the jus civile [. . .]', transl. MacCormack in Watson, *Digest of Justinian* [n. 21]); Ulrike Babusiaux, "Die Rechtsschichten," in *Handbuch des Römischen Privatrechts*, ed. Ulrike Babusiaux et al. (Tübingen: Mohr Siebeck, 2023): 114–91, 128.

117 Jakob Fortunat Stagl, "Die Funktionen der utilitas publica," *Zeitschrift der Savigny-Stiftung für Rechtsgeschichte, Romanistische Abteilung* 134 (2017): 514–23; and Jakob Fortunat Stagl, "El pueblo del derecho es también el pubelo de las leyes?," in *Legum multitudo: La presencia de las leyes públicas en el derecho privado romano*, ed. Dario Mantovani (Valencia: Tirant Lo Blanch, 2022): 123–58.

118 D. 1.3.16 Paul. l. s. de iure singulari.

law we are not supposed to draw legal rules' (*In his, quae contra rationem iuris constituta sunt, non possumus sequi regulam iuris*).[119] Otherwise the entire system of Roman law would have imploded. Ultimately, *ius singulare* represented a technique for incorporating new rules without having to change the old ones.

There are two sources that confirm the qualification of the rules produced by *favor libertatis* as *ius singulare*, the first being D. 40.5.24.10 (Ulp. 5 fideicomm.):

> D. 40.5.24.10 (Ulpian libro quinto fideicommissorum): Si quis servo pignerato directam libertatem dederit, licet videtur iure suptili inutiliter reliquisse, attamen quasi et fideicommissaria libertate relicta servus petere potest, ut ex fideicommisso liber fiat: favor enim libertatis suadet, ut interpretemur et ad libertatis petitionem procedere testamenti verba, quasi ex fideicommisso fuerat servus liber esse iussus: nec enim ignotum est, quod multa contra iuris rigorem pro libertate sint constituta.

> D. 40.5.24.10 (Ulpian, Fideicommissa, book 5): If someone has directly given freedom to his pledged slave, the slave may, even though by a strict interpretation of the law his manumission is void, claim liberty as if he had been given fideicommissary liberty, so he may be free due to the *fideicommissum*. For liberty's sake (*favor libertatis*) the text of the testament is to be interpreted in such a way as to render possible the claim of liberty, [that is to say] as if the slave had been given fideicommissary liberty: For it is not unknown that many rules have been established against the rigour of the law for the sake of liberty.[120]

A debtor manumits in his will a slave to whom he has previously pledged liberty. This manumission is void insofar as it would diminish the creditor's position, but it can be reinterpreted as a *fideicommissum* with the consequence that the slave can claim liberty after his master's death, 'because', as the text says literally 'the *favor libertatis* requires' this reinterpretation. 'Since it is not unknown that many rules have been established against the rigour of the law in favour of liberty (*favor libertatis*)'.

Surprisingly the second text (Pap. 9 resp.) is from the same title, 'On fideicomissarial liberties', D. 40.5.23.3, a text which echoes the above mentioned case of Julian in D. 40.4.16:

> D. 40.5.23.3 (Papinianus libro nono responsorum): Etiam fideicommissaria libertas a filio post certam aetatem eius data, si ad eam puer non pervenit, ab herede filii praestituta die reddatur: quam sententiam iure

> D. 40.5.23.3 (Papinian, replies, book 9): Moreover, fideicommissary freedom, which is due from the son when he reaches a certain age, should be granted as due on the fixed day by the son's heir, if the boy did not live to that age; but this principle is regarded as conveying an

119 Stagl, *Camino* (n. 22): 318, 327; *contra* Mario Varvaro, "La dote, il ius singulare e il 'sistema didattico' di Gaio," *Seminarios Complutenses de Derecho Romano* 39 (2016): 409. A reply can be found in Jakob Fortunat Stagl, "Caesars Koch oder das Schweigen der Quellen: Zur Kritik Varvaros am didaktischen System des Gaius," *Zeitschrift der Savigny-Stiftung für Rechtsgeschichte, Romanistische Abteilung* 135 (2018): 582–91.
120 Transl. Brunt in Watson, *Digest of Justinian* (n. 21).

singulari receptam ad cetera fideicommissa relicta porrigi non placuit.

exceptional right, and it has been decided that it does not extend to other fideicommissary gifts.[121]

If liberty has been given to a slave after the son has reached a certain age and the son does not reach that age, the heir taking the son's place must nevertheless manumit the slave.

5 The Rationale of *favor libertatis*

Having explained the origin of *favor libertatis* from a family of *leges publica*, of which the *lex Iunia Petronia* and the *lex Iunia Norbana* are two conspicuous exponents, we have not yet explained the intellectual and social reasoning behind this legislation, nor why it was implemented – apparently willingly.[122] Otherwise, it would never have gained its momentum, remembering Horace's famous observation: *Quid leges sine moribus / vanae proficient.*[123]

As a starting point for our disquisition, we should turn to the legal consequences of giving freedom to a slave. As stated above, the slave acquired either limited citizenship or just the status of *Latinus Iunianus*, depending on the formality of the manumission; only their children were *ingenui*, that is to say, Roman citizens in the full meaning of the word. These were ramifications in the sphere of *ius publicum*. In the sphere of *ius privatum* the status of liberty was also ambiguous. The *libertini* (a term describing the status in general) were not simply *liberi*; rather, they owed *obsequium* to their former masters who now had become their *patroni*; with regard to these obligations they are called *liberti*. Slaves could, incidentally, purchase their freedom with the help of their *peculium*.[124] The *obsequium* owed by freedmen to their *patroni* consisted not just in respectful behaviour, but above all in the legal obligation to work a certain amount of time each year for the *patronus* (*operae*),[125] and to leave a part of their inheritance to the *patronus* or his heirs (*bona libertorum*).[126] Manumitting a slave created, in other

121 Transl. Brunt in Watson, *Digest of Justinian* (n. 21).

122 An example is D. 40.5.50 Marcian. 7 inst.: [. . .] *in obscuro libertatem praevalere. quae sententia mihi quoque verior esse videtur* ('[. . .] but that if it were unclear [. . .] the grant of freedom takes precedence. In my view, too, this opinion is more correct.', transl. Brunt in Watson, *Digest of Justinian* [n. 21]). On this see Boulvert and Morabito, "Le droit de l'esclavage" (n. 15): 121.

123 Hor. carm. 3.24 ('What use are all these empty laws/without the behaviour that should accompany them', transl. A.S. Kline, "Horace: The Odes, Book 3," *Poetry in Translation*, 2003 https://www.poetryintranslation.com/PITBR/Latin/HoraceOdesBkIII.php#anchor_Toc40263869 [accessed 01.09.2022]).

124 Kaser, *Das Römische Privatrecht*, vol. 1 (n. 5): 297 at n. 83.

125 Carla Masi Doria, *Civitas Operae Obsequium. Tre studi sulla condizione giuridica dei liberti* (Naples: Jovene, 1993): 18–26.

126 Masi Doria, *Civitas* (n. 126): 27–54; Boulvert and Morabito, "Le droit de l'esclavage" (n. 15): 113.

words, just a new form of dependency[127] and therefore was not such a big loss for the heir; being *patronus* of a *libertus* was an asset.[128] Due to this situation, there existed a enhaced form of manumission, which was freedom without freedman status (*ius anuli aurei*[129]). More radical was the option of *natalium restitutio*,[130] a fictional declaration that conferred freeborn status. Another feature distinguished a will from any legal act *inter vivos;* its defects only appeared *post mortem*, when they could no longer be redressed. The fact that the bulk of three books in the Digest is dedicated only to the interpretation of legates and *fideicommissa* (D. lib. 30–32 'De legatis et fideicommissis') shows that it was precisely in this field that the art of the jurists was needed most. For these reasons, wills are the legal transactions where *favor libertatis* was most likely to be necessary to mend a knotty situation. And the death of the master was, as we saw above, the moment where the idea of temporal property could best be implemented.

5.1 Interest

The interest in enfranchising slaves is first and foremost that of self-preservation (Marcell. D. 29.5.16):

D. 29.5.16 (Marcellus libro 12 digestorum): Domino a familia occiso servus communis necem eius detexit: favore libertatis liber quidem fieri debet, pretii autem partem sibi contingentem socium consequi oportet.	D. 29.5.16 (Marcellus, Digest, book 12): Where a master was killed by his household slaves, a slave held in common exposed his murder; he certainly must be freed in order to favor freedom (favor libertatis), but the co-owner ought to obtain the value of the share which falls to him.[131]

This text should be understood in the context of the *senatus consultum Silanianum*,[132] which stipulated that all the slaves of a household were to be put to death if one of them had killed the master.[133] We know from Tacitus that this law was enforced in the case of a household of more than 400 slaves, albeit not without a prior

127 Boulvert and Morabito, "Le droit de l'esclavage" (n. 15): 100.

128 This explains Gaius' lengthy disquisition on this topic in inst. 3.39–54.

129 Ulp. 5 *ad ed.* D. 2.4.10.1; Ulp. 40 *ad ed.* D. 38.2.3 pr.

130 Ulp. 40 *ad ed.* D. 38.2.3.1.; Diocl. C. 6.8.2; for these phenomena see Theodor Mommsen, *Römisches Staatsrecht*, vol. 1 (Leipzig: Hirzel, 1877): 398; Robleda, *Il diritto* (n. 15): 172.

131 Transl. Gordon in Watson, *Digest of Justinian* (n. 21).

132 Otto Lenel, *Palingenesia iuris civilis*, vol. 1 (Leipzig: Bernhard Tauchnitz, 1887): col. 650.

133 Danilo Dalla, *Senatus Consultum Silanianum* (Milan: Giuffrè, 1994); Jill Diana Harries, "The Senatus Consultum Silanianum: Court Decisions and Judicial Severity in the Early Roman Empire," in *New Frontiers: Law and Society in the Roman World*, ed. Paul J. du Plessis (Edinburgh: Edinburgh University Press, 2013): 51–72.

debate in the senate.[134] The fear felt by masters of their slaves was proverbial: *totidem servi, tot hostes* ('one has many foes as one has slaves').[135] The truth of this proverb was proved beyond doubt during the slave revolts.

Servile peaceableness and obedience were achieved not only by means of punishments and threats but also benefits: above all, the promise of freedom after long and honourable service. Our text looks at the question of how to act when the crime committed against the master is being exposed by a slave held in common: he is to be enfranchised in accordance with *favor libertatis*; the heir must compensate the co-owner. We may deduce from this that the idea behind *favor libertatis* was the creation of an incentive for slaves not to seek to kill their masters[136] or to develop behaviour like a tendency to escape or to commit suicide, both of which are detrimental to a slave's performance from an economic point of view. In a rescript from Antoninus Pius (86–161 CE), there is direct proof for this kind of reasoning (Coll. 3.3):[137]

Coll. 3.3.5–6: [. . .] Servorum obsequium non solum imperio, sed et moderatione sufficientibus praebitis et iustis operibus contineri oportet. Itaque et ipse curare debes iuste ac temperate tuos tractare, ut ex facili requirere eos possis, ne, si apparuerit vel inparem te inpediis esse vel atrociore dominationem saevitia exercere, necesse habeat proconsul, ne quid tumultuosius contra accidat, praevenire et ex mea iam auctoritatem te ad alienandos eos conpellere.	Coll. 3.3.5–6: [. . .] The obedience of slaves must be maintained not merely by the exercise of authority, but by reasonable treatment satisfaction of their necessities, and a fair apportionment of tasks. You should, on your part, therefore, take care to treat your slaves fairly and with moderation, so that you may without difficulty be able to claim them back. Otherwise, on it transpiring that their maintenance is beyond your resources, or that you exercise authority with revolting cruelty, the Proconsul may be under the necessity of preventing the mischief of a possible outbreak by forcing you, with my sanction, to part with your slaves'.[138]

A lesser evil for the master but nonetheless a great preoccupation, even a 'visceral fear' in the words of Boulvert and Morabito, was the possibility that slaves might

134 Tac. *ann.* 14.44.
135 Probably a simplification of *totidem hostes esse quot servos*. Sen. *epist.* 47.5.
136 Huchthausen, "Freiheitsbegünstigung" (n. 18): 62; Ettore Ciccotti, *Il tramonto della schiavitù nel mondo antico* (Turin: Bocca, 1899): 270. For the public interest in legislation, see Jakob Fortunat Stagl, "Utilitas publica, ius naturale y protección de la natura," *Revista General de Derecho Romano* 33 (2019).
137 On this text see Gamauf, "Sklaven (servi)" (n. 3): 92–135: on 126–29 there is a discussion of the rationale behind this legislation which Gamauf interprets in a purely pragmatic way while rejecting any ideological, philosophical or ethical considerations.
138 Transl. H. Hyamsom, *Mosaicarum et romanarum legum collatio* (London/New York: H. Frowde/ Oxford University Press, 1913).

escape, and all kinds of countermeasures were taken against this, *sit venia verbo*, 'natural' tendency.[139]

5.2 The Link with Augustan Demographic Policies

The *lex Iunia Petronia* must be seen in connection with the demographic measures adopted by the Julio-Claudian emperors, especially their legislation to restrict manumissions, because there is, superficially at least, a contradiction between *favor liberatis* on the one hand and restrictions on manumission on the other.

The *lex Fufia Caninia de manumissionibus*[140] of 2 CE and the *lex Aelia Sentia de manumissionibus*[141] of 4 CE, both of which were passed under the aegis of Augustus, imposed massive restrictions on the manumission of slaves and prescribe severe sanctions for transgressions.[142] In order to understand that both the *lex Iunia Petronia* and the *leges Fufia Caninia* and *Aelia Sentia* are closely related to them,[143] we must call to mind another, much better-known and arguably more significant law: the *lex Iulia et Papia*. This pivotal piece of Augustan social policy sought to confine Roman citizens in marriages so as to raise the number, the quality and the morals ('Zahl, Niveau und Moral', as Max Kaser wrote) of Rome's citizenry.[144] It mainly targeted the *élite*, i.e. senators and knights.[145]

If we keep this prime concern of Augustus in mind, the individual parts combine effortlessly to forge a harmonious whole. Let us look first at the motivation for the abovementioned *senatus consultum Sillanianum* in Tacitus (*ann.* 14.44):

Tac. annales 14.44: Suspecta maioribus nostris fuerunt ingenia servorum etiam cum in agris aut domibus isdem nascerentur caritatemque dominorum statim acciperent. postquam vero nationes in familiis habemus, quibus diversi	Tac. annales 14.44: To our ancestors the temper of their slaves was always suspect, even when they were born on the same estate or under the same roof, and drew in affection for their owners with their earliest breath. But

139 Boulvert and Morabito, "Le droit de l'esclavage" (n. 15): 106; for details see Gamauf, "Sklaven (servi)" (n. 3): 39–42.

140 Paul. *lib. sing. ad leg. Fuf.* D. 35.1.37; Paul. *lib. sing. ad leg.* D. 50.16.215; and P. Hamb. 1.72r l. 6 (II–III d. C.); Paul. Sent. 4.14.3; Mantovani, *Legum multitudo* (n. 59): 43.

141 Tit. D. 40.9; Alex. C. 7.2.5; 7.11.1; Mantovani, *Legum multitudo* (n. 59): 43.

142 Robleda, *Il diritto* (n. 15): 149–153.

143 As is argued by Schulz, *Principios* (n. 1): 143 and Kaser, *Das Römische Privatrecht*, vol. 1 (n. 5): 297.

144 Kaser, *Das Römische Privatrecht*, vol. 1 (n. 5): 318.

145 Jochen Bleicken, *Lex publica: Gesetz und Recht in der römischen Republik* (Berlin: De Gruyter, 1975): 508.

ritus, externa sacra aut nulla sunt, conluviem istam non nisi metu coercueris.	now that our households comprise nations – with customs the reverse of our own, with foreign cults or with none, you will never coerce such a medley of humanity except by terror.'[146]

The masters had become suspicious of the slaves who had 'other customs', 'foreign cults or 'none at all': the first emperor did not want such people to intermingle with the citizens of Rome whom he had restored, and so he legislated against manumissions. This concern plagued him to the end: in his political testament, he urged Tiberius to prevent Rome from filling up with such a 'motley crowd' (ἵνα μὴ παντοδαποῦ ὄχλου τὴν πόλιν πληρώσωσι).[147]

Favor libertatis and the laws to curb manumissions are two sides of the same coin.[148] But is there not a contradiction between the *lex Iunia Petronia* and the restrictions on manumission?[149] No, – quite the contrary;[150] manumission as such was needed to control the 'motley crowd': it was the carrot that complemented the stick.[151] But in order to fulfil its purpose, only deserving slaves could be manumitted, and not large numbers.[152] The limit placed on *manumissio* served the interests not only of the masters – for whom it was a means of retaining control over citizenship – but also the freedmen, who were thus enabled in terms of holding on to the exclusivity of their position. A freedman such as M. Antonius Pallas, who under the emperor Claudius had amassed one of the empire's largest private fortunes,[153] would hardly wish to share his status with too many others. *Favor libertatis* did not come to the aid of slaves in general: only to those for whom it was right that they should enjoy freedom, i.e. the deserving slaves whose manumission would be a just reward for their life-long labours. If there arose difficulties that were primarily of a technical nature, *favor libertatis* helped to overcome them. Denying a slave his freedom after a lifetime of honourable service merely on the grounds of a *subtilitas iuris* would have violated the implicit agreement between master and slave. Such disloyalty

146 Transl. John Jackson, *The Annals*, vol. 4, *Tacitus* (London/Cambridge: William Heinemann/Havard University Press, 1956): 179.
147 Cass. Dio 56.33.3.
148 Kaser, *Das Römische Privatrecht*, vol. 1 (n. 5): 285, 296; Schulz, *Principios* (n. 1): 143.
149 Both Huchthausen, "Freiheitsbegünstigung" (n. 18): 53 and Imbert, "Favor Libertatis" (n. 15): 277 n. 2, argue that there is.
150 Schulz, *Principios* (n. 1): 240.
151 Boulvert and Morabito, "Le droit de l'esclavage" (n. 15): 118.
152 Huchthausen, "Freiheitsbegünstigung" (n. 18): 59.
153 Stewart Irvin Oost, "The Career of M. Antonius Pallas," *The American Journal of Philology* 79, no. 2 (1958): 113; Alföldy, *Sozialgeschichte* (n. 3); Paul Veyne, *La société romain* (Paris: POINTS, 2001); Aloys Winterling, "'Staat' und 'Gesellschaft' in der römischen Kaiserzeit: Zwei moderne Forschungsprobleme und ihr antiker Hintergrund," *Zentrum für interdisziplinäre Forschung der Universität Bielefeld, Mitteilungen* 3 (1998): 5.

would have destabilised the entire system of slavery, which, as I said above, was held together by both the use of the stick and the carrot.

In this way, *favor libertatis* achieved a balance between the need for manumission – whether for loyalty or self-preservation –, the need to control citizenship, and – for the freed – the desire to defend their status *vis-à-vis* those further down the ladder.[154]

From a sociological point of view, we must distinguish between the 'patriarchal' household slaves and those slaves used for agricultural or industrial production. They served different purposes – convenience and profit, respectively – and the way their masters related to them was wholly different: household slaves were humanised, while slaves in agriculture and industry were treated like cattle.[155] *Favor libertatis* concerns the household slaves, while the ban on manumission targets the slaves who are a mere means of production.

5.3 Equity and Humanity

It would, however, simplify matters unduly if we were to reduce such laws merely to the selfish interests of the masters:[156] *favor libertatis* is also the consequence of a humane approach towards slavery, or *humanitas* in Roman terms.[157] The high regard in which the Roman jurists held *humanitas* is well attested,[158] especially in Ulpian.[159] This arch-Roman concept is in essence a 'vehicle' for stoic anthropocentrism.[160] Take, for example, Ulp. D. 34.5.10.1:

D. 34.5.10.1 (Ulpianus libro sexto disputationum): Plane si ita libertatem acceperit ancilla: 'si primum marem pepererit, libera esto', et haec uno utero marem et feminam peperisset,

D. 34.5.10.1 (Ulpian, Disputations, book 6): It is clear that if a female slave has received freedom on the following terms, "let her be free if the first child she bears is male" and she gives

154 Bleicken, *Lex publica* (n. 145): 511, underscores the elite's need for safety.

155 Padgug, "Problems" (n. 19): 26; Boulvert and Morabito, "Le droit de l'esclavage" (n. 15): 118, 126–36.

156 A point that spoils the otherwise brilliant book by Ciccotti, *Il tramonto della schiavitù* (n. 136).

157 Castello, "'Humanitas'" (n. 48): 2175–89.

158 Heinz Haffter, "Die römische Humanitas," *Neue Schweizer Rundschau* 21 (1953/54): 719 = Hans Oppermann, ed., *Römische Wertbegriffe* (Darmstadt: Wissenschaftliche Buchgesellschaft, 1967): 468; Carlo A. Maschi, *Humanitas come motivo giuridico con un esempio nel diritto dotale romano* (Trieste: Universita di Trieste, 1949); Wolfgang Schadewaldt, "Humanitas Romana," in *Aufstieg und Niedergang der römischen Welt*, pt. 2, *Principat*, vol. 4, *Philosophie und Künste*, ed. Hildegard Temporini and Wolfgang Haase (Berlin: De Gruyter, 1973): 43–62.

159 Tony Honoré, *Ulpian: Pioneer of Human Rights* (Oxford: Oxford University Press, 2002); *contra* Aldo Schiavone, *Ius. La invención del derecho en Occidente* (Buenos Aires: Adriana Hidalgo, 2012): 451.

160 Henryk Kupiszewski, "Humanitas et le droit romain," in *Scritti minori*, ed. Henryk Kupiszewski (Naples: Jovene, 1997): 335–45.

si quidem certum est, quid prius edidisset, non debet de ipsius statu ambigi, utrum libera esset, necne; sed nec filiae, nam, si postea edita est, erit ingenua. Sin autem hoc incertum est, nec potest nec per subtilitatem iudicialem manifestari, in ambiguis rebus humaniorem sententiam sequi oportet, ut tam ipsa libertatem consequatur, quam filia eius ingenuitatem, quasi per praesumtionem priore masculo edito.

birth at the same confinement to two children, one male and one female, then, provided that it is certain which child was born first, there is no reason for doubt to arise either about her status, that is, whether or not she is free, or about that of the female child, since, if she was the second to be born she will be of free birth. However, if there is uncertainty as to the order of the births and no clarification can be secured even by careful judicial investigation, then, since the circumstances are controversial, the more humane view should be adopted whereby the slave obtains her freedom and her daughter the status of being freeborn on the presumption that the male child was the firstborn.[161]

A female slave is to be manumitted on the condition that the first child she gives birth to is a boy – if she meets the condition, this child will be freeborn (*ingenuus*[162]). It should be pointed out here that freeborn status was preferable by far, which was why there existed a separate *favor ingenuitatis*.[163] Our slave gives birth to a boy and a girl; the order of the births is known. In this case, there can be no doubt about the status of the mother as a freedwoman and the freeborn status of her daughter, the younger twin. But what if we cannot determine the order of the births? In such uncertain cases, the jurist's opinion runs, we should adopt the 'more humane view' and assume that the first-born child was the boy. The decision ultimately amounts to this: for the sake of *humanitas*, in the case of twin birth, the mother is to be granted liberty and her children freeborn status.[164]

The value of *humanitas* cited here as a motive for the decision is a quintessentially Roman idea[165] and pervaded the whole of Roman law, as Fritz Schulz pointed out.[166] 'Humaneness', as we might translate it, is inextricably related to nature, and in consequence to natural law for the reason that humanity is a part of nature:

161 Transl. Tuplin in Watson, *Digest of Justinian* (n. 21).

162 Kaser, *Das Römische Privatrecht*, vol. 1 (n. 5): 298.

163 Diocl. and Max. C. 8.50.15; also Ulp. 12 *ad Sab*. D. 38.16.1.4; for this phenomenon, see Buckland, *Law of Slavery* (n. 3): 312.

164 Constantin Willems, *Justinian als Ökonom: Entscheidungsgründe und Entscheidungsmuster in den 'quinquaginta decisiones'* (Cologne: Vandenhoeck & Ruprecht, 2017): 312.

165 Waldstein, "Entscheidungsgrundlagen" (n. 22): 3, 89; and Aldo Schiavone and Dario Mantovani, eds., *Testi e problemi del giusnaturalismo romano* (Pavia: IUSS Press, 2007); Stagl, *Camino* (n. 22): 96.

166 Schulz, *Principios* (as above, n. 1): 201–203; whose historical scope includes the Christian era, Jean Gaudemet, "Des 'droits de l'homme' ont-ils été reconnus dans l'Empire romain?," in *Labeo* 33 (1987): 5–23.

D. 1.1.1.3 (Ulp. 1 inst.): Ius naturale est, quod natura omnia animalia docuit: nam ius istud non humani generis proprium, sed omnium animalium, quae in terra, quae in mari nascuntur, avium quoque commune est. hinc descendit maris atque feminae coniunctio, quam nos matrimonium appellamus, hinc liberorum procreatio, hinc educatio: videmus etenim cetera quoque animalia, feras etiam istius iuris peritia censeri.

D. 1.1.1.3 (Ulpian, Institutes, book 1): *Jus naturale* is that which nature has taught to all animals; for it is not a law specific to mankind but is common to all animals-land animals, sea animals, and the birds as well. Out of this comes the union of man and woman which we call marriage, and the procreation of children, and their rearing. So we can see that the other animals, wild beasts included, are rightly understood to be acquainted with this law.[167]

The difference between *humanitas* and *ius naturale* consists, we could conclude, in that the former is by definition restricted to human beings whereas the latter comprises all living creatures. There are several instances where *favor libertatis* is presented as an upshot of *humanitas*:

First case: What if a fugitive slave becomes by chance a praetor? Are his legal deeds as praetor valid? Ulpian's answer is affirmative: 'This [solution] is more humane: Since the People of Rome could bestow this function upon him [not knowing he was a slave], it would have set him free had it known he was a slave' (*hoc enim humanius est: cum etiam potuit populus Romanus servo decernere hanc potestatem, sed et si scisset servum esse, liberum effecisset*).[168] In other words, the humane interpretation is that the Roman People would have set him free when they wanted him as a magistrate.

Another case: Mother and son die in a shipwreck; it is important to know who died first in order to establish who is the heir of whom; which in turn is the precondition to establish the share of the surviving relatives in the inheritance. 'Granted the impossibility of determining which of them died first, it is more generous to regard the son as having lived longer'.[169] This reasoning is based on the – natural – course of events that children outlive their parents.[170]

A direct link between *humanitas* and *favor libertatis* can be found in the third example:

167 Transl. MacCromick in Watson, *Digest of Justinian* (n. 21).

168 D. 1.14.3 Ulp. 38 ad Sab. On this case see Natale Rampazzo, *Quasi praetor non fuerit. Studi sulle elezioni magistratuali Roma repubblicana tra regola ed eccezione* (Naples: Satura Editrice, 2008): 357–552; and Rolf Knütel, "Barbatius Philippus und seine Spuren," in *Ausgewählte Schriften: Rolf Knüttel*, ed. Holger Altmeppen, Sebastian Lohsse, Ingo Reichard and Martin Josef Schermaier (Heidelberg: C.F. Müller, 2021): 871–91.

169 D. 34.5.22 Iav. 5 ex Cass: cum explorari non possit, uter prior exstinctus sit, humanius est credere filium diutus vixisse (transl. Tuplin in Watson, *Digest of Justinian* [n. 21]).

170 Theophilus Gaedke, *De iure commorentium ex disciplina Romanorum* (Rostock: 1830): 38; Palma, *Humanior interpretatio* (n. 37): 35.

D. 48.23.4 (Paulus libro 17 quaestionum): In metallum damnata mulier eum quem prius conceperat edidit, deinde a principe restituta est. humanius dicetur etiam cognationis iura huic restituta videri.

D. 48.23.4 (Paul, Views, book 1): A woman who had been condemned to the mines gave birth to a child whom she had conceived beforehand and was then reinstated by the emperor. It will be more humane to say that the rights of blood relationship [to the child] appear to be restored to her also.[171]

The persons who were condemned to the mines (*in metallum*) became *servi poenae*, a special type of slave. In this case the woman had conceived before her sentence, she gave birth while being a *serva poenae*.[172] At that point, her sentence was overturned. Since her child was born by a slave, it was to be considered a slave.[173] But it was 'more humane' to consider not only herself personally free but also her kinship relations like those of a free person, with the consequence that her child was considered to be freeborn. Out of humaneness, the child was to share freedom and kinship with its mother.[174] Justinian finally states that slaves in a certain context are entitled to freedom 'for liberty's sake and with regard to humanity' (*libertatis favore et humanitatis intuitu*).[175] *Favor libertatis* can, therefore, be understood as an emanation of the Roman doctrine pertaining to natural law, which amounts to the same thing as saying that it is a requirement of *humanitas*.[176] As we established above, the Roman jurists held that slavery was against natural law since man is born free and the deprivation of liberty and the ensuing subjection to another person 'against nature';[177] from the point of view of nature, 'all men are created equal' – an echo of Ulp. D. 50.17.32:

D. 50.17.32 (Ulpianus libro 42 ad Sabinum): Quod attinet ad ius civile, servi pro nullis habentur: non tamen et iure naturali, quia, quod ad ius naturale attinet, omnes homines aequales sunt.

D. 50.17.32 (Ulpian, Sabinus, book 43): As far as concerns the civil law slaves are regarded as not existing, not, however, in the natural law, because as far as concerns the natural law all men are equal.[178]

171 Transl. Robinson in Watson, *Digest of Justinian* (n. 21).

172 Aglaia McClintock, *Servi della pena. Condannati a morte nella Roma imperiale* (Naples: Edizioni Scientifiche Italiane, 2010): 13–58.

173 Gai. 1.89–91.

174 Jacques Cuiacius, *Opera omnia in decem tomos distributa*, vol. 5 (Prato, 1838): col. 1810; the new literature can be found in Alice Cherchi, "Riflessioni sulla condizione giuridica delle metallariae nel tardo impero. A proposito di C. 11.7(6).7," *Annali del seminario giuridico dellauniversità di Palermo* 59 (2016): 223–25; McClintock, *Servi della pena* (n. 172): 109.

175 C. 3.31.12.2b Iust.

176 Essential commentary in Robleda, *Il diritto* (n. 15): 96, 102; see also Wacke, "Der favor libertatis" (n. 15): 926.

177 Gai. 1.89 (but see also 2.69 where slavery is justified with *naturalis ratio*); Ulp. 1 inst. D. 1.1.4; Flor. 9 inst. D. 1.5.4 pr-1; I. 1.2.2; I. 1.5 pr.

178 Transl. Crawford in Watson, *Digest of Justinian* (n. 21).

On a theoretical level, the jurists tried to overcome the apparent contradiction between natural freedom and societal slavery by blaming slavery on *ius gentium*, which amounts to saying, 'Everybody else does it, why shouldn't we?' But neither the emperors nor the jurists stopped at that rather feeble justification; instead they revived a concept stemming from Halcyon days, namely *favor libertatis*. By doing so, they created a compromise[179] between an institution without which life in antiquity simply was on the one hand not imaginable – it is commonly held that Spartacus and his comrades wanted to abolish their condition as slaves and not the institution as such[180] – and which on the other hand produced fear in some,[181] uneasiness in others and even pangs of bad conscience in very sensitive individuals – it was nothing but a 'hex' that condemned one of the suckling babies to serfdom. This discomfort was inserted into the theory by jurists who had probably been inspired by stoicism,[182] which thus claimed an initial and natural state of freedom, against which slavery then offended. By establishing this theoretical basis, they not only helped the emperors in their legislative activity *in favorem libertatis*, but also justified their own extensive interpretation of statutes and wills. *Favor libertatis* is a compromise between slavery and the abolition of slavery; between an institution deeply ingrained in Roman society, economy and law on the one hand, and philosophical ideas pointing towards a brotherhood of man as symbolized by the two suckling twins Romulus and Remus on the other. And this compromise was not static but dynamic, which can be deduced from the emperors' legislation to alleviate the condition of the slaves: I have already mentioned the *lex Iunia Petronia* and a rescript against maltreatment. Those slaves abandoned due to their frailty were given Iunian status, as we have seen;[183] Claudius and Hadrian intervened against the killing of slaves by their masters;[184] killing the slaves of others was also made punishable,[185] as was castration;[186] the slave who had bought his freedom can force his master by law to manumit him;[187] the *praefectus urbi* takes care of the

179 Boulvert and Morabito, "Le droit de l'esclavage" (n. 15): 119 speak of a 'true policy' ('véritable politique').

180 There is something like a *consensus sapientium* on this point see Baldwin, "Two Aspects" (n. 72): 294; Bellen, *Studien* (n. 68): 156; Gamauf, "Sklaven (servi)" (n. 3): 7; Alfred Heuss, "Das Revolutionsproblem im Spiegel der antiken Geschichte," *Historische Zeitschrift* 216, no. 1 (1973): 1, 51.

181 Boulvert and Morabito, "Le droit de l'esclavage" (n. 15): 103.

182 Tony Honoré, "Ulpian, Natural Law and Stoic Influence," *Tijdschrift voor Rechtsgeschiedenis* 78, no. 1–2 (2010): 199–208. A sound discussion of this problem can be found in Jakub Urbanik, "On the Uselessness of It All: The Roman Law of Marriage and Modern Times," *Fundamina* 20, no. 2 (2014): 948–54.

183 Mod. D. 40.8.2; Iust. C. 7.6.1.3.

184 Suet. Claud. 25.2; SHA Hadr. 18.7.

185 Gai. 3.213; Marci. D. 48.8.1.2.

186 Ven. Sat. D. 48.8.6; Hadr-Ulp. D. 48.8.4.2.

187 Divi fratres/Ulp. D. 40.1.4pr.

slaves who justly claim to be maltreated by their masters.[188] This tendency of imperial legislation continues after the Barracks Emperors, that is to say, in the third century CE.[189]

To neglect the importance of *favor libertatis* as a phenomenon of legislation and legal practice, and to ridicule its philosophical underpinning in the form of *ius naturale*, is a projection of modern ideas into antiquity and must be rejected as methodologically unjustified. It is based first on a more or less overt rejection of the concept of *ius naturale*, even though the authenticity of the texts featuring this concept can no longer be put into doubt.[190] It is impossible for historians to neglect the testimony of the texts reviewed in this paper, and the testimony of *ius naturale* as a rationale for the legislation and ensuing interpretation by jurists which cannot be sidelined[191] – whether or not this seems convincing from a modern point of view. The opinion that the Scipionic Circle, where *humanitas* was introduced into the mindset of the Roman ruling class, must be an invention by Cicero for the reason that Scipio Africanus was capable of harsh measures to maintain discipline in the field[192] is nothing more than a projection of one's own prejudices and craving for a world without contradictions onto the sources – which is the antithesis of what a historian can and should do. The fact that the result of the compromise between *servitus* and *libertas* is not clear-cut, and the existence of contradictions, are probably very 'human', as well as a characteristic of Roman law[193] which developed not by revolution but by evolution.[194] And it this second characteristic which is the other hidden motive for neglecting *favor libertatis* and marginalizing natural law. As a compromise, *favor libertatis* is a sort of vehicle for a slow, tantalisingly slow evolutionary process, the polar opposite of 'revolution', which has been the shibboleth of political thinking and legal doctrine since the eighteenth century.[195] Roman law is instead characterised by its traditionalism, by rejecting the new: for that sort

188 Ulp. D. 1.12.1.8.

189 Kaser, *Das Römische Privatrecht*, vol. 1 (n. 5): 125–29.

190 Fundamental in this respect is Waldstein, "Entscheidungsgrundlagen" (n. 22): 78–88; for confirmation see the results of the Cedant-seminar on natural law: Mantovani and Schiavone, *Testi e problemi* (n. 165).

191 Palma, *Humanior interpretatio* (n. 37): 151 ('no trascurabile'); see also Sebastiano Tafaro, "Schiavitù," in *Festschrift für Rolf Knütel zum 70. Geburstag*, ed. Holger Altmeppen, Ingo Reichard and Martin Josef Schermaier (Heidelberg: C.F. Müller, 2009): 1227–68.

192 See the references in Schadewaldt, "Humanitas" (n. 158): 52.

193 Jakob Fortunat Stagl, "L'ambiguïté existentielle du droit romain: Une faille de la codification justinienne," *Revue historique de droit français et étranger* 95, no. 4 (2017): 455–65.

194 Tomasz Giaro, "Dogmatische Wahrheit und Zeitlosigkeit in der römischen Jurisprudenz," *Bullettino dell'istituto di diritto romano Vittorio Scialoja* 29 (1987): 1–105.

195 Just consider Marx's phrase that revolutions are the 'locomotives' of history; Karl Marx, "Die Klassenkämpfe in Frankreich 1848 bis 1850," in *Marx-Engels-Werke*, vol. 7, ed. Institut für Marxismus-Leninismus beim ZK der SED (Berlin: Dietz, 1973): 9, 85. On the acceleration of the perception of time, especially after the French Revolution, see Rainer Kosseleck, "'Erfahrungsraum' und

of legal thinking this kind of compromise, of not changing things outwardly, was just adequate: treating *favor libertatis* as *ius singulare* served exactly this purpose. Just think of Jhering's dictum that progress in Roman law hobbled on the 'crutches' of fictions,[196] that is to say, a legal technique bringing about change, even revolution, without having to change one iota in the authoritative texts. It is simply a hermeneutical error to project one's own philosophy of history or one's own craving for a world of logical order free of contradiction onto sources that have nothing to do with this. If Roman emperors and lawyers based themselves on natural law as the theoretical basis of their doing, we have to accept this and not try to brush it aside.

6 *Opus legis scriptum in cordibus*

Tryphoninus calls a decision which does not respect *favor libertatis* 'unjust and contrary to the favour of liberty established by our forebears' (*iniquum et contra institutum a maioribus libertatis favorem*),[197] the word *aequum* refers to natural law, especially to the idea of equality,[198] and consequently, anything *iniquum* is against natural law.[199] But natural law acts as a political and philosophical doctrine, not as a legal principle capable of overriding established law, not even partially – and especially not a *lex publica*.[200] We do not know of even a single case of Romans believing that natural law was powerful enough to supersede established law; instead we have testimonies according to which *ius*, even if it is *iniquum*, that is to say against natural law, is valid under the condition that it was created by due process.[201] That does, of course, not prevent those who, as the Apostle Paul wrote, carry the 'work of the law written in

'Erwartungshorizont': Zwei historische Kategorien," in *Vergangene Zukunft*, ed. Rainer Kosseleck (Berlin: Suhrkamp, 1979): 349.

196 Rudolf von Jhering, *Geist des römischen Rechts auf den verschiedenen Stufen seiner Entwicklung*, vol. 3/1 (Leipzig: Breitkopf und Härtel, 1865): 305.

197 Tryph. 4 disp. D. 49.15.12.9.

198 Isid. orig. 10.7; on this see Dario Mantovani, "L'aequitas romana: Una nozione in cerca di equilibrio," in *Antiquorum Philosophia: An International Journal* 11 (2017): 1–22.

199 Jakob Fortunat Stagl, "Die Ausgleichung von Vorteil und Nachteil als Inhalt klassischer aequitas," in *Testi e problemi del giusnaturalismo romano*, ed. Aldo Schiavone and Dario Mantovani (Pavia: IUSS Press, 2007): 675–713.

200 Even Waldstein, "Entscheidungsgrundlagen" (n. 22): 86, must concede that natural law was not strong enough to prevail against slavery, and cites no example where it overrides a statute. *Ius singlare*, which by definition is *contra rationem iuris*, i.e. natural law, by its mere existence excludes such a possibility.

201 Paul. 14 ad Sab. D. 1.1.11: [. . .] *praetor quoque ius reddere dicitur etiam cum inique decernit, relatione scilicet facta non ad id quod ita praetor fecit, sed ad illud quod praetorem facere convenit.* ('The praetor is also said to render legal right [jus] even when he makes a wrongful decree, the

their hearts' (*opus legis scriptum in cordibus*)[202] from battling to see their convictions transformed into law, a 'general compact of the body politic' (*communis rei publicae sponsio*) as Papinian's definition of *lex publica* goes, which renders unto Caesar that which is Caesar's, and unto God those things that are God's.[203] We may conclude that the strange species of slaveholders fighting for the freedom of slaves existed;[204] the human heart is full of contradictions and eludes attempts at categorisation by overzealous philosophers, past and present.

reference, of course, being in this case not to what the praetor has done, but to what it is right for a praetor to do.', transl. MacCormack in Watson, *Digest of Justinian* [n. 21]); Gai. 1.83: *Animadvertere tamen debemus, ne iuris gentium regulam vel lex aliqua vel quod legis vicem optinet, aliquo casu commutaverit* ('Yet we must consider whether there are any circumstances in which some statute or other thing having the force of statute has modified the rule of the law of all peoples', transl. Gordon and Robinson, *The Institutes of Gaius* [n. 1]: 63) refers to *ius gentium*, which is not exactly the same.

202 Vulg. Rom. 2.15. On this see D'Ors, *Los romanistas* (n. 56): 17 '*ius naturale catholicum*'; Cf. Lucia di Cintio, *'Ordine' e 'Ordinamento': Idee e categorie giuridiche nel mondo romano* (Milan: LED Edizioni Universitarie, 2019): 36–39.

203 Vulg. Mt. 22.21. On the abolition of slavery, see Stagl, *Camino* (n. 22): 103, 141.

204 Boulvert and Morabito, "Le droit de l'esclavage" (n. 15): 115, speak of 'la fraction la plus éclairée des esclavagistes'.

Martin Schermaier

Neither Fish nor Fowl: Some Grey Areas of Roman Slave Law

1 Law is Written for Those Who Possess

Anyone who ventures into the *Corpus iuris civilis* in hopes of learning about Roman slave law is overwhelmed by the sheer mass of sources. How to find one's way through them? How to discover something about the legal position of slaves, about their rights and duties? Such questions are understandable but pointless. There is no uniform law on slavery, or even slave law as distinct from other areas of law, in the Roman legal sources. This is due to the fact that most of the relevant sources address the legally decisive questions not from the point of view of a slave but from that of an entitled party, such as a slave owner or a creditor. As slaves were unable to own anything and could be creditors only in a loose understanding of the term, a text may mention slaves but not in terms of their rights or duties. Anyone who does not study large portions of Roman property law will learn little about the law of Roman slavery.

More accessible are those texts that address the legal capacity of slaves, or manumission and its legal consequences. These topics were of interest to Justinian's compilers for systematic reasons and because they concerned property law so that they were arranged in clusters under specific titles: the most important are D. 1.5 (*de statu hominum*) and the twelve titles contained in D. 40 that address general questions of manumission (*manumissio*) and other reasons for freeing slaves. In the *Codex Iustinianus*, book D. 40 corresponds to titles C. 7.1–24. In the first book of his *Institutiones*, Gaius discusses the law of persons (in inst. 1.9–54) as well as the law on slaves and freedmen.

But by far the largest number of legal texts from which we can infer information about the social reality of slavery is scattered throughout the compilation of Justinian and other sources. Slaves feature in these texts where jurists discuss the acquisition, loss or the compass of a master's rights, or questions such as whether or under what circumstances slaves were able to make acquisitions for their masters or place them under obligation. A typical example is D. 41.1 (*de adquirendo rerum dominio*), which covers various matters about the acquisition of ownership. Every other fragment[1] contained in it addresses the question of whether and how a *dominus* acquired property through those in his power, either children *in potestate* or

1 These fragments are strangely interlinked with others in which someone becomes an original owner (i.e. without acquiring the right from a former owner). This allows us to draw conclusions as to the work of the compilers but is irrelevant to the question under discussion.

https://doi.org/10.1515/9783110987195-009

slaves. By far the biggest number of fragments concerns the acquisition of ownership by slaves. Something similar is repeated in title D. 41.2 (*de adquirenda vel amittenda possessione*), which deals with the acquisition and loss of possession by free men but also cases in which slaves or others *in potestate* participated.[2]

But we should not expect these texts to be concerned only with formulaic sentences or simple facts.[3] They discuss at length such questions as whether someone who was free but considered himself a slave was able to acquire for his master;[4] or what would happen if a slave owned in common should acquire,[5] or one in whom another person may have exercised a usufructuary right.[6] Of course, we can gain more knowledge from this than the simple fact that a slave was unable himself to be a proprietor.[7] This we can learn from the following sentence by the classical jurist Julian:

D. 41.1.37.6 (Iul. 44 dig.): Si, cum mihi donare velles, iusserim te servo communi meo et Titii rem tradere isque hac mente acciperet, ut rem Titii faceret, nihil agetur: nam et si procuratori meo rem tradideris, ut meam faceres, is hac mente acceperit, ut suam faceret, nihil agetur. quod si servus communis hac mente acceperit, ut duorum dominorum faceret, in parte alterius domini nihil agetur.

D. 41.1.37.6 (Julian, Digest, book 44): You wish to make me a gift, and I tell you to make delivery to the slave whom I own in common with Titius, and the slave receives the thing with the intention of acting only for Titius; the transaction is void; for even if you deliver a thing to my procurator to make it mine and he receives it as for himself, the transaction is void. If, on the other hand, a common slave should receive a thing with the intention of making it the property of both his owners in similar circumstances, the transaction will be void in respect of the other owner.[8]

---

2 Cf. D. 41.2.1.5 (Paul. 54 ad ed.): *Item adquirimus possessionem per servum aut filium. qui in potestate est. et quidem earum rerum. quas peculiariter tenent* [. . .] ('Similarly, we acquire possession through a slave or son in our power and, indeed, in the case of those things which they hold in peculium', transl. Thomas in Alan Watson, *The Digest of Justinian*, vol. 1–4 [Philadelphia: University of Pennsylvania Press, 1985]: vol. 4, 502).

3 For a detailed discussion of the various problems see Wolfgang Krüger, *Erwerbszurechnung kraft Status. Eine romanistisch-vergleichende Untersuchung* (Berlin: Duncker & Humblot, 1979).

4 Such as D. 41.1.23 (Ulp. 43 ad Sab.); D. 41.1.40 (Afr. 7 quaest.); D. 41.1.43 pr. (Gai. 7 ad ed. prov.); D. 41.1.54 (Mod. 31 ad Quint. Muc.).

5 Such as D. 41.1.37.1–6 (Iul. 33 dig.); D. 41.1.45 (Gai. 7 ad ed.); D. 41.1.63. 1–2 (Tryph. 7 disp.).

6 Cf. D. 41.1.47 (Paul. 50 ad ed.); D. 41.1.49 (Paul. 9 ad Plaut.); D. 41.1.63.3 (Tryph. 7 disp.).

7 Cf. Orlando Patterson, *Slavery and Social Death. A Comparative Study* (Cambridge, MA: Harvard University Press, 1982): 182: 'The fundamental feature of slavery, in law, was the fact that the slave could not be a proprietor: he or she was, quintessentially, a property-less person.'

8 Transl. Thomas in Watson, *Digest of Justinian*, vol. 4 (n. 2): 496.

This text is not about contracting a donation but about transferring ownership by means of a donation. Three cases are discussed, but the setting is the same in all three: A wants to transfer a thing to B by the help of B's slave. B himself has asked A to hand the thing over to his slave. In the first case, the slave is owned by B and Titius. If the slave receiving the thing is of the opinion that the thing is destined for Titius, the transfer of ownership fails. Only if he is willing to accept it on behalf of B does B become the owner. This is difficult to explain from a modern perspective:[9] the slave is only passively engaged, like an automaton which accepts something on behalf of its owner. But in the very case that he is slave of two co-owners, the slave's opinion is decisive: he decides who of the two masters is to acquire possession. The slave's will directs the allocation of the thing. As long as we do not know whether B or someone else acquires possession, ownership will not pass on. Using his slave, B acquires possession only if the slave accepts the thing on behalf of B.

The second case is even more surprising. Here, the recipient is B's manager (*procurator*). If he receives the thing as assigned to him, B does not acquire ownership. This sounds as if the manager were a free person able to acquire ownership for himself. But depending on the context, he could also be a slave as in the first and the third examples. Though slaves were not able to own or to possess from a strictly legal point of view, jurists agreed that slaves could have their own belongings.[10] The third case is definitely about a slave. If a slave of two co-owners accepts the thing on behalf of both, B becomes owner only to 50%. The other part remains with A.

In terms of its form, this piece is typical for classical legal texts: the jurists decided cases without arguing. In order to grasp the *ratio decidendi*, we have to be aware of at least two premises: first, the transfer of ownership depended on the transfer of possession. Second, the acquisition of possession presupposed both the will to possess (*animus possidendi*) and factual possession.[11] B wants to possess the thing, but as long as the slave has not received it, B does not possess at all. And once the slave has received the thing, possession by B remains unclear as long as we do not know the slave's intent. Only if the slave accepts the thing on behalf of B does B gain possession and therefore becomes owner. The opinion or will of the slave to hold the thing for B bridges the *animus possessionis* of B with the factual possession of the slave. This construction is quite close to the model of indirect possession as it is

---

9 And even from a modern perspective of Roman law, cf. William Warwick Buckland, *The Roman Law of Slavery. The Condition of the Slave in Private Law from Augustus to Justinian* (Cambridge: Cambridge University Press 1908): 387–93.

10 D. 40.12.32 (Paul. 6 reg.); see below 257.

11 Discussed in Max Kaser, *Das römische Privatrecht*, vol. 1, *Das altrömische, das vorklassische und klassische Recht*, 2nd ed. (Munich: C.H. Beck, 1971): 390–95; Christian Baldus, "Possession in Roman Law," in *The Oxford Handbook of Roman Law and Society*, ed. Paul J. du Plessis, Clifford Ando and Kaius Tuori (Oxford: Oxford University Press, 2014): esp. 537–38.

known for tenants or custodians. The opinion or will of the slave does not replace the *animus possidendi*, but it makes possession imputable.

Similar texts referring to the discretion of the slave occur in cases of *peculia*, such as the one of Gaius, in D. 41.1.43.2 (7 ad ed. prov.):[12] if a slave has two *peculia*, one from his owner, another from the usufructuary, and if he buys a thing, ownership passes to that master from whose *peculium* the sales price has been paid. Here, too, the slave's decision allocates ownership.[13] Texts like those of Gaius and Julian refer to the fact that slaves were held to be not things but human beings. They had a *mens*, an opinion or an intention, which could be decisive in allocating goods. But in cases like this one Roman jurists did not assume a kind of general 'agency' of slaves. They were only interested in the question of who eventually acquired possession or ownership of the thing in question. In doing so, they naturally assumed that a slave would have his own opinion about the ownership of the thing, and that this opinion was legally relevant for assigning possession and ownership. However, not all jurists shared this opinion. Ulpian, who discussed the same cases, denied that allocation of the acquired thing depended on the will of the slave,[14] arguing instead that a slave always acquired for the master to whom the donor wanted to give the thing in question. The relation in which this text stands to Julians's decision is a matter of

12 D. 41.1.43.2 (Gaius 7 ad ed. prov.): *Cum servus, in quo alterius usus fructus est, hominem emit et ei traditus sit, antequam pretium solvat, in pendenti est, cui proprietatem adquisierit: et cum ex peculio, quod ad fructuarium pertinet, solverit, intellegitur fructuarii homo fuisse: cum vero ex eo peculio, quod proprietarium sequitur, solverit, proprietarii ex post facto fuisse videtur.* ('When a slave, in whom another has a usufruct, buys and takes delivery of a slave, the question for whom he acquires him is in suspense until he pays the price; if he pays it out of a peculium from the fructuary, he is deemed to acquire for the fructuary, but should he use a peculium which follows his actual owner, the slave purchased, by relation back, is held to belong and to have belonged to his owner'; transl. Thomas in Watson, *Digest of Justinian*, vol. 4 [n. 2]: 497).

13 On that texts and related ones see Fritz Sturm, "Sklavenkasse entscheidet über Eigentumserwerb: Zu Gaius D. 41.1.43.2 und Ulpian D. 7.1.25.1," in *Sklaverei und Freilassung im römischen Recht. Symposium für Hans Josef Wieling zum 70. Geburtstag*, ed. Thomas Finkenauer (Berlin/Heidelberg: Springer Verlag, 2006): 223–41.

14 D. 39.5.13 (Ulp. 7 disp.): *Qui mihi donatum volebat, servo communi meo et Titii rem tradidit: servus vel sic accepit quasi socio adquisiturus vel sic quasi mihi et socio: quaerebatur quid ageret. et placet, quamvis servus hac mente acceperit, ut socio meo vel mihi et socio adquirat, mihi tamen adquiri: nam et si procuratori meo hoc animo rem tradiderit, ut mihi adquirat, ille quasi sibi adquisiturus acceperit, nihil agit in sua persona, sed mihi adquirit.* ('Somebody who wished to make me a gift handed the property in question to a slave jointly owned by me and Titius. The slave received it, understanding that he was getting it either for my co-owner or for both of us together. The question arose of what the legal result of the transaction was. It is agreed that although the slave received the property on the understanding that he was getting it either for my co-owner or for both of us together, nonetheless, he got it for me; for in the case also in which the donor handed the property to a procurator of mine on the understanding that the latter was getting it for me but the procurator received it as though he were getting it for himself, the latter achieves nothing in his own person but gets the property for me', transl. Tuplin in Watson, *Digest of Justinian*, vol. 3 [n. 2]: 410).

some dispute.[15] What is however obvious is that the Roman jurists did not draw the line between free and slave on the basis of a general theory of action.

Things are different today. Jurists only examine in the case of persons[16] whether someone can trigger legal consequences through self-determined action.[17] In Roman antiquity, the concept of *persona* was less exclusive;[18] it was not beyond the legal imagination that a person might be treated like an asset. These days, the boundary between legal subjects and legal objects is very strictly drawn. According to Kant, a human being can only ever be an end in itself, never a means to an end: this is how personhood is expressed.[19] Modern (German) legal doctrine takes up this thought:[20] in law, a human being can never be treated as an object, a thing. This is why texts such as D. 41.1.37.6 challenge our modern terminology. They show that Roman jurists saw slaves as persons who thought and acted independently. Even so, the slaves were objects and, as such, the instruments of their masters: the texts appear to be interested in the legal consequences of servile actions only from the masters' perspective.

2 Slave Protection and Proprietors' Interests

a) Matters are not greatly different in our next example, even though it seems to change perspective. At first, the following text sounds as though the jurist, Ulpian, was concerned about the welfare of slaves to whose usufruct a third party was entitled.

---

15 See for example Fabian Klinck, *Erwerb durch Übergabe an Dritte nach klassischem römischen Recht* (Berlin: Duncker & Humblot, 2004): 113–14 and 237 (with further references).

16 The typical reflex is therefore to treat artificial intelligences legally as (independent) persons: see already Lawrence Byard Solum, "Legal Personhood for Artificial Intelligences," *The North Carolina Law Review* 70, no. 4 (1992): 1231–86; recently Visa A.J. Kurki and Tomasz Pietrzykowski, eds., *Legal Personhood: Animals, Artificial Intelligence and the Unborn* (Berlin/New York: Springer Verlag, 2017); Jaana Sild, "Legal Capacity of Artificial Intelligence," *L'Europe Unie* 13 (2018): 74–78.

17 We therefore speak of legal capacity, see for example Article 12 (2) of the UN Convention on the Rights of Persons with Disabilities (2006); see also §§ 104 ff. (German) BGB.

18 Cf. already above, Schermaier, Without rights.

19 Immanuel Kant, *Die Metaphysik der Sitten*, vol. 2, *Metaphysische Anfangsgründe der Tugendlehre* (Königsberg: Nicolovius, 1797): § 38 (p. 140): 'Die Menschheit selbst ist eine Würde; denn der Mensch kann von keinem Menschen [. . .] bloß als Mittel, sondern muss jederzeit zugleich als Zweck gebraucht werden und darin besteht seine Würde (die Persönlichkeit) [. . .]'.

20 Josef Wintrich, "Über Eigenart und Methode verfassungsgerichtlicher Rechtsprechung," in *Verfassung und Verwaltung in Theorie und Wirklichkeit. Festschrift für Herrn Geheimrat Professor Dr. Wilhelm Laforet anlässlich seines 75. Geburtstages* (Munich: Isar Verlag, 1952): 227–49, 235–36.

D. 7.1.15.1–2 (Ulp. 18 ad Sab.): Mancipiorum quoque usus fructus legato non debet abuti, sed secundum condicionem eorum uti: nam si librarium rus mittat et qualum et calcem portare cogat, histrionem balniatorem faciat, vel de symphonia atriensem, vel de palaestra stercorandis latrinis praeponat, abuti videbitur proprietate. (2) Sufficienter autem alere et vestire debet secundum ordinem et dignitatem mancipiorum.

D. 7.1.15.1–2 (Ulpian, Sabinus, book 18): If the usufruct left as a legacy is one of slaves, the usufructuary must not put them to a wrong use; his use of them must correspond to their respective characters. For example, if he sends a scribe into the country and makes him carry a basket of lime, or if he makes an actor do the work of a bath attendant or a singer perform the duties of a household servant or if he takes a man from the wrestling arena and sets him to clean out the latrines, he will be held to be making a wrong use of the property of the bare owner. [2] He must also provide the slaves with sufficient food and clothing, each according to his rank and worth.[21]

This text limits a usufructuary's choice how to use the slaves who were left to him in a will. If a slave was trained for a highly skilled job, he could not command him to do physical work. If he did so anyway, the owner was entitled to claim damages on the grounds of *cautio usufructuaria*, the obligation every usufructuary had to render when a slave was handed over to them. On the other hand, this shows that at least § 1 did not primarily protect the slave himself but rather his owner who might want to have him back in the future. Ulpian's decision corresponds to the principle that a usufructuary was entitled to use the thing *salva rerum substantia* only, without diminishing its state and value.[22]

But what about § 2? In it, Ulpian states that the usufructuary had to feed and clothe the slaves according to their rank and dignity. Would it have diminished the value of a slave if the usufructuary had clothed him in a worse manner than that corresponding to his rank? It is hard to imagine. Did the Roman jurists read a usufructuary's handing out of poor clothing to a slave as disrespect towards the slave's master?[23] Usufruct placed a one-sided, regular burden on a proprietor and excluded them from their proprietary rights for a long period of time, so the law at any rate set narrow limits for a usufructuary, as the following sentence shows.

21 Transl. Fergus in Watson, *Digest of Justinian*, vol. 1 (n. 2): 221.

22 Cf. D. 7.1.1 (Paul. 3 ad Vitell.): *Usus fructus est ius alienis rebus utendi fruendi salva rerum substantia.* ('Usufruct is the right to use and enjoy the things of another without impairing their substance', transl. Fergus in Watson, *Digest of Justinian*, vol. 1 [n. 2]: 216).

23 This is the explanation suggested by Andreas Wacke in "Die Menschenwürde von Sklaven im Spiegel des Umgehungsgeschäfts nach Sextus Pedius. Si alii rei homo accedat und D. 21,1,44 pr.," in *Iurisprudentia univeralis. Festschrift für Theo Mayer-Maly*, ed. Martin Schermaier, Michael J. Rainer and Laurens Winkel (Cologne/Weimar/Vienna: Böhlau, 2002): 811–36, 832 n. 105.

D. 7.1.15.3 (Ulp. 18 ad Sab.): Et generaliter Labeo ait in omnibus rebus mobilibus modum eum tenere debere, ne sua feritate vel saevitia ea corrumpat: alioquin etiam lege Aquilia eum conveniri.

D. 7.1.15.3 (Ulpian, Sabinus, book 18): Labeo states as a general rule that in the case of movable property of every kind, the usufructuary is bound to observe due moderation, so as not to spoil it by rough or harsh usage; indeed, if he does not, the Aquilian action can be brought against him.[24]

Referring to Labeo, Ulpian says that the usufructuary must not spoil (*corrumpere*) the things left to him. If he did, he was not only liable under the *cautio* but also under tort law (*ex lege Aquilia*). It emerges from this general explanation that in § 2 Ulpian is not merely concerned with slaves being fed or clothed less lavishly than they would have been by their master. Rather, the jurist thinks of cases in which malnutrition or insufficient clothing caused slaves to suffer damage to their bodies or their health. So, this sentence is, again, probably not primarily concerned with the rights of slaves, but with protecting their owners' rights in them.

Even so, D. 7.1.15.2 is remarkable because the text appears to contradict Patterson's argument that enslavement caused the complete loss of honour and dignity. This loss, Patterson writes, was characteristic of 'social death'.[25] But even though the text is an important piece in the mosaic of Roman slavery, it poses no real challenge to Patterson's argument.[26] Ulpian writes about the rank of slaves among themselves,[27] which he does not measure against the masters' *ordo* and *dignitas*.[28] His doing so proves that jurists paid attention to social differentiation among slaves. To reduce our takeaway from the text merely to the slaves in § 2 reflecting their masters' *ordo* and *dignitas* is out of the question. It is their own 'ranks' that are at issue, even if an owner were just as interested in a usufructuary treating his slaves as befitting their respective ranks as the slaves were themselves – possibly even more.

The situation was similar for the sanctioning of an assault on a slave's dignity, or *iniuria*. Only a *dominus* was entitled to bring an action against the wrongdoer, so we might assume that it was the owner's honour that was offended by a slave being

24 Transl. Fergus in Watson, *Digest of Justinian*, vol. 1 (n. 2): 221.

25 Patterson, *Slavery and Social Death* (n. 7): 77–101.

26 Which could be different in case of D. 21.1.44 pr. (Paul. 2 ad aed. cur.), where Sextus Pedius argues that slaves could not be a 'give-away' in sales contracts because of the *dignitas hominum*. On that text Wacke, "Menschenwürde" (n. 23): 812–14 and 827–34.

27 Similarly Bürge, who writes about the 'Sozialisation der Sklaven', cf. Alfons Bürge, "Cibaria. Indiz für die soziale Stellung des römischen Arbeitnehmers?," in *Ars boni et aequi. Festschrift für Wolfgang Waldstein zum 65. Geburtstag*, ed. Martin Schermaier and Zoltán Végh (Stuttgart: Franz Steiner Verlag, 1993): 63–78, 72 n. 56.

28 So also Stefan Knoch, *Sklavenfürsorge im Römischen Reich. Formen und Motive zwischen humanitas und utilitas* (Hildesheim: Georg Olms Verlag, 2005): 26–28.

beaten (*verberatus*).[29] But the jurists made a clear distinction between an *iniuria* against a slave occurring in order to injure the master, and one that targeted the slave himself.[30] This seemed important to Ulpian, especially in cases of physical attack, as it was the slave who experienced the pain.[31] That was why differences were made according to the slave's social status to decide on this basis which *iniuria* against him entitled the *dominus* to sue: in the case of a higher-ranking slave – such as an *ordinarius* or a *dispensator* –, an invective was sufficient grounds;[32] in the case of a socially lower-ranked slave, the threshold for what constituted an insult was much higher:

D. 47.10.15.44 (Ulp. 77 ad ed.): Itaque praetor non ex omni causa iniuriarum iudicium servi nomine promittit: nam si leviter percussus sit vel maledictum ei leviter, non dabit actionem: at si infamatus sit vel facto aliquo vel carmine scripto puto causae cognitionem praetoris porrigendam et ad servi qualitatem: etenim multum interest, qualis servus sit, bonae frugi, ordinarius, dispensator, an vero vulgaris vel mediastinus an qualisqualis. et quid si compeditus vel male notus vel notae extremae? habebit igitur praetor rationem tam iniuriae, quae admissa dicitur, quam personae servi, in quem admissa dicitur, et sic aut permittet aut denegabit actionem.

D. 47.10.15.44 (Ulpian, Edict, book 77): Thus, the praetor does not promise an action for every affront in respect of a slave; if the slave be lightly struck or mildly abused, the praetor will not give an action; but if he be put to shame by some act or lampoon, I think that the praetor's investigation into the matter should take into account the standing of the slave; for it is highly relevant what sort of slave he is, whether he be honest, regular, and responsible, a steward or only a common slave, a drudge or whatever. And what if he be in fetters, branded, and of the deepest notoriety? The praetor, therefore, will take into account both the alleged affront and the person of the slave said to have suffered it and will grant or refuse the action accordingly.[33]

29 Cf. D. 47.10.15.34 (Ulp. 77 ad ed.): *Praetor ait: Qui servum alienum adversus bonos mores verberavisse deve eo iniussu domini quaestionem habuisse dicetur, in eum iudicium dabo. Item si quid aliud factum esse dicetur, causa cognita iudicium dabo.* ('The praetor says: "Where a man shall be said to have thrashed another's slave or to have submitted him to torture, contrary to sound morals, without the owner's consent, I will give an action. Equally, if it be said that something else be done, I will, having heard the circumstances, give an action."'; transl. Thomas in Watson, *Digest of Justinian*, vol. 4 [n. 2]: 778); for more details see Richard Gamauf, "Öffentliche Ordnung und Injurienrecht: Sozialgeschichtliche Beobachtungen anhand des Edikts de iniuriis quae servis fiunt," in *Scritti per Alessandro Corbino*, vol. 3, ed. Isabella Piro (Tricase: Libellula, 2016): 221–45; see also Jan Dirk Harke, *Corpus der römischen Rechtsquellen zur antiken Sklaverei*, vol. 3, *Die Rechtsposition der Sklaven*, pt. 2, *Ansprüche aus Delikten am Sklaven* (Stuttgart: Franz Steiner Verlag, 2013).
30 So for example D. 47.10.15.35 und 45 (Ulp. 77 ad ed.).
31 And again D. 47.10.15.35: [. . .] *hanc enim et servum sentire palam est* ('[. . .] for it is obvious that the slave himself feels such things.', transl. Thomas in Watson, *Digest of Justinian*, vol. 4 [n. 2]: 778).
32 On this text see also Gamauf, "Dispensator" (in this volume).
33 Transl. Thomas in Watson, *Digest of Justinian*, vol. 4 (n. 2): 779.

So, it was a slave's status that decided the measure of honour and respect he was due. Of course, this criterion could also be articulated from the point of view of the *dominus*: a master's interest in the integrity of his slave depended on the role this slave performed in the household. However, the Roman jurists did care about the slave personally,[34] as we can see from the case of a slave committing an *iniuria*: it is a greater outrage to be insulted by a slave than by a free person, and the former case warrants a lawsuit against the slave's master more than the latter.[35]

b) There is a further dimension to protection for a slave in the interests of their master, which we find reflected in numerous surviving cases: when slaves were sold, it often happened that the previous owner entered into the contract on the condition that the buyer treated the slave in a specific way, such as manumitting (*ut manumittatur*) or not prostituting them (*ne prostituatur*).[36] Such covenants could be enforced by a contractual penalty,[37] but the form regularly employed was a conditional construction that enabled the seller to reclaim the slave if the buyer did not comply with the agreed arrangement. Such arrangements had an effect *in rem* if they were based on additional agreements in the context of *mancipatio* which was necessary for the transfer of slaves: in such cases, if a buyer resold the slave, the original seller was able to demand their return even from the third buyer.[38] In the event of an agreement *ut manumittatur* not being honoured, a rescript of Marcus Aurelius' granted the slave immediate liberty.[39] The same applied to a slave who had been sold under the condition *ne prostituatur*. If this condition had been worded in such a way that she would

34 Richard Gamauf is sceptical, see "Slavery: Social Position and Legal Capacity," in *The Oxford Handbook of Roman Law and Society*, ed. Paul J. du Plessis, Clifford Ando and Kaius Tuori (Oxford: Oxford University Press, 2016): 386–401, 396.

35 D. 47.10.17.3 (Ulp. 77 ad ed.): *Quaedam iniuriae a liberis hominibus factae leves (non nullius momenti) videntur, enimvero a servis graves sunt: crescit enim contumelia ex persona eius qui contumeliam fecit.* ('Some affronts which, perpetrated by freemen, are regarded as slight (of no consequence) are serious if perpetrated by slaves. For the outrage is enhanced by the station of the person responsible.', transl. Thomas in Watson, *Digest of Justinian*, vol. 4 [n. 2]: 780).

36 Collated exhaustively in Thomas McGinn, "Ne serva prostituatur. Restrictive Covenants in the Sale of Slaves," *Zeitschrift der Savigny-Stiftung für Rechtsgeschichte, Romanistische Abteilung* 107 (1990): 315–53 (= Thomas McGinn, *Prostitution, Sexuality, and the Law in Ancient Rome* [New York: Oxford University Press, 1998]: 288–319); on this topic see also Matthew J. Perry, *Gender, Manumussion and the Roman Freedwoman* (New York: Cambridge University Press, 2014).

37 See overall Rolf Knütel, *Stipulatio poenae. Studien zur römischen Vertragsstrafe* (Cologne/ Vienna: Böhlau, 1976): on D. 18.7.6 pr. (Pap. 27 quaest.) at 357–61, on D. 45.1.122.2 (Scaev. 28 dig.) at 172–74.

38 See McGinn, "Ne serva prostituatur" (n. 36): 316–20.

39 Cf. D. 40.1.20.2 (Pap. 10 resp.); D. 40.8.6 (Marc. sing. ad form. hypoth.); for further references see Buckland, *Law of Slavery* (n. 9): 71.

be free immediately if the seller violated the agreement,[40] it is likely that Vespasian had already granted her (Latin) freedom.[41]

Such arrangements by which a seller wanted to secure manumission or protect a slave from being prostituted at first glance appear to be drawn up in favour of the slaves.[42] But if we include comparable agreements that obviously only protected the interests of the seller, we gain a different perspective. These include well-known agreements such as the one which obliged the buyer to take the slave abroad (*ut exportetur*),[43] or prohibited him from freeing the slave (*ne manumittetur*).[44] For this reason, Tom McGinn argued that even the arrangements favourable to slaves – especially those that stipulated *ne prostituatur* – were in fact concluded in the interests of the seller, i.e. the former master, because the agreement *ne prostituatur* increased the seller's moral standing.[45] McGinn sees this as confirmation of Patterson's findings that slaves themselves lacked honour, but that the master acquired honour through the slave.[46] Lastly, McGinn regarded such covenants as instruments of social control:[47] arguing that while they placed a burden on the new owner and reduced the price for the seller, they stabilised the system of slavery.[48] By contrast, Matthew Perry recently emphasised the privileged position of a slave sold under such an agreement, which in his view made her

40 This seems to have been a frequent arrangement, cf. D. 2.4.10.1 (Ulp. 5 ad ed.); D. 21.2.34 pr. (Pomp. 27 ad Sab.); C. 4.56.2.

41 Cf. D. 37.14.7 pr. (Mod. sing. de manumissionibus); cf. McGinn, "Ne serva prostituatur" (n. 36): 324–37; Buckland, *Law of Slavery* (n. 9): 70–71.

42 This – at least for for *ne prostituatur* – is the argument of Buckland, *Law of Slavery* (n. 9): 70: 'This restriction is imposed in the interest for morality, and of the ancilla'; similarly Johannes M. Rainer, "Zur Prostitution von Sklavinnen in Rom," in *Inter cives necnon peregrinos. Essays in Honour of Boudewijn Sirks*, ed. Jan Hallebeek et al. (Göttingen: V&R unipress, 2014): 627–40, 635–37.

43 For some relevant examples see D. 18.7 (*de servis exportandis*).

44 Such as D. 29.5.3.15 (Ulp. 50 ad ed.); D. 30.44.7 (Ulp. 21 ad Sab.); D. 40.1.9 (Paul. sing. reg.); D. 40.9.9.2 (Marc. 1 inst.); D. 49.15.12.16 (Tryph. 4 disp.); Adam Wilinski, "Ricerche sull'alienazione degli schiavi nel diritto romano: Vendita dello schiavo con la clausola ne manumittatur," *Index* 5 (1974): 321–28; see most recently Fabian Klinck, "Papinian D. 18,7,6 pr. und die Sanktionierung von Freilassungs- und Prostitutionsverboten bei Sklavenverkäufen," in *Argumenta Papiniani. Studien zur Geschichte und Dogmatik des Privatrechts*, ed. Jan Dirk Harke (Berlin/Heidelberg: Springer Verlag, 2013): 79–89.

45 McGinn, "Ne serva prostituatur" (n. 36): 345–51.

46 Patterson, *Slavery and Social Death* (n. 7): 97–101 citing Hegel; cf. McGinn, "Ne serva prostituatur" (n. 36): 347–48.

47 Cf. already Keith R. Bradley, *Slaves and Masters in the Roman Empire. A Study in Social Control* (Brussels: Latomus, 1984).

48 McGinn, "Ne serva prostituatur" (n. 36): 340–45; similarly now Jacobo Rodriquez Garrido, "Ne serva prostituatur. Exlavitud, prostitución y los limites de la dominica potesetas en la Roma Antigua," *Dialogues d'historie ancienne* 46, no. 1 (2020): 173–96; Jakob Stagl argues in a similar vein in his contribution on *favor libertatis* (in this volume).

safe from sexual exploitation for life: 'The application of a *ne serva prostituatur* covenant effectively allowed for a sense of sexual honor for female slaves'.[49]

These points, rather than being contradictory, complement one another: the covenant *ut manumittatur* or *ne prostituatur* benefitted the slave but were concluded in the interest of the seller; at the same time, they stabilised the system of slavery because all slaves could hope for these or similar arrangements in case they were sold.

But what about the jurists who decided these cases? What motives led them to enhance the effectiveness of such covenants? On the whole, Roman jurists were sparing with reasons. When they did give them, we can often draw socio-historical conclusions. Papinian, for example, explained that the agreement *ne prostituatur* served to protect a female slave from 'disgrace' (*contumelia*) and grew out of her old master's 'affection' (*affectio*) and 'tact' (*verecundia*). The fragment is lengthy but worth quoting in full:

D. 18.7.6 pr. (Pap. 27 quaest.): Si venditor ab emptore caverit, ne serva manumitteretur neve prostituatur, et aliquo facto contra quam fuerat exceptum evincatur aut libera iudicetur, et ex stipulatu poena petatur, doli exceptionem quidam obstaturam putant, Sabinus non obstaturam. sed ratio faciet, ut iure non teneat stipulatio, si ne manumitteretur exceptum est: nam incredibile est de actu manumittentis ac non potius de effectu beneficii cogitatum. ceterum si ne prostituatur exceptum est, nulla ratio occurrit, cur poena peti et exigi non debeat, cum et ancillam contumelia adfecerit et venditoris affectionem, forte simul et verecundiam laeserit: etenim alias remota quoque stipulatione placuit ex vendito esse actionem, si quid emptor contra quam lege venditionis cautum est fecisset aut non fecisset.

D. 18.7.6 pr. (Papinian, Questiones, book 27): Suppose a vendor to have sold a slave-woman, extracting from the purchaser an undertaking that she will not be manumitted nor put to prostitution and, through some act contrary to this proviso, she is evicted or becomes free, and the penalty arising from the stipulation is claimed; there are those who think that the plaintiff may be met with the defense of fraud, though Sabinus denies this. But reason requires that the stipulation should not be binding at law if the provision be that there should be no manumission; for it is incredible that the parties should have deliberated upon the act of the manumitter and not on the effects of the benefit. But if the provision be that a slave-woman should not be put to prostitution, there is no ground on which the penalty should not be claimed and exacted; for the woman herself and the vendor's feelings are outraged, and, it may be, modesty is offended. Indeed, leaving aside the stipulation, it became accepted that the action on sale will lie if the purchaser acts or is guilty of an omission in contravention of a term of the sale.[50]

49 Perry, *Gender* (n. 36): 35; cit. 36.
50 Transl. Thomas in Watson, *Digest of Justinian*, vol. 2 (n. 2): 542.

The facts of the case are complex and require explanation.[51] The seller of a slave woman extracted from the buyer the promise, safeguarded by a contractual penalty, that she would neither be freed nor prostituted. After the former contingency did, in fact, occur, the woman was vindicated by a third party or recognised as a free woman in a lawsuit. Papinian found that the seller was unable to demand payment of the contractual penalty on the grounds either of eviction or because the woman had in the meantime attained her freedom, because the buyer had not himself manumitted the slave: as such, he had not violated the covenant. Prostituting the slave was a different matter, however: for this the buyer would have to answer, regardless of whether the slave had attained her freedom or not.

Papinian's opinion takes into account both the slave and her former master. His arguments of *affectio* and *verecundia* focus on the master's honour, which Papinian links to the sexual integrity of the slave. This confirms the argument of Patterson and McGinn. But at the same time the jurist underlines the fact that the slave woman, too, suffered disgrace (*cum et ancillam contumelia adfecerit*) by having been prostituted in breach of the agreement. So, his argument is also about her reputation, not just her former master's. Social historians may read this as a reflection or plausibilisation of the master's interest. However, this reference to the slave's own self-interest would have been superfluous for a legally viable justification of why the promised *poena* had been forfeited. The fact that it was made despite the habitual terseness of the classical jurists in general and Papinian in particular[52] is significant. For him, the slave's protection was worth mentioning not on legal but on social and moral grounds. This may be an indication for his sympathetic stance towards the enslaved.[53] It certainly demonstrates that the protection of slaves was an accepted topos in classical legal discourse.[54]

c) We can only indirectly deduce from the legal sources the fact that slaves were accorded both a social rank and an interest in maintaining it – examples include D. 7.1.15.2 und D. 18.7.6 pr. If this rank suffered violation or impairment, it was at

51 See for more detail Klinck, "Papinian D. 18.7.6 pr." (n. 44): 80–83.

52 Papinian is notorious for his terseness. Ulrich Manthe ("Votum parentium: Pap. D. 29.4.26," in *Quaestiones Iuris. Festschrift für Joseph Georg Wolf zum 70. Geburtstag*, ed. Ulrich Manthe and Christoph Krampe [Berlin: Duncker & Humblot, 2000]: 163–81) regards Papinian as the 'in seiner Ausdrucksweise präziseste(n) aller römischen Juristen' (163), while Andreas Wacke opines that his writings showcase the Roman jurists' 'lakonische Kürze [. . .] in gesteigerter Form.' See Andreas Wacke, "Die sorgfältige Klagen-Auswahl durch den Käufer bei umgekehrter Eviktion (Papinian Dig. 21,2,66 pr.): Da mihi facta, dabo tibi ius?," in *A bonis bona discere. Festgabe für János Zlinszky*, ed. Orsolya M. Péter and Béla Szabó (Miskolc: Bibor Verlag, 1998): 63–89, quote at 64.

53 Cf. Alberto Toso, "Emilio Papiniano e le influenze cristiane nell'evoluzione del diritto romano classico," *Acta Iuridici Internationalis* 2 (1935): 21–35.

54 See also Ulrike Babusiaux, *Papinians Quaestiones. Zur rhetorischen Methode eines spätklassischen Juristen* (Munich: C.H. Beck, 2011): 234, who understands this *amplificatio* of the opinion as a rhetorical device.

most the master but never the slave who had grounds for a claim. So, from a legal point of view, 'slave honour' was subsumed in the master's honour. In D. 18.7.6 pr., the penalty had been promised by the buyer to the former owner and not to the slave. Even so, a slave's honour was perceived as a legally protected value itself. This reflects a social consensus with a significance that goes beyond the individual cases of benevolent treatment for slaves that we know from the literature.

3 Grey Areas Between Law and Social Practice

a) If the jurists ascribed significance to the rights of slaves, even if the latter had no legal rights of their own, we are in a normative grey area. In the classical system of formulary procedure, a subjective right was defined as that which was protected by legal action: as such, slaves were without rights. Being excluded from formulary procedure, they could not seek legal protection for formal reasons alone. This resulted in the paradoxical situation, discussed elsewhere,[55] that a slave could owe a debt but not be sued for it. The Roman jurists employed the makeshift remedy of referring to such situations as *naturaliter debere* or *naturalis obligatio*.[56] Whiles such *obligationes* were not actionable, they were nevertheless treated like effective obligations: they could be discharged, they could be offset for or against a claim, and they could be secured by a guarantee.[57] The legal concept of *obligatio naturalis* served also to delineate the grey area between non-enforceability and effective obligation. The term alleged the existence of gradations in the legal validity of obligations. It created an institutionalised form of reduced legal protection for certain obligations, which survived in different forms in a number of modern legal systems.[58]

So, the Roman jurists recognised, in principle, the legal capacity of slaves, but denied them their own claims due to the servile lack of legal capacity; this precluded the pursuit of claims in formal procedure. Despite the existence of *extraordinaria cognitio*, the imperial type of legal proceedings controlled by government officials which constituted a less formalised and therefore more flexible form of litigation, obligations

---

55 On D. 15.1.41 see Schermaier, "Without Rights?" (in this volume, 16–17).

56 See for example D. 44.7.14 (Ulp. 7 disp.). For numerous other sources see Kaser, *Das römische Privatrecht*, vol. 1 (n. 11): 480–81; Reinhard Zimmermann, *The Law of Obligations. Roman Foundations of the Civilian Tradition* (Oxford: Oxford University Press, 1996): 7–10; Phillip Louis Landolt, *'Naturalis Obligatio' and Bare Social Duty* (Vienna/Cologne/Weimar: Böhlau, 2000); Götz Schulze, *Die Naturalobligation: Rechtsfigur und Instrument des Rechtsverkehrs einst und heute – zugleich Grundlegung einer Forderungslehre im Zivilrecht* (Tübingen: Mohr Siebeck, 2008): 49–82.

57 Cf. Kaser, *Das römische Privatrecht*, vol. 1 (n. 11): 481; Buckland, *Law of Slavery* (n. 9): 693–701.

58 For German law see for example § 214 para 2 BGB (even a claim that is now statute-barred may be validly discharged); § 516 para 1 and § 518 (even an informal promise to make a gift creates a dischargeable obligation).

involving slaves remained unenforceable. Where property claims by and against slaves were concerned, there was an unwillingness to deprive the *dominus* of his chance of controlling them. However, where a slave's interest in his liberty was at stake, the *cognitio extraordinaria* could in certain cases be an option. This follows from the above-mentioned right of slaves to sue an heir for the liberty bequeathed to them,[59] and from the same right to proceed with their own means against a buyer in breach of a covenant to manumit.[60]

This option was not available in cases where a third party had a claim against a slave. Nor did the *peculium*, the special property granted slaves by their masters which they could use independently according to their tasks, establish a servile legal capacity, whether active or passive. The *peculium* was instead – rather like the *naturalis obligatio* – an institutionalised compromise:[61] the circumstances in which masters employed their slaves sometimes required that a slave decided independently on the acquisition and disposal of goods. Ancient custom dictated, however, that because slaves themselves were the property of their *dominus*, they were unable to have either ownership or possession. By means of the *peculium*, a master granted his slaves at least the right to dispose of parts of the *peculium* like an owner. In this way, slaves could dispose of and acquire by their own decision. Formally, these transactions were apportioned to the master, but de facto they were 'property of the slave'.[62]

These two examples, *peculium* and *naturalis obligatio*,[63] show how specific legal concepts bridged the grey area between social practice and strict law. Both concepts were institutionalised early on, probably because they were also used for the benefit of other persons *in potestate* – especially children under *patria potestas*.[64] But in contexts that concerned only slaves, classical law often remained ambiguous: respecting certain servile relationships or transactions but without legally undergirding them. However, a slave's legal claims to their *peculium* or against third parties could become fully valid if the slave was later freed and the *peculium* was left to them (which was common). This applied at all levels: family and inheritance law, debt and property law, and in litigation. If a slave was manumitted together with his *peculium*, he became the master of the slaves he had previously controlled as his *servi vicarii*.[65] The

59 See above p. 10.
60 See below p. 266.
61 See in more detail Richard Gamauf, "Peculium" (in this volume).
62 So Ulrike Roth, "Food, Status, and the Peculium of Agricultural Slaves," *Journal of Roman Archaeology* 18 (2005): 278–92, 278.
63 Buckland, *Law of Slavery* (n. 9): 683: 'The recognition (i.e. of naturalis obligatio) is doubtless connected with that of debts to and from the peculium.'
64 For a discussion of the concept of *naturalis obligatio* see Buckland, *Law of Slavery* (n. 9): 683–84.
65 Cf. D. 33.8.6.2 (Ulp. 25 ad Sab.); D. 33.8.15 (Alf. Var. 2 dig. a Paulo epit.); D. 33.8.25 (Cels. 19 dig.); for a different case (joint ownership) in the case of competing orders, cf. D. 33.8.21 (Scaev. 8 quaest.) and D. 33.8.22.1 (Labeo 2 post. a Iav. epit.). On the rights of slave *vicarii* see esp. Heinrich Erman, *Servus vicarius. L'esclave de l'esclave romain. Extrait du Recueil publié par la Faculté de*

claims between him and his master were now settled as if the recent freedman had always been free.[66] Any property inherited by or bequeathed to the slave now actually belonged to the freedman.[67] The fungibility of legal personality went so far that while the case was pending, a slave litigating a manumission case was treated as a free person in their legal relations with third parties.[68] Some of these rules seem strange from today's perspective. We shall take a closer look at some of them.

b) The legal grey area inhabited by Roman slaves touched, for example, on their relationships with their own blood relatives (*cognati*). If the laws were applied strictly, slaves were not related to anyone at all, not even their own parents or their own children. This, Patterson has argued, was an expression of their social isolation.[69] But during the empire, if not already earlier, this isolation decreased considerably. Masters accepted, at times even encouraged, their slaves' marital unions, if for no other reason than the fact that home-born offspring (*vernae*) saved them the purchase cost of buying in slaves.[70] We should not discount the possibility that this was connected to the dwindling slave supply from prisoners of war under the empire.[71] In any case, the extant inscriptions from the imperial era show numerous family ties among slaves.[72] Columella even recommends that the *vilicus* – the estate manager, generally a slave – has a wife to support him.[73]

Droit de l'Université de Lausanne, à l'occassion de l'Exposition national suisse, Genève, 1896 (Lausanne: F. Rouge, 1896 ; repr. Naples: Jovene, 1986): 391–532.

66 There are numerous references in D. 15.1 (De peculio), e.g. D. 15.1.7.4–7 (Ulp. 29 ad ed.); D. 15.1.17 (Ulp. 29 ad ed.), but also D. 33.8.16 pr.–1 (Afr. 5 quaest.).

67 E.g. D. 15.1.3.1 (Ulp. 29 ad ed.); Gai. inst. 2.189; D. 28.5.6.2 (Ulp. 4 ad Sab.); on these and other texts see Wolfram Buchwitz, *Servus alienus heres. Die Erbeinsetzung fremder Sklaven im klassischen römischen Recht* (Vienna/Cologne/Weimar: Böhlau, 2013): 674–78.

68 Cf. D. 40.12.24 (Paul. 51 ad ed.).

69 See in general Patterson, *Slavery and Social Death* (n. 7): 38–45; with less emphasis 189.

70 The seminal works are Elisabeth Herrmann-Otto, *Ex ancilla natus. Untersuchungen zu den 'hausgeborenen' Sklaven und Sklavinnen im Westen des römischen Kaiserreiches* (Stuttgart: Franz Steiner Verlag, 1994): esp. 231–398; Henrik Mouritsen, "The Families of Roman Slaves and Freedmen," in *A Companion to Families in the Greek and Roman Worlds*, ed. Beryl Rawson (Chichester/Malden, MA: Wiley-Blackwell, 2011): 129–44, esp. 133–37.

71 See Elemér Pólay, *Die Sklavenehe und das römische Recht*, Acta Juridica et Politica. Universitatis Szegediensis 14/7 (Szeged: Universitätsverlag der Universität Szeged, 1967): 46–47; see also Herrmann-Otto, *Ex ancilla* (n. 70): 250–68.

72 See for example Marleen B. Flory, "Family in familia: Kinship and Community in Slavery," *American Journal of Ancient History* 3 (1978): 78–95; Susan Treggiari, "Contubernales in CIL 6," *Phoenix* 35 (1981): 42–69.

73 Colum. 1.8.5: *Sed qualicumque villico contubernalis mulier assignanda est, quae contineat eum, et in quibusdam rebus tamen adiuvet* ('But be the overseer what he may, he should be given a woman companion to keep him within bounds and yet in certain matters to be a help to him'; transl. Harrison

Slaves could not enter into a valid marriage (*matrimunium iustum*) under Roman law;[74] their children were not considered legitimate, and male slaves were not entitled to exercise *patria potestas*. A quasi-marital union between slaves or between a male slave and a freedwoman, if it had been approved by the master, was called *contubernium*. The standardised designation reveals the institutionalisation of such unions.[75] They were not only social facts, but also produced legal consequences, about which we only hear in individual cases. There was no general 'law' of *contubernium*. The cases discussed here do not explicitly refer to *contubernia*. Even so, these individual cases strengthen the impression that – as Helmholz put it – 'law did not altogether match the facts'.[76]

We must assume that the setting up of servile families always required the consent of the slaves' master or masters; as such, the legal consequences are to be explained by the *consensus domini*.[77] This can be seen above all from the testamentary dispositions which provide information about the fate of servile marriages and families. Two wills recounted by Scaevola are revealing:

D. 32.41.2 (Scaev. 22 dig.): [. . .] 'omnibus autem libertis meis et quos vivus et quos his codicillis manumissi vel postea manumisero, contubernales suas, item filios filias lego, nisi si quos quasve ad uxorem meam testamento pertinere volui vel ei nominatim legavi legavero.' [. . .]	D. 32.41.2 (Scaevola, Digest, book 22): [. . .] "To all my freedmen whom I have manumitted both in my lifetime and in this codicil or shall manumit in future, I bequeath their partners and their sons and daughters, with the exception of such persons of either sex that I have desired in my will to belong to my wife, or have bequeathed or shall bequeath to her by name." [. . .][78]

B. Ash, *Columella. On Agriculture*, vol. 1, Loeb Classical Library [Cambridge, MA: Harvard University Press, 1941]: 87). Similarly Varro rust. 1.17.5; see for example Pólay, *Die Sklavenehe* (n. 71): 14–16.

74 Ulp. reg. 5.5: *cum servis nullum est conubium* ('With slaves there is no right to marry'); *conubium* is the right to conclude a marriage according to civil law. See the brief remarks in Pólay, *Die Sklavenehe* (n. 71): 49–50.

75 See most recently Marcel Simonis, *Cum servis nullum est conubium. Untersuchungen zu den eheähnlichen Verbindungen von Sklaven im westlichen Mittelmeerraum des Römischen Reiches* (Hildesheim: Georg Olms Verlag, 2017); for a survey of the relevant legal texts see Reinhard Willvonseder, *Stellung des Sklaven im Privatrecht*, vol. 1, *Eheähnliche Verbindungen und verwandtschaftliche Beziehungen*, Corpus der römischen Rechtsquellen zur antiken Sklaverei 4 (Stuttgart: Franz Steiner Verlag 2010).

76 Richard H. Helmholz, "The Law of Slavery and the European Ius Commune," in *The Legal Understanding of Slavery – From the Historical to the Contemporary*, ed. Jean Allain (Oxford: Oxford University Press, 2014): 17–39, 29.

77 For this reason, Kaser's statement that *contubernia* were not acknowledged 'vom Recht' is too sweeping, cf. Kaser, *Das römische Privatrecht*, vol. 1 (n. 11): 284.

78 Transl. Braun in Watson, *Digest of Justinian*, vol. 3 (n. 2): 84.

D. 34.1.20 pr. (Scaev. 3 resp.): 'Stichus nutricis meae nepos liber esto: cui decem aureos annuos dari volo.' qui deinde interpositis nominibus eidem Sticho contubernalem eius et liberos legavit hisque, quae vivus praestabat. [. . .]	D. 34.1.20 pr. (Scaevola, Replies, book 3): "Stichus, my nurse's grandson, is to be free, and I wish him to be paid ten aurei per annum"; then, having made other entries, [the testator] has left the same Stichus his wife and children and has left them the things he was accustomed to provide for them in his lifetime. [. . .][79]

In both wills[80] the testators stipulated that the heirs must give to the freedman or freedmen their wives and children (as their slaves). They thus took care to ensure that the servile families would remain together even after the testators' deaths.[81] Such or similar stipulations seem to have been so common that Ulpian wanted to apply them even where a testator had not explicitly expressed them:

D. 33.7.12.7 (Ulp. 20 ad Sab.): Uxores quoque et infantes eorum, qui supra enumerati sunt, credendum est in eadem villa agentes voluisse testatorem legato contineri: neque enim duram separationem iniunxisse credendus est.	D. 33.7.12.7 (Ulpian, Sabinus, book 20): It should also be held that the testator wanted the wives and children too of those enumerated above, if they live in the same villa, to be included in the legacy; for it is not credible that he would have imposed a harsh separation.[82]

What Ulpian has in mind, however, are not legacies in favour of slaves or freedmen but rather legacies of estates and their equipment. Alfenus Varus had stated that human beings could not be accessories, but Ulpian disagreed (D. 33.7.12.2): *constat enim eos, qui agri gratia ibi sunt, instrumento contineri.*[83] If a slave was *instrumentum* (a piece of equipment), he was bequeathed together with the estate. In that case, his wife and children were also part of the bequest. A little later, but in the same text, Ulpian quotes Iuventius Celsus, who was of the opinion that a legacy consisting of an estate included all the slaves who worked there, not just the agricultural labourers. Ulpian repeats:

---

79 Transl. Jameson in Watson, *Digest of Justinian*, vol. 3 (n. 2): 147.

80 On both see Pólay, *Die Sklavenehe* (n. 71): 27–28.

81 Herrmann-Otto, *Ex ancilla* (n. 70): 262, regards the death of a *dominus* as the greatest threat to the continued existence of a slave family.

82 Transl. Seager in Watson, *Digest of Justinian*, vol. 3 (n. 2): 126; on this text Pólay, *Die Sklavenehe* (n. 71): 28.

83 D. 33.7.12.2 (Ulp. 20 ad Sab.): 'Alfenus says, however, that if a man legated some of his slaves to others, the rest, who were on the farm, are not included in the *instrumentum*, because he held that no living creature counts as *instrumentum*. This is not true; for it is agreed that those who are there for the sake of the land are included in the *instrumentum*.' (transl. Seager in Watson, *Digest of Justinian*, vol. 3 [n. 2]: 125).

D. 33.7.12.33 (Ulp. 20 ad Sab.): Contubernales quoque servorum, id est uxores, et natos, instructo fundo contineri verum est.

D. 33.7.12.33 (Ulpian, Sabinus, book 20): It is true that the companions and children of slaves are also included in a fundus *instructus*.[84]

With this interpretation, Celsus and Ulpian made it possible for servile families to continue to live together if they formed part of a larger inheritance. But this solution, with its welcome outcome for the slaves, probably only rarely applied in cases where smaller estates were divided among several heirs or among the legatees.[85] Not until Constantine (C. 3.8.11) was there a rule stipulating that in the division of properties care had to be taken for families of slaves and *coloni* not to be separated. For this reason, is it not clear how far Ulpian's interpretation of the will, which ensured the continued existence of the servile family unit, actually applied. That it goes back to the classical era[86] is confirmed by a parallel thought in the rescinded transaction of a contract of sale due to a defect:

D. 21.1.35 (Ulp. 1 ed. cur. aed.): Plerumque propter morbosa mancipia etiam non morbosa redhibentur, si separari non possint sine magno incommodo vel ad pietatis rationem offensam. quid enim, si filio retento parentes redhibere maluerint vel contra? quod et in fratribus et in personas contubernio sibi coniunctas observari oportet.

D. 21.1.35 (Ulpian, Curule Aediles' Edict, book 1): Healthy slaves are generally returned on account of those who are diseased when they cannot be separated without great inconvenience or affront to family ties. Suppose that I wish to return the parents but keep their son or vice versa. The same is true in respect of brothers and those linked in a servile quasi-matrimonial relationship.[87]

The decision[88] was based on the following facts: someone had bought a slave who had an illness. This entitled the buyer to *actio redhibitoria*, through which they could rescind the contract of sale, i.e. demand that the purchase price be returned to them. In exchange, the buyer had to return the slave: but not just the one slave in cases where, for example, the item purchased had been a slave family of whom only the son was ill. In this and similar cases, Ulpian argues, the claim for restitution covered the entire family. What applied to the bond between parents and their children also applied to siblings and to spouses living together in a *contubernium*. So according to

84 Transl. Seager in Watson, *Digest of Justinian*, vol. 3 (n. 2): 127.

85 This might be why, in comparable inheritance cases, Roman jurists advocated the separation of slave families; for examples see Knoch, *Sklavenfürsorge* (n. 28): 32–33.

86 The dispute about this question in the scholarship of the last century is briefly discussed in Pólay, *Die Sklavenehe* (n. 71): 29.

87 Transl. Thomas in Watson, *Digest of Justinian*, vol. 2 (n. 2): 614.

88 On this and similar decisions in detail Thomas Finkenauer, "Filii naturales: Social Fate or Legal Privilege?" (in this volume): section 4 and Thomas Finkenauer, "Der Schutz der Sklavenfamilie im klassischen römischen Recht," *Revue Internationale des Droits de l'Antiquité* 67/68 (2020/2021): 82–88.

Ulpian, spouses, siblings and families could only be restituted together. In the jurist's logic, however, this presupposed that they had also been bought together. Even so, Ulpian's solution is the best example for the law regarding servile families as units, and for its willingness to preserve these units – at least in certain contexts.

Ulpian's motive, however, remains unclear: on the one hand, 'great inconvenience' was to be prevented by keeping the family together; while any other solution would violate *pietas*. Was Ulpian concerned with protecting the interests of the owner, or those of the family[89]? Some scholars believe the reference to *pietas* to be a later, postclassical addition;[90] and it is true that the phrase starting *vel ad . . .* sounds somewhat like an afterthought. But, as Bodel has pointed out, we should not underestimate the influence of social norms on the behaviour of individual *domini*, especially in the context of marriage and family life.[91]

The reference to *magnum incommodum* is equally puzzling. Applied to the master, it could only mean that Ulpian considered the market value of a family to be higher than that of its individual members. In that case, rigorous economic calculation lay behind the apparently humane solution. But perhaps this is not a contradiction. We might even doubt that altruism and philanthropy can manage at all without economic calculation.[92] Even if the Roman jurists intended to use the protection for servile families only as a means of increasing their motivation to work, the texts bear witness to the gradual 'juridification' of what had initially been a mere social practice in a legal vacuum. Although in such cases the slaves themselves could not bring any claims, their private interests were at least indirectly taken into account.

Where they did discuss servile kinship relations, the Roman jurists always employed the terms customary for Roman families.[93] The prohibitions of marriage that

---

89 On the latter cf. Johanna Filip-Fröschl, "Gefühle und Recht. Gedanken zur rechtlichen Relevanz von Gefühlen, ausgehend von den Bestimmungen zur römischen Sklavenfamilie," in *Vis ac potestas legum. Liber amicorum Zoltán Végh*, ed. Michael Rainer (Frankfurt am Main: Peter Lang Verlag, 2010): 9–33.

90 Discussed in Herrmann-Otto, *Ex ancilla* (n. 70): 263–64. n. 74; Pólay, *Die Sklavenehe* (n. 71): 29; Finkenauer, "Filii naturales" (in this volume): section 4.1.

91 John Bodel, "Death and Social Death in Ancient Rome," in *On Human Bondage. After Slavery and Social Death*, ed. John Bodel and Walter Scheidel (Oxford: Wiley-Blackwell, 2016): 87: 'How far moral censure and legal exemptions go toward demonstrating societal recognition of the validity of slave marriages can be debated, but the inhibiting influence of social norms on the behaviour of individual masters toward their slaves should not be underestimated.'

92 See for example David A. Kennett, "Altruism and Economic Behavior, I: Developments in the Theory of Public and Private Redistribution," *The American Journal of Economics and Sociology* 39, no. 2 (1980): 183–98; see also Oded Stark, *Altruism and Beyond. An Economic Analysis of Transfers and Exchanges Within Families and Groups* (Cambridge: Cambridge University Press, 1995).

93 See for example D. 38.10.10.5 (Paul. sing. de gradibus): *Non parcimus his nominibus, id est cognatorum, etiam in servis: itaque parentes et filios fratresque etiam servorum dicimus: sed ad leges serviles cognationes non pertinent* ('We do not refrain from using these names, that is, the names of

applied to free Romans were equally applied to freedpersons, thus taking into account the natural kinship ties they had formed as slaves.[94] These are pragmatic rather than fundamental solutions, which can at best be interpreted as preliminary stages for the juridification of the personal circumstances of slaves.

c) A different matter are business transactions between slaves in which they acted in their own interests rather than in their masters' interests. In one of his letters, the younger Pliny describes his practice of allowing his slaves to buy and trade with each other and to make provisions for each other in their wills.

Plin. epist. 8.16: Solacia duo nequaquam paria tanto dolori, solacia tamen: unum facilitas manumittendi – videor enim non omnino immaturos perdidisse, quos iam liberos perdidi –, alterum quod permitto servis quoque quasi testamenta facere, eaque ut legitima custodio. [2] Mandant rogantque quod visum; pareo ut iussus. Dividunt donant relinquunt, dumtaxat intra domum; nam servis res publica quaedam et quasi civitas domus est.	Plin. letters. 8.16: Two facts console me somewhat, though inadequately in trouble like this: I am always ready to grant my slave their freedom, so I don't feel their death is so untimely when they die free men, and I allow even those who remain slaves to make a sort of will which I treat as legally binding. (2) They set out their instructions and requests as they think fit, and I carry them out as if acting under orders. They can distribute their possessions and make any gifts and bequests they like, within the limits of the household: for the house provides a slave with a country and sort of citizenship.[95]

Pliny describes a social practice that did not create any legal ties at all. He respected the contracts and wills of his slaves because for the slaves the household (*domus*) in which they lived was a *quasi civitas*. For the slaves, it represented that which for the

cognate relatives, even in the case of slaves; and so we talk about the parents and sons and brothers of slaves too, but servile relationships do not belong to [the realm of] the laws;' transl. Jameson in Watson, *Digest of Justinian*, vol. 3 [n. 2]: 353).

94 D. 23.2.14.2 (Paul. 22 ad ed.): *Serviles quoque cognationes in hoc iure observandae sunt. igitur suam matrem manumissus non ducet uxorem: tantundem iuris est et in sorore et sororis filia. idem e contrario dicendum est, ut pater filiam non possit ducere, si ex servitute manumissi sint, etsi dubitetur patrem eum esse. unde nec volgo quaesitam filiam pater naturalis potest uxorem ducere, quoniam in contrahendis matrimoniis naturale ius et pudor inspiciendus est: contra pudorem est autem filiam uxorem suam ducere.* ('Blood relationship between slaves must be considered in connection with this rule. So, on manumission a man cannot marry his own mother, and the rule is the same for a sister and a sister's daughter. On the other hand, it must be said that a father cannot marry his daughter, if they have been manumitted, even where it is doubtful whether he is her father. So a natural father cannot marry his daughter who was born out of wedlock, because natural law and decency must be taken into consideration in marriage, and it is indecent to make a daughter into your wife;' transl. McLeod in Watson, *Digest of Justinian*, vol. 2 [n. 2]: 659).

95 Transl. Betty Radice, *Pliny the Younger: Letters*, vol. 2, Loeb Classical Libary (Cambridge, MA: Harvard University Press, 1969): 47–48.

citizens was the state that ensured their peaceful coexistence. Who, if not the master of the house, could set the necessary legal framework? His reasoning therefore testifies not only to Pliny's philanthropy but also to his awareness that his slaves – at least as far as this type of interactions was concerned – were wholly at his mercy.

But there is a second side to this story: what should the slaves have wanted to bequeath to one another if all they had to dispose of was a *peculium* (and even this was true only for a selected few of them)? This *peculium* could not have been included among the *quasi testamenta* because the decision of who the *peculium* was to go to after the slave's death was made not by the slave but the master.[96] A master wanted the *peculium* to be in the hands of a slave who he could expect to increase his wealth. We must therefore assume that the slaves had their own belongings, perhaps jewellery, crockery or tools that belonged to them personally. The existence of such personal possessions, most of which were probably modest, is made plausible by a text of the jurist Paulus:

D. 40.12.32 (Paul. 6 reg.): De bonis eorum, qui ex servitute aut libertate in ingenuitatem vindicati sunt, senatus consultum factum est, quo cavetur de his quidem, qui ex servitute defensi essent, ut id dumtaxat ferrent, quod in domo cuiusque intulissent: in eorum autem bonis, qui post manumissionem repetere originem suam voluissent, hoc amplius, ut, quod post manumissionem quoque adquisissent non ex re manumissoris, secum ferant, cetera bona relinquerent illi, ex cuius familia exissent.

D. 40.12.32 (Paul, Rules, book 6): In regard to the property of those who had made good a claim to be freeborn, when reputed slaves or freedmen, the senate passed a decree which provides in the case of those whose claim had been made when they were in reputed slavery, that they should take only what they had brought into the household concerned; as to the property of those who had wished to reclaim their original status after manumission, it added that they were to take with them what they had also acquired after manumission but not from the assets of the manumitter, and to leave other property to the person whose household they had left.[97]

This text takes us into the complicated world of freedom trials.[98] Such trials concerned slaves or freedmen who litigated over their free birth. Slaves, who were barred from bringing actions, could do so only with the aid of a (free) *adsertor in libertatem*, a fiduciary who brought the trial in their stead.[99] Paul recounts a senate decision according to which the person whose freedom had been established in such a trial could take

96 Woldemar von Uxkull-Gyllenband, "s.v. peculium," in *Paulys Realencyclopädie der classischen Altertumswissenschaft* 19/1, ed. Wilhelm Kroll (Stuttgart: J.B. Metzler, 1937): 13–16, at 16, takes a different position, without providing an explanation.

97 Transl. Brunt in Watson, *Digest of Justinian*, vol. 3 (n. 2): 482.

98 See most recently Miriam Indra, *Status quaestio. Studien zum Freiheitsprozess im klassischen römischen Recht* (Berlin: Duncker & Humblot, 2011); unfortunately she does not reference this text.

99 This is discussed in Buckland, *Law of Slavery* (n. 9): 655–56; Indra, *Status quaestio* (n. 98): 123–63.

with them no more and no less than what they had brought into the household of their last master. Paul therefore seemed to expect slaves to have personal property because the text includes the possibility that the person whose freedom had just been established had come into the household of their last *dominus* as a slave.

Such private property stayed below the radar of Roman legal texts. From a civil law perspective, slaves could own nothing and have no property. Where there is mention of slave property, what the legal texts discuss is always a *peculium*. Might the *senatus consultum* in D. 40.12.32 mean a case where a slave had been acquired together with his *peculium* and then shown to be an *ingenuus* in a freedom trial? This hardly seems likely. The person who had acquired a slave plus *peculium* had bought this *peculium* and so acquired ownership of it. It would be strange if the buyer had then to hand over this *peculium* to the person proven to be free. And there is nothing at all in this 'dark text'[100] about what the (presumed) slave had acquired during their time with their *dominus*.

So, reading Pliny and Paul in parallel, we can assume that slaves had personal assets which they could take with them when they went from one owner to another. These were undoubtedly not riches. But social practice accepted a form of 'having' that was not legally recorded until the slave was freed or could prove in a trial that they had been free all along.

d) A very similar constellation can be inferred from a text by Ulpian in which he mentions a dowry among slaves:

D. 23.3.39 pr. (Ulp. 33 ad ed.): Si serva servo quasi dotem dederit, deinde constante coniunctione ad libertatem ambo pervenerint peculio eis non adempto et in eadem coniunctione permanserint, ita res moderetur, ut, si quae ex rebus corporalibus velut in dotem tempore servitutis datis exstiterint, videantur ea tacite in dotem conversa, ut earum aestimatio mulieri debeatur.

D. 23.3.39 pr. (Ulpian, Edict, book 33): If a female slave gives property as if it were a dowry to a male slave, and afterward while they are still together, they both gain their freedom without their peculium being withdrawn, and their relationship continues, matters are arranged so that if anything remains of the corporeal property which was given as if it were a dowry while they were slaves, it will be held to have been converted into a real dowry, so that a valuation of it will be due to the woman.[101]

A slave woman was unable to provide a regular Roman dowry (*dos*) to her husband for the simple reason that the two could not contract a legal marriage (*matrimonium iustum*).[102] But the example shows the power of social norms: by using her own means the woman was determined to demonstrate how seriously she took the

---

100 Buckland, *Law of Slavery* (n. 9): 666.

101 Transl. McLeod in Watson, *Digest of Justinian*, vol. 2 (n. 2): 675.

102 See the brief discussion in Jakob Fortunat Stagl, *Favor dotis. Die Privilegierung der Mitgift im System des römischen Rechts* (Vienna/Cologne/Weimar: Böhlau, 2009): 11.

commitment to enter into a *contubernium.*[103] So she acted just like proper Romans did in this situation by handing over to her husband a small fortune from which he could pay part of the *onera matrimonii*, the financial burdens of marriage.[104] It should be remembered that even for free Romans there was no legal obligation to provide a husband with a dowry. But it was regarded as a social duty, and as such may have been observed even more strictly than if the husband had had an actual claim to the dowry.

We may consider this text as evidence that – as we have already observed[105] – slaves could have some small personal property, even though legally they could be neither owners nor possessors. We cannot rule out the possibility that even female slaves may have been given *peculia*;[106] perhaps this was the case here. If we do not want to assume either the existence of a *peculium* or of some other small personal funds of the woman in this case, there are two other possible explanations. She may have been given the funds from the *peculium* of one of her fellow slaves. In that case the text would prove that a slave could dispose of their *peculium* at their own discretion and for their own purposes. Or she may have got the funds from a free person. This is unlikely but not impossible. If the woman had been the *filia naturalis* of a free man, i.e. born by a slave woman but fathered by a free man, her father may have provided her with a dowry.

But the appointment of the dowry always remained a symbolic act because the rules established for a husband's use of the *dos* and for the wife's claims for restitution did not apply in this case. This changed if both were manumitted. If the manumission occurred *constante coniunctione*, i.e. while the quasi-marital union still existed, the funds that had been given over to the husband were considered to have turned tacitly into a regular dowry (*tacite in dotem conversa*). In the event of divorce, the husband was then liable for restitution of the *dos* or – as the text suggests – for restitution of its estimated value. However, this presupposes that the husband had also been given the *peculium* assigned to him by his former *dominus*. Only in that case would the assets at the husband's disposal as a free man be considered identical to those given to him as a slave. Liability followed property, only

---

103 Note D. 23.3.1 (Paul. 14 ad Sab.): *Dotis causa perpetua est, et cum voto eius qui dat ita contrahitur, ut semper apud maritum sit.* ('The right to a dowry is perpetual, and in accordance with the wishes of the person who provides it, an agreement is made to the effect that it will always remain in the husband's possession.', transl. McLeod in Watson, *Digest of Justinian*, vol. 2 [n. 2]: 668).

104 Cf. D. 23.3.56.1 (Paul. 6 ad Plaut.); D. 23.3.76 (Tryph. 9 disp.); on this and other indications see Stagl, *Favor dotis* (n. 102): 22–25; auch Percy E. Corbett, *The Roman Law of Marriage* (Oxford: Clarendon Press, 1969): 147.

105 See above 256–58.

106 Such as in D. 15.1.27 pr. (Gai. 9 ed prov.); certainly Pólay, *Die Sklavenehe* (n. 71): 38, assumes that slave women had *peculia*.

the identity of the liable person changed: had her husband remained a slave, the wife – if she had been manumitted – could have reclaimed her funds from his *dominus*.[107] The same would probably apply if the husband had been freed, but his *peculium* been retained by his master.

But this text is more than proof that liability followed property. Firstly, the debtor's identity was decisive: what someone had done as a slave was later, after he had been freed, apportioned to him as though he had always been free. This is indicated by the legal consequence which Ulpian granted the wife, but which needs an explanation: she could demand an *aestimatio* after the end of the marriage. This statement is ambiguous. Either Ulpian merely meant that the husband was liable for the value of the *dos* in case he should culpably be unable to restitute it. But it is also possible that the dowry had been given as a *dos aestimata* from the start.[108] In this case the husband's liability was only for the restitution of the value at which it had been estimated at the time. In this form, it would have strengthened the wife's claim for restitution. The husband was not liable because he still possessed the dowry, but because he had previously received it. Ulpian's reference to the *peculium* only had the purpose of securing the wife's claim. If the *dominus* had retained it, the husband's obligation to repay would have been apportioned to him – just as if there had been no manumission.

First and foremost, then, liability followed the person who incurred it. This had originally been the slave husband himself. His manumission 'cured' the fact that he could not legally be held liable. He was the same person who is now being held liable for acts he had performed then. This was self-evident for tortious acts committed by a slave. If a slave had caused damage to a third party, they continued to be liable after manumission: *noxa caput sequitur*.[109] Similarly, anyone who had caused damage to a third party while being free was still liable as a slave.[110] What applied to tort liability also applied to claims and obligations a slave had incurred before their release. Ulpian stated:

---

107 Cf. D. 24.2.23.13 (Ulp. 33 ad ed.); Otto Lenel, *Palingenesia iuris civilis*, vol. 2 (Leipzig: Bernhard Tauchnitz, 1889, repr. Aalen: Scientia Verlag, 2000): 644, assumes that this text in Ulpian's commentary was directly related to our passage. He therefore lists both texts (together with D. 26.7.11) as Ulpian no 956.

108 See for example Kaser, *Das römische Privatrecht*, vol. 1 (n. 11): 340; Stagl, *Favor dotis* (n. 102): 51–254.

109 Buckland, *Law of Slavery* (n. 9): 106–30; see also Adriaan Johan Boudewijn Sirks, "Noxa caput sequitur," *Tijdschrift voor Rechtsgeschiedenis* 81, no. 1–2 (2013): 81–108.

110 CF. the illustrative passage in Gai. inst. 4.77: *Omnes autem noxales actiones capita sequuntur.* ('All noxal actions attach to the delinquint.', transl. William M. Gordon and Olivia F. Robinson, *The Institutes of Gaius* [London: Duckworth, 1988]: 465).

D. 44.7.14 (Ulp. 7 disp.): Servi ex delictis quidem obligantur et, si manumittantur, obligati remanent: ex contractibus autem civiliter quidem non obligantur, sed naturaliter et obligantur et obligant. denique si servo, qui mihi mutuam pecuniam dederat, manumisso solvam, liberor.

D. 44.7.14 (Ulpian, Disputations, book 7): Indeed, slaves are liable in delict, and remain liable, if they are manumitted; however, they are not civilly liable for their contracts, but are both bound and bind others naturally. Furthermore, if I pay a manumitted slave who gave me money on loan, I am released.[111]

This text also explains why in D. 23.3.39 pr. the freedman was liable to his wife for repayment of the dowry. The last sentence seems to go even further: a person who borrowed money from a slave and paid it back after manumission was released from their obligation. We are told nothing about whether the slave had a *peculium*, and if so, if he had been given it upon manumission. But that is not what matters here. The sentence does not protect the slave but the debtor, who may not have known that his creditor had in the meantime been freed.

e) The phenomenon known to the classical sources as *emptio suis nummis*, 'purchase from [the slave's] own money',[112] is probably also closely related to *peculium*. Numerous legal texts attest to cases in which slaves bought their freedom from their masters. Often a free person was involved who bought the slave from their *dominus* and then manumitted them.[113] The money required was provided by the slave themselves. It usually came from the slave's *peculium* but could also be procured from a fourth party[114] or through the slave's own labour for the purchaser.[115] The initial case was presumably the purchase with proceeds from the *peculium*. Related agreements were those between slaves and masters in which the master promised freedom once the slave had generated a certain sum in profit.[116] We also know of numerous cases in which a master in his will ordered the manumission of a slave after the latter had paid a certain amount to the heir.[117] All of these cases offered to

111 Transl. Beinart in Watson, *Digest of Justinian*, vol. 4 (n. 2): 643; see the discussion, with further references, Buckland, *Law of Slavery* (n. 9): 677.

112 See recently Susanne Heinemeyer, *Der Freikauf des Sklaven mit eigenem Geld – Redemptio suis nummis* (Berlin: Duncker & Humblot, 2013); Rolf Knütel, "Freikauf mit eigenem Geld," in *Handwörterbuch der antiken Sklaverei*, ed. Heinz Heinen et al. (Stuttgart: Franz Steiner Verlag, 2012): 1095–97; Thomas Finkenauer, "Anmerkungen zur redemptio servi suis nummis," in *Festschrift für Rolf Knütel zum 70. Geburtstag*, ed. Holger Altmeppen, Ingo Reichard and Martin Josef Schermaier (Heidelberg: C.F. Müller, 2009): 345–57; Buckland, *Law of Slavery* (n. 9): 636–40.

113 See for example D. 5.1.67 (Ulp. 6 disp.); D. 40.1.4 (Ulp. 6 disp.).

114 Cf. D. 40.1.4.1 (Ulp. 6 disp.).

115 Cf. D. 40.1.4.10 (Ulp. 6 disp.).

116 See for example D. 4.3.7.8 (Ulp. 11 ad ed.); D. 15.1.11.1 (Ulp. 29 ad ed.); D. 40.1.6 (Alf. 4 dig.); D. 45.1.104 (Iav. 11 ex Cass.).

117 See for example D. 12.4.3.7 (Ulp. 26 ad ed.); D. 12.6.53 (Proc. 7 epist.); D. 40.7.3.7 (Ulp. 27 ad Sab.); D. 40.7.14 pr. (Alf. 4 dig.); D. 40.7.20.2 (Paul. 16 ad Plaut.).

the slaves an incentive to work to increase their *peculium* and thereby gain their freedom. However, they differ in their legal construction.

Let us concentrate on those cases that involved agreements made with the slaves, such as the 'purchase from [the slave's] own money'.[118] Such agreements shared the unattractive characteristic that they were – provisionally, at least – non-binding under civil law. The same applied – again, provisionally[119] – for the instruction given by a slave to a free third party to purchase the slave's freedom: *cum servus extero se mandat emendum, nullum mandatum est.*[120] So if the slave gave the third party money from his *peculium* to purchase his freedom, the third party was not thereby obliged to actually buy the slave. If the purchase did go ahead, the slave was then unable to force the purchaser to set him free. If the buyer failed to manumit the slave as agreed, only the seller could demand that the buyer do so.[121] For this reason, the seller was granted a counteraction on the slave's mandate to the third party that they buy and release him. This was explained by the fact that the seller had consented to the slave's mandate to purchase the slave's freedom. After all, the seller had agreed to receive money from the slave's *peculium* as purchase price; in other words, to be paid with his, the seller's, own money. But the original mandate given by the slave only worked in favour of the seller not of the purchaser: the latter could now not assert the counteraction (*actio mandati contraria*) against the seller.[122] This prevented the buyer from recovering the purchase price from the seller after the slave had been freed. The mandate to purchase given by the slave was only effective in terms of achieving the objective pursued – i.e. manumission of the slave. However, only the purchaser could bring the corresponding action against the seller not the slave.

This somewhat strange construction well demonstrates that – insofar as the slave's manumission was concerned – the legal corset was not as tightly cut as some historians have assumed. From the legal constructions surrounding the 'purchase from [the slave's] own money' it has been concluded that slaves had been 'faktisch ein Stück Rechtsfähigkeit zugebilligt'.[123] Finkenauer qualified this by

118 Cf. for example D. 33.8.8.5 (Ulp. 25 ad Sab.): [. . .] *si servus com domino de libertate pactus fuerit* [. . .] ('[. . .] if a slave has made an agreement with his owner concerning his freedom [. . .]'; transl. Seager in Watson, *Digest of Justinian*, vol. 3 [n. 2]: 134).

119 An example for the discharging of an obligation entered into by a slave after manumission is D. 45.1.104 (Iav. 11 ex Cass.).

120 D. 17.1.54 pr. (Pap. 27 quaest.): 'When a slave gives a mandate to a third party to buy him, the mandate is of no effect.' (transl. Gordon and Robinson in Watson, *Digest of Justinian*, vol. 2 [n. 2]: 495).

121 This is expressly stated in D. 17.1.54 pr.; cf. Heinemeyer, *Freikauf* (n. 112): 241–54; Rolf Knütel, "Das Mandat zum Freikauf," in *Mandatum und Verwandtes. Beiträge zum römischen und modernen Recht*, ed. Dieter Nörr and Shigeo Nishimura (Berlin/Heidelberg: Springer Verlag, 1993): 353–74, 368–71.

122 See D. 17.1.54 pr., as well as D. 17.1.19 (Ulp. 43 ad Sab.).

123 Knütel, "Mandat" (n. 121): 353; similarly Knütel, *Freikauf* (n. 112): 1096.

arguing that mandates for manumission were hardly ever concluded without the *dominus*' consent,[124] positing that in his view, behind this consent usually lay the master's special interest in the slave being freed without imposition on him of the usual duties of a *libertus*. This could be achieved by the slave being manumitted by a buyer who had not had to make a financial sacrifice of his own to acquire the slave.[125] Finkenauer assumes that this was especially the case with the manumission of *filii naturales*, children fathered by the master with one of his slave women.[126]

Finkenauer's argument is plausible. It is hardly imaginable a slave would have been permitted to conclude, without the consent of the *dominus*, a *mandatum* with a buyer that was at least partially effective. But neither should we overstate this consent. Because viewed from the point of view of the slave's previous master, the latter would consent to a mandate intended for the purchase of his own thing (i.e. his slave). Such a mandate, however, was generally not valid.[127] This is why it was essential for the slave to take the initiative to buy their freedom and commission a third party[128] rather than the *dominus* himself – even if, based on the mandate, the *dominus* was granted the right to demand from the third party that they free the slave.

The strange construction of a mandate issued by a slave, which was effective only in favour of the slave's earlier master, is fascinating to legal historians. Non-jurists are likely be surprised, however, above all about the fact that the previous owner was willing to accept a purchase price that had already belonged to him. But in this respect the law, as Ulpian put it, 'closed both eyes':

D. 40.1.4.1 (Ulp. 6 disp.): Et primo quidem nummis suis non proprie videtur emptus dici, cum suos nummos servus habere non possit: verum coniventibus oculis credendum est suis nummis eum redemptum, cum non nummis eius, qui eum redemit, comparatur. proinde sive ex peculio, quod ad venditorem pertinet, sive ex adventicio lucro, sive etiam amici beneficio vel liberalitate vel prorogante eo vel repromittente vel se delegante vel in se recipiente debitum redemptus sit, credendum est

D. 40.1.4.1 (Ulpian, Disputations, book 6): Now at first sight the expression "purchased with his own cash" seems improper, since a slave cannot have cash of his own; but we are to close our eyes and suppose him to have been bought with his own cash, when it is not the cash of the purchaser which is used to pay the price. So then whether he has been purchased with his peculium, which belongs by right to the vendor, or from profit obtained by chance, or by the kindness or generosity of a

124 Finkenauer, "Anmerkungen zur redemptio" (n. 112): esp. 351–55.

125 See Finkenauer, "Anmerkungen zur redemptio" (n. 112): 349–51; Wolfgang Waldstein, *Operae libertorum. Untersuchungen zur Dienstpflicht freigelassener Sklaven* (Stuttgart: Franz Steiner Verlag, 1986): 201–4.

126 Finkenauer, "Anmerkungen zur redemptio" (n. 112): 353–54; see also his paper in this volume.

127 D. 17.1.19 (Ulp. 43 ad Sab.) in fine; cf. also Finkenauer, "Anmerkungen zur redemptio" (n. 112): 348; Knütel, "Mandat" (n. 121): 363–68.

128 Even such a mandate considered in isolation would have been ineffective, cf. D. 17.1.54 pr. (Pap. 27 quaest.).

suis nummis eum redemptum: satis est enim, quod is, qui emptioni suum nomen accommodaverit, nihil de suo impendit.	friend, or by the slave's carrying a charge to his own account, or giving an undertaking, or accepting a liability or the obligation to pay a debt, we are to suppose that he was purchased with his own cash; it is enough that the nominal purchaser laid out no money of his own.[129]

A slave was unable to have his own money. So, when he ransomed himself (with the help of a third party), he could only pay with the money in his *peculium:* but the *peculium* belonged to his master in any case (*ad venditorem pertinet*). Strictly speaking, then, the slave paid his purchase price with the seller's – his master's – money. How, then, can there be talk of a slave buying his freedom 'with his own money'? According to Ulpian, this could only be imagined *coniventibus oculis*, i.e. by (a jurist) turning two blind eyes (literally, by squeezing both eyes shut).

These examples show that for Ulpian, the purchase price belonged to the slave – in economic, if not in legal terms. He included *adventicium lucrum*, profit accruing to the slave or that which he obtained through the generosity of friends who provided or vouched for him. These examples are unusual because at least *lucrum adventicium* (profit accruing to the slave) would automatically have become part of the *peculium*; we might think of inheritances or legacies bestowed on a slave by third parties.[130] Only if the purchase price were paid by a third party – such as a friend or benefactor – would it bypass the *peculium* and so could be apportioned directly to the slave. Ulpian could compare both cases side by side because it was important to him that the third party who had been commissioned to purchase and manumit would not have to expend any of their own funds (*satis est enim, quod is, qui emptioni suum nomen accommodaverit, nihil de suo impendit*). Seen from the perspective of the seller – i.e. the slave's former master – both cases were in fact the same: regardless of whether the contribution by a third party was to be considered part of the slave's *peculium*, it had not been generated *from* the *peculium*, but had been given to the slave for his own benefit. So, in economic terms it was indeed the slave's 'own money': the sum he had been given to purchase his freedom belonged to the slave – not legally, but de facto.[131]

But even where a slave took the purchase price from his *peculium*, it can be understood as his money, i.e. the money he generated. This was all the more true in cases where the *dominus* consented to the operation and gave the *peculium* to the freedman to secure his existence.[132] Viewed in retrospect, the freedman really had paid the purchase price from the assets he now owned. A *dominus* would only grant a *peculium* to those slaves to whom he held out the prospect of manumission, and

129 Transl. Brunt in Watson, *Digest of Justinian*, vol. 3 (n. 2): 421.

130 See in more detail Wolfram Buchwitz, "Giving and Taking" (in this volume).

131 As Uxkull-Gyllenband aptly put it, see, "peculium" (n. 96): 16.

132 Cf. frg. Vat. 261, but probably also D. 33.8.8.5 (Ulp. 25 ad Sab.).

whom he therefore wanted to encourage to particular industriousness in order to increase their *peculium*.[133] In economic terms it was immaterial whether *dominus* and slave had agreed that the slave would pay the ransom from the profits he had generated, or whether he would hand them to a third party who would ransom him with them. In both cases the *dominus* would keep the profits and free the slave. If he had already given the capital over to the slave (minus the profits), in the *dominus*' calculations the *peculium* had stopped being part of his own assets from the time he had handed it over to the slave.[134] Whether he had lost it from a legal point of view depended on the slave's degree of success: if he was successful, the profits would go to the *dominus* in the shape of the purchase price; otherwise his master was left with ownership of the slave and the remainder of the *peculium*.

So, we see that the 'purchase' of a slave with their own money was usually made from the profits generated by the slave. From the master's point of view, these profits were extraneous, even if they had been generated with his own assets. It is therefore not surprising that some jurists referred to the *peculium* as the slave's (*quasi*) *patrimonium*.[135] Ulpian only had to turn two blind eyes where the legal classification of the money as the slave's 'own' was concerned. It had been regularly earned by the slave, originating from their own labour, and thus was indeed, in economic terms, their 'own money'. Ulpian articulates the contradiction between the legal and the economic attribution, and indicates that it was the latter that mattered in the cases of slaves ransoming themselves with their own money.[136] But neither he nor any other jurist goes so far as to change the *peculium*'s legal attribution. Because it was not only the rules of the acquisition of possession and ownership that rested on it, but above all the reason why a *dominus* was liable for his slave's transactions up to the amount of the *peculium*.

From our modern perspective, a slave buying his freedom with his own money is a peculiar legal construct. But it testifies like almost no other Roman legal concept to its origin in the *peculium*'s social and economic function: it was a 'special asset' assigned to a slave not legally but economically.[137] Anything they generated with it was apportioned to them even if it did not belong to them.

---

133 It is against this background that the Parable of the Talents should be understood (Vulg. Mt. 25.14–30 and Vulg. Luc. 19.12–27).

134 This is the reason for separate accounting, cf. Richard Gamauf, "s.v. peculium," in *Handwörterbuch der antiken Sklaverei*, ed. Heinz Heinen et al. (Stuttgart: Franz Steiner Verlag, 2012) and above (in this volume).

135 See for example D. 15.1.47.6 (Paul. 4 ad Plaut.); D. 15.1.32 pr. (Ulp. 2 disp.); cf. also Isid. etym. 5.25.5; CIL IX 4112; on this topic see in brief Gamauf, "peculium" (n. 134).

136 See already Okko Behrends, "Prinzipat und Sklavenrecht. Zu den geistigen Grundlagen der augusteischen Verfassungsschöpfung," in *Rechtswissenschaft und Rechtsentwicklung*, ed. Ulrich Immenga (Göttingen: Schwartz, 1980): 60.

137 See Roth, "Food" (n. 62): 278–92; and in more detail Richard Gamauf, in this volume.

In addition to this 'de facto' entitlement of a slave to the profits they had generated, mention should also be made of a slave's specific procedural entitlement in connection with self-ransoming. This is what Behrends and Knütel mean when they refer to a slave's 'Teilrechtsfähigkeit'[138] or 'relativen Rechtsfähigkeit' (i.e. a 'partial' or 'relative' legal capacity).[139] It is true that it was possible for a *dominus* to force the buyer to manumit the slave (by way of bringing an action founded on the mandate),[140] but slaves themselves had not originally been entitled to such a claim. The emperors Marcus Aurelius and Lucius Verus, however, instructed Urbius Maximus, presumably the urban prefect of Rome,[141] to grant slaves themselves an action against the buyer if, contrary to the agreement, they had not been freed.[142] The emperors' instruction could only refer to the legal proceedings controlled by imperial officials known as *cognitio extraordinaria*, in which there was no legal hurdle to admitting a slave to a lawsuit.[143]

Even so, the granting of a specific action is remarkable: manumission thereby was qualified as a slave's own interest in need of protection. Unlike in cases of testamentary manumission – which could also be brought before the *extraordinaria cognitio* by slaves themselves (and heard by the *praetor fideicommissarius*)[144] – in cases of a mandate for manumission there was at least the former owner who could demand the slave's freeing not by bringing an *actio mandati* but also an *actio empti*. But the *divi fratres* wanted to enable slaves to enforce manumission themselves, without having to be dependent on their former *dominus* or his heirs. The similarity of interests to the fideicommissum for manumission is likely to have favoured this decision: just as was the case with the fideicommissum, the former *dominus* charged the buyer with freeing the slave they had bought.

4 Conclusion

The master would release the slave once the latter had generated a specified amount. It was a simple, mutually beneficial calculation. His investment had brought profit to the master; by manumitting the slave he avoided future risks that might arise from

138 Cf. Knütel, "Freikauf" (n. 112): 1096; Behrends, "Prinzipat" (n. 136): 58.
139 Behrends, "Prinzipat" (n. 136): 58.
140 Cf. again D. 17.1.54 pr. (n. 120 and 121).
141 This is argued by Finkenauer in "Anmerkungen zur redemptio" (n. 112): 346, with reference to Lothar von Seuffert, "Der Loskauf von Sklaven mit ihrem Geld," in *Festschrift für die Juristische Fakultät in Gießen zum Universitäts-Jubiläum*, ed. Reinhard Frank (Gießen: De Gruyter, 1907): 1–20, 3–4.
142 Cf. D. 40.1.4 pr. (Ulp. 6 disp.); D. 5.1.67 (Ulp. 6 disp.).
143 Cf. above p. 249 sq.
144 See in brief Schermaier, "Without rights?" (in this volume, n. 60).

ownership of the slave. The slave experienced social advancement and, if he had been given the *peculium*, now had a basis for his own economic subsistence. The fact that this plausible practice was not given an elegant legal framework, but only legally tolerated by 'turning blind eyes', arouses mistrust in the efficiency of Roman law. But what we can observe here, in the case of slaves purchasing freedom with their own money, applies just as much to other social circumstances: the institutions and persons involved in the system of formulary procedure unswervingly adhered to traditional rules, resorting to exceptions, fictions or makeshift constructions where this was required by new conflicts. Not until the empire and the advent of the *extraordinaria cognitio* did entirely new ways of conflict resolution open up. There are countless examples for this 'conservatism' of the classical era. They include the unconditional upholding of the categorical distinction between free and slave,[145] and the principle that any person under the authority of another (*persona alieni iuris*) was a propertyless person.[146]

The *peculium* was one of the institutions particularly well suited to bridge this gap between Roman institutional traditionalism and the requirements of a diversified economy.[147] Although the *peculium* belonged to the *dominus*, who alone as the person in authority was able to be owner and proprietor, it enabled slaves (and sons *in potestate*) to make their own economic dispositions, which legally were treated as if they had been transacted by the *dominus*. Formally, slaves remained without property: de facto they were regarded as proprietors.

Modern scholars of slavery are well aware of this difference.[148] But they tend to focus on the formal, strictly legal side: 'The fundamental feature of slavery, in law, was the fact that the slave could not be a proprietor: he or she was, quintessentially, a property-less person'.[149] Such general sentences ignore the fact that, in special cases, the Roman jurists provided slaves with legal remedies to secure their social and proprietary position. It is true that such special cases always depended on the consent of the *dominus*. But once he had given his consent – if, for example, he had permitted manumission or provided for it in his will – the slave could force it to be put into practice.

When Honoré, incidentally with good reason, describes the legal position of slaves by saying that, as slaves, our lives could be 'disrupted without our consent

145 See above p. 251–56.

146 Cf. Gai. inst. 1.48: *nam quaedam personae sui iuris sunt, quaedam alieno iuri sunt subiectae* ('Some people are independent and some are subject to others.', transl. Gordon and Robinson, *The Institutes of Gaius* [n. 110]: 45).

147 See already for a similar argument Alfons Bürge, "Lo schiavo (in)dipendente e il suo patrimonio," in *Homo, caput, persona: La construzione giuridica dell'identità nell'esperienza romana; dall'epoca di Plauto a Ulpiano*, ed. Alessandro Corbino, Michel Humbert and Giovanni Negri (Pavia: IUSS Press, 2010): 386–90.

148 Cf. just Patterson, *Slavery and Social Death* (n. 7): 182–86.

149 Patterson, *Slavery and Social Death* (n. 7): 182.

by the decision of an individual in whose power we find ourselves',[150] we need to qualify this description with respect to Roman law: once given to a slave, the master's word was legally binding. This put slaves on an equal footing with their masters – not only in economic but also in legal terms. However, this qualification cannot be generalised: the legal safeguarding of some servile social conditions did not develop until the second century. We cannot claim it for Roman antiquity as a whole. Moreover, only a few slaves benefited from this evolution, almost always those who played an important role in their master's household and finances. So, the legal sources do not draw a representative picture of the social and legal position of Roman slaves, because it is most often those privileged slaves we find in their pages.

There can be a number of reasons to explain the fact that Roman law of the classical era gradually began to address servile social conditions. One is the sympathetic stance towards the enslaved under the Antonine dynasty, which may – especially under Marcus Aurelius – have philosophical motives. We should also not discount economic reasons: in an economy with a strong division of labour but no differentiated (free) labour market, slaves by necessity had to occupy positions that required them to make independent decisions and in that sense to act autonomously.[151] We must also bear in mind the fact that the number of slaves in Rome declined from the second century onwards; this must have had deflationary effects which increased the value of slaves not only in material terms. It can finally be argued that the legal protection of servile social conditions stabilised the system of slavery: it increased the incentive for slaves to work to the best of their ability for the benefit of their masters. If we return to our last example, a slave purchasing his freedom with his own money, however, our argument fails: here, protection for the slaves clearly came at the expense of the *dominus* who had – perhaps even rashly or thoughtlessly – set the process of self-purchase in motion.

The result of this review of Roman slave law (especially of the classical period), boils down to a slender, but not an unimportant, proposition: the social differences that we can observe among slaves were given legal recognition in some areas. Anyone who uses Roman slave law as a source for the study of ancient slavery must pay heed to those nuances and always put general statements into context. Otherwise, they risk missing important details.

150 Tony Honoré, "The Nature of Slavery," in *The Legal Understanding of Slavery – From the Historical to the Contemporary*, ed. Jean Allain (Oxford: Oxford University Press, 2014): 14.

151 See for example Andrea di Porto, *Impresa collettiva e schiavo "manager" in Roma antica (II sec. a. C.-II sec. d. C.)* (Milan: Giuffrè, 1984); Bürge, "Lo schiavo" (n. 147): 384–85; Andreas M. Fleckner, *Antike Kapitalvereinigungen. Ein Beitrag zu den konzeptionellen und historischen Grundlagen der Aktiengesellschaft* (Vienna/Cologne/Weimar: Böhlau, 2010): 217–38.

Bibliography

Abatino, Barbara, and Giuseppe Dari-Mattiacci. "Agency Problems and Organizational Costs in Slave-Run Business," *Amsterdam Law School Legal Studies Research Paper* No. 2011–40/ *Amsterdam Center for Law & Economics Working Paper* No. 2011–13, 13.10.2011, https://papers.ssrn.com/sol3/papers.cfm?abstract_id=1942802 [accessed 02.09.2022].

Aellen, Christian. *A la recherche de l'ordre cosmique. Forme et fonction des personnifications dans la céramique Italiote*, vol. 1–2 (Kilchberg/Zurich: Akanthus, 1994).

Affolter, Friedrich. *Die Persönlichkeit des herrenlosen Sklaven. Ein Stück aus dem römischen Sklavenrecht* (Leipzig: Von Veit, 1913).

Albers, Gregor. *Perpetuatio obligationis, Leistungspflicht trotz Unmöglichkeit im klassischen Recht* (Cologne: Böhlau, 2019).

Albertario, Emilio. "I Tribonianismi avvertiti dal Cuiacio," *Zeitschrift der Savigny-Stiftung für Rechtsgeschichte, Romanistische Abteilung* 31 (1910): 158–75.

Albertario, Emilio. "Conceptus pro iam nato habetur," *Bullettino dell'Istituto di Diritto Romano* 33 (1924): 1–77.

Albertario, Emilio. "D. 21,1,35. 'Ulpian L. 1 ad edictum aedilium curulium'. Esempio di decomposizione di un testo giustinianeo nei suoi elementi costitutivi," in *Studi in onore di Salvatore Riccobono*, vol. 1, ed. (Palermo: Arti Grafiche Cav. Giuseppe Castiglia, 1936): 641–51.

Albrecht, Michael von. *Geschichte der römischen Literatur: Von Andronicus bis Boethius und ihr Fortwirken*, 3rd ed. (Berlin: De Gruyter, 2012).

Alföldy, Geza. *Römische Sozialgeschichte*, 4th ed. (Stuttgart: Franz Steiner Verlag, 2011).

Allain, Jean. "The Definition of Slavery in International Law," *Howard Law Journal* 52, no. 2 (2009): 239–75.

Amarelli, Francesco. *Vetustas – innovatio. Un'antitesi apparente nella legislazione di Costantino* (Naples: Jovene, 1978).

Ambrosino, Rodolfo. "Vel fratres (In margine all'editto degli Edili curuli)," *Studia et Documenta Historiae et Iuris* 16 (1950): 290–94.

Andreau, Jean. *Banking and Business in the Roman World* (Cambridge: Cambridge University Press, 1999).

Andreau, Jean. "Freedmen in the Satyrica," in *Petronius: A Handbook*, ed. Jonathan R.W. Prag and Ian D. Repath (New York: Wiley-Blackwell, 2009): 114–24.

Ankum, Hans. "Der Ausdruck favor libertatis in den Konstitutionen der römischen Kaiser," in *Sklaverei und Freilassung im römischen Recht: Symposium für Hans Josef Wieling zum 70. Geburtstag*, ed. Thomas Finkenauer (Berlin/Heidelberg: Springer Verlag, 2006): 1–17

Ankum, Hans, Marjolijn van Gessel-de Roo and Eric Pool. "Die verschiedenen Bedeutungen des Ausdrucks in bonis alicuius esse/in bonis habere im klassischen römischen Recht (I)," *Zeitschrift der Savigny-Stiftung für Rechtsgeschichte: Romanistische Abteilung* 104 (1987): 238–436.

Ankum, Hans, Marjolijn van Gessel-de Roo and Eric Pool. "Die verschiedenen Bedeutungen des Ausdrucks in bonis olicuius esse/in bonis habere im klassischen römischen Recht (III)," *Zeitschrift der Savigny-Stiftung für Rechtsgeschichte: Romanistische Abteilung* 107 (1990): 155–215.

Astolfi, Riccardo. *Studi sull'oggetto dei legati in diritto romano*, vol. 2 (Padua: Cedam, 1969).

Astolfi, Riccardo. *La 'lex Iulia et Papia'* (Padua: Cedam, 1996).

Aubert, Jean-Jacques. *Business Managers in Ancient Rome: A Social and Economic Study of Institores, 200 B.C.–A.D. 250* (Leiden: Brill, 1994).

https://doi.org/10.1515/9783110987195-010

Aubert, Jean-Jacques. “Dumtaxat de peculio: What’s in a Peculium, or Establishing the Extent of the Principal’s Liability,” in *New Frontiers: Law and Society in the Roman World*, ed. Paul J. du Plessis (Edinburgh: Edinburgh University Press, 2013): 192–206.

Avenarius, Martin. *Der pseudo-ulpianische liber singularis regularum: Entstehung, Eigenart und Überlieferung einer hochklassischen Juristenschrift. Analyse, Neuedition und deutsche Übersetzung: Quellen und Forschungen zum Recht und seiner Geschichte* (Göttingen: Wallstein-Verlag, 2005).

Avenarius, Martin. “Marc Aurel und die Dogmatik des römischen Privatrechts. Kaiserliche Rechtspflege im System der Rechtsquellen und die Ausfüllung von Gestaltungsspielräumen in einer Übergangszeit der Rechtsentwicklung,” in *Selbstbetrachtungen und Selbstdarstellungen*, ed. Michael van Ackeren and Jan Opsomer (Wiesbaden: Reichert, 2012): 203–84.

Avenarius, Martin, ed. *Stellung des Sklaven im Privatrecht*, vol. 3, *Erbrecht. Aktive Stellung: Personeneigenschaft und Ansätze zur Anerkennung von Rechten*, Corpus der römischen Rechtsquellen zur Sklaverei 4 (Stuttgart: Franz Steiner Verlag, 2017).

Babusiaux, Ulrike. *Papinians Quaestiones. Zur rhetorischen Methode eines spätklassischen Juristen* (Munich: C.H. Beck, 2011).

Babusiaux, Ulrike. “Funktionen der Etymologie in der Juristischen Literatur,” *Fundamina: A Journal of Legal History* 20, no. 1 (2014): 39–60.

Babusiaux, Ulrike, et al., eds. *Handbuch des Römischen Privatrechts* (Tübingen: Mohr Siebeck, 2023).

Bagnani, Gilbert. “The House of Trimalchio,” *American Journal of Philology* 75, no. 1 (1954): 16–39.

Bagnani, Gilbert. *Arbiter of Elegance: A Study of the Life and Works of C. Petronius* (Toronto: University of Toronto Press, 1954).

Balch, David K., and Carolyn Osiek, eds. *Early Christian Families in Context: An Interdisciplinary Dialogue* (Grand Rapids: Eerdmans, 2003).

Baldus, Christian. “Possession in Roman Law,” in *The Oxford Handbook of Roman Law and Society*, ed. Paul J. du Plessis, Clifford Ando and Kaius Tuori (Oxford: Oxford University Press, 2016): 41.1–41.6.

Baldwin, Barry. “Two Aspects of the Spartacus Slave Revolt,” *The Classical Journal* 62, no. 7 (1967): 289–94.

Barchiesi, Alessandro. “Extra legem: Consumo di letteratura in Petronio, Arbitro,” in *La letteratura di consumo nel mondo greco-latino: Atti del convegno internazionale Cassino, 14–17 Settembre 1994*, ed. Michael Paschalis and Stelios Panayotakis (Eelde: Groningen University Library, 2013): 189–208.

Barney, Stephen A., W.J. Lewis, J.A. Beach and Oliver Berghof, eds. *The Etymologies of Isidore of Seville* (Cambridge: Cambridge University Press, 2006).

Bechmann, August. *Das Ius Postliminii und die Lex Cornelia: Ein Beitrag zur Dogmatik des römischen Rechts* (Erlangen: Verlag von Andreas Deichert, 1872).

Beggio, Tommaso. *Paul Koschaker (1879–1951). Rediscovering the Roman Foundations of European Legal Tradition*, 2nd ed. (Heidelberg: Winter, 2018).

Beggio, Tommaso. *Contributo allo studio della ‘servitus poenae’* (Bari: Cacucci Editore, 2020).

Behrends, Okko. “Prinzipat und Sklavenrecht. Zu den geistigen Grundlagen der augusteischen Verfassungsschöpfung,” in *Rechtswissenschaft und Rechtsentwicklung*, ed. Ulrich Immenga (Göttingen: Schwartz, 1980): 417–55 [= in *Institut und Prinzip*, vol. 1, ed. Martin Avenarius (Göttingen: Wallstein Verlag, 2004): 417–55].

Behrends, Okko, Rolf Knütel, Bertold Kupisch and Hans Hermann Seiler. *Corpus Iuris Civilis, Text und Übersetzung*, vol. 4 (Heidelberg: C.F. Müller, 2005).

Bellen, Heinz. *Studien zur Sklavenflucht im römischen Kaiserreich* (Stuttgart: Franz Steiner Verlag, 1971).

Bellieni, Camillo. *Enfiteusi, schiavitù e colonato in Sardegna all'epoca di Costantino* (Cagliari: Edizioni della Fondazione Il nuraghe, 1930).

Bellodi Ansaloni, Anna. *Ad eruendam veritatem: Profili metodologici e processuali della quaestio per tormenta* (Bologna: Bononia University Press, 2011).

Berg, Peter van den. "Slaves: Persons or Property? The Roman Law on Slavery and Its Reception in Western Europe and Its Overseas Territories," *Osaka Law Review* 63 (2016): 171–88.

Berger, Adolf. *Encyclopedic Dictionary of Roman Law* (Philadelphia: American Philosophical Society, 1953).

Beseler, Gerhard. *Beiträge zur Kritik der römischen Rechtsquellen*, vol. 4 (Tübingen: Mohr Siebeck, 1920).

Beseler, Gerhard. "Aequissimus," *Zeitschrift der Savigny-Stiftung für Rechtsgeschichte, Romanistische Abteilung* 45 (1925): 455–56.

Beseler, Gerhard. "Unklassische Wörter," *Zeitschrift der Savigny-Stiftung für Rechtsgeschichte, Romanistische Abteilung* 57 (1937): 1–51.

Biondi, Biondo. *Il diritto romano cristiano*, vol. 2 (Milan: Giuffrè, 1952).

Biondi, Biondo. *Il diritto romano cristiano*, vol. 3 (Milan: Giuffrè, 1954).

Blackburn, Robin. "The Old World Background to European Colonial Slavery," *The William and Mary Quarterly* 54, no. 1 (1997): 65–102.

Bleicken, Jochen. *Lex publica: Gesetz und Recht in der römischen Republik* (Berlin: De Gruyter, 1975).

Blume, Fred H. *The Codex of Justinian: A New Annotated Translation* (Cambridge: Cambridge University Press, 2016).

Bodel, John. "Trimalchio and the Candelabrum," *Classical Philology* 84, no. 3 (1989): 224–31.

Bodel, John. "The cena Trimalchionis," in *Latin Fiction: The Latin Novel in Context*, ed. Heinz Hofmann (London: Routledge, 1999): 38–51.

Bodel, John. "Slave Labour and Roman Society," in *The Cambridge World History of Slavery*, vol. 1, *The Ancient Mediterranean World*, ed. Keith R. Bradley and Paul Cartledge (Cambridge: Cambridge University Press, 2011): 311–36.

Bodel, John. "Death and Social Death in Ancient Rome," in *On Human Bondage. After Slavery and Social Death*, ed. John Bodel and Walter Scheidel (Oxford: Wiley-Blackwell, 2016): 81–108.

Bonfante, Pietro. *Corso di diritto romano*, vol. 1 (Rome: Attilio Sampaolesi publisher, 1925; repr. Milan: Giuffrè, 1963).

Bonfiglio, Barbara. *Corruptio servi* (Milan: Giuffrè, 1998).

Bonin, Filippo. "Tra ius antiquum, lex Iulia e Lex Papia: Il complesso destino die caduca in età Augustea," *Teoria Storia del diritto Privato* 12 (2019), https://dialnet.unirioja.es/servlet/articulo?codigo=7236855 [accessed 05.08.2022].

Boschung, Dietrich. *Antike Grabaltäre aus den Nekropolen Roms* (Bern: Stämpfli, 1987).

Boulvert, Gérard. "Les esclaves et les affranchis impériaux sous le Haut-Empire romain" (PhD diss., CRDP Aix-en-Provence, 1964).

Boulvert, Gérard. *Esclaves et affranchis impériaux sous Haut-Empire. Rôle politique et administratif* (Naples: Jovene, 1970).

Boulvert, Gérard. *Domestique et fonctionnaire sous le Haut-Empire romain: La condition de l'affranchi et de l'esclave du prince* (Paris: Les Belles Lettres, 1974).

Boulvert, Gérard, and Marcel Morabito. "Le droit de l'esclavage sous le Haut-Empire," in *Aufstieg und Niedergang der römischen Welt*, pt. 2, *Principat*, vol. 14, *Recht*, ed. Hildegard Temporini and Wolfgang Haase (Berlin: De Gruyter, 1982): 98–182.

Bradley, Keith R. *Slaves and Masters in the Roman Empire: A Study in Social Control* (Brussels: Latomus, 1984).

Bradley, Keith R. "Roman Slavery and Roman Law," *Historical Reflections/Réflexions Historiques* 15, no. 3 (1988): 477–95.
Bravo García, Antonio. "El 'Satiricón' como reflejo de la esclavitud de su tiempo," *Cuadernos de filología clásica* 6 (1974): 195–208.
Breitenstein, Natalie. *Petronius: 'Satyrica 1–15': Text, Übersetzung, Kommentar* (Berlin: De Gruyter, 2009).
Brinkhof, Johannes Jacobus. *Een studie over het peculium in het klassieke Romeinse recht* (Meppel: Krips Repro B.V., 1978).
Browning, Robert. Review of *Arbiter of Elegance: A Study of the Life and Works of C. Petronius*, by Gilbert Bagnani, *The Classical Review* 6, no. 1 (1956): 45–47.
Brunt, Peter Astbury. *Roman Imperial Themes* (Oxford: Oxford University Press, 1990).
Bruun, Christer. "Slaves and Freed Slaves," in *The Oxford Handbook of Roman Epigraphy*, ed. Christer Bruun and Jonathan Edmondson (New York: Oxford University Press, 2015): 605–26.
Buchwitz, Wolfram. "Fremde Sklaven als Erben: Sozialer Aufstieg durch Dritte," in *Homo, caput, persona: La costruzione giuridica dell'identità nell'esperienza romana; dall'epoca di Plauto a Ulpiano*, ed. Alessandro Corbino, Michel Humbert and Giovanni Negri (Pavia: IUSS Press, 2010): 393–425.
Buchwitz, Wolfram. *Servus alienus heres. Die Erbeinsetzung fremder Sklaven im klassischen römischen Recht* (Vienna/Cologne/Weimar: Böhlau, 2012).
Buchwitz, Wolfram. "Servus servo heres: Testierfreiheit für Sklaven," in *Fontes Iuris: Atti del VI Jahrestreffen Junger Romanistinnen und Romanisten Lecce, 30–31 marzo 2012*, ed. Pierangelo Buongiorno and Sebastian Lohsse (Naples: Edizioni Scientifiche Italiane, 2013): 141–59.
Buckland, William Warwick. *The Roman Law of Slavery. The Condition of the Slave in Private Law from Augustus to Justinian* (Cambridge: Cambridge University Press, 1908).
Buján, Antonio Fernández de. "Conceptos y dicotomías del ius," *Revista Jurídica Universidad Autónoma de Madrid* 3 (2000): 9–43.
Buongiorno, Pierangelo. *Senatus consulta Claudianis temporibus facta. Una palingenesi delle deliberazioni senatorie dell'età di Claudio (41–54 d.C.)* (Naples: Edizioni Scientifiche Italiane, 2010).
Buongiorno, Pierangelo. *Claudio, Il principe inatteso* (Palermo: 21 Editore, 2017).
Bürge, Alfons. "Vertrag und personale Abhängigkeiten im Rom der späten Republik und der frühen Kaiserzeit," *Zeitschrift der Savigny-Stiftung für Rechtsgeschichte, Romanistische Abteilung* 97 (1980): 105–56.
Bürge, Alfons. "Cum in familia nubas. Zur wirtschaftlichen und sozialen Bedeutung der familia libertorum," *Zeitschrift der Savigny-Stiftung für Rechtsgeschichte, Romanistische Abteilung* 105 (1988): 312–33.
Bürge, Alfons. "Cibaria: Indiz für die soziale Stellung des römischen Arbeitnehmers?," in *Ars boni et aequi: Festschrift für Wolfgang Waldstein zum 65. Geburtstag*, ed. Martin Josef Schermaier and Zoltán Végh (Stuttgart: Franz Steiner Verlag, 1993): 63–78.
Bürge, Alfons. *Römisches Privatrecht: Rechtsdenken und gesellschaftliche Verankerung. Eine Einführung* (Darmstadt: Wissenschaftliche Buchgesellschaft, 1999).
Bürge, Alfons. "Lo schiavo (in)dipendente e il suo patrimonio," in *Homo, caput, persona: La costruzione giuridica dell'identità nell'esperienza romana; dall'epoca di Plauto a Ulpiano*, ed. Alessandro Corbino, Michel Humbert and Giovanni Negri (Pavia: IUSS Press, 2010): 369–391.
Buti, Ignazio. *Studi sulla capacità patrimoniale dei 'servi'* (Naples: Jovene, 1976).
Buti, Ignazio. "Si serva servo quasi dotem dederit. Matrimoni servili e dote," in *Schiavi e dipendenti nell'ambito dell''oikos' e della 'familia': Atti del 22. Colloquio Girea: Pontignano (Siena), 19–20 novembre 1995*, ed. Mauro Maggi and Giuseppe Cordiano (Pisa: ETS, 1997): 289–306.

Bydraes, Kort. "The Young Trimalchio," *Acta Classica* 36 (1993): 143–46.
Cantarella, Eva. *Gli amori degli altri: Tra cielo e terra, da Zeus a Cesare* (Milan: La nave di Teseo, 2018).
Capogrossi Colognesi, Luigi. "Das Eigentum in Rom vom Ende der patriarchalischen Ordnung bis zur Blütezeit der Sklavereiordnung," in *Eigentum. Beiträge zu seiner Entwicklung in politischen Gesellschaften. Werner Sellnow zum 70. Geburtstag*, ed. Jens Köhn and Burkhard Rode (Weimar: Böhlau, 1987): 117–39.
Carlsen, Jesper. *Vilici and Roman Estate Managers until A.D. 284* (Rome: L'Erma di Bretschneider, 1995).
Carlsen, Jesper. *Land and Labour. Studies in Roman Social and Economic History* (Rome: L'Erma di Bretschneider, 2013).
Castagnetti, Sergio. *Le 'leges libitinariae' flegree: Edizione e commento* (Naples: Satura Editrice, 2012).
Castello, Carlo. "'Humanitas' e 'favor libertatis'. Schiavi e liberti nel I secolo," in *Sodalitas. Scritti in onore di Antonio Guarino*, vol. 5, ed. Antonio Guarino and Vincenzo Giuffrè (Naples: Jovene, 1984): 2175–89.
Champlin, Edward. *Final Judgements: Duty and Emotion in Roman Wills, 200 B.C.-A.D. 250* (Berkeley: University of California Press, 1991).
Chantraine, Heinrich. *Freigelassene und Sklaven im Dienst der römischen Kaiser* (Wiesbaden: Franz Steiner Verlag, 1967).
Charlin, Frédéric. "Droit romain et Code Noir. Quelques réflexions a posteriori," *Clio@Themis. Revue électronique d'histoire du droit* 8 (2015), https://publications-prairial.fr/cliothemis/index.php?id=1491?id=1491#toc [accessed 08.09.2022].
Chausson, François. "De Domitia Longina aux Antonins: Le règne de Nerva," *Bulletin de la Société nationale des Antiquaires de France* 2002 (2008): 201–6.
Chelotti, Marcella. "Rubi," in *Supplementa Italica*, vol. 5, ed. Unione Accademica Nazionale (Rome: Quasar, 1989).
Cherchi, Alice. "Riflessioni sulla condizione giuridica delle metallariae nel tardo impero. A proposito di C. 11.7(6).7," *Annali del seminario giuridico dellauniversità di Palermo* 59 (2016): 223–25.
Chiusi, Tiziana, Johann Filip-Fröschl and Johannes Michael Rainer, eds. *Corpus der römischen Rechtsquellen zur antiken Sklaverei* (*Corpus of Roman Legal Sources on Ancient Slavery*) (Stuttgart: Mainz Academy, since 1999), https://www.adwmainz.de/index.php?id=712&L=4 [accessed 08.09.2022].
Ciccotti, Ettore. *Il tramonto della schiavitù nel mondo antico* (Turin: Bocca, 1899).
Cintio, Lucia di. *L''interpretatio Visigothorum' al 'Codex Theodosianus'* (Milan: LED Edizioni Universitarie, 2013).
Cintio, Lucia di. *'Ordine' e 'Ordinamento': Idee e categorie giuridiche nel mondo romano* (Milan: LED Edizioni Universitarie, 2019).
Clarke, John R. *Art in the Lives of Ordinary Romans: Visual Representation and Non-Elite Viewers in Italy, 100 B.C.-A.D. 315* (Berkeley: University of California Press, 2003).
Cloud, J.D. "Parricidium: From the lex Numae lo the lex Pómpela de parricidiis," *Zeitschrift der Savigny-Stiftung für Rechtsgeschichte, Romanistische Abteilung* 88 (1971): 1–66.
Coleman, Kathleen M. "Fatal Charades: Roman Executions Staged as Mythological Enactments," in *Journal of Roman Studies* 80 (1990): 44–73.
Columella, Lucius Junius Moderatus. *Columella: On Agriculture*, transl. E.S. Forster and Edward H. Heffner, vol. 1, Loeb Classical Library (Cambridge, MA: Harvard University Press, 1941).
Columella, Lucius Junius Moderatus. *Columella: On Agriculture*, transl. Harrison Boyd Ash, vol. 2, Loeb Classical Library (Cambridge, MA: Harvard University Press 1954).

Conklin, Carli N. *The Pursuit of Happiness in the Founding Era. An Intellectual History* (Missouri: University of Missouri, 2019).
Coppola Bisazza, Giovanna. *Lo iussum domini e la sostituzione negoziale nell'esperienza romana* (Milan: Giuffrè, 2003).
Corbett, Percy E. *The Roman Law of Marriage* (Oxford: Clarendon Press, 1969).
Costa, Emilio. *Il diritto privato romano nelle commedie di Plauto* (Turin: Bocca, 1890).
Courtney, Edward. *Musa Lapidaria: A Selection of Latin Verse Inscriptions* (Atlanta: Scholars Press, 1995).
Courtney, Edward. *A Companion to Petronius* (Oxford: Oxford University Press, 2001).
Crook, John A. *Law and Life of Rome, 90 B.C. – A.D.* 212 (New York: Cornell University Press, 1967).
Crook, John A. "'Si parret' and a Joke in Petronius," in *Sodalitas: Scritti in onore di Antonio Guarino*, vol. 3, ed. Antonio Guarino and Vincenzo Giuffrè (Naples: Jovene, 1984): 1353–56.
Cujacius, Jacques. *Opera omnia*, vol. 7 (Naples: Michael Aloysius Mutius, 1758).
Cuiacius, Jacques. *Opera omnia in decem tomos distributa*, vol. 5 (Prato, 1838).
D'Arms, John H. *Commerce and Social Standing in Ancient Rome* (Cambridge: Harvard University Press, 1981).
D'Ors, Álvaro. *Los romanistas ante la actual crisis de la ley* (Madrid: Ateneo, 1952).
Dalla, Danilo. *Senatus Consultum Silanianum* (Milano: Giuffrè, 1994).
Daube, David. "The Compilers' Use of a Revised Paul and Ulpian," *Zeitschrift der Savigny-Stiftung für Rechtsgeschichte, Romanistische Abteilung* 90 (1973): 359–60.
Daube, David. *Collected Studies in Roman Law*, ed. David Cohen and Dieter Simon (Frankfurt am Main: Klostermann, 1991).
de Ligt, Luuk. "Legal History and Economic History: The Case of the actiones adiecticiae qualitatis," *Tijdschrift voor Rechtsgeschiedenis* 67, no. 3–4 (1999): 205–26.
de Melo, Wolfgang. *Plautus: The Merchant. The Braggart Soldier. The Ghost. The Persian* (Cambridge: Harvard University Press, 2011).
de Vaan, Michiel. *Etymological Dictionary of Latin and the Other Italic Languages* (Leiden: Brill, 2008).
Debray, Louis. "Pétrone et le droit privé romain," *Nouvelle revue historique de droit français et étranger* 43 (1919): 5–70 (part 1); 127–86 (part 2).
Deissler, Johannes. "Cold Case? Die Finley-Vogt-Kontroverse aus deutscher Sicht," in *Antike Sklaverei: Rückblick und Ausblick. Neue Beiträge zur Forschungsgeschichte und zur Erschließung der archäologischen Zeugnisse*, ed. Heinz Heinen (Stuttgart: Franz Steiner Verlag, 2010): 77–94.
Delacampagne, Christian. *Die Geschichte der Sklaverei* (Dusseldorf/Zurich: Artemis und Winkler Verlag, 2004).
Dell'Oro, Aldo. *Le cose collettive nel diritto romano* (Milan: Giuffrè, 1963).
Diederich, Silke. "Sklaverei bei den römischen Agrarschriftstellern," in *Unfreie Arbeit: Ökonomische und kulturgeschichtliche Perspektiven*, ed. Mustafa Erdem Kabadayi and Tobias Reichardt (Hildesheim: Georg Olms Verlag, 2007): 149–65
Dolganov, Anna. "Imperialism and Social Engineering: Augustan Social Legislation in the Gnomon of the Idios Logos," in *Studien zum Gnomon des Idios Logos': Beiträge zum Dritten Wiener Koloquium zur Antiken Rechtsgeschichte*, ed. Thomas Kruse (Vienna: Holzhausen, 2022): 1–39.
du Plessis, Paul J. "The Slave in the Window," in *By the Sweat of Your Brow: Roman Slavery in Its Socio-Economic Setting*, ed. Ulrike Roth (London: Institute of Classical Studies, University of London, 2010): 49–60.
du Plessis, Paul J. "Trouble at the Baths," *RIDROM* 26 (2021): 308–33, https://ruidera.uclm.es/xmlui/bitstream/handle/10578/28461/touble.pdf?sequence=1&isAllowed=y [accessed 26.08.2022].

Duff, Arnold Mackay. *Freedmen in the Early Roman Empire* (Oxford: Clarendon Press, 1928; repr. 1958).
Dumont, Jean Christian. *Servus: Rome et l'esclavage sous la république* (Rome: École française de Rome, 1987).
Dupont, Clémence. *Les constitutions de Constantin et le droit privé au début du IVe siècle* (Lille: Université de Lille, 1937).
Eck, Werner. *Information Regarding Paul Weaver's Repertorium of Imperial Freedmen and Slaves* (Cologne: Universität zu Köln, 2005), https://alte-geschichte.phil-fak.uni-koeln.de/personal/ehemalige-emeriti/eck-prof-dr-werner/weaver-repertorium [accessed 12.09.2022].
Eck, Werner. "Grabmonumente in Rom und im Rheinland: Reflex von sozialem Status und Prestige?," in *Social Status and Prestige in the Graeco-Roman World*, ed. Annika B. Kuhn (Stuttgart: Franz Steiner Verlag, 2015): 165–88.
Edmondson, Jonathan. "Slavery and the Roman Family," in *The Cambridge World History of Slavery*, vol. 1, *The Ancient Mediterranean World*, ed. Keith R. Bradley and Paul Cartledge (Cambridge: Cambridge University Press, 2011): 337–61.
Eigler, Ulrich. "Familiariter cum servis vivere: Einige Überlegungen zu Inhalt und Hintergrund von Senecas Epistel 47," in *Seneca: philosophus et magister*, ed. Thomas Baier, Gesine Manuwald and Bernhard Zimmermann (Freiburg im Breisgau: Rombach, 2005): 63–79.
Erman, Heinrich. "Servus vicarius. L'esclave de l'esclave romain," in *Recueil publié par la Faculté de Droit de l'Université de Lausanne, à l'occassion de l'Exposition national suisse* (Lausanne: F. Rouge, 1896; repr. Naples: Jovene, 1996).
Esposito, Roberto. "Il dispositivo della persona," in *Homo, caput, persona. La costruzione giuridica dell'identità nell'esperienza romana*, ed. Alessandro Corbino, Michel Humbert and Giovanno Negri (Pavia: IUSS Press, 2010): 50–63.
Esposito, Roberto. *Le persone e le cose* (Turin: Giulio Einaudi Editore, 2014).
Fabre, Georges. *Libertus. Recherches sur les rapports patron-affranchi à la fin de la république romaine* (Rome: École française de Rome, 1981).
Fanizza, Lucia. "Il parricidio nel sistema della 'lex Pompeia'," *Labeo* 25, no. 3 (1979): 267–89.
Fantham, Elaine, ed. *Seneca: Selected Letters* (Oxford: Oxford University Press, 2010).
Ferrary, Jean-Louis. "La législation augustéenne et les dernières lois comitiales," in *Leges publicae. La legge nell'esperienza giuridica romana*, ed. Jean-Louis Ferrary (Pavia: IUSS Press, 2012): 569–92.
Ferretti, Paolo. *Complicità e furto nel diritto romano* (Milan: Giuffrè, 2005).
Field, James A. "The Purpose of the Lex Iulia et Papia Poppaea," *The Classical Journal* 40, no. 7 (1945): 398–416.
Filip-Fröschl, Johanna. "Gefühle und Recht. Gedanken zur rechtlichen Relevanz von Gefühlen, ausgehend von den Bestimmungen zur römischen Sklavenfamilie," in *Vis ac potestas legum. Liber amicorum Zoltán Végh*, ed. Michael Rainer (Frankfurt am Main: Peter Lang Verlag, 2010): 9–33.
Finkenauer, Thomas. "Anmerkungen zur redemptio servi suis nummis," in *Festschrift für Rolf Knütel zum 70. Geburtstag*, ed. Holger Altmeppen, Ingo Reichard and Martin Josef Schermaier (Heidelberg: C.F. Müller, 2009): 345–57.
Finkenauer, Thomas. *Die Rechtsetzung Mark Aurels zur Sklaverei* (Stuttgart: Franz Steiner Verlag, 2010).
Finkenauer, Thomas. "Die römischen Juristen und die Gerechtigkeit," in *Recht und Gerechtigkeit*, ed. Otfried Höffe (Freiburg im Breisgau/Berlin: Rombach, 2014): 11–46.
Finkenauer, Thomas. "Pönale Elemente der lex Aquilia," in *Ausgleich oder Buße als Grundproblem des Schadenersatzrechts von der lex Aquilia bis zur Gegenwart. Symposium zum 80. Geburtstag von Herbert Hausmaninger*, ed. Richard Gamauf (Vienna: Manz, 2017): 35–71.

Finkenauer, Thomas. "Der Schutz der Sklavenfamilie im klassischen römischen Recht," *Revue Internationale des Droits de l'Antiquité* 67/68 (2020/2021): 82–88.
Finley, Moses I. "Between Slavery and Freedom," *Comparative Studies in Society and History* 6, no. 3 (1964): 233–49.
Finley, Moses I. *Ancient Slavery and Modern Ideology* (New York: The Viking Press, 1980).
Finley, Moses I. *Ancient Slavery and Modern Ideology*, 2nd ed. (New York: Markus Wiener, 1980).
Flaig, Egon. *Weltgeschichte der Sklaverei*, 3rd ed. (Munich: C.H. Beck, 2018).
Fleckner, Andreas M. *Antike Kapitalvereinigungen. Ein Beitrag zu den konzeptionellen und historischen Grundlagen der Aktiengesellschaft* (Vienna/Cologne/Weimar: Böhlau, 2010).
Fleckner, Andreas M. "The Peculium: A Legal Device for Donations to personae alieno iuri subiectae?," in *Gift Giving and the 'Embedded' Economy in the Ancient World*, ed. Filippo Carlà and Maja Gori (Heidelberg: Winter, 2014): 213–39.
Flobert, Pierre. "Considérations intempestives sur l'auteur et la date du Satyricon sous Hadrien," in *Petroniana: Gedenkschrift für Hubert Petersmann*, ed. József Herman and Hannah Rosén (Heidelberg: Winter, 2003): 109–22.
Flory, Marleen. "Family in familia: Kinship and Community in Slavery," *American Journal of Ancient History* 3 (1978): 78–95.
Foucault, Michel. *Histoire de la sexualité*, vol. 3, *Le souci de soi* (Paris: Gallimard, 1984).
Friedländer, Ludwig. *Darstellungen aus der Sittengeschichte Roms in der Zeit von August bis zum Ausgang der Antonine*, vol. 1, 9th ed., ed. Georg Wissowa (Leipzig: Hirzel, 1919).
Friedländer, Ludwig. *Darstellungen aus der Sittengeschichte Roms in der Zeit von August bis zum Ausgang der Antoninen*, vol. 3 (Leipzig: Hirzel, 1920).
Fronto, Marcus Cornelius. *The Correspondence of Marcus Cornelius Fronto*, vol. 1, Loeb Classical Library, ed. and transl. C.R. Haines (Cambridge, MA: Harvard University Press, 1919; repr. 1955).
Fuhrmann, Christopher J. *Policing the Roman Empire: Soldiers, Administration, and Public Order* (Oxford: Oxford University Press, 2012).
Gaedke, Theophilus. *De iure commorentium ex disciplina Romanorum* (Rostock: 1830).
Gaius. *The Institutes of Gaius*, transl. W.M. Gordon and O.F. Robinson (London: Duckworth/Cornell University Press, 1988).
Galeotti, Sara. *Mare monstrum. Mare nostrum. Note in tema di pericula maris e trasporto marittimo nella riflessione della giurisprudenza romana (I secolo a.C. – III secolo d.C.)* (Naples: Jovene, 2020).
Gamauf, Richard. *Ad statuam licet confugere: Untersuchungen zum Asylrecht im römischen Prinzipat* (Frankfurt am Main: Peter Lang Verlag, 1999).
Gamauf, Richard. "'Cum aliter nulla domus tuta esse possit . . .': Fear of Slaves and Roman Law," in *Fear of Slaves – Fear of Enslavement in the Ancient* Mediterranean. *Peur de l'ésclave – Peur de l'ésclavage en mediterranée ancienne (Discours, representations, pratiques)*, ed. Anastasia Serghidou (Besançon: Presses Universitaires de Franche-Comté, 2007): 145–64.
Gamauf, Richard. "Petronius 97: Quaestio lance et licio oder Rechtspraxis des ersten Jahrhunderts?," in *Fides humanitas ius: Studii in onore di Luigi Labruna*, vol. 3, ed. Cosimo Cascione and Carla Masi Doria (Naples: Editoriale Scientifica, 2007): 2037–45.
Gamauf, Richard. "Aliquid de iure gustare: Portrayal and Criticism of Lawyers in Petronius," in *Ius Romanum Schola Sapientiae: Pocta Petrovi Blahovi k 70. narodeninám*, ed. Peter Mach, Matúš Nemec and Matej Pekarik (Trnava: Právnická fakulta Trnavskej university, 2009): 151–65.
Gamauf, Richard. "Slaves Doing Business: The Role of Roman Law in the Economy of a Roman Household," *European Review of History/Revue européenne d'histoire* 16, no. 3 (2009): 331–46.

Gamauf, Richard. "Kindersklaven in klassischen römischen Rechtsquellen," in *Kindersklaven – Sklavenkinder: Schicksale zwischen Zuneigung und Ausbeutung in der Antike und im interkulturellen Vergleich: Beiträge zur Tagung des Akademievorhabens Forschungen zur antiken Sklaverei (Mainz, 14. Oktober 2008)*, ed. Heinz Heinen (Stuttgart: Franz Steiner Verlag, 2012): 231–60.

Gamauf, Richard. "Erro: Suche nach einem verschwundenen Sklaven: Eine Skizze zur Interpretationsgeschichte des ädilizischen Edikts," in *Inter cives necnon peregrinos: Essays in Honour of Boudewijn Sirks*, ed. Jan Hallebeek et al. (Göttingen: V&R unipress, 2014): 269–87.

Gamauf, Richard. "Onesimus: fugitivus errove. Einsichten für die Bibelexegese aus der Digestenexegese? (Rechtshistorische Anmerkungen zum Umgang mit römischen Rechtstexten in der neueren Philemon-Auslegung," in *Constans et perpetua voluntas: Pocta Petrovi Blahovi k 75. narodeninám*, ed. Peter Mach, Matej Pekarik and Vojtech Vladár (Trnava: Právnická fakulta Trnavskej university, 2014): 159–76.

Gamauf, Richard. "Öffentliche Ordnung und Injurienrecht: Sozialgeschichtliche Beobachtungen anhand des Edikts de iniuriis quae servis fiunt," in *Scritti per Alessandro Corbino*, vol. 3, ed. Isabella Piro (Tricase: Libellula, 2016): 221–45.

Gamauf, Richard. "Slavery: Social Position and Legal Capacity," in *The Oxford Handbook of Roman Law and Society*, ed. Paul J. du Plessis, Clifford Ando and Kaius Tuori (Oxford: Oxford University Press, 2016): 386–401.

Gamauf, Richard. "De nihilo crevit. Freigelassenenmentalität und Pekuliarrecht," in *Der Bürge einst und jetzt: Festschrift für Alfons Bürge*, ed. Ulrike Babusiaux, Peter Nobel and Johannes Platschek (Zurich: Schulthess, 2017): 225–53.

Gamauf, Richard. "Ideal Freedmen-Lives? On the Construction of Biographies in the Cena Trimalchionis," in *Le realtà della schiavitù: Identità e biografie da Eumeo a Frederick Douglass. Les réalités de l'esclavage: Identités et biographies d'Eumée à Frederick Douglass. Atti del XL Convegno internazionale del GIREA (Napoli, 18–20 dicembre 2017)*, ed. Francesca Reduzzi Merola, Maria Vittoria Bramante and Adelaide Caravaglios (Naples: Satura Editrice, 2020): 273–93.

Gamauf, Richard. "Dispensator: Sozialprofil eines Sklavenberufes in den Satyrica und römischen Juristentexten," Index 49 (2021): 112–42.

Gardner, Jane F. *Frauen im antiken Rom* (Munich: C.H. Beck, 1995).

Garland, Andrew. "Cicero's Familia Urbana," *Greece & Rome* 39, no. 2 (1992): 163–72.

Gaudemet, Jean. "Des 'droits de l'homme' ont-ils été reconnus dans l'Empire romain?," *Labeo* 33 (1987): 5–23.

Gaurier, Dominique. *Les 50 livres du Digeste de l'Empereur Justinien. Edition traduite et annotée*, vol. 2 (Paris: Éditions La Mémoire du Droit, 2017).

George, Michele. "The Lives of Slaves," in *The World of Pompeii*, ed. John J. Dobbins and Pedar W. Foss (London: Routledge, 2007): 538–49.

Giaro, Tomasz. "Dogmatische Wahrheit und Zeitlosigkeit in der römischen Jurisprudenz," *Bullettino dell'Istituto di Diritto Romano 'Vittorio Scialoja'* 29 (1987): 1–104.

Giaro, Tomasz. *Römische Rechtswahrheiten. Ein Gedankenexperiment* (Frankfurt am Main: Klostermann, 2007).

Giliberti, Giuseppe. *Legatum kalendarii. Mutuo feneratizio e struttura contabile del patrimonio nell'età del principato* (Naples: Jovene, 1984).

Giltaij, Jacob. *Mensenrechten in het Romeinse recht?* (Nijmegen: Wolf Legal, 2011).

Heineccius, Johann Gottlieb. *Antiquitatum Romanarum iurisprudentiam illustrantium syntagma*, 1st ed. (Halle: 1719).

Gröschler, Peter. "Die pompejanischen und herkulanensischen Urkunden als Erkenntnisquelle für das römische Recht," in *Hermeneutik der Quellentexte des Römischen Rechts*, ed. Martin Avenarius (Baden-Baden: Nomos, 2008): 44–63.

Grosso, Giuseppe. *I legati nel diritto romano. Parte generale*, 2nd ed. (Turin: Giappichelli, 1962).

Grotius, Hugo. *De jure belli et pacis*, vol. 2 (Utrecht: Ex officina Ioannis a Schoonhoven & Soc., 1625).

Guarino, Antonio. *Storia del diritto romano* (Naples: Jovene, 1998).

Gummerus, Herman. *Der Ärztestand im römischen Reiche nach den Inschriften* (Helsingfors: Societas Scientiarum Fennica, 1932).

Günther, Rosmarie. *Frauenarbeit – Frauenbindung* (Munich: Wilhelm Fink, 1987).

Hadden, Sally. "The Fragmented Laws of Slavery in the Colonial and Revolutionary Eras," in *The Cambridge History of Law in America*, vol. 1, *Early America (1580–1815)*, ed. Michael Grossberg and Christopher Tomlins (Cambridge: Cambridge University Press, 2008): 253–87 and 646–57.

Haffter, Heinz. "Die römische Humanitas," *Neue Schweizer Rundschau* 21 (1953/54): 719 [= *Römische Wertbegriffe*, ed. Hans Oppermann (Darmstadt: Wissenschaftliche Buchgesellschaft, 1967): 468].

Hafner, Markus. *Lucians Schrift 'Das traurige Los der Gelehrten'. Einführung und Kommentar zu De Mercede Conductis Potentium Familiaribus, lib. 36*, Hermes Einzelschriften 110 (Stuttgart: Franz Steiner Verlag, 2017).

Hagemann, Matthias. *Iniuria: Von den XII-Tafeln bis zur Justinianischen Kodifikation* (Cologne: Böhlau, 1998).

Harke, Jan Dirk. *Corpus der römischen Rechtsquellen zur antiken Sklaverei*, vol. 3, *Rechtspositionen am Sklaven*, pt. 2, *Ansprüche aus Delikten am Sklaven* (Stuttgart: Franz Steiner Verlag, 2013).

Harper, Kyle. *Slavery in the Late Roman World, A.D. 275–425* (Cambridge: Cambridge University Press, 2011).

Harries, Jill Diana. "The Senatus Consultum Silanianum: Court Decisions and Judicial Severity in the Early Roman Empire," in *New Frontiers: Law and Society in the Roman World*, ed. Paul J. du Plessis (Edinburgh: Edinburgh University Press, 2013): 51–72.

Harris, William V. "Demography, Geography and the Sources of Roman Slaves," *Journal of Roman Studies* 89 (1999): 62–75.

Hartnett, Jeremy. *The Roman Street: Urban Life and Society in Pompeii, Herculaneum, and Rome* (Cambridge: Cambridge University Press, 2017).

Heinemeyer, Susanne. *Der Freikauf des Sklaven mit eigenem Geld. Redemptio suis nummis* (Berlin: Duncker & Humblot, 2013).

Heinen, Heinz, et al., eds. *Handwörterbuch der antiken Sklaverei*, vol. 1–3 (Stuttgart: Franz Steiner Verlag, 2017).

Helmholz, Richard H. "The Law of Slavery and the European Ius Communem," in *The Legal Understanding of Slavery. From the Historical to the Contemporary*, ed. Jean Allain (Oxford: Oxford University Press, 2014): 17–39.

Herrmann-Otto, Elisabeth. *Ex ancilla natus: Untersuchungen zu den 'hausgeborenen' Sklaven und Sklavinnen im Westen des römischen Kaiserreiches* (Stuttgart: Franz Steiner Verlag, 1994).

Herrmann-Otto, Elisabeth. "Sklaven und Frauen unter Konstantin," in *Konstantin der Große*, ed. Alexander Demandt and Josef Engemann (Trier: Philipp von Zabern Verlag, 2006): 83–95.

Herrmann-Otto, Elisabeth. "Die Sklaverei in antiken Theorien und deren Bedeutung für die moderne Menschrechtsdiskussion," in *Grundlagen der antiken Sklaverei. Eine Institution zwischen Theorie und Praxis*, ed. Elisabeth Herrmann-Otto (Hildesheim: Georg Olms Verlag, 2015): 39–58.

Heumann, Hermann Gottlieb, and Emil Seckel, eds. *Handlexikon zu den Quellen des römischen Rechts*, 9th ed. (Jena: G. Fischer, 1914; 11th ed., Jena: Akademische Druck- und Verlagsanstalt, 1971).

Heuss, Alfred. "Das Revolutionsproblem im Spiegel der antiken Geschichte," *Historische Zeitschrift* 216, no. 1 (1973): 1–72.
Hickey, Robin. "Seeking to Understand the Definition of Slavery," in *The Legal Understanding of Slavery. From the Historical to the Contemporary*, ed. Jean Allain (Oxford: Oxford University Press, 2012): 220–41.
Hilliard, Kathleen M. *Masters, Slaves, and Exchange: Power's Purchase in the Old South* (New York: Cambridge University Press, 2014).
Hirschfeld, Otto. *Die kaiserlichen Verwaltungsbeamten bis auf Diocletian*, 2nd ed. (Berlin: Weidmann, 1905).
Höbenreich, Evelyn, and Giunio Rizzelli. *Scylla: Fragmente einer juristischen Geschichte der Frauen im antiken Rom* (Vienna: Böhlau, 2003).
Hofmann, Heinz. "Petronius, Satyrica," in *A Companion to the Ancient Novel*, ed. Edmund P. Cueva and Shannon N. Byrne (Chichester: Wiley-Blackwell, 2014): 96–118.
Holzberg, Niklas. *Petronius Arbiter: Satyrische Geschichten* (Berlin: Akademie-Verlag, 2013).
Honoré, Tony. "Ownership," in *Oxford Essays in Jurisprudence*, ed. Anthony Gordon Guest (Oxford: Oxford University Press, 1961): 107–47.
Honoré, Tony. *Emperors and Lawyers* (Oxford: Clarendon Press, 1994).
Honoré, Tony. *Ulpian: Pioneer of Human Rights* (Oxford: Oxford University Press, 2002).
Honoré, Tony. "Justinian's Digest: The Distribution of Authors and Works to the Three Committees," *Roman Legal Tradition* 3 (2006): 1–47.
Honoré, Tony. "Ulpian, Natural Law and Stoic Influence," *Tijdschrift voor Rechtsgeschiedenis* 78, no. 1–2 (2010): 199–208.
Honoré, Tony. "The Nature of Slavery," in *The Legal Understanding of Slavery. From the Historical to the Contemporary*, ed. Jean Allain (Oxford: Oxford University Press, 2014): 9–39.
Hooper, William Davis, and Harrison Boyd Ash, eds. *Marcus Porcius Cato: On Agriculture. Marcus Terentius Varro: On Agriculture* (Cambridge, MA: Harvard University Press, 1935).
Hopkins, Keith. *Death and Renewal*, Sociological Studies in Roman History 2 (Cambridge: Cambridge University Press, 1983).
Hornum, Michael B. *Nemesis, the Roman State and the Games* (Leiden/New York/Cologne: Brill, 1993).
Horsfall, Nicholas. "'The Uses of Literacy' and the Cena Trimalchionis II," *Greece & Rome* 36, no. 2 (1989): 194–209.
Horvat, Marijan. "'Servi' e 'legatum fundi' nella giurisprudenza classica," in *Antologia giuridica romanistica ed antiquaria*, vol. 1 (Milan: Giuffrè, 1968): 211–22 [= in *Studi in onore di Edoardo Volterra*, vol. 5 (Milan: Giuffrè, 1971): 89–97].
Huchthausen, Liselot. "Zum Problem der Freiheitsbegünstigung (favor libertatis) im römischen Recht," *Philologus* 120, no. 1 (1976): 47–72.
Imbert, Jean. "Favor libertatis," *Revue historique de droit français et étranger* 26 (1949): 274–79.
Impallomeni, Giambattista. *L'editto degli edili curuli* (Padua: Cedam, 1955).
Indra, Miriam. *Status quaestio. Studien zum Freiheitsprozess im klassischen römischen Recht* (Berlin: Duncker & Humblot, 2011).
Isola, Lisa. "Überlegungen zur Litiskreszenz bei der actio ex testamento," *Zeitschrift der Savigny-Stiftung für Rechtsgeschichte, Romanistische Abteilung* 137 (2020): 106–35.
Jacobelli, Luciana. *Gladiatori a Pompei* (Rome: L'Erma di Bretschneider, 2003).
Jakab, Éva. *Praedicere und cavere beim Marktkauf: Sachmängel im griechischen und römischen Recht* (Munich: C.H. Beck, 1997).
Jaschke, Kathrin. *Die Wirtschafts- und Sozialgeschichte des antiken Puteoli* (Rahden: Leidorf, 2010).
Jhering, Rudolf von. *Geist des römischen Rechts auf den verschiedenen Stufen seiner Entwicklung*, vol. 3/1 (Leipzig: Breitkopf und Härtel, 1865).

Johnston, David. “Peculiar Questions,” in *Thinking Like a Lawyer: Essays on Legal History & General History for John Crook on His Eightieth Birthday*, ed. Paul McKechnie (Leiden: Brill, 2002): 5–13.

Johnston, David. “Suing the Paterfamilias: Theory and Practice,” in *Beyond Dogmatics: Law and Society in the Roman World*, ed. John W. Cairns and Paul J. du Plessis (Edinburgh: Edinburgh University Press, 2007): 173–84.

Jones, Arnold H.M., John Robert Martindale and John Morris. *The Prosopography of the Later Roman Empire*, vol. 1, *A.D. 260–395* (Cambridge: Cambridge University Press, 2001).

Joshel, Sandra R. *Slavery in the Roman World* (Cambridge: Cambridge University Press, 2010).

Joshel, Sandra R. “Slavery and Roman Literary Culture,” in *The Cambridge World History of Slavery*, vol. 1, *The Ancient Mediterranean World*, ed. Keith R. Bradley and Paul Cartledge (Cambridge: Cambridge University Press, 2011): 214–40.

Kant, Immanuel. *Die Metaphysik der Sitten*, vol. 2, *Metaphysische Anfangsgründe der Tugendlehre* (Königsberg: Nicolovius, 1797).

Karlowa, Otto. *Römische Rechtsgeschichte*, vol. 1 (Berlin: Von Veit, 1885).

Kaser, Max. *Eigentum und Besitz im älteren römischen Recht* (Weimar: Hermann Böhlaus Nachfolger, 1943).

Kaser, Max. “rec. of Scritti in onore di Contardo Ferrini pubblicati in occasione della sua beatificazione, Milano 1947,” *IURA* 2 (1951): 160–79.

Kaser, Max. *Das Römische Privatrecht*, vol. 1, *Das altrömische, das vorklassische und klassische Recht* (Munich: C.H. Beck, 1955; 2nd ed. 1971).

Kaser, Max. *Das Römische Privatrecht*, vol. 2, *Die nachklassischen Entwicklungen* (Munich: C.H. Beck, 1959; 2nd ed. 1975).

Kaser, Max. Review of *The Law of Persons in the Later Roman Republic*, by Alan Watson, *Tijdschrift voor Rechtsgeschiedenis* 36, no. 3 (1968): 429–33.

Kaser, Max. *Zur Methodologie der römischen Rechtsquellenforschung*, Österreichische Akademie der Wissenschaften, Philosophisch-historische Klasse, Sitzungsberichte 227/5 (Vienna/Cologne/Graz: Böhlau, 1972).

Kaser, Max. *Ius gentium* (Cologne/Vienna: Böhlau, 1993).

Kaser, Max, and Karl Hackl. *Das römische Zivilprozeßrecht*, 2nd ed. (Munich: C.H. Beck, 1997).

Kaser, Max, Rolf Knütel and Sebastian Lohsse. *Römisches Privatrecht: Ein Studienbuch*, 22nd ed. (Munich: C.H. Beck, 2021).

Kehoe, Dennis P. “Agency and Growth in the Roman Economy,” in *New Frontiers: Law and Society in the Roman World*, ed. Paul J. du Plessis (Edinburgh: Edinburgh University Press, 2013): 177–91.

Kehoe, Dennis P. “Agency, Roman Law, and Roman Social Values,” in *Ancient* Law, *Ancient Society*, ed. Dennis P. Kehoe and Thomas McGinn (Ann Arbor: University of Michigan Press, 2017): 105–32.

Kelsen, Hans. *Reine Rechtslehre*, 2nd. ed. (Vienna: Franz Deuticke, 1960).

Kennett, David A. “Altruism and Economic Behavior, I: Developments in the Theory of Public and Private Redistribution,” *The American Journal of Economics and Sociology* 39, no. 2 (1980): 183–98.

Kierdorf, Wilhelm. “Imagines maiorum,” in *Der neue Pauly: Enzyklopädie der Antike*, vol. 5, ed. Hubert Cancik and Helmuth Schneider (Stuttgart: J.B. Metzler, 1998): 946–47.

Kindler, Martin. *Affectionis aestimatio. Vom Ursprung des Affektionsinteresses im römischen Recht und seiner Rezeption* (Berlin: Duncker & Humblot, 2012).

Kirschenbaum, Aaron. *Sons, Slaves and Freedmen in Roman Commerce* (Jerusalem: Hebrew University Magnes Press, 1987).

Kleiter, Tobias. *Entscheidungskorrekturen mit unbestimmter Wertung durch die klassische römische Jurisprudenz* (Munich: C.H. Beck, 2010).

Klinck, Fabian. *Erwerb durch Übergabe an Dritte nach klassischem römischem Recht* (Berlin: Duncker & Humblot, 2004).

Klinck, Fabian. "Papinian D. 18,7,6 pr. und die Sanktionierung von Freilassungs- und Prostitutionsverboten bei Sklavenverkäufen," in *Argumenta Papiniani. Studien zur Geschichte und Dogmatik des Privatrechts*, ed. Jan Dirk Harke (Berlin/Heidelberg: Springer Verlag, 2013): 79–89.

Klingenberg, Georg. *Corpus der römischen Rechtsquellen zur antiken* Sklaverei, vol. 10, *Juristisch speziell definierte Sklavengruppen 6: Servus fugitivus* (Stuttgart: Franz Steiner Verlag, 2005).

Knoch, Stefan. *Sklavenfürsorge im Römischen Reich: Formen und Motive zwischen humanitas und utilitas* (Hildesheim: Georg Olms Verlag, 2005; 2nd ed. 2017).

Knothe, Hans-Georg. "Das gemeine Kindesvermögensrecht: Zur Anwendung römischer Rechtsquellen unter gewandelten Familienstrukturen und Berufsbildern," *Zeitschrift der Savigny-Stiftung für Rechtsgeschichte, Romanistische Abteilung* 98 (1981): 255–302.

Knütel, Rolf. *Stipulatio poenae. Studien zur römischen Vertragsstrafe* (Cologne/Vienna: Böhlau, 1976).

Knütel, Rolf. "Das Mandat zum Freikauf," in *Mandatum und Verwandtes: Beiträge zum römischen und modernen Recht*, ed. Dieter Nörr and Shigeo Nishimura (Berlin/Heidelberg: Springer Verlag, 1993): 353–74.

Knütel, Rolf. "Rechtsfragen zu den Freilassungsfideikommissen," in *Sklaverei und Freilassung im römischen Recht: Symposium für Hans Josef Wieling zum 70. Geburtstag*, ed. Thomas Finkenauer (Berlin: Springer Verlag, 2006): 131–51.

Knütel, Rolf. "Uxores constrictae," *Fundamina* 20, no. 1 (2014): 467–74.

Knütel, Rolf. "Barbatius Philippus und seine Spuren," in *Ausgewählte Schriften: Rolf Knüttel*, ed. H. Altmeppen, Sebastian Lohsse, Ingo Reichard and Martin Josef Schermaier (Heidelberg: C.F. Müller, 2021): 871–91.

Knütel, Rolf, Berthold Kupisch, Thomas Rüfner and Hans Hermann Seiler. *Corpus Iuris civilis. Text und Übersetzung*, vol. 5, *(Digesten 28–34)* (Heidelberg: C.F. Müller, 2012).

Kobusch, Theo. *Die Entdeckung der Person. Metaphysik der Freiheit und modernes Menschenbild* (Darmstadt: Herder Verlag, 1997).

Kosseleck, Rainer. "'Erfahrungsraum' und 'Erwartungshorizont': Zwei historische Kategorien," in *Vergangene Zukunft*, ed. Rainer Kosseleck (Berlin: Suhrkamp, 1979): 349.

Krüger, Hugo. "Die humanitas und die pietas nach den Quellen des römischen Rechtes," *Zeitschrift der Savigny-Stiftung für Rechtsgeschichte, Romanistische Abteilung* 19 (1898): 6–57.

Krüger, Hugo. "Testamenti factio," *Zeitschrift der Savigny-Stiftung für Rechtsgeschichte, Romanistische Abteilung* 53 (1933): 505–8.

Krüger, Wolfgang. *Erwerbszurechnung kraft Status. Eine romanistisch-vergleichende Untersuchung* (Berlin: Duncker & Humblot, 1979).

Kunkel, Wolfgang. *Herkunft und soziale Stellung der römischen Juristen*, 2nd ed. (Graz/Weimar: Hermann Böhlaus Nachfolger, 1967).

Kunkel, Wolfgang. *Die Magistratur*, vol. 2, *Staatsordnung und Staatspraxis der römischen Republik* (Munich: C.H. Beck, 1995).

Kupisch, Berthold. "Der Sklave als Zwangs-Erbe, Ulpian/Julian 4 ad Sab. (D. 28,5,6,4)," *Tijdschrift für Rechtsgeschiedenis* 84, no. 3–4 (2016): 379–400.

Kupiszewski, Henryk. "Humanitas et le droit romain," in *Scritti minori*, ed. Henryk Kupiszewski (Naples: Jovene, 2000): 335–45.

Küppers, Arndt. "Humanität, II. Sozialethisch," *Staatslexikon online*, 04.01.2021, https://www.staatslexikon-online.de/Lexikon/Humanit%C3%A4t [accessed 04.08.2022].

Kurki, Visa A.J., and Thomas Pietrzykowski, eds. *Legal Personhood: Animals, Artificial Intelligence and the Unborn* (Berlin/New York: Springer Verlag, 2017).

Kyle, Donald G., *Spectacles of Death in Ancient Rome* (London/New York: Routledge, 1998).

Labruna, Luigi. "Gérard Boulvert (1936–1984)," *Index* 15 (1987): XIII–XVII.

Laes, Christian. "Desperately Different? Delicia Children in the Roman Household," in *Early Christian Families in Context: An Interdisciplinary Dialogue*, ed. David K. Balch and Carolyn Osiek (Grand Rapids: Eerdmans, 2003): 298–326.

Lamberti, Francesca. "Fideicommissa libertas ancillae data," in *Femmes-esclaves. Modèles d'interpretation anthropologique, économique, juridique*, ed. Francesca Reduzzi Merola and Alfredina Storchi Marino (Naples: Jovene, 1999): 2385–94.

Landolt, Phillip Louis. *'Naturalis Obligatio' und Bare Social Duty* (Vienna/Cologne/Weimar: Böhlau, 2000).

Langenfeld, Hans. *Christianisierungspolitik und Sklavengesetzgebung der römischen Kaiser von Konstantin bis Theodosius II* (Bonn: Habelt-Verlag, 1977).

Langer, Vera Isabella. *Declamatio Romanorum: Dokument juristischer Argumentationstechnik. Fenster in die Gesellschaft ihrer Zeit und Quelle des Rechts?* (Frankfurt am Main: Peter Lang Verlag, 2007).

Lauffer, Siegfried. Review of *Struktur der antiken Sklavenkriege*, by Joseph Vogt, *Vierteljahrschrift für Sozial- und Wirtschaftsgeschichte* 46, no. 3 (1959): 395.

Laureys, Marc, and Rolf Lessenich. "Humanität," in *Bonner Enzyklopädie der Globalität*, ed. Ludger Kühnhardt and Tilman Mayer (Wiesbaden: Springer Verlag, 2017): 1379–88.

Leicht, Pier Silverio. "Il matrimonio del servo," in *Scritti in onore di Contardo Ferrini*, vol. 1, ed. Università cattolica del Sacro Cuore (Milan: Vita e pensiero, 1947): 305–17.

Leist, Burkard Wilhelm. *Ausführliche Erläuterung der Pandecten nach Hellfeld, ein Commentar begründet von D. Christian Friedrich von Glück*, vol. 4, Serie der Bücher 37/38 (Erlangen: Palm & Enke, 1879).

Lenel, Otto. *Palingenesia iuris civilis*, vol. 1–2 (Leipzig: Bernhard Tauchnitz, 1889).

Lenel, Otto. *Palingenesia iuris civilis*, vol. 2 (Leipzig: Bernhard Tauchnitz, 1889; repr. Aalen: Scientia Verlag, 2000).

Lenel, Otto. *Das Edictum Perpetuum: Ein Versuch zu seiner Wiederherstellung*, 3rd ed. (Leipzig: Bernhard Tauchnitz, 1927).

Lenski, Noel. "Framing the Question: What is a Slave Society?," in *What Is a Slave Society? The Practice of Slavery in Global Perspective*, ed. Noel Lenski and Catherine M. Cameron (Cambridge: Cambridge University Press, 2018): 15–58.

Lewis, Andrew. "Slavery, Family and Status," in *The Cambridge Companion to Roman Law*, ed. David Johnston (Cambridge: Cambridge University Press, 2015): 151–74.

Liebs, Detlef. "Töchter klassischer Juristen," in *Festschrift für Ernst von Caemmerer zum 70. Geburtstag*, ed. Hans Claudius Ficker et. al. (Tuebingen: Mohr Siebeck, 1978): 21–44.

Liebs, Detlef. "Jurisprudenz," in *Handbuch der lateinischen Literatur der Antike*, vol. 8/5, *Restauration und Erneuerung: Die lateinische Literatur von 284 bis 374 A.D.*, ed. Reinhart Herzog and Peter Lebrecht Schmidt (Munich: C.H. Beck, 1989): 66.

Liebs, Detlev. "Römische Provinzialjurisprudenz," FreiDok plus: Universitätbibliothek Freiburg, https://freidok.uni-freiburg.de/fedora/objects/freidok:10556/datastreams/FILE1/content [accessed 25.08.2022].

Ligios, Maria Antonietta. *Interpretazione giuridica e realtà economica dell''instrumentum fundi' tra il I sec. a.C. e il III d.C* (Naples: Jovene, 1996).

Ligios, Maria Antoinetta. "'Ademptio peculii' e revoca implicita del legato: Riflessioni su D. 34.4.31.3 (Scaev. 14 dig.)," *Index* 34 (2006): 501–50.

Lo Cascio, Elio. "La vita economica e sociale delle città romane nella testimonianza del Satyricon," in *Studien zu Petron und seiner Rezeption/Studi su Petronio e sulla sua fortuna*, ed. Luigi Castagna and Eckard Lefèvre (Berlin: De Gruyter, 2007): 3–14.

Lohsse, Sebastian. "Die Beerbung des Kriegsgefangenen. Entwicklungsstufen der Auslegung der lex Cornelia de confirmandis testamentis," in *Facetten des römischen Erbrechts*, ed. Jan Dirk Harke (Berlin/Heidelberg: Springer Verlag, 2021): 79–111.

López Barja de, Quiroga, Pedro Manuel. "Latinus iunianus una aproximación," *Studia Historica. Studia Antigua* 4–5 (1986–1987): 125–26.

Lotmar, Philipp. "Marc Aurels Erlaß über die Freilassungsauflage," *Zeitschrift der Savigny-Stiftung für Rechtsgeschichte, Romanistische Abteilung* 33 (1912): 304–82.

MacLean, Rose. *Freed Slaves and Roman Imperial Culture* (Cambridge: Cambridge University Press, 2018).

Maddalena, Linda De. "Spuren des römischen Rechts im Code Noir," in *Sklaverei und Recht: Zwischen römischer Antike und moderner Welt*, Berner Universitätsschriften 61, ed. Iole Fargnoli and Thomas Späth (Bern: Haupt Verlag, 2018): 85–99.

Maganzani, Lauretta. "Appunti sui concetti di dignità umana alla luce della casistica giurisprudenziale romana," *Studia et documenta historiae et iuris* 77 (2011): 521–43.

Mahaffy, John Pentland. "The Slave Wars against Rome," *Hermathena* 7, no. 16 (1890): 167–82.

Maiuro, Marco. *Res Caesaris. Ricerche sulla proprietà imperiale nel principato* (Bari: Edipuglia, 2012).

Manna, Lorena. *Actio redhibitoria e responsabilità per i vizi della cosa nell'editto de mancipiis vendundis* (Milan: Giuffrè, 1994).

Manthe, Ulrich. "Votum parentium: Pap. D. 29,4,26," in *Quaestiones Iuris. Festschrift für Joseph Georg Wolf zum 70. Geburtstag*, ed. Ulrich Manthe and Christoph Krampe (Berlin: Duncker & Humblot, 2000): 163–81.

Mantovani, Dario. "Mores, leges, potentia. La storia della legislazione romana secondo Tacito (Annales III 25–28)," in *Letteratura e civitas. Transizioni dalla Repubblica all'Impero. In ricordo di Emanuele Narducci*, ed. Mario Citroni (Pisa: ETS, 2012): 353–404.

Mantovani, Dario. "L'aequitas romana: Una nozione in cerca di equilibrio," *Antiquorum Philosophia: An International Journal* 11 (2017): 27–55.

Mantovani, Dario. *Les juristes écrivains de la Rome antique: Les oeuvres des juristes comme literature* (Paris: Les Belles Lettres, 2018).

Mantovani, Dario. *Legum multitudo: La presencia de las leyes públicas en el derecho privado romano* (Valencia: Tirant Lo Blanch, 2022).

Manuwald, Gesine. "Der Dichter in der Gemäldegalerie: Zur Diskussion über Kunst und Literatur in Petrons Satyrica," in *Studien zu Petron und seiner Rezeption/Studi su Petronio e sulla sua fortuna*, ed. Luigi Castagna and Eckard Lefèvre (Berlin: De Gruyter, 2007): 253–66.

Marotta, Valerio. *Multa de iure sanxit. Aspetti della politica del diritto di Antonino Pio* (Milan: Giuffrè, 1988).

Martino, Francesco de. *Storia della costituzione romana*, vol. 4, 2nd ed. (Naples: Jovene, 1974).

Martino, Francesco de. *Wirtschaftsgeschichte des alten Rom* (Munich: C.H. Beck, 1985).

Marx, Karl. "Die Klassenkämpfe in Frankreich 1848 bis 1850," in *Marx-Engels-Werke*, vol. 7, ed. Institut für Marxismus-Leninismus beim ZK der SED (Berlin: Dietz, 1973): 9, 85.

Maschi, Carlo A. *Humanitas come motivo giuridico con un esempio nel diritto dotale romano* (Trieste: Universita di Trieste, 1949).

Masi Doria, Carla. *Civitas Operae Obsequium: Tre Studi sulla condizione giuridica dei liberti* (Naples: Jovene, 1993).

Masterson, Mark. "Studies of Ancient Masculinity," in *A Companion to Greek and Roman Sexualities*, ed. Thomas K. Hubbard (Hoboken: Wiley-Blackwell, 2014): 19–32.

Mateo, Antonio. "La consideración clásica de la 'cognatio servilis' en la venta de esclavos (a propósito de D. 21,1,35)," *Bullettino dell'Istituto di Diritto romano* 101–102 (2005): 335–83.
Maxey, Mima. *Occupations of the Lower Classes in Roman Society as Seen in Justinian's Digest* (Chicago: University of Chicago Press, 1938).
Mazza, Mario. "Il breve regno (in)felice di Publio Elvio Pertinace: Considerazioni sull'impero romano alla svolta dell'età severiana," in *Fides Humanitas Ius, 9 maggio 2007*, ed. Cosimo Cascione and Carla Masi Doria (Naples: Editoriale Scientifica, 2008).
McClintock, Aglaia. *Servi della pena. Condannati a morte nella Roma imperiale* (Naples: Edizioni Scientifiche Italiane, 2010).
McClintock, Aglaia. "Nemesis, dea del νόμος. Modalità e simboli della repressione criminale nei primi secoli dell'impero," *Revue Internationale des Droits de l'Antiquité* 62 (2014): 289–306.
McClintock, Aglaia. "Giustizia senza dèi," in *Giuristi nati. Antropologia e diritto romano*, ed. Aglaia McClintock (Bologna: Il Mulino, 2016): 73–95.
McClintock, Aglaia. "The Concept of servus poenae in Roman Law and Its Reception in the Early Modern Period," in *Le realtà della schiavitù: Identità e biografie da Eumeo a Frederick Douglass. Atti del XL Convegno Internazionale GIREA Napoli, 18–20 dicembre 2017*, ed. Francesca Reduzzi Merola, Maria Vittoria Bramante and Adelaide Caravaglios (Naples: Satura Editrice, 2020): 519–31.
McGinn, Thomas. "Ne serva prostituatur. Restrictive Covenants in the Sale of Slaves," *Zeitschrift der Savigny-Stiftung für Rechtsgeschichte Romanistische Abteilung* 107 (1990): 315–53.
McGinn, Thomas. *Prostitution, Sexuality and the Law in Ancient Rome* (New York: Oxford University Press, 1998).
McGinn, Thomas. "Celsus and the Pauper: Roman Private Law and the Socio-Economic Status of Its Consumers," in *Scritti per Alessandro Corbino*, vol. 4, ed. Isabella Piro (Tricase: Libellula Edizioni, 2016): 619–45.
Meillassoux, Claude. *L'esclavage en Afrique précoloniale* (Paris: François Maspero, 1975).
Melillo, Generoso. *Categorie economiche nei giuristi romani* (Naples: Jovene, 2000).
Melluso, Marco. *La schiavitù nell'età giustinianea* (Paris: Presses Universitaires Franc-Comtoises, 2000).
Meloni, Piero. *L'ammistrazione della Sardegna da Augusto all'invasione vandalica* (Rome: L'Erma di Bretschneider, 1966).
Memmer, Michael. "Ad servitutem aut ad lupanar . . .," *Zeitschrift der Savigny-Stiftung für Rechtsgeschichte, Romanistische Abteilung* 108 (1991): 21–93.
Mencacci, Francesca. "Relazioni di parentela nella comunità servile. Gli schiavi gemelli," in *Schiavi e dipendenti nell'ambito dell''oikos' e della 'familia': Atti del 22. Colloquio Girea: Pontignano (Siena), 19–20 novembre 1995*, ed. Mauro Maggi and Giuseppe Cordiano (Pisa: ETS, 1997).
Menner, Josef. "D. 33,7,18,4 – vilicus und vilica als Objekte des Erbschaftsstreits," in *Sklaverei und Freilassung im römischen Recht. Symposium für Hans Josef Wieling zum 70. Geburtstag*, ed. Thomas Finkenauer (Heidelberg: Springer Verlag, 2006): 153–87.
Mette-Dittmann, Angelika. *Die Ehegesetze des Augustus: Eine Untersuchung im Rahmen der Gesellschaftspolitik des Princeps* (Stuttgart: Franz Steiner Verlag, 1991).
Metzger, Ernest. *Litigation in Roman Law* (Oxford: Oxford University Press, 2005).
Mevius, David. *Ein kurtzes Bedencken über die Fragen so von dem Zustand, Abfoderung und verwiederter Abfolge der Bawrsleute zu welchen iemand Zuspruch zu haben vermeynet, bey jetzigen Zeiten entstehen und vorkommen* (Stralsund: Zachariä, 1645).
Meyer-Zwiffelhofer, Eckhard. *Im Zeichen des Phallus: Die Ordnung des Geschlechtslebens im antiken Rom* (Frankfurt am Main: Campus Verlag, 1995).
Mignot, Dominique A. "Le droit romain et la servitude aux Antilles," *Bulletin de la Société d'Histoire de la Guadeloupe* 127–128, no. 1–2 (2001): 25–46.

Mignot, Dominique A. “Du ‘ius vetus’ au code noir: Le délit de l’esclave aux îles françaises d’Amérique (XVIIe – XVIIIe siècle),” *Latomus* 64, no. 3 (2005): 733–41.
Millar, Fergus. *The Emperor in the Roman World, 31 B.C.-A.D. 337* (London: Duckworth, 1977).
Minaud, Gérard. *La comptabilité à Rome: Essai d’histoire économique sur la pensée comptable commerciale et privée dans le monde antique romain* (Lausanne: Presses polytechniques et universitaires romandes, 2005).
Mommsen, Theodor. *Römisches Staatsrecht*, vol. 1 (Leipzig: Hirzel, 1877).
Mommsen, Theodor. “Observationes epigraphicae,” in *Ephemeris epigraphica: Corporis inscriptionum Latinarum supplementum*, vol. 5, ed. Instiuti Archaeologici Romani (Romae-Berolini: apud Georgium Reimerum, 1884).
Mommsen, Theodor. *Römisches Strafrecht* (Leipzig: Duncker & Humblot, 1899).
Mommsen, Theodor. *Gesammelte Schriften*, vol. 7, *Philologische Schriften*, 3rd ed (Zurich: Weidmann, 1994).
Morabito, Marcel. “Les esclaves privilégiés à travers le Digeste témoins et acteurs d’une société en crise,” *Index* 13 (1985): 477–90.
Moreau, Philippe. “Loi Iulia de maritandis ordinibus,” *Leges Populi Romani*, 12.03.2020, http://telma.irht.cnrs.fr/outils/lepor/notice449/ [accessed 01.09.2022].
Mouritsen, Henrik. “The Families of Roman Slaves and Freedmen,” in *A Companion to Families in the Greek und Roman World*, ed. Beryl Rawson (Chichester/Malden, MA: Wiley-Blackwell, 2011): 129–44.
Mouritsen, Henrik. *The Freedman in the Roman World* (Cambridge: Cambridge University Press, 2011).
Mouritsen, Henrik. “Slavery and Manumission in the Roman Elite: A Study of the *Columbaria* of the Volusii and the Statilii,” in *Roman Slavery and Roman Material Culture*, ed. Michele George (Toronto: University of Toronto Press, 2013): 43–68.
Muñiz Coello, Joaquín. “Officium dispensatoris,” *Gerión. Revista de Historia Antigua* 7 (1989): 107–20.
Naiden, F.S. “Embola Petroniana,” *Classical Quarterly* 53, no. 2 (2003): 637–39.
Nettis, Anita Vittoria. “Padroni, sesso e schiavi,” *Index* 28 (2000): 155–72.
Niort, Jean-François. *Le Code Noir. Idées reçues sur un texte symbolique* (Paris: Le Cavalier Bleu, 2015).
Noodt, Gerardus. *Probabilium Juris Civilis*, vol. 4, 3rd ed. (Lugduni Batavorum: Ex officiana Fredericum Haaring, 1705).
Nörr, Dieter. *Recht und Gesellschaft: Festschrift für H. Schelsky zum 70. Geburtstag* (Berlin: Duncker & Humbolt, 1978) [= *Historia iuris antiqui: Gesammelte Schriften*, 3 vols., ed. Tiziana J. Chiusi, Wolfgang Kaiser and Hans-Dieter Spengler (Goldbach: Keip, 2003)].
Nörr, Dieter. “C. Cassius Longinus: Der Jurist als Rhetor (Bemerkungen zu Tacitus, Ann. 14.42 – 45),” in *Historiae iuris antiqui: Gesammelte Schriften*, vol. 3, ed. Tiziana J. Chiusi, Wolfgang Kaiser and Hans-Dieter Spengler (Goldbach: Keip, 2003): 1585–620 [= *Althistorische Studien: Hermann Bengtson zum 70. Geburtstag dargebracht von Kollegen und Schülern*, ed. Heinz Heinen, Karl Stroheker and Gerold Walser (Wiesbaden: Franz Steiner Verlag, 1983): 187–222].
Nougués, Juan Manuel Blanch, and Carmen Palomo Pinel. “Ius publicum y ius priuatum en la experiencia histórica del derecho. Un ejemplo insólito en las distinciones de Bártolo expuestas a través de esquemas,” *Revista General de Derecho Romano* 18 (2012): 1–68.
Olshausen, Eckart. “Soziokulturelle Betrachtungen zur Cena Trimalchionis,” in *Studien zu Petron und seiner Rezeption/Studi su Petronio e sulla sua fortuna*, ed. Luigi Castagna and Eckard Lefèvre (Berlin: De Gruyter, 2007): 15–31.
Oost, Stewart Irvin. “The Career of M. Antonius Pallas,” *The American Journal of Philology* 79, no. 2 (1958): 113–39.

Orestano, Riccardo. "La valutazione del prezzo nel fedecommesso e nel legato di res aliena e nella fideicommissaria libertas," *Annali della Facoltà di Giurisprudenza. Università degli Studi di Camerino*, vol. 10 (Naples: Jovene, 1936): 225–56.

Ortu, Rosanna. "Costantino e la tutela giuridica della 'servorum agnatio'," in *Philia. Scritti per Gennaro Franciosi*, vol. 3, ed. Frederico Maria D'Ippolito (Naples: Satura Editrice, 2007): 1887–926.

Otto, Carl E., Bruno Schilling and Carl F.F. Sintenis. *Das Corpus Juris Civilis in's Deutsche übersetzt*, vol. 3 (Leipzig: G. Focke, 1831).

Owens, Leslie Howard. *This Species of Property. Slave Life and Culture in the Old South* (New York: Oxford University Press, 1976).

Padgug, Robert A. "Problems in the Theory of Slavery and Slave Society," *Science & Society* 40, no. 1 (1976): 3–27.

Palma, Antonio. *Humanior interpretatio. 'Humanitas' nell'interpretazione e nella normazione da Adriano ai Severi* (Turin: Giappichelli, 1992).

Palmer, Vernon V. "Essai sur les origines et les auteurs du Code Noir," *Revue internationale de droit comparé* 50, no. 1 (1998): 111–40.

Parker, Holt Neumon. "Free Women and Male Slaves, or Mandingo Meets the Roman Empire," in *Fear of Slaves – Fear of Enslavement in the Ancient* Mediterranean. *Peur de l'ésclave – Peur de l'ésclavage en mediterranée ancienne (Discours, representations, pratiques)*, ed. Anastasia Serghidou (Besançon: Presses Universitaires de Franche-Comté, 2007): 281–98.

Parker, Holt Neumon. "Sex, Popular Beliefs, and Culture," in *Cultural History of Sexuality in the Classical World*, ed. Mark Golden and Peter Toohey (London: Bloomsbury, 2014): 123–44.

Patterson, Orlando. *Slavery and Social Death. A Comparative Study* (Cambridge, MA: Harvard University Press, 1982).

Paulus, Christoph. *Die Idee der postmortalen Persönlichkeit im römischen Testamentsrecht. Zur gesellschaftlichen und rechtlichen Bedeutung einzelner Testamentsklauseln* (Berlin: Duncker & Humblot, 1992).

Pellecchi, Luigi. "Loi Iunia Norbana sur l'affranchissement," *Leges Populi Romani*, 15.04.2020, http://telma.irht.cnrs.fr//outils/lepor/notice490/ [accessed 01.09.2022].

Penner, James E. "The 'Bundle of Rights' Picture of Property," *UCLA Law Review* 43 (1995/1996): 711–820.

Penner, James E. "The Concept of Property and the Concept of Slavery," in *The Legal Understanding of Slavery. From the Historical to the Contemporary*, ed. Jean Allain (Oxford: Oxford University Press, 2012): 242–52.

Pernice, Alfred. *Labeo: Das römische Privatrecht im ersten Jahrhunderte der Kaiserzeit*, vol. 1 (Halle: Verlag der Buchhandlung des Waisenhauses, 1873).

Perozzi, Silvio. *Istituzioni di diritto romano*, vol. 1, 2nd ed. (Rome: Athenaeum, 1928).

Perry, Matthew J. *Gender, Manumission, and the Roman Freedwoman* (New York: Cambridge University Press, 2014).

Pesaresi, Roberto. *Ricerche sul peculium imprenditoriale* (Bari: Cacucci Editore, 2008).

Petersen, Lauren Hackworth. *The Freedman in Roman Art and Art History* (Cambridge: Cambridge University Press, 2006).

Pfaff, Ivo. *Ein Beitrag zur Lehre vom favor libertatis* (Vienna: Manz, 1894).

Pflaum, Hans-Georg. "Préface," in *Domestique et fonctionnaire sous le haut-Empire romain*, vol. 3, ed. Gérard Boulvert (Paris: Les Belles Lettres, 1974).

Pharr, Clyde. *The Theodosian Code* (Princeton: Princeton University Press, 1952).

Pinzone, Antonino. "Naufragi, fisco e trasporti marittimi nell'età di Caracalla (su CJ 11,6,1)," *Quaderni Catanesi* 4, no. 7 (1982): 64–109.

Platschek, Johannes. "Das Nebengut der Ehefrau in D. 23.3.9.3 (Ulp. 31 Sab.): Quae Gaiae peculium appellantur," *Quaderni Lupiensi* 5 (2015): 125–38.
Pliny the Younger. *Letters*, vol. 2, transl. Betty Radice, Loeb Classical Library 59 (Cambridge, MA: Harvard University Press, 1969).
Polaček, Adalbert. "Diritti dell'uomo nell'epoca costantiniana," in *Atti dell'Accademia Romanistica Costantiniana*, vol. 8, ed. G. Crifò and S. Giglio (Naples: Edizioni Scientifiche Italiane, 1990).
Poláček, Vojtěch. "Randbemerkungen zur Forschung über Staat und Recht im Altertum," in *Studi in onore di Edoardo Volterra*, vol. 3 (Milan: Giuffrè, 1971): 201–36.
Pólay, Elemér. *Die Sklavenehe und das römische Recht*, Acta Juridica et Politica, Universitatis Szegediensis 14.7 (Szeged: József Attila Tudományegyetem Szeged, 1967).
Pool, Eric. "Lateinische Syntax und juristische Begriffsbildung: In bonis 'alicuius' esse und bonitarisches Eigentum im klassischen römischen Recht," *Zeitschrift der Savigny-Stiftung für Rechtsgeschichte, Romanistische Abteilung* 102 (1985): 470–81.
Porto, Andrea di. *Impresa collettiva e schiavo 'manager' in Roma antica (II sex. a. C.-II sex. d. C.)* (Milan: Giuffrè, 1984).
Prachner, Georg. "Zur Bedeutung der antiken Sklaven- und Kolonenwirtschaft für den Niedergang des römischen Reiches (Bemerkungen zur marxistischen Forschung)," *Historia: Zeitschrift für Alte Geschichte* 22 (1973): 732–56.
Prag, Jonathan R.W. "Cave Navem," *Classical Quarterly* 56, no. 2 (2006): 538–47.
Prag, Jonathan R.W., and Ian D. Repath, eds. *Petronius: A Handbook* (New York: Wiley-Blackwell, 2009).
Pringsheim, Fritz."Ius aequum und ius strictum," *Zeitschrift der Savigny-Stiftung für Rechtsgeschichte, Romanistische Abteilung* 42 (1921): 643–55.
Puglisi, Angelo. "Servi, coloni, veterani e la terra in alcuni testi di Costantino," *Labeo* 23 (1977): 305–17.
Puglisi, Gaetano. "Il microcosmo di C. Pompeius Trimalchio Maecenatianus: Schiavi e liberti nella casa di un mercante romano (Petr. 27–78)," *Index* 15 (1987): 207–26.
Puliatti, Salvatore. *Callistratus: Opera* (Rome: L'Erma di Bretschneider, 2019).
Quadrato, Renato. "Maris atque feminae coniunctio," *Index* 38 (2010): 223–52.
Raber, Fritz. "Zum 'pretium affectionis'," in *Festgabe für Arnold Herdlitczka*, ed. Franz Horak and Wolfgang Waldstein (Munich/Salzburg: Wilhelm Fink, 1972): 197–213.
Raditsa, Leo Ferrero. "Augustus' Legislation Concerning Marriage, Procreation, Love Affairs and Adultery," in *Aufstieg und Niedergang der römischen Welt* pt. 2, *Principat*, vol. 13, *Recht*, ed. Hildegard Temporini and Wolfgang Haase (Berlin: De Gruyter, 1980): 278–339.
Rainer, Johannes M. "Humanität und Arbeit im römischen Recht," *Zeitschrift der Savigny-Stiftung für Rechtsgeschichte, Romanistische Abteilung* 105 (1988): 745–70.
Rainer, Johannes M. "Zur Prostitution von Sklavinnen in Rom," in *Inter cives necnon peregrinos. Essays in Honour of Boudewijn Sirks*, ed. Jan Hallebeek et al. (Goettingen: V&R unipress, 2014): 627–40.
Rampazzo, Natale. *Quasi praetor non fuerit. Studi sulle elezioni magistratuali Roma repubblicana tra regola ed eccezione* (Naples: Satura Editrice, 2008): 357–552.
Reduzzi Merola, Francesca. *'Servo parere'. Studi sulla condizione giuridica degli schiavi vicari e dei sottoposti a schiavi nelle esperienze greca e romana* (Naples: Jovene, 1990).
Reduzzi Merola, Francesca. "I vari livelli della dipendenza: Il vicarius vicarii," in *I diritti degli altri in Grecia e a Roma*, ed. Alberto Maffi and Lorenzo Gagliardi (Sankt Augustin: Academia Verlag, 2011): 249–54.
Riccobono, Salvatore, Vincenzo Arangio-Ruiz and Giovanni Baviera, eds. *Fontes iuris Romani antejustiniani*, vol. 3 (Florence: S.A.G. Barbera, 1968).

Richlin, Amy. *Slave Theater in the Roman Republic: Plautus and Popular Comedy* (Cambridge: Cambridge University Press, 2017).
Riedlberger, Peter. *Prolegomena zu den spätantiken Konstitutionen* (Stuttgart-Bad Cannstatt: Frommann-Holzboog Verlag, 2020).
Rieks, Rudolf. “Humanitas,” in *Historisches Wörterbuch der Philosophie*, vol. 3, ed. Joachim Ritter, Karlfried Gründer and Gottfried Gabriel (Basel: Schwabe, 1973): 1231–32.
Rimell, Victoria. “Petronius’ Lessons in Learning: The Hard Way,” in *Ordering Knowledge in the Roman Empire*, ed. Jason König and Tim Whitmarsh (Cambridge: Cambridge University Press, 2007): 108–32.
Rimell, Victoria. “Letting the Page Run On. Poetics, Rhetoric, and Noise in the Satyrica,” in *Petronius: A Handbook*, ed. Jonathan R.W. Prag and Ian D. Repath (New York: Wiley-Blackwell, 2009): 65–81.
Robinson, Olivia F. “Slaves and the Criminal Law,” *Zeitschrift der Savigny-Stiftung für Rechtsgeschichte, Romanistische Abteilung* 98 (1981): 213–54.
Robinson, Olivia F. *The Criminal Law of Ancient Rome* (London: Duckworth, 1995).
Robleda, Olís. *Il diritto degli schiavi nell’antica Roma* (Rome: Pontificia Universita Gregoriana, 1976).
Rodak, Dominik. *Entwicklungslinien des militärischen Sonderguts (peculium castrense) von Augustus bis Hadrian* (Göttingen: V&R unipress, 2022).
Rodriquez Garrido, Jacobo. “Ne serva prostituatur. Exlavitud, prostitución y los limites de la dominica potesetas en la Roma Antigua,” *Dialogues d’historie ancienne* 46, no. 1 (2020): 173–96.
Rolfe, John Carew. *Suetonius: Lives of the Caesars*, vol. 2, *Julius. Augustus. Tiberius. Gaius. Caligula* (Cambridge, MA: Harvard University Press, 1914).
Rosati, Gianpiero. “Trimalchio on Stage,” in *Oxford Readings in the Roman Novel*, ed. Stephen J. Harrison (Oxford: Oxford University Press, 1999): 85–104.
Roth, Hans-Jörg. *Alfeni Digesta: Eine spätrepublikanische Juristenschrift* (Berlin: Duncker und Humblot, 1999).
Roth, Ulrike. “Food, Status, and the Peculium of Agricultural Slaves,” *Journal of Roman Archaeology* 18 (2005): 278–92.
Roth, Ulrike. “Peculium, Freedom, Citizenship: Golden Triangle or Vicious Circle? An Act in Two Parts,” in *By the Sweat of Your Brow: Roman Slavery in Its Socio-Economic Setting*, ed. Ulrike Roth (London: Institute of Classical Studies, University of London, 2010): 91–120.
Roth, Ulrike. “An(other) Epitaph for Trimalchio: Sat.30.2,” *Classical Quarterly* 64, no. 1 (2014): 422–25.
Roth, Ulrike. “Liberating the cena,” *Classical Quarterly* 66, no. 2 (2016): 614–34.
Rotondi, Giovanni. *Leges publicae populi Romani* (Hildesheim: Georg Olms Verlag, 1990).
Ruden, Sarah. *Petronius: Satyricon* (Indianapolis: Hackett Publishing, 2000).
Ruden, Sarah. *The Golden Ass: Apuleius* (New Haven: Yale University Press, 2011).
Ruffing, Kai, and Hans-Joachim Drexhage. “Antike Sklavenpreise,” in *Antike Lebenswelten: Konstanz – Wandel – Wirkungsmacht: Festschrift für Ingomar Weiler zum 70. Geburtstag*, ed. Peter Mauritsch, Werner Petermandl, Robert Rollinger and Christoph Ulf (Wiesbaden: Harassowitz, 2008): 321–51.
Russel, Donald A. *Quintilian: The Orator’s Education*, vol. 3, *Books 6–8* (Cambridge, MA: Harvard University Press, 2001).
Saccoccio, Antonio. “Römische Sklaverei zwischen ius gentium und ius naturale,” in *Sklaverei und Recht: Zwischen römischer Antike und moderner Welt*, Berner Universitätsschriften 61, ed. Iole Fargnoli and Thomas Späth (Bern: Haupt Verlag, 2018): 41–54.
Salerno, Francesco. *Ad metalla: Aspetti giuridici del lavoro in miniera* (Naples: Jovene, 2003).

Saller, Richard P. "Familia, Domus, and the Roman Conception of the Family," in *Phoenix* 38, no. 4 (1984): 336–55.
Saller, Richard P. *Patriarchy, Property and Death in the Roman Family* (Cambridge: Cambridge University Press, 1994).
Sánchez-Moreno Ellart, Carlos M. "Die fictio legis Corneliae in P. Berol. 11753 A and 21294 A," *Archiv für Papyrusforschung und verwandte Gebiete* 67, no. 1 (2021): 102–9.
Sanders, Thomas Collett. *The Institutes of Justinian*, 5th ed. (London: Longmans, 1874)
Santalucia, Bernardo. *Studi di diritto penale romano* (Rome: L'Erma di Bretschneider, 1994).
Santalucia, Bernardo. *Diritto e processo penale nell'antica Roma*, 2nd ed. (Milan: Giuffrè, 1998).
Sargenti, Manlio. *Il diritto privato nella legislazione di Costantino* (Milan: Giuffrè, 1938).
Scapini, Nevio. *La confessione nel diritto romano*, vol. 1, *Diritto classico* (Turin: Giappichelli, 1973).
Schadewaldt, Wolfgang. "Humanitas Romana," in *Aufstieg und Niedergang der römischen Welt*, pt. 2, *Principat*, vol. 4, *Philosophie und Künste.*, ed. Hildegard Temporini and Wolfgang Haase (Berlin: De Gruyter, 1973): 43–62.
Schäfer, Christoph. "Die Rolle der actores in Geldgeschäften," in *Fünfzig Jahre Forschungen zur antiken Sklaverei an der Mainzer Akademie 1950–2000: Miscellanea zum Jubiläum*, ed. Heinz Bellen and Heinz Heinen (Stuttgart: Franz Steiner Verlag, 2001): 211–23.
Scheidel, Walter. "Quantifying the Sources of Slaves in the Early Roman Empire," *Journal of Roman Studies* 87 (1997): 156–69.
Scheidel, Walter. "The Roman Slave Supply," in *The Cambridge World History of Slavery*, vol. 1, *The Ancient Mediterranean Worlds*, ed. Keith Bradley and Paul Cartledge (Cambridge: Cambridge University Press, 2011): 287–310.
Schermaier, Martin. Review of *Humanior interpretatio. 'Humanitas' nell'interpretazione e nella normazione da Adriano ai Severi*, by A. Palma, *Iura: Rivista internazionale di diritto romano e antico* 44 (1993/1996): 343–51.
Schermaier, Martin. "Dominus actuum suorum. Die willenstheoretische Begründung des Eigentums und das römische Recht," *Zeitschrift der Savigny-Stiftung für Rechtsgeschichte, Romanistische Abteilung* 134 (2017): 49–105.
Schiavone, Aldo. *Ius: La invención del derecho en Occidente* (Buenos Aires: Adriana Hidalgo, 2012).
Schiavone, Aldo, and Dario Mantovani, eds. *Testi e problemi del giusnaturalismo romano* (Pavia: IUSS Press, 2007).
Schiemann, Gottfried. "Pietas und patria potestas. Bemerkungen zu Marcian D. 48,9,5," in *Interpretationes Iuris Antiqui. Dankesgabe für Shigeo Nishimura*, ed. Thomas Finkenauer and Adriaan Johan Boudewijn Sirks (Wiesbaden: Harrassowitz, 2018): 311–22.
Schmall, Sabine. *Patrimonium und Fiscus. Studien zur kaiserlichen Domänen- und Finanzverwaltung von Augustus bis Mitte des 3. Jahrhunderts n. Chr.* (PhD diss., Universität Bonn, 2011).
Schmeling, Gareth L. *A Commentary on the Satyrica of Petronius* (Oxford: Oxford University Press, 2011).
Scholz, Markus. "Verdammter Dieb. Kleinkriminalität im Spiegel von Fluchtäfelchen," in *Gefährliches Pflaster: Kriminalität im Römischen Reich*, ed. Marcus Reuter and Romina Schiavone (Mainz: Philipp von Zabern Verlag, 2011): 89–105.
Schulz, Fritz. *Prinzipien des römischen Rechts* (Berlin: Duncker & Humblot, 1934).
Schulz, Fritz. *Principios de derecho romano*, transl. Manuel Abellan Velasco (Madrid: Universidad Complutense, 1990).
Schulze, Götz. *Die Naturalobligation. Rechtsfigur und Instrument des Rechtsverkehrs einst und heute – zugleich Grundlegung einer Forderungslehre im Zivilrecht* (Tuebingen: Mohr Siebeck, 2008).

Schumacher, Leonhard. *Servus index: Sklavenverhör und Sklavenanzeige im republikanischen und kaiserzeitlichen Rom* (Wiesbaden: Franz Steiner Verlag, 1982).
Schumacher, Leonhard. *Sklaverei in der Antike: Alltag und Schicksal der Unfreien* (Munich: C.H. Beck, 2001).
Schumacher, Leonhard. "On the Status of Private Actores, Dispensatores and Vilici," in *By the Sweat of Your Brow: Roman Slavery in Its Socio-Economic Setting*, ed. Ulrike Roth (London: Institute of Classical Studies, University of London, 2010): 31–47.
Scott, Rebecca J. "Under Color of Law Siliadin v France and the Dynamics of Enslavement in Historical Perspective," in *The Legal Understanding of Slavery. From the Historical to the Contemporary*, ed. Jean Allain (Oxford: Oxford University Press, 2012): 152–64.
Seeck, Otto. *Regesten der Kaiser und Päpste für die Jahre 311 bis 476 A.D.* (Stuttgart: J.B. Metzler, 1919).
Seiler, Hans Hermann. *Der Tatbestand der negotiorum gestio im römischen Recht* (Cologne: Böhlau, 1968).
Sergeenko, M.E. "Villicus," in *Schiavitù e produzione nella Roma repubblicana*, ed. Iza Biezunska-Malowist (Rome: L'Erma di Bretschneider, 1986): 191–207.
Seuffert, Lothar von. "Der Loskauf von Sklaven mit ihrem Geld," in *Festschrift für die Juristische Fakultät in Gießen zum Universitätsjubiläum*, ed. Reinhard Frank (Giessen: De Gruyter, 1907): 1–20.
Seyfarth, Wolfgang. *Soziale Fragen der spätrömischen Kaiserzeit im Spiegel des Theodosianus* (Berlin: Akademie-Verlag, 1963).
Shearer, David R. "Stalinism, 1928–1940," in *The Cambridge History of Russia*, vol. 3, *The Twentieth Century*, ed. Ronald Grigor Suny (Cambridge: Cambridge University Press, 2006): 192–216.
Sherwin-White, Adrian Nicholas. *The Letters of Pliny: A Historical and Social Commentary* (Oxford: Clarendon Press, 1966).
Shinomori, Daisuke. "Testamentum porcelli: Ein von Sklaven errichtetes Testament?," in *Aus der Werkstatt römischer Juristen: Vorträge der Europäisch-Ostasiatischen Tagung 2013 in Fukuoka*, ed. Ulrich Manthe, Shigeo Nishimura and Mariko Igimi (Berlin: Duncker & Humblot, 2016): 353–74.
Sicari, Amalia. *Leges venditionis. Uno studio sul pensiero giuridico di Papiniano* (Bari: Cacucci Editore, 1996).
Siedentop, Larry. *Inventing the Individual. The Origins of Western Liberalism* (London: The Belknap Press, 2014).
Sild, Jaana. "Legal Capacity of Artificial Intelligence," *L'Europe Unie* 13 (2018): 74–78.
Silla, Francesco Maria. *La 'cognitio' sulle 'libertates fideicommissae'*, L'Arte Del Diritto 11 (Padua: Cedam, 2008).
Simon, Dietrich V. "Zum Einfluß des Christentums auf die Gesetzgebung Kaiser Konstantins des Großen," in *Rom, Recht, Religion. Symposium für Udo Ebert zum siebzigsten Geburtstag*, ed. Kristian Kühl and Gerhard Seher (Tuebingen: Mohr Siebeck, 2011): 73–88.
Simonis, Marcel. *Cum servis nullum est connubium: Untersuchungen zu den eheähnlichen Verbindungen von Sklaven im westlichen Mittelmeerraum des Römischen Reiches* (Hildesheim: Georg Olms Verlag, 2017).
Sirks, Adriaan Johan Boudewijn. "The lex Junia and the Effects of Informal Manumission and Iteration," *Revue Internationale des Droits de l'Antiquité* 30 (1983): 211–92.
Sirks, Adriaan Johan Boudewijn. "Der Zweck des Senatus Consultum Claudianum von 52 n. Chr.," *Zeitschrift der Savigny-Stiftung für Rechtsgeschichte, Romanistische Abteilung* 122 (2005): 138–49.

Sirks, Boudewijn. "Noxa caput sequitur," *Tijdschrift voor Rechtsgeschiedenis* 81, no. 1–2 (2013): 81–108.
Skinner, Marilyn B. *Sexuality in Greek and Roman Culture* (Malden: Blackwell, 2005).
Smith, Martin S., ed. *Petronius: Cena Trimalchionis* (Oxford: Oxford University Press, 1975).
Solazzi, Siro. *Il concorso dei creditori nel diritto romano*, vol. 2 (Naples: Jovene, 1938).
Solazzi, Siro. "Il rispetto per la famiglia dello schiavo," *Studia et Documenta Historiae et Iuris* 15 (1949): 187–92.
Solin, Heikki. "Abuso dell'onomastica nella ricerca epigrafica," in *Usi e abusi epigrafici. Atti del Colloquio Internazionale di epigrafia latina (Genova 20–22 settembre 2001)*, ed. Maria Grazia Angeli Bertinelli and Angela Donati (Rome: Quasar, 2003).
Söllner, Alfred. "Bona Fides – Guter Glaube," *Zeitschrift der Savigny-Stiftung für Rechtsgeschichte, Romanistische Abteilung* 122 (2005): 1–61.
Solum, Lawrence Byard. "Legal Personhood for Artifical Intelligences," *The North Carolina Law Review* 70, no. 4 (1992): 1231–86.
Spengler, Hans-Dieter. "Zugleich Person und Sache – vielleicht Arbeitstier oder Unternehmer: Rechtliche Aspekte der römischen Sklaverei," in *Recht der Wirtschaft und der Arbeit in Europa. Gedächtnisschrift für Wolfgang Blomeyer*, ed. Rüdiger Krause, Winfried Veelken and Klaus Vieweg (Berlin: Duncker & Humblot, 2004): 271–83.
Splett, Jörg. "Humanität, I. Philosophisch," *Staatslexikon online*, 04.01.2021, https://www.staatslexikon-online.de/Lexikon/Humanit%C3%A4t [accessed 04.08.2022].
Spranger, Peter P. *Historische Untersuchungen zu den Sklavenfiguren des Plautus und Terenz*, 2nd ed. (Stuttgart: Franz Steiner Verlag, 1984).
Stagl, Jakob Fortunat. "Die Ausgleichung von Vorteil und Nachteil als Inhalt klassischer aequitas," in *Testi e problemi del giusnaturalismo romano*, ed. Aldo Schiavone and Dario Mantovani (2007): 675–713.
Stagl, Jakob Fortunat. *Favor dotis. Die Privilegierung der Mitgift im System des römischen Rechts* (Vienna/Cologne/Weimar: Böhlau, 2009).
Stagl, Jakob Fortunat. "Eine Flucht nach Rom: Der geistige Weg Ernst Rabels," *Tijdschrift voor Rechtsgeschiedenis* 79, no. 3–4 (2011): 533–52.
Stagl, Jakob Fortunat. "Das 'testamentum militare' in seiner Eigenschaft als 'ius singular'," *Revista de Estudios Histórico-Jurídicos* 36 (2014): 129–57.
Stagl, Jakob Fortunat. "Glanz der Rhetorik und Finsternis der Logik in einer Entscheidung Marc Aurels (Marcell. D. 28, 4, 3 pr.–1)," in *Meditationes de iure et historia: Essays in Honour of Laurens Winkel.* [= *Fundamina: A Journal of Legal History* 20], ed. Rena van den Bergh et al. (Pretoria: Unisa Press, 2014): 871–80.
Stagl, Jakob Fortunat. "Die Funktionen der utilitas publica," *Zeitschrift der Savigny-Stiftung für Rechtsgeschichte, Romanistische Abteilung* 134 (2017): 514–23.
Stagl, Jakob Fortunat. "Caesars Koch oder das Schweigen der Quellen: Zur Kritik Varvaros am didaktischen System des Gaius," *Zeitschrift der Savigny-Stiftung für Rechtsgeschichte, Romanistische Abteilung* 135 (2018): 582–91.
Stagl, Jakob Fortunat. "Utilitas publica, ius naturale y protección de la natura," *Revista General de Derecho Romano* 33 (2019).
Stagl, Jakob Fortunat. "L'ambiguïté existentielle du droit romain: Une faille de la codificationjustinienne," *Revue historique de droit français et étranger* 95, no. 4 (2017): 455–65.
Stagl, Jakob Fortunat. *Camino desde la servidumbre* (Madrid: Editorial Dykinson, 2021).
Stagl, Jakob Fortunat. "El pueblo del derecho es también el pueblo de las leyes?," in *Legum multitudo: Sobre la presencia de las leyes públicas en el derecho privado de la antigua Roma*, ed. Dario Mantovani (Valencia: Tirant Lo Blanch, 2022): 123–58.

Stampp, Kenneth M. *The Peculiar Institution: Slavery in the Ante-Bellum South* (New York: Vintage Books, 1956).
Star, Christopher. *The Empire of the Self: Self-Command and Political Speech in Seneca and Petronius* (Baltimore: Johns Hopkins University Press, 2012).
Starace, Pia. *Lo statuliber e l'adempimento fittizio della condizione. Unostudio sul favor libertatis fra tarda Repubblica ed età antonina* (Bari: Cacucci Editore, 2006).
Starace, Pia. "Venuleio, il parricidio, i servi, la natura," in *Testi e problemi del giusnaturalismo romano*, ed. Dario Mantovani and Aldo Schiavone (Pavia: IUSS Press, 2007): 497–518.
Stark, Oded. *Altruism and Beyond. An Economic Analysis of Transfers and Exchanges Within Families and Groups* (Cambridge: Cambridge University Press, 1995).
Stelzenberger, Barbara. *Kapitalmanagement und Kapitaltransfer im Westen des Römischen Reiches* (Rahden: Leidorf, 2008).
Stiegler, Herwig. "'Konkubinenkind', 'privignus', 'parricidium'," in *Sodalitas. Scritti in onore di Antonio Guarino*, vol. 7, ed. Antonio Guarino and Vincenzo Giuffrè (Naples: Jovene, 1984): 3191–214, 3208.
Sturm, Fritz. "Sklavenkasse entscheidet über Eigentumserwerb: Zu Gaius D. 41,1,43,2 und Ulpian D. 7,1,25,1," in *Sklaverei und Freilassung im römischen Recht Symposium für Hans Josef Wieling zum 70. Geburtstag*, ed. Thomas Finkenauer (Berlin/Heidelberg: Springer Verlag, 2006): 223–41.
Sturm, Fritz. "Ius gentium. Imperialistische Schönfärberei römischer Juristen," in *Römische Jurisprudenz – Dogmatik, Überlieferung, Rezeption. Festschrift für Detlef Liebs zum 75. Geburtstag*, ed. Karlheinz Muscheler (Berlin: Duncker & Humboldt, 2011): 663–69.
Sullivan, J.P. "Petronius' 'Satyricon' and Its Neronian Context," in *Aufstieg und Niedergang der römischen Welt*, pt. 2, *Principat*, vol. 32.3, *Sprache und Literatur (Literatur der julisch-claudischen und der flavischen Zeit)*, ed. Hildegard Temporini and Wolfgang Haase (Berlin: De Gruyter, 1985): 1666–86.
Tafaro, Sebastiano. "Schiavitù," in *Festschrift für Rolf Knütel zum 70. Geburstag*, ed. Holger Altmeppen, Ingo Reichard and Martin Josef Schermaier (Heidelberg: C.F. Müller, 2009): 1227–68.
Talbert, Richard J.A. *The Senate of Imperial Rome* (Princeton, NJ: Princeton University Press, 1984).
Thesaurus Linguae Latinae, vol. 1 (Leipzig: Teubner, 1909–1934); vol. 2 (Leipzig: Teubner, 1900–1906).
Thilo, Ralf Michael. *Der Codex accepti et expensi im Römischen Recht: Ein Beitrag zur Lehre von der Litteralobligation* (Goettingen: Muster-Schmidt, 1980).
Toso, Alberto. "Emilio Papiniano e le influenze cristiane nell'evoluzione del diritto romano classico," *Acta Iuridici Internationalis* 2 (1935): 21–35.
Treggiari, Susan. "Contubernales in CIL 6," *Phoenix* 35 (1981): 42–69.
Treggiari, Susan. *Roman Marriage: 'Iusti Coniuges' from the Time of Cicero to the Time of Ulpian* (Oxford: Oxford University Press, 1991).
Treggiari, Susan. "Questions on Women Domestics in the Roman West," in *Schiavitù, manomissione e classi dipendenti nel mondo antico*, Pubblicazioni dell'istituto di storia antica 13, ed. Maria Capozza (Rome: L'Erma di Bretschneider, 1997): 185–201.
Urbanik, Jakub. "On the Uselessness of It All: The Roman Law of Marriage and Modern Times," *Fundamina* 20, no. 2 (2014): 948–54.
Varvaro, Mario. "La dote, il ius singulare e il 'sistema didattico' di Gaio," *Seminarios Complutenses de Derecho Romano* 39 (2016): 409–39.
Végh, Zoltán. "Ex pacto ius," *Zeitschrift der Savigny-Stiftung für Rechtsgeschichte, Romanistische Abteilung* 110 (1993): 184–295.

Venturini, Carlo. "Der dominus, der servus und die muliercula – Anmerkungen zu D. 11,3,16," in *Sklaverei und Freilassung im römischen Recht: Symposium für Hans Josef Wieling zum 70. Geburtstag*, ed. Thomas Finkenauer (Berlin: Springer Verlag, 2006): 243–50.

Verboven, Koenraad. "A Funny Thing Happened on My Way to the Market: Reading Petronius to Write Economic History," in *Petronius: A Handbook*, ed. Jonathan R.W. Prag and Ian D. Repath (New York: Wiley-Blackwell, 2009): 125–39.

Verboven, Koenraad. "Dispensator," in *The Encyclopedia of Ancient History*, vol. 4, ed. Roger S. Bagnall et al. (Malden: Wiley, 2013): 2166–67.

Veyne, Paul. "Vie de Trimalcion," *Annales: Histoire, Sciences Sociales* 16 (1961): 213–47.

Veyne, Paul. *La société romain* (Paris: POINTS, 2001).

Veyne, Paul. *Sexe et pouvoir à Rome* (Paris: Tallandier, 2005).

Vigorita, Spagnuolo. *Casta Domus. Un seminario legislazione matriminiale augustea* (Indiana: Indiana University Press, 2002).

Vittinghoff, Friedrich. "Die Theorie des historischen Materialismus über den antiken Sklavenhalterstaat," *Saeculum* 11 (1960): 89–131.

Vitucci, Giovanni. "Libertus," in *Dizionario Epigrafico*, vol. 4/1. (Rome: L'Erma di Bretschneider, 1958): 905–46.

Voci, Pasquale. *Diritto ereditario romano*, vol. 1 (Milan: Giuffrè, 1960).

Voci, Pasquale. *Diritto ereditario romano*, vol. 2, 2nd ed. (Milan: Giuffrè, 1963; 2nd ed., 1967).

Voci, Pasquale. *Nuovi studi sulla legislazione romana del tardo impero* (Padua: Cedam, 1989).

Vogt, Joseph. *Struktur der antiken Sklavenkriege* (Stuttgart: Franz Steiner Verlag, 1957).

Vogt, Joseph. *Sklaverei und Humanität: Studien zur antiken Sklaverei und ihrer Erforschung* (Wiesbaden: Franz Steiner Verlag, 1983).

Völker, Thomas, and Dirk Rohmann. "Praenomen Petronii: The Date and Author of the Satyricon Reconsidered," *Classical Quarterly* 61, no. 2 (2011): 660–76.

Volterra, Edoardo. *Senatus consulta*, ed. Pierangelo Buongiorno, Annarosa Gallo and Salvatore Marino (Stuttgart: Franz Steiner Verlag, 2017).

Wacke, Andreas. "Faktische Arbeitsverhältnisse im Römischen Recht? Zur sogenannten 'notwendigen Entgeltlichkeit', besonders bei Arbeitsleistungen vermeintlicher Sklaven," *Zeitschrift der Savigny-Stiftung für Rechtsgeschichte, Romanistische Abteilung* 108 (1991): 123–54.

Wacke, Andreas. "Der favor libertatis: Skizze eines Forschungsvorhabens," in *Vorträge gehalten auf dem 28. Deutschen Rechtshistorikertag Nimwegen 23–27 September 1990*, ed. Paul Nève and Chris Coppens (Nimwegen: Gerard Nood Instituut, 1992): 21–23.

Wacke, Andreas. "Die adjektizischen Klagen im Überblick. Erster Teil: Von der Reeder- und der Betriebsleiterklage zur direkten Stellvertretung," *Zeitschrift der Savigny-Stiftung für Rechtsgeschichte, Romanistische Abteilung* 111 (1994): 280–362.

Wacke, Andreas. "Die sogfältige Klagen-Auswahl durch den Käufer bei umgekehrter Eviktion (Papinian Dig. 21,2,66 pr.): Da mihi facta, dabo tibi ius?," in *A bonis bona discere. Festgabe für Janos Zlinsky*, ed. Orsola M. Péter and Bela Szaabo (Miskolc: Bibor Verlag, 1998): 63–89.

Wacke, Andreas. "Manumissio matrimonii causa. Die Freilassung zwecks Heirat nach den Ehegesetzen des Augustus," in *Fünfzig Jahre Forschungen zur antiken Sklaverei an der Mainzer Akademie: 1950–2000. Miscellanea zum Jubiläum*, ed. Heinz Bellen and Heinz Heinen (Stuttgart: Franz Steiner Verlag, 2001): 133–58.

Wacke, Andreas. "Die Menschenwürde von Sklaven im Spiegel des Umgehungsgeschäfts nach Sextus Pedius. Si alii rei homo accedat und D. 21,1,44 pr.," in *Iurisprudentia universalis Festschrift für Theo Mayer-Maly*, ed. Martin J. Schermaier, J. Michael Rainer and Laurens C. Winkel (Cologne/Weimar/Vienna: Böhlau, 2002): 811–36.

Wacke, Andreas. "Erbrechtliche Sukzession als Persönlichkeitsfortsetzung?," *Zeitschrift der Savigny-Stiftung für Rechtsgeschichte, Romanistische Abteilung* 123 (2006): 197–296.
Wacke, Andreas. "Die libera administratio peculii: Zur Verfügungsmacht von Hauskindern und Sklaven über ihr Sondergut," in *Sklaverei und Freilassung im römischen Recht: Symposium für Hans Josef Wieling zum 70. Geburtstag*, ed. Thomas Finkenauer (Berlin: Springer Verlag, 2006): 251–316.
Wacke, Andreas. "Das Affektionsinteresse: Heute und in römischen Rechtsquellen," in *Ars iuris. Festschrift für Okko Behrends*, ed. Martin Avenarius, Rudolf Meyer-Pritzl and Cosima Müller (Göttingen: Wallstein Verlag, 2009): 555–88.
Wagner, Herbert. *Voraussetzungen, Vorstufen und Anfänge der römischen Generalverpfändung* (Marburg: N.G. Elwert, 1968).
Walde, Alois, and Johann Baptist Hofmann. *Lateinisches Etymologisches Wörterbuch*, vol. 1, Indogermanische Bibliothek, 2. Reihe: Wörterbücher (Heidelberg: Carl Winter, 1938).
Waldstein, Wolfgang. *Untersuchungen zum römischen Begnadigungsrecht. Abolitio – indulgentia – venia*, Commentationes Aenipontanae 18 (Innsbruck: Universitätsverlag Wagner, 1964).
Waldstein, Wolfgang. "Entscheidungsgrundlagen der römischen Juristen," in *Aufstieg und Niedergang der römischen Welt*, pt. 2, *Principat*, vol. 15, *Recht*, ed. Hildegard Temporini and Wolfgang Haase (Berlin: De Gruyter, 1976): 3–100.
Waldstein, Wolfgang. *Operae libertorum. Untersuchungen zur Dienstpflicht freigelassener Sklaven* (Stuttgart: Franz Steiner Verlag, 1986).
Waldstein, Wolfgang. "Schiavitù e Cristianesimo da Costantino a Teodosio II," in *Atti dell'Accademia Romanistica Costantiniana*, vol. 8 (Naples: Edizioni Scientifiche Italiane, 1990): 123–45.
Waldstein, Wolfgang. "Zur 'Teilrechtsfähigkeit der Sklaven nach Kaiserrecht'," in *Ars Iuris. Festschrift für Okko Behrends zum 70. Geburtstag*, ed. Martin Avenarius, Rudolf Meyer-Pritzl and Cosima Möller (Göttingen: Wallstein Verlag, 2009): 589–602.
Watson, Alan. *The Law of Persons in the Later Roman Republic* (Oxford: Oxford University Press, 1967).
Watson, Alan. *The Digest of Justinian*, vol. 1–4 (Pennsylvania: University of Pennsylvania Press, 1985).
Watson, Alan. *Roman Slave Law* (Baltimore/London: Johns Hopkins University Press, 1987).
Watson, Alan. *Slave Law in the Americas* (Athens: University of Georgia Press, 1989).
Watson, Alan. "Seventeenth-Century Jurists, Roman Law, and the Law of Slavery," *Chicago-Kent Law Review* 68, no. 3 (1992): 1343–54.
Watson, Alan. "Religious and Gender Discrimination. St. Ambrose and the Valentiniani," *Studia et Documenta Historiae et Iuris* 61 (1995): 313–26.
Weaver, Paul Richard Carey. "The Status Nomenclature of the Imperial Freedmen," *Classical Quarterly* 13, no. 2 (1963): 272–78.
Weaver, Paul Richard Carey. "Augustorum libertus," *Historia* 13, no. 2 (1964): 188–89
Weaver, Paul Richard Carey. "Irregular Nomina of Imperial Freedmen," *Classical Quarterly* 15, no. 2 (1965): 323–26.
Weaver, Paul Richard Carey. "Social Mobility in the Early Roman Empire: The Evidence of the Imperial Freedmen and Slaves," *Past & Present* 37 (1967): 3–20.
Weaver, Paul Richard Carey. *Familia Caesaris: A Social Study of the Emperor's Freedmen and Slaves* (Cambridge: Cambridge University Press, 1972).
Weaver, Paul Richard Carey. "Repertorium Familiae Caesarum," *Universität zu Köln*, 09.07.2013, https://alte-geschichte.phil-fak.uni-koeln.de/personal/ehemalige-emeriti/eck-prof-dr-werner/weaver-repertorium [accessed 23.08.2022].

Weiß, Alexander. *Sklave der Stadt: Untersuchungen zur öffentlichen Sklaverei in den Städten des Römischen Reiche*, Historia Einzelschriften 173 (Stuttgart: Franz Steiner Verlag, 2004).
Welch, Katherine E. *The Roman Amphitheatre. From Its Origins to the Colosseum* (Cambridge/New York: Cambridge University Press, 2007).
Wenger, Leopold. *Die Quellen des römischen Rechts* (Vienna: Holzhausen, 1953).
Wesenberg, Burkhardt. "Zur Wanddekoration im Hause des Trimalchio," in *Studien zu Petron und seiner Rezeption/Studi su Petronio e sulla sua fortuna*, ed. Luigi Castagna and Eckard Lefèvre (Berlin: De Gruyter, 2007): 267–83.
Whittuck, Edward Arthur, ed. *Gai Institutiones or Institutes of Roman Law by Gaius*, 4th ed. (Oxford: Clarendon Press, 1904).
Wieacker, Franz. *Römische Rechtsgeschichte: Quellenkunde, Rechtsbildung, Jurisprudenz und Rechtsliteratur*, vol. 1, *Einleitung, Quellenkunde, Frühzeit und Republik* (Munich: C.H. Beck, 1988).
Wieacker, Franz. *Römische Rechtsgeschichte*, vol. 2, *Die Jurisprudenz vom frühen Prinzipat bis zum Ausgang der Antike* (Munich: C.H. Beck, 2006).
Wieacker, Franz. *A History of Private Law in Europe, with Particular Reference to Germany*, transl. Tony Weir (Oxford: Clarendon Press, 1995).
Wiedemann, Thomas E.J. "The Regularity of Manumission at Rome," *Classical Quarterly* 35, no. 1 (1985): 162–75.
Wiedemann, Thomas E.J. *Emperors and Gladiators* (London/New York: Routledge, 1992).
Wieling, Hans. *Testamentsauslegung im römischen Recht* (Munich: C.H. Beck, 1972).
Wieling, Hans. Review of *Festgabe für Arnold Herdlitczka zu seinem 75. Geburtstag, dargebracht von seinen Schülern und Freunden*, ed. Franz Horak und Wolfgang Waldstein, *Zeitschrift der Savigny-Stiftung für Rechtsgeschichte, Romanistische Abteilung* 89 (1972): 464–71.
Wieling, Hans. "Grundbesitz I (rechtsgeschichtlich)," in *Reallexikon für Antike und Christentum*, vol. 12, ed. Theodor Klauser (Stuttgart: Anton Hiersemann Verlag, 1983): col. 1172–96.
Wiese, Marion. *Leibeigene Bauern und Römisches Recht im 17. Jahrhundert. Ein Gutachten des David Mevius* (Berlin: Duncker & Humblot, 2005).
Wilinski, Adam. "Ricerche sull'alienazione degli schiavi nel diritto romano: Vendita dello schiavo con la clausola ne manumittatur," *Index* 5 (1974): 321–28.
Willems, Constantin. *Justinian als Ökonom: Entscheidungsgründe und Entscheidungsmuster in den 'quinquaginta decisiones'* (Cologne: Vandenhoeck & Ruprecht, 2017).
Williams, Craig A. *Roman Homosexuality* (Cary: Oxford University Press, 2010).
Willvonseder, Reinhard. *Stellung des Sklaven im Privatrecht*, vol. 1, *Eheähnliche Verbindungen und verwandtschaftliche Beziehungen*, Corpus der römischen Rechtsquellen zur antiken Sklaverei 4 (Stuttgart: Franz Steiner Verlag, 2010).
Winterbottom, Michael. *Seneca the Elder: Declamations*, vol. 1, *Controversiae Books 1–6: Suasoriae, Fragments*, Loeb Classical Library 464 (Cambridge, MA: Harvard University Press, 1974).
Winterling, Aloys. "'Staat'und 'Gesellschaft' in der römischen Kaiserzeit: Zwei moderne Forschungsprobleme und ihr antiker Hintergrund," *Zentrum für interdisziplinäre Forschung der Universität Bielefeld, Mitteilungen* 3 (1998): 5–23.
Winterling, Aloys. *Aula Caesaris: Studien zur Institutionalisierung des römischen Kaiserhofes in der Zeit von Augustus bis Commodus (31 v. Chr.–192 n. Chr.)* (Munich: C.H. Beck, 1999).
Wintrich, Josef. "Über Eigenart und Methode verfassungsgerichtlicher Rechtsprechung," in *Verfassung und Verwaltung in Theorie und Wirklichkeit. Festschrift für Herrn Geheimrat Professor Dr. Wilhelm Laforet anlässlich seines 75. Geburtstages* (Munich: Isar Verlag, 1952): 227–49.

Wissowa, Georg, et al., eds. *Paulys Realencyclopädie der classischen Altertumswissenschaft (RE)*, vol. IV 2 (Stuttgart: J.B. Metzler 1901), vol. V 1 (Stuttgart: J.B. Metzler, 1905), vol. XII (Stuttgart: J. B. Metzler, 1925), vol. XIX 1 (Stuttgart: Metzler, 1937), vol. XX 1 (Stuttgart: J.B. Metzler, 1941).

Wolf, Joseph Georg. *Das Senatusconsultum Silanianum und die Senatsrede des C. Cassius Longinus aus dem Jahre 61 n. Chr.* (Heidelberg: Winter, 1988).

Wolf, Joseph Georg. *Neue Rechtsurkunden aus Pompeji: Tabulae Pompeianae Novae: Lateinisch und deutsch* (Darmstadt: Wissenschaftliche Buchgesellschaft, 2010).

Wolf, Joseph Georg. "Interpolationen in den Digesten," *Studia et Documenta Historiae et Iuris* 79 (2013): 3–80.

Wubbe Felix B.J. *Res aliena pignori data* (Leiden: Universitaire pers Leiden, 1960).

Wycisk, Tonia. *Quidquid in foro fieri potest: Studien zum römischen Recht bei Quintilian* (Berlin: Duncker & Humblot, 2008).

Wyke, Maria. "Mistress and Metaphor in Augustan Elegy," in *Sexuality and Gender in the Classical World: Readings and Sources*, ed. Laura K. McClure (Oxford: Blackwell, 2002): 193–219.

Yardley, John, and Anthony Barret. *Cornelius Tacitus: The Annals. Reigns of Tiberius, Claudius, and Nero* (Oxford: Oxford University Press, 2008).

Zannini, Pierluigi. "In tema di regolamento di confini della sfera di risarcibilitá del danno aquiliano. Una lezione dei prudentes," in *Valori e principii del diritto romano*, vol. 3, ed. Andrea Trisciuoglio (Naples: Edizioni Scientifiche Italiane, 2009): 117–27.

Żeber, Ireneusz. *A Study of the Peculium of a Slave in Pre-Classical Roman Law* (Wrocław: Wydawnictwo Uniwersytetu Wrocławskiego, 1981).

Zimmermann, Reinhard. *The Law of Obligations. Roman Foundations of the Civilian Tradition* (Oxford: Oxford University Press, 1996).

Zoz de Biasio, Maria Gabriella. "Nota minima sulla tutela dei nuclei familiari servili," in *Studi in onore di Arnaldo Biscardi*, vol. 4, ed. Franco Pastori (Milan: Istituto Editoriale Cisalpino-La Goliardica, 1983): 537–44.

Zwalve, Willem J. "Callistus's Case: Some Legal Aspects of Roman Business Activities," in *The Transformation of Economic Life under the Roman Empire: Proceedings of the Second Workshop of the International Network Impact of Empire (Roman Empire, c. 200 B.C.–A.D. 476), Nottingham, July 4–7, 2001*, ed. Lukas de Blois and John Rich (Amsterdam: J.C. Gieben, 2002): 116–27.

Authors

Wolfram Buchwitz, born 1980, is Professor of Civil Law, Roman Law, Legal History, and Civil Procedure at the University of Würzburg. He graduated from the University of Münster in 2005, completed postgraduate studies at La Sapienza University of Rome in 2006, and doctoral studies at the University of Bonn. His main research interests are Classical Roman Law and Dispute Resolution Law.

Pierangelo Buongiorno, is Professor for Roman Law at the University of Macerata. He worked in the Universities of Mainz, Lecce, Münster. He was awarded with the Gérard Boulvert Award (2010) and with the Sofja Kovalevskaja Award (2014). His main research fields are the legal activity of the Roman Senate, the prosopography of the Roman jurists and the history of romanistic historiography.

Thomas Finkenauer, born in 1968, studied law and history in Trier, Geneva and Rome. Since 2005 Professor of Private Law, Roman Law, and European Private Law (tenured) at the University of Tübingen. Visiting professor in Montpellier, Palermo, Milan, and Bern. Research interests are Roman Law, History of Law, German and European Civil Law.

Richard Gamauf, born in 1964, is Professor of Roman Law and Ancient Legal History at the University of Vienna. He was awarded with the Kupiszewski-Award of the Centro romanistico internazionale Copanello (2001). His main research interests are the social aspects in the sources of Classical Roman Law and Roman slave law.

Aglaia McClintock, jurist and historian, is Professor of Roman Law at the University of Sannio. She is Life Member of Clare Hall, University of Cambridge. She was awarded the Special Prize «Furio Diaz» of the Fondazione Cassa Risparmi di Livorno (2013). Her research focuses on criminal law and slavery; the legal condition of women; the iconographic and religious representations of Roman justice; madness in Roman law.

Martin Schermaier, born in 1963, is Professor of Civil Law and Roman Law at the University of Bonn. He was awarded with the "Premio Gérard Boulvert" (1993), is member of the *Nordrhein-Westfälische Akademie der Wissenschaften und der Künste* (since 2007) and is principal investigator in the Cluster of Excellence "Beyond Slavery and Freedom." His main research interests are Classical Roman Law, Legal History and modern Civil Law.

Jakob Fortunat Stagl, born in 1971, is professor of Roman Law at the University of Warsaw since 2020. Before he held positions in Chile and Germany. He is principal investigator of the research project 'The Temple of Justice. A Foundation of a systematic Interpretation of the Digest', financed by the National Science Centre (NCN) of Poland. He is writing on Roman law as well as on legal history and civil law.

https://doi.org/10.1515/9783110987195-011

Index of Sources

I. Inscriptions, Papyri, Collections etc.

AE (Année épigraphique)

1916, 116 182 n. 43
1973, 471 156 n. 197
1975, 232 156 n. 197
1980, 247 156 n. 197
1985, 143 183, 184
1990, 51 148 n. 139, 156 n. 197
1993, 911 147 n. 132
2005, 1107 156 n. 197
2006, 173 81
2009, 1256 137 n. 64

CIL (Corpus Inscriptionum Latinarum)

II-07 981 113 n. 136
III 3172 137 n. 64
III 3658.7 46 n. 127
III 4797 156 n. 197
III 6998 102 n. 79
III 13652 102 n. 79
IV 9246b 140
V 2176.4 46 n. 127
V 5050 74 n. 27
VI 239 156 n. 197
VI 278 139 n. 75
VI 376 83
VI 1747 149 n. 147
VI 2225.8 46 n. 127
VI 2307 176
VI 2354 183
VI 3687 131 n. 30
VI 3739 156 n. 197
VI 5197 158 n. 215
VI 8634 84
VI 9320 156 n. 197
VI 11390 176
VI 12533 80
VI 15317 81
VI 19175 102 n. 79
VI 24316 81
VI 26007 85 n. 57
VI 26008 85 n. 57
VI 39568 156 n. 197
VIII 7076 183, 184
VIII 12922 81
IX 313 81
IX 825 149 n. 147
IX 3028 149 n. 147
IX 4112 265 n. 135
IX 4186 139 n. 75
IX 5177 156 n. 197
X 26 137 n. 64
X 4687 184
X 6318 80
XI 3612 68
XI 5898 85 n. 57
XI 6314 113 n. 136
XI 7092 156 n. 197
XII 5130.6 46 n. 127
XIII 5194 156 n. 197
XIV 2856 156 n. 197
XIV 3033 156 n. 197

CLE (Carmina Latina Epigraphica)

CLE 12.3 46 n. 127
CLE 371.2 46 n. 127

Epigraphic Database Roma (EDR)

000144 83
104467 81
127089 80
138067 85
151983 81
158684 85
171345 84
177121 80
179457 83

ILS (Inscriptiones Latinae Selectae)

206 74 n. 27
1514 158 n. 215
1967 84
2815 80
3670 83
7367 149 n. 147

https://doi.org/10.1515/9783110987195-012

Papyrus Hamburgensis (P. Hamb.)
1.72r l. 6 227 n. 140

Papyrus Zenon (P. Zen.)
3.59398 147 n. 137

Res gestae divi Augusti
22 193 n. 12

Vulgata (Vulg.)
Luc. 19.12–27 265 n. 133
Mt. 22.21 236 n. 203
Mt. 25.14–30 265 n. 133
Rom. 2.15 236 n. 202

II. Ancient Legal Sources

1. Ius anteiustinianum

Codex Theodosianus
2.25.1 43, 44, 47, 55–60
5.17.1 58

Collatio legum Mosaicarum et Romanarum (Coll.)
3.3.5–6 226

Fragmentum Dositheanum (frg. Dos.)
5 217 n. 92
15 205 n. 11

Fragmenta Vaticana (frg. Vat.)
261 264 n. 132
283 221 n. 113

Gaius
– Gai Institutiones (Gai.)
1.2 212 n. 55, 216 n. 84
1.7 137 n. 66
1.8 8
1.9 8, 97
1.9–54 237
1.13 195 n. 20
1.19 30
1.20 29 n. 29
1.37 118 n. 168
1.38 29 n. 30
1.39 29 n. 30
1.41 205 n. 11
1.44 205 n. 11
1.47 118 n. 168
1.48 267 n. 146
1.49 12 n. 69
1.51 94
1.52 12 n. 68, 94 n. 34
1.55 12 n. 68, 137 n. 60, 217 n. 87
1.58 211 n. 43
1.83 236 n. 201
1.84 82
1.89–91 232 n. 177
1.102 137 n. 66
1.108–115b 12 n. 69
1.119 136
1.120 136
1.121 136
1.122 136, 137 n. 59
1.150 137 n. 66
1.173 137 n. 66
1.176 137 n. 66
2.13 9 n. 48, 94 n. 34, 204 n. 5
2.69 232 n. 177
2.87 94 n. 35, 121 n. 182, 168 n. 9
2.96 94 n. 35, 121 n. 182
2.153 169
2.185 168, 170
2.189 251 n. 67
2.202 38 n. 77
2.229 219 n. 103
2.239 151 n. 164
2.262 38 n. 77
2.263–266 204 n. 10
2.267 204 n. 8
2.282 38 n. 76
3.42 172 n. 17
3.56 217
3.160 133
3.213 233 n. 185
3.222 157 n. 207
4.9 38 n. 76
4.14 203, 208 n. 29, 213 n. 60

4.72a 174 n. 22
4.74a 87 n. 2
4.77 260 n. 110
– Gai epitome (Gai. ep.)
1.6.4 25 n. 7

Leges
– Lex Cumana libitinaria
face A, col. II, ll. 3–5 194 n. 18

Pauli sententiae (PS)
1.1b.1 27 n. 18
2.10.6 26 n. 9
2.19.6 176 n. 26
2.23.2 208 n. 29
2.24.2 208 n. 29
3.6.38 45 n. 121
4.8.22 21 n. 117
4.13.3 153 n. 176
5.1.3 78 n. 37

Ps. Ulpian, Liber singularis regularum
1.12 75
1.25 151 n. 164
2.4 109
5.5 26 n. 9, 252 n. 73
20.10 121 n. 182
20.16 183

2. Corpus Iuris Civilis

Institutiones Iustiniani (Inst.)
1.2.2 232 n. 177
1.2.12–1.3 pr. 8 n. 46
1.5 pr. 232 n. 177
1.5.3 205 n. 13, 217
1.6.5 30 n. 36
1.14.1 153 n. 176
1.16 200
2.7.4 207
2.9.3 121 n. 182
2.12.5 20 n. 109
2.20.20 89 n. 11
3.11.1 208 n. 29
3.26.10 134

Digesta (D.)
1.1.1.2 212 n. 51
1.1.1.3 46 n. 122, 231
1.1.4 5 n. 29, 97 n. 54, 100 n. 67, 211, 232 n. 177
1.1.7 216 n. 84
1.1.7.1 222 n. 116
1.1.10 219 n. 104
1.1.11 235 n. 201
1.2.2.41 17 n. 90
1.3.1 213 n. 58
1.3.15 222
1.3.16 222 n. 118
1.3.17 210 n. 39
1.3.20 214 n. 64
1.3.28 213 n. 57
1.4.1 pr. 207 n. 27
1.5 237
1.5.1 8 n. 46, 204 n. 4
1.5.3 8 n. 46, 97
1.5.3.1 211 n. 42
1.5.4 100 n. 67
1.5.4 pr. 206, 233 n. 177
1.5.4.1 11 n. 66, 64 n. 235, 97 n. 54, 206, 221 n. 114, 233 n. 177
1.5.5 pr. 157 n. 205
1.5.5.1 12 n. 66, 221 n. 114
1.7.46 23
1.12.1.8 234 n. 188
1.14.3 98 n. 57, 231 n. 168
1.19.1.2 75
2.4.4.1.2 27 n. 17
2.4.4.3 28
2.4.6 27
2.4.8 pr. 28 n. 19
2.4.10.1 225 n. 129, 246 n. 40
3.2.4.2 147 n. 135
3.2.23 45 n. 116
3.5.5.8 157 n. 200
4.3.7.8 261 n. 116
4.4.24.1 45 n. 115
4.5.1 8
4.5.3.1 7
4.5.4 8

4.7.3.1 208 n. 29
4.8.32.7 208 n. 29
5.1.19.3 118 n. 169
5.1.67 261 n. 113, 266 n. 142
6.1 17 n. 91
6.1.41.1 91 n. 17
6.1.49.1 12 n. 70
7.1.1 242 n. 22
7.1.15.1 141 n. 94, 242
7.1.15.2 242–243, 248
7.1.15.3 141 n. 94, 243
7.1.68 pr. 65 n. 237
7.7.6.2 67 n. 218
8.1.4 221 n. 113
9.2.23.3 109 n. 111
9.2.23.4 163 n. 253
9.2.33 pr. 62
9.2.52.4 145 n. 122, 154 n. 182
9.4.38.1 12 n. 67
11.3.1.4 146 n. 126
11.3.1.5 89 n. 11, 119 n. 172
11.3.16 92 n. 21
12.6.64 11 n. 66
13.4.2.6 135 n. 52–53
13.7.11.5 130 n. 26
14.1.1.12 130 n. 26
14.1.1.13 130 n. 26
14.1.5.1 95 n. 43
14.2.4 76
14.3.5.10 147 n. 133, 149 n. 147
14.3.12 131 n. 30
14.3.13 118 n. 169
14.3.17.1 97 n. 50
14.3.17.1.4 97 n. 50
15.1 87 n. 1–2, 106, 251, n. 66
15.1.3.1 251 n. 67
15.1.3.3 152 n. 170
15.1.3.4 107 n. 106
15.1.4.1 94 n. 36
15.1.4.2 117 n. 159
15.1.4.6 107 n. 105, 115 n. 147
15.1.5.3 101, 106 n. 96
15.1.5.4 90, 92, 95 n. 38, 101, 105, 137 n. 62
15.1.6 107 n. 105, 115 n. 147
15.1.7.1 107 n. 106, 137 n. 63
15.1.7.4 91 n. 17, 95 n. 37, 101 n. 73, 251 n. 66
15.1.7.5 174, 251 n. 66
15.1.7.6–7 251 n. 66
15.1.8 94 n. 36
15.1.11.1 261 n. 116
15.1.16 94 n. 36, 106 n. 103, 137 n. 63
15.1.17 147 n. 136, 251 n. 66
15.1.18 102 n. 76, 106 n. 101
15.1.19.1 91 n. 18
15.1.21 pr. 93 n. 24
15.1.24 137 n. 63
15.1.25 94 n. 29
15.1.27 pr. 259 n. 106
15.1.29.1 97 n. 50
15.1.32 pr. 91 n. 18, 265 n. 135
15.1.37.3 95 n. 38
15.1.39 106
15.1.40.1 94 n. 29
15.1.41 16, 17, 249 n. 55
15.1.41 pr. 107 n. 109
15.1.46 137 n. 63
15.1.47 pr. 97 n. 50
15.1.47.6 91 n. 18, 265 n. 135
15.1.48 pr. 119 n. 171, 137 n. 63
15.1.48.1 137 n. 63
15.1.49 pr. 107 n. 106
15.1.49.2 17 n. 90, 89 n. 11
15.3 87 n. 2
15.3.3.1 94 n. 28
15.3.3.3 94 n. 28
15.3.3.4 106
15.3.3.5 89 n. 11
15.3.3.7 94 n. 28
15.3.3.9 135 n. 49
15.3.3.10 94 n. 28
15.3.7 pr. 156
15.3.16 106 n. 103
16.3.1.8 147 n. 135
16.3.27 45, 92 n. 22
17.1.12.12 153 n. 171
17.1.12.16 131 n. 26
17.1.19 262 n. 122, 263 n. 127
17.1.29.3 133 n. 44
17.1.34 pr. 131 n. 26

17.1.54 pr. 32, 32 n. 44, 63, 262 n. 120–122, 263 n. 128, 266 n. 140
18.1.5 98 n. 56
18.1.42 216 n. 81, 217
18.7 246 n. 43
18.7.6 pr. 245 n. 37, 247–249
18.7.9 208 n. 29
18.7.10 34 n. 53
19.1.30 pr. 117 n. 159
19.5.5.4 131 n. 26, 135 n. 52
20.1.6 37
20.1.7 37
20.1.8 36, 37
20.3.1.1 137 n. 62
21.1.1 pr. 215 n. 70
21.1.1.1 42 n. 100
21.1.4.2 119 n. 172
21.1.17.4 151 n. 163
21.1.17.5 151 n. 163
21.1.17.7 119 n. 173
21.1.17.10 94 n. 34
21.1.34 pr. 42 n. 101
21.1.34.1 42 n. 102
21.1.35 21 n. 94, 40 n. 89, 42–43, 44 n. 110, 46, 52 n. 155, 61, 254
21.1.38.14 43, 47 n. 131
21.1.39 43
21.1.40 43
21.1.44 pr. 109 n. 111, 243 n. 26
21.1.65 119 n. 172
21.2.34 pr. 246 n. 40
22.1.28.1 65 n. 237
22.1.37 45 n. 115
22.4.6 45
23.2.8 27 n. 16
23.2.14.2 27, 64 n. 234, 256 n. 94
23.2.56 27 n. 16
23.3.1 259 n. 103
23.3.2 212 n. 54
23.3.9.3 103 n. 81
23.3.39 46 n. 123, 92 n. 22
23.3.39 pr. 258, 261
23.3.56.1 259 n. 104
23.3.76 259 n. 104
24.1.9.1 102 n. 76
24.2.23.13 260 n. 107
24.3.1 212 n. 54
26.2.28 pr. 180–181
26.7.11 260 n. 107
26.7.37.1 130 n. 26, 131 n. 26
28.1.3 18 n. 98
28.1.8 18 n. 97
28.1.16 pr. 166, 168, 170, 176
28.1.19 18 n. 97
28.1.20.7 17
28.1.28 18 n. 97
28.4.3 208 n. 30, 219
28.4.3 pr.-1 219 n. 102
28.5.6.2 251 n. 67
28.5.31 pr. 167 n. 4
28.5.35.3 118 n. 169, 141 n. 91
28.5.42 75
28.7.15 46 n. 126
28.7.21 80, 171, 173
28.8.1 18
29.2.25.2 75 n. 29
29.2.25.3 75 n. 29, 189
29.2.71 208 n. 29
29.4.26 pr. 181 n. 40
29.5.2 46 n. 127
29.5.3.15 246 n. 44
29.5.16 208 n. 29, 225
30.44.7 246 n. 44
30.71.3 38
30.71.4 38
31.14 208 n. 29
31.83 171
32.14.2 38 n. 78, 40 n. 84
32.29.4 208 n. 31
32.30.6 38 n. 78, 39 n. 82
32.37.7 48 n. 140, 50
32.41.2 45, 51, 61, 252
32.41.5 50 n. 147
32.79.1 103 n. 81
33.1.18.1 153 n. 173
33.1.21.2 153 n. 173
33.5.21 49 n. 141, 54 n. 172
33.7.8 pr. 53 n. 161
33.7.12.2 43 n. 161, 253, 253 n. 83
33.7.12.3 149 n. 147
33.7.12.5 53 n. 164, 54 n. 166

33.7.12.6	54 n. 165	37.5.3.2	179, 181
33.7.12.7	45 n. 121, 52 n. 155, 54, 61 n. 213, 253	37.11.2.9	177
		37.14.7 pr.	246 n. 41
33.7.12.31	37 n. 70	37.14.10	8 n. 44
33.7.12.33	55 n. 178, 254	37.15.1.1	45, 46 n. 124
33.7.17	109 n. 111	38.2.3 pr.	225 n. 129
33.7.18.4	50 n. 147	38.2.3.1	225 n. 130
33.7.19.1	118 n. 170	38.8.1.2	26 n. 11
33.7.20.1	48	38.8.1.4	25 n. 5, 6
33.7.20.4	45 n. 121, 49 n. 144	38.10.10.5	26 n. 12, 255 n. 93
33.7.27.1	51 n. 150	38.16.1 pr.	20 n. 111
33.8	87 n. 1	38.16.1.4	230 n. 163
33.8.6	91 n. 17	38.17.1.6	208 n. 30
33.8.6.2	250 n. 65	39.5.13	240 n. 14
33.8.6.3	102 n. 76	40	237
33.8.6.4	89 n. 11	40.1.3	210
33.8.8.2	102 n. 76, 106 n. 101	40.1.4	261 n. 113
33.8.8.5	262 n. 118, 264 n. 132	40.1.4 pr.	31 n. 41, 233 n. 187, 266 n. 142
33.8.14	102 n. 76, 106 n. 101		
33.8.15	250 n. 65	40.1.4.1	32 n. 43, 107–108, 113, 261 n. 114, 263
33.8.16	93 n. 25		
33.8.16 pr.	149 n. 145, 251 n. 66		
33.8.16.1	251 n. 66	40.1.4.8	33
33.8.21	250 n. 65	40.1.4.10	261 n. 115
33.8.22.1	117 n. 162, 250 n. 65	40.1.6	89 n. 11, 102 n. 76, 106 n. 101, 261 n. 116
33.8.23 pr.	102 n. 76, 106 n. 101		
33.8.23.1	89 n. 11		
33.8.25	250 n. 65	40.1.7	145 n. 122
34.1.14.1	45 n. 116	40.1.9	246 n. 44
34.1.20 pr.	48 n. 140, 253	40.1.19	33
34.2.1 pr.	141 n. 92	40.1.20.2	245 n. 39
34.5.10.1	208 n. 30, 229	40.1.24 pr.-1	215
34.5.22	231 n. 169	40.2.4	208 n. 29
34.8.3	75 n. 29	40.2.12	30 n. 35
34.8.3 pr.	189	40.2.13	30–31, 45
35.1.37	227 n. 140	40.2.14.1	30 n. 33
35.1.40.3	89 n. 11	40.2.16 pr.	31 n. 39
35.1.57	102 n. 76	40.2.20.3	30 n. 34
35.1.59	20, 22	40.4.1	208 n. 29
35.1.59.2	19	40.4.5	50 n. 146, 208 n. 31
35.1.71.1	153 n. 178	40.4.10.1	208 n. 29
35.2.32.5	208 n. 29	40.4.11.2	209
35.2.61	38 n. 78	40.4.16	208 n. 29, 209, 223
35.2.63 pr.	62 n. 223	40.4.17.2	208 n. 29
36.1.11.2	48 n. 140	40.4.24	151 n. 165
36.1.17 pr.	102, 106 n. 97	40.4.26	208 n. 29
36.1.18.4	66	40.4.29	208 n. 29
36.1.26.2	208 n. 29	40.5.4.16	208 n. 29
36.1.80.12	102 n. 79	40.5.12 pr.	153 n. 174

40.5.21 153 n. 174
40.5.23.3 223
40.5.24.10 208 n. 29, 223
40.5.26 208 n. 29
40.5.31.1 98 n. 55
40.5.35 151 n. 165
40.5.37 208 n. 30
40.5.41.1 153 n. 174, 154
40.5.41.10 208 n. 30
40.5.41.15 129 n. 19, 152 n. 169
40.5.50 50 n. 146, 216 n. 80, 224 n. 112
40.7.3.2 89 n. 11
40.7.3.7 261 n. 117
40.7.3.16 208 n. 31
40.7.4.6 208 n. 29
40.7.9.3 208 n. 29
40.7.14 pr. 106 n. 103, 261 n. 117
40.7.17 102 n. 76
40.7.19 208 n. 29
40.7.20.2 261 n. 117
40.7.20.3 208 n. 29
40.7.20.6 45 n. 115
40.7.21 pr. 113, 129 n. 19
40.7.28 208 n. 29
40.7.34.1 19 n. 107
40.7.39.2 94 n. 36
40.7.40.1 113
40.7.40.3 102 n. 76, 106 n. 101
40.8.2 233 n. 183
40.8.3 34 n. 53
40.8.6 245 n. 39
40.8.9 208 n. 29
40.9 227 n. 141
40.9.4 210 n. 39
40.9.9.2 246 n. 44
40.9.10 118 n. 168, 169
40.11.2 100 n. 67
40.12.9.2 98 n. 55
40.12.24 251 n. 68
40.12.30 98 n. 55, 208 n. 29
40.12.32 239 n. 10, 257–258
40.12.38.1 208 n. 29
41.1 17 n. 91, 237
41.1.10.1 121 n. 182
41.1.23 238 n. 4
41.1.37.1 89 n. 11, 238 n. 5
41.1.37.2–5 238 n. 5
41.1.37.6 238 n. 5, 241
41.1.40 238 n. 4
41.1.43 pr. 238 n. 4
41.1.43.2 240
41.1.45 238 n. 5
41.1.47 238 n. 6
41.1.49 238 n. 6
41.1.54 238 n. 4
41.1.54.4 94 n. 35
41.1.63.1–2 238 n. 5
41.1.63.3 238 n. 6
41.2 238
41.2.1.5 95 n. 38, 133 n. 42, 137 n. 62, 153 n. 171, 238 n. 2
41.2.1.14 118 n. 169
41.2.3.18 133 n. 42
41.2.24 95 n. 38
41.2.38 pr. 205 n. 11
41.2.44.1 95 n. 41
41.2.49.1 95 n. 38
41.3.44 pr. 98 n. 56
41.7.2 12 n. 67
42.5.38 pr. 35
42.8.17.1 26 n. 10
43.29.3.9 208 n. 29
44.4.5.3 130 n. 26
44.7.14 249 n. 56, 261
45.1.38.7 95 n. 38
45.1.73 pr. 135 n. 52
45.1.104 261 n. 116, 262 n. 119
45.1.122.2 245 n. 37
45.1.131.4 132 n. 39
45.1.141.4 118 n. 169, 129 n. 20, 135, 136
46.1.16.4 107 n. 109
46.3.35 102 n. 76
46.3.51 132
46.3.62 134, 155 n. 183
46.3.84 102 n. 76
47.2.67.3 130 n. 26
47.2.68.4 117 n. 159
47.4.1.7 19 n. 107
47.9.3.8 77 n. 32
47.9.6 76
47.9.7 75, 76
47.10.15.15 158 n. 216
47.10.15.34 244 n. 29
47.10.15.35 244 n. 30–31

47.10.15.44	128 n. 17, 244
47.10.15.45	244 n. 30
47.10.15.48	158 n. 208
47.10.17.3	245 n. 35
47.17	147 n. 135
48.2.12.4	29 n. 25, 64 n. 234
48.8.1.2	233 n. 185
48.8.4.2	233 n. 186
48.8.6	233 n. 186
48.8.11.1	196
48.9.5	46 n. 125
48.10.7	19, 208 n. 29
48.11.1.1	217 n. 85
48.11.7. pr.-1	8 n. 44
48.19.7. pr.	189
48.19.29	190
48.19.31 pr.	196
48.23.4	232
49.14.12	75 n. 29, 188
49.15.12.9	208 n. 29, 235 n. 197
49.15.12.16	246 n. 44
49.15.18	20 n. 109
49.15.22. pr.	20 n. 111
49.17.19.5	208 n. 29
49.17.20	208 n. 29
50.1.17.7	131 n. 26
50.6.6.3	76
50.6.6.4	76
50.6.6.5	76
50.6.6.6	76
50.16	98
50.16.49	12 n. 70, 99–100
50.16.66	9 n. 51
50.16.166	141 n. 92, 142 n. 96
50.16.182	94 n. 35, 98
50.16.195.2	94 n. 33
50.16.207	9 n. 52, 24 n. 125
50.16.215	11–12, 227 n. 140
50.16.220.1	50 n. 147
50.16.220.3	50 n. 147
50.17	22
50.17.20	207, 208 n. 29
50.17.32	15, 65 n. 236, 100 n. 67, 232
50.17.107	16, 18 n. 101, 174 n. 21
50.17.118	94 n. 35
50.17.122	208 n. 29
50.17.179	208 n. 29
50.17.209	22–23

Codex (C.)

3.8.11	254
3.28.11	197
3.31.12.2b	232 n. 175
3.38.11	59–61
4.6.9	208 n. 29
4.26.10 pr.	91 n. 17
4.56.2	246 n. 40
4.57.2	34
6.8.2	225 n. 130
6.27.2	208 n. 30
6.37.26	222 n. 113
7.1–24	237
7.2.5	227 n. 141
7.2.6	208 n. 29
7.4.9	154 n. 179
7.4.10	208 n. 29
7.6.1.3	233 n. 183
7.11.1	227 n. 141
7.11.2	102 n. 76
7.16.12	33
7.22.2	208 n. 29
8.16.1	38
11.6.1	77 n. 35
11.7(6).7	232 n. 174

III. Literary Sources

Apuleius
– metamorphoses

8.22	137 n. 65, 144 n. 113

Augustine of Hippo
– de civitate dei

19.5	187 n. 2
22.6.28	218 n. 98

Cassius Dio
– historia Romana

54.2.4	193 n. 12
56.33.3	228 n. 147
57.11.6	195
58.19.6	73 n. 23
59.10.1	193 n. 15

Cato, Marcus Portius (censor)
– de agri cultura
1.4 15 n. 83
5.1 149 n. 152
5.56–59 116 n. 158

Catullus, C. Valerius
– carmina
25 123 n. 189

Cicero, Marcus Tullius
– de legibus
2.52 80
– de officiis
1.31 46 n. 129
– epistulae ad Atticum
15.15.3 132 n. 37
– in L. Pisonem oratio
67 150 n. 156
– pro P. Quinctio oratio
15.4 35 n. 59
– topica
18 8 n. 42
29 8 n. 42

Columella, L. Iunius Moderatus
– de re rustica
1.8 149 n. 149
1.8.5 41 n. 97, 251 n. 73
1.8.10 149 n. 147
1.8.15 148 n. 143
1.8.16 148 n. 143
1.8.17 148 n. 143
11.1.24 106 n. 103
11.1.25 148 n. 140

Diodorus Siculus
– bibliotheca historica
5.28.1 191 n. 9

Ennius, Q.
– tragoediae
Alexander, 69–71 191 n. 8

Fronto, M. Cornelius
– epistulae
Ad M. Caes. 2.1.2 194 n. 16

Gellius, A.
– noctes Atticae
5.19.9 216 n. 78

Historia Augusta
Hadr. 18.7 233 n. 184
Elag. 49.3. 148 n. 138

Horatius, Q.
– carmina
3.24 224 n. 123
– epistulae
1.14.15 119 n. 172

Isidore of Seville
– etymologiarum sive originum libri
5.25.4 100
5.25.5 100, 105, 110, 265 n. 135
– origines
10.7 236 n. 198

Lactantius, L. Caecilius Firmianus
– divinae institutiones
5.15.3 58 n. 194

Lucian of Samosata
– de mercede conductis
36 5 n. 26
39 5 n. 27

Martialis, M. Valerius
– epigrammata
6.39 144 n. 108
6.73.1 142 n. 96
6.73.2 142 n. 96
7.71 152 n. 171
8.23 150 n. 156
11.39.6 152 n. 171

Ovid, P.
– metamorphoses
1.89–94 100 n. 66
1.127–131 100 n. 66

Pausanias
– graeciae descriptio
1.33.3 198 n. 24

Petronius, T. (arbiter)
8.2–4 104 n. 86
27.5 142 n. 99
27.6 141 n. 87
28.7 112 n. 127, 150 n. 154
28.8 158 n. 217
29.3 138 n. 72
29.4 138 n. 72
30.1 156 n. 195
30.2 131 n. 28
30.3 131 n. 28
30.7 103 n. 84, 131 n. 28, 147 n. 131
30.8 103 n. 84, 131 n. 28, 147 n. 131
30.9 103 n. 84, 131 n. 28, 147 n. 131, 158 n. 214
30.10 103 n. 84, 131 n. 28, 144 n. 110, 147 n. 131
30.11 158 n. 217
31.2 157 n. 199
37.6 148 n. 142
45.4 142
46.3 139 n. 73, 161 n. 239
46.4 161 n. 239
46.5 161 n. 239
46.6 161 n. 239
46.7 161 n. 239
46.8 161 n. 239
47.12 148 n. 140
47.13 148 n. 140
49.6 150 n. 158
50.1 150 n. 158
52.4 150 n. 158
52.5 150 n. 158
52.6 150 n. 158
53 103 n. 84
53.1 148 n. 139
53.2 91 n. 17, 127 n. 11
53.6–8 117 n. 164
53.10 142 n. 96–97, 146, 149 n. 152, 163 n. 253
54.3 150 n. 158
57.4 150 n. 158, 160 n. 232
57.6 141 n. 87
57.9 159 n. 218
58.7 139 n. 73
69.3 140–141
70.5 149 n. 152
71.3 153 n. 173
71.5 127 n. 8
71.6 127 n. 8
71.7 127 n. 8
71.8 127 n. 8
71.9 127 n. 8
71.10 127 n. 8
71.11 127 n. 8
71.12 127 n. 8
75.3 103 n. 85, 161 n. 239
75.4 103 n. 84, 116 n. 156, 139 n. 73, 161 n. 239
75.10 138 n. 68
75.11 138 n. 68, 141
76.1 138 n. 68, 144 n. 110
76.7 103 n. 81
76.8 103 n. 85

Plautus, T. Maccius
– Asinaria
276 112 n. 132
– Captivi
5.4 191 n. 9
– Casina
103 149 n. 147
– Mostellaria
661 15 n. 83
15 n. 83
– Persa
192 112 n. 133
– Pseudolus
1140 15 n. 83
– Rudens
929 117 n. 161, 118 n. 167
– Trinummus
413 117 n. 159
– Truculentus
461–462 117 n. 159

Plinius, C. (minor)
– epistulae
8.16 86 n. 59, 119 n. 175, 181, 256

Plutarch
– Cato maior
4.4 115 n. 149
21.2 149 n. 150
21.3 150 n. 156, 150 n. 161
21.7 115 n. 145
– de sera numinis vindicta
25 (564 e-f) 198 n. 25
25 (565 a) 198 n. 26

Quintilianus, M. Fabius (vel Ps.-Quintilianus)
– declamationes minores
16.4 219 n. 99
345.10 136 n. 55
388 163 n. 256
– institutio oratoria
6.3.93 154 n. 182, 162 n. 249

Seneca, L. Annaeus (maior)
– controversiae
4 praef. 10 139 n. 79
5.5.1 149 n. 147

Seneca, L. Annaeus (minor)
– de beneficiis
3.18–20 6 n. 30
3.21.2 46 n. 129
– de clementia
1.18.1 46 n. 129, 149 n. 147
1.18.2 3 n. 9
1.21.2 194 n. 17
– de ira
3.29.1 141 n. 93
– epistulae morales ad Lucilium
47 6 n. 30
47.1 64 n. 233
47.5 226 n. 135
47.13 46 n. 129
122.15 162 n. 152

Statius, P. Papinius
– Thebais
5.626–28 46 n. 129

Suetonius, C.
– Caligula
47.1 74 n. 27
– divus Claudius
12.1 86 n. 60
25.2 233 n. 184
28 73 n. 22
– divus Iulius
27.1 177
– divus Tiberius
15.2 175
– Galba
20.2 163 n. 256
– Otho
5.2 161 n. 241

Tacitus, P. Cornelius
– annales
12.60.1 74, 86 n. 60
14.42.1 121 n. 182, 122
14.43.1 123 n. 191, 152 n. 168
14.43.2 123 n. 191
14.43.4 122
14.44 152 n. 168, 226 n. 134, 227
14.44.2 124
14.45.1 124 n. 192
16.17 125 n. 1
16.18 125 n. 1
16.19 125 n. 1, 150 n. 161
– historiae
1.49.1 163 n. 256

Tertullianus, Q. Septimius Florens
– apologeticum
27.7 187 n. 2

Valerius Maximus
– facta et dicta memorabilia
6.8.2 46 n. 129

Varro, M. Terentius
– res rusticae
1.2.17 110
1.13.2 112 n. 127
1.16.5 112 n. 127, 149 n. 149, 150 n. 154
1.17 214 n. 69
1.17.5 41 n. 95, 149 n. 147, 252 n. 73
1.17.7 110
1.19.3 110
2.10.6–7 41 n. 95

IV. Modern Legal Sources

Bürgerliches Gesetzbuch, Germany (BGB)

§§ 104 sqq.	241 n. 17
§ 214	249 n. 58
§ 516	249 n. 58
§ 518	249 n. 58
§ 903	12 n. 71
§ 1632	9, 12

Slavery Convention of the League of Nations (1926)

Article 1	12, 14

UN Convention on the Rights of Persons with Disabilities (2006)

Article 12	241 n. 17

Bei Fragen zur Produktsicherheit wenden Sie sich bitte an:
If you have any questions regarding product safety,
please contact:

Walter de Gruyter GmbH
Genthiner Straße 13
10785 Berlin
productsafety@degruyterbrill.com